People Resourcing and Talent Planning

STEPHEN PILBEAM

AND

MARJORIE CORBRIDGE

People Resourcing and Talent Planning

HRM in Practice

FOURTH EDITION

**Financial Times
Prentice Hall
is an imprint of**

Harlow, England • London • New York • Boston • San Francisco • Toronto • Sydney • Singapore • Hong Kong
Tokyo • Seoul • Taipei • New Delhi • Cape Town • Madrid • Mexico City • Amsterdam • Munich • Paris • Milan

Pearson Education Limited
Edinburgh Gate
Harlow
Essex CM20 2JE
England

and Associated Companies throughout the world

Visit us on the World Wide Web at:
www.pearsoned.co.uk

First published 1998
Second edition 2002
Third edition 2006
Fourth edition published 2010

© Stephen Pilbeam and Marjorie Corbridge 2010

ISBN 978-0-273-71954-0

British Library Cataloguing-in-Publication Data
A catalogue record for this book is available from the British Library

Library of Congress Cataloging-in-Publication Data
A catalog record for this book is available from the Library of Congress

10 9 8 7 6 5 4 3 2
14 13 12 11 10

Typeset in 9.5/12pt Sabon by 35
Printed and bound by Ashford Colour Press Ltd., Gosport

Brief Contents

Contents

List of Figures and Tables

List of Exhibits

EVOLUTION OF THE TITLE OF THE BOOK AND RELATIONSHIP TO THE 2010 CIPD MODULE – RESOURCING AND TALENT MANAGEMENT

The first edition of this book was titled *Employment Resourcing*, rather than the Chartered Institute of Personnel and Development's *Employee Resourcing*, quite simply because not all those who work in organisations are employees. Therefore, employment resourcing was considered to be a more holistic and contemporary term. The 2002 revision of the CIPD Professional Standards produced the title *People Resourcing* and we were comfortable with this. In the third edition we stretched the title of the book to *People Resourcing: Contemporary HRM in Practice*, to reflect the applied nature of our approach and contemporary developments in HRM. For the fourth edition, the HR lexicon has changed again and the terms *Talent Management* and *Talent Planning* are now common parlance. As Chapter 4 contends, the definition of talent management and planning is perspectival and depends on whether a narrow approach is taken, with an exclusive focus on high potentials and future leaders and concerned primarily with succession planning, or a broader and more inclusive approach is taken, which regards all employees as 'talent' and therefore worthy of developing, rewarding, performance managing and retaining due to the critical contribution of people performance to organisational sustainability. In the latter case, this broad view of talent management and planning is about the strategic alignment of HR activity with the business direction of the organisation.

'People resourcing and talent planning' is a highly contextual and contingent activity and this is recognised throughout the book. We do not believe that there is 'one right way' to resource organisations with talent, as it all depends on the contingent character-istics of the organisation and the people. The contextual nature of HR activity makes it necessary for managers to be aware of influences in the internal and external environments – context is key. This book therefore addresses the *breadth* of HR issues and includes all the activities essential for the acquisition, management and retention of talent from HR planning through to release from employment. Therefore, the aim of the book is:

> to describe and to analyse contemporary HR practice and developments in people resourcing and talent planning with full regard to context.

This people resourcing text more than meets the knowledge and understanding requirements for the CIPD's Resourcing and Talent Management module, and the CIPD module content has been matched against the chapters in this book (see below). In addition, the chapters on reward, relations and development, *inter alia*, offer a useful summary for other CIPD modules. It is therefore a multipurpose CIPD text.

As well as serving the needs of CIPD students, the book is sufficiently comprehensive in scope to be attractive to tutors and students on other management or business-related programmes who are seeking an applied and integrated HR text to contribute to the exploration of fundamental aspects of managing talent in contemporary organisations. Units of HRM study, particularly on degree and postgraduate programmes, invariably have a high people resourcing element. We were again encouraged by the reviewers' comments on the third edition and it is evident from these that the book continues to be used not only on professional programmes but also on Level 3 undergraduate units and on Masters programmes. We are aware that the book is used as underpinning knowledge for NVQs and it has also claimed a place on the bookshelf of HR practitioners.

CHANGES IN THE 2010 EDITION

This text has been updated to reflect:

- The continuing development of the HR role in terms of business partnership, added-value and strategic awareness.
- Increasing interest in organisational sustainability through the integration of HR activity with business objectives.
- Significant changes in employment and related law since 2006, particularly in the areas of equality and managing discipline at work.
- Contemporary HR issues such as: changes in the world of work, the reconfiguration of HR activity which exploits e-HR, the war for talent and talent management, and employee well-being.
- Further demand for additional case study and illustrative material.

In addition to updating and adding new material to existing chapters, we have a new chapter on human resource development. The challenge has again been to constrain the size of a textbook that is broad in scope. The international dimension of HR is generally beyond the scope of this generalist text and more specialist texts are increasingly available. In any case, the distinction between a multinational organisation managing ex-pats and local employees on the one hand, and international aspects of HR practice specific to particular regions or countries on the other, already generates two foci for the study of international HRM – we could not hope to explore this fully.

STYLE AND APPROACH

- The functions of effective people resourcing and talent planning are examined while seeking a balance between academic rigour and practitioner relevance.
- Prescriptive solutions are avoided and critical evaluation is encouraged to enable HR practitioners and line managers to make informed HR choices.
- The chapters and areas of HRM covered progress logically and, while necessarily having to divide the book into topic areas, we have aimed to avoid the disintegration of what we see as an integrated subject.

Each chapter begins with multi-level learning outcomes and ends with a summary of the main learning points. Other pedagogical features include illustrative exhibits, discussion topics, assignments, in-class activities, coursework opportunities and case studies. Relevant references enable the reader to pursue lines of enquiry. Our overall approach reflects our experience as HR practitioners as well as HR teachers, and we are evidently straddling the practitioner/academic 'divide' – we get compliments and criticisms from both camps. This encourages us to continue with this approach in the hope that we offer something readable and distinctive.

RELATIONSHIP OF THE BOOK TO THE CIPD RESOURCING AND TALENT PLANNING MODULE

The content of this book is mapped against the CIPD Resourcing and Talent Management module. Relevant chapters are indicated against each dimension of the indicative module content.

Indicative module content	Chapter/s
1 **Analyse the major features of the employment markets from which organisations source staff and how these markets evolve or change.** Ways in which employment markets vary and the implications for organisations. Current and future demand and supply of skills. Identifying and assessing the role of employment market competitors. Key national and international employment market and demographic trends.	1, 2, 4
2 **Play a leading role in the development and evaluation of resourcing and talent management strategies, diversity management and flexible working initiatives.** Ensuring that the organisation remains competitive in its major employment markets having regard to organisational objectives, resource constraints and the need to enhance flexibility. Positioning an organisation in the market. Work–life balance initiatives, employer branding exercises, setting terms and conditions, job analysis and design, flexible working. Managing skills shortages. Managing diversity. Ethical working practices.	3, 4, 8, 14
3 **Manage recruitment, selection and induction activities effectively, efficiently, lawfully and professionally.** Critical analysis of the major methods used in recruiting and selecting people in national and international settings. Efficient recruitment administration. Job advertising, employment agencies, education liaison. Reliability and validity of different selection methods. Psychometric testing, selection interviewing, assessment centres. Design and delivery of timely and effective staff induction.	6, 7
4 **Undertake long- and short-term talent planning and succession planning exercises with a view to building long-term organisational performance.** Reconciling demand for and supply of skills. Workforce planning, scenario planning, succession planning. Enhancing functional and numerical flexibility. Outsourcing, subcontracting and using external consultants.	4, 11
5 **Gather and analyse information on employee turnover as the basis for developing robust staff retention strategies.** Measuring, recording and analysing turnover data, diagnosing the principal drivers of unwanted turnover. Developing, operationalising and evaluating actions aimed at increasing employee retention.	4, 5, 9, 10, 12
6 **Manage retirement, redundancy and dismissal practices fairly, efficiently and in accordance with the expectations of the law, ethical and professional practice.** Understanding of how to manage the release of employees efficiently, ethically and lawfully. Professional practice in disciplinary procedure, redundancy selection, and severance compensation. Pre-retirement planning and training. Phased retirement. Legal restraints and rights.	11, 17, 18, 19

RELATIONSHIP OF THE BOOK TO OTHER CIPD MODULES

CIPD module	Chapter/s
HRM in context	1, 2, 3 and 4
Performance management	11
Reward management	9 and 10
Managing employment relations	13, 14, 15 and 16
Employment law	8, 13, 17, 18 and 19
HR information services	5
Learning and talent development	12
Designing, delivering and evaluating learning and development	12

Acknowledgements

We thank our families for their continued support and encouragement. In this edition we acknowledge the invaluable contributions of our colleagues at the University of Portsmouth – Derek Adam-Smith, Sylvia Horton, David Farnham and Val Anderson.

PUBLISHER'S ACKNOWLEDGEMENTS

We are grateful to the following for permission to reproduce copyright material:

Figures
Figure 4.2 from *Talent: strategy, management, measurement.* CIPD (Tansley, C., Turner, P., Foster, C., Harris, L., Sempik, A., Stewart, J., and Williams, H. 2007), with the permission of the publisher, the Chartered Institute of Personnel and Development, London (www.cipd.co.uk); Figure 4.3 from *Talent: strategy, management, measurement. London:* CIPD. (Tansley, C.,Turner, P., Foster, C., Harris, L., Sempik, A., Stewart, J., and Williams, H. 2007), with the permission of the publisher, the Chartered Institute of Personnel and Development, London (www.cipd.co.uk); Figure 12.4 from Exploring strategic maturity in HRD: Rhetoric, aspiration or reality?, *Journal of European Industrial Training*, 24(8), 425–462 (McCracken, M. and Wallace, M. 2000), © Emerald Group Publishing Limited all rights reserved; Figure 12.6 from Seeking success through strategic management development, *Journal of European Industrial Training*, 27 (6), 292–303 (Brown, P. 2003), © Emerald Group Publishing Limited all rights reserved.

Exhibits
Exhibit 3.1 adapted from *The Competent Manager: A model for effective performance*, Wiley (Boyatzis, R. 1982), reproduced with permission of John Wiley and Sons Inc.; Exhibit 3.6 adapted from Table 15: Main use of competency frameworks, *Learning Development Survey*, 2007, 19 (CIPD 2007), CIPD, with the permission of the publisher, the Chartered Institute of Personnel and Development, London (www.cipd.co.uk); Exhibit 16.1 adapted from *Inside the Workplace: Findings from the 2004 Workplace Employment Relations Survey*, Routledge (Kersley, B., Alpin, C., Forth, J., Bryson, A., Bewley, H., Dix, G. and Oxenbridge, S. 2006), reproduced under the terms of the Click-Use Licence.

The Financial Times
Exhibit 19.1 adapted from Coping with redundancy (if you stay), *Financial Times*, 6 March 2005 (Kellaway, L.).

In some instances we have been unable to trace the owners of copyright material, and we would appreciate any information that would enable us to do so.

Chapter 1

People Resourcing: the changing world of work and contemporary human resource management

LEARNING OUTCOMES: TO BE ABLE TO

- Appreciate the contingent nature of talent planning and people resourcing
- Describe changes in the world of work and examine how these changes impact on organisations and management
- Evaluate the contemporary human resource management trends and the HR role
- Explain the fundamentals of HR strategy

INTRODUCTION

People resourcing is that part of human resource management (HRM) which focuses on the recruitment and release of individuals from organisations, as well as the management of their performance and potential while employed by the organisation. In contemporary HR parlance this is 'talent planning and resourcing'. The path through this book is intended to be logical and integrated and is based on three practical questions – How can organisations resource talent into the organisation? How can organisations manage talent effectively? How can organisations release talent from the organisation? Yes, talent sometimes needs to be released.

This chapter also addresses changes in the world of work in so far as they affect organisations, human resource management activity and human resource (HR) practitioners. The aim is to highlight some of the features of these changes while, in the spirit of contextuality and the exercising of informed managerial or practitioner choice, leaving it to the reader to assess the extent of the changes and the impact on their role within the current or future organisational context. This approach also seeks to recognise that while we are bombarded with stories of organisational turbulence and change, this may be subject to exaggeration. We may live in a dynamic organisational world, but there are degrees of stability too and we need to recognise that change is evolutionary as well as revolutionary. Changes in the world of work have implications for both HR practitioners and line managers, and the role and competencies expected of them in organisations, because HR management is a shared activity between HR specialists and line managers. For HR specialists in particular there are increasing expectations that they should demonstrably add value in pursuit of competitive advantage and organisational sustainability. For line managers there are increasing expectations that they should have responsibility for managing their human resources, as well as other resources. Add to this the potential of e-enabled HR and HR outsourcing opportunities and it is evident that HR professionals, and line managers with responsibility for people, have been experiencing change. Whether HR practitioners have entered a new era or are merely contending with inevitable professional adaptation is also worthy of some debate. Traditionalists – personnel luddites – will underplay the rate of change and the impact on the HR profession, and conversely the plethora of excitable commentators – HRM zealots – will trespass into exaggeration, while the thinking practitioner or manager will make their own informed judgements.

It is beyond the scope of this generalist text to pursue in depth the full range of contemporary HR issues, but in this chapter we introduce the important themes of the nature of human resource management, the reconfiguration of the role of the HR specialist, including the rise of the HR business partner and the relationship between HR strategy and business performance.

A CONTINGENT APPROACH

A fundamental contention of this book is that people resourcing activity is contingent upon particular organisational circumstances and the organisational context. A specific type of HR practice or a particular approach to the management of people is not assumed. People resourcing is enacted by specialist HR practitioners and by line managers. The precise role of an HR function within an organisation, and the distribution of HR responsibilities and activities, is influenced by contingency factors which include:

- the ownership, sector, size, tradition and stage of development of an organisation;
- the degree of turbulence or dynamism in the competitive or task environment and the influence of the political, economic, social, technological, international and legal (PESTIL) contexts external to the organisation;
- the attitude and imagination of the chief executive, or the most senior person, towards the management of human resources;
- the enactment of a unitary, neo-unitary or pluralistic approach to the employment relationship (*see* Chapter 15);
- the competence, reputation and track record of HR job-holders and the existence or absence of the skills and capacity to resource talent effectively.

A contingent approach to talent planning and people resourcing is therefore proposed with the aim of enabling managers to make informed choices about people resourcing activities. This is in accord with the CIPD's notion of 'an HR professional who applies a critically thoughtful approach to their job in order to make a contribution to the survival, profitability, vision and strategic goals of their organisation' (Whittaker and Johns, 2004) and also with the findings of a major research project on the 'changing HR function' (CIPD, 2007) which concluded that 'the idea that there is something called best practice, which if implemented will always result in superior performance is flawed . . . context does appear to be king'. Opportunities are provided by this text for HR professionals and managers to select and apply people resourcing techniques in the specific organisational context within which they operate. For example, in recruitment and selection the appropriateness of standard recruitment and selection procedures is questioned, as the professional recruiter needs to be aware of the strengths, weaknesses and implications of recruitment methods and selection devices so that they can be chosen and utilised appropriately and effectively. In employee reward systems a contingent attitude was neatly summarised by Murlis some time ago (1991), who suggested that there is no 'Holy Grail' in pay and reward, only 'horses for courses'. A knowledge of reward components, an awareness of the often conflicting aims of a reward strategy, recognising the need to integrate reward strategy with other HR practices, and also with corporate objectives, and the ability to be critically evaluative about pay and reward alternatives will promote informed choice based on the understanding and interpretation of organisational contingencies. Sisson and Storey (2000: 252) make this point well: 'policies and practices configured or tailored to the organisation's specific circumstances are likely to be much more effective than those plucked off the shelf or bought from a consultant. HR is not a technological area where there is an automatic best practice solution.' There are no HR simple solutions or universal right answers, 'HRM practice [is] not amenable to universal models based on rational actors. Behaviour is cued and enacted according to specific organisational, cultural and institutional contexts' (Newell and Scarborough, 2002).

The elements of people resourcing are exposed in Figure 1.1. A horizontally integrated approach to people resourcing incorporates human resource development, the employment relationship and reward. Figure 1.1 demonstrates this holistic approach to the effective resourcing of the organisation with people and provides a framework

Figure 1.1
An integrated
approach to people
resourcing

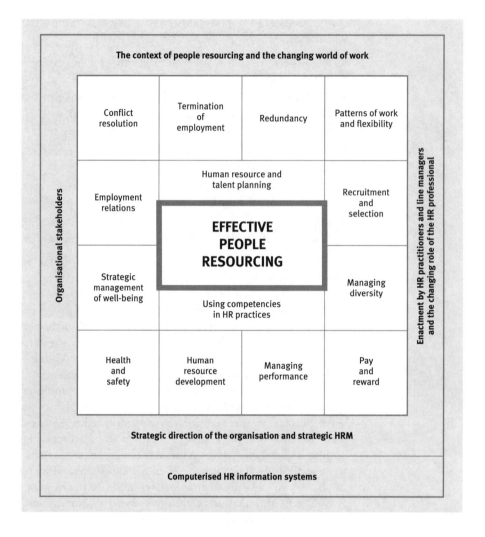

for this book. The basic proposition is that in order to effectively resource the organisation with people HR activities need to be complementary to each other and with the strategy, if one exists, of the organisation.

A CRITICAL PERSPECTIVE AND NO RIGHT HR ANSWERS!

A critically evaluative approach to people resourcing decisions, including a healthy scepticism towards evangelical rhetoric and the latest jargon, is encouraged. Caution is urged in relation to energetic, assertive and overused terminology. The aim is to stimulate debate and prompt a healthy questioning of the concepts. Some indicative illustrations of this language include quality and excellence, vision, empowerment, people are our most valuable resource, world class, delighting our customers, the customer is king, business process re-engineering, human capital reporting, employer branding, the employer of choice, and so on. The fundamental question is – What do these words mean and how is the worthy rhetoric translated into reality and practice? It was some time ago, although it still resonates today, that Moss Kanter, Harvard Professor of Business Administration, exhibited this healthy scepticism, particularly in relation to management gurus, in indicating that she did not like:

> glib, easy answers and popular fads of the moment; trying to create social movements around ideas as opposed to providing information and enabling people to make up their own minds . . . there is a whole lucrative realm of business and management books with billboard jackets and shouty titles that offer more miracle cures than a television evangelist.   (Moss Kanter, 1996)

Peters and Waterman's *In Search of Excellence* (1982) triggered interest in the 'big idea', distilling the 12 golden rules of management from research into 40 organisations with outstanding corporate performance. The reality is that two-thirds of these organisations have gone bankrupt or been taken over, which does cast some doubt on the efficacy of the golden rules. Legge (2005) draws attention to Marks & Spencer and BA being presented as exemplars of the development of cultures of excellence, but 'in both cases, complacency born of the Icarus paradox[1] and the misreading of the marketplace have allowed competitors to outstrip them in profitability and growth in market share'. To some extent these British icons recovered their position, but the 2009 recession generated further setbacks. As long ago as 1995 Marchington was also critical of obedience to management fads when he argued that 'we are fed a diet of simplistic solutions that are based on assumptions of happiness and peace where conflict and organisational politics are aberrations instead of being the norm'. He also pointed out that HR conclusions are frequently based on an unrepresentative sample of case study organisations. Management terms of the new millennium are used conservatively in this text and attention is drawn to the need for a reflective engagement with contemporary language. Engage contemporary ideas, but make up your own mind about how effective they might be in your organisation. A critical approach need not be negative or cynical, because in the search for excellence new HR ideas need to withstand robust scrutiny in pursuit of continuous improvement.

This book provides insights rather than the 'right answers' or 'the one best way'. This approach can be disturbing for some students and managers who may be comfortable with, or accustomed to, more prescriptive and assertive approaches. Practitioner and academic experience leads the authors to the inevitable conclusion that people resourcing is characterised by uncertainty and diversity. Embracing this uncertainty, adopting a critical perspective and seeking a fit with particular organisational circumstances are much more practical and productive. It is useful to begin our people resourcing exploration by examining contemporary changes in the world of work.

CHANGES IN THE WORLD OF WORK

The competitive environment is a major driver of change in the world of work:

> The pressures on organisations to add value, achieve sustained competitive advantage, and respond and adapt quickly and flexibly to new challenges and

---

[1] Overconfidence in own strength.

opportunities are relentless. The responses to these pressures have taken many forms, including new types of organisation, lean, delayered, flexible, process- or project-based, increasing reliance on information technology, and an emphasis on continuous improvement in terms of performance, quality and customer service. The quality of the human or intellectual capital possessed by organisations is seen generally as the key factor in differentiating them from their rivals and achieving superior results. The focus is on the development of business strategies to achieve longer-term goals, and the part played by human resource strategies in general, and reward strategies in particular, in supporting their achievement is now well recognised.   (Armstrong and Brown, 2001)

Clearly some organisations can survive on fairly traditional hierarchical structures to deliver standardised ranges of products and service, but increasingly customer orientation, product differentiation and service support require new forms of organisation. This is requiring no more than 'horses for courses' but it does draw attention to the fact that there is no guarantee that today's organisations will exist indefinitely in their present form, or indeed exist at all. Therefore, there is a case for organisational strategists to recognise drivers for change and for managers to diagnose and be able to act upon the implications of these drivers, because organisational survival may depend on it. This impacts on approaches to managing people and the demands made on people managers, whether they are line managers or HR professionals. It is the context within which people are managed that is changing and HR managers have had to reposition themselves 'in the ever-changing environment of global competition, new technology, and new methods of working and organising work' (Armstrong, 2000). Private sector mantras are sustainable competitive advantage, added value, core competencies and strategic capability, while in the public sector the driving force has been 'best value' and from 2010 cuts in public spending.

Organisational transience, employability and the transactional psychological contract

Organisational fluidity and transience, the 'here today gone tomorrow' perspective, has impacted on employees' feelings of job security. While it may still be statistically possible to demonstrate that in many cases jobs are relatively secure, the expression of organisational and environmental uncertainty, together with the managerially projected imperative of adaptation and change, together with the global recession of 2009, have impacted upon employee perceptions of job permanence. It has also impacted upon the mutuality of obligation between employer and employee with regard to traditional career patterns. The end of the job for life may have been subject to hyperbole, but career patterns are different and twenty-first-century workers may need to engage in continuous development and the refurbishing of skills in order to maintain employability. This tends to promote a loyalty to self rather than intensifying loyalty to the organisation. Worker loyalty may therefore have to be purchased by the employer through the currency of self-development opportunities. Promoting self-development is not just about offering training courses but encompasses lateral career moves, development appraisal and employer responsiveness to worker employability needs. These ideas have links to the concept of the 'war for talent' where employers compete with each other to recruit and retain valuable employees. This competition involves offering not only appropriate financial rewards but also non-financial rewards. Armstrong and Brown

(2001) contend that managers should not underestimate the significance of pay as a means of attracting, retaining and providing tangible rewards to people, because it is essential to get this right since much damage can be done if it is wrong. But as a means of generating long-term commitment and motivation they argue that pay has to be regarded as only part of a whole and that 'it is the non-financial rewards that will ultimately make the difference'. For Armstrong and Brown non-financial rewards include 'recognition, scope to achieve and exercise responsibility, opportunities for growth and development, the intrinsic motivation provided by the work itself and the quality of working life provided by the organisation'. These ideas are explored further in the reward chapters.

This refocusing of the employer–employee relationship can create the transactional psychological contract, replacing a relational psychological contract, whereby both parties sustain the employment relationship all the time there is 'something in it for them'; it is self-centred rather than familial.

Customer aspirations and power

Although phrases like 'the customer is king' and 'delighting our customers' can be accused of being trite, there is little doubt that, among other things, organisations have had to become more customer-focused in order to survive and prosper in competitive environments. Excellence in customer service has always been a differentiating factor, but perhaps what is different now is that customers have had their expectations fuelled and are encouraged to feel empowered to demand quality products and good service. Customers are also more inclined to exercise their power through either the withdrawal of custom or the pursuit of compensation or restitution. Philpott (2001) sums up this customer power: 'intense competition in global and domestic markets forces businesses to keep labour costs in check and/or raise their game in terms of product quality, because empowered consumers want ever-better goods at ever-lower prices.' This rise in customer aspirations is not only a private sector phenomenon, because citizen consumers of public services have also been encouraged, principally through public policy, to perceive themselves as fully fledged customers. It is not for this section to debate the legitimacy of the customer-driven organisation, nor to say how it should be achieved, but merely to draw attention to an issue which has implications for the world of work. Customer aspirations and power are influencing the way organisations are structured and managed and have significant implications for workers who have to contend with the increased emphasis on satisfying customer needs through being more responsive and more flexible, and providing emotional labour – 'the management of emotions and provision of behavioural displays associated with feelings in interactions with customers/clients' (Legge, 2005). Managers need to be aware that emotional labour can lead either to worker alienation, caused by perceived employee inequality in relation to the customer and the managerial imposition of rules on how employees are allowed to feel (Korczynski, 2002), or it can be a major source of job satisfaction where employees have some autonomy in the expression of emotional labour and have socially embedded relationships with customers, for example in the caring services.

The war for talent and the new paternalism

Where shortage labour markets exist they confer power to workers, as sellers of their labour, and enable a greater degree of choice to be exercised over whom to work for and on what terms. This is one element of the war for talent – employers having to compete with each other to secure their human resource needs. The war for talent goes beyond this, as the name suggests, and it is argued that in order to survive in competitive product and service markets employers need to attract and retain the most talented workers, even in difficult macroeconomic conditions. It is through securing the expertise, creativity and innovation of talented people that the organisation will prosper. In service-based and knowledge economies employees are not only the major operating cost but also the source of competitive advantage. Studies by Goleman in the USA, reported by Brown (2001), found that in low-skill work the highest-performing workers contributed twice to three times as much as average workers, while in professional jobs top performers were capable of adding ten times as much value as their co-workers. Kets de Vries, in summing up the competition for talent (Williams, 2000), created an interesting metaphor: 'Today's high performers are like frogs in a wheelbarrow, they can jump out at any time.' The implication is that organisations need to prevent talented employees from escaping. To extend the metaphor, this does not mean putting a lid on the wheelbarrow, it means making the wheelbarrow a sufficiently attractive place to stay. This attractiveness cannot be defined in any generic way because this rather depends on what the frogs want. Williams argues that the answer resides in talent management processes which go beyond ensuring that financial rewards are market competitive and encompasses the whole range of non-financial and environmental rewards. The work environment, depending on the type of work, might include opportunities to exercise discretion, to engage in innovative work, to have opportunities for self-development, to work with interesting people and to be able to share in success in the broadest sense. These features would be in addition to what might be considered more traditional non-financial rewards such as recognition, responsibility and being treated with respect. The role of managers in talent management is to exercise empowering leadership and deploy competencies related to coaching, mentoring and feedback.

In the war for talent the aim of the organisation is to become the employer of choice and seek to project the employer brand to the labour market. Employer branding is defined as 'a targeted, long term strategy to manage the awareness and perceptions of employees, potential employees and related stake-holders with regards to a particular firm' (Backhaus and Tikoo, 2004). Employer branding aims to differentiate the organisation's characteristics as an employer from its competitors in the labour market through highlighting and marketing the unique aspects of the employment package, known as 'the value proposition' – the value/total rewards offered to employees in return for joining and staying with the organisation, and producing high work performance. Some employers seem to be going to extraordinary lengths to retain people and this can be termed the 'new paternalism'. Examples of this include schemes for accumulating supermarket-style reward points, leisure zones at the office, 'duvet days' and concierge services. Concierge services might involve collecting dry cleaning, renewing road tax and buying birthday cards and presents (Cooper, 2000b). Chaudhuri (2000) quotes a new economy organisation as saying:

> If you want to keep staff then you have to look after them. That is why we try and create a campus atmosphere at our office. We have top quality gourmet food available and in the evenings we run cookery classes. You also get Waitrose Direct, a grocery shopping service – who wants to waste their spare time by pushing a supermarket trolley? Every morning workers are offered free fruit with breakfast.

The new paternalism and the war for talent may be fought principally in the dot.com or new economy sectors, despite the recent travails of those sectors. However, the underlying principle in shortage labour markets is that employers need to offer an attractive financial and non-financial rewards package, which incorporates personal choice and flexibility, if they are to compete effectively in the labour market and secure and retain the services of talented people.

Economic recession – a war on talent management strategies?

The extent to which organisations are changing their talent management strategies in the face of a recession was examined by the CIPD late in 2008 and clearly the economic conditions prevailing in 2009 represented a significant change in the world of work. This resulted in both negative and positive effects on talent management activity. So, was it a war *on* talent management strategies? For some organisations the economic challenges were such that development budgets were cut, recruitment was frozen and redundancies became the order of the day (CIPD, 2009b). Changes made to reward strategies included restricted pay increases, or in some cases pay reductions, an increased focus on rewarding top performers only and further interest in individual performance-related pay. The economic conditions also placed pressure on employer branding initiatives, as return on investment in talent management strategies came under closer scrutiny. However, some organisations continued to see talent management as a key survival strategy to differentiate them from competitors and to position the organisation to benefit from an economic upturn. In these cases the economic circumstances sharpened the priorities in relation to:

- developing in-house talent through using the internal labour market;
- focusing on essential development related to business needs;
- seizing opportunities provided by the labour market to recruit key talent; and
- increasing the focus on employee retention,

whilst subjecting cost-effectiveness to greater scrutiny. There is no escape from contingency in talent planning, even in a recession. Surplus labour markets confer power on employers, and whilst the war for talent may pause during a recession, at some stage it is likely that 'employers will be faced with skill shortages, an ageing UK population and limits on immigration' (Taylor, 2009) and the power balance may change again. This view is endorsed by the Economist Intelligence Unit (2008):

> Finding and retaining talent is tough and is going to get tougher. While a global economic slowdown, with its attendant lay-off, may provide temporary respite in some industries, falling birth-rates, an increasingly demanding workforce and greater competition for talent from emerging-market firms will continue to pile.

We have endeavoured to draw attention, no more than that, to a number of contextual features in the changing world of work and by way of summary these are listed, with others, in Exhibit 1.1. These have been given limited treatment in this chapter principally because further changes in the world of work might render them obsolete. It is up to the informed practitioner or manager to keep up to date and be able to analyse changes in the world of work and anticipate the implications for organisations, for managers and for workers. The evolution of HR can be attributed to the changing business environment and changes in the world of work (Ulrich *et al.*, 2008) and HR

EXHIBIT 1.1 Changes in the world of work: a summary

- Job insecurity perceptions and organisational transience
- New career patterns, concern with employability and the transactional psychological contract
- Customer aspirations and power
- The war for talent, employer branding and the new paternalism
- Globalisation and internationalisation of goods, service, finance, information and workers
- Continuing demographic and labour market change
- ICT exploitation and diffusion, including e-commerce
- Continuing corporate restructuring, takeovers and mergers
- Global recession of 2009 and public spending cuts

professionals are now expected to be business focused and add value to their organisation – knowledge of context is key.

HUMAN RESOURCE MANAGEMENT (HRM)

Changes in the world of work have been matched by developments in HRM practice and it is useful to examine briefly HRM origins and development and contemporary HRM characteristics, before examining the reconfiguration of HR practice and HR roles.

HRM origins and development

Elements of contemporary HRM can be traced back to the human relations movement of the 1930s and the discovery of the social needs of workers, and also the developments in the body of knowledge associated with job satisfaction, motivation and leadership in the 1950s and 1960s in pursuit of increased human performance at work. HRM as a term and an approach to managing people originated in the USA in response to global competitive pressure. In particular, the impressive performance of Japanese organisations stimulated management interest in the ideas of employee commitment and loyalty and their impact on productivity. UK organisations also came under competitive pressures from developed and emerging countries and one response was to import American and Japanese ideas associated with 'human resource management'. These global competitive factors and the rise of the Conservative 'New Right' in the UK in the 1980s contributed to the emergence of a British version of HRM through creating an employment climate based on hostility to collectivism, the deregulation of labour markets and the reassertion of the 'right to manage'. This climate was conducive to the individualist and unitary emphasis of the HRM philosophy. Managerial aspiration became effective human resource utilisation and HRM claimed to put people at the heart of the business, which was something of an indictment, and suggestive of failure, for personnel management practitioners. The 1980s emergence of HRM provoked a long-running debate about whether HRM was a new and distinct, and more

Figure 1.2
A continuum
of personnel
management activity

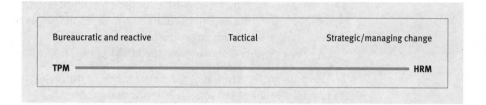

Legge goes on to say that the major HRM debate of the twenty-first century is how
to conceptualise and test the links between HR practice and business performance.
This is not to suggest that HR practice has not changed, because it has; it is just that
these debates about personnel management and HRM differences are now sterile.
However, it does remain useful to identify the characteristics and key elements of contemporary HRM practice in the twenty-first century.

effective, form of managing people, and generated many models which juxtaposed
'traditional' personnel management with 'new' HRM. A common theme was that
personnel management was associated with short-term, tactical practices and HRM
emphasised strategic issues and the HR contribution to the business (Figure 1.2). This
continuum was largely an academic construction because business-focused, strategic
personnel management (SPM) could substitute for the term HRM. These debates are
interesting from a historical perspective, but the debate has now moved on and Legge
(2005) crystallises this view:

> Clearly debates that were central to UK HRM research even 10 years ago – for
> example 'is HRM different from personnel management?', 'Why has HRM emerged?'
> – are now moribund. This is partly due to US dominance in setting research agendas
> . . . and partly due to an established consensus on the issues involved. There is little
> point in discussing the niceties of the differences between personnel management
> and HRM when, in the US, HRM is just another term for personnel management.
> In any case it was a bit of a straw man debate. Whether HRM was considered to be
> different from personnel management – in the UK at least – largely depended on
> the point of comparison.

Legge goes on to say that the major HRM debate of the twenty-first century is how
to conceptualise and test the links between HR practice and business performance.
This is not to suggest that HR practice has not changed, because it has; it is just that
these debates about personnel management and HRM differences are now sterile.
However, it does remain useful to identify the characteristics and key elements of contemporary HRM practice in the twenty-first century.

The characteristics and key elements of contemporary HRM

Contemporary HRM practice tends to exhibit philosophical characteristics that may
include:

- the belief that investment in people is good business, because *people* make the
  difference to organisational performance;
- an emphasis on the alignment of the objectives of the individual employee with
  those of the organisation;
- the right to manage is legitimised by the need for organisations to survive in
  competitive environments;
- a unitary or neo-unitary employment relations frame of reference consisting of
  harmony, consensus, commitment and shared employer and employee interests;
- the alignment of the HR function firmly with managerial interests, requiring the
  HR practitioner to enact a 'business partnership' role.

There is clearly a contrast here with pluralistic frames of reference that are based more on the inherent nature and inevitability of conflict in the employment relationship and focus on how conflict can be productively reconciled.

Five key elements emanate from the HRM philosophy:

1 The strategic integration of HR management with corporate strategy.
2 The devolution of HR activities to line managers.
3 The pursuit of employee commitment and engagement.
4 Extending worker flexibility.
5 The active management of corporate culture.

The strategic integration of HR management

The aim of strategic integration is to achieve a close relationship between business strategy and HR strategy (vertical integration) and also to ensure that HR activities are mutually reinforcing (horizontal integration) – in other words, the pursuit of business-focused HR management which creates and sustains competitive advantage. HR management is therefore directly concerned with the managerial needs and not primarily with the needs of employees. The managerial argument is that the benefits of corporate success based on employee alignment with managerial interests 'trickle down' to employees, so creating a mutuality of interests and benefits. Strategic integration can elevate the standing and influence of the HR function, spice up the image and provide a stark contrast to perceptions of HR as a 'trash can' administrative and welfare function which hinders line managers through procedural control.

The devolution of HR activities to line managers

The devolution rationale is that HR management is critical to effective business performance and therefore needs to be enacted by empowered line managers who are responsible for coordinating and directing all resources, including human resources, towards organisational success. Responsibilities for HR activities, such as recruitment and selection, reward, grievance and discipline, managing diversity and so on, are devolved to line managers who exercise greater autonomy and authority. This clearly has implications for HR practitioners. It can be perceived as a threat to the HR function by removing a *raison d'être*, with negative consequences in terms of power and influence, or it can be viewed as liberating by freeing up HR practitioners to adopt an expert advisory and consultancy role and a strategic people management focus (Storey, 1995; Harris *et al.*, 2002; CIPD, 2007). As far back as 1998 Hall and Torrington reported that HR managers tended to be enthusiastic about the transfer of activities to line managers, although some concerns were expressed about letting go of familiar and enjoyable tasks only to be faced with the vulnerability and uncertainties of the advisory and consultancy role. Line manager perspectives can also be mixed, with devolution of HR activities being perceived as either empowering or merely unwelcome extra work. Devolution to line managers can have dysfunctional HR consequences, such as a lack of opportunity to learn from HR specialists, inefficiency and duplication as each line manager invents new methods of HR management, lack of consistency in employee treatment and working conditions, and unstructured *ad hoc* HR practices. Successful devolution therefore requires competent and confident line managers, advisory support from HR professionals and continuous management development. Devolution to the line is unlikely ever to be total in anything but very small organisations and the extent of devolution will be contingent upon organisational circumstances. HR activities have always been devolved to some degree and it remains a question of achieving an appropriate balance. Some corporate-level HR activity is always necessary in order to ensure compliance with the law, fairness and consistency in treatment, and the dissemination of effective practice (Harris *et al.*, 2002); indeed, it can be argued that increased employment regulation and a willingness by employees to litigate produces a counter-force to the devolution of HR by reinforcing the HR specialist role in keeping the organisation out of trouble and away from employment tribunals. The demise of the HR profession is not an inevitable consequence of devolution; in fact, it may bring HR specialists and line managers closer together through having to work in partnership.

Employee commitment and engagement

This is pursued on the assumption that committed employees will willingly engage with corporate goals and work flexibly to achieve them. Employee commitment is delivered by a psychological contract which is nurtured through individualistic involvement practices, increasingly given a positive spin and referred to as modern human resource practices or progressive people management practices (Caulkin, 2001), and based on shared values which incorporate the internalisation of organisational objectives. The performance lever of management is therefore the commitment rather than the control of employees. However, because employee commitment is consciously secured through managerial interventions, contemporary HR practice faces the charge of being more controlling than is at first apparent – is it really 'employee manipulation dressed up as mutuality'? (Fowler, 1987; Pfeffer, 2007). The requirement for committed employees is also evident in the quality movement with its emphasis on employee identification with corporate values, the pursuit of continuous improvement and excellence, and the need for high individual performance levels.

Extending worker flexibility

Based on the idea that adaptive organisations need adaptive workers, this requires workers to be flexible about the 'what', 'how', 'when' and 'why' of performing work in order that activity can be managerially directed towards the achievement of organisational objectives. Flexibility occurs in many interrelated forms, including functional, numerical, temporal and financial, and these together with concepts of core, periphery and tertiary workers are discussed in Chapter 4. Flexibility has the potential to be an important HR lever for the effective utilisation of human resources, but the extent to which it is a strategic response or a collation of reactive, *ad hoc* and cost-driven measures is problematic to establish. There are inherent tensions and problems associated with the pursuit of flexibility. Flexible workforces and flexible working may actually contribute to instability, discontinuity and fragmentation by creating status divides between groups of workers, who may be contracted on different arrangements, and also by demanding a flexibility commitment from employees which is perceived as excessive and therefore dysfunctional to the employment relationship. In other words, flexibility demands on employees can damage the psychological contract. This is not to say that worker flexibility is a bad thing, but just to draw attention to the possibility that in excess it could undermine the organisational cohesion which may be necessary for optimum quality and performance.

The management of corporate culture

Culture is 'taken for granted assumptions, beliefs, meanings and values enacted and shared by organisational members' (Gowler and Legge, 1986). Culture is the glue which holds together contemporary HR management practice and therefore needs to be actively managed to secure the identification of employee interests with those of the organisation. Managing corporate culture means creating shared values and a sense of purpose. The creation of these shared values and the communication of the corporate vision are invariably dependent on strong, often charismatic leadership and hence the contemporary HR emphasis on the quality, and the reward, of senior managers. The adherence to corporate values by employees is encouraged through the reward strategy and supported by HR policies which communicate the cultural values desired by management, and indeed seek to limit 'deviant' worker behaviour. The management of culture harbours tensions because there are doubts about the extent to which culture can actually be managed. While *corporate culture* and the associated values can be projected by management, the *organisational culture* is created and sustained by individuals and groups working in the organisation. Organisational cultures are not necessarily homogeneous and in reality there may be a collection of subcultures with some exhibiting 'resigned behavioural compliance' to projected corporate values, because the alternative is unemployment or diminished rewards (Legge, 2005). A second cultural tension is between a strong culture and the adaptive organisation – a strong corporate culture may militate against responsiveness to environmental influences through being resistant to change. Nonetheless, the management of corporate culture is a strong plank of contemporary HRM.

THE CHANGING ROLE OF THE HR PROFESSIONAL

HR business partnership, as a concept, emerged from Ulrich's *Human Resource Champions* (1997). Far from seeing business partners as a select group of strategists Ulrich describes business partnership as 'an overriding feature of the key roles that HR professionals play in organisations'. The key message was that instead of focusing on what *HR does*, HR professionals should focus on what *HR delivers* in terms of results that enrich the organisation's value to customers, investors and employees. For Ulrich the question was not 'Should we do away with HR?' but 'What should we do with HR?' and he advocated creating a new role and agenda that focused not on traditional HR activities, but on business outcomes. More specifically, Ulrich argued that HR could deliver organisational excellence in four ways:

1 HR should become a partner with senior and line managers in strategy execution.

2 HR should become an expert in the way HR work is organised and executed.

3 HR should become a champion for employees, representing employee concerns to senior management and working to increase employee commitment to the organisation and their ability to deliver business results.

4 HR should become an agent of continuous transformation, shaping processes and a culture that together improve an organisation's capacity for change.

Ulrich recognised that this was a radical departure from a mainly 'policy policing and regulatory watchdog role' and that the new agenda would mean that 'every one of HR's activities would need, in some concrete way, to help the company better serve its customers or increase shareholder value'. Armstrong (2000) was helpful in articulating the notion of the business partnership, and also pointed out that it was not a new idea:

> Another concept often associated with HRM is that of the HR director as a business partner or manager. This idea is generally attributed to Ulrich but was advanced many years before by Tyson who suggested that: 'Personnel specialists as business managers integrate their activities with top management and ensure that they serve a long term strategic purpose and have the capacity to see the broad picture and to see how their role can help to achieve the company's business objectives'. In 1993 the HR director of Motorola stated that, 'I have agreed with my teams that we will be business partners in each business; we will have the understanding of what is going on to converse knowledgeably with any of the business people'.

But the notion of being a business partnership has risen in prominence:

> There have been a number of dimensions to the changing face of the HR function over recent years . . . there has been a move to increase the value HR offers its business customers. This has often centred on the desire for the function to be more strategic and business-focused in its contribution. One of the factors that allegedly has held back the function is that too much time has been devoted to administrative activities and insufficient time to transformational ones.   (CIPD, 2007)

In essence the philosophy of the business partner HR role concerns being a business manager first and a functional HR specialist second. From this perspective there is no intrinsic value in HR activities *per se*; it is in supporting business objectives that the HR specialist establishes a *raison d'être*. Clearly a prerequisite of a business partnership role is to ensure that HR policies and processes are characterised by effective administration, fairness and equity, compliance with the law and effective practice, all of which requires high levels of professional competence; but, in order to add real value, it is argued, the HR business partner is expected to appreciate and understand corporate strategy, identify with the objectives of their managerial colleagues and contribute to the optimisation of people performance, and thereby organisational performance. Business results are therefore the dominant concern of the HR business partner. Business partnership is not confined to director-level HR roles; it is an HR philosophy that can be adopted by all levels of HR practitioner.

Within the business partnership model, line managers and senior managers become the internal customers of the HR practitioner and the HR function, and managerial needs therefore take precedence over the needs of other stakeholders. The business partnership role for HR practitioners therefore requires the adoption of a managerial ideology and the HR practitioner firmly plants his or her feet in the managerial camp, and consequently needs to demonstrate added value to the business. This tends to intensify some of the ambiguities of the HR role, because being a business partner is potentially in conflict with ideas associated with being an employee champion (the HR role often perceived by employees) and is not entirely compatible with notions of professional status since the HR business partner's allegiance is primarily to the employing organisation rather than to a profession. The business partnership role may enable the HR practitioner to jettison some of the functional activities, such as recruitment, training and discipline, through devolving them to line managers. This may create space to be a key player in performance management, quality and continuous improvement, reward strategy, organisational development and driving change. Extracts from HR job advertisements illustrate this (emphasis added):

HR Manager – You will work in **partnership with the business managers** to develop and implement a **proactive** HR function. This is a highly challenging role which will test your ability to deliver best in class HR solutions that **add value** to a demanding and **quality focused** business.

Human Resources Associate – Reporting to the HR Group Leader and **working closely with line management**, you will provide **value added support to the business**.

Human Resources Manager – You will ensure that HRM initiatives **complement the company's strategies and business plans**.

HR Business Partner – of vital importance will be your ability **to build relationships with line managers**, helping them to become self-sufficient on HR issues.

HR Business Partners – **think strategically** and have first class **influencing, interpersonal and change management skills** to ensure that HR is aligned to business needs.

Ulrich and Brockbank (2005a) proposed a consolidated HR framework which incorporates five HR roles – HR leader (at the centre), strategic partner, human capital developer, functional expert and employee advocate. In contrast to the business partner concept Ulrich and Brockbank's argument is that *each* of the five roles needs to be enacted by the HR professional in order to deliver value to the organisation.

HR leaders lead and value their own function and develop other leaders in the organisation. Effective HR leadership involves setting clear goals, being decisive, communicating effectively, managing change and defining results in terms of value added for investors, customers, line managers and employees.

Strategic partners bring know-how about business change, consulting and learning to their relationships with line managers. They partner managers in reaching their goals through strategy formulation and direction.

Human capital developers recognise people as critical assets and are concerned with developing this human capital through promoting learning opportunities to enable employees, and the organisation, to be successful in the future.

Functional experts possess a body of HR knowledge and an HR toolkit which enable them to provide HR solutions aligned to business needs now and in the future. Some HR practices are delivered through administrative efficiency, including the exploitation of e-HR, and others are delivered through policies and interventions.

Employee advocates listen to employee concerns and empathise with them, while at the same time adopting a customer, shareholder and managerial perspective and communicating to employees what is expected of them to be successful in creating value. Advocacy involves maintaining a reputation for fairness, equity, managing diversity and promoting mutual respect.

Clearly the degree of enactment of each of the roles will be influenced by the precise nature of the HR role and the organisational contingencies. However, Arkin (2007) reports that Ulrich describes 'business partnership as an overriding feature of all the key roles that HR professionals play in organisations'. The apparent reconfiguration of the HR role, however described, does appear to have 'a clear direction of travel from a function historically focused on rules, administration and service provision to a function based on business issues and working with line managers to deliver performance targets' (CIPD, 2003). Brown and Emmott (2003) expressed something similar: 'The traditional, reactive, fire-fighting mode of HR is being eroded in favour of a more high powered function displaying specialist expertise and a clear business strategy mission.' In order to stimulate further debate, and by calling upon the research of the writers referenced in this chapter, we have synthesised a summary of past and future behaviours of the HR role in Exhibit 1.2.

EXHIBIT 1.2 HR behaviours

Past HR role behaviours	Future HR role behaviours
Personnel management as a functional specialism	The HR function to be integrated with other business functions
Concern with administration and personnel processes	Exploitation of e-HR, self-service HR and HR outsourcing
Policing the line managers	Enabling the line managers
Obsession with legal compliance, rules and procedures	An adding-value business focus that aims to minimise bureaucracy
Ensuring employees receive a fair day's pay for a fair day's work	Rewarding performance, desired employee behaviours and the exercise of discretionary effort
Caring for employees	Valuing employees as human capital
Delivering training	Unlocking talent through multiple learning interventions
HR as a matter of faith and a focus on *what HR does*	Concern with HR performance indicators and HR metrics that measure *what HR delivers*
Concern with 'doing things right' in the here and now	Concern with 'doing the right things' now and in the future to contribute to organisational sustainability

Criteria for HR success

According to the CIPD (2004) three broad areas are essential to HR's success: the support of senior management, the alignment of HR strategy with the organisation's strategy, and line management support. These criteria are not mutually exclusive.

Senior management support. The perception of the HR function will influence the importance given to HR and will affect HR focus and ability to deliver. According to Maxwell and Farquharson (2008) having an understanding of the attitude of senior managers towards the HR function is important and, as Purcell (2001: 4) put it, 'what HR can do, is to a degree, a function of what it is allowed or invited to do by the dominant coalition in the firm'. The HR strategy of the organisation will not only be determined by management perceptions of HR roles, but also on the attitude and perception of the HR professional.

The alignment of HR and organisational strategy. Integrating HR and business strategy is 'fundamental to achieving business excellence' (Briggs and Keogh, 1999) and the effective management of talent is key to ensuring that stakeholders' expectations are met, and is therefore a source of sustained competitive advantage (CIPD, 2004). Somewhat surprisingly Caldwell (2008) declared that despite the advantages of the integration of HR and business strategy, organisations have been slow on the uptake and there remains limited empirical evidence to demonstrate its presence in organisational practice.

Line management support. As HR becomes more strategic in focus, line management support is crucial to success in strategy development and execution, and ultimately in its ability to create value to the organisation. However, the devolution of HR activities to the line is viewed with mixed reaction, with some line managers enthusiastic about taking on HR responsibilities, whereas others are displeased at the prospect (Gautam and Davis, 2007). For devolution to be successful, line managers must be given the necessary training, support and time to carry out HR activities. Francis and Keegan (2006) argue that HR runs the risk of losing employee confidence and trust by releasing transactional HR activities to line managers who may be unprepared or unwilling to take on the responsibilities. However, the trend for devolution continues and, according to Ulrich and Brockbank (2005b), 'HR must sensitise line managers to the importance of their role in achieving business objectives'.

Measuring HR performance through using HR metrics is also important and Exhibit 1.3 provides a case study approach in the NHS – see also Exhibit 11.2 and the balanced scorecard.

The HR professional map – HR for the twenty-first century

According to the CIPD there has been a significant shift in the focus of HR. Whilst recognising that the profession is at its most mature point yet, the CIPD assert that the concern should be with improving organisational performance by building sustainable capability, not just delivering on the day-to-day HR part of the role, although that remains important. An extensive programme of consultation with senior HR professionals and other leaders in business, the public services and management education informed the development of an HR professional map in 2009 and the clear message is that in order to deliver 'sustainable capability', HR practitioners need to:

EXHIBIT 1.3   Workforce scorecard metrics for business-focused HR performance reporting

Portsmouth Hospitals NHS Trust (PHT) is a large acute trust with an annual turnover of £400m, a multi-professional workforce of 7000 employees and provides emergency, general and specialist healthcare to more than 250 000 people each year, across three geographically displaced sites. The requirement to consistently meet national access targets and to deliver recurrent financial surpluses creates a significant challenge for the senior leadership team. For those charged with the effective utilisation of the Trust's diverse workforce, this challenge is manifest in the need to establish a business-focused HR performance reporting system. The aim of this system is to ensure there is a clear 'line of sight' between the Trust's HR interventions and the impact the workforce has on service reform, productivity improvement (and hence patient care), and overall organisational efficiency. Adopting a metrics reporting system that is more scientifically based, well presented and aligned with core business objectives raises the profile of the HR function and increases its organisational impact. A persuasive argument for establishing business-focused metrics is that they enable HR practitioners to converse better in the language of business, by providing a basis for defining:

- key measures associated with the workforce;
- trends in performance, over time, as the metrics are tracked;
- measurable workforce outputs and areas of weakness or underperformance;
- feedback about measurement methods and the metrics to be tracked;
- and also determining appropriate interventions to address deteriorating or under-achievement.

Therefore, the development of any reporting metrics needs to be based upon the priorities of the strategic plan and objectives. These define the key business drivers and, in turn, provide the criteria for those metrics that managers most desire to monitor. Processes must also be designed to collate data relevant to the metrics and reduce them to numerical form for presentation and analysis. If the chosen reporting metrics are to be effective in informing and initiating improvements, action must follow analysis – there is little value in measuring and presenting performance data if this information is then not acted upon. The application of the management concept associated with balanced scorecard methodology to human resource management supported the development of a 'workforce scorecard', the objectives of which were threefold, namely:

- to align local workforce strategies and HR interventions with organisational goals;
- to measure the contribution of these strategies and interventions to improved organisational performance and patient and staff experience;
- to support efficiency improvements: increased productivity linked with financial improvement.

PHT metrics are associated with four key perspectives, or 'domains'. These domains are directly linked to the delivery of the Workforce Strategy and all directly influence the Trust's ability to achieve its business objectives, and all are interdependent. This interdependency, together with the strategic aims associated with measuring each of the four domains, is shown below:

(Box continued)

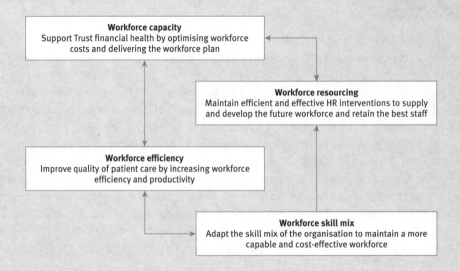

In determining the individual metrics to be included within each of the four domains, a systematic approach was taken. As an essential first step it was necessary to revisit the organisation's core business objectives, since these provide the anchor point for any reporting framework that aims to inform and support the process of continuous improvement. This analysis was conducted in parallel with a review of the Workforce Strategy, to ensure synergy between the two. Having established this alignment, the number and type of metrics to be reported upon was carefully considered. Informed by the views of senior clinical staff and general managers, the collective advice at this stage was 'make it relevant and keep it simple'. This view supported the underpinning principle associated with scorecard methodology, which contends that data should be clearly presented and not overly complex. In other words, the true value of the data lies in their relative simplicity and ability to focus on key measures that really matter. Therefore, only those measures that could demonstrate the 'line of sight' with the achievement of the business objectives, and which could be presented in a straightforward manner and effectively benchmarked, were selected.

Applying this testing process eventually reduced the number of key metrics to four within each domain. Broadly, these are:

substantive workforce; temporary workforce; overtime; total workforce capacity; sickness absence; turnover; unit staff costs; workforce productivity; percentage of staff at particular bands/grades, by specialty (i.e. skill mix); percentage of professionally qualified clinical workforce; recruitment effectiveness; workforce stability; diversity profile; and essential skills training.

For the first time, a measure of the overall 'cost-effectiveness' of the workforce is being provided through both the unit staff costs and workforce productivity metrics. The latter is the product of the total monetary value of all healthcare delivered by the Trust, over the defined period, divided by the total workforce capacity for the same period, and is defined as a monetary value. Supporting a much greater focus on improving workforce productivity through the redesign of services and traditional roles, the skill mix metrics provide an essential starting point for highlighting opportunities for redistributing/rebalancing skills across the organisation.

Source: Adapted from Power, M. (2007) 'Workforce scorecard metrics for business focused HR performance reporting', *CIPD Portsmouth Group HR Bulletin: research and practice*, 2 (3), pp. 11–13. Mark Power, Head of Workforce Performance, Portsmouth Hospitals NHS Trust.

- know their organisations inside out through understanding the drivers of sustainable business performance, and the barriers to achieving it;
- know the main ways in which HR expertise can make an impact and contribute beyond the confines of the traditional role;
- have the behavioural skills to turn knowledge into effective action.

This represents 'a shift from a primary focus on supporting line managers to manage their people well, to a primary focus on ensuring the organisation has the sustainable capability it needs to deliver its aims both today and in the future' (Orme, 2009). The HR map charts the profession from three perspectives: functional specialisms/ professional areas, levels of competence and key behaviours. This provides the basis for development programmes and qualifications, and the map is also used as a diagnostic tool and for career planning. The functional specialisms/professional areas are:

1 Strategy, insights and solutions
2 Leading and managing the function
3 Organisation design
4 Resourcing and talent planning
5 Organisation development
6 Learning and talent development
7 Performance and reward
8 Employee relations
9 Employee engagement
10 Information and service delivery

There are four levels of competence stretching from Band 1 for an entry-level professional to Band 4 to reflect the essential expertise for a director-level professional. Within each band there is a description of the knowledge (what you need to know) and activities (what you need to be able to do), but complemented with a definition of 'how' it needs to be done (the behaviours).

The eight key behaviours are: curious; decisive thinker; skilled influencer; driven to deliver; collaborative; personally credible; courage to challenge; and role model. Each behaviour is then broken down into various components, which are called upon in different ways depending on the seniority of the role. The behaviour 'courage to challenge' is illustrated in this example:

Band 4 (HR director)   Acts as a 'mirror' to colleagues, challenging actions that are inconsistent with espoused values, beliefs and promises.

Band 3   Holds own position determinedly and with courage when it is the right thing to do, even when those in power have divergent views.

Band 2   Observes, listens, questions and challenges to ensure a full discussion.

Band 1 (entry level)   Uses questions to explore and understand others' viewpoints.

By bringing the 10 professional areas, the 8 behaviours and the 4 bands of competence together, the CIPD claim to have created the most comprehensive picture yet of contemporary and business-focused HR activity (www.cipd.co.uk/hr-profession-map).

HR STRATEGY AND PEOPLE RESOURCING – THE FUNDAMENTALS

Perspectives and theories relating to HR strategy are explored in the next chapter but it is useful to introduce the fundamentals of a strategic HR approach from a managerial perspective. These are as follows:

1   Linking HR practices to the achievement of corporate strategy and business objectives.

2   Deploying HR practices to lever employee contribution and performance in a desired direction; for example, performance management and culture management in the areas of customer focus and responsiveness to change.

3   Linking HR practices to each other to create complementarities in the pursuit of synergy and increased potency.

4   Aligning the HR function with the business, reinforcing managerial prerogative and emphasising that organisations are employer and not employee led.

5   A belief that proactive 'good' HR practices are critical to organisational success and the ability to compete and survive; a 'people make the difference' philosophy.

Strategic integration can be vertical and horizontal. Vertical integration means that HR practices and activities are designed to support the achievement of corporate objectives and horizontal integration relates to the internal coherence of HR practices so that HR practices are complementary and 'bundled' rather than in conflict; for example, broad-banded pay structures that are complementary to flatter organisational structures and to career and development imperatives. It is not necessary to have a grand plan to be strategic, although clearly a plan provides direction. Torrington and Hall (1998) were quite revealing on HR strategy (emphasis added):

> The influence of business need was also apparent in the nature of the strategy that was produced. Few organisations looked towards the personnel function to produce an integrated HR strategy in response to business needs, but looked towards a strategic response to identified key business issues. HR strategy thus tended to be in many cases reactive rather than proactive, and was built up in a piecemeal rather than holistic way. None of our interviewees identified HR strategy as driving business strategy, but many identified business strategy as driving HR strategy. This demonstrates the personnel function being responsive to business need, and moves

us on from the situation of the personnel manager hankering after a nicely-packaged HR strategy driven by lofty ideals distinct from commercial imperatives. The internally integrated, proactive HR strategy seems no more than an ideal to dream of. *A stream of strategic decisions is needed rather than a strategy*. We found *evidence of strategic thinking rather than written HR strategy*. The critical issue is whether what constitutes the HR strategy, piecemeal as it is, is simply directed by the business strategy or whether other influences are recognised and incorporated, so that a distinct, authoritative line of thinking on HR issues is integrated with business strategy.

In its broadest sense, therefore, HR strategy is fundamentally about adopting a strategic state of mind, rather than necessarily being extensively engaged in strategic activities or in the design of a grand strategic plan. This strategic state of mind can be enacted at different levels depending on the HR position and the potential of the individual:

Level 1   Strategic awareness
Level 2   Strategic thinking
Level 3   Strategic decision-making
Level 4   Strategic planning

Strategic awareness is actively seeking knowledge of the corporate strategy, and HR strategy if it exists; strategic thinking is building this acquired knowledge into day-to-day HR activities; and strategic decision-making is actively incorporating strategic knowledge into making HR decisions. Strategic planning is thinking ahead and predicting the strategic consequences of any HR action.

ADDING VALUE THROUGH HR PRACTICES

HR practitioners may have always known intuitively that well-managed people will work better and thereby influence the financial performance of the organisations in which they are employed, but HR practitioners are under pressure to demonstrate that they add value and contribute to the bottom line. As Wright *et al.* (2004) put it, 'HR practitioners have increasingly become concerned with being able to demonstrate and convince managers that HR is providing added-value in order to gain equal footing in the decision making process.' Nirvana for the HR profession must therefore be evidence of a demonstrable and causal link between people management and organisational performance. The search for proof is being pursued with energy and vigour. There is a distinction between line manager HR activity and functional activity by HR specialists; as Guest and King (2001) put it, 'good people management was as much about the way front line supervisors, team leaders and middle managers engaged with their staff as it was about implementing particular HR practices'. In this vein Purcell *et al.* (2000) are assertive about the link: 'The existence of a link between the way people are managed and business performance is now well established.' Guest and King (2001) agree: 'There is a link between all types of financially successful UK firms and the presence of an HR function.' Having said that, Guest and King go on to say that despite this finding, chief executives perceive line managers as the key to effective people management. This casts HR practitioners firmly in the role of supporting the line.

Purcell *et al.* (2003) present a 'People and Performance Model' (also discussed in Chapter 2 in relation to human resources strategy), which asserts that employee performance is a function of Ability + Motivation + Opportunity (AMO). For people to perform better they must have the *ability* to do so because they have the necessary knowledge and skills, must be *motivated* to do the work well and be given the *opportunity* to deploy their skills in contributing to team and organisational success. The Purcell *et al.* research identified that high AMO was stimulated by 11 interrelated HR policies: sophisticated recruitment and selection, learning and development, teamworking, an emphasis on providing career opportunities, information sharing and two-way communication, involvement in decision-making, performance and development appraisal, pay satisfaction, job security, job challenge and autonomy, and work–life balance opportunities. Purcell *et al.* identified that line managers had a critical role in implementing and enacting these policies through effective leadership and where this was the case employees became committed to the organisation, were motivated and had job satisfaction which in turn encouraged the exercise of discretionary effort and high performance. The Purcell *et al.* model is therefore also making the case for the deployment of HR practices as the route to organisational success. Purcell *et al.* recognise that an assertion that the existence and the quality of HR policies *per se* causes the chain reaction to desirable outcomes would be naïve, because the line managers, as the employment relations interface, need effective HR management skills in order to effectively apply the HR policies. Line managers are therefore critical in creating and transmitting impressions of the organisation, making jobs interesting, dispensing autonomy and encouraging employees to feel valued. The Purcell *et al.* research resonates with research into high performance work practices (HPWP). A widely accepted definition of HPWP is that they are:

> a set of complementary work practices covering three broad areas and cover *high involvement practices* such as self-directed teams, quality circles and the sharing of company information; *human resource practices* such as sophisticated recruitment processes, performance appraisals, work redesign and mentoring; and, *reward and commitment practices* such as a range of financial rewards, family friendly policies, job rotation and flexible working.   (DTI, 2005)

The DTI research illustrated that high HPWP adoption was linked to higher organisational performance, while recognising that different sectors need to adopt different bundles of HPWPs to achieve the different business outcomes.

What do we make of this research so far? First, that the profession is even more convinced that effective HR practices and a professional HR function add value and contribute to bottom-line performance. Second, others, including senior managers, are still to be entirely convinced. Third, we are still some way towards articulating the bundle of HR practices that will lift corporate performance. Although, much of the current HR research appears to be pointing in the same direction – good HR equals good business.

e-HR, THE THREE-LEGGED MODEL AND THE OUTSOURCING OF HR ACTIVITIES

e-HR is also addressed in Chapter 5, but as part of the exploration of the changing HR role it is useful to introduce it in this scene-setting chapter, together with a brief

Figure 1.3 Three-legged model

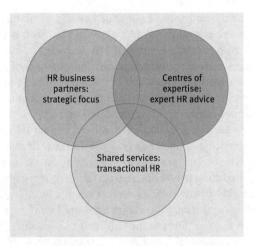

discussion on HR outsourcing. Clearly, for small to medium-sized businesses the potential of e-HR is constrained, whereas in multi-site, multinational organisations (the ones we tend to hear about in relation to e-HR) the potential for exploitation of the technology is much greater. Fundamentally e-HR is about using email, the Internet and organisational intranets to facilitate and mediate HR activities, as well as exploiting it as a learning and development medium. e-HR tends to be linked to a restructuring of HR activities to include HR shared service centres, where call centres provide HR services to employees and managers, and it may therefore be more appropriate to use the term e-enabled HR. This has led to the reconfiguration of HR activity in some organisations to what has become known as the 'three-legged model' (Reilly, Tamkin and Broughton, 2007). This is exposed in Figure 1.3 and the three legs are:

1 *Shared HR services* – administrative and transactional HR activities, including employee enquiries, which are call centre and web based. Business units 'share' the HR services with potential cost benefits through economies of scale.

2 *HR business partners* – HR professionals focused on strategic development and change management through working closely with senior managers and business units.

3 *Centres of excellence* – HR experts offer specific expertise and advice in HR activities such as recruitment, reward, employee relations, and learning and development in order to provide specialist support to front line managers, to business partners and to shared HR services (Reilly *et al.*, 2007).

The shared services leg has been adopted more by 'larger organisations needing strong, effective and efficient delivery of transactional HR, through a call centre and web portal. The *centres of excellence* have come to represent teams with specific HR expertise that can develop products and services to meet the needs of the organisation' (Griffin *et al.*, 2009). The third leg of the business partner 'can cover anyone from a single individual providing strategic advice to an organisation's top leadership team, to a simply re-branded HR adviser' (Griffin *et al.*, 2009).

Outsourcing as a term means no more than resourcing an HR activity outside the organisation. There has always been outsourcing, prime examples being the use of recruitment agencies and training consultants. The reasons for outsourcing are generally related to cost-efficiency or to the buying in of expertise not available within the organisation. The current emphasis on the strategic role of the HR function provides another driver, and that is to outsource a range of HR activities in order to liberate the HR function to operate as a strategic business partner unencumbered with routine HR work. Within the changing world of work and the hunger for economic efficiency the outsourcing of activities to bring corporate advantage has become a normal managerial pursuit. Organisations outsource cleaning, catering, security, IT support, accounting, legal advice and marketing, *inter alia* – HR activity is no different. HR outsourcing is an opportunity rather than a universal solution and constitutes a part of the ongoing evaluation of the HR role and contribution to the business. In any case, the in-house HR team needs to maintain professional expertise in order to manage and retain jurisdiction over external HR providers. The adoption of a three-legged model of HR provides an outsourcing opportunity in relation to shared services. Ulrich and Brockbank (2005b) argue that large organisations will tend to outsource 'large bundles of HR transactions to increasingly viable vendors, while smaller firms will probably outsource discrete practices'.

CASE STUDY   Call centres in the financial services sector – just putting you on hold . . .

UniBank

UniBank was founded in the West Midlands during the late nineteenth century and by 1990 had become a traditional national high-street bank with branches in most UK towns and cities. Its main business is in personal banking and financial services for individual customers and small businesses. It has subsidiary business units which handle personal insurance, mortgages and share-dealing, but these are managed separately from the high-street banking concern.

The development of UniCall

By the mid 1990s all traditional banks were feeling the pressure of fierce competition in financial services, intensified by the arrival of new entrants such as supermarkets and other well-known brands. With an eye to the growing commercial success of direct line banking organisations, UniBank decided to enter the telephone banking sector, and has recently been able to improve shareholder value by switching a significant proportion of its general account management and enquiry activity to a dedicated call centre, named UniCall. This resulted in the closure of many smaller, unprofitable branches and the consequent need for redundancies. UniBank attempted to redeploy existing employees where possible, but also needed to recruit new staff to work in the national call centre. True to its origins, and mindful of the relatively high unemployment rates in the West Midlands, UniBank decided to locate UniCall just outside Birmingham. However, none of this was achieved easily, since the press and public expressed concern and dismay at the closure of so many small local branches, and there was strong trade union resistance to the job losses. Thus is it true to say that currently staff morale is low, that there is considerable anxiety and discontent with the new arrangements, and that the staff at UniCall itself are beginning to feel somewhat exposed as the debate about branch closures rages in the media.

The work at UniCall

At present UniCall employs 150 staff and operates 24 hours a day, 7 days a week on a 4-shift system. The majority of staff work on the daytime shifts. Staff work at sets of 4 desks, wear headsets with microphones to take the calls and operate terminals with access to all the required account and product information. Supervisors are responsible for each shift and there are two call centre managers and a deputy manager, one of whom is always either available at the centre or can be contacted by mobile phone. Pay scales are standardised; there is a starting rate of £15 000 which applies to newly recruited staff during their 6 months probationary period, after which they are placed at the bottom of a 4-point scale which rises by increments to £20 000. Employees proceed up the scale by annual increments until they reach the top point, after which further increases are dependent on promotion to supervisory or managerial work. Supervisory grades start at £22 000 and rise similarly to £27 500. There is no performance management system in place, and as yet the idea of an appraisal system has not been developed. UniCall is located in pleasant, airy open-plan offices which are nicely decorated and have good basic facilities including a snack and sandwich service, a rest room, a separate smoking room, and a kitchenette for the preparation of hot drinks and snacks; thus the 'hygiene' factors are fairly good.

Problems with UniCall

The history of UniCall has been mixed. After a patchy first 6 months, it seems to be picking up business very rapidly as customers begin to see the advantages of this service. While this is encouraging, it has led to a new range of problems. The existing number of UniCall staff is now clearly inadequate for the growing demands for the telephone banking service. Recruitment is under way but this is likely to place existing induction and initial training programmes under strain. Complaints are beginning to be heard from customers who are being 'put on hold' for anything from 30 seconds to 5 minutes during busy periods (especially early in the evenings and at weekends).

There are also problems associated with the use of the computer system itself; these centre on the apparent inability of some staff to extract accurate information about relatively simple enquiries, or the length of time that such interrogations take. Monitoring systems which measure the number and duration of different types of call add weight to these complaints, with enquiries relating to standing orders and direct debit arrangements appearing to take up to 50 per cent longer than they should according to the authors of the software. There have been customer complaints about rudeness, staff's apparent inflexibility when dealing with complex account problems and the fact that different operators seem to give different answers to the same questions. There are additional knock-on effects for customers who prefer to visit their local branch. Here the problem seems to be that branch staff themselves have to telephone the call centre in order to deal with certain very simple transactions such as opening new accounts, and that they too are often kept 'on hold' to the annoyance of clients and their own considerable frustration.

The call centre staff are also beginning to complain about aspects of the work. UniBank carried out a staff survey 6 months after the start of the operation and again after a further 3 months and the findings of the second survey reflect the increased pressures by revealing a higher degree of discontent than that noted in the first survey. Workers say that they often feel very isolated from their colleagues, which leads to a certain unhealthy rivalry both within and between shifts. Many feel that they are 'like battery hens', working in an intensive manner, with little control over the number and type of calls which they receive

(Box continued)

and limited opportunity to recover from one call before receiving the next. They are also under constant surveillance, with calls being monitored both to determine the productivity of the operators, and to check the accuracy of the information given and general quality of their work. This causes some resentment, and it appears that the operators often find informal ways to control the number of calls they receive and the time between calls. Some groups have worked out a method by which calls can be redirected to one of their number, thus allowing them all to appear busy while only one is actively taking calls. This way they take it in turns to give themselves an informal break from calls while still giving the appearance of working. On occasion this technique has been used to 'soak' new or unpopular members of staff, who find themselves the victims of such redirection, not realising that they are the only person on their team who is actually busy and appears to have a backlog. Supervisors are aware that this is happening, but find it very difficult to detect.

Some of the redeployed staff remain unhappy with the type of service they are being asked to give and find it too impersonal. On the other hand, some of the new recruits, especially in the younger age groups, believe that they work better and more effectively than other staff, and are beginning to feel that the standardised pay structure does not recognise or reward their individual skills and efficiency. Some are concerned about their employability and want formal recognition for their skills which would be transferable to other similar employers, of which there is an increasing number in the region. Indeed, UniCall has already lost a number of its staff to other local call centres which have a more varied clientele and better career prospects.

UniCall and UniLine, the future strategy

UniBank remains aware of the way in which the banking and personal finance sector is likely to develop and management recently decided to expand the service at UniCall to include the provision of mortgages and insurance, thus providing more of an integrated 'one-stop shop' service. Furthermore, work has already started on the development of an online banking system, 'UniLine', in parallel with the telephone service. UniBank has been somewhat late in its realisation of the importance of online banking, and thus finds itself at something of a disadvantage here. The new operation, UniLine, is located in the same set of buildings as UniCall, and urgently needs both programming staff and others with knowledge of banking and financial services who can help both to develop and run the initial trials of UniLine. It is also clear that if the local labour market is unable to supply this type of expertise at a competitive rate, then UniBank will have to consider alternative approaches.

UniBank and unions

UniBank recognises the UNIFI trade union. Membership increased at the start of the branch closure programme, but has been affected by redundancies and is starting to decline. Membership was always low at UniCall, where the workforce is relatively transitory and predominantly female (10–12 members on average). In addition, workers at UniCall felt that the union was concentrating too hard on resisting the branch closure programme to take an interest in the call centre, particularly since the call centre was partly responsible for job losses at the branches. However, there have been rumours about the possibility of further job losses, this time at UniCall. This is because competitors in the banking and financial services industry continue to outsource work abroad, and because UniLine is likely to take over more of UniCall's business and this is causing UNIFI to start recruiting more steadily at UniCall.

Questions

1   Identify the key HRM issues at UniCall.

2   Recommend and justify HRM interventions that will improve business performance.

Contributed by Gill Christy, University of Portsmouth.

BRAVE NEW WORLD OR MORE OF THE SAME?

This chapter exposes changes in the world of work and the influences on contemporary HR practice. While recognising that change is taking place, it is important not to become too excitable and suggest that we are entering some kind of brave new HRM world. Armstrong (2000) summed this up:

> The notion that personnel practitioners became involved in strategy formulation and implementation after HRM was invented is a travesty of the facts. Perhaps the word 'strategy' was not bandied around as much then as now but personnel specialists could not deliver effective services unless they understood the business context within which they were operating – where the business was going, what its needs were. To imply that until they travelled along the road to Damascus in the mid-1980s they were unaware of the need to innovate and think ahead is an insult to the many able personnel practitioners who were doing just that before the 1980s.

This is not meant to suggest that there is no change, but to encourage a balanced perspective. It is all a question of degree – line managers have always undertaken the management of human resources, but they may be doing more of it; the HR practitioner has always had to have a business orientation, but perhaps it is sharper now; the HR professional has always had to be aware of strategy, but perhaps there is now a greater emphasis on this. Perhaps the HR profession is in crisis with threats and opportunities being provided by e-enabled HR, shared HR services and outsourcing developments; perhaps it is not: 'What we see is a variety of approach rather than a clear consensus about the appropriate way to organise the [HR] function. HR specialists have a propensity for navel-gazing and neurosis about their role but on this occasion it seems ill founded. No doubt, however, observers will continue to tell the healthy patient that he or she is ill' (Torrington, 1998). Armstrong (2000), in concluding his analysis in 'The name has changed but has the game remained the same?' states:

> This means that HR practitioners must be aware of evolving business needs and how new ideas and good practice might fit those needs, however they are described. In its essentials the game has remained the same but the way it is being played has altered. Whether or not the name has changed is immaterial. New [HR] practices are developed and operated individually or 'joined up' because they meet the needs of the situation. What matters is what works.

We conclude that we may be in a new era but not necessarily a brave new world, but make up your own mind. To end this chapter we provide in Exhibit 1.4 'The shape of HRM in the twenty-first century?' and below we summarise 10 key HRM themes.

1 There is an emergent body of research that good HR practices equals good business – but what are the good HR practices and what is the role of the line manager in turning HR strategy into effective practice?

2 It is increasingly being recognised that people are the organisation's principal sustainable source of competitive advantage.

3 Technical HR competence is no longer enough; HR practices need to add value in the pursuit of corporate objectives and organisational sustainability – raising the question of how added value can be measured.

4 In pursuit of competitive advantage, HR policies and practices need to be aligned with corporate strategy and with each other – vertical integration and internal coherence.

5 Compliance with employment law is essential but this does not on its own add value to the organisation – compliance is a critical failure factor, but added value is the critical success factor for HR practice.

6 'Best practice' HR still needs to be applied contingently to fit the organisation – there are no simple HR solutions.

7 Proactivity in HR delivery is necessary rather than just reacting to events.

8 Outsourcing of HR activities – a threat to the HR function or an opportunity to engage in beneficial partnerships?

9 Harnessing the potential of 'shared services' and 'e-enabled HR' may enable a reconfiguration of HR functional activity.

10 HR professionals perhaps need to be business managers first and functional specialists second.

Perhaps this is all summed up by Roden and Fairhurst (2007) who state that: 'HR professionals need to put their organisations first and HR second if they are to deliver a world class service, HR won't be taken seriously by the top team if it isn't contributing to the bottom line. And, it's not been good at demonstrating its value. Instead, HR needs to prioritise the organisation over the discipline, get a deep understanding of the organisation's work and become part of the team that fuels the organisation's engine'. They suggest there are three main components to achieving world-class HR:

- Employee engagement.
- Aligning HR strategy to the business strategy.
- Investing in HR practices and processes that make strategy happen.

The CIPD Chief Executive, Jackie Orme, echoes this perspective:

> **I've always said if you want to join HR, don't do it because you like dealing with people. You have to have fantastic people skills, but you also have to be driven to succeed. There are some big challenges ahead of us and the first is cementing our discipline as an excellent business discipline and not just a people discipline.**
>
> (Logan, 2008)

EXHIBIT 1.4 HRM in the twenty-first century?

Personnel administration	>>>>	Outsource, devolve, exploit e-HR
Employee-centric HR activity	>>>>	Devolve/share with line managers and exploit e-HR and shared services
The contemporary HR role	>>>>	Business focus, talent management and organisational transformation

SUMMARY LEARNING POINTS

The perspective of this book encompasses the following contentions:

1   People resourcing and talent planning consists of a set of integrated HR activities which are enacted by HR practitioners and by line managers.

2   People resourcing decisions and activities are contingent upon particular organisational circumstances, and prescriptive and universal people management solutions are to be treated with caution.

3   The world of work is changing, and while the rate of change may sometimes be exaggerated it is important for informed practitioners and managers to be aware of and able to react to the changes.

4   Organisational fluidity and transience coupled with exhortations to self-manage careers can result in workers giving primacy to their own employability concerns.

5   There is no doubt that customer aspirations and power are increasing and resulting in customer-driven organisations. This has significant implications for workers and for managers.

6   Employers may have to compete for good workers through offering competitive financial rewards and attractive non-financial rewards, and through deploying talent management strategies.

7   Contemporary HRM trends feature a business orientation for HR professionals and the pursuit of HR practices strategically aligned to corporate objectives.

8   There are changes in the role of the HR professional encompassing business partnership, e-enabled HR, the reconfiguration of HR services and the potential for outsourcing HR activities. These influences should not be perceived as universal, because the role of the HR practitioner is dependent on the fit with organisational circumstances.

REFERENCES AND FURTHER READING

Arkin, A. (2007) 'Street Smart', *People Management*, 5 April, 24–7.

Armstrong, M. (2000) 'The name has changed but has the game remained the same?' *Employee Relations*, 22(6), 576–93.

Armstrong, M. and Brown, D. (2001) *New Dimensions in Pay Management*. London: CIPD.

Backhaus, K. and Tikoo, S. (2004) 'Conceptualising and researching employer branding', *Career Development International*, 9(5), 501–17.

Beattie, D. (2001) *CIPD Annual Report*. London: CIPD.

Briggs, S. and Keogh, W. (1999) 'Integrating human resource strategy and strategic planning to achieve business excellence', *Total Quality Management*, 10(4/5), 447–53.

Brown, D. (2001) 'Lopsided view', *People Management*, 22 November, 36–7.

Brown, D. and Emmott, M. (2003) 'Happy days', *People Management*, 23 October, 16–17.

Caldwell, R. (2008) 'HR business partner competency models: re-contextualising effectiveness', *Human Resource Management Journal*, 18(3), 275–94.

Caulkin, S. (2001) *Performance through People, the New People Management – the Change Agenda*. London: CIPD.

Chaudhuri, A. (2000) 'Perk practice', *The Guardian: Management*, 30 August, 10–11.

CIPD (2003) *HR: Where we are, where we're heading*. London: CIPD.

CIPD (2004) *Business Partnering – a new direction for HR*. London: CIPD.

CIPD (2006) 'The changing HR function: the key questions', *Change Agenda*. London: CIPD.

CIPD (2007) 'The changing HR function', *Survey Report*. London: CIPD.

CIPD (2009a) 'The HR Profession Map', www.cipd.co.uk/hr-profession-map, accessed 3 June 2009.

CIPD (2009b) 'The war on talent: talent management under threat in uncertain times', *Hot topic*. London: CIPD.

Cooper, C. (2000a) 'HR and the bottom line: in for the count', *People Management*, 12 October, 28–34.

Cooper, C. (2000b) 'Concierge services: chore competency', *People Management*, 7 December, 22–5.

DTI (2005) 'High performance work practices: linking strategy and skills to performance outcomes', *Achieving best practice in your business* (in association with the CIPD). London: DTI.

Economist Intelligence Unit (2008) *Talent Wars: the struggle for tomorrow's workforce*. SAP.

Fowler, A. (1987) 'When chief executives discover HRM', *Personnel Management*, 19(1).

Francis, H. and Keegan, A. (2006) 'The changing face of HRM: in search of balance', *Human Resource Management Journal*, 16(3), 231–49.

Futures: the Industrial Society (2000) 'Most wanted: the quiet birth of the free worker', www.theworkfoundation.com/publications.

Gautam, D.K. and Davis, A.J. (2007) 'Integration and devolvement of human resource practices in Nepal', *Employee Relations*, 29(6), 711–26.

Gowler, D. and Legge, K. (1986) 'Images of employees in company reports: do company chairmen view their most valuable asset as valuable?' *Personnel Review*, 15(5), 9–18.

Griffin, E., Finney, L., Hennessy, J. and Boury, D. (2009) *Maximising the value of HR business partnering: A practical research based guide.* Horsham: Roffey Park Institute.

Guest, D. (1989) 'Personnel and HRM: can you tell the difference?' *Personnel Management*, January.

Guest, D. and King, Z. (2001) 'HR and the bottom line: personnel's paradox', *People Management*, 14 October, 30–8.

Hall, L. and Torrington, D. (1998) *The Human Resource Function: Dynamics of change and development.* London: FT Pitman Publishing.

Harris, L., Doughty, D. and Kirk, S. (2002) 'The devolution of HR responsibilities – perspectives from the UK's public sector', *Journal of European Industrial Training*, 26(5), 218–29.

Hendry, C. and Pettigrew, A. (1990) 'HRM: an agenda for the 1990s', *International Journal of HRM*, 1(1).

IRS Employment Trends 721 (2001) 'e-HR: personnel tomorrow', February, 6–13.

Korczynski, M. (2002) *HRM in the Service Sector.* Basingstoke: Palgrave.

Legge, K. (1995) *Human Resource Management: Rhetorics and Realities.* Basingstoke: Macmillan.

Legge, K. (2005) *HRM: rhetorics and realities.* Basingstoke: Palgrave.

Logan, G. (2008) 'CIPD vows to raise HR profile with Government', *Personnel Today*, 7 October, 4.

Marchington, M. (1995) 'Fairytales and magic wands: new employment practices in perspective', *Employee Relations*, 17(1), 51–66.

Maxwell, G. and Farquharson, L. (2008) 'Senior managers' perceptions of the practice of human resource management', *Employee Relations*, 30(3), 304–22.

Morgan, S. (2001) 'How to manage outsourcing', *People Management*, 3 May, 44–5.

Moss Kanter, R. (1996) *World Class: Thriving locally in global economy.* London: Simon & Schuster.

Murlis, H. (1991) *The Future for Total Remuneration Packages*, IPM Conference, October.

Newell, H. and Scarborough, H. (2002) *HRM in Context.* Basingstoke: Palgrave.

Orme, J. (2009) 'A route map for the HR profession', *People Management*, 15 January, 16–17.

Peters, T.J. and Waterman, R.H., Jr (1982) *In Search of Excellence: Lessons from America's best-run companies.* New York: Warner.

Pfeffer, J. (2007) 'Human Resources from an organizational perspective: some paradoxes explained', *Journal of Economic Perspectives*, 21(4), 115–34.

Philpott, J. (2001) 'The informed vote: the emerging political economy of work', *People Management*, 11 January, 42–3.

Purcell, J. (2001) 'Personnel and human resource managers: power, prestige and potential', *Human Resource Management Journal*, 11(3), 3–4.

Purcell, J., Kinnie, N., Hutchison, S. and Rayton, B. (2000) 'HR and the bottom line: inside the box', *People Management*, 26 October, 30–8.

Purcell, J., Kinnie, N., Hutchinson, S., Rayton, B. and Swart, J. (2003) *Understanding the People and Performance Link: Unlocking the black box*. London: CIPD.

Reilly, P., Tamkin, P. and Broughton, A. (2007) 'The Changing HR function: Transforming HR'? London: CIPD.

Renwick, D. (2003) 'HR managers – guardians of employee well-being?' *Personnel Review*, 32(3), 341–59.

Roden, N. and Fairhurst, D. (2007) cited in 'Put organisations first to kick off HR's finest hour', *People Management*, 4 October, 9.

Sisson, K. and Storey, J. (2000) *The Realities of HRM*. Buckingham: Open University Press.

Storey, J. (1995) *Human Resource Management: A critical text*. Oxford: Blackwell.

Taylor, S. (2009) in 'Recession puts employer branding in the spotlight', *Impact: update on CIPD policy and research*, Issue 27, p. 16, 7 May, London: CIPD.

Torrington, D. (1998) 'Crisis and opportunity in HRM', in Sparrow, P. and Marchington, M. (eds) *HRM – the New Agenda*. London: FT Pitman Publishing.

Torrington, D. and Hall, L. (1998) 'How human resource strategy is put into practice', *Employee Relations Review*, Issue 4. Croners.

Ulrich, D. (1987) 'Strategic human resource planning: why and how?' *Human Resource Planning*, 10(1), 37–56.

Ulrich, D. (1992) 'Strategic human resource planning: linking customers and employees', *Human Resource Planning*, 15(2), 47–62.

Ulrich, D. (1996) 'Transforming the HR function', *Journal of Gemini Consulting Group*, Spring.

Ulrich, D. (1997) *Human Resource Champions: the next agenda for adding value and delivering results*. Boston, MA: Harvard Business School Press.

Ulrich, D. (1998) 'A new mandate for human resources', *Harvard Business Review*, January/February, 124–34.

Ulrich, D. and Brockbank, W. (2005a) 'Role Call', *People Management*, 16 June, 24–28.

Ulrich, D. and Brockbank, W. (2005b) *The HR value proposition*. Harvard Business School Press.

Ulrich, D., Brockbank, W., Johnson, D., Sandholtz, K. and Younger, J. (2008) *HR Competencies: Mastery at the Intersection of People and Business*. Society for Human Resource Management.

Whittaker, J. and Johns, T. (2004) 'Standards deliver', *People Management*, 30 June, 32–4.

Williams, M. (2000) 'Retention strategies: transfixed assets', *People Management*, 3 August, 29–33.

Wright, P., McMahan, G., Snell, S. and Gerhart, B. (2004) 'Comparing line and HR executives' perceptions of HR effectiveness', *HRM Journal*, 40, 111–24.

ASSIGNMENTS AND DISCUSSION TOPICS

1 In small groups brainstorm 10 contemporary HRM terms which are in common usage and discuss what they mean in practice.

2 Is the devolution of HR activities to line managers a good or a bad thing, first, for the HR profession and, second, for organisational effectiveness? Examine the way that HR activity has developed within your organisation. Where do HR activities take place and who does them?

3 The changing world of work: in groups, discuss the following two questions and be prepared to feed back into a whole-class discussion. First, in what way is the world of work changing compared to 10–15 years ago and what changes do you anticipate in the next decade? You can refer to Exhibit 1.1 if this is helpful. Second, what are the implications of the changing world of work for employees, for managers and for the HR professional?

4 What is meant by 'added value' and 'business partnership' in relation to the HR role? How should HR professionals respond to the demands of their internal customers, normally line management colleagues?

5 To what extent is it possible to measure the contribution of HR activities to organisational success and what measures should be used?

6 Analyse the eight CIPD 'key behaviours' required by HR professionals and comment on how they can be developed. To what extent does the specific organisational role of the HR practitioner determine the mix of behaviours required? Illustrate your answer with practical examples, using your own role and that of other students.

7 Is e-enabled HR a threat or an opportunity for the HR profession? Justify your point of view with practical examples.

8 The outsourcing (or externalisation) of HR activities can be defined as the use of consultants or specialist providers to supply HR activities or services previously undertaken by the organisation's own HR specialists. It can be viewed as the HR equivalent of facilities management – the facility in this case is 'the human resource'. Using the taxonomy of HR activities below, or one of your choice, analyse a number of organisations and identify which HR activities are currently outsourced. You should make some quantitative assessment of the extent of the outsourcing of each category.

HR strategy development	Human resource planning
Work and job design	Recruitment
Selection	Reward strategies and systems
Job evaluation	Payroll administration
Performance management	Internal communications
Quality initiatives	Diversity initiatives
Employee relations	Health and safety
Employee assistance programmes	Training
Management development	Careers advice and planning
Redundancy and/or dismissal	Outplacement
Employment law advice	HR advisory service to line managers
Organisation development	

In relation to your findings consider the following questions. What are the reasons for the outsourcing? What are the challenges associated with outsourcing? What evidence is there for an increase in HR outsourcing in the next three years? If so, which areas do you think will increase and why? Write a report and/or give a presentation on the state of play in HR outsourcing which reflects your research.

9　Business partnership on trial – 2-hour debate

This student-led activity develops knowledge and understanding of the business partnership concept by putting it 'on trial' through critically evaluating research originally presented by Helen Francis and Ann Keegan at the CIPD Professional Standards Conference in 2005. Students will need to engage in pre-reading and lead a facilitated debate that will also utilise their HR knowledge and experience to contextualise the discussion.

The learning outcomes of this activity are to be able to:

- Analyse the 'business partnership' concept.
- Critically evaluate the concept within the context of contemporary HR practice.

In preparation for the activity, students need to read the *HRMJ* and *People Management* articles by Helen Francis and Anne Keegan and write brief notes addressing the following questions:

(a)　What are the characteristics of the business partnership approach to HR activity in theory?

(b)　What is the reality of the business partnership concept in practice?

(c)　What are the potential and actual advantages and disadvantages of the business partnership concept to organisations, HR professionals, front line managers and employees?

The activity

During the activity students will work in three groups:

- Group A – will present the case *for* the business partnership concept.
- Group B – will present the case *against* the business partnership concept.
- The jury, who will deliver a verdict.

Groups A and B preparation time for presenting the case – 30 minutes.
The jury will spend the same 30 minutes discussing the questions above.

First, Group A will present its case *for* the business partnership concept – 15 minutes.
The jury will then ask questions of Group A – 15 minutes.

Second, Group B will present its case *against* the business partnership concept – 15 minutes.
The jury will then ask questions of Group B – 15 minutes.

Third, the jury will then spend up to 20 minutes openly discussing the two cases presented before coming to a decision at the end of the seminar *for* or *against* the business partnership concept.

Finally, the facilitator wraps up the activity using the guidance from the Lecturer's Guide – 10 minutes.

Francis, H. and Keegan, A. (2005) 'Slippery slope', *People Management*, 30 June, 26–31.
Francis, H. and Keegan, A. (2006) 'The changing face of HRM: in search of balance', *Human Resource Management Journal*, 16(3), 231–49.

This activity was designed and first delivered by Dr David Hall, University of Portsmouth.

Chapter 2

Human Resources Strategy: perspectives and theories

by David Farnham

LEARNING OUTCOMES: TO BE ABLE TO

- Explain the concept of strategy
- Recognise how HR activities relate to the strategic drivers of organisations
- Evaluate the possible contribution of the HR function to the strategic process and barriers to converting HRS into practice
- Critique the different approaches to HRS

INTRODUCTION

Since the 1980s academics and practitioners have shown acute interest in human resources strategy (HRS) and in its relationship to corporate performance, but there is no generic definition of the term. Some time ago HRS was explained as 'the intentions' of an organisation 'toward its employees, expressed through philosophies, policies and practices' (Tyson, 1995). Prior to this Hendry and Pettigrew (1986) provided a wider definition, claiming that the strategic aspect of human resource management (HRM) within organisations consists of four key elements:

- planning
- a coherent approach to the managing of people underpinned by a core 'philosophy'
- matching HRM activities and policies to some explicit strategy
- seeing people as a 'strategic resource' for achieving 'competitive advantage'.

The Hendry and Pettigrew framework suggests that those responsible for developing effective HR strategies, and linking these to business strategy, have to adopt a conceptual and reflective approach to the task. Determining an appropriate HRS in organisations is not simply about applying set techniques or simplified rules to the process, since there are no generally agreed tools of analysis or 'magic bullets' for action in this area of HR management. Indeed, both research and practice point in a number of different and conflicting directions. Given the controversial nature of strategic management and the complexities of HRS, this chapter adopts a theory-building, analytical and critical approach to the topic. The aim is to guide readers towards an appreciation of the research literature in the field and its implications for practice. The chapter outlines some of the debates and ambiguities in this area of HRM, explores the role of HRS in contributing to organisational effectiveness and provides some basic critiques of the main HR strategic models identified in the research literature (Salaman, Storey and Billsberry, 2005).

STRATEGY: MISCONCEPTIONS, CONCEPTS AND TYPOLOGIES

The noun 'strategy' and the adjective 'strategic' are used extensively in business literature, business education and 'management speak' today. Thus we have 'corporate strategy', 'strategic planning', 'business strategy', 'strategic management', 'strategic thinking', 'strategic analysis', 'strategic objectives', 'strategic human resource management', 'human resource strategy' and many other expressions of strategy and strategic intent. Yet while we intuitively understand that 'strategy' is something about 'setting one's goals and finding ways of achieving them', there is no universally agreed definition or conceptualisation of the term, despite the claims of some self-professed management gurus. Indeed, as Whittington (2001: 1f) pointed out, 'there is not much agreement about strategy' and 'strategy isn't easy', while Markides (2000: vii) has concluded that 'we simply do not know what strategy is or how to develop a good one'.

Clearly, business strategy has always existed but was traditionally assumed to be a rational, logical, self-evident and profit-centred process. As the former President of General Motors confidently asserted in his autobiography nearly 50 years ago

(Sloan, 1963: 49): 'The strategic aim of a business is to earn a return on capital, and if in any particular case the return in the long run is not satisfactory, the deficiency should be corrected or the activity abandoned.' But 'strategy' is not as simplistic as this. So why is there such interest, even obsession, with the strategic dimensions of organisational life in the business, public service and voluntary sectors? And what sense can be made of 'strategy', in an increasingly postmodern age that is sceptical of rationality, receptive to individualism and values local contexts?

The answer to the first question lies in the 'new' globalisation and changing nature of the world economy, emergence of large, transnational business corporations and impact of information and communication technologies on the world of work and organisational systems over the past 30 years. The answer to the second question can be found in the search for 'strategy' by top managers in response to the increasing complexity of the contemporary business environment. This includes the pursuit of growth and reduction of market insecurity in an increasingly dynamic free-market, international economy (Farnham, 2005).

There is, then, no single model of 'strategy' but, because of intensified competition in product markets in the private sector, and greater accountability and competition in the public sector, top managers are looking for appropriate strategic responses likely to ensure organisational survival and enterprise success in conditions of change, market turbulence and rising customer expectations. There are different approaches to this task. A central issue in the debate about strategy determination is whether organisational leaders are in control of their organisations' destinies or whether the environment is the determining factor. Human agency theory posits that strategies and patterns of organisational actions derive out of a leader's will, intellect and administrative skills. Determinist views of strategy, in contrast, focus on the determinants of organisational structures within which business leaders are constrained in taking strategic decisions (Farnham, 2005).

Whittington (2001) has summarised the debate, neatly and convincingly. He argued that those creating strategy do so from two dimensions. They have to consider the *outcomes* of strategy and the *processes* by which it is made. The outcomes are either 'profit-maximising' or 'pluralist' ones (i.e. other than profit-making alone such as ethical choices, social goals or stakeholder interests); the processes are either 'deliberate' (i.e. planned) or 'emergent' (i.e. they come about by accident, muddle or inertia). This results in four 'idealised' perspectives of strategy, although in the practical world there can be hybrid, overlapping systems which interact and merge one into another:

- deliberate and profit-maximising (classical)
- emergent and profit-maximising (evolutionary)
- emergent and pluralist (processual)
- deliberate and pluralist (systemic).

These perspectives, or theories of strategy, are often neither explicit nor formalised but are short cuts to managerial action and getting things done in organisations in the search for market success, efficiency and profitability.

Where strategic emphasis is on profit-making outcomes and deliberate processes, we have the 'classical' approach to business strategy. This focuses on analysing, planning and commanding from the top and is typically found in mature, capital-intensive industries tending to monopoly or oligopoly in the UK, United States and Australasia.

The 'evolutionary' approach to strategy is based on profit-making outcomes and emergent processes and is rooted in keeping production costs low and business options open. It is commonly found in small firms, new industries and Anglo-Saxon conglomerates. The 'processual' approach to strategy aims at pluralist outcomes and uses emergent processes. It stays 'close to the ground', goes 'with the flow' and is typically found in protected bureaucracies and knowledge-based firms. The 'systemic' approach to strategy is based on pluralist outcomes and deliberate processes and plays by 'local rules'. It is typically found in non-Anglo-Saxon businesses and family firms and state enterprises in France, Germany and parts of the Far East.

The heyday of classical school thinking was the 1960s, where strategic success or failure was determined internally through managerial planning, rational analysis and rigorous calculation. The influence of the processual perspective was strongest during the 1970s. It too was inward-looking but its concerns were with political bargaining and the building of core managerial skills and competencies within organisations. The evolutionary school of strategy typified the 1980s and emphasised the external demands on organisations such as the impact of markets and economic factors on business decisions, as well as survival of the fittest in the marketplace. And, most recently, the systemic school of theory, which came to the fore during the 1990s and remains so now, has argued that to understand what is happening in organisations, and among business competitors, requires corporate strategists to be socially sensitive to the diversity of contemporary economic and business practices.

To sum up, each of these four perspectives of strategy is based on differing assumptions about its outcomes and processes, which leave managerial strategists with hard choices to make in practice. Certainty is replaced by uncertainty, simplicity by complexity, and prescription by contingency. As Whittington (2001: 118) concludes:

> Classical confidence in analysis, order and control is undermined by Processual scepticism about human cognition, rationality and flexibility. The incrementalist learning of Processualists is challenged in turn by the impatient markets of Evolutionists. But even Evolutionary markets can be bucked if, as Systemic analysts of social systems allege, the state is persuaded to intervene.

STRATEGY, BUSINESS PERFORMANCE AND HUMAN RESOURCES MANAGEMENT

Establishing measurable links between corporate strategy and HRS is problematic. In the small and medium-sized enterprise sector, for example, there may be no effective connection between corporate strategy and HRS, simply because corporate strategy might be essentially reactive and there may be no explicit HRS at all. In other sectors, corporate strategy may drive HRS or, less likely, HRS may drive corporate strategy. In yet other cases corporate strategy and HRS may be integrated in that a holistic strategy incorporates a number of sub-strategies, including HR issues. Such an approach is rooted in the belief that HRS is critical to business profitability and efficiency and is an organisational end in itself (Boxall, 1996 and 2007).

Establishing measurable links between HRS and effective business performance is also problematic. However, as Torrington *et al.* (2008) have pointed out, 'there is a strong lobby propounding the view that human resources are *the* source of competitive advantage for the business, rather than, say, access to capital or use of technology'. Also, Boxall and Steeneveld (1999) claimed it is self-evident that the quality of HRM is a critical influence on the performance of firms and managing people. Their study, for example, concluded, first, that successful firms enact those HR strategies enabling them to survive as credible members of their industry or sector. The fundamental strategic priority of those leading HRM activities should be to ensure that management takes a lead in those HR actions that are vital for supporting the viability of the firm, as it faces challenges of change and competition in its sector. They view alignment of organisational and employee interests as the basic congruence problem in managing employment relations. The second, more difficult task is to perceive and enact those HR strategies that might generate some kind of competitive advantage for the business.

There are a number of approaches attempting to link strategy, business performance and HRS. Although there are some overlaps, the three general categories are 'best-practice' models, 'best-fit' models and the 'resource-based' model (Exhibit 2.1), each of which is examined below (Salaman, Storey and Billsberry, 2005). In practice, however, when it comes to implementing an HRS, there are frequently conflicts and contradictions within the ranks of management itself, both hierarchically and functionally. Marchington and Wilkinson (2005) have identified five separate sets of reasons why middle managers and supervisors might not implement HR strategies in the ways desired by senior colleagues:

- lack of identification with employer goals
- problems of work overload
- limited investment in training and development
- the value of retaining some flexibility at workplace level
- failure to apply organisational rules.

EXHIBIT 2.1 Best practice, best fit and RBV of the firm – a summary

Best practice – universal and inherently good HR strategy and practices can be prescribed; requiring senior management to commit to key (best) HR practices as a route to superior organisational performance.

Best fit – contingencies and context determine HR strategy and practices; this requires the HR strategy to be aligned with the competitive strategy and complementary to internal and external contextual factors.

The resource-based view (RBV) of the firm – people are one component in an 'exploitable' portfolio of organisational resources; this exploitation recognises people as a valuable human capital in the pursuit of competitive advantage and requires the recruitment and retention of core competencies, and also the active management of tacit and explicit employee knowledge.

BEST-PRACTICE MODELS

There has been much interest in the concept of 'best-practice' models of HRS in both the UK and United States. These are sometimes called 'high performance work systems' (HPWS), 'high commitment' HR, or 'high involvement'. Basically, the idea is that a particular set of HR practices has the potential to bring about improved performance for all organisations and that certain 'bundles' of HR practices can contribute to improved employee attitudes and behaviours, lower levels of absenteeism and labour turnover, and higher levels of productivity, quality and customer service. These HR bundles, in turn, are seen as generating higher levels of profitability.

Supporters of 'best-practice' models of HRS argue that there are certain HR practices which help organisations achieve competitive advantage in the marketplace. They suggest there is a positive link between HRS and business performance but argue that the effect is only optimised where 'best' HR policies are used. All of them suggest that the same basic HR policies and practices universally enhance business performance in every organisation, irrespective of particular product markets, business goals and organisational circumstances. This optimisation, they argue, takes place through a variety of mechanisms such as enhancing the competence of employees, gaining their commitment, motivating them and adopting appropriate methods of job design. According to Guest (2000: 2), for example, best practice borrows from expectancy theory and implies that all the above – competence, commitment, motivation and effective job design – need to be present to ensure the best organisational outcomes. 'Positive employee behaviour should in turn impact upon establishment level outcomes such as low absence, quit rates and wastage, as well as high quality and productivity.'

In a much earlier paper Guest (1989) proposed four sets of HR policy goals: *strategic integration, commitment, flexibility* and *quality*. These relate to specific HRM policies, such as managing change, that are expected to result in desirable outcomes for organisations. Strategic integration means making sure that HRM is fully integrated into strategic planning (vertical integration), that HR policies are consistent with one another (horizontal integration) and that line managers use appropriate HR practices in their daily work. Commitment aims to ensure that employees feel bound to the organisation and are committed to high performance. Flexibility requires an adaptable organisational structure and functional flexibility based on multi-skilling. Quality is expected to result in high quality products or services delivered through high quality flexible employees. The HR policies claimed to facilitate this are linked with organisational and job design, the management of change, recruitment, selection and internal socialisation, appraisal, training and development, rewards and communication. Expected organisational outcomes include high levels of job performance, problem-solving, innovation, change and cost-effectiveness, matched by low levels of labour turnover, absence and grievances.

The Harvard model

One path-finding 'best-practice' approach is the Harvard model, proposed by Beer, Spector, Lawrence, Quinn Mills and Walton (1984). They suggest that managerial HR policy choices are influenced by stakeholder interests and the particular situational factors interacting on them. The strategic task of management is to take policy choices in the light of these circumstances. Such choices result in certain HR outcomes and long-term consequences for individuals, organisations and society at large. The stakeholder interests identified include shareholders, management, employees, government, the community and trade unions. The situational factors impacting upon the organisation's stakeholders are workforce characteristics, business strategy, management philosophy, the labour market, task technology, laws and societal values. Four clusters of HRM policy choices are seen to be critical and these relate to the degree and nature of influence that employees are likely to have. These are 'employee influence', 'human resource flow', 'reward systems' and 'work systems'. Perceived HR outcomes are the four Cs: *commitment, competence, congruence* and *cost-effectiveness*. The long-term consequences are identified as individual well-being, organisational effectiveness and societal well-being.

Superficially, the Harvard model seems to allow for some variation of HR strategies and choices, thus appearing to contrast itself with situational determinism. But, in reality, its analysis of strategic choice has strong prescriptive overtones. For example, the specified desirable outcomes – the four Cs – are attempting to elevate one particular type of strategic approach over others. Indeed, the Harvard approach appears to suggest that there is one preferred set of HR policy choices that are superior to all others – those incorporated within its own framework.

Many of the policies and practices typically associated with the Harvard model, as with other best-practice approaches, though not explicitly stated, are rooted in neo-human relations theory (Maslow, 1943; Herzberg *et al.*, 1957; McGregor, 1960). Thus some of their underlying beliefs and ideas include widespread use of the 'team' analogy in the models, assumptions about high levels of trust within enterprises, and perceptions of HRM as central to business strategy. Senior managers are presumed to be highly visible and able to provide a 'vision' for the future of their organisations that employees can identify with and share, while middle managers are seen as inspiring, encouraging and facilitating change by harnessing the commitment and cooperation of employees. Best-practice models also assume federal, decentralised corporate structures, where job design is congruent with organisation structure, technology and HR policies and where work teams enjoy large measures of autonomy, with a great deal of task flexibility.

The implicit HR policies incorporated within the Harvard model and best-practice approach comprise six key elements. The first is numerical flexibility, temporal flexibility and single status. The second is selection processes emphasising attitudes as well as skills. Third, appraisal is assumed to be open and participative, with two-way feedback between managers and employees. Fourth, training and development of core employees are central to this model, with lateral as well as upward career advancement and an emphasis on general as well as specific employability. Fifth, reward systems utilise individual and group performance-related pay, skill-based pay, profit and gain sharing, share ownership and flexible benefits packages. Sixth, participation and employee involvement are based on extensive use of two-way communication and problem-solving groups. Trade union organisation, while not necessarily excluded from best-practice models, is not central to this approach to HRS.

The partnership approach

Unions do have some legitimacy in another best-practice model, however. This is the 'partnership' approach, which has been on the HRS agenda for many years. The partnership model has been extolled by a variety of interests such as the Department of Trade and Industry and the Trades Union Congress. Even here, though, the union role is somewhat ambiguous. Indeed, it is especially controversial whether partnership is in essence about the relationship between the organisation and the individual or the organisation and the trade union. There is no agreed definition of partnership but six key principles underpin it:

- Shared commitment to the success of the organisation, including support for flexibility and replacement of adversarial employment relations by cooperative ones.
- Recognition that the interests of the partners (employer and union; employer and staff) may legitimately differ.
- Employment security, including measures to improve the employability of staff, as well as limiting compulsory redundancy.
- Focus on quality of working life.
- Commitment to managerial transparency, openness to discussing future plans, genuine consultation and willingness to listen to the business case for alternative strategies.
- Adding value, by drawing on resources not previously accessed.

The partnership best-practice model, in short, is contemporary HRM combined with some form of collective representation or employee voice, with or without trade unions.

There are three main sources of the partnership model. First, there was the 'new industrial relations' literature in the United States during the 1980s, which emphasised the common interests of employers and unions in the employment relationship in contrast to adversarialism. A second source was mainland Europe, with its version of 'social partnership' or 'concertation' among employers, unions and governments at national level in many EU countries. This was complemented by 'social dialogue' at EU level, involving employer and union confederations, public employers and EU institutions, so as to promote both social policy for citizens and modernisation of work organisations to advance competitive success. Third, in the UK, debates over the 'new realism' during the 1990s suggested that unions should develop a joint approach with employers, thereby creating the conditions for both economic success and social cohesion.

There is some evidence to show that partnership works. Both survey and case study evidence points to there being some positive links between partnership arrangements and business performance. Both management and unions have had to adapt to the partnership model. Management has had to change its style from one of 'doing' to 'facilitating', to act more openly and change its approach to the unions by adopting a problem-solving methodology. Unions, in turn, have had to accept the need for joint communication and recognise that the long-term interests of their members are best served by helping organisations be successful and not by opposing change for its own sake. They have also had to give away collective bargaining power.

High commitment HR practices

In an influential North American study at the end of the last century, Pfeffer (1998) identified seven basic components of best-practice/high commitment HR practices.

His underpinning analysis is based on the importance of the 'human equation' in organisations, enabling 'profits' to be 'built' by putting 'people first'. His seven components are:

- *Employment security and internal labour markets.* These underpin the other six practices. This is on the grounds that it is unrealistic to ask employees to work hard and with commitment without some expectation of job security and concern for their future careers.

- *Selective hiring and sophisticated selection.* Recruiting and retaining outstanding people is seen as an effective way to achieve sustained competitive advantage and involves using psychometric tests, structured interviews and work sampling. Competencies sought include trainability, commitment, drive, persistence and initiative.

- *Extensive training, learning and development.* Here employers need to ensure that 'outstanding talent' remains at the forefront of their field. This includes product knowledge, working in teams and interpersonal relations, with employers needing to synergise the contributions of talented and exceptional employees in the organisation.

- *Employee involvement, information sharing and worker voice.* This feature rests on the view that open communications about financial matters, strategy and operational problems ensure employees are informed about organisational issues. Also for team working to be successful, employees need information to provide a basis from which to make suggestions and contribute to organisational performance.

- *Self-managed teams/teamworking.* Teamwork is seen as leading to better decision-making and the achievement of more creative solutions to operational problems.

- *High compensation contingent upon performance.* There are two elements to this practice: higher than average compensation and performance-related reward (PRR). PRR can be based on an individual, team, departmental or establishment-wide basis.

- *Reduction of status differentials/harmonisation.* This is seen as encouraging employees to offer ideas within an 'open' management culture. The principal point behind moves to single status and harmonisation is that it aims to break down artificial barriers among different groups of staff, thus encouraging teamworking and flexibility.

Searching for the 'black box'

Not all studies present positive links between best-practice HR and organisational performance. Some have doubts about the precise sorts of HR practices making up the high commitment bundle, about their synergy with one another and their universal applicability. Research by Purcell and his colleagues (2003) sought to open up this 'black box'. These studies were undertaken over a 30-month period in 10 organisations from different business sectors, comprising a wide range of employment contexts, with interviews being conducted with HR, line managers and non-managerial staff. The results were, first, that the research team used the 'AMO' model. This argues that in order to perform better, people must have the *ability* and skills to work with others, be *motivated* to work and want to do it well, and have the *opportunity* to deploy their skills in the job and contribute to workgroup and organisational success. Second, each organisation was recognised as operating with a 'big idea'. This was embedded within the organisation and served to glue it together and make it successful. Third, line managers were identified as being critically important in achieving high performance work. Finally, measures of performance were adapted to be relevant for each organisation. Indeed, it makes sense to vary measures of best-practice bundles depending on the workplace, since workers are likely to stress different practices due to their occupational status, age or gender (Harney and Jordan, 2008).

Critiques of best-practice models

The universal application of best-practice models is contested by some writers. Purcell (1999), for example, is particularly sceptical about the claim that bundles of 'best-practice' or high commitment HR practices are universally applicable. He claims that it leads down a 'utopian *cul-de-sac*'. What is needed is to identify the circumstances of where and when high commitment HR strategies are best used, explain why some organisations do or do not adopt them and how some organisations seem to have more appropriate HR systems than others.

One concern, for example, is that 'best practice' seems to work on the assumption that employers take a long-term perspective of their organisations' prospects. In practice, this may not be the case. For example, instead of employers cutting back on training when business is difficult, they are urged to spend more on training in lean times, when it is easier to release employees from other duties. There are good economic reasons for doing this but what is actually done depends on business leaders taking a long-term perspective and looking to the prospect of future market growth, which they may not be prepared to do.

Second, it is easier to engage in high commitment practices when labour costs are low as a proportion of total costs. But when labour costs make up a high proportion of total costs, as in many service-sector organisations, it is more difficult for managers to persuade those controlling an organisation's financial resources that there are long-term benefits in 'investing in human capital'. There is little incentive for employers to invest in high commitment HR, for example, if supply-chain contracts are of limited length and organisations are expected to compete on reducing costs.

Third, it depends on what types of staff employers recruit. Innovative HR practices are likely to contribute to improved performance when employees have skills that managers lack, when employees are motivated to apply these skills through discretionary effort, and when the firm's business strategy can only be achieved when employees make this discretionary effort.

Fourth, growth of 'non-standard' employment contracts has led some commentators to question if flexible employment is compatible with best-practice HR and whether or not it can be applied to all employees in an organisation, irrespective of their occupational status or labour market value. For example, employers might want to nurture long-serving employees but not those on short-term employment contracts or subcontracted workers.

BEST-FIT MODELS

'Best-fit' models are based on the proposition that different types of HRS are suitable for different types of business conditions. The best-fit approach claims that there is a link between HRS and competitive advantage but that HRS is contingent upon the particular circumstances of each enterprise. Organisations need to identify the HR strategies which 'fit' their enterprises in terms of their product markets, labour markets, size, structures, strategies and other factors. What is 'right' for one organisation is not appropriate for others. In other words, best-fit HRS is based on the idea that HR practices vary between organisations, depending on business strategy or product-market circumstances. Best-fit models may be described as 'outside-in' theories. There are three main types of best-fit models. One links HR strategic choices to different stages in a firm's business cycle. Another relates them to the different strategic and structural configurations of organisations. And the third matches HR strategies to different business strategies.

The business life cycle model

The first of these, the business life cycle model, tries to link HR policy choices with the varying needs of firms at different stages in their life cycles from start-up, through growth, maturity and decline. At each stage, it is claimed, a firm has different business priorities which, in turn, demand different HR strategies. The recruitment, selection and staffing, compensation and benefits, training and development, and employee relations functions need to make different responses at different stages in an organisation's business cycle. During a firm's start-up stage, for instance, the training and development (T and D) function needs to define the company's future skill requirements and begin establishing career ladders for staff. During a firm's period of growth, however, T and D needs to maintain an effective management team through appropriate management development and organisational development activities. In a firm's maturity, T and D focuses on maintaining flexibility and the skills of an ageing workforce. And finally, in a firm's decline the T and D function has to focus on retraining and providing career consulting services to its staff.

The structural configuration model

The second best-fit model, linking HRS to the strategy and structure of firms, is exemplified by Fombrun *et al.* (1984: 37) in their basic model for analysing strategic HRM. In their view, effective systems for managing human resources lead to increased effectiveness within organisations and these HR systems can be internally 'fitted' to business strategy. Their model provides a set of frameworks for conceptualising HRM and explores the link between HRM and the formulation and implementation of strategic and business objectives. They have elaborated the traditional view of how managers should think about strategic management by including HRM as an integral tool which they can use in strategy determination. For Fombrun and his colleagues (*ibid.*: 37), 'the critical managerial task is to align the formal structure and human resource systems so that they drive the strategic objectives of the organisation'.

The model of Fombrun *et al.* identifies a range of appropriate HR strategic choices, in terms of selection, appraisal, rewards and development that are dependent upon an organisation's strategic/structural configurations. These configurations range from single product strategies with functional structures, through diversified product strategies linked to multi-divisional structures and multiple product strategies operating globally. Thus a business depending on a single product strategy and a functional structure is likely to pursue basic HR policies, which are largely functional, subjective and unsystematic. Businesses following a diversification strategy within a multi-divisional structure, in contrast, are likely to be characterised by an HRS driven by impersonal, systematic HR processes adaptable to different parts of the organisation. In terms of selection, for example, this is likely to be functionally and generalist oriented, with systematic criteria being used. Appraisal will be impersonal and based on returns on investment and productivity, with subjective assessments of contribution to the business. Rewards, in turn, could incorporate large pay bonuses based on profitability, linked with subjective assessments of contribution to business performance. Finally, T and D would be cross-functional, cross-divisional and cross-business.

Once management has articulated a philosophy about managing people, Fombrun *et al.* argue, it can then focus on designing the HR system. They identify four generic functions performed by HR managers, which they call the 'Human Resource Cycle', with performance being a function of all HR components. These are:

- selecting the people best able to perform the jobs defined by the structure
- appraising their performance to ensure equitable distribution of rewards
- motivating employees by linking rewards to high level performance
- developing employees to enhance their performance at work.

They argue that success in implementing strategic objectives depends on how well organisations carry out the human resource cycle. This means selecting the right people, measuring appropriate behaviours, rewarding progress against strategic objectives and developing skills to ensure success of the strategy. The strength of this approach is that it provides a basic framework showing how selection, appraisal, rewards and development can be mutually linked to encourage appropriate employee behaviour. However, this 'internal fit' model, while useful, raises questions about the model's simplistic responses to organisational strategy. Further, the model has also been criticised because of its dependence on a rational, deliberate approach to strategy formulation, its unitary assumptions about the employment relationship and its lack of recognition of employee interests in the equation.

The matching model

The third best-fit model matches business strategy with HRS. These theories draw on Porter's distinction among innovation, quality enhancement and cost-reduction strategies (Porter, 1985). This model links the competitive strategies of firms with HRM practices and conceives HRS in terms of generating the kinds of desired employee 'role' behaviours required to fulfil given business strategies, and then identifying HR policies and practices to achieve and reinforce such behaviours. Where the strategy goal is 'quality enhancement', for example, then high concern for quality by employees can be generated by relatively egalitarian treatment of staff and some guarantees of employment security. Quality enhancement also requires a moderate amount of cooperative, interdependent employee behaviour. The sorts of HRM policies encouraging this are likely to incorporate mixes of individual and group criteria for performance appraisal, which is mainly short-term and results oriented.

Where 'cost reduction' is a strategy goal, however, desired employee behaviour demands moderate concern for quality of output but high concern for quantity. The HRM policies supporting these behaviours are close monitoring of market pay levels when making payment decisions and minimal levels of training and development. While agreeing that success or failure of firms does not turn entirely on their HRM practices, this model elevates HRM to having a crucial influence.

Critiques of best-fit models

A number of critiques have been made of best-fit models. First, these models are deterministic and 'top-down' in orientation. Each assumes that it is possible to 'read off' a preferred HRS from an understanding of business strategy or a firm's competitive prospects. Yet many organisations do not have clear business strategies, so it is not possible to claim that there are links with HR where no strategy exists. Also contingency approaches adopt the classical perspective on strategy (i.e. one of rational, logical, sequential decision-making), which is often an unrealistic assumption.

Second, organisations are pluralistic entities, with multiple influences acting on them. Each best-fit model puts a primacy on a single but different contextual factor and assumes that this determines patterns of HR practices and strategies. Problems arise if different factors, external to the organisation, suggest the adoption of different types of HR strategy. As Boxall and Purcell (2007) note: 'the strategic goals of HRM are plural. While they do involve the firm's competitive objectives, they also involve meeting employee needs and complying with social requirements for labour management . . . The firm is after all a network of stakeholders.'

Third, managers do not have complete control over employees. But each best-fit model is based on scientific management principles that assume managers are all-knowing, all-powerful agents in dealing with those lower down organisational hierarchies. In practice, it is impossible for senior managers to have sufficient information to make effective judgements that take account of all possible effects and scenarios within their organisations.

Fourth, these models are static ones and do not focus on the processes of change. All these models try to relate two sets of variables together in a static way, without taking account of the processes involved. Evidence suggests, for example, that organisations do not move in the direction indicated by the life cycle model but through a series of recurrent crises as they grow and develop.

Fifth, these models neglect how institutional forces shape HR policy and strategy. The principal focus of research on best-fit models is at the level of the organisation and the assumption is made that employers are 'free agents' able to make decisions based only on their own assessment of the situation. However, as Boxall and Purcell (2003: 61) have shown: 'firms are "embedded" in societies which regulate and influence them while also providing social capital of varying quality. The firm can never be the complete author of its own HRM.'

Sixth, categorising 'real' organisations can be difficult. Thus, while differences in HR practices between diverse organisations in different sectors can be apparent and clear to observe, assessing differences between two organisations in separate (or the same) segments of the same broad product market is more problematic. Hence it is sometimes difficult to apply best-fit models to real-life organisations.

THE RESOURCE-BASED MODEL

The resource-based model has emerged as one of the dominant perspectives in strategic management. The origins of the resource-based model of HRS are located within the business strategy literature, which was influential in initiating developments in pay systems, training and development and other HR issues. The essence of the 'resource-based' argument is that organisations comprise unique bundles of assets (including 'human assets') and that access to these, and the firm's ability to make effective use of them, provides the source of its competitive advantage in the marketplace. The resource-based view (RBV) of the firm concentrates on its internal resources, strategy and business performance, where the contribution of a firm's human resources is to promote competitive advantage through developing 'human capital' rather than just aligning human resources to the firm's strategic goals. The focus is not just on the behaviour of human resources but on the skills, knowledge, attitudes and competencies which people bring into the organisation, thus promoting sustained competitive advantage and corporate growth. As Sisson and Storey (2000: 34) argued: 'such an approach to understanding strategy places managers' role in identifying, utilizing and renewing such assets centre-stage'. The RBV of the firm is useful because it focuses on an organisation's internal resources and the specific factors enabling organisations to remain viable in the market and to achieve competitive advantage. In contrast to the best-fit model, the RBV of the firm is an 'inside-out' model.

The RBV of the firm is rooted in the business economics literature, where theories of profit and competition have identified the internal resources of the firm as the major determinants of competitive success. Proponents of this model, such as Barney (2007), define 'resources' as 'all assets, capabilities, organisational processes, firm attributes, information, knowledge etc. controlled by a firm that enable the firm to conceive of and implement strategies that improve its efficiency and effectiveness'. He classifies them into three categories: physical capital, organisational capital and human capital, where 'human capital resources' include the experience, judgement and intelligence of individual managers and workers in the firm.

In the RBV of the firm, competitive advantage occurs when a firm implements a value-creating strategy that is not being simultaneously implemented by its competitors. But this only occurs in situations of 'resource heterogeneity' (i.e. where resources vary across firms) and 'resource immobility' (i.e. where competing firms are unable to obtain resources from other firms).

Sustained competitive advantage, in turn, only exists when other firms are incapable of duplicating the benefits of competitive advantage. Hence a competitive advantage is not considered sustained until all efforts by competitors to duplicate the advantage have ceased. According to Barney (1991), 'the resource-based model of strategic management suggests that organisation theory and organisational behavior may be a rich source of findings and theories concerning rare, non-imitable, and non-substitutable resources in firms' (*ibid*.: 116). He identified four criteria that indicate whether the resource is getting a sustained advantage. The resource must:

- add positive value to the firm
- be unique or rare among competitors
- be inimitable
- not be substituted with another resource by competing firms.

Wright *et al.* (1994: 308), built on this in discussing how human resources meet the above criteria for sustained competitive advantage. First, by drawing on 'utility analysis' literature, they conclude that human capital resources do provide value to firms, as well as providing methods for estimating this value. Second, since cognitive ability is normally distributed in populations, they argue that human resources with high ability are rare. Thus 'it is safe to say that firms with high average levels of cognitive ability relative to their competitors possess more valuable human capital resources than those of their competitors'. Third, they also argue that, since HR advantages are most frequently characterised by unique historical conditions, causal ambiguity and social complexity, human capital is almost always inimitable. A potential problem with this is the notion that human resources are highly mobile. But Wright and his colleagues conclude that this is not the case, because of the high transaction costs in moving from one employer to another. Fourth, while accepting that it might be possible to substitute other resources in the short term, they suggest that it is very unlikely that such substitution could result in sustained competitive advantage. This is because, to the extent that the resource offsetting the advantage of human resources is not itself rare, inimitable or non-substitutable, it will not be imitated and human resources will again constitute a competitive advantage.

The role of human resources in sustained competitive advantage

Turning to the role of human resources in sustained competitive advantage, it is asserted, first, that firms with high levels of human capital have relative productivity advantages over their competitors (Baron and Armstrong, 2007). This is because they develop more efficient means of accomplishing their tasks. Such firms also have greater capacity to respond to external changes, through sensing the need for change and developing strategies to adapt to it. Second, HR practices help in developing human resources as a source of sustained competitive advantage by creating and developing a pool of high quality human capital. Third, those firms in an industry developing effective mixes of selection and reward systems have strategic advantage because human resources are not perfectly mobile. Fourth, having the correct mix of HR practices is a necessary condition for maximising the effectiveness of the human resource capital pool. Thus, although HR practices are not themselves sources of sustained competitive advantage, they play an important role in developing sustained capital advantage through developing the human capital pool. Also by affecting HR behaviour, HR practices moderate the relationship between this pool and sustained capital advantage.

In summary, the RBV of the firm suggests the need to integrate human resources in the formulation stage of a firm's strategy. This approach also provides a framework for examining the potential for a given pool of human capital to carry out a given strategy. It is claimed that the resource-based view of HRS demonstrates that strategies are not universally applicable but are contingent on having an HR base necessary to implement them. The view of human resources as a pool of capital implies a change in treating the costs incurred in HR interventions. If human resources are a source of sustained capital advantage, then they are better viewed as investment in a capital asset rather than as an outgoing expense.

Critiques of the RBV of the firm

At least five issues have been identified as arising from the application of the RBV of the firm to HRS. First, there are questions whether the RBV of the firm relates to the entire 'human capital' pool of an organisation or just senior managers. Although the latter are likely not only to be rarer in quality but also to have the potential to exert greater influence over organisational performance, it can also be argued that 'value' is dispersed throughout an organisation.

Second, questions have been asked whether the RBV of the firm relates to human resources/human capital practices or processes that employers use to manage employment relationships. Boxall (1996) made the distinction between 'human capital advantage' (a stock of exceptional human talent) and 'organisational process advantage' (socially complex, historically evolved processes) that emerge and are difficult to imitate. Combined together they form 'human resource advantage' or the idea that competitive advantage can be achieved by employing better people, using better HR processes.

Third, there is the issue of 'path dependency'. The RBV of the firm provides a particularly useful framework for analysing HRS because it recognises the importance of historical conditions and the different paths taken in organisations over time, as well as industry movements. The degree of trust that develops over time among different organisational actors is a good example. Also informal relations emerging at workplace level over time are particularly difficult to imitate.

Fourth, because the RBV of the firm focuses on organisational level, it downplays the significance of institutional arrangements at national level, industry level and networks beyond the firm. As Boxall and Purcell (2003) have made clear, some firms have immediate advantage in international competition because they are located in societies with much better educational and technical infrastructures than others. HR choices are fashioned by not only managers but also external forces.

Fifth, there has been a tendency to focus almost exclusively in the literature on the RBV of the firm on industry leadership and competitive advantage. However, as Boxall and Purcell (2000: 15) have argued: 'caution is needed before we get too carried away with the idea of differentiation. It is easy to exaggerate the differences between firms in the same sector.' In their view, 'all viable firms in a sector need some similar resources in order to establish their identity and secure some legitimacy.'

CASE STUDY   Polygon University – the challenges of developing a human resources strategy

Polygon University is a new university in a large conurbation in the Midlands, with over 20 000 students and 3000 academic staff and 1000 support staff, where there is also an older established university of similar size. The mission of Polygon University is to be a centre of excellence in education, research and consultancy services, and to prepare its students for their lives after leaving university. The key strategic objectives of the university are to offer high quality teaching, achieve excellence in selected areas of research, and provide high quality consultancy services to business and community organisations. It also seeks to optimise its income streams. The university depends on the commitment and performance of its staff to achieve these objectives. It recognises unions for academic staff and support staff and negotiates core pay and conditions nationally. Senior managerial and professorial staff are on personal contracts and performance-related pay. Given the competitive nature of student recruitment, research funding and other funding opportunities, university management, led by a new vice-chancellor, is planning to revise the institution's HRS which is currently largely a reactive one. Looking to the future, the HR aims of the institution include reviewing staffing needs, addressing staff recruitment and retention difficulties, preparing staff for future job demands, promoting equal opportunity targets, rewarding good performance and dealing with poor performance.

Question

Using this basic information about this organisation, imagine that you are an HR consultant who has been asked to advise university management which model or variant of HRS (or strategies) – best-practice, best-fit, or RBV of the firm – this organisation might usefully adopt to achieve its overall objectives. Drawing on the material provided in this chapter, and the case material, outline the advice that you would give and why you would give it. In determining your answer, you can make any reasonable assumptions about the organisation, provided that the case study is not changed in any way by what is added.

DEVELOPING AN EMERGENT HUMAN RESOURCE STRATEGY

Because many managers view the above models as somewhat abstract and unreal, as well as being very time-intensive to operate, they are more attracted to developing HRS pragmatically and incrementally. Where they do this, HR managers, in association with senior managers, are more likely to do so by relying on a human resource planning (HRP) or talent management (TM) approach (*see* Chapter 4). This enables them to take account of organisational circumstances and the firm's unique human resources, rather than drawing on any of the particular models outlined above. This suggests that they are likely to adopt a more contingent approach, so as to configure or tailor HRS to particular corporate conditions.

Sisson and Storey (2000) argued that the first step in developing an HRS is identifying the strengths and weaknesses of the current strategy, if one exists. In conducting a strategic HRM audit five main questions can usefully be asked:

- Is there a clearly understood HRS?
- Are people seen as a strategic resource by senior management?
- Are there clearly understood strategies for the main elements of HRM?
- Does human resource planning take account of internal and external environmental factors?
- Does the HR function have a strategic role in HRM?

HRS and HRP

Since employing the right people in the right place at the right time is essential for any organisation, the second step in developing an HRS is applying human resource planning (HRP) techniques to the task. This involves calculating the demand for human resources, starting with the organisation's business plan (however short term and limited it might be) and using a range of forecasting techniques. This is followed by planning human resource supply through auditing the current structure of the workforce. This requires tracking those employed, transferring internally and leaving the organisation. The matching process seeks to link the demand and supply processes together. From this an HR gap analysis can be derived and policy options reviewed. This quantitative data needs supplementing by qualitative data about staff competencies, career preferences and performance ratings obtained from internal documentation where this is available.

Subsequent stages of HR strategic planning are less clear-cut, less easy to articulate and less easy to operationalise. But several observers stress the importance of organisational 'vision' and 'mission' in establishing the values underpinning strategic choices in HR policy and practice. These seek to link the direction in which the organisation is heading with its key business objectives, HR objectives, HRS and HR policies. It is sometimes argued that managing culture change is also an essential element in developing a new HRS. Culture change is associated with the attempted reconstructing of employee behavioural patterns built around the interlocking concepts of organisational vision, mission, values, customer orientation and quality and performance management.

The final element that has to be considered in developing an emergent HRS is integration. This requires horizontal (or internal) integration of the resultant HR policies and practices. There is also the need for vertical (or external) integration to ensure that HR strategies are compatible with business strategy in turn (see Figure 2.1).

Organisational complexity

Ultimately, any analysis of HRS and HRP/TM needs to take account of organisational complexity. This includes the role of institutional forces and internal politics and how these shape managerial actions. In particular, as noted above, employer goals may be adapted, ignored or resisted by managers at lower levels in the organisational hierarchy or in different departments. As Marchington and Wilkinson (2008) have written: 'To conceive of management as a coherent, omnipotent and omniscient entity is clearly unrealistic as different managerial functions typically fight for influence within organisations.'

Figure 2.1 Corporate and HR strategy: an illustration of an integrated approach

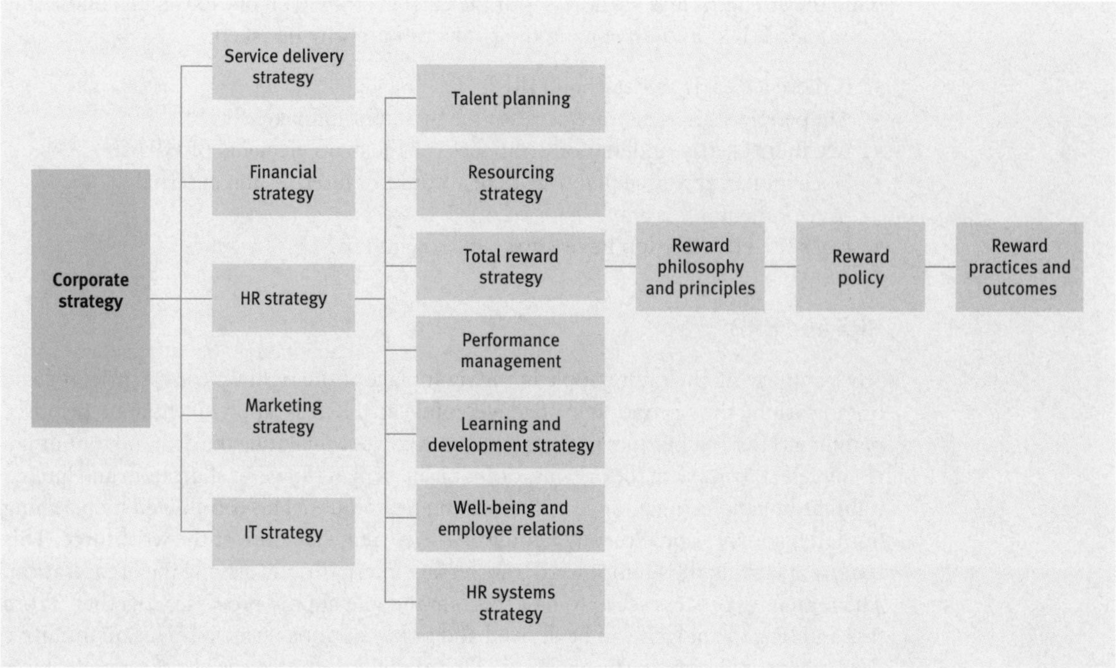

SUMMARY LEARNING POINTS

1   There is no single model of strategy, but four perspectives can be identified based on the outcomes of strategy and the processes by which it is made.

2   Although it is difficult to establish measurable links between strategy, business performance and HRS, there is growing evidence that HRS is critical in ensuring organisational success and effectiveness.

3   There are substantive reasons why middle managers and supervisors might not implement HR strategies in the ways desired by senior managers.

4   Best-practice models of HRS (HPWS or high commitment HR) assume that a universal set of HR policies and practices (including the partnership model) are conducive to high organisational performance, irrespective of the competitive strategy of organisations. A major critique of best-practice models is that they are not universally applicable to all organisations.

5   Best-fit models of HRS focus on the need to align HR policies and practices with the requirements of business strategy and assume that different HR strategies are suited to different business strategies. A major critique of best-fit models of HRS is that they neglect how institutional forces shape HR policy and strategy.

6   The resource-based model of HRS focuses on promoting sustained competitive advantage through developing human capital resources rather than just aligning

human resources to corporate strategy. A major critique of the resource-based model of HRS is that the individual organisation has only a limited degree of autonomy in determining its future.

7   Developing an emergent HRS is more likely to be a pragmatic activity and can be processed by identifying the strengths and weaknesses of existing strategy, data collecting for HRP purposes, while taking account of corporate vision, culture and horizontal and vertical integration. Finally, any analysis of HRS/HRP needs to take account of the complexities and the internal contradictions of organisational life.

REFERENCES AND FURTHER READING

Ansoff, H. (1965) *Corporate Strategy*. Harmondsworth: Penguin.

Appelbaum, E., Bailey, T., Berg, P. and Kallenberg, A. (2000) *Manufacturing Competitive Advantage: The effects of high performance work systems on plant performance and company outcomes*. NY: Cornell University Press.

Barney, J. (1991) 'Firm resources and sustained competitive advantage', *Journal of Management*, 17(1), 99–120.

Barney, J. (2007) *Resourced-Based Theory: creating and sustaining competitive advantage*. Oxford: OUP.

Baron, A. and Armstrong, M. (2007) *Human Capital Management: achieving added-value through people*. London: CIPD.

Beer, M., Spector, B., Lawrence, P., Quinn Mills, D. and Walton, R. (1984) *Managing Human Assets*. New York: Free Press.

Boxall, P. (1996) 'The strategic HRM debate and the resource-based view of the firm', *Human Resource Management Journal*, 6(3), 59–75.

Boxall, P. and Purcell, J. (2000) 'Strategic human resource management: where have we come from and where are we going?' *International Journal of Management Reviews*, 2(2), 443–63.

Boxall, P. and Purcell, J. (2003) *Strategy and Human Resource Management*. London: Palgrave Macmillan.

Boxall, P. and Purcell, J. (2007) *Strategy and Human Resource Management*. London: Palgrave Macmillan.

Boxall, P. and Steeneveld, M. (1999) 'Human resource strategy and competitive advantage: a longitudinal study of engineering consultancies', *Journal of Management*, 36(4), 443–63.

Chandler, A. (1962) *Strategy and Structure: Chapters in the history of American industrial enterprise*. Cambridge, MA: MIT Press.

Collins, M. (ed.) (1991) *Human Resource Management Audit*. Birmingham: North Western and West Midlands Regional Health Authority.

Connock, S. (1991) *HR Vision*. London: Institute of Personnel Management.

Cyert, R. and March, J. (1963) *A Behavioral Theory of the Firm*. Englewood Cliffs, NJ: Prentice-Hall.

De Wit, B. and Meyer, R. (1999) *Strategy Synthesis*. London: Thomson.

Department of Trade and Industry (1997) *Partnerships with People*. London: DTI.

European Commission (1997) *Green Paper: Partnership for a New Organisation of Work*. Luxembourg: Office for the Official Publications of the European Communities.

Farnham, D. (1994) *Employment Relations and the Rebirth of History*. University of Portsmouth Inaugural Lectures.

Farnham, D. (2005) *Managing in a Strategic Business Context*. London: CIPD.

Fombrun, C., Tichy, N. and Devanna, M. (1984) *Strategic Human Resource Management*. New York: Wiley.

Grant, R. (1991) 'The resource-based theory of competitive advantage: implications for competitive advantage', *California Management Review*, Summer, 114–35.

Guest, D. (1987) 'Human resource management and industrial relations', *Journal of Management Studies*, 24(5), 503–21.

Guest, D. (1989) 'Personnel management and HRM: can you tell the difference?' *Personnel Management*, January.

Guest, D. (2000) 'Human resource management, employee well-being and organisational performance', paper presented at CIPD Professional Standards Conference, University of Warwick.

Guest, D. (2001) 'Human resource management: when research confronts theory', *International Journal of Human Resource Management*, 12(7), 1092–106.

Harney, B. and Jordan, C. (2008) 'Unlocking the black box: line managers and HRM-performance in a call centre context', *International Journal of Productivity and Performance Management*, 57(4), 275–96.

Hendry, C. and Pettigrew, A. (1986) 'The practice of human resource management', *Personnel Review*, 15(5), 3–8.

Herzberg, F., Mausner, B. and Snyderman, B. (1957) *The Motivation to Work*. New York: Wiley.

Industrial Partnership Association (1992) *Towards Industrial Partnership*. London: IPA.

Industrial Partnership Association (1997) *Towards Industrial Partnership: New ways of working in British companies*. London: IPA.

Kochan, T. and Barrocci, T. (1985) *Human Resource Management and Industrial Relations*. Boston, MA: Little, Brown.

Kochan, T., Katz, H. and McKersie, R. (1986) *The Transformation of American Industrial Relations*. New York: Basic Books.

Legge, K. (1995) *Human Resource Management: Rhetoric and Reality*. London: Macmillan.

MacDuffie, J. (1995) 'Human resource bundles and manufacturing performance: Organisational logic and flexible production systems in the world auto industry', *Industrial and Labor Relations Review*, 48, 197–221.

Marchington, M. and Wilkinson, A. (2005) *Human Resource Management at Work: People management and development* (3rd edn). London: CIPD.

Marchington, M. and Wilkinson, A. (2008) *Human Resource Management at Work: People management and development* (4th edn). London: CIPD.

Markides, C. (2000) *All the Right Moves: A guide to crafting breakthrough strategy*. Boston, MA: Harvard Business School Press.

Maslow, A. (1943) 'A theory of human motivation', *Psychological Review*, May.

McGregor, D. (1960) *The Human Side of Enterprise*. New York: McGraw-Hill.

Mintzberg, H. (1979) *The Structuring of Organizations*. Englewood Cliffs, NJ: Prentice-Hall.

Penrose, E. (1958) *The Theory of the Growth of the Firm*. New York: Wiley.

Pettigrew, A. (1973) *The Politics of Organisational Decision-Making*. London: Tavistock.

Pfeffer, J. (1998) *The Human Equation: Building profits by putting people first*. Boston: Harvard Business School.

Porter, M. (1985) *Competitive Advantage: Creating and sustaining superior performance*. New York: Free Press.

Purcell, J. (1999) 'The search for best practice and best fit in human resource management: chimera or cul-de-sac?' *Human Resource Management Journal*, 9(3), 26–41.

Purcell, J., Kinnie, N., Hutchinson, S., Rayton, B. and Swart, J. (2003) *Understanding the People and Performance Link: Unlocking the black box*. London: CIPD.

Salaman, G., Storey, J. and Billsberry, J. (2005) *Strategic Human Resource Management: theory and practice*. London: Open University Press.

Schuler, R.S. and Jackson, S.E. (1987) 'Linking competitive strategies with human resource management', *The Academy of Management Executive*, 1(3), 207–19.

Sisson, K. and Storey, J. (2000) *The Realities of Human Resource Management*. Buckingham: Open University Press.

Sloan, A. (1963) *My Years with General Motors*. London: Sidgwick & Jackson.

Thomas, C. and Wallis, B. (1998) 'Welsh Water: a case study in partnership', in Sparrow, P. and Marchington, M. (eds) *HRM: The new agenda*. London: FT Pitman Publishing.

Torrington, D., Hall, L. and Taylor, S. (2008) *Human Resource Management* (7th edn). Harlow: Financial Times Prentice Hall.

Torrington, D., Hall, L., Taylor, S. and Atkinson, C. (2009) *Fundamentals of Human Resource Management*. Harlow: Financial Times Prentice Hall.

TUC (1999) *Partnerships for Progress*. London: TUC.

Tyson, S. (1995) *Human Resource Strategy*. London: Pitman.

Whittington, R. (2001) *What is Strategy – and does it matter?* London: Thomson Learning.

Williamson, O. (1985) *The Economic Institutions of Capitalism*. New York: Free Press.

Wood, S. (1999) 'Getting the measure of the transformed high-performance organisation', *British Journal of Industrial Relations*, 37(3), 391–418.

Wright, P., McMahan, G. and McWilliams, A. (1994) 'Human resources and sustained competitive advantage: a resource-led perspective', *International Journal of Human Resource Management*, 5(2), 301–26.

ASSIGNMENTS AND DISCUSSION TOPICS

1 What is business strategy? Why has business strategy become so important for organisations in recent years? Why is it so difficult to provide a universal model of business strategy to guide strategists in undertaking a strategic review in their own organisation?

2 Identify and discuss the necessary conditions for determining a business strategy in an organisation you work for or one with which you are familiar. What is the case for including HR issues within a business strategy?

3 What are the strengths and weaknesses of (a) the resource-based model of HRS, (b) the Harvard model and (c) the partnership model?

4 Distinguish between the 'business life cycle' model, the 'strategic and structural configuration' model and the 'matching' model of HRS.

5 Drawing upon the models discussed in this chapter, what sort of HRS (or mix of them) does the organisation you work for have (or in an organisation with which you are familiar)? Critically review it, indicating how it might be changed to achieve the organisation's business goals more effectively.

6 A new chief executive has been appointed to an organisation where people management has traditionally had a low priority and weak influence. She has asked you to provide an outline paper justifying the introduction of a new HRS. Do this, indicating the sort of issues that the HRS might address and how this might be done.

7 Identify, assess and evaluate the competencies and skills needed by an HR strategist.

Chapter 3

Competencies in People Resourcing

by Sylvia Horton

LEARNING OUTCOMES: TO BE ABLE TO

- Explain the origins of the competency movement
- Distinguish between the different meanings of competency
- Evaluate different ways of constructing competency frameworks
- Critique the use of competency frameworks in HRM
- Contribute to the development of a competency management approach

INTRODUCTION

The emergence of contemporary HRM, with its emphasis on strategic HR approaches and recognition of people as the organisation's most important resource, paved the way for the development of competency management. Competency management reflects a change from a job-based to a person-based approach to people resourcing and grew, in the 1980s, out of an economic context of greater globalisation and increasing competitiveness in world markets, the emergence of a knowledge-based service economy, flatter organisational structures and greater decentralisation, more emphasis on team working, and the need for both functional and personal flexibility within organisations. Organisations in both the private and public sectors have adopted competency frameworks that are designed to reflect the missions and goals of the organisation and to integrate organisational and HR strategies both horizontally and vertically. Competency management is not without its difficulties, although its benefits are still widely acclaimed. This chapter examines the debates surrounding the concept and describes the ways in which it is currently used in people resourcing.

DEFINITIONS AND CONCEPTS

What are competencies?

There are many different meanings, definitions and spellings and at least two distinct concepts to which the word competence is attached. There is also a range of foci, which can be the basis for developing competency frameworks; these include jobs, tasks, roles, persons and organisations. Furthermore, competencies can relate to different levels within an organisation – strategic, supervisory and operational. As the research report on *Competency Frameworks in UK Organisations* (CIPD, 2001) states:

> The terms 'competence', 'competences', 'competency' and 'competencies' are used almost interchangeably leading to some confusion not least regarding whether the term refers to an activity, a personality trait, a skill or even a task.   (CIPD, 2001: 2)

Having given this 'health warning', we will begin by making a distinction (reflected in spelling) between **competency(ies)** which refers to

> The behavioural characteristic of an individual which is causally related to effective or superior performance in a job   (Boyatzis, 1982)

and **competence(s)** which is

> The ability to perform activities within an occupation to a prescribed standard.
>   (Fletcher, 1991)

These two definitions reflect a difference in focus: the first relates to the inputs that help achieve successful performance at work and the second to the outcomes of competence. These are often described as 'behavioural competencies' and 'outcome-based competences'. The simplest way to describe the difference is that competencies are about the people who do the work, while competences are about the work and its achievement. These two approaches are sometimes identified as the American and British respectively but today they are often found in combination or hybrid forms and the terms are used interchangeably.

What is competency management?

Competency management is an integrated set of activities concentrated on implementing and developing competencies of individuals, teams and organisations in order to realise the mission and the goals of the organisation and improve the performance of its staff. It is a particular approach to identifying, attracting, developing and rewarding the competencies necessary to realise the mission, goals, objectives and targets of the organisation.

What is a competency framework?

A competency framework is both a list of competencies and a tool by which competencies are expressed, assessed and measured (Strebler *et al.*, 1997). Competency frameworks are generally based either on the 'behavioural' model, where competencies are expressed as the behaviours that individuals need to demonstrate their competency, and the 'minimum standards' model, which relates to *'the ability to perform activities within an occupation to a prescribed standard'* (Fletcher, 1997).

Core competence

The term 'core' competence also has several meanings. One use of the concept differentiates the essential (must have) from the subsidiary (might have) competencies that individuals need to do a job. A second use of the word is to refer to the common competencies that employees within an organisation need to have, irrespective of the role or the level at which they are operating. A third use by Hamel (1991) relates to organisations rather than individuals. He describes a core competence as 'a messy accumulation of learning', comprising tacit and explicit knowledge, skills and technologies, which gives an organisation a competitive advantage. Core competencies of an organisation make a significant contribution to 'customer'-perceived value and 'customer' benefits. It is the core competency, which makes the organisation competitively unique and creates gateways to new markets. Organisations may have different types of core competencies. They may be market-access competencies (management of brand development, sales and marketing, technical support), integrity-related competencies (quality, cycle time management, just-in-time inventory management) that enable the organisation to do things quicker and more reliably than competitors, or functionally related competencies (skills that enable unique functionality). It is the 'core' competence that makes an organisation distinctive and gives it that competitive edge over its rivals. This idea of the 'core competency' has been central to academic and practitioner thinking on strategic management for the last decade.

To add to this complexity of competency lexicography, Strebler *et al.* (1997) highlight further terminological confusion as businesses adopt 'capabilities' or 'key success factors' to describe what, in effect, are competencies. The word capabilities is also now widely used in the public sector where capability reviews of all central government departments were conducted in 2007 to identify shortfalls in key organisational competencies (Audit Office, 2009). Such variety alerts the reader to recognise that different terms may indicate differences about the focus (person versus job), the level of performance (competent versus effective or superior) and the object (role or organisation). To understand the subtle differences between the definitions and their use, one needs to trace the origins of the competency movement.

THE COMPETENCY MOVEMENT

The skills gap

By the late 1960s the economies of the USA and UK were experiencing pressures caused by globalisation, increased international competition and technological change. Both countries responded to these external forces in similar ways. First, there was a move to improve the standards and performance of the educational system, which was seen to be failing both business and individuals by not meeting the needs of the labour market or equipping young people with appropriate knowledge and skills to gain employment and do a good job. Reforms of the educational system occurred first in the USA and then in the UK. Both proceeded to transform their teacher training system and subsequently all three sectors of education. In the UK standard attainment tests (SATs), along with a national curriculum and output assessment, were introduced in primary and secondary schools during the 1980s. In the 1990s league tables and quality ratings entered higher education.

Second, there was a move to raise the level of training in the workplace. Britain's worsening economic performance during the 1980s led the government to initiate a number of investigations and reports, which emphasised the need for a flexible and adaptable workforce that could respond to economic change (Manpower Services Commission, 1981) and a comprehensive training programme based on new standards of occupational competence (MSC/NEDO, 1986). The British government put in place a system for setting standards across all sectors of industry. Industry Lead Bodies were created to develop the new standards and a National Council of Vocational Qualifications (NCVQ) was appointed to coordinate their work within a national framework. National Vocational Qualifications (NVQs) were seen as alternatives to the traditional educational qualifications conferred by academic examination bodies.

An NVQ comprises units of competence, each of which can be separately achieved and certificated. The NVQ process involved establishing the precise definition of the skills required to do particular jobs, assigning jobs to appropriate levels and evolving rigorous tests to assess whether people met the standards. It is not confined to manual and technical occupations but is fully comprehensive, covering all manual, clerical, technical, administrative, professional and managerial positions.

> The NVQ Framework covers five levels from the basic competence required to undertake elementary, routine and predictable work activities (Level 1) through intermediate skills and competences required for supervisory work (Level 3), to competences involving the application of complex principles in unpredictable contexts associated with responsibility for substantive resources (Level 5).
>
> (Winterton and Winterton, 1999)

Reports by Handy (1987) and Constable and McCormack (1987) indicated the particularly low standing and training of British management compared to its major competitors. The development of the chartered or professional manager, which began with the Management Charter Initiative in 1987 (MCI, 1990) was intended to encourage training and accreditation of recognised management skills that were subsequently developed within an NVQ framework.

During the 1990s the American government turned its attention to setting down national skill standards across all occupations and was clearly influenced by what had been happening in the UK. The Clinton Administration set up the National Skills

Standards Board (NSSB) in 1994 to encourage the development of a voluntary national system of skill standards that may be assessed and certified 'to ensure the development of a high skill, high quality, high performance workforce, including the most skilled frontline workforce in the world' (NSSB, 1998, sec. 502). The NSSB was replaced by the National Skills Standards Board Institute (NSSBI) in 2003, by which time nearly 60 per cent of American industry was covered by standards frameworks. The process is still continuing.

In the UK the emphasis on skills has also continued unabated but in the late 1990s the infrastructure was reformed. Learning and Skills Councils were created (these are now pending abolition in 2011), Sector Skills Councils (SSCs) replaced the Lead Bodies, and the NCVQ became part of a new Quality and Curriculum Agency in 1997. There was a shift in focus from NVQs to National Occupational Standards and National Professional Standards for professional groups. This reflected the growing comprehensiveness of the approach, which was no longer applicable to lower level occupations, but increasingly to professional organisational groups including teachers, healthcare professionals and the police etc. This also reflected the government's concern about the quality of professional preparation and professional practice. The 25 SSCs are employer-led independent bodies that have four key goals:

1. To reduce skill gaps and shortages
2. To improve productivity in business and public sector performance
3. To increase opportunities to improve the skills and productivity of the workforce
4. To improve the supply of skilled personnel and national occupational standards.

At the time of writing, the SSCs are being rigorously assessed by the National Audit Office to obtain re-licensing. The re-licensing framework and process are available on www.ukces.org.uk. Skills policy is in a permanent state of revision and refinement and the latest initiative is the creation of skills academies (Payne, 2008).

Managerial competencies

The second strand in the Anglo-American response to declining competitiveness was the investigation of management excellence. Some argue that the real father of the managerial competency movement is McClelland (1973) who argued that traditional exams and tests were no good as predictors of whether people could do a job well and that there were other ways to look for competencies that would predict success. His approach to identifying competencies and his methodology of 'behavioural event interviewing' (*see* below) took off in a consultancy group, McBer Associates, which he founded in 1963. For the next decade, McBer was busy developing competency models for many of America's top companies.

In 1982 the American Management Association commissioned Richard Boyatzis, of McBer Associates, to undertake research into 'successful' managers and to identify their attributes and features. Boyatzis (1982) concluded that there were 19 generic competencies that outstanding managers tend to have. These included personal traits, experience, motives and other attributes rather than specific skills. Boyatzis adopted the term 'competency', plural 'competencies', to describe an:

> underlying characteristic of an individual that is causally related to effective or superior performance in a job.   (Boyatzis, 1982)

Boyatzis observed 2000 managers in 41 different management jobs and 12 organisations. He found a great deal of commonality but emphasised that context was also important. He argued that it was necessary to construct a specific competency framework for each organisation even though the competencies are generic. His competency model, shown in Exhibit 3.1, groups managerial competencies into clusters which relate to the major functions of managers within any organisation. These are achieving the

EXHIBIT 3.1 Boyatzis' competency model

Goal and action management cluster	Human resource management cluster
Concerned with impact: being concerned with symbols of power to have impact on others, concerned about status and reputation	*Use of socialised power*: ability to use influence to build alliances, networks, coalitions and teams
Diagnostic use of concepts: identifying and recognising patterns from an assortment of information by bringing a concept to the situation and attempting to interpret events through use of the concept	*Managing group process*: stimulating others to work effectively in groups
	Accurate self-assessment: seeing personal strengths and weaknesses and knowing one's own limitations (threshold competency)
Efficiency orientation: being concerned to do something better	*Positive regard*: having a belief in others, being optimistic and valuing others
Proactivity: being disposed to take action to achieve something	**Focus on others cluster**
Leadership cluster	*Perceptual objectivity*: avoiding bias or prejudice
Conceptualisation: ability to construct concepts out of data and information	*Self-control*: being able to subordinate self-interest in the interest of the organisation
Self-confidence: having presence and being decisive, knowing what you are doing, believing in it and doing it well	*Stamina and adaptability*: being able to maintain energy and commitment and showing flexibility and orientation to change
Oratorical skills: making articulate and well-communicated presentations to large and small groups	**Directing subordinates cluster**
Logical thought: placing events in causal sequence, being orderly and systematic (threshold competency)	Threshold competencies of developing others, spontaneity and use of unilateral power

Source: From *The Competent Manager* by Boyatzis, R. © 1982 John Wiley & Sons, Inc. This material is used by permission of John Wiley & Sons, Inc.

goals of the organisation, providing leadership, managing people and controlling and directing others. What is significant about this model is the emphasis on what managers *can do* and *how they do things*, in other words on how they behave rather than what skills or knowledge they have. Boyatzis showed what made some managers exceptional and others not.

Core competencies

During the 1970s and 1980s, American academics turned their attention to strategic management as the key to competitive success. The work of Porter (1980, 1985) focused on the need to know and understand the market opportunities present in the fast changing environment and how to select from options to diversify, decentralise, integrate or merge. Ideas on strategic management revolved particularly around PESTEL (political, economic, social, technological, environmental/ecological and legal contexts) and SWOT (strengths, weaknesses, opportunities and threats) analysis (Andrews, 1980). In an important article in the *Harvard Business Review* (1990), however, Prahalad and Hamel suggested that companies need to understand their core competencies and capabilities in order to successfully exploit their resources. All organisations have different types of resources that enable them to develop different strategies, but they have a distinctive advantage if they can develop strategies that their competitors are unable to imitate. The ability of managers to identify and exploit these special or 'core' competencies spells excellence. The competency movement in the US was greatly advanced by the work of Prahalad and Hamel's perception of core competencies:

> Core competencies are the collective learning in the organisation especially how to co-ordinate diverse production skills and integrate multiple streams of technologies
> (Prahalad and Hamel, 1990: 82)

and Hamel's view that real competition today is the competition over competencies:

> conceiving of the firm as a portfolio of core competencies and disciplines suggests that inter-firm competition, as opposed to inter-product competition, is essentially concerned with the acquisition of skills.   (Hamel, 1991: 83)

Today, many organisations no longer define themselves as a collection of business units but as a portfolio of competencies.

Later thinking on competencies related to an organisation's ability to learn and acquire new capabilities and competencies as a more important determinant of its competitive position than its current endowment of unique resources, or the industry structure it currently faces. Sustainable competitive advantage in the long run is seen to arise from the superior ability to identify, build and leverage new competencies. The concept of the learning organisation, therefore, builds upon the ideas central to the competency movement outlined above and also continuing professional development which became more prominent in the first decade of the twenty-first century.

Differences between American and British approaches to competencies

What, therefore, are the differences, if any, between the American and British approaches so often referred to in the HR literature? First, there are differences between the behavioural or 'worker-oriented' approach (American) and the standards or work-oriented approach (British) found in the opening definitions. Second, there is the difference between the emphasis on excellence or superior performance (American) and the benchmark standard performance (British). As Roberts (1997: 70) expresses it, 'It is the difference between drivers of performance and standards of work.' Although these distinctions are conceptually clear-cut, in practice both approaches are found in each country and within individual organisations. This is partly because the companies that first developed a competency approach in the UK were subsidiaries of American corporations. It is also because of criticisms of the UK's 'flawed model' and the need to combine both norm and criterion referenced approaches (Adams, 1998). From the outset, there were serious criticisms of the NVQ system (Wilson, 1999) as it initially ignored explicit and tacit knowledge in favour of demonstrated skills. Many of those criticisms, however, have now been met and the concept has been widened and revised:

> Occupational competence is defined as the ability to apply knowledge, understanding, practical and thinking skills to achieve effective performance to the standard required in employment. This includes solving problems and being sufficiently flexible to meet demands. (NCVQ, 1997)

The occupational standards approach, which has succeeded NVQs at the higher levels, is now much broader and incorporates the idea of the reflective practitioner but NVQs are still used for lower-level staff. There are now many criticisms of behavioural models of competency, in particular the difficulty of identifying and operationalising the concept of competency, especially core competency, and of assessing and measuring it. In the civil service, there has been a return in part to the standards approach with the creation of the Professional Skills in Government framework. This was developed in collaboration with the Government Skills Council to ensure that all civil servants have managerial skills, knowledge and behaviours relevant to the job of public management.

WHO USES COMPETENCY FRAMEWORKS?

Although no comprehensive national surveys have been undertaken, there is widespread evidence that large private and public organisations, particularly in the service sector, are using competency frameworks and adopting competency management (Matthewman, 1995; Strebler and Bevan, 1996; Industrial Society, 1996; Winterton and Winterton, 1999; CIPD, 2001). According to the 2007 CIPD annual *Learning and Development Survey*, competency frameworks are still gaining ground:

> Sixty per cent of organisations have a competency framework in place for their staff and just under half of those who haven't, say they intend to introduce one in the next two years. (CIPD, 2007)

Competencies have become one of the 'big ideas' in HRM on a par with management by objectives (MBO) and total quality management (TQM), and competency management is fast becoming a prominent HR strategy not only in the UK and the USA but also internationally (Horton *et al.*, 2002: 205).

Many organisations have adopted the occupational standards developed by the NCVQ and now the LSSs, although their use is not as widespread as expected. Others have linked personal professional development to the standards set by the old Lead

Bodies such as the CIPD, the BIM, NMC and APM (Association for Project Management). Gaining accredited Investors in People (IiP) status has also been a major factor in adopting a structured competency-based training and development strategy, although this has been more important in the public than in the private sector because of a government commitment to IiP. There has also been pressure from the European Union and the British government to invest in human capital as the foundation for business success in the twenty-first century (DfEE, 1998; DfES, 2005). The emergence of an industry of private consultancy firms promoting competency management has been a further factor. A dedicated journal, *Competency and Emotional Intelligence*, published by Industrial Relations Services, is devoted entirely to the theory and practice of competencies and to disseminating information and good practice. It undertakes an annual survey on competency management, showing the increase in its uptake, and this is an important source of information on the growth and spread of its practice. The CIPD and British Institute of Management (BIM) have fully embraced the competency approach and as Lead Bodies also disseminate good practice and the latest ideas on HR issues. Both Lead Bodies have been particularly active in promoting performance management, and competencies are clearly at the centre of performance.

WHY DO EMPLOYERS USE COMPETENCY FRAMEWORKS?

In various surveys carried out to establish why employers adopt a competency-based approach to management, the reasons given tend to be the same. One survey (Wustemann, 1999) revealed that employers introduce competencies because they think it will:

- Improve individual performance (92 per cent)
- Support corporate values and objectives (82 per cent)
- Facilitate cultural change (60 per cent)
- Improve individuals' technical skills (44 per cent)
- Improve retention of staff (18 per cent)
- Improve recruitment and selection (6 per cent).

Many employers cite the need to develop the future skills required by the business as the main reason, while others believe that competencies will provide a common language and facilitate cultural change. Research carried out in the civil service (Horton and Farnham, 2000) showed the reasons for adopting competency management there were that it:

- enabled a common language and standard criteria to be applied across a range of HR functions;
- assisted both managers and employees in identifying training and development needs;
- enabled the organisation to promote its values, goals and objectives;
- assisted in the management of change;
- enabled employees to know what was expected of them;
- was a corollary of performance management.

This last point is important as it provides an explanation for the almost universal use of competency management in the civil service and its widespread use in other government organisations, including the NHS, local government, police and judicial system. Performance management has been imposed by central government on the public sector over the last 30 years (Massey and Pyper, 2005). All organisations now operate within clearly defined goals and objectives, performance targets and quality standards. This rationalistic and economistic approach requires that all resources, including human resources, are selected and used to ensure maximum performance. Competency frameworks are clearly an adjunct to performance management as they offer a means of identifying the skills, knowledge and attitudes required by staff to achieve the organisation's stated purpose.

A recent research report for the European Academy of Business in Society, *Leadership Qualities and Management Competencies for Corporate Responsibility* (Wilson, Lenssen and Hind, 2006), states that most world-class organisations use competencies to define and drive high performance. An interesting change of focus can be observed in the CIPD Change Agenda, which focuses on the learner and concludes that competencies are of central importance in providing a framework for the learner to take responsibility for their own learning (CIPD, 2003). Competency frameworks are often found in organisations without highly developed performance management systems, especially where they are used for staff development. An interesting rationale for adopting a competency approach is indicated by NASA, the American space agency: 'Competency Management allows you to systematically measure and monitor the knowledge base of the workforce. Thus enabling you to staff the right people with the right skills at the right time' (NASA Competency Management System Awareness Briefing, 2003). NASA deployed competency management to move from the 'Current State' to the 'Desired State'.

The current state was characterised by:

- Lack of 'One NASA' approach to knowledge requirement across the Agency.
- No Agency-level system allowing senior managers to get a more accurate picture of the Agency-wide competency strengths and weaknesses.
- Limited flexibility for management to develop options to resolve imbalances.
- Limited data available to enable workforce shaping and modelling for desired future programme directions and changes in technology.

The desired state was characterised by:

- Improved accuracy of data to better enable workforce planning across the Agency.
- Integration of human capital competencies with workforce-related business processes.
- Workforce competencies strategically linked to Agency programme/project requirements.
- Measurement and assessment of competency gaps for continuous improvement of human capital management.

The claims made for competency management are impressive and are often the reason why organisations in the private, public and voluntary sectors are adopting this fashionable idea. The claims, however, are often anecdotal with very little evidence to verify them or to measure their value added. There is also a question over whether this is a fad that will pass into the ether of organisational developments like MBO and TQM (Page, Hood and Lodge, 2005).

HOW TO CONSTRUCT A COMPETENCY FRAMEWORK

We have seen that a competency framework is a list of skills and competencies that identify and describe the behaviours and technical skills necessary to perform a particular role or task at a particular level within an organisation. In the past, organisations used very mechanistic approaches to job profiling by breaking jobs down into activities and processes, responsibilities and scope and identifying skills, experience or qualifications needed to do the job. Job analysis was in turn the basis for job descriptions and person specifications that would match the job, and for grading structures. Today the construction of job descriptions and person specifications is more sophisticated. Emphasis is placed on ensuring they are organic rather than static, encompass 'soft' people skills and competencies and are future rather than backward oriented. Triangulation is also normally used in the information-gathering stage.

Is constructing a competency framework any more than an aggregation of job profiles? The answer is *yes*. A competency framework defines the competency requirements relating to the tasks and roles within an organisation and puts them together into 'job families' and 'levels'. Job families refer to groups of jobs where the competencies are common irrespective of which part of the organisation the job is located or, in the case of generic skills frameworks, which organisation. Such frameworks usually comprise 'core competencies' that all people working within the organisation or type of job require. They may also include 'specific' competencies that are technical and relate to a particular role. Levels relate to the hierarchical position of the jobs and roles.

Competencies then are usually grouped into behavioural and technical categories. Behavioural competencies look at the way people behave or go about their work. They describe 'softer' attributes and traits and are therefore harder to observe and measure. Despite this, behavioural competencies are typically at the heart particularly of managerial competency frameworks. Technical competencies involve cognitive and practical skills that employees can demonstrate. These are frequently related to a specific role. They can only be used in a core framework, which covers similar workers, or they have to be added to core competencies for specific jobs. One way round this is to use '*competency to obtain technical knowledge*' which is often found in frameworks developed in the civil service, where a wide range of specialists and generalists work together in one organisation. In many organisations, technical competencies are written into specific job descriptions and are kept separate from the competency framework.

A competency framework, then, can be based on behaviours or on substantive knowledge and skills or on a combination of the two (*see* Exhibit 3.2). The emphasis, however, is always on what needs to be done and how it should be done. The various components of competencies are identified by Sparrow and Hilltop (1993: 402) as follows.

- *Body of knowledge*: what an employee needs to know in order to be able to do the job and achieve the objectives the job specifies. This includes information in specific content areas.
- *Skills*: what an employee needs to possess in order to perform the tasks associated with the job; can be applied to a range of situations.
- *Attitudes, values and self-image*: what an employee needs to display in connection with achieving the tasks; attitudes that predict behaviour in the short or long term.
- *Traits*: characteristics or qualities that are associated with effectiveness. These may be physical characteristics or consistent responses to situations.

EXHIBIT 3.2 Individual competencies

Knowledge	Expertise	Motivation	Values	Behaviour
To know		To want to know		To be able to
Technical competencies			Behavioural competencies	

- *Motives*: drives or thoughts that are related to a particular goal; the things a person consistently thinks about or wants that cause him or her to act with commitment.
- *Self-image*: the understanding that a person has of himself or herself in the context of values held by others.
- *Social role*: the perception of social norms and behaviours that a person needs to adopt in order to fit in.

Many writers differentiate between 'threshold' and 'superior' competencies. Threshold competencies are those that are essential to performing a job but are not causally related to superior job performance, while superior competencies are those that are causally linked to excellent performance. Boyatzis (1982), in his research into management competencies, identified 6 threshold and 15 superior competencies (*see* Exhibit 3.1).

The 10 most common competencies found in competency frameworks in the 1990s (Wood and Payne, 1998: 27) were:

- communication
- achievement/results orientation
- customer focus
- teamwork
- leadership
- planning and organisation
- commercial/business awareness
- problem-solving
- analytical thinking
- building relationships.

There appears, therefore, to be very little change over the last 10 years as, according to the CIPD (2007), the most popular competencies now are:

- communication skills
- people management
- team skills
- customer service skills
- results orientation
- problem-solving

Exhibit 3.3 is an example of a competency framework which illustrates many of the points made above.

EXHIBIT 3.3 The competency framework of a large housing association

Core competencies	Specific competencies
These apply to every job within the association	Each job will have specific competencies and these will vary according to level. There is an appropriate level for the relevant competencies attached to each job. Each level subsumes those below it
Achievement approach: is the desire to work well against a standard of excellence which is self driven and monitored. A competent individual will demonstrate how they: • Contribute fully to meeting targets or standards and achieve results, making best use of their own and others' skills • Constantly review own and others' performance to gain further improvements	**Thinking approach** *Decision making and initiative* (i) Systematically analyse causes of problems and identify solutions (ii) Ensure processes adapted, respond to pressure while noting policy and strategy (iii) Initiate action to improve/enhance job results or find /create new initiatives *Strategic thinking* (iv) Maintain a broad overview of business challenges and drive the business towards achieving long-term goals
Customer care: is the desire and willingness to address the needs of the internal and external customers. A competent individual will demonstrate how they: • Provide rapid and effective responses to their customers' needs and expectations • Determine priority according to those needs and recognise customer satisfaction as central to the business • Continually look to improve quality and promote excellence	**Relationships** *Oral communication* (i) Good, clear, convincing speech (ii) Good listener, understands others *Written communication* (iii) Conveys information clearly, accurately and convincingly *Teamwork* (iv) Contributes actively to working environment in which people work together, participate and take ownership of decisions: resolves conflict and build cooperation within and between teams *Influence and negotiating* (v) Uses variety of techniques to consistently gain agreement or acceptance of ideas or action plans

(Box continued)

People management approach: is the way an employee gives greater consideration to the needs of the individual in the organisation in order to contribute to its role as a caring employer. A competent performer will demonstrate how they: • Place value on the individual's and the team's contribution to the Association	**Organisation and managerial** *Organising and planning* (i) Thinks ahead and schedules activities (ii) Selects and uses techniques to measure, review and improve performance (iii) Participates and leads on projects, balances priorities and manages resources *People management and development* (iv) Motivates, inspires and supports others (v) Achieves results through delegation (vi) Collaborates across functions (vii) Identifies strengths and weaknesses (viii) Provides training, coaching and development resources to improve performance
Values: this approach is about being open and honest in dealing with colleagues and external contacts. A competent individual will demonstrate how they: • Are seen as fair and non-judgemental • Balance business priorities with customer needs and high professional standards • Recognise, accept and build upon the diversity of cultural values, generating commitment to corporate goals	**Technical** *Information management* (i) Retrieve relevant information quickly and efficiently (ii) Analyse data to show business trends and use in decision making *Financial and numerical application* (iii) Understand the financial implication of actions on day-to-day operations and on the business plan (iv) Plan budgets and business activities (v) Ensure financial and management control systems are effective *Professional competence* (vi) Apply appropriate knowledge and professional skills to meet job requirements

The competency framework in Exhibit 3.3 is linked to levels and each of the competencies is expressed in more specific terms according to the level. An example of 'achievement approach', which is a core competency, is described at different levels as shown in Exhibit 3.4.

EXHIBIT 3.4 Achievement approach competency by level

Level 1 Administrative assistant
- Completes tasks set according to standards prescribed by the manager or the organisation

Level 5 Middle management
- Achieves set targets, and proactively identifies and pursues new, stretching targets and opportunities
- Sets priorities or choose goals based on information about inputs and outputs
- Are actively interested in the overall business results
- Tries to improve performance by looking for new opportunities or revising working methods

Level 8 Senior management
- Is geared towards achieving results for the organisation, setting ambitious goals and objectives for self and other staff
- Generates a results-oriented working environment by motivating others and communicating the importance of achieving results
- Ensures that the necessary resources are in place to achieve corporate objectives

TECHNIQUES FOR CONSTRUCTING COMPETENCY FRAMEWORKS

There are several techniques that can be used to identify competencies and construct competency maps that fill in the details and describe all the different behaviours associated with specific and general competencies. These include repertory grids, critical incident analysis, skill questionnaires, diaries and benchmarking.

Repertory grids involve asking managers to divide their employees into 'good' and 'less good' performers. Two good and one less good performer are identified, and what makes the two good performers similar and distinguishes them from the poor performer is noted. This process is repeated several times until all the major differences have been identified. Managers are then asked questions to identify why the behaviours are different. The information is then categorised on a grid highlighting the range of behaviours in a variety of circumstances. This process results in a framework of behaviours that good performers might display.

Critical incident analysis involves collecting observed incidents that have proved to be very important or critical to performance. What emerge are the elements of job performance that make the difference between success and failure in a job. This process involves interviewing people who have observed or experienced at first hand the incidents being recorded. These anecdotal accounts are used to derive and build up a composite picture of job behaviours.

Skill questionnaires involve using a survey designed to find out, from a representative population, what are recognised as the requisite skills to perform a job well. Some involve the use of Likert scales to assess the relative importance attached to particular skills. Skills can range from cognitive through technical to interpersonal and personal skills.

Diaries involve asking people to keep a record of what they have done over a period of days to identify what tasks and what skills they needed to accomplish those tasks.

Benchmarking involves examining what other companies or organisations are doing and comparing your own practice against 'best practice' organisations. This can give an insight into what makes them successful or what is building success in your own organisation. Additionally it helps to see how a framework can work in practice. This is a very popular method either in isolation or combined with one or other of the methods identified above.

Competency frameworks are difficult and costly to construct. Some organisations do develop them from scratch, although often with the help of consultants. Many organisations draw upon lists that have been constructed in support of occupational standards, for example the CIPD, or Occupational Skills frameworks and adapt them. Others just buy off-the-shelf packages. Ideally competency frameworks should 'fit' the organisation. When preparing a competency framework it is important to take account of legislation, such as the sex, race and disability Acts, to ensure that none of the competencies discriminate against any particular group of employees or potential employees.

The CIPD (2007) *Learning and Development Survey* revealed that the majority, 65 per cent, of frameworks in their sample were designed in-house or in-house with consultants. Only 8 per cent used frameworks produced by external organisations such as trade associations or government bodies. What is interesting, however, is that the content of most competency frameworks is very similar and the core and technical competencies often have the same headings. This is particularly true in the UK where there are significant similarities across both public and private organisations. It is less the case in Continental European countries where there are greater differences between the public and private sectors.

ASSESSING COMPETENCIES

A major criticism of the use of competencies is that they are not observable and measurable, i.e. they are not SMART. Some mechanism, therefore, is essential for assessing competencies. One approach is to draw up clear descriptors of what is expected and give examples of desirable and undesirable behaviours. This was done by the senior civil service when they constructed their competency framework in 2001 – Exhibit 3.5 illustrates selected examples. 'Softer' skills, such as teamworking and interpersonal skills are notoriously difficult to measure objectively but a number of ways are increasingly used. These include:

- assessment centres
- development centres
- field assessment (360-degree feedback)
- self-assessment
- computer aided simulation
- questionnaire predicting competencies.

EXHIBIT 3.5 Senior Civil Service Competency Framework – leadership for results

1 Giving purpose and direction: Creating and communicating a vision of the future

Effective behaviour	*Ineffective behaviour*
Is clear what needs to be achieved	Looks to others to provide direction
Involves people in deciding what has to be done	Takes an overly cautious approach
Communicates a compelling view of the future	Assumes people know what is required of them without being told
Sets clear short- and long-term objectives	Loses sight of the big picture
Creates practicable and achievable plans	Allows a culture which is intolerant of diversity
Establishes standards of behaviour which promote diversity	
Agrees clear responsibilities and objectives to deliver results	
Initiates change to make things happen	

2 Making a personal impact: Leading by example

Effective behaviour	*Ineffective behaviour*
Visible and approachable to all	Says one thing and does another
Acts with honesty and integrity	Takes contrary views as a personal criticism
Is valued for sound application of knowledge and expertise	Fights own corner, ignoring wider interests
Resilient and determined	Accepts the status quo
Challenges and is prepared to be challenged	Aloof and arrogant
Says what people may not want to hear	Aggressive, not assertive
Takes difficult decisions and measured risks	
Accepts responsibility for own decisions	
Takes personal responsibility for making progress in equality and diversity	
Implements corporate decisions with energy and commitment	

(Box continued)

3 Thinking strategically: Harnessing ideas and opportunities to achieve goals

Effective behaviour	*Ineffective behaviour*
Sensitive to wider political and organisational priorities	Works only from own perspective or assumptions about the world
Assimilates and makes sense of complex or conflicting data and different perspectives	Fails to make connections between ideas or people
Finds new ways of looking at issues	Focuses solely on the detail
Homes in on key issues and principles	Focuses on intellectual debate at the expense of action
Considers the potential and impact of technology	Fails to consider the needs of a diverse community
Identifies opportunities to improve delivery through partnership	
Anticipates and manages risks and consequences	
Gives objective advice based on sound evidence and analysis	
Communicates ideas clearly and persuasively	

The whole framework, which is still in use, can be found in Pilbeam and Corbridge (2006).

An IDS study in 1997 showed how British Sugar included a measure of team feedback within its competency assessment: 'Each team member rates their colleagues against the performance criteria for each competency.' A similar approach was adopted with 360-degree assessment by Anglian Water where employees and managers agreed a number of objectives each year that would demonstrate achievement across the range of core competencies including 'soft' ones (Incomes Data Services, 1997a). There are now many software packages available that assist in staff appraisals and enable appraiser, appraisee, peers and subordinates to provide 360-degree appraisals electronically, but there is no information yet on how many companies or organisations in the UK are using them.

USING COMPETENCIES

The scope for using competency-based systems is wide-ranging. Figure 3.1 demonstrates the areas of HRM where competency frameworks can be used. They can also be used to integrate and link an organisation's main HR processes to its business

Figure 3.1 Using
competencies in HRM

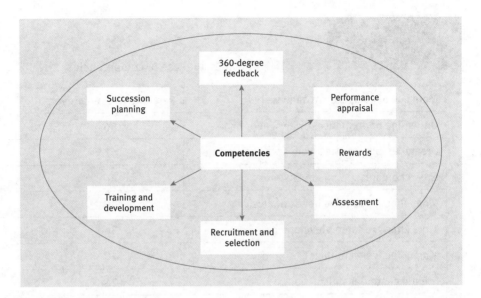

strategy. If used systematically, competencies tie together all HR processes from recruitment and induction to appraisal, training and development, and rewards, so that they focus on the same key expectations and objectives and provide mutual reinforcement to each other (Matthewman, 1998). The ability to use competency frameworks in this holistic way depends on the degree of HR sophistication and the HR policies, processes and practices that are in place (Hefferman and Flood, 2000). The adoption of competency frameworks is generally associated with organisations possessing well-developed HRM processes rather than more basic HR systems. The use of competency frameworks is also affected by organisational factors such as size, ownership and environment, as Hefferman and Flood (2000) found in their survey of 500 organisations in Ireland.

Most organisations tend to start using competency approaches in an *ad hoc* way in specific HR activities and focus on managers. The most popular areas to start with are training and development, staff appraisal and recruitment and selection (Horton, 2000; Rankin, 2001). A survey undertaken for *Competency and Emotional Intelligence* (Rankin, 2003) reported that the top five uses of competencies were – appraisal/performance management, training and development, selection, recruitment and promotion.

There is less evidence of competency-based reward systems, although some organisations have or are still using them. The civil service has had performance-related pay systems since the late 1980s and in 2001 a new pay and performance system was introduced in the senior civil service (SCS) linked in part to a new competency framework. Outside the SCS individual departments and agencies determine their own pay and reward systems and link their appraisal system and PRP to their competency framework. PRP has not been particularly popular (Horton, 2009: 130) and there has been some movement away from individual PRP in the public sector, especially in local government. In contrast, PRP and competency management are becoming more popular in the public sectors in other OECD countries (Horton *et al.*, 2002; OECD, 2005).

EXHIBIT 3.6 Employers' use of competencies

Main use of competency frameworks	Percentage of employers
Underpins performance reviews/appraisals	56
Greater employee effectiveness	47
Greater organisational effectiveness	44
More effective training needs analysis	36
More effective career development	36
More effective recruitment	28
Greater customer satisfaction	26
Better job design	19
Other	3

Source: CIPD (2007) Learning and Development Survey. London: CIPD. p19

More recently competency frameworks are seen primarily as a tool for managing performance and progression more effectively (Whiddett and Hollyford, 2007). A CIPD Annual Survey Report on learning and development (2007) found that the three main applications of competency frameworks are: underpinning performance reviews/appraisal; greater employee effectiveness and greater organisational effectiveness – see Exhibit 3.6.

- underpinning performance reviews/appraisal
- greater employee effectiveness
- greater organisational effectiveness
- more effective training needs analysis
- more effective career management.

Managers and individuals, however, often find it difficult to link their goals or the goals of the organisation to the competency framework, and therefore resist using it in a performance management context. Whiddett and Hollyforde (2007) suggest that to ensure a competency framework is fit for purpose there is a need to ensure that employees and managers:

- understand the purpose of the framework and how behaviours contribute to organisational and personal success;
- are clear about the mission and the goals and objectives of the organisation;
- ensure that the structure and the culture of the organisation support the behaviours in the competency framework;

- ensure that the employees have the basic knowledge and skills, which underpin the behaviours;
- keep the competency framework simple;
- train people in how to use the competency framework.

Recruitment and selection

The arguments for using competency-based approaches to recruitment and selection are, first, that it focuses on the knowledge, skills and aptitudes that people require to do a job rather than their qualifications; second, that it permits more objective assessment of job candidates because it is based upon a clear profile of the job; and, third, that it meets equity and diversity principles because the same criteria are applied in rating each candidate. Farnham and Stevens (2000) compare the traditional approach to recruitment in a local authority with a newly developed competency-based one and conclude that selection decisions are now more evidence-based and more objective and assessment of candidates is more rigorous. In addition to developing more relevant selection criteria, improving interviewing and assessment techniques, the competency approach can provide a link through to post entry training and development. Studies reveal that when recruiting externally greater emphasis is placed on 'soft', transferable skills, while in internal selection the emphasis is more on technical competencies (IES, 1997a, b, c, 2000, 2001). There is also some evidence that using competency-based recruitment and selection can reduce labour turnover and recruit higher-performing staff (CIPD, 2001). In the CIPD (2009a) *Recruitment Survey* 69 per cent of respondents use competency-based interviews in their selection process. The benefits of using a competency-based recruitment and selection process are that:

- it improves the accuracy in assessing people's suitability or potential for different jobs;
- it facilitates a closer match between a person's skills and interests and the demands of the job;
- it prevents assessors from making 'snap' decisions or basing decisions on factors irrelevant to the job;
- it underpins the full range of assessment and development techniques – application forms, interviews, tests, assessment centres and appraisal ratings;
- through disaggregating an individual's profile into specific skills and characteristics, development plans can more accurately be targeted to areas of true development need. (Wood and Payne, 1998: 23)

In addition it ensures that the process is more objective and all candidates are assessed in the same way and using the same criteria. It also ensures that the organisation does not contravene the discrimination legislation and is better able to justify its selection choice in the event of an appeal.

Performance management

Competencies are increasingly being used as a central feature of performance management systems, as the framework can provide a foundation for the whole performance cycle, from objective setting to appraisal and longer-term development (IDS, 1997a). Each competency identified in the framework at the appropriate level can be used as a basis of assessment in appraisals. Many organisations now expect employees to demonstrate their competency achievements. 'Soft' competencies that are very difficult to measure objectively can be assessed through 360-degree feedback. This is now being used increasingly in the civil service and the NHS, as well as some private organisations. However, most organisations tend to use a balanced approach to performance assessment where competencies are only one element, along with other performance criteria including output targets and objectives.

Training and development

Among those organisations that have adopted competence-based management (CBM) it is almost universally applied in the area of training and development. The major reasons are that organisations see the importance of competency frameworks in identifying skill and ability gaps, training needs and designing training programmes. In most organisations, competency-based training is business driven and aimed at immediate job needs (Strebler *et al.*, 1997), but in some it is oriented towards personal development. In the personal development review process competency frameworks are used to

- compare and identify
- discuss and agree
- undertake training and development
- review and evaluate.

Personal development, in most organisations, is still kept separate from performance management; although where competency management is holistic they are integrated. It is also kept separate from pay because it is felt it discourages people from admitting to development and training needs. Competency-based developmental approaches are more often used with managerial and white-collar staff than with technical and manual workers. A CIPD Research Report (2001) found that most organisations in their survey preferred to develop their own frameworks for training and development rather than use the MCI or other occupational standards. However, Loan-Clarke *et al.* (2000) found SMEs using NVQs and MCI. And today smaller organisations use the SSCs' standards. In the civil service, all departments and agencies are being encouraged to use the new Professional Skills in Government framework (www.civilservice.gov.uk).

Appraisal

Competency frameworks are being used increasingly in the appraisal process, especially in performance and development appraisals. They are particularly useful in identifying the development needs of individuals and mapping out routes to career advancement and progression. Clear objectives in terms of developing and enhancing competencies can be set and strategies for achieving these objectives can be agreed. Today the emphasis is increasingly on personal development and employees are expected to decide what development they need and how they could achieve it. Competency profiles help employees to see what is expected from them and how they can move up in the organisation. They also assist managers in talent spotting and planning for succession and ensuring that staffs are prepared to fill senior roles. They also enable managers to spot poor performance and it is often claimed that dealing with under and poor performance is one of the biggest challenges especially where employees have employment rights. An interesting development in the SCS, in response to poor performance, is the use of personal improvement plans (PIPs). A PIP is agreed between the civil servant, who has failed to achieve the objectives set or display the necessary competencies, and the line manager. The official is closely monitored over a six-month period and failure to improve is followed by a change of job, training or termination of contract (Horton, 2005).

Rewards

In 2000, one in eight companies was using competence-related pay and another 20 per cent were considering it (Pay and Benefits Bulletin, 2000). In 2009 (CIPD, 2009b) around one-third of employees received some form of performance bonus. There is wide diversity, however, in the ways that organisations link rewards to competencies. The most common method is to link individual PRP to competencies, although this tends to be a subordinate factor compared to output targets. In a survey of competence-related award systems, Adams (1999) (cited in CIPD, 2001) identified four main ways in which employers made the link:

- 76 per cent used competencies in the design of grading structures
- 80 per cent used them in promotion
- 88 per cent used them to determine pay rises or cuts
- 56 per cent used them to determine how an overall pay rise should be divided into shares.

Employers give the main reasons for using competency-based rewards as:

- to motivate people and to encourage better performance
- to increase flexibility among the workforce
- to change employee behaviour
- to give employees access to job progression and to allow some form of job progression where no other form of promotion opportunities exists.

The CBI recorded similar reasons in their 1999 report (CBI, 1999):

> Although there was a move in both the public and private sectors to link pay to competencies and performance during the 1990s, there is now a reversal of that trend. The reasons for the change of policy include, first, the effect on other uses of the competency framework such as development and training; second, the effect of individual performance-related pay on team working; and, third, the potential for demotivating employees who are not rewarded. There is also the so-called crowding out effect of extrinsic monetary rewards on the intrinsic motivating factors especially in the public services.   (Frey and Jegen, 2001)

ACTIVITY   The competency framework of a large housing association

1   Critically review the competency framework in Exhibit 3.3.

2   Exhibit 3.4 outlines the core competency of achievement approach at three levels –
    administrative assistant, middle management and senior management. Take the other three core
    competencies of customer care, people management and values and draft detailed descriptions
    for each of the three levels to provide the criteria for assessing performance.

3   Comment on the reliability and validity of using a competency framework for the assessment of
    individual performance.

THE PROS AND CONS OF COMPETENCY MANAGEMENT

The need for continuous improvement in performance has never been greater, whether it is in the NHS, local government, the prison service, the Prime Minister's office, Lloyds TSB or Marks & Spencer. During a period of recession, the need to improve performance and operate with a smaller workforce puts even more pressure on HRM. There are pressures on organisations not only to obtain and retain the 'skilled' staff that is needed to achieve organisational 'success' (Armstrong and Baron, 2005), but also to retain skilled staff while shedding the less skilled. Competencies have caught on as a 'catch all' term to encompass what are a bundle of aptitudes, skills, abilities, orientations and behaviours that make up a 'good' or 'excellent' employee. Especially in the area of management, organisations no longer need stable, conscientious and reliable employees, although all those qualities are desirable. They want exceptional, enterprising, innovating and able people to lead the organisation in a highly competitive and fast-changing environment. Competency frameworks and competency management have been marketed as the latest good idea to take on board to help management identify good staff and to manage them effectively.

It is also acknowledged that a competency approach assists in the integration of corporate, business and human resource strategies, both horizontally and vertically, and provides a means of integrating human resource activities at every level too.

Horton and Farnham's (2000) research in the civil service found unanimous recognition, by the human resource managers, of the benefits of the competency approach for organisations, managers and individual staff. Specifically, competency frameworks clarify what is expected of staff, provide more objective measures of performance and can be constructed and used to carry through cultural and organisational change. The CIPD identify the main benefits of a competency-based system as:

- employees have a set of objectives to work towards and are clear about how they are expected to perform their jobs;
- the appraisal and recruitment systems are fairer and more open;
- there is a link between organisational and personal objectives;
- processes are measurable and standardised across organisational and geographical boundaries. (CIPD, 2005)

Competency management, however, is not without its critics. The most common criticisms are that competency frameworks are generally over-elaborate and bureaucratic. The language used to describe competencies is often unclear and off-putting and also difficult to operationalise. More substantive issues are: the extent to which generalised, transorganisational competency frameworks such as MCI and occupational standards have wrenched them from their context and hence the tacit knowledge that contributes so significantly to good performance. Further related concerns are:

- Can competence or discrete competencies be separated from their contexts and interrelationships and from tacit knowledge?
- Is it even meaningful to seek to identify competencies as common to a range of jobs, and if this can be done what are the most significant competencies in, say, a manager's job?
- Can competence be effectively measured and if so against what criteria?
- How meaningful are the frameworks produced, e.g. for the SCS, the housing association or your own organisation?
- In the approaches to competence, what assumptions are being made about the nature of reality and the appropriate ways to study it, e.g. epistemological and philosophical frameworks?
- How far does the concept of competence incorporate both tacit and formal knowledge ('know how' and 'know what')?
- Do they eliminate subjectivity and bias? Are the models gender, ethnic, or age biased?
- A further critique is that competencies can be seen as producing clones and being static.
- Competency frameworks get out of date quickly, may be difficult to change and become an end in themselves rather than a means to an end!

The CIPD (2005) has raised concerns about competency frameworks being based on what good performers have done in the past and that this approach works against rapidly changing circumstances. What we need now are people with the right skills and attitudes for new ways of working. Organisations do not want clones but teams with mixed skills who balance each other's strengths and weaknesses. Competency frameworks need to be continually updated, revised or replaced. If competency frameworks are not the answer, then what is?

SUMMARY LEARNING POINTS

1 There are many definitions and spellings of competency, there are 'person-focused' and 'job-focused' approaches, core, generic and specific forms.

2 The competency movement developed because of increased competition from globalisation, changes in the structures and processes of organisations, work and HRM.

3 In the 1980s, training and skills were seen as the key to competitive advantage, and a national vocational qualifications (NVQ) framework was created and occupational standards established in both the UK and the US.

4 In the US, however, managerial excellence was also seen as the key to competitive advantage and this led to the development of competency frameworks based on behavioural characteristics of above-standard or excellent managers and later to the idea of core competencies of organisations.

5 Competency frameworks can be constructed in a number of ways using repertory grids, critical incident analysis, questionnaires, focus groups and job analysis.

6 First companies and then public organisations thought that using competency frameworks would bring significant organisational benefits, although there is little empirical evidence to substantiate this.

7 Competency frameworks are used most frequently in recruitment and selection, training and development, appraisal and performance management, but more recently to bring about cultural change and to assist employees in personal development and CPD.

8 There are criticisms of the competency approach, which include the difficulty of constructing frameworks, cost and time, a tendency to become over-bureaucratic, and the reduced ability of organisations to adapt to the future and innovate because of 'cloning'.

REFERENCES AND FURTHER READING

Adams, K. (1998) 'Peddling a flawed model', *Competency*, 5(3), 27–9.

Andrews, K. (1980) *The Concept of Corporate Strategy*. New York: Irwin.

Armstrong, G. and Baron, A. (2005) *Managing Performance: Performance management in action*. London: CIPD.

Audit Office (2009) *Assessment of the Capability Reviews*. London: The Stationery Office.

Boyatzis, R. (1982) *The Competent Manager: A model for effective performance*. New York: Wiley.

CBI (1998) *Employment Trends Survey*. London: CBI.

CIPD (2001) *Competency Frameworks in UK Organisations* (Research Report). London: CIPD.

CIPD (2003) *Focus on the Learner*. London: CIPD.

CIPD (2005) *Competency and Competency Frameworks*. London: CIPD.

CIPD (2007) *Learning and Development Survey*. London: CIPD.

CIPD (2009a) *Recruitment, Retention and Turnover Survey Report*. London: CIPD.

CIPD (2009b) *Reward Management: Annual Survey Report*. London: CIPD.

Constable, J. and McCormack, R. (1987) *The Making of British Managers*. British Institute of Management and Confederation of British Industry.

Department for Education and Employment (1998) *The Learning Age: A renaissance for a new Britain* (Cm 3790). London: HMSO.

Department for Education and Skills (2005) *White Paper Skills: Getting on in Business: getting on at work*. London: The Stationery Office.

Farnham, D. and Stevens, A. (2000) 'Developing and implementing competence-based recruitment and selection in a social services department', *International Journal of Public Sector Management*, 13(4), 369–82.

Fletcher, S. (1991) *NVQs, Standards and Competence: A practical guide for employers, managers and trainers*. London: Kogan Page.

Fletcher, S. (1992) *Competence-based Assessment Techniques*. London: Kogan Page.

Fletcher, S. (1997) *Analysing Competencies*. London: Kogan Page.

Frey, B. and Jegen, R. (2001) 'Motivation Crowding Theory', *Journal of Economic Surveys*, 15(5), 589–611.

Hamel, G. (1991) 'Competition for competence and inter-partner learning within international strategic alliances', *Strategic Management Journal*, 12, 83.

Handy, C. (1987) *The Making of Managers: A report on management education and training and development in the United States, West Germany, France, Japan and the UK*. London: Manpower Services Commission, National Economic Development Office and Confederation of British Industries.

Hefferman, M. and Flood, P. (2000) 'An exploration of the relationship between the adoption of managerial competencies, organisational characteristics and human resources sophistication and performance in Irish organisations', *Journal of European Industrial Training*, 24, 123–36.

Horton, S. (2000) 'Competency management in the British Civil Service', *International Journal of Public Sector Management*, 13(4), 354–68.

Horton, S. (2005) 'Performance Management in the British Civil Service'. Paper delivered at the Institute of Public Administration, Dublin, January.

Horton, S. (2009) 'Human Resource Management in the Public Sector', in Bovaird, T. and Loffler, E. *Public Management and Governance* (2nd edn). London: Routledge.

Horton, S. and Farnham, D. (1999) *Public Management in Britain*. London: Macmillan.

Horton, S., Hondeghem, A. and Farnham, D. (2002) *International Perspectives on Competency-based Management in the Public Sector*. Brussels: IOS.

IES (1997a) *From Admin to Strategy: The changing face of the HR function* (IES Report 332). Brighton: Institute for Employment Studies.

IES (1997b) *Skills, Competencies and Gender: Issues for pay and training* (IES Report 333). Brighton: Institute for Employment Studies.

IES (1997c) *Getting the Best out of your Competencies* (IES Report 334). Brighton: Institute for Employment Studies.

IES (2000) *Employee Returns: Linking HR performance to business strategy* (IES Report 365). Brighton: Institute for Employment Studies.

IES (2001) *Performance Review: Balancing objectives and content* (IES Report 370). Brighton: Institute for Employment Studies.

Incomes Data Services (1997a) *Performance Management, Study No. 626*. London: IDS.

Incomes Data Services (1997b) *Developing Competency Frameworks, Study No. 639*. London: IDS.

Industrial Society (1996) *Management Competencies: Managing Best Practice Report 21*. London: Industrial Society.

Institute of Personnel and Development (2000) *Recruitment* (IPD Survey Report No. 14). London: IPD.

Loan-Clarke, J., Boocock, G., Smith, A. and Whittaker, J. (2000) 'Competence-based management development in small and medium-sized enterprises: a multi-stakeholder analysis', *International Journal of Training and Development*, 4(3), 76–95.

Management Charter Initiative (1990) *Management Competencies: The Standards Project*. London: MCI.

Manpower Services Commission (1981) *A New Training Initiative: Agenda for action*. London: MSC.

Massey, A. and Pyper, R. (2005) *Public Management and Modernisation in Britain*. Basingstoke: Palgrave/Macmillan.

Matthewman, J. (1995) 'Trends and developments in the use of competency frameworks', *Competency*, 2(4), 1–20.

Matthewman, J. (1998) 'Competencies in practice: the 5th HR-BC/IRS Annual Survey', *Journal of Performance Through People*, 5(2), 2–10.

McClelland, D. (1973) 'Testing for competence rather than intelligence', *American Psychologist*, 28(1), 1–40.

MSC/NEDO (1986) *A Challenge to Complacency*. London: MSC/NEDO.

National Skills Standards Board (1998) www.ed.gov/legislation/GOALS2000/The Act/sec502.html.

NCVQ (1997) *Criteria for National Vocational Qualifications*. London: Qualifications and Curriculum Authority.

OECD (2005) *Performance-related Pay Policies for Government Employees*. Paris: OECD.

Page, E. (2005) A Symposium on Competencies and Higher Civil Servants, *Public Administration*, 8(4), 779–860.

Page, E., Hood, C. and Lodge, M. (2005) 'Conclusion: Is competency management a passing fad?' *Public Administration*, 83(4), 853–60.

Payne, J. (2008) *Skills policy in England and Scotland after Leitch*. SKOPE Issue Paper 18 Nov.

Porter, M. (1980) *Competitive Strategy*. New York: Free Press.

Porter, M. (1985) *Competitive Advantage*. New York: Free Press.

Prahalad, C. and Hamel, G. (1990) 'The core competence of the corporation', *Harvard Business Review*, 79–91.

Rankin, N. (2001) 'Raising performance through people: the eighth competency survey', *Competency and Emotional Intelligence – Annual Benchmarking Survey 2000/01*, 2–21. London: IRS.

Rankin, N. (2003) 'Raising performance through competencies', *Competency and Emotional Intelligence – the 10th Benchmarking Survey*. London: IRS.

Rankin, N. (2004) 'The new prescription for performance: the eleventh competency benchmarking survey', *Competency and Emotional Intelligence*, Benchmarking Supplement 2004/5. London: IDS.

Roberts, G. (1997) *Recruitment and Selection: A competency approach*. London: IPD.

Sanchez, R. and Heene, A. (1996a) *Dynamics of Competence-based Competition: Theory and practice in the new strategic management*. Oxford: Elsevier.

Sanchez, R. and Heene, A. (1996b) *Strategic Learning and Knowledge Management*. Chichester: Wiley.

Senge, P. (1990) *The Fifth Discipline: The art and practice of the learning organisation.* New York: Doubleday/Random House.

Sparrow, P. and Hilltop, J.-M. (1993) *European Human Resource Management in Transition.* Cambridge: Cambridge University Press.

Strebler, M. and Bevan, S. (1996) *Competence-based Management Training.* Brighton: Institute for Employment Studies.

Strebler, M., Robinson, D. and Bevan, S. (1997) *Getting the Best out of Competencies* (IES Report 334). Brighton: Institute for Employment Studies.

Whiddett, S. and Hollyforde, S. (2003) *A practical guide to competencies: How to enhance individual and organisational performance* (2nd edn). London: CIPD.

Whiddett, S. and Hollyforde, S. (2007) 'How to get your competency framework right', *People Management*, July, 44–5.

Wilson, D. (1999) 'The development of national standards in the USA', *Competence and Emotional Intelligence*, 6(3), 38–44.

Wilson, A., Lenssen, G. and Hind, P. (2006) *Leadership Qualities and Management Competencies for Corporate Responsibilitie*s. A Report for the European Academy and the Europen Academy of Business in Society, Hertfordshire: Ashridge.

Winterton, J. and Winterton, R. (1999) *Developing Managerial Competence.* London: Routledge.

Wood, R. and Payne, T. (1998) *Competency-based Recruitment and Selection.* Chichester: Wiley.

Wustemann, L. (1999) 'The way that UK employers are paying for competencies', *Competency and Emotional Intelligence – Annual Benchmarking Survey 1999/2000*, 46. London: IRS.

ASSIGNMENTS AND DISCUSSION TOPICS

1 What are the differences between the American and British approaches to competencies? Discuss why competency management has become an international phenomenon.

2 Identify the major problems in constructing a competency framework and evaluate three ways in which a competency framework can be constructed.

3 Find out to what extent competency frameworks are used in your organisation or one you have researched. Is it an *ad hoc* or a holistic approach?

4 Why do you think competency-based management of rewards is the least popular area of use?

5 Can managers be trained to use competencies? If so, how would you design, deliver and evaluate a training programme?

Chapter 4

Human Resource Planning, Talent Planning and Worker Flexibility

LEARNING OUTCOMES: TO BE ABLE TO

- Define human resource planning and evaluate systems for the effective forecasting of human resource supply and demand

- Critically review the characteristics of different labour markets

- Define talent planning and examine strategies for the management of talent

- Contribute to the design of strategies for retaining talented employees

- Examine the nature and implications of flexibility at work and flexible working

- Evaluate a range of patterns of work from employer and employee perspectives

INTRODUCTION

The effective resourcing of the organisation with workers (or talent in contemporary parlance) relies on the identification and definition of human resource requirements. For this to be achieved the organisation needs to know, first, where it is now in terms of market position or service provision; second, its objectives in the medium and long term; and, third, have a clear vision of its future development – in other words it needs a strategic plan. The strategic plan should take account of the workers already in the organisation, or available to the organisation, and the workforce behaviour in terms of length of stay and progression through the organisation. Human resource planning is a strategic opportunity, contributes to strategic decisions and shapes the development of the organisation. There are many ways of 'getting the work done', not only through the direct employment of workers, but also through outsourcing of activities and using contract labour. A variety of patterns of work and various forms of workforce flexibility can be utilised to meet the strategic requirements of the organisation and these are important elements of human resource planning. Talent management can be considered a contemporary manifestation of human resource planning, and a rebranding of HR activity, and talent planning and management are also explored in this chapter.

HUMAN RESOURCE PLANNING

Human resource planning (HRP) seeks to ensure that organisational objectives are achieved through the development and implementation of a human resource strategy. When considering HRP it is important to be clear what is meant by the term. The numerical, extrapolative method, usually referred to as workforce planning, is often termed a *hard* approach and focuses primarily on the number of staff in the organisation. Numerical indicators, such as number of staff in the different grades, labour turnover, stability, cohort analysis together with a precise definition of the organisational manpower system are used to create a numerical picture of the structure of the organisation and the movement of staff within it. This can be developed into a sophisticated mathematical model, but however sophisticated it becomes it remains a mechanistic approach which seeks to identify numerical shortfalls or excesses, or gaps, and seeks quantitative corrective action. It is probably best viewed as a sub-set of the broader HRP approach. HRP, in contrast, is more strategic, less focused on numbers and takes account of the competencies and skills of the workforce together with the HR policies and practices needed to meet strategic objectives. This is termed the *soft* approach. The IPM Statement on Human Resource Planning (1992) stands the test of time and reflects this broad view of HRP:

> Human resource planning is the systematic and continuing process of analysing an organisation's human resource needs under changing conditions and integrating this analysis with the development of HR policies appropriate to meet those needs. It goes beyond the development of policies on an individual basis by embracing as many aspects of managing people as possible with a key emphasis on planning to meet the skill and development needs of the future.

This definition exposes the holistic, strategic focus of HRP. This is not to deny the value of *hard* workforce planning, but to identify that it may be too narrow a perspective in dynamic organisational contexts and environments. HRP is also a logical and convenient starting point for examining people resourcing in practice. It provides the necessary signposts and a rational framework for the broad range of HR issues to be considered when seeking to resource the organisation effectively.

THE PROCESS OF HUMAN RESOURCE PLANNING

There is a need for good, accurate and up-to-date information for the quantitative and qualitative analysis of people needs and this is undoubtedly assisted through the use of a suitable HR information system (*see* Chapter 5). Bramham (1994) provided a useful framework for this analysis (Figure 4.1). The model has been adapted to give an increased profile to the resourcing dimension and identifies four main components of HRP activity:

1 Investigation and analysis – internal and external.
2 Forecasting to determine an HR imbalance or 'talent gap'.

Figure 4.1 The process of human resource planning *Source*: Adapted from Bramham J. (1994) *Human Resource Planning*, London: CIPD. Reproduced by permission of the publisher.

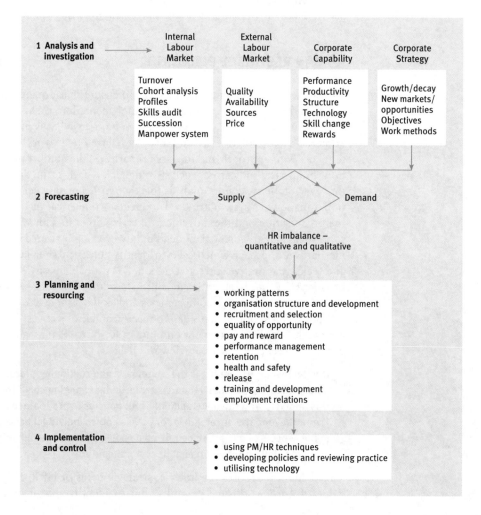

3 Planning, resourcing and retention activities.
4 Utilisation and control through HR techniques, policies and IT.

Investigation and analysis

Investigation and analysis are time-consuming, detailed and fundamental activities involving the accumulation of organisational and external information. Data are required from internal and external sources of labour availability, and the organisation needs to be assessed in terms of *what* work needs to be done and *how* it should be done to achieve corporate objectives efficiently and effectively. The analysis focuses on determining the *supply* of labour available from internal and external sources and the *demand* for labour based on assessment of internal organisational needs and external competition or constraints. This knowledge of labour supply and labour demand enables the identification of the quantitative HR imbalance or *talent gap* but it can also provide an indication of the quality of the labour demanded or the supply of labour available to the employer. Knowledge of the *talent gap* informs people resourcing decisions and shapes the planning, resourcing and development activities needed for determining contractual arrangements for employment, for recruitment and selection, for managing, motivating, training and rewarding performance and for achieving employee release from the organisation. HR techniques, employment policies and IT are the tools for the implementation and control of the resourcing plans.

The internal labour market

In order to develop a sound understanding of how the internal labour market operates, it is important that the organisation considers not only the quantitative measures, such as labour turnover, workforce profiles and cohort analysis, which will provide indicators of the behaviour of the workforce, but also the more qualitative measures such as skills audits and succession planning.

Labour turnover or wastage

This is a measure of the rate at which employees leave the organisation. It is needed not only as a measure of organisational wastage as a whole, but also, and more significantly, to identify areas of concern. A total wastage figure will provide an indication of attrition within the organisation as a whole, which is important for benchmarking. However, the figure may be meaningless in providing organisational information on which to act, as it can conceal significant differences in departments or occupational groupings. To be of value in the planning process different measures of labour turnover are needed to enable the HR planner to identify areas in the organisation with high or low turnover. High labour turnover can be costly and result in a poorly skilled workforce because employees may leave once they are trained and consequently more valuable. Investment in training will not pay off if employees do not remain long enough to return the investment. Low labour turnover can also be dysfunctional since it may lead to a static or depressed internal labour market and inhibit the entry of new blood into the organisation. Some departure from the organisation, such as retirement, can be planned, but it is the unplanned and unforeseen departure that is often problematic.

Different measures of labour turnover are available and it is important to be consistent in the measures used. It is also necessary to know what measures other organisations are using if benchmarking comparisons are to be made. Two common measures of wastage are the *transition method* and the *central method*. The transition method is a useful forecasting measure and compares the number of employees in post at the start of a period and the number of that group that leave during the period. It does not take account of other staff who start and leave during the period.

$$\text{Transition Rate (\%)} = \frac{\text{Leavers from the group in post at the start}}{\text{Total employees in the group at the start}} \times 100$$

The central method includes employees who join in the period and relates the total leavers to the average number of employees in a given period.

$$\text{Central Rate (\%)} = \frac{\text{Total leavers from the group}}{\text{Average number of employees in the group}} \times 100$$

These two measures give different results and when compared can indicate if employees are leaving within a short time of being recruited. Workforce stability can also be measured through calculating the percentage of employees with certain lengths of service – one, two or five years, for example. This is a reflection of accumulated knowledge, skill and experience.

$$\text{Stability Rate (\%)} = \frac{\text{Number of employees with service of one year}}{\text{Average number of employees in the group}} \times 100$$

In calculating labour turnover or stability it is important to use employee groupings that are meaningful such as occupational group, department or other logical grouping. Group size needs to be sufficient to give a meaningful result as small numbers distort the measure.

Cohort analysis

This describes the observation and recording of the behaviour and movement of a similar group of employees who join the organisation together. Wastage, transfer and promotion measures of this group provide information about the pathway through the organisation of those who stay and when and where the leavers go. Cohort analysis is a useful measure for those organisations that recruit relatively large numbers of the same type of employees at one time, for example new graduates or call centre staff. A thorough understanding of the rate at which individual members of the cohort leave, transfer or are promoted helps the planner to understand the organisation's need for employees of this type to meet future requirements.

Staff profiles

These provide additional indicators such as:

- Age distribution – useful in planning retirements, identifying age clusters and generally recognising and anticipating problems associated with imbalances in the age profile.

- Gender or ethnic distribution – useful in monitoring the effectiveness of equal opportunity initiatives and in identifying gender and ethnic segregation.
- Skills audits – provide clear indications of shortages or surpluses of key skills within the organisation. The collection and recording of skills is a complex and challenging activity as skills have to be defined clearly in terms of both content and level if the information is to be useful for planning purposes.

The manpower system

This is another element in quantitative workforce planning. In broad terms it involves the detailed identification of the different manpower systems operating in the organisation, the measurement of people stocks at the different levels and the flows through the organisation. It is essential to know the main entry points into the organisation and the main outflow points. This analysis can help in the targeting of recruitment activity and also at identifying internal blockages to progression – the key points at which larger numbers of staff are leaving.

Analysis involves looking at promotion and transfer rates and the wastage from the system. This provides useful information on progression and bottlenecks that lead to employees leaving the organisation and also on the behaviour and movement within the groups.

The external labour market

The external labour market has to be investigated to assess the availability of labour outside the organisation. The external labour market includes all those working or actively seeking work. Labour markets are dynamic. People usually enter the market from full-time education, or they may return to the labour market after a period of non-participation, for example following a period of caring or travelling. People may leave the market through retirement, illness or injury or a decision to no longer participate in the labour force. Referring to the external labour market implies there is only one external labour market, while in reality there are many. The managerial skill is in knowing the specific labour markets that need to be accessed by the organisation. The number and quality of people available externally is dependent on the nature, size, sector and geographical location of the organisation. External labour markets are defined by factors such as the nature of the work, the level of pay, the degree of organisational flexibility, the travel to work time and the number of hours for the job.

The local labour market, or travel to work area, is influenced by the attractiveness or otherwise of these pay, work and contractual factors, and other external issues such as transport and infrastructure. All of these define the distance an individual is prepared to travel to work and will shape the boundaries of the local labour market.

The global, national or regional labour market is delineated by geographical boundaries. The jobs included in a global, national or regional labour market are normally higher paid and more specialised. They usually require national qualifications or significant high-level experience, which command higher status and higher rewards. The more specialised the job requirements and the higher the job level, the wider the geographical boundaries of the labour market. The provision of home-working blurs the boundaries of the geographical labour markets as improved technology and the increasing availability of remote working change the boundaries of the labour market and give organisations access to workers who previously would have lived too far away.

Occupational or professional labour markets are defined by the qualifications required to practise or participate in a particular occupation.

It is important for the organisation to fully analyse the labour market for the different jobs within the business, to know how the markets behave and to recognise that these markets are different and have different features over time. Scanning the labour markets for information can be done through job advertisement analysis, professional networking and benchmarking, exit interviews with employees who are leaving (*see* Chapter 7) and accessing labour market information generated by government agencies and other specialist providers.

The nature and structure of labour markets

The participation rate – This is a measurement of 'who' is in a particular labour market. The recruiter needs to know which people are in the relevant labour market and how they can be attracted. The DWP, local authorities, the Careers Service, the Offices of Population, Censuses and Surveys and the Employment Service all provide access to a range of information on participation rates for different groups, for example by age, educational attainment, gender and socio-economic grouping.

Flows from education – These measure the profile of those leaving education. It is important for the HR planner to have a clear picture of the skills and qualifications of labour market entrants from all stages of education. Quantitative and qualitative changes in those exiting at different points in the education system will be significant to the organisation and influence decisions relating to recruitment, rewards and investment in training.

Competition in the labour market – This also affects the nature and structure of the labour market. A large number of organisations in a particular location seeking a workforce with similar skills will lead to a seller's market or a shortage labour market where competition for labour is high and the power in the employment relationship may move more towards the employee. This situation will affect some resourcing policies such as family-friendly policies, reward strategies and worker flexibility as organisations look for initiatives which will give them a competitive edge in the recruitment and retention of labour. A small number of organisational competitors may lead to a surplus or buyer's market where there are many applicants for jobs and the balance of power returns to the employer.

Several other issues influence the nature of labour markets. The level of unemployment affects labour mobility. High unemployment may make individuals more concerned for job security and more fearful of the reduction in statutory employment protection when starting a new job. This influences job change decisions and contributes to a more static labour market. It cannot be assumed that all labour markets will react to high levels of unemployment in the same way, as there will still be areas of skill shortage. Whether there exists a shortage (labour demand exceeds supply) or a surplus (labour supply exceeds demand), the labour market has a bearing on the balance of power in employment relationships between the sellers of labour (employees) and the buyers of labour (employers). Demographic changes influence labour markets because age and gender profiles and ethnic composition change over time. Demographic indicators and information on social trends increase the information available to the HR planner.

An analysis of the internal and external labour markets therefore generates considerable information about the supply, availability and cost of labour. The next stage of analysis and investigation is to consider the demand for labour within the organisation.

Corporate capability

Overall corporate performance needs to be disaggregated to highlight areas of strength and weakness. Targets and indicators are needed to identify how well the organisation is performing. Comparative techniques such as benchmarking can be used both internally and externally to compare activities and functions and to assess overall performance. Useful indicators include market share, profitability, financial turnover and other measures such as total output, product or service quality, employee productivity, employee retention and environmental auditing. The type of technology used within the organisation should be assessed. Investment in new technology may affect the demand for labour. It may increase demand by enabling the organisation to produce a higher quality product, to increase the market share and increase output. Alternatively the introduction of new technology may change the skills profile required and create the need for more investment in training the current workforce, or a need to release those without the required skills and replace them with employees with the 'right' skills. New technology can also result in labour substitution and reduce the number of employees needed.

Other measures of the HR aspects of corporate capability include an assessment of human capital. The issue of human capital has had an increased focus in recent years. The Department of Trade and Industry (DTI) set up the Accounting for People (AfP) task force which reported in 2003 that 'people and their related skills, knowledge and experience are a significant source of organisational wealth and competitiveness' and the task force recommended that the operating and financial review (OFR) should include non-financial measures in annual reports from 2005. This reporting will include information on employees and customers and provides stakeholders with a better understanding of the potential for future performance of the business. Mayo (2005) comments that 'there is now disappointment that the OFR regulations from the DTI are playing down these recommendations'. He goes on to say that 'it has stimulated focus on people related measures. But this is an area that is confused. Most organisations have some measures but they are often a jumble of metrics that lack purpose.' An analysis of corporate capability using, for example, the framework of measurements of human capital promoted in the CIPD report (2005a) *Human Capital Reporting – an internal perspective* will help in enabling the HR business partners to better understand the issue of corporate capability through factoring in the people indicators. The organisational structure can be examined for appropriateness for future developments. More flexible structures, promoting employee empowerment, re-engineering business processes, and decentralisation are indicative of the range of issues that might feature in the organisational assessment, which informs the human resource plan.

Corporate strategy

Organisations may benefit from a clear vision of their development in the medium to long term. The rate of change in many business sectors is high; nonetheless, even in dynamic times organisations must seek to retain control over their strategic development. A significant change in retailing has been an increase in 24-hour opening in the supermarket sector. Key participants in this sector will continue to review whether they compete or not and assess the impact of that decision on their market share. The progression in financial services from online banking to online purchase of financial products such as insurance and mortgages is a further example of changes in the strategic direction of these sectors. Strategic decisions have major, concomitant operational implications with associated and significant HR implications. Hence the importance of understanding the links between the corporate strategy and the human resource plans. Although the HR function may not be able to change the corporate strategy, early involvement in the planning process will facilitate the identification of the primary HR issues and thereby enable more effective human resource planning.

Forecasting

The forecasting stage of the HRP process involves the comparison between the identified supply of labour and the quantified demand for labour in terms of the skills and competencies needed to achieve the corporate aims. This stage is often an iterative process with a bottom-up forecast, from the line manager, often different from the top-down forecast, from the senior team, and questions of affordability are raised. There is almost inevitably an imbalance at this stage with an HR surplus or a shortfall identified. The mechanism for restoring the HR balance is the development and effective deployment of a range of HR policies and practices – the planning and resourcing stage.

Planning and resourcing

The development of a range of HR policies and practices enables the human resource plan to be achieved. A clear direction is needed to ensure that the HR policies are integrated with the corporate strategy to secure the best fit. These HR policies determine how the organisation is to be resourced with people and include not only recruitment and release policies to achieve numerical and skill set balance but also a range of policies related to the effective management of people at work. These HR policies are also significant retention tools and include patterns of work and flexibility, reward strategies, performance management, training and development and the effective management of the employment relationship – all of these are addressed in this text.

Implementation and control

The final stage in the HRP model is the approach to implementation and control. This focuses on the skills and competencies needed as well as internal HR expertise to ensure that the management of the organisation is both competent and confident in the design and operation of the resourcing policies. Policies need to be regularly reviewed to ensure compatibility with the corporate strategy and also coupled with the exploitation of information technology to enable the integration of the corporate strategy and the human resource plan. If people really are to make a difference and to contribute fully to corporate success, human resource planning is a vital and integrative element of HR strategy.

DEVELOPMENTS IN HUMAN RESOURCE PLANNING

Workforce planning reached its peak in the relative stability of the 1970s when unemployment was low and organisations needed to focus on identifying their supply of labour and retaining existing labour. Since the 1990s there has been less of a focus on the quantitative approach and increasingly a more holistic HRM approach is being adopted. Castley (1996) indicates that one of the main reasons for the move away from mechanistic workforce planning is that the traditional approach was more 'concerned with *head count* rather than with *head content* which prevented it from being flexible enough to meet the changing conditions'. Successful organisations now acknowledge that the need for human resource planning is greater than ever. The need to maximise employee contribution through the development of skills and competencies and to define employee objectives in terms that reflect the strategic direction of the organisation are essential if the organisation is to achieve continuous improvement and, through that, business success. The pace of change makes it problematic to identify all the changes that may occur in the business world but some prediction of workforce changes is possible; for example, the need for highly skilled knowledge workers, greater competition for talent, increased diversity in the workforce and the number of retirees exceeding labour market entrants. These factors provide encouragement for organisations to revisit human resource planning processes in order to better manage the changing corporate scenarios (White, 2002; Melymuka, 2002; Sullivan, 2002a).

Organisations providing round the clock services, such as emergency services and armed services, may use complex workforce planning models. This will include operational planning in the human resource planning processes in order to ensure appropriate staffing levels at particular periods, and complexity may be necessary for this distinctly operational HRP dimension. Reilly (1996), discussed in IES (2003), contends that:

> most organisations and most planning situations do not require a complicated technique or complicated software . . . it is unlikely that organisations will use complex statistical models because the environment is too unstable and cannot specify demand with any precision.

What business is looking for is flexibility and approaches to planning which enable the organisation to respond rapidly to external and internal change.

Scenario planning

One approach to human resource planning that has been around since the 1970s but which is now gaining in popularity is the idea of scenario planning. According to the IES (2003), 'Shell used scenario planning [in the 1970s] to generate a number of possible options for the future, with associated workforce implications. This approach was very beneficial to the company during the oil price crisis that followed, for which Shell's competitors were completely unprepared.' As the UK Minister for Transport said in 2006, 'we can either stumble into the future and hope it turns out all right, or we can try and shape it. To shape it, the first step is to work out what it might look like.' Scenario planning is an attempt to limit the criticisms of traditional human resource planning by developing an approach which is more flexible and which can be adjusted to take account of external or internal changes that may occur so that any future uncertainty has less impact on the organisation. Wheeler (2004) identifies five elements of scenario planning development. First, a team of managers and HR professionals should come together to develop scenarios for future strategic directions or business developments. The team aims to identify the type of employees, in terms of skills and competencies needed for each scenario and by doing this they are able to identify and develop 'talent pools' to meet these needs. Second, examine the available organisational skills to identify any shortages and build future skill or talent characteristics as desirable criteria into recruitment profiles to anticipate the need. Third, develop multi-talent pipelines, to support entry to or progression within the organisation. The organisational intranet can be used to 'paint a picture' of future talent needs and to generate interest in the organisation. Fourth, spend time building talent pools rather than searching for specific candidates, and recruit for potential. Fifth, build relationships with potential applicants through newsletters, online chat rooms or instant messaging (m-HR) to keep interesting and interested people on board.

Armstrong (2001) identifies the key advantages of a more flexible approach to human resource planning and scenario planning as:

- the anticipation of problems of shortage or surplus
- the development of a flexible workforce able to adjust to uncertainty and change
- less reliance on external recruitment
- improvements in the utilisation of labour through increased flexibility.

The skill in successful scenario planning is to generate a sufficient number of scenarios to increase the likelihood that the organisation will identify 'the right one' and not so many that there is information overload. This approach to HRP encourages creativity by facilitating the process of thinking outside the box, taking into account organisational strengths and weaknesses and supporting an element of beneficial risk-taking.

Succession planning

Succession planning is defined by Hirsch (2000) as 'a process by which one or more successors are identified for key posts (or groups of similar posts), and career moves and/or development activities are planned for these successors. Successors may be ready to do the job, short term successors, or seen as having longer term potential, long term successors.' Succession planning can be seen as a subset of human resource planning, management development, talent management and skills analysis. Hirsch goes on to describe what organisations are looking for in succession planning and she identifies four main objectives. First, the ability to improve job filling for key positions, together with faster decision-making. Second, processes which support an active development of longer-term successors. Third, the generation of information through a regular audit of the talent pool within the organisation. Fourth, fostering a corporate culture through the development of a group of people who are seen as a corporate resource. Succession planning can be criticised as being inflexible and of failing to acknowledge the changes that are apparent within organisations. CIPD (2009a) report that in the past succession planning was about organisational needs and failed to recognise that *people* make career decisions, not organisations. Just as the idea of organisational commitment to 'a job for life' has gone, it may no longer be realistic to expect that those identified as having the potential to fill key posts, and hence be highly desirable employees, will remain within the organisation.

TALENT PLANNING AND TALENT MANAGEMENT

Tansley *et al.* (2007) argue that persistent skill shortages, changing UK demographics, an increase in diversity and concerns with work–life balance have contributed to greater competition for employees who are capable of making a difference to organisational sustainability, thus raising the issue of talent acquisition, development, management and retention high on the corporate and HR agenda. According to Guthridge and Lawson (2008) 'a McKinsey Quarterly survey revealed that finding talented people was the single biggest managerial preoccupation of the next five years' and that few organisations were getting it right with the main barriers to effective talent planning and talent management being:

> short termist mindsets, minimal collaboration and talent sharing between business units and a lack of clarity of the role of HR in talent planning and the management of talent.

The changes in the world of work, increased globalisation, demographic changes, the emerging economies and the increase in knowledge workers highlight the need for managers and specialists to work anywhere in the world and the need for local staff with an international mindset. Guthridge and Lawson (2008) also explore the changes that have occurred since the publication of *The War for Talent* (Chambers *et al.*, 1998) and the way in which the talent planning and talent management strategies can be developed. First, they suggest that *talent should be targeted at all levels*; this extends the focus on talent from solely on the 20 per cent of top performers and recognises the contribution of a larger proportion of the workforce, illustrated by 'the insurer Aviva, with its strategy to manage the vital many'. Second, they stress the importance of developing *multiple value propositions*, recognising that there is no longer a single way of selling the employer brand and that careful articulation of a range of alternative paths for progression within the organisation enables the organisation to compete for talent using a range of very clear messages that appeal to a variety of potential employees. Third, they found that those organisations that *rotated talent across units* through 'the development of strong global talent management practices tended to outperform those with weaker practices'. This was especially apparent in multinationals where a period of time working overseas is often seen as a prerequisite for promotion. Fourth, they suggest that *HR should have 'more influence over business strategy'*. They express concern over the extent to which 'critical functional capability, such as workforce planning has been neglected' and also the need for HR to have a greater understanding of the business and higher visibility within it.

Definitions of talent are perspectival (Hughes and Rog, 2008) and according to Tansley *et al.* (2007) 'talent definitions (are) organisationally specific and influenced by the type of industry and the nature of its work dynamic'. CIPD research (2006b) excavated different perspectives on the nature of 'talent' and 'talent management', from which two definitions were distilled:

> Talent consists of those individuals who can make a difference to organisational performance, either through their immediate contribution or in the longer term by demonstrating the highest levels of potential

and

> Talent management is the systematic attraction, identification, development, engagement/retention and deployment of those individuals with high potential who are of particular value to an organisation.

This is similar to the position of Baron and Armstrong (2007), who define talent management as:

> A comprehensive and integrated set of activities to ensure that the organisation attracts, retains, motivates and develops the talented people it needs now and in the future.

Baron and Armstrong's (2007) definition of talent management implies a common starting point, but different organisations may have different definitions of talent, for example case study evidence (CIPD, 2006b) suggests it could be any of these:

- The top-performing 1 per cent of executives.
- The top 10 per cent of high-performers, whatever their role or level.
- Executives with potential for board-level appointments together with high-potential individuals who are identified as future leaders.
- Graduate trainees with potential for top leadership.
- *Each and every* employee is considered to be talent and is included in talent management activities – a 'total talent pool'.

The CIPD (2006c) *Learning and Development Survey* revealed that while more than half of the respondents declared that they undertook 'talent management activities' only 20 per cent had formally defined what they meant by talent. In order to be effective talent management needs to be aligned with the strategy of the organisation and supported by integrated HR processes.

Talent planning

Talent management starts with effective talent planning and this requires consideration of the corporate strategy. A clearly articulated corporate strategy allows a talent strategy to be developed and both quantitative and qualitative HR information related to the talent requirements to be identified. The approach to talent management is significantly influenced by the *definition* of talent appropriate to the business: an exclusive, inclusive, or a hybrid model. Developing and communicating a common understanding of talent within an organisation is critical to success and Tansley *et al.* (2007) draw attention to these inclusive and exclusive approaches to talent management, arguing that the approach will determine the size of the talent pool to be talent managed. An exclusive approach focuses on the high performers and the key positions for succession planning, usually located in a single talent pool. An inclusive approach recognises that there are employees at all levels who have talent which is useful for the organisation, and that making use of all talent can make a positive contribution to the business; this approach is normally characterised by multiple talent pools. Tansley *et al.* (2007) identify the pros and cons of an exclusive and an inclusive approach (Figure 4.2), but also state that:

Figure 4.2 The pros
and cons of exclusive
and inclusive
approaches to talent
management

An exclusive approach to talent management	
Pros	*Cons*
• Provides an identifiable, strategic resource for succession planning if aimed at the future leaders of an organisation • Targets resources: financial and non-financial • More opportunity to offer individualised development programmes to the talent pool • Easier to track and evaluate benefits	• High potential for reduced engagement and increased turnover among staff not included in the designated talent pool • Less scope to increase diversity • Reduced development opportunities and resources for those not on a talent programme • If focused on one occupational group or grade, other types of talent may be overlooked
An inclusive approach to talent management	
Pros	*Cons*
• Wider employee engagement if entire organisation has access to a talent pool • Supports succession planning for all key roles, not just senior management • Encourages the development of a more diverse workforce • More opportunity to benefit from all the talents in the workforce	• Learning and development and other resources are spread too thinly • Increased competition for progression which requires managing • Individuals with skills core to the business may receive less investment, to the detriment of the organisation's strategic goals

Source: from *Talent: strategy, management, measurement*. CIPD (Tansley, C., Turner, P., Foster, C., Harris, L., Sempik, A., Stewart, J., and Williams, H. 2007), with the permission of the publisher, the Chartered Institute of Personnel and Development, London (www.cipd.co.uk).

the research suggests that most organisations have hybrid views of talent that bring together aspects of both. In reality these approaches may be opposite ends of a spectrum with practice in organisations lying somewhere along that line as appropriate to the needs of that organisation.

A 'talent pool' is a term for a collective resource of talented employees, with selection for membership of a talent pool being based on performance review, assessment centre, 360 degree appraisal or line manager nomination. Transparency in selection for a talent pool will contribute to diversity objectives. Talent pools are not static; membership can change as business needs change and as talent supply changes. There are challenges to managing talent pools. Assigning an employee to a particular talent pool creates expectations for that employee. The employee will expect career progression, and in some organisations this may be defined in setting up the talent pool. Failure to deliver on this expectation may lead to employee frustration, ultimately causing them to leave the organisation. It is important, therefore, for the numbers and types of talent pools to be sustainable within the planned organisational growth or development. The talent strategy and plan needs to take into account the organisational context and the external context in defining the demand for and the supply of talent in order to forecast the talent requirements. The talent management strategy is implemented through the talent management pipeline, and the collection of integrated HR and management processes (*see* Figure 4.3).

A strategic talent management approach informs the quantitative and qualitative HR forecast to ensure that talent management activities are closely aligned with the business direction of the organisation. This is very similar to the process of human

Figure 4.3 Linking corporate and talent management strategies

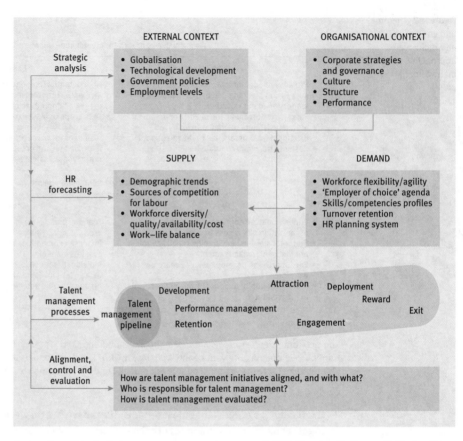

Source: from *Talent: strategy, management, measurement*. CIPD (Tansley, C., Turner, P., Foster, C., Harris, L., Sempik, A., Stewart, J., and Williams, H. 2007), with the permission of the publisher, the Chartered Institute of Personnel and Development, London (www.cipd.co.uk).

resource planning and is most recently illustrated by the *Linking corporate and talent management strategies* framework (Tansley *et al.*, 2007) – *see* Figure 4.3. This framework has many similarities with HRP models, such as Bramham (1994). Tansley *et al.* (2007) also identified that succession planning was frequently quoted by senior managers as being fundamental to talent management strategy, particularly where the talent management processes were focused on the pipeline for future leaders. Aligning talent strategy with business direction is a critical success factor and requires identification of the business strategies that have talent management implications, analysing internal talent supply and assessing external talent markets. The talent management framework in Figure 4.3 provides a step-by-step process for identifying talent pools and deciding upon talent management activities of succession planning, talent attraction, talent reward, talent development, talent performance management and talent retention.

Attracting talent

Analysis and forecasting of talent requirement indicates whether an organisation needs to attract in talent from outside the organisation. Talented employees are in demand,

EXHIBIT 4.1 Talent management in Cargill

Cargill is a large multinational company that employs just under 150 000 people in more than 60 countries. Its core business has five elements: crops and livestock; food; health and pharmaceuticals; financial and risk management; and industrial. Cargill has expanded rapidly, in particular its international expansion has been significant and its need for talented managers and leaders is increasing. Cargill has a corporate talent management team that is driving talent management in an integrated way, using recruitment, performance management and development to achieve high-level results. It brings together representatives from across the businesses globally twice a year to look at how talent might be managed and talent succession planned within the changing business context. Cargill has global definitions of leadership and talent that apply to every business unit in every location and a leadership model which is used by the whole business.

Cargill has different talent pools. For example, it has a 'corporate pool' that has 300 members and the responsibility for the careers of these members and their development lies with the top leaders in the organisation from across the world. It also has a high-impact performers (HIPs) definition that focuses on the high-performing 'thought leaders' who are critical to Cargill growth.

Benefits that Cargill have seen from their talent management initiative include: managers who can think and act globally; increased mobility of talent across the business; and talent with not just business knowledge, but also cultural awareness.

so consideration needs to be given to how to attract them. Striving to becoming an 'employer of choice', creating a strong employer brand and multiple employee value propositions (EVPs), to show the range of opportunities available, will contribute to the ability to attract talented employees. Having created a strong brand, it is essential to deliver and fulfil the expectations created in the psychological contract or employees will be disappointed and withdraw. Brand performance is strongly influenced by what actually happens in relation to talent management and development activities. The brand can be damaged by any mismatch between brand identity and employees' perception of the brand, and the brand's reputation.

Developing talent

Membership of a talent pool creates expectations of a structured, perhaps individualised and formal development process. Many organisations may include structured and formal development programmes often linked to qualifications such as the MBA into their management programmes but these are resource intensive and expensive options which may not be accessible to all, nor meet the needs of all those in the pool. Secondments, special projects and international assignments can each provide excellent opportunities for development. Less formal development opportunities may be provided through coaching. A performance coaching and development system introduced in PwC (2008) requires every member of staff to have a coach:

> Formal coach-coachee meetings, which are facilitated through our Performance Coaching and Development tool, happen at least three times a year. At the start of

the fiscal year, the coach and coachee establish a development plan. Mid-year, they conduct a progress check. At year-end, they have a formal review to discuss goals, career direction, strengths and challenges, feeding into the following year's plan. Through informal and formal coaching, our people receive ongoing feedback essential to their growth and development.

Rewarding talent

A strong employer brand and focused development are clearly important factors in managing talent. However, reward is a critical issue if the organisation is to retain the talent it has attracted and developed. Rees (2008) cites the Innecto study, which:

> established that the new generation of talent is focused on financial reward. Sixty eight per cent of those in the survey said that pay was their number one motivator. By contrast HR professionals identified personal pride as the number one motivator for talented people followed by competitive and challenging environment with financial reward placed third.

Much of the research on talent management focuses on the process of managing talent and little on rewarding talent, but this is a fundamental part of the effective management of talent. Organisations need to be clear about their strategic objectives and the part that talent plays in achieving the strategy in order to develop a total reward strategy that supports the talent. Rees (2008) identifies two types of talent for the purpose of developing base pay: those who are 'high performers' *now*, and who are making a significant contribution to organisational success; and those who are identified as 'high potentials'. She argues that the base pay aspect of reward should be different for these two groups. Failure to meet the expectations of the high performers may result in members of this group being enticed away by greater financial reward with a competitor. The high potential group is less likely to be attractive to the competitor as they have not yet demonstrated achievement of results so the use of intrinsic rewards, together with bonuses or long-term incentives may be appropriate. This is a complex issue and is raised here to place it firmly on the talent management agenda. Total reward strategies are discussed in Chapter 9, and it is unlikely that a single reward strategy will meet the needs to effectively reward high performers and high potentials without some adjustment; 'another new mindset is required to challenge the reward strategy for talented individuals' (Rees, 2008).

Talent management in changing economic times

The war for talent has focused on the competition for labour and the shortages experienced by organisations at a time of economic growth, but it is important to acknowledge the economic cycle and to recognise that a key feature is its cyclical nature. This means there are likely to be times when economic growth slows and that will have an impact on the labour market and the competition for talent. However, organisations that can retain their focus on talent planning and talent management may find that they are better placed for success when growth resumes. A CIPD survey (2009b) reports that over one-quarter of respondents have changed their approach to talent management in the light of the changing economic times. They report both positive and negative responses to the challenge; with just under half indicating that their training and development budgets are being cut, some are reporting the frustration being felt that their talent management programmes are being adversely affected, while others are reporting that they are having to get more value from the budget by '*doing things differently*' including less use of external providers, a more holistic approach to developing talent and examining the talent management systems. Others are reporting a shift of focus to retention of talent and are also acknowledging that talent management is a longer-term strategy and consequently striving to maintain their investment in talent. The uncertain times have encouraged more creativity with over half the organisations identifying and growing internal talent with an emphasis on targeted development. Others are still recruiting talent but are changing their recruitment practices with less use of recruitment agencies and more focus on new media as a cost-effective way to recruit. While the uncertainties can be seen as a threat, some organisations see this as an opportunity and there is evidence from the report that some organisations are looking for talent that has been shed by competitors.

EMPLOYEE RETENTION

Labour turnover rates vary in the UK from region to region and from industry to industry. Results from the CIPD *Recruitment, retention and turnover survey* (2009c) indicate that the aggregate rate of labour turnover for the UK was 16 per cent, a little lower than in 2008 when it was 17 per cent. Geographic variations indicate that high labour turnover rates are more likely to occur in regions where unemployment rates are lower and it is easier for employees to find alternative work. The survey also shows that labour turnover rates are highest in the private sector where the aggregate is around 18 per cent and lowest in the public sector at around 13 per cent. However, even these figures hide significant differences between industries and type of jobs. With these significant differences it is important that organisations identify their benchmark organisations accordingly with comparisons made on a geographic, industry and job group basis. A level of labour turnover can have positive benefits for organisations. Replacement of those who leave the organisation brings in 'new blood' and 'new ideas', providing the opportunity to reflect on how things are done, to develop new initiatives and implement new ideas. New employees can also bring in new and valuable competencies that can add value to the business. The difficulty lies in deciding at what level labour turnover stops being a benefit and becomes dysfunctional.

The problems of labour turnover

The most significant factors in determining whether levels of labour turnover are unacceptable are, first, the costs associated with replacement of an effective employee who leaves the organisation and, second, the availability of suitable potential employees within the labour market.

Costs of labour turnover

Despite the costs of labour turnover being significant it remains a measure that is rarely calculated. This is a lost HR opportunity because a more convincing case for new initiatives could be made if the costs of turnover are presented alongside the cost for retention strategies through proactivity in developing turnover costing models. Costing turnover is complex and will need to be tailored to the organisation, but costs may include:

- *The management and administration of voluntary resignations*: the processing of the resignation including responding to the letter, notification of payroll, exit interviewing.
- *Recruitment of replacements*: job analysis, review and preparation of job description and person specification, advertising costs, corresponding with applicants.
- *Selection of replacements*: shortlisting, administration of the selection process, management and administration time spent in applying the selection methods.
- *Administration associated with starting employees*: the letter of appointment, drawing up the contract of employment, preparation of new starter pack.
- *Induction of new employees*: the costs of central, departmental and job-specific induction.
- *Training of new employees*: on-the-job and off-the-job training, mentoring, appraisal, review, monitoring required until the new employee reaches acceptable performance standards.
- *Cover for the job while positions are unfilled*: the costs of temporary employees, the administration of the acquisition of temporary workers, the management of the temporary workers.

In addition to these basic costs it is also important to identify organisation-specific costs which may be relevant for the particular organisation or the post being filled. Indicative factors which can be considered here are the nature of the business, the contractual obligations and the impact on market share. If the nature of the business requires the provision of a 24/7 service and at any one time a defined number of staff to be fully operational, for example in the health and residential social services, education and emergency services, there will be no alternative to covering the post either through the allocation of overtime or through incurring the costs associated with acquiring temporary workers. Business deadlines may be contractually applicable and missed deadlines may incur additional costs. An inability to compete effectively due to staff shortages may impact on market share and diminish reputation. In practice the HR business partner has an opportunity to identify the key factors and develop models that will give a more accurate cost of labour turnover and thereby add value to the business through retention strategies.

Availability of suitable potential employees

Labour market conditions will determine the availability of suitable potential applicants. Knowledge of the prevailing labour market conditions, for the range of staff employed within the organisation, will determine the extent to which high turnover is a problem for the organisation. The CIPD survey (2009c) indicates that skill shortages are seen by employers as a problem, reporting that 81 per cent of organisations experienced recruitment difficulties. The principal reasons for these difficulties are skills shortages, lack of experienced applicants and level of pay. Recruiting in shortage labour markets presents particular challenges but lowering selection criteria without putting in place support for new recruits such as training, mentoring, coaching or shadowing may only serve to exacerbate the problem. Recruiting inappropriate people by overselling the job, appointing a candidate without the ability or potential to do the job or providing inadequate induction or support to learn the job to a level where successful performance is achieved can contribute to increased labour turnover because new employees will leave the organisation, and potentially compound the problem by impacting adversely on the reputation of the organisation as an employer.

Retaining talent

Given the issues associated with labour turnover there is a case for organisations to develop and implement a retention strategy. The CIPD (2009c) survey shows that the number of organisations experiencing retention problems has fallen to 69 per cent from 80 per cent in 2008. In order to fully understand the retention issues within an organisation, there is a critical need to identify why people leave. It is useful to analyse the reasons for leaving and to identify the 'push' and 'pull' factors. Push factors are those less desirable dimensions of the job or organisation that push people to look for a new employer and may include lower levels of pay, the nature of the supervision, limited potential for progression, lack of training opportunities, limited availability of flexible working or an absence of employee voice mechanisms. Pull factors, in contrast, are those dimensions which are attractive in alternative employers and may include a desirable working environment, a more convenient geographical location, an extensive range of benefits or an employer of choice brand. The aim is to enhance the less attractive push factors and to counterbalance the attractive pull factors, while recognising that some reasons for leaving are unavoidable, such as relocation with a partner or changing domestic circumstances. A key process in collecting information about why people leave is the exit interview and, while this is not without its problems, it remains a potentially valuable source of data. Exit interviews are discussed further in Chapter 7.

Why do employees leave?

The exit interview can provide data on why employees are leaving the organisation and identify the extent to which push factors or pull factors are exerting influence on employee retention. A survey by Hay (2002) suggests that the main driver to leave an organisation is the level of job satisfaction, with those planning to leave experiencing lower satisfaction levels. In examining the relationship between job satisfaction and turnover, the survey reports that of those who were satisfied in their job 83 per cent felt that their skills and abilities were being used, 66 per cent indicated that they had opportunities to develop new skills and 74 per cent were confident in their senior management. The respective figures for those employees who had low job satisfaction and were planning to leave were considerably lower at 49 per cent, 38 per cent and 41 per cent. The CIPD recruitment and retention survey (2009c) asked the respondents to identify the method they used to ascertain why employees leave the organisation: 89 per cent use exit interviews and 28 per cent use exit surveys, which they describe as anonymous questionnaires; 25 per cent use 'word of mouth' with 23 per cent collecting their information through staff surveys. The key reasons why employees leave are cited as: perceived shortcomings in promotion opportunities; change of career; a lack of development opportunities; redundancy; retirement; and level of pay. The survey reports a range of steps that organisations have taken to address employee retention together with the percentage of respondents adopting the various retention interventions:

47 per cent	Increased learning and development opportunities
45 per cent	Improved induction process
42 per cent	Increased pay
42 per cent	Improved selection techniques
39 per cent	Improved line management HR skills
35 per cent	Improved employee involvement
32 per cent	Improved benefits
24 per cent	Offered coaching and/or mentoring or buddy system
21 per cent	Better promotion to employees of employer brand
19 per cent	Improved physical working conditions
19 per cent	Revised reward systems to better recognise effort
18 per cent	Redesigned jobs to increase job satisfaction
18 per cent	Changed career management processes
15 per cent	Offered secondments
15 per cent	Better publicised levels of pay and conditions
13 per cent	No initiatives undertaken
13 per cent	Removed age-related policies
11 per cent	Increased diversity of staff
8 per cent	Offered flexible bonus
8 per cent	Used recruitment/induction bonuses

This is no more than a menu and clearly retention interventions need to be targeted at the reasons identified in the particular organisation rather than slavishly doing what other organisations do.

Why do employees stay?

While there is evidence (CIPD, 2009c) that many organisations try to identify why people leave, there is less evidence that organisations try to find out why people stay. Perhaps the easiest way to collect this information is through a regular staff survey and it should be possible to include questions in the survey that enable the organisation to identify the key factors which successfully retain employees. The data generated from asking why people stay will enable the employer to develop, target and implement interventions that not only improve retention rates but also improve the organisation's image as an employer of choice, with a potentially positive impact on recruitment as well as retention. The Hay survey (2002), in showing a significant difference in labour turnover, absenteeism and requests for transfer between high-satisfaction and low-satisfaction employees, concludes that an important 'way to nurture good people is to recognise that high achievers require a job that stretches their talents'. Investment in training and development to broaden and deepen the skills of their employees provides organisations with the opportunity to 'be forward thinking and improve retention by taking a long term perspective'. The DTI and Reed

Consultancy survey (2002) indicated that half of the 4000 respondents identified flexible working as the benefit that they would look for most in their next employment with a third saying that they would choose flexible hours rather than a pay increase of £1000 per year. Hertfordshire County Council was identified in *Human Resource Management International Digest* (2003) as developing an award-winning work–life balance initiative which has benefited both employers and employees and which has resulted in cash savings from, among other things, reduced recruitment costs, lower sickness absence rates and improved staff morale.

FLEXIBILITY AT WORK

The changing political, economic, social and global contexts of organisations have become catalysts for stimulating changes in the way in which work is organised. One adaptive response to these influences can be identified in trends in the changing patterns of work. The argument for continuous and broad human resource planning, in contrast to numerically focused workforce planning, is also a response to more turbulent organisational contexts. Traditional approaches to work organisation based on hierarchy, formalised structures, job definition, demarcation of activities and bureaucratic control may be less suitable for uncertain and unpredictable environments. Dynamic working environments require more organic responses and the pursuit of flexibility at work, in all its forms, can be viewed as another functional adaptation by the organisation to these external environmental influences.

Stimulants to the development of wider organisational flexibility also include:

- The pursuit of competitive advantage through organisational differentiation on people performance, hence the concept of the lean organisation.
- A shift from Fordist mass production techniques to flexible specialisation in production processes (Horton, 2000).
- Demographic and social changes, such as a changing age profile in UK employment, increasing female participation in the labour market, concern with work–life balance and lifestyle changes including an increased expectation of a 24/7 society.
- Globalisation and its impact on how organisations define their market and source their workforce.
- The deregulation of labour markets and the reassertion of the right to manage by managers to include managing employee flexibility.
- Changes in technology, particularly e-based and m-based technologies.
- The search for economic efficiency and the satisfaction of shareholder financial demands.
- Increasing number of service sector jobs and escalating customer aspirations and power.

Flexibility means different things to different people and is examined from two, but related, perspectives. The two perspectives are, first, the pursuit of *employee flexibility* at work by employers in order to maximise productivity and to secure economic efficiency and, second, the enhancement of *flexible working* opportunities to promote employee work–life balance. The first is principally an employer perspective and the second is principally an employee perspective, although clearly there are potential benefits to the employer in terms of the recruitment and retention of talented employees who are able to have their work–life balance needs accommodated. This second perspective of flexible working is mainly addressed through the deployment of different patterns of work or contractual working arrangements. The underlying meaning of flexibility implies adaptability and responsiveness to change, a positive feature. The CIPD (2009d) identify the two most cited reasons for organisations to make use of flexible working as 'to help retain staff' and 'to meet employee needs', followed by 'to comply with legislation'.

Forms of flexibility from the employer perspective

Flexibility at work can be defined as:

> the ability of the organisation to adapt the size, composition, responsiveness and cost of the people inputs required to achieve organisational objectives.

Various forms of flexibility exist and common categories include functional, numerical and financial (Leopold and Harris, 2009; Beardwell and Claydon, 2007; Redman and Wilkinson, 2006; Atkinson, 1996; Bramham, 1994). Categorisation should not suggest that the forms of flexibility are mutually exclusive and many forms of overlapping flexibility exist (Figure 4.4). Managers need to distinguish between these forms of flexibility in order to be able to seize opportunities for increasing organisational flexibility, but they should also be aware of the problems.

Figure 4.4
Overlapping forms of flexibility

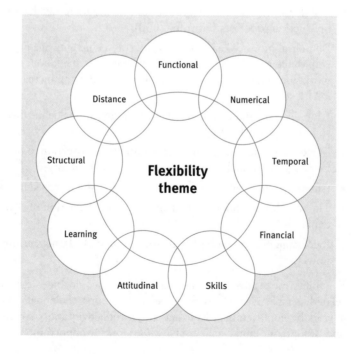

Functional flexibility

This relates to the employer's ability to deploy people in response to work priorities and demands. It can be either horizontal or vertical. Horizontal implies a reduction in demarcation between activities and tasks at the same level while vertical functional flexibility involves the acceptance and performance of tasks and activities by employees at either a lower or a higher job level. Functional flexibility is closely associated with skills flexibility (in order that employees are capable of performing the required tasks), with attitudinal flexibility and the redesign of work processes, equipment and layout. Reward systems need to be compatible with functional flexibility objectives so that task demarcations are not perpetuated or reinforced. Working practices which incorporate elements of functional flexibility include teamworking, empowerment, multi-skilling, re-skilling and project working.

Numerical flexibility

This is the scope to expand or contract labour supply through altering the number of people employed in proportion to product or service demand. It relies on the quick and easy engagement and release of people through rapid recruitment responses and the use of fixed, short-term or temporary contracts. Numerical flexibility also involves the increased use of agency staff and the subcontracting of work. It requires an acceptance by management that using employee redundancy is a legitimate human resource practice.

Temporal flexibility

This is concerned with restructuring working hours to increase organisational responsiveness to work demands. It has the aim of maximising productive time and minimising unproductive time and may be formal or informal. Formal temporal flexibility can be achieved through the use of annual hours arrangements and through zero- or core-hours contracts. Flexitime arrangements constitute temporal flexibility, but in this case they are primarily responsive to employee, rather than employer, needs. Informal temporal flexibility includes employee discretion to adapt working hours to work demands and also the growing expectation that employees should work 'beyond contract' when necessary (the concept of elastic working hours).

Financial flexibility

This increases the ability of the organisation to control employment expenditure. It is pursued in a number of ways. First, through the use of local market rates to determine the commercial worth and the reward package of employees to ensure value for money in employing staff. Second, through the use of individual pay arrangements instead of collectively regulated and uniform pay levels. For example, performance-related pay and profit-related pay. Third, through shifting from national or central bargaining to local bargaining arrangements to intensify the linkage between employment costs and local affordability. Fourth, through the use of non-consolidated bonus pay and non-pensionable payments to avoid those payments which relentlessly and permanently increase the pay bill.

Skills flexibility

This incorporates not only skills development and acquisition, but also employee receptiveness to the updating and extension of the skills necessary to reduce job demarcation and promote employee versatility. Skills flexibility may be vertical or horizontal through a deepening or a widening of the employee's skill base. Skills flexibility can be promoted through the use of competencies, which emphasise what people actually have to do, and to what level or standard.

Attitudinal flexibility

This infers a specific focus on the encouragement of flexible employee attitudes characterised by a receptiveness to learning new skills, a willingness to engage in functional flexibility and a responsiveness to changes in working practices or management approaches. Flexible attitudes and behaviour can be recognised, rewarded and reinforced through integrated human resource practices and the management of corporate values.

Learning flexibility

This has links to the concept of the learning organisation, broadly defined as an organisation which continuously transforms itself through the ability of its members to learn. The development of learning flexibility by employees includes a willingness to transfer learning from the familiar and comfortable ways of working to include embracing new ways of getting things done. Learning flexibility is associated with contemporary HRD philosophies, quality management and Investor in People standards.

Structural flexibility

As an objective, this is a response to concern that organisational hierarchy may reinforce job specialisation and restrictive working practices and consequently inhibit flexible working and organisational responsiveness. Teamworking, matrix organisations, project working, lateral job moves, delayering, empowerment and process re-engineering offer opportunities for increasing flexibility through fluidity of organisation structure.

Distance flexibility

This is achieved through better use of technology. Work may be undertaken in locations remote to the work organisation through teleworking and the exploitation of electronic mail, mobile technology and videoconferencing – effectively making the location of the worker irrelevant.

The flexible firm

Many of these forms of flexibility can be identified within the model of the flexible firm, reproduced in Figure 4.5. Atkinson developed the model of the flexible firm in the 1980s and, old though it is, the model is still valuable in bringing together different forms and

Figure 4.5 The flexible firm

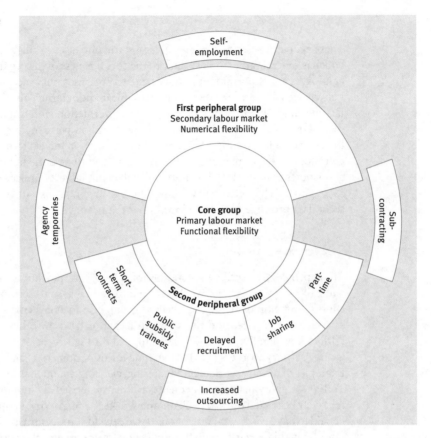

Source: Atkinson (1984), Institute of Manpower Studies, University of Sussex.

dimensions of flexibility and in providing a framework for understanding and analysing alternative ways to achieve flexibility and of identifying some of the implications of the flexible workforce. The flexible firm concept broadly divides the workforce into a core group, a first peripheral group and a second peripheral group. Alternative labels, in the context of the labour market, are primary, secondary and tertiary.

The primary group

This group is ascribed core status and tends to comprise full-time, permanent, career employees. It will normally include knowledge workers, managers and other professional and technical staff. This group can be considered critical to organisational success through the possession of the essential skills and knowledge which differentiate the organisation in competitive environments. Primary workers are insulated, or offered some protection, against market fluctuations in demand for their labour. This group of employees will normally be well rewarded and relatively secure and tend to have access to development and career opportunities in order to secure their long-term commitment to the organisation. In return, core status implies employee willingness and ability to engage in multi-forms of flexibility in order to contribute significantly to the achievement of organisational success. Core workers have careers.

The secondary group

These people are ascribed first peripheral status and have a skills and knowledge profile which is general rather than specific to the core business of the organisation. Secondary employees are important, but not critical, to organisational success, as their skills and knowledge will normally be readily available in the external labour market. Examples include administrative, secretarial, sales, production and supervisory staff. This secondary group of employees can be employed on permanent contracts, but with a lower level of job security than core employees, or on longer-term fixed or temporary contractual arrangements. Patterns of work tend to be non-standard, and this group contributes to numerical flexibility through being subject to release and reengagement as required. They effectively buffer the core against insecurity. Employees in the secondary group tend to have jobs rather than careers.

The tertiary group

These people are ascribed second peripheral or external status and consist of 'beck and call' or 'as and when' workers, exemplified by casual, zero-hours or core-hours contracts of employment. This tertiary group also includes labour provided through contracts for services and the subcontracting of work to other organisations or to self-employed individuals. Workers supplied through agencies can also be part of this group. Tertiary workers provide dynamic forms of numerical and financial flexibility. Examples of tertiary work include catering, cleaning, maintenance and assembly work. Tertiary employment arrangements are characterised by minimal job security, a relatively restricted reward package and worker disposability. People in this group can be said to have work rather than jobs or careers. In stark contrast it is possible to recognise also in this tertiary group those elite portfolio workers who possess skills for which there is high demand, who provide work on a paid-for-results or a consultancy basis, and where the correspondingly high rewards compensate for any lack of employment security or regularity. Perhaps this elite group are best described as core externals and include specialist providers of information technology support, change process consultants, interim managers and even chief executives.

The flexible firm model is a conceptual model, which helps our understanding, but it is not a prescription or a blueprint for the structuring of organisations. There is no rigid definition of the types of work which constitute each segment, nor is there guidance on the relative size of the segments in relation to organisational contingency factors. The model is a visual, analytical tool and allows a probing of the different forms of flexibility, an analysis of the varying patterns of work and employment packages, and a consideration of the relative size and managerial implications of the primary, secondary and tertiary elements. Handy (1989) proposes an alternative, but parallel flexible model consisting of a professional core, a flexible labour force and a contractual fringe to form what he terms 'a shamrock organisation'. This trinity of organisational 'leaves' are distinct groups and are managed, organised and rewarded differently based on their differing expectations of and commitment to the employment relationship. In common with Atkinson's model (1984), the shamrock concept is silent on the most appropriate distribution of work between the three groups, but it does provoke further critical evaluation of organisational activity and consideration of how it can most effectively be resourced.

There is a debate about whether the ideas associated with the flexible firm and shamrock organisation represent a strategic human resource response or whether it more appropriately represents an operational level response as a pragmatic reaction to the intensification of competitive pressures and the managerial opportunities presented by the deregulation of labour markets. The positive flexibility thesis is that it provides a buffer in increasingly turbulent organisational environments, increases the strategic responses available to address the issue of competitive pressure, and enables the optimum utilisation of people in the pursuit of corporate objectives. The negative flexibility thesis is that it capitalises on or exploits the labour market vulnerability of employees, is a managerial lever to intensify work demands, reintroduces disharmony in terms and conditions between different groups of workers which results in tensions and disintegration into subcultures, and inhibits the development of the committed employment relationships and healthy psychological contracts which are essential to organisational success. Legge (1998) expresses the view that 'flexible employment largely benefits the employer at the expense of the employee' by giving primacy to the need of the organisation to survive in competitive environments through the satisfaction of escalating customer demands and the financial demands of shareholders. This exposes a potential contradiction, which was expressed by Geary (1992) as:

> The peripheralisation of a significant element of the labour force would seem to have little in common with one of the main dictums of HRM – to value and develop employees as an organisation's key resource.

A balanced view of flexibility at work is advocated and this needs to be based on, first, an awareness of the different forms of flexibility and, second, an appreciation of the potential for positive and negative consequences of flexibility initiatives. Ultimately the complexity and inherent contradictions in the flexible firm approach require active management and demand a diverse range of human resource and employment relations skills.

Forms of flexibility from the employee perspective

The employee seeks flexibility at work not just from enhancement to the work itself but also from the range of options available to get the work done. Sparrow (2008) comments that 'flexible working is a growing phenomenon, and government plans to increase the right to request flexible hours . . . are set to accelerate the trend'. However, this is not the only stimulus: the last significant increase in flexible working was in the 1970s at a time of recession, and economic pressure may lead to an increase again in flexible working. Sparrow quotes Peter Thomson, of Henley Management School, who says, 'there is no magic rule that says knowledge work must be done in an office', and also Alex Reeve of Microsoft who contends that 'work is a thing that you do, not a place you go to'. The environmental impact of travelling to a place to work and the rising cost of office space may also be triggers for change. Thomson predicts that 'from being seen as a family-friendly employee benefit, flexibility will become a business and productivity-friendly strategy', and adds that 'flexible working is more productive, staff are more loyal, there is less absenteeism, and employers feel that they can attract and retain them at a time and a place that suits their lifestyle'. He also puts forward the view that 'conventional working rewards inefficiency. Results based working rewards productivity.'

PATTERNS OF WORK

In the last 40 years UK labour markets have undergone significant change. In the post-war era employment was not regulated and employers had the power to 'hire or fire' at will. Employment contracts were normally full time and the standard pattern of work was 40 to 48 hours a week from Monday to Friday; in the early part of that period, Saturday working was also included. Some industries worked in shifts, but this was mainly in the continuous production or the personal service industries. The contractual options for 'getting the work done' were relatively few and simple. This is no longer the case and increased flexibility can be achieved through an array of patterns of work which are available to employers and, by definition, to employees. 'Patterns of work have always been subject to change but the pace of change is now more rapid than ever. The driving force for this change comes from both organisations who want to change the way their employees' work is organised to better suit their business needs and from individuals who want to achieve a better balance between work and home life' (ACAS, 2005) – see Exhibit 4.2.

EXHIBIT 4.2 Changing patterns of work

Employment status of the population: changing patterns 1975–1993 (Gregg and Wadsworth, 1995, *Oxford Review of Economic Policy*)

- The number of full-time (FT) permanent employees fell by 33 per cent
- The number of workers on FT, fixed-term or temporary contracts trebled
- The number of employees on PT contracts increased by 25 per cent

WERS: *Inside the Workplace* (Kersley *et al.*, 2005)

- 27 per cent of workers on PT contracts (public sector 33 per cent, private sector 25 per cent)
- More than 30 per cent of workplaces are using fixed-term or temporary contracts
- Annual hours contracts in 6 per cent of workplaces

The European Commission (2006)

'Fixed term contracts, part time contracts, on-call contracts, zero hours contracts, contracts for temporary workers hired via employment agencies and freelance consultants have become a feature of European labour markets, with non-standard contracts now covering 40 per cent of the EU25 workforce.'

First, there is a choice between contracts of employment, where the worker has employed status and associated employment rights, and contracts for services, which enable the organisation to get the work done without having direct employees. Workers with contracts for services contribute to numerical flexibility for the organisation and have more limited but increasing employment rights. Second, there are a significant number of variations to the standard, full-time contract; these are termed non-standard or atypical arrangements. However, as less than 50 per cent of the working population has a traditional full-time, 'permanent' job with an employment contract, perhaps this arrangement should no longer be termed standard. An increasing range of atypical contracts and patterns of work have developed primarily in response to concerns for competitiveness and the need to control costs by resourcing people in line with demand but also to meet the needs of an increasingly diverse workforce with differing needs. Diverse working arrangements produce diverse employment challenges and the human resource planner needs to be aware of these. Imaginative use of a variety of contractual options enables employers and employees to work towards the flexibility that is so often needed to maximise the benefits to the employer while allowing the employee to choose working arrangements that fit with their out-of-work requirements. However, there are criticisms of flexible working (Guest *et al.*, 1998) which include the difficulties of managing the variety of contracts, which Guest calls 'contract chaos', and perceptions of fairness in terms of who has access to flexibility, but with good systems and transparency of operation these potential problems can be overcome.

The CIPD report (2005b) on the impact and implementation of flexible working surveyed 585 organisations 'to explore how organisations are making use of flexible working practices, their motives for doing so and the effects they are seeing on their businesses'. They found that organisations offer a combination of both formal and informal arrangements with part-time working being the most prevalent, with 90 per cent offering this option; around 40 per cent enhance the statutory right to request flexible working (available to parents of young children – *see* Chapter 8); employee retention and meeting employees' needs are given as the most common reasons for offering flexible working, with around 25 per cent citing business and customer needs as important factors. The most significant perceived effects of flexible working identified by the respondents are employee retention, employee motivation and enhancement of recruitment opportunities.

Temporary work

WERS (Kersley *et al.*, 2006) found that over 30 per cent of organisations surveyed employed workers on temporary or fixed-term contracts, that temporary working arrangements were much more prevalent in larger organisations and that the majority of organisations showed an increase in the use of temporary working. A temporary employment contract is for a limited time and the expectation of both the employer and the employee is that the employment will cease. A temporary contract can be terminated by either side giving notice and temporary workers have statutory employment protection rights which accrue to the employee at various points (*see* Chapters 8 and 18). A fixed-term contract is also temporary, but the period of employment is normally defined and the contract expires at a fixed point in time without a need for notice.

Temporary contracts have been common in organisations to cover specific requirements such as maternity leave or long-term sick absence, but the increase in use is largely attributable to the need to match staffing to workload demand to achieve numerical and financial flexibility. Temporary working among graduates has increased and there is evidence that a substantial number of temporary workers have a university degree. The popular image of temporary work being concentrated in the unskilled and unqualified population is therefore not entirely accurate.

There are challenges on both sides of the contract. Employers may perceive temporary workers as less reliable and characterised by high labour turnover. This may not be surprising, as reliability and stability can be correlated with employee commitment and it is more difficult for an employee to commit to an organisation where the organisational commitment is temporary. Workers accept temporary work for a number of reasons. The choice may be between temporary work or no work or it may offer an entry point to the organisation with the potential to become a permanent employee.

Part-time work

A part-time worker is anyone contracted to work less than the normal full-time hours. Some government bodies regard 30 hours as the qualifying figure. The majority of part-time workers are in hotel and catering, health and social work, distribution and retailing and in education (ACAS, 2005). The service sector, including retailing, banking, finance, tourism and catering, has been the fastest-growing sector of the UK economy with a consequential increase in part-time workers. ACAS (2005) reports that 'about a quarter of employees in Britain work part-time and over 80 per cent of these are women', with *WERS* reporting a similar figure. Increasingly evident in the part-time labour market are students and this is partially attributable to the introduction of loans in higher education. Students need to work not only to live, but also to constrain debt.

The use of part-time staff has benefits for the employer. It enables the organisation to have workers available for busy periods and to avoid paying staff when the demand for work is slack. This is very evident in the retail sector where an increase in out-of-town shopping, the introduction of Sunday trading and longer opening hours each day has significantly increased the total staffing hours in each week and produced more slack periods overall. The managerial response to fluctuating, but predictable, work demands is to staff the stores with workers on a variety of part-time contracts appropriate to the staffing need. There are some disadvantages to the employer. The use of more part-time staff increases the total number of workers employed, pushing up training, administrative and recruitment costs. Managerial challenges are presented in relation to staffing continuity, holiday arrangements, and communicating with, managing and motivating employees who come to work at different times. In order to raise the perceived status of part-time workers they are sometimes referred to as key-time workers.

Ethically and legally, part-time workers are entitled, on a *pro rata* basis, to the same pay and benefits as full-time workers. The Part-time Workers (Prevention of Less Favourable Treatment) Regulations 2000 prohibit employers from treating part-time workers, not just employees, less favourably than full-time workers unless such treatment can be objectively justified. The right not to be treated less favourably is based on the *pro rata* principle in comparison to a full-time worker working for the same employer and having the same type of contract. The employer is obliged to provide pro-rated equality for pay and benefits, promotion and training opportunities, pensions and holiday entitlement and equal treatment in relation to discipline, grievance, redeployment and redundancy selection. The employer has only two defences against a claim of less favourable treatment: first, that the unfavourable treatment was not connected to a worker's part-time status or, second, that there is a valid and objective business reason which justifies less favourable treatment.

Variations on the part-time working theme are core-hours contracts and term-time contracts. Core-hours contracts guarantee a minimum numbers of hours per week, or none in the case of zero-hours contracts, with the implicit right of the employer to flex the hours upwards in order to secure appropriate staffing levels for the business. In this case the employee is something of a 'beck and call' worker and is only likely to be sustained by this type of contract if it meets work–life balance needs as well as financial needs. Ethically the core-hours worker should receive appropriate notice and be able to reasonably refuse the offer of extra hours. Term-time contracts are aimed at those workers who have caring responsibilities for school-age children and enable workers to be at home during school holidays. The holiday periods will either be covered by other workers, perhaps extending their hours, or require the recruitment of short-term workers, frequently from the student labour market.

Job sharing

Job sharing is a specific form of part-time work where two people share a full-time job. The tasks, duties and responsibilities of the job are divided in a way that meets the needs of the two individuals and the organisation. The pay and benefits of the full-time job are shared. The division can be:

- split days – one employee works mornings and the other works afternoons;
- split weeks – the two employees work one week on and one week off, with a changeover in the middle of the week;
- alternate weeks – the two employees work whole weeks, one week on and one week off.

Advantages of a job share include: the opportunity for built-in cover for leave which provides continuity of work; retaining trained and committed employees who wish to reduce their working hours; also, two people can bring a wider range of skills, ideas and experience to the job. Disadvantages associated with job share include: increased training and administration costs through some duplication in these areas; potential for conflict if there are different performance standards between the job-holders; issues can occur if the job share is a management job where there may be increased difficulties experienced by staff who may find it difficult to work for two managers with different management styles and abilities; and it can be problematic to replace one member of the job share duo if he or she leaves. Careful recruitment and selection of the two employees to look for people who are compatible is important and also it can be beneficial to include the remaining worker in the recruitment of a new employee if one of the job sharers leaves. Effective communication between the job-sharing employees is essential and this can be facilitated through a handover period or the logging of significant events. It is also essential to match the two workers to ensure compatibility and complementary skills.

Annual hours

Annual hours working involves specifying the contractual hours to be worked as an annual rather than as a weekly figure and is a method of matching staffing to work demands which fluctuate on an annual cycle. Advantages of annual hours working include: increased employee and employer flexibility and the control of costs because employees work longer hours at peak times and shorter hours when demand is low without adjustments in pay. Employee pay is unaffected by the fluctuation in weekly hours worked and is stabilised over the year as a whole, within the limits of the Working Time Regulations 1998. Employers need to take the nominal full-time hours per week and compute an annual equivalent allowing for annual leave and bank holidays. A specific challenge of annual hours contracts is complexity of management and administration, including, for example, sickness absence payment calculations, training days allowance, the implications of unplanned leave and the hours and pay of workers who leave or join the organisation part way through the contractual year.

A change from weekly hours to annual hours will have to be developed, agreed and implemented sensitively as employees may be suspicious of managerial motives and feel they will lose out. The productivity advantages of annual hours to the organisation may mean that employees can be offered compensatory benefits; for example, an overall reduction in total contractual hours or increased job security due to an increase in competitive advantage for the organisation.

Remote working

Variously referred to as teleworking or home working, the essence of remote working is that a worker does not necessarily report to a corporate place of work on a daily basis. Most frequently this involves working at home for some or all of the time. For the purposes of its Labour Force Survey, the Office of National Statistics (ONS) defines teleworkers as 'people who work mainly in their own home or mainly in different places using home as a base, who use both a telephone and a computer to carry out their work at home' (CIPD, 2008a). There has been a significant increase in the proportion of employees who spend some or all of their time working from home. Figures from the Labour Force Survey indicate that they represented 2.2 million or 7 per cent of all people in employment in 2001 (Hotopp, 2002). The ONS report that between 1997 and 2005 there was a 150 per cent increase in the number of workers classified as teleworkers, and put the figure at 8 per cent of all workers (CIPD, 2008a). The CIPD's *Labour market outlook* found that 60 per cent of employers offered teleworking (CIPD, 2008b). Working from home (CIPD, 2008b) has grown in recent years because of:

- *Technology*: Teleworking could not have developed without the ablity to communicate with the office base via computers and mobile phones. The spread of broadband and cheaper digital technology means that this ability has increased and will continue to do so. And, of course, the general population is becoming much more IT-literate.

- *Cost savings*: Some employers introducing home working hope to be able to save on office space and 'hot desk' employees on their visits to the office.

- *Improving productivity*: There is some evidence that working from home improves productivity, and reduces absence and labour turnover.

- *Work–life balance*: By cutting travel, reducing stress and enabling people to work when it suits them, it is argued that working from home is a means of harmonising work and family commitments.

- *Green issues*: Reducing travel should reduce pollution. With growing concern about global warming, this is likely to be increasingly cited as a further reason for introducing home working, and will be used by organisations wanting to promote a green image.

Remote working may only be possible for certain types of job and successful home working will depend on the worker having suitable facilities in terms of space and technology in the home. The primary benefits that employers gain are increased organisational flexibility, a reduction in office space costs and the recruitment and retention of workers who are unable or do not wish to take up standard office employment because of either personal preference or personal circumstances. The benefits for the worker are increased flexibility over working times and a reduction in travel times and costs as well as the stress caused by commuting (Rankin, 2003). It can therefore be argued that remote working enhances the work–life balance but this must be countered by the increased difficulties of separating home and work and the potential for physical and psychological intrusion into home life.

The government has embraced the European framework agreement on guidance for home working, which encourages the implementation of home working arrangements that are mutually beneficial to employer and employee. And the CBI, the TUC and CEEP UK (a group which represents public sector employees) jointly produced guidance on teleworking to support employers in developing policies to support the further extension of home working. This guidance includes: health and safety issues, financial issues such as taxation, allowances and expenses, HR issues such as recruitment, training and career development, personal support for home workers to reduce isolation and security issues to ensure the confidentiality of information. Dwelly and Bennion (2003) identify a number of ways to make home working work. These include:

> developing a business case for homeworking, do not just see it as an afterthought; ensure integration of HR policies, for example performance management systems which are based on outputs not hours; ensure that line managers have the skills to manage and maintain relationships with homeworkers; evaluate homeworking on an organisational basis against corporate goals not just on an individual basis; develop communications, consultation and representation mechanisms which include homeworkers and ensure that risk assessment, data protection and confidentiality processes operate effectively and that remote working systems meet homeworking needs and are supported reliably.

It is important to recognise that remote workers retain the employment rights associated with their contract regardless of where the work is located, and also that remote working requires high trust relationships between managers and workers. Remote working need not be all or nothing because it can be used in combination with office-based working, on either a specified or an *ad hoc* basis.

A flexible approach to employee working patterns

Each pattern of work has advantages and disadvantages for the employer and the employee. The pattern of work and the associated contractual arrangements are determined by considering factors such as: complexity of administration and relative cost, attractiveness of the work and the contractual arrangements to quality recruits, surpluses or shortages in the labour market, the degree of worker commitment required for and associated with the type of work, organisational concerns for equity and fairness and acceptability to employee representatives.

EXHIBIT 4.3 Fenland District Council: a joined-up approach to flexibility

Fenland District Council has embraced the opportunities that increased flexibility offers and around 60 per cent of its employees work part-time. According to the Change and Development Manager, Shari Kahn, the Council offers flexibility in terms of times of work, days of work and location, with compressed hours and home working available to all employees. She goes on to explain that to meet the needs of the employees who work flexible patterns the council has to provide flexible learning opportunities. Fenland use the government agency Learndirect for a range of skills training and NVQs in management, together with 'bite-sized chunks' of e-learning, a resource library and tutor-led sessions. A rating of 'excellent' in the Comprehensive Performance Assessment she puts down to the success of this flexible approach and more than 80 per cent of employees said that they were proud to work for Fenland District Council.

A flexible approach to working patterns may manifest itself in empowering employees to exercise some discretion over when, where and how they work. It can be defined as 'the exercise of employee choice in relation to personal circumstances and work demands but compatible with the achievement of business objectives'. The employer benefits are the potential for improved employee effectiveness and performance and the recruitment and retention of talented workers. This can be an element in being perceived as an employer of choice through offering scope for individual talent to prosper and opportunities for work–life balance. Like remote working it requires high trust, output-driven performance management and the overcoming of traditional cultural and managerial barriers. Employers continue to strive for flexibility and, according to the CIPD (2005b), the main reasons are: to improve the retention of employees, to meet employee needs, to comply with legislation, to support the needs of the business, to increase customer satisfaction and to maximise the use of organisational assets. Recent findings from the authoritative ACAS and DTI-sponsored *Workplace Employment Relations Survey* (*WERS*) (Kersley *et al.*, 2005) report home working up from 16 per cent to 28 per cent, term-time-only working up from 14 per cent to 28 per cent, flexitime up from 19 per cent to 26 per cent, job sharing up from 31 per cent to 41 per cent and switching from full-time to part-time working up from 46 per cent to 64 per cent between 1998 and 2004. Interestingly *WERS* reports that:

> The increase in the availability of flexible working is reflected elsewhere in the survey, with managers showing more understanding of employees' responsibilities outside work. In 1998, 84 per cent of managers believed that it was up to an individual employee to balance their work and family responsibilities. This has now reduced to around two thirds (65 per cent).

There is a range of options which organisations can use to increase flexibility and the most common is the use of a variety of employment contracts. However, there is no one prescriptive solution; employers should examine their business, their employees and their customers to construct a business case which supports their choices.

CASE STUDY   Introducing flexible working at Safelife Insurance Limited

Safelife Insurance Limited is a UK-based insurance company offering the full range of personal insurance including life insurance, home insurance, car insurance and travel insurance, among other products. It is based in the Thames/M4 corridor and also has extensive online sales as well as 24-hour telephone contact facilities for sales and claims. It employs around 10 000 staff.

Flexible working and Safelife Limited

Following the legislative changes in 2003 enabling parents to request flexible working, Safelife has taken the strategic decision that all staff should be able to request flexible working, although there is no commitment that staff will necessarily be granted the option of flexible working. This strategic decision was taken for the following reasons:

- The need to retain knowledgeable staff in a highly competitive labour market.
- The wish to increase the motivation of employees by giving them more control over their work.
- The expectation that this will positively impact sickness absence levels.
- To provide a high level of customer service.

The organisation believes that flexible working, which can include any reasonable request from a variation in start and finish times to remote working, also has benefits for staff as it can be used to meet employees' needs to fit with home responsibilities and to enable staff to have a better work–life balance. Teams as well as individuals are encouraged to review their objectives and current patterns of work and to devise a business case for changes to working arrangements, which meet the needs of the team members and also ensure excellent customer service.

In order to ensure fair treatment and transparency in taking the decision to allow flexible working, Safelife has devised a procedure to be followed by all employees making a request. This procedure requires those requesting flexible working to develop a business case which includes details of the proposed changes, costs and performance levels and spells out the customer benefits of the changes.

Activity

In your role as the HR business partner at Safelife Insurance Limited you have been asked to prepare a briefing sheet for staff on the introduction of the policy on flexible working. The briefing note should include:

1 The strategic rationale for the introduction of flexible working.

2 Details of eligibility for flexible working, which includes those with statutory rights, and the company policy for all staff.

3 Details of the process for requesting flexible working.

4 A framework for the development of the business case including recommended structure of the case.

5 Details of the process for assessing the business case including the criteria which will be used.

SUMMARY LEARNING POINTS

1 Planning for the future requirements of the organisation in terms of workers is not a 'one-off' annual activity; it is a systematic, holistic, proactive and continuing process which needs constant review. Human resource planning is a strategic HR opportunity.

2 Hard workforce planning is best considered as a sub-set of holistic human resource planning. HRP contributes to the achievement of strategic organisational objectives through planning the acquisition of an appropriately skilled workforce. Acquiring the right number of workers is only one factor and the ability to resource the organisation with high-quality staff with the skills and competencies required by the organisation is of equal importance.

3 Knowledge of the diverse nature of labour markets is fundamental to the HRP process and to understanding the labour supply.

4 A strategic corporate plan contributes to a common understanding of organisational direction and informs human resource planning.

5 Employers are looking for an approach to human resource planning that provides them with maximum flexibility and scenario planning may enable a more effective assessment of future staffing needs to be made.

6 Annual reporting on the people aspects of organisational capability through human capital management is not yet a requirement for organisations but it is a mechanism for assessing human resource requirements. Systems for human capital management are being developed and could provide a useful additional tool for inclusion in the human resource planning process.

7 The war for talent continues and the development of talent planning initiatives supported by the talent management activities of attracting talent, developing talent and rewarding talent are key to the acquisition and retention of talented employees who contribute to organisational sustainability.

8 Employee retention is a key issue for many UK organisations and better understanding of why employees leave and why employees stay through the use of exit interviews and staff attitude surveys will allow employers to develop, target and implement appropriate retention strategies.

9 Changes in the external environments within which work organisations operate are stimulating flexible responses to the structuring of work. Flexibility initiatives can take many forms and these forms overlap.

10 The concepts of the flexible firm and the shamrock organisation provide opportunities to analyse flexible approaches to work organisations, but they do not prescribe the 'one best way'. Worker flexibility can have positive and negative consequences and requires proactive and skilled HR management.

11 There has been a significant increase in atypical workers. The full-time, Monday to Friday contract has declined and a variety of contractual arrangements and patterns of work are available to the employer.

12 Patterns of work have always been subject to change but the pace of change is now more rapid. The driving force for this change comes both from

organisations seeking to change the way that employees' work is organised to better suit business needs and from individuals seeking a better balance between work and home life.

REFERENCES AND FURTHER READING

Advisory, Conciliation and Arbitration Service (2002) *Controlling labour turnover*. London: ACAS.

Advisory, Conciliation and Arbitration Service (2005) *Changing Patterns of Work: Advisory booklet* (periodically revised). London: ACAS.

Advisory, Conciliation and Arbitration Service (2009) *Flexible working and work-life balance*. London: ACAS.

Aikin, O. (2000) 'Everyday rights for part-time staff', *People Management*, 25 May, 23–4.

Armstrong, M. (2001) *Human Resource Management Practice*. London: Kogan Page.

Atkinson, J. (1984) 'Manpower strategies for flexible organisations', *Personnel Management*, August, 28–31.

Atkinson, J. (1996) *Temporary Work and the Labour Market*. London: IES.

Baron, A. and Armstrong, M. (2007) *Human Capital Management: Achieving added value through people*. London: CIPD.

Beardwell, J. and Claydon, T. (2007) *Human Resource Management: A contemporary approach*. Harlow: Financial Times Prentice Hall.

Berger, L. and Berger, D. (2008) *The compensation handbook*. Maidenhead: McGraw-Hill.

Bramham, J. (1994) *Human Resource Planning*. London: CIPD.

Castley, R.J. (1996) 'Policy-focused approach to manpower planning', *International Journal of Manpower*, 17(3), 15–24.

Chambers, E., Foulon, M., Handfield-Jones, H., Hankin, S. and Michaels III, E. (1998) 'The war for talent', *The McKinsey Quarterly*, 3, 44–57.

Christensen, J. and E., Rog, E. (2008) 'Talent management: a strategy for improving employee recruitment, retention and engagement within hospitality organisations', *International Journal of Contemporary Hospitality Management*, 20(7), 743–57.

CIPD (2004) *Employee turnover and retention – Factsheet*. London: CIPD.

CIPD (2005a) *Human Capital Reporting – an internal perspective*. London: CIPD.

CIPD (2005b) *Flexible Working: Impact and implementation, an employer survey*. London: CIPD.

CIPD (2006a) *Talent Management*. London: CIPD.

CIPD (2006b) *Talent Management: understanding the dimensions*. London: CIPD.

CIPD (2006c) *Learning and Development*. London: CIPD.

CIPD (2008a) *Flexible Working: Factsheet*. London: CIPD.

CIPD (2008b) 'Focus: working from home', *Labour market outlook*, May, 10–13, www.cipd.co.uk/subjects/hrpract/hrtrends/_qtrends.htm.

CIPD (2008c) *Talent Management: an overview*. London: CIPD.

CIPD (2009a) *Succession Planning*. London: CIPD.

CIPD (2009b) *The War on Talent? Talent management under threat in uncertain times*. London: CIPD.

CIPD (2009c) *Recruitment, retention and turnover: Annual Survey*. London: CIPD.

CIPD (2009d) *Flexible Working: Factsheet*. London: CIPD.

CIPD (2009e) *Flexible Working: Impact and implementation, an employer survey*. London: CIPD.

Cowie, J. (2004) *Improving Staff Retention*, Incomes Data Services Study 765, June. London: IDS.

Cranfield School of Management (2008) *Flexible working and performance*. London: Working Families.

Cully, M. (1999) *Britain at Work as Depicted by WERS*. London: Routledge.

Davies, R. (2001) 'How to boost staff retention', *People Management*, April 2001.

DTI/Reed Press Release (30 December 2002) 'More people want flexible hours than cash, company cars or gym', retrieved 14 November 2005 from www.gnn.gov.uk.

Dwelly, T. and Bennion, Y. (2003) *Time to go home: Embracing the homeworking revolution*. The Work Foundation.

European Commission (2006) 'Modernising labour law to meet the challenges of the 21st century', *Green Paper*, Com. 708.

Geary, J. (1992) 'Employment flexibility and HRM: the case of three American electronics plants', *Work, Employment and Society*, 6(2), 250–70.

Glen, C. (2006) 'Key skills retention and motivation: The war for talent still rages and retention is the high ground', *Industrial and Commercial Training*, 38, 37–44.

Gregg, P. and Wadsworth, J. (1995) 'A short history of labour turnover, job tenure, and job security: 1975–93', *Oxford Review of Economic Policy*, 11, 73–90.

Guest, D., MacKenzie Davey, K. and Smewling, C. (1998) *Innovative employment contracts: Flexible friend or fashionable foe*, retrieved from www.flexibility. co.uk/flexwork/contract/birkbeck.htm, May 2005.

Guthridge, M., Komm, A.B. and Lawson, E. (2008) 'Making talent management a strategic priority', *The McKinsey Quarterly*, January, 49–59.

Guthridge, M. and Lawson, E. (2008) 'Divide and survive', *People Management*, September, 40–44.

Handy, C.B. (1989) *The Age of Unreason*. London: Business Books.

Hay, M. (2002) 'Strategies for survival in the war for talent', *Career Development International*, January, 52–5.

Hay Group (2005) *Talent management – what the best organisations actually do*, Hay Group Inc.

Hirsch, W. (2000) 'Succession planning demystified', *IES Report 372*. Brighton: IES.

Horton, S. (2000) 'The changing context of employee relations', in Farnham, D. (ed.) *Employee Relations in Context*. London: CIPD.

Hotopp, U. (2002) 'Teleworking in the UK', *Labour Market Trends*, June, 311–18.

Human Resource Management International Digest (2003) 'Everyone's a winner at Hertfordshire County Council', 11(7), 7–11.

Hughes, C.J. and Rog, E. (2008) 'Talent management: A strategy for improving employee recruitment, retention and engagement within hospitality organisations', *International Journal of Contemporary Hospitality Management*, 20(7), 743–57.

Hutchinson, S. and Purcell, J. (2003) *Bringing policies to life: The vital role of front-line managers in people management*, Executive Briefing. London: CIPD.

Incomes Data Services (2002) *Flexitime schemes – IDS Study 725*. Brighton: IDS.

Incomes Data Services (2002) *Teleworking – IDS Study 729*. Brighton: IDS.

Industrial Society (2001) *Flexible work patterns – managing best practice 85*. London: Industrial Society.

Innecto Reward Consulting (2006) *High Flyer Trend Report*. London: www.innecto-group.co.uk.

Institute for Employment Studies (2003) *Workforce Planning, the Wider Context: A literature review*, July. Brighton: IES.

IPM Statement on Human Resource Planning (1992) Brighton: IPM.

IRS (2005) 'Recruitment and retention: Yesterday, today and tomorrow', *IRS Employment Review*, June.

Kersley, B., Alpin, C., Forth, J., Bryson, A., Bewley, H., Dix, G. and Oxenbridge, S. (2006) *Inside the Workplace: First Findings of the Workplace Employment Relations Survey (WERS 2004)*. London: DTI.

Legge, K. (1998) 'Flexibility: the gift-wrapping of employment degradation', in Sparrow, P. and Marchington, M. (1998) (eds) *HRM: The new agenda*. London: FT Pitman.

Leopold, J. and Harris, L. (2009) *The strategic managing of human resources*. Harlow: FT Prentice Hall.

Mayo, A. (2005) 'Serious Behaviour', *People Management*, 7 April, 23.

Melymuka, K. (2002) 'Don't just stand there – get ready', *Computerworld*, 36, 48–9.

Michaels, E., Handfield-Jones, H. and Axelrod, B. (2001) *The war for talent*. Boston: Harvard Business School Press.

PwC (2008) *Performance Coaching and Development*. PriceWaterhouseCoopers. www.pwc.com/extweb/aboutus.nsf/docid/7345C78C3AE7AD7B85257274007E3A61, 6 March 2009.

Rankin, N. (2003) 'Measuring and managing labour turnover', *IRS Employment Review*, 773, 4 April, 32–8.

Redman, T. and Wilkinson, A. (2006) *Contemporary Human Resource Management*. Harlow: FT Prentice Hall.

Rees, D. (2008) '*Using compensation to win talent wars*', in Berger, L. and Berger, D. (eds) *The compensation handbook*. Maidenhead: McGraw-Hill.

Reilly, P. (1996) 'Human Resource Planning: An Introduction', *IES Report 312*. Brighton: IES.

Robinson, D. (1997) *HR Information Systems: Stand and Deliver, IES Report 335*. Brighton: IES.

Sparrow, S. (2008) 'Flexible working: bouncing back', November, retrieved 28 July 2009, www.personneltoday.com/articles/2008/11/10/48207/flexible-working-bouncing-back.html.

Stredwick, J. and Ellis, S. (2004) *Flexible Working*. London: CIPD.

Sullivan, J. (2002a) *VP of HR: Stop being surprised (workforce planning Part 1 of 2)*, www.drjohnsullivan.com/newsletter/072402.

Sullivan, J. (2002b) *Before you try it, understand why workforce planning fails*, 12 August, www.erexchange.com/articles.

Sullivan, J. (2002c) *Why workforce planning fails*, 19 August, www.erexchange.com/articles.

Tansley, C., Turner, P., Foster, C., Harris, L., Sempik, A., Stewart, J. and Williams, H. (2007) *Talent: strategy, management, measurement*. London: CIPD.

Taylor, S. (2002) *The Employee Retention Handbook*. London: CIPD.

Torrington, D., Hall, L. and Taylor, S. (2008) *Human Resource Management*. Harlow: FT Prentice Hall.

Truss, C., Soane, E. and Edwards, C. (2006) *Working life: Employee attitudes and engagement*. London: CIPD.

Ulrich, D. (2008) 'Not-so-standard deviation', *People Management*, August, 32–33.

Wheeler, K. (2004) *5 steps to getting started in talent scenario planning*, www.erexchange.com/articles, 15 April.

Wheeler, K. (2005) *Reframing traditional workforce planning*. www.erexchange.com/articles, 15 April.

White, M. (2002) 'Paying more than lip service to diversity', *Chief Executive*, October.

ASSIGNMENTS AND DISCUSSION TOPICS

1 In order to undertake the first stage of the HRP model, the analysis, it is necessary to collect internal and external information. What information does an HR planner need to collect? Categorise under the headings of, first, business information and, second, HR information.

2 Identify and discuss the defining labour market characteristics for specified jobs in your organisation.

3 Is there a talent management strategy in your organisation, or an organisation with which you are familiar? If there is a formal strategy:

   (i)   describe the objectives of the strategy
   (ii)   identify the key features of the strategy
   (iii) comment on whether the strategy is successful

   If there is no formal strategy, are there any indicators within your organisation that talent is valued? Detail the indicators you have identified and comment on the role these play in the management of talent.

4 Investigate the rate of labour turnover in your organisation (or an organisation with which you are familiar). Comment on whether the rate is high or low, taking into account your geographical location, your industry and the types of job within the organisation. Prepare a report which outlines HR interventions for the more effective retention of talented employees.

5 Identify whether the costs associated with labour turnover are measured effectively within your organisation. To what extent are these costs considered at strategic level in developing HR policies and procedures?

6 Using the overlapping forms of flexibility identified in Figure 4.4, analyse the extent to which your organisation displays the characteristics associated with each form. Discuss the advantages and limitations of flexibility initiatives in your organisation.

7 To what degree does your organisation correspond to the model of the flexible firm? Using the three categories of primary, secondary and tertiary workers, discuss the characteristics of the workers in each category and comment on the nature of intrinsic and extrinsic rewards that are appropriate for each.

8 What patterns of work are used in your organisation, and why? Where and how are the decisions made about the pattern of work and the contractual arrangements to be offered?

9 Consider the suitability of a job in your organisation for remote working. What conditions will be necessary for it to be a successful pattern of work for the employer and for the employee? Are there any cultural and managerial barriers to be overcome?

Chapter 5

HR Information Systems and e-enabled HR

INTRODUCTION

The information available to organisations is growing at an exponential rate and that information explosion is evident in all parts of our lives. Instant access to 'what we want to know, when we want to know it' is central to many things that we do. Business organisations are no exception. The Internet is embedded in most organisations with many businesses able to provide goods or services to any part of the world through the development of e-business systems in a way that would not have been possible a few years ago. In addition, organisations can source labour in locations remote from the home business and enable the worker to work at a time and a place which suits both the employer and the employee through the exploitation of electronic and mobile technology. The HR function has not escaped these changes and employers and employees increasingly expect access to HR services on a 24-hour basis. The chapters so far have highlighted some of the challenges facing organisations, and accurate and timely information is an essential requirement for effective decision-making. People are a complex resource to manage and the variety of employee contractual terms, attendance patterns, skills and experience demand increasingly sophisticated HR information if the organisation is to maximise the competence and flexibility of employees. Manual systems are unable to meet all but simple demands for information and if the HR function is to continue to develop in partnership with managers, and add value at all levels of the organisation, more sophisticated systems which provide accurate and timely information are needed. These systems need to be sufficiently robust to ensure that HR services can be developed and delivered to meet the expectations of the business partners and make a positive contribution to successful business development. Evidence from a CIPD survey (2005) 'shows that less than one-fifth of HR information systems are integrated with an organisation wide IT system and almost half of the respondents said their systems were difficult for the HR department to use'. Smethurst (2005) quotes Martyn Sloman, the CIPD Adviser, Learning, Training and Development, as saying that:

> the survey showed the profession was in danger of not being sufficiently ambitious in its use of IT . . . Competitive advantage in organisations lies at the interface of HR and IT and that we [the HR profession] should be dictating the future pattern of HRIS.

INFORMATION NEEDS

The pressure on organisations for increased efficiency and effectiveness demands that all organisational resources are used to maximum effect. A mechanistic managerial approach may be appropriate for physical or financial resources, but human resources have a view of what they want from work and bring attitudes, beliefs and aspirations to the workplace. Data collected and held on HR information systems may include not only factual data about the organisation and the employee but also the expectations, ambitions and opinions of the employee together with a managerial view on the ability and potential of that employee. Planning takes place at different organisational levels and these levels of planning and managerial activity will have different information needs. Effective planning needs to be supported by effective management information systems. Information systems should be designed, developed or chosen to meet organisational needs – a standard system cannot be prescribed. Provided the right data is collected and stored, modern information systems are able to provide the right information at the right time in response to a variety of managerial needs. The structure and culture of the organisation will have an impact on which information system is the most suitable, with a centralised and highly controlled organisation having different requirements to one which has more devolved structure and decision-making. Managerial choice needs to be exercised in deciding on the most appropriate information system. One certainty is that manual information systems will not meet the needs of all but very small organisations.

Data requirements for HR information systems

A temptation in the development of HR information systems is to collect every piece of data about the organisation and every worker, to enable any and all information needs to be met. Significant costs are associated with the collection, storage and processing of large amounts of data. Therefore the information needs of the business should specifically determine the data requirements and the establishment of information priorities will maximise cost-effectiveness. An analysis of information needs will enable appropriate data to be identified in detail so that a suitable database can be developed and maintained. Personal data required from individual employees should be collected, stored and processed in line with legal requirements. The data requirements need to be reviewed regularly to ensure that the data continues to meet changing information needs.

A key factor in ensuring the effectiveness and usefulness of HR information systems is the interface between the manual systems and the IT systems. Support systems need to be developed and responsibilities assigned for the collection, input and maintenance of the data. These manual systems should be regularly reviewed to ensure that the potentially large task of data capture and data input is effectively managed. Data should ideally be collected and input into the system as close to the point of capture as possible because this will reduce the need for extensive systems for the manual transfer of data, and also reduce the potential for error. The feasibility of devolving the capture, input and maintenance responsibility will reflect the culture of the organisation and the extent to which responsibility and ownership of data and information are centralised or decentralised. In a decentralised organisation, where many HR activities are devolved to line managers, the responsibility for the collection and input of personal data is also logically devolved to the line manager as the most likely person to know of a change to the personal or contract details of the employee. In many organisations, where all employees have access to IT, the maintenance and responsibility for accuracy of individual personal details may be devolved to individual employees. For example, employees who change their address or their marital status or who change from part-time to full-time working will need to have their record updated to reflect this change. If this can be done by the line manager at the point of the change it will simplify the system and will need limited supporting manual systems. In organisations where the HR information system is centralised there will need to be supporting manual systems for notifying a central function, often the HR department, of any changes, and responsibility for updating the record will have to be assigned within the central department. There is the potential for tension between the line manager and the HR function on the assignment of responsibility for system update. The successful resolution of this tension will ensure that both parties have a clear understanding of the aims and objectives of the HR information system and the benefits to management decision-making of ensuring an up-to-date management tool. Differences in practice of HR devolution or centralisation are at the heart of this debate, and the outcome of any discussion will undoubtedly reflect the relationship between line management and HR practitioners, and also the positioning of the HR function within the organisation.

HR INFORMATION AND BUSINESS PARTNERING

An important factor in the successful development of the HR professional as a business partner is the contribution the HR professional can make to the effective management of human resources. The HR business partner's knowledge and understanding of the key people behaviour and performance indicators will enable the HR professional to contribute to effective management at all levels. Knowledge such as the profile of the workforce, the levels of labour turnover and absence, the factors which impact on an employee's decision to leave the organisation or which support the employee's decision to stay, the profile of skills, together with other factors such as age, sex and ethnic profile and the features of the workforce flows will enhance the relationship between HR and the manager and enable them to work in partnership to the benefit of the business. Mastering this information, together with knowledge of the internal and external labour markets, professional expertise in HR management and skills in developing and implementing effective HR practices, will enable the business partnership to develop. CIPD research on business partnering (2005) focuses on the need for the HR business partner to 'tackle business issues' and 'moves them away from an unhealthy preoccupation with administrative processes and regulatory compliance'. It also 'reinforces ways for HR to engage with strategic processes that relate to both the direction and the delivery of business objectives'. Knowledge of business objectives and business processes is vital to that development but information about the availability and behaviour of the human resource is important complementary and supplementary knowledge, which will enhance contribution and add value to the business. In addition to information needed to manage the organisation effectively there is also an increase in the need for good information and communication systems for all employees. The e-revolution has created increased employee expectations with regard to access to information. The development of organisational intranets with 24/7 availability can lead to a change in the way that HR services are provided.

e-HR AND THE TRANSFORMATION OF HR SERVICES

e-HR is difficult to define because of a multiplicity of models depending on organisational circumstances but it has been defined by Kettley and Reilly (2003) as 'the application of conventional, web and voice technologies to improve HR administration, transactions and process performance'. The development of this technology goes beyond simply HR applications, and organisations that have embraced e-developments are most likely to include e-HR in their delivery of HR services. Organisations may develop an e-HR approach for several reasons. Kettley and Reilly (2003) identify the following reasons for organisations to adopt e-HR:

- HR service improvement, in particular a move to a more strategic and business focus.
- Cost cutting and organisational efficiency.
- The desire of the HR function to change its relationship with line managers (towards business partnering).
- The transformation of HR to a customer-focused and responsive function.
- To offer a level of service that fits the changing world of work.
- To produce comprehensive and more timely management information.

To capitalise on these e-developments the HR function needs to embrace changing technology and provide both transactional and transformational services. In facilitating transactional and transformational HR service, e-HR can be analysed at basic, intermediate and top levels.

Transactional services may be defined as maintenance services – the exchange of information between a range of customers. These customers are managers and employees within the organisation, as well as potential employees. This is *basic-level e-HR*, which might incorporate the intranet provision of, first, live information on training courses, vacancies, employee benefits entitlement and the staff handbook; second, the online availability of HR policies and procedures such as discipline, grievance and health and safety; third, interactive facilities such as changes in employee details, management reporting and requests for basic information on staff turnover or pay rates; and, fourth, the corporate Internet provision of information on job vacancies and career opportunities accessible to those outside the organisation. This activity is termed disintermediation, whereby there is no personal intermediary between the information and its recipient. The benefits being sought are quick and easy access to information and a reduction in the resources required to provide it. Employers are seeking productivity gains, reduction in HR costs in the provision of HR transactional services, and a freeing-up of HR capacity to focus more on advisory and strategic roles. These basic-level HR transactions, estimated by some commentators as 60 to 80 per cent of the HR load, can be handled in real time by e-HR, enabling the more important HR activities to be escalated to the intermediate level.

Intermediate-level e-HR may comprise business unit-level HR practitioners in the field or in a shared services centre. These HR staff are subject experts able to provide online e-HR support through advisory and consultancy services to line managers in specialist areas such as employment law, compensation and benefits, and performance management.

Transformational services are those services which the HR function can provide to managers to support the effective management of the business. This often needs the HR professional to collect, process and analyse data from both inside and outside the organisation and to provide and present the resultant information in the most appropriate way and in the most appropriate forum to add value to strategic or operational decisions. It is this aspect of e-HR which leads to both the transformation of the HR function and the transformation of the business. Reddington (2003) interestingly indicates that:

> for many HR functions, the response to the pressures [to add value] will be found in e-HR led transformation . . . Technology is only a tool – an enabler – for supporting more effective ways of working and managing the human dimension in organisations. Before any technology can be effectively deployed, fundamental approaches to

people management must be transformed. In most cases this involves changing the way HR management is done in organisations and repositioning the HR function.

This *top-level e-HR* consists of HR strategic business partners working with line managers to provide business solutions through the most effective development and resourcing of the organisation.

e-HR is also related to the Ulrich (2005) three-legged framework of shared services, centres of excellence and business partners (*see* Chapter 1). The development of an HR intranet supports shared services through freeing-up HR time spent on administrative functions, allowing HR to increase its business capabilities and to change its functional model. As Holbeche (2001) states:

> if the basic HR processes such as administrative activities are not in good order, especially on sensitive issues such as . . . pay, no strategic contribution is likely to be considered of value until the administrative problem is fixed.

However, Reddington (2008) argues that 'the adoption of e-HR in this way involves more displacement or devolution of traditional HR activities to the line manager through the use of web-based self-service tools'. The transformation of HR to achieve the strands of 'centres of excellence' and 'business partners' may only be achieved through the effective devolution of appropriate HR activities to the line manager and this needs consultation with the managers and training to develop line manager HR skills. e-HR therefore has significant implications for line managers who, by definition, have to accept even more responsibility for managing their people. Goodge (2001) identifies this as a huge shift of responsibility from the HR department to line managers with 'the intelligent IT systems underpinning e-HR removing routine transactional processes from the HR function by providing line managers with the information, advice and help they once received from HR'. There are also implications for the employees, who to a greater extent may also be disintermediated from HR professionals. While e-HR facilitates the redefinition of HR roles and capacity, there are links also with the added value, business orientation and strategic aspirations for the HR function.

EXHIBIT 5.1 **The impact of e-HR**

Shared services at Southwest One

The change in the world economic situation in 2008 resulted in local authorities in the UK looking for ways of reducing costs with minimum impact on the service provision. One way is through the development of shared services, supported by effective IT systems. One such example is that of Southwest One, where Somerset County Council, Taunton Deane Borough Council, Avon and Somerset Police and IBM have come together to provide HR, IT and finance services to the public sector members of the partnership. The 10-year deal is predicted to save £17 million a year and Somerset County Council were able to levy a below average council tax increase as a result of this initiative. The development of shared services along this model relied heavily on robust supporting IT systems. One of the major concerns about shared services and supporting IT systems is the impact

(Box continued)

on the development of HR professionals. According to Andy Cook, Managing Director of Marshall-James, 'In another ten years, organisations will be struggling to find senior HR people with the skills and experience to continue providing high level strategic input into the organisation.'

Brockett, J. (2009) 'More councils look to shared services to keep them afloat', *People Management*, 26 February, 12.

Birmingham City Council – HR restructuring

Birmingham City Council is seeking £185 million saving through the introduction of a £100 million three-year 'excellence in people management programme' including a £45 million IT system. The assistant HR director explains that 'under the new structure managers will take on more responsibility for employee training and absence levels, and staff can access their own personal records. HR has business partners in all service areas and the HR function . . . will be made up mainly of specialists in areas such as recruitment and workforce planning.'

Phillips, L. (2009) 'HR reforms at Birmingham City Council aim to boost efficiency', *People Management*, 4 June, PM Online.

MANAGERIAL DECISION-MAKING AND THE HRIS

The 2004 CIPD survey, *Is HR getting the best out of IT?* alleged that 'significant changes were being made to the role of HR professionals and the ways in which they work. The HRIS is a key part of that transformation, helping to improve the efficiency of HR administration and enabling a greater focus on making a strategic contribution to the business.' The survey showed that three-quarters of organisations have an HRIS in place, with 100 per cent in central government, utilities and call centres and less than half in food and drink organisations. The HRIS is used most extensively in operational functions such as absence management and recruitment and selection, but also features as a strategic tool in HR planning and HR strategy.

The collection, storage and processing of data allows information to be produced to meet the needs at the different levels of managerial decision-making within the organisation – strategic, functional/tactical and operational (Figure 5.1).

Strategic level

Information is needed in aggregated form about the whole organisation for medium- and long-term corporate planning. This includes, for example:

- age profiles of employees and wastage rates for human resource planning
- profile of employment arrangements to maximise flexibility and ensure effective resourcing
- gender, ethnic, disability and other profiling to monitor trends for policy review
- skills and competencies profiling for product or service planning (Exhibit 5.2).

Figure 5.1 Data to information and the decision-making levels

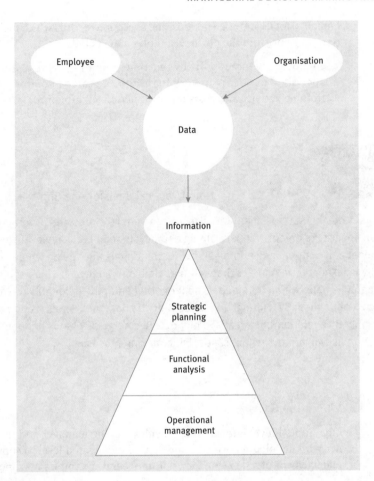

EXHIBIT 5.2 Strategic decision-making

Following the merger of two large financial services organisations, the senior management team need to see the employee profile of the new organisation to match this against the business needs for both the skills and competencies of staff as well as the staff availability required to build a successful new business providing a round-the-clock service. This may present a challenge in that data may be on two HR systems which are unable to interface. However, the HR function can add value to the business by combining the data and converting it into information which is available in a useful and easily accessible form.

Functional/tactical level

Information provides middle managers with analysis of trends, indications of where the organisation is going and how it is doing. Functional managers need summary reports, limited to totals and aggregations, and exception reports, which highlight unusual events or deviations from the norm. Examples may include:

- employee absence reports by function or unit for trend analysis and comparisons
- analysis of accidents at work for health and safety monitoring or risk assessment
- training activity and costs for the function (Exhibit 5.3).

EXHIBIT 5.3 Functional/tactical decision-making

An organisation is due for reassessment for 'Investors in People' status and a working party is undertaking an analysis of organisational training and development. It is reviewing policies on staff development and performance appraisal, but information is needed on where, what and when training activity is taking place. An HRIS that captures data on training activities and events can produce comparative data by function, department or other grouping to identify the extent, nature, clustering or cost of training. By 'cutting' and presenting the data in different ways and through generating comparative information a realistic picture will emerge of what is happening in the organisation and this will inform the tactical decision-making process.

Operational level

Operational-level information provides the line manager and the HR business partner with detailed reports at individual or aggregated level to support the day-to-day management of a department or business unit. Examples may include:

- diary reports of due appraisals
- skills and competencies analysis for staffing a departmental project
- contractual information on staff to ensure appropriate staffing levels
- individual employee attendance record for counselling (Exhibit 5.4).

EXHIBIT 5.4 Operational decision-making

An organisation has introduced a new policy on the management of absence. Line managers are tasked with managing absence and attendance within their department and therefore need to be able to extract a variety of reports to assist in this managerial task. Aggregated reports on numbers of employees absent in a period, numbers and patterns of days absent and lists of individual staff with the number and frequency of days absent will provide the manager with an overview of the situation in the department, identify problem areas and inform plans to manage the employee absence at an operational level.

Although illustrations of information needs have been provided, specific information needs will be diverse and will be dependent on organisational contingencies. However, a good HRIS will enable the HR practitioner to contribute effectively as a business partner at different levels of the organisation and support the business manager in making effective decisions on issues such as human resource planning, attendance, selection, reward, progression, development and performance.

THE BENEFITS OF AN HRIS

The benefits of e-HR and an HRIS are derived from the effective application of HR information to the resourcing challenges facing the organisation. These challenges change over time and vary between organisations. Parry *et al.* (2007), in a research report for the CIPD, argue that:

> As technology improves, organisations are using HR information systems to support and manage an increasing number of HR processes and functions. Where e-HR was at one time simply a tool used for administrative and recording processes, it can now encompass a variety of applications, for example recruitment and selection, e-learning, flexible benefits. It also supports integrated call centres, shared services and self-service environments. It can be an important aspect of any changes to the structural design and operation of the HR function.

The important requirement is to identify the relevant issues and be mindful of the fact that accurate HR information assists the decision-making process, allowing options to be investigated, compared and costed. The following examination of specific HR activities is indicative of the benefits that can accrue from effective HR information systems.

Human resource and talent planning

Planning for the effective resourcing of the organisation with people requires information from inside the organisation about the strategic direction and corporate goals and about the human resources available to achieve these goals, and from outside the organisation about the available resources in the external labour market. An HRIS can be used to provide information such as a skills audit, labour turnover, workforce profiles and succession planning to assist in the planning and decision-making process.

A skills audit of the workforce – This requires data on identified key skills, specialist skills and skill levels (appropriately coded for ease of reporting) and data on the current employee skills in order to provide reports which identify the skills gap and help to shape plans to close the gap, either through the development of existing employees or through recruiting the skills externally.

Labour turnover – Data on employee headcount and leavers will provide rates of labour turnover and identify trends and areas of the organisation where it is difficult to retain staff; this can be further analysed to identify possible causes of labour turnover and appropriate responses developed.

Workforce profiles – Profiling can identify, for example, potential problems with age clusters which may mean a large number of skilled staff leaving in a short time or, alternatively, reduced opportunities for challenge or promotion. Internal information can be combined with external information such as the number of school or university leavers, major competitors in the area and the local and national employment levels to enable options to be identified and included in the planning process.

Succession planning – The identification of key positions and effective planning for the replacement of those positions through the identification and development of suitable employees is an important aspect of human resource planning. This requires the collection and storage of key data which can be used to track performance and development of those staff and appropriate selection to be made at the time when a replacement is needed.

Recruitment and selection

The implementation of a specialist recruitment package allows the recruitment and selection process to be streamlined and managed more effectively. An organisation which undertakes a substantial amount of recruitment or receives many speculative applications may gain significant benefits from computerising the process. Recruitment and selection administration is labour-intensive and costs may be reduced and a higher-quality service provided by a good IT system. Information to be generated and processed may include details of the vacancy and the sources of recruitment used, together with associated costs and key dates. In addition, personal details such as age, sex, ethnic origin and disability can be captured for equal opportunities monitoring purposes. The system will allow the tracking of candidates through 'the recruitment and selection system' so that candidate enquiries can be efficiently and effectively handled. Reports produced to monitor recruitment and selection activity can include numbers of applications from each recruitment source, equal opportunity reporting to provide a profile of applicants by age, sex, ethnic origin and disability, and recruitment costs. The recruitment process is streamlined through the production of standard letters to applicants and candidates, with copies to the interviewing manager. This not only speeds up the process but can also be good public relations in projecting an efficient organisational image. The availability of information allows recruitment and selection activity to be targeted and potentially increases cost-effectiveness. The electronic scanning of CVs can be matched to predetermined criteria in order to reduce the time spent on shortlisting candidates. The Internet provides a useful source of recruitment in some industries and web technology allows quick and easy posting of vacancies either through specialist recruitment agency web pages or through the organisational web page. It is now common for many organisational web pages to contain a current vacancies hyperlink. The principal benefit of e-recruitment is the speed of access to potential recruits. However, it is not a suitable recruitment source for all labour markets and therefore labour market intelligence relating to the predisposition of potential applicants, together with an assessment of likely Internet access, is a prerequisite to the effective deployment of online recruitment. The equal opportunities dimension also requires an assessment of the potential for the unlawful, and undesirable, exclusion of a particular labour market segment.

Equal opportunities

The regular review of an equal opportunities policy is needed to monitor policy effectiveness. The HRIS can provide information to identify trends and to highlight areas for more detailed investigation. Information to be generated and processed may include the age, sex, ethnic origin, age and disability profile of the organisation, data on training completed, which can be used to monitor access to training for part-time staff or identify the need for positive action for under-represented staff, information on promotion decisions to observe trends and assess transparency of decisions, appraisal ratings to monitor distributions and ensure fairness. The information can be combined in different ways and used to review the operation of the policy. Barriers to entry to the organisation and progression within the organisation can be identified and appropriate adjustments made to the policy or training given to employees. The advantage of having good information is that action can be targeted at identified problems with some confidence because action is not based solely on assumptions being made about problems. Policies are more likely to be reviewed and action taken when good-quality information is used to inform policy-making.

Pay and reward

Reward strategies are becoming increasingly complex and constant review is necessary to ensure that reward strategy objectives are being achieved. Information from market surveys needs to be analysed and stored. HRIS reports can be used for reward comparisons, to monitor the operation of the reward policy and to assess value for money. The impact of pay increases can be projected to determine affordability. Appropriate information can be produced to support equal pay reviews and audits and the reports can be scrutinised to look for clusters of gendered jobs to ensure that any difference in pay is defendable in terms of the demands of the job. Internal pay comparisons can be undertaken to identify and investigate any potential problem areas and adjustments made. It is also easy for individual pay increases to be accessed to ensure fair treatment in pay decisions. Reward reporting may include salary profiles of employees, percentage increase profiles to examine distribution of pay increases and salary profiles by sex for equal pay comparison, and information can be examined to look at the impact of different percentage increases on the total pay bill. IT job evaluation packages incorporating competence-based or points-rating schemes can accelerate the process of job evaluation and dispense with the need for individual calculation of job scores. The preparation of information to inform pay negotiations can identify a range of options and a variety of combinations of pay, hours and benefits to form the basis of the negotiating position.

Performance management

Benefits derive from monitoring the performance management system. This can take the strategic approach, which may include value for money, comparisons against benchmarks and return on investments. At operational level the HRIS can store individual objectives and measures of performance following performance appraisal. Under- and over-achievers can be identified and development opportunities, such as coaches, mentors or challenging projects, assigned to support personal development. Performance management information to be processed may consist of individual or team objectives, competency frameworks, performance indicators, departmental targets, individual potential and development needs, and individual ambitions – identified by the employee and details of succession plans. Information can be produced which identifies individual, team and departmental performance trends. Objectives can be analysed for fairness and assessed to see if they are achievable, with agreed adjustments made where necessary. Individual ambitions and organisational opinions of potential can be evaluated and expectations of both parties managed. Expert systems can be used to combine data for promotion (performance, salary and development) and identify those employees ready for promotion.

Training and development

The development of employees is costly and in order to ensure that appropriate training and development takes place and that the organisation gets value for money, training activity needs to be focused and managed effectively. Training and development needs can be identified and details stored within the HRIS, and these can then be assessed against strategic objectives. Training and development can then be provided to meet individual and organisational needs. Centralised access and aggregation of the data will identify collective development needs. Training information for processing may include individual training needs, team training requirements, actual training undertaken, training costs, allocation of training and the generation of appropriate information for comparison with the strategic plan. In addition, forward planning can take place to identify competency frameworks, which can then be used for many aspects of people management. The data combinations are extensive and innovation is needed to recognise the potential for the information on employee training and development, and to combine it in creative ways.

Health and safety

An HRIS can contribute to the effective management of health and safety in the storage and analysis of data on individual employee health and on accidents at work, and also through recording the findings and outcomes of risk assessment. Analysis of employee health and absence records can identify health issues before they develop into major attendance problems and the stored outcomes of effective risk assessment can contribute to the development of safe systems of work which will help to prevent injuries and ill health. Information to be processed may include the volume, pattern and distribution of employee sick absence, reasons for absence, actions taken to manage attendance, details of accidents and injuries and information on hazardous occurrences at work. Recurring health and safety problems can be identified through HRIS reports, or clusters of sick absence may emerge from the analysis. Investigations can then focus on causes rather than just on symptoms.

Employment relations and conflict management

An HRIS also offers benefits in the management of the employment relationship. The analysis of aggregated data on disciplinary occurrences may identify common problems that point to poor communication, particularly relating to the communication of organisational rules. Through providing clearer statements on regulations and managerial expectations, the induction of new employees and the training of existing employees can be improved and should result in a reduction in disciplinary offences and action. Similarly, the analysis of formal employee grievance expressions and the identification of common problems that give rise to employee dissatisfactions can be identified through the HRIS and should result in clearer policy statements and reduce the potential for conflict in the employment relationship.

Redundancy

A redundancy situation is potentially emotionally charged for employees and for managers. The increased objectivity and transparency, which computer listings give to redundancy selection, can ease the situation. The HRIS may allow alternative redundancy options to be modelled, investigated and costed in pursuit of the most appropriate solution. Information to be processed may include details of age and length of service, redundancy payment entitlement, pension entitlement, skills or competency profiles, performance rating and absence records. Alternative selection criteria can be defined and costed prior to consultation with employees so that the impact on the organisation can be projected. Early retirement, 'last in first out', or a multi-variant matrix (measured factors in combination) of performance and skills indicators can be considered, weightings produced and calculations performed to produce a rank order of redundancy action. This may appear impersonal, but the depersonalisation of the redundancy activity may be a strength in facilitating the redundancy process and in objectively defending redundancy decisions.

The potential benefits of HRIS are extensive; they cover all areas of people resourcing and, in order to be realised, require commitment, innovation, knowledge, expertise and IT skills. They support the identification and development of business partnering and should enable the HR professional to maximise the opportunities to add value to the business. Many of the benefits may be operational but the potential remains for significantly greater creativity in the exploitation of the HRIS. In conclusion, the HRIS is no longer limited to simple databases but is expanding to include expert systems, decision support systems, intranets and web technology. All of this requires the HR professional to be skilled in the exploitation of the technology, creative and innovative in the development of the technology and prepared to use the technology to enhance the business partner role.

CASE STUDY Young People's Fashion PLC and HRIS

Background information to Young People's Fashion PLC

Young People's Fashion PLC is a retail fashion company located in the north of England. It was established in the mid 1990s and has grown steadily, and in 2009 is expected to have 25 stores and employ over 600 people. The company has clearly espoused values with a strong focus on the people it employs.

(Box continued)

As the shops are spread over quite a wide geographical area the company strives to put together a management team before opening a new shop to ensure that the organisational values are embedded within the culture of the new shop from the start. So far, more that 80 per cent of its current stores are managed by people who have been promoted from within. As with many new businesses its systems are mainly manual and the HR director recognises that if the company were to continue to grow then, in order to sustain its values and its desire to continue to give power to the store manager, it would need to invest in technology which would support that vision. The management team within the organisation identified its information priorities so that this would form the basis of the assessment and purchase of a new HRIS. The team identified two overriding priorities that were required from the system:

- First, the system should support the line manager by providing easy access to information for the day-to-day management of the store.
- Second, the system should provide quality strategic information to allow the directors to monitor progress.

Information needs

The organisation undertook a high-level analysis to determine the main criteria for selecting an HRIS. This analysis identified three main criteria. First, that the system should be able to manage the growing volume of data without requiring the organisation to make changes to its business processes. Second, the company wanted a single database to include both HR and payroll, which was centrally managed but accessible by all managers to enable capture of the data at source. Third, a sophisticated reporting system which allowed managers at all levels to have access to information appropriate to their decision-making level.

Questions

Young People's Fashion PLC has now to start the process of purchase and implementation of the new system. If you, as an HR business partner, were a participant in the working party to complete this project, how would you address the following questions?

1 What research should the working party do to identify a shortlist of suppliers?

2 What team should be brought together to view the systems demonstrated by the shortlisted suppliers?

3 List the range of issues that you think should be explored with the suppliers at the demonstrations.

4 When the organisation has made the decision on the purchase of a system the issues associated with implementation must be addressed. If you, as an HR business partner, were a member of the implementation team, how would you analyse the following requirements?
   (a) Who would you expect to be on the implementation team?
   (b) How would you establish the baseline data for the new system?
   (c) What training needs can you identify and how will these be addressed?
   (d) What criteria for success will the implementation team set and how will these be measured?

SECURITY OF PERSONAL DATA

Two significant and interrelated issues are associated with the security of personal data, whether it is kept manually or processed electronically by an HRIS: first, assuring confidentiality in possession and use of data; and, second, determining who should have access to data. This concern for confidentiality is often heightened when the records are kept electronically, but even the safekeeping of manual employee files is a legal requirement and therefore the security of personal data should be of intense concern to all managers and HR practitioners. There exist significant organisational variations in how and where manual files are kept, with some organisations permitting employee personal files to be left on desks unattended even overnight. Other organisations have a 'clear desk' policy, which requires that all files are returned to safekeeping when the desk is unattended, potentially making the data more secure. All personally identifiable information is required by law to be secure. Commercial software normally has built-in and sophisticated security systems which allow individual user profiling to ensure that access is on a need-to-know basis. The system developer should be looking for a system that features a password, user control definition for every user, individual profiling to the level of the field – meaning that fields such as those relating to pay could be blanked out on the screen, allowing extensive access to the system to the data-inputter for purposes of updating, while sight of sensitive data remains accessible only to those with a particular access profile – and an audit trail which tracks access to the system and any changes made. The management of decentralised systems where there are many users can be complex, and responsibility for this task has to be clearly defined and assigned to ensure confidence in the security of the system. Disclosure of passwords and leaving an HRIS 'logged-on' while away from the workstation may need to be identified as disciplinary offences, as these actions impact adversely on the security of the data.

The increased flexibility in the way that employees work, and where they work, creates security of data issues. Organisations clearly need to balance the necessity of sharing information with the need to keep data secure; this can be done through an information security policy which clarifies roles and responsibilities for all employees. High-profile cases of data sticks left in pub car parks and commuters working with confidential information while on the train surrounded by onlookers demonstrate how easily data can become 'insecure'. In addition to policies to address who can take data where, consideration needs to be given to what data employees may have in 'portable' form. In relation to those employees leaving the business, a data security policy needs to address the security and use of not only client data but also personally identifiable employee data. Employees with remote access to corporate systems also pose a threat to data security.

DATA PROTECTION – RIGHTS, ACCESS AND SECURITY

A raft of legislation provides protection for individuals and ensures that information given in confidence remains confidential and cannot be disclosed without consent unless it is in the public interest. The legislation includes:

- Human Rights Act 1998
- Public Interest Disclosure Act 1998

- Data Protection Act 1998
- Freedom of Information Act 2000
- The Telecommunications (Lawful Business Practice) Regulations 2000.

Human Rights Act 1998

In 2000 the Human Rights Act brought into UK law the European Convention on Human Rights. Among other things the convention states that everyone has the right to respect for their private and family life, home and correspondence. Aspects of this are important both to the actions of employers and for the protection of employees, particularly with regard to confidentiality and the holding of information. Many organisations use email systems as mainstream communication systems and the Human Rights Act requires organisations to respect the privacy of employees with regard to interception of email and of telephone conversations. However, it may be useful for this right to be protected formally within the organisation through the development of clear policies on the personal use of the Internet and email.

Public Interest Disclosure Act 1998

The Public Interest Disclosure Act is designed to give greater protection to whistleblowers and protects employees against being treated unfairly because of the disclosure of information which is in the public interest. The Act applies only to protected disclosures, which include health and safety issues, employers' legal obligations, environmental damage and criminal offences. The Act requires that in order to obtain protection the employee must first disclose the information to the employer. If the employee fears either that the employer will not take appropriate action in the light of the disclosure or that they will be victimised by the employer, then the employee may go public with the information. Employers should make sure that they have in place processes and routes for disclosure that protect employees and provide mechanisms for action and for feedback to the employee.

Data Protection Act 1998

The Data Protection Act (DPA) regulates all individually identifiable data relating to a living person and contained in a readily accessible filing system. This includes employment files and any individual informal files kept by line managers. The DPA covers not just electronically held data but also manually held data. Chubb (2008) quotes Alan Warner from Hertfordshire County Council as saying, 'data protection is desperately important to the employer-employee relationship . . . complacency is the enemy here. HR's role in data protection is crucial . . . the way an organization treats access to and security of employees' personal information will dictate the extent to which someone trusts their employer.' There are eight enforceable principles for the obtaining, holding and disclosing of personal data. These principles, which must be complied with, state that the data must be:

- lawfully and fairly processed
- processed for specified purposes
- adequate, relevant and not excessive
- accurate and kept up to date

- not be kept for longer than is necessary
- processed within the rights of the data subject
- held securely
- not transferred outside the EU to countries without adequate protection.

The DPA established the Data Protection Commissioner, now the Information Commissioner, and all organisations holding data are required to notify the Information Commissioner. Notification is a statutory requirement and failure to notify is a criminal offence. The Information Commissioner reports directly to Parliament and is responsible for the dissemination of information, promotion of good practice and ensuring compliance with both the Data Protection Act and the Freedom of Information Act. The Information Commissioner has the power to: check if organisations are complying with the requirements of the DPA; serve information notices requiring organisations to provide information when requested; serve enforcement notices and 'stop now' orders where there has been a breach of the Act; prosecute those committing a criminal offence under the Act; conduct audits to assess whether organisations processing personal data follow good practice; report to Parliament of data protection areas of concern. The DPA requires the identification of a designated data controller with responsibility for ensuring compliance. In the event of a breach of the legislation the data controller will be personally responsible unless he or she can demonstrate that reasonable steps have been taken to ensure compliance. Reasonable steps include a reliable audit system, an appropriate data protection policy, suitable training available to those who collect, store and retrieve information and well-documented communication processes. Links with the disciplinary and grievance procedures need to make clear the responsibilities of employees with access to personal data, as well as their rights of access to data held on them. The data subject, that is the identifiable person about whom data is held, has the right to know what data is held on them, where data is being processed, why the data is being held, who might receive the data and also have confidence that decisions relating to that individual will not be taken solely on processed data. Any data subject request for information is required to be in writing and contain sufficient information for the employer to be able to identify and provide the information. The information requested is to be supplied within 42 days and the employer may charge a fee for supplying the data.

The DPA identifies sensitive data which can only be held with the explicit consent of the individual. Employers may seek this consent from new employees within the contract of employment and existing employees may be asked to give their explicit consent. Sensitive data includes ethnic origin, religious beliefs, trade union membership, sexual life, physical or mental health and criminal history. An area of concern to employers is the provision of confidential information by a third party. The most common information of this type in the employment relationship is a reference, which may be requested and provided prior to employment. The key factor is whether the employee has the right of access to this information, which is held in the employment record. The most important factor in this instance is the status of the reference and this hinges on whether the reference was requested and provided **in confidence**. The referee can withhold disclosure by supplying the reference to the employer in confidence. The employer must ensure compliance and therefore must ensure that there are procedures in place that protect the confidential status of the reference. Alternatively, the employer should state that the individual may have access to the reference and, as a consequence, the referee supplies the reference in the full knowledge that the individual may see it. Whatever approach is taken by the employer, appropriate systems must be in place to protect the supplier of the reference and the rights of access of the individual.

The Information Commissioner has responsibility for issuing Codes of Practice which offer guidance on the practical aspects of implementation and compliance with the DPA. There are currently Employment Practices Data Protection Codes on Recruitment and Selection, Employment Records, Monitoring at Work, and Information about Workers' Health. These codes identify benchmark standards regarding the collection, storage and processing of personal data and provide useful information for organisations to support the development of procedures which will ensure that organisational practice complies with the law.

Freedom of Information Act 2000

The Freedom of Information Act provided a general right of access to all types of recorded information held by public authorities from January 2005. This extends the right of access to information under the DPA from individual data to all types of information held by public bodies, including information supplied by third parties, although public authorities will have to be mindful of the DPA before disclosing individual data. The Freedom of Information Act is enforced by the Information Commissioner who therefore has responsibility which includes both the Freedom of Information Act and the DPA. The Act requires Codes of Practice to be issued which provide guidance to public bodies on the development of 'desirable practice' in implementing the legislation.

The Telecommunications (Lawful Business Practice) Regulations 2000

These regulations were issued in order to comply with the Telecommunications Directive, which covers all types of communications on public and private systems. The regulations allow employers to intercept telephone, email, fax etc. with the employee's consent. The employer can also intercept communication without the employee's consent in order to establish facts, for quality control and training purposes, to comply with regulatory procedures, for system maintenance or to detect unauthorised use. It is therefore important that employers put in place policies and procedures that govern the use of telecommunications for personal use.

Data protection policies and procedures

The far-reaching data protection legislation raises a number of issues for the organisation. In order to ensure compliance with this extensive legislation employers need to devise and implement policies and procedures that communicate to employees and guide employers' actions. Areas for consideration in the development and implementation of policies will include the appointment of an information controller; an audit of information systems which identifies what information is held and why; a review of data security including an assessment of compliance of data collection and data transmission outside the EU; a review of policies and procedures regarding the requesting and holding of employment references; the development and communication of a policy statement on the use of telephones, the Internet and email; a policy statement together with procedures on reporting under the Public Interest Disclosure Act; and details of employee access to information procedures.

It is essential to ensure that managers understand the extent of the legislation, the rights of employees and the need to have a controlled and disciplined approach to the recording and use of information about employees. Organisations need to decide where information is held. If all information is to be held centrally, it may be easier to control if it is held in computer records rather than on extensive, dispersed manual files where security may be a high risk, from the point of view of both data collection and security of access to the data.

EMPLOYEE INTERNET AND EMAIL POLICIES

The prevalence of the Internet in the workplace and the ease of access to this resource by employees, together with the use of email as a communication tool, raise issues about organisational control of these resources. The organisation should have an agreed strategy for use of this technology and a policy to inform employees and to guide management action. The 'Employment Practices Code' issued by the Information Commissioner provides guidance on the employer's right to monitor employee actions. The Code recommends carrying out an impact assessment to ensure that Internet and email monitoring complies with the DPA. This should confirm the purpose of monitoring, the benefits of monitoring and the risks of any adverse impact. The policy should state what is prohibited, including access to areas of the Internet such as pornographic material, and the disciplinary consequences of breaching the policy. The organisation's position on browsing the Internet and the use of social networking sites, such as Facebook, at work needs to be communicated and consideration needs to be given to the potential impact of sites such as YouTube. The policy options range from a complete ban on employees posting any entry to these sites through to allowing non-work-related entries. Other areas for policy consideration include the downloading of information which may breach copyright legislation or introduce virus infections to the employer network, and the use of a work email address for personal communication. The DPA provides employer guidance on the monitoring of employee emails. Technology is constantly changing and the speed of transmission of information far exceeds that of just a few years ago. This acceleration will continue and employers will need to be rigorous in protecting the business as well as acting fairly and reasonably towards employees by having clear rules on use and on monitoring.

SUMMARY LEARNING POINTS

1 Accurate and timely information informs strategic planning and encourages the effective deployment of staff. The information explosion increases managerial expectations about the availability of information, and the HR function can enhance its status and influence through utilising the potential of an HRIS to contribute to the strategic planning process.

2 Different combinations of data provide information for all levels of decision-making:
   - strategic decision-making and planning
   - tactical decision-making and monitoring
   - operational decision-making and control.

3   An effective HRIS will support the HR business partner and the line manager in working together to deliver HR services to the organisation.

4   Organisational structure and culture, together with the degree of centralisation or devolution of HR activities, will influence the type of HRIS implemented and the extent of user access. Line manager HRIS access can facilitate organisational change and promote line manager ownership of the system.

5   Effective HRIS have a role in all areas of HR management, and HR practitioners are encouraged to be innovative in exposing managers to the more sophisticated analysis that enhances decision-making.

6   HRIS and the provision of e-HR services can support the delivery of HR information to both employees and managers or can go beyond the basics to act as a mechanism for transforming the HR function.

7   e-HR solutions can provide a creative and cost-effective way of delivering HR services and can be a tool in HR transformation.

8   The security of all individual data is regulated by the Data Protection Act 1998, which requires organisations to appoint an information controller, notify the Information Commissioner and comply with the eight enforceable principles.

9   A raft of legislation protects the rights of individuals with respect to privacy and access to information, and employers must develop appropriate policies and procedures to inform employees and guide employers' actions.

10 Employers need Internet and email use policies to protect the business and the employee.

REFERENCES AND FURTHER READING

Aikin, O. (2004) 'The exempt files?' *People Management*, 26 February, 18–19.

Chubb, L. (2008) 'Why we're all still stuck on protecting data, 10 years on', *People Management*, 10 July, 14–15.

CIPD (2004) *Is HR getting the best out of IT?* People and Technology Survey report. London: CIPD.

CIPD (2005) *Business Partnering: a new direction for HR*, CIPD Guide. London: CIPD.

CIPD (2007) *Internet and e-mail policies*, CIPD Factsheet. London: CIPD.

CIPD (2009) *Data Protection*, CIPD Factsheet. London: CIPD.

Daniels, K. (2004) *Employment Law for HR and Business Students*. London: CIPD.

Data Protection Guidance www.informationcommissioner.gov.uk, retrieved October 2004.

Emmott, M. (2003) 'Seeing sense', *People Management*, 10 July, 23.

Goodge, P. (2001) 'e-HR pure and simple', *People Management*, 8 March, 51.

Holbeche, L. (2001) *Aligning Human Resources and Business Strategy*. Oxford: Butterworth Heinemann.

Kettley, P. and Reilly, P. (2003) 'e-HR: An introduction', *Institute of Employment Studies Report 398*. Brighton: IES.

Parry, E., Tyson, S., Selbie, D. and Leighton, R. (2007) *HR and technology: Impact and advantages*, Research into Practice Report. London: CIPD.

Reddington, M. (2003) *e-HR Led HR Transformation*, www.roffeyparkresearch.com, retrieved October 2004.

Reddington, M. (2008) *The impact of e-HR on HR and line manager capability*, www.bluefinsolutions.com, October.

Smethurst, S. (2005) 'Profession lacking in IT ambition', *People Management*, 16 June, 10.

Spencer, S. (2003) 'Set the record straight', *People Management*, 28 August, 14–15.

Temperton, E. and Norbury, A. (2004) 'Off the record', *People Management*, 15 January, 18–19.

Trapp, R. (2001) 'Of mice and men', *People Management*, 28 June, 24–32.

ASSIGNMENTS AND DISCUSSION TOPICS

1 What types of HRIS are used in your organisation? Where does ownership lie and how does this affect the use of the system? What enhancements to your HRIS would you like to see and how might these changes impact on the HR role?

2 What contribution does HR information make to the decision-making processes in your organisation? Identify the different levels of decision-making and the way that information is developed and presented to meet these different requirements.

3 How far has your organisation gone in the development and use of e-HR in the delivery of HR services? Identify areas where e-HR is used for transactional services and areas where e-HR is used for transformational purposes.

4 How well does the HRIS meet the needs of the 'users' in your organisation? Identify the barriers to effective use of information and examine ways to overcome these barriers.

5 How secure is personal data in your organisation? What systems are in place to ensure security of data and how are these systems monitored and reviewed?

6 Review the impact of legislation on the obtaining, holding and disclosing of individual data in your organisation. What policies and procedures have been developed to ensure that the rights of individuals to access and the rights of individuals to privacy are protected?

7 Examine the policies in your organisation related to the control and monitoring of Internet and email. How are these policies communicated to staff? What systems are in place to monitor staff use of the Internet and how do you know whether the policies work?

Chapter 6

Recruitment: attracting the right people

LEARNING OUTCOMES: TO BE ABLE TO

- Analyse recruitment and selection processes as a system of inputs, outputs and interrelated sub-systems

- Subject organisational recruitment and selection processes to robust scrutiny in pursuit of business-focused continuous improvement

- Undertake job analysis and identify significant labour market characteristics

- Evaluate alternative methods of recruitment and make informed choices of method

INTRODUCTION

Effective human resource planning can predict HR gaps and promote a focus on recruiting the right people to deliver business objectives. The recruitment and selection process is a matching activity between applicant and job, which is dependent, first, on the organisation clearly defining and specifying a need; second, on utilising appropriate recruitment methods and selection techniques effectively; and, third, on reviewing, evaluating and modifying the recruitment and selection system in the light of experience. Recruitment and selection, while being systematic, need not be inflexible and as well as the candidate fitting the job, the job may need to fit the candidate to some extent – a degree of job malleability and person malleability will lubricate the matching process. The recruitment and selection of workers is fundamental to the functioning of an organisation and there are compelling reasons for getting it right. Inappropriate selection decisions reduce organisational effectiveness, invalidate reward and development strategies, are frequently unfair on the individual recruit and can be distressing for managers who have to deal with unsuitable employees. Inappropriate recruitment is also expensive. If the overall costs of leaving, including payroll and administration, recruitment and selection time and fees, induction, training, unproductive time and any indirect loss of business or customer satisfaction, are taken into account, the estimated cost per leaver can be around £4000, and £10 000 for managers and professionals (CIPD, 2009b). Recruitment is addressed in this chapter and selection in the next chapter.

CONTINGENCY IN RECRUITMENT AND SELECTION METHODS

Good recruitment and selection is important because well-thought-out, agreed and communicated policies, procedures and practices can significantly contribute to effective organisational performance, to good employee relations and to a positive public image. Ineffectiveness in recruitment and selection may lead to poor work performance, unacceptable conduct, internal conflict, low morale and job satisfaction and dysfunctional labour turnover. Good recruitment is more than just filling vacancies and human resource planning is the route to forecasting HR requirements and ensuring that the recruitment and selection activity is directed at getting the right people, in the right place, at the right time with the right skills to achieve the business objectives. Recruitment and selection is therefore an essential part of HR strategy. Recruitment and selection processes should be effective, efficient and fair – effective in generating candidates of appropriate quality and quantity and distinguishing between the suitable and the unsuitable; efficient in being timely and resource effective; fair by dealing equitably, honestly and courteously with all applicants and providing a positive framework within which diverse candidates can demonstrate their abilities (ACAS, 2006). A contingent approach to recruitment and selection is advocated, while recognising that this may be constrained in practice by standard (self-imposed) organisational procedures. Standard procedures may contribute to fairness and consistency, but some flexibility is also desirable to ensure a business-focused recruitment process. Recruiters should be aware of the range, strengths and limitations of recruitment methods and selection techniques, as this will enable informed choices to be made.

The extent to which the functional elements of recruitment and selection are distributed between line managers and HR practitioners will be contingent upon organisational circumstances. The division of recruitment and selection responsibilities will be determined by factors such as organisational size, administrative resources, locus of professional expertise and the HR strategy on HR devolution to line managers. A strategy to devolve recruitment and selection responsibility to line managers will invariably be a question of *the degree of devolution* and rarely results in absolute decentralisation of recruitment and selection functions. Whether increased devolution is perceived by line managers as liberating or merely an abdication by HR specialists, and extra unsolicited work, is subject to continuing debate – although the argument that line managers should be responsible for their human as well as other resources is compelling. Regardless of the division of responsibilities, a manager who is not closely involved in the recruitment process and the selection decision is less likely to be committed to the outcome or accept full responsibility for the performance of the recruit. All involved in recruitment and selection, whether as a direct participant or as an adviser, will benefit from a knowledge and understanding of the range of options and also from an exposure to effective practice and professional principles. While there may be effective practice and professional principles in recruitment and selection, there is no one best way and prescriptions are to be avoided. These recruitment and selection chapters adopt a systems approach, emphasise choice and flexibility, identify and discuss the functional elements in recruitment and selection, and stress the importance of critical review and evaluation of the business-focused recruitment and selection processes in the pursuit of continuous improvement.

RECRUITMENT, SELECTION AND THE SYSTEMS APPROACH

It is useful for analytical purposes to distinguish between recruitment and selection.

- *Recruitment* is a process which aims to attract appropriately qualified candidates for a particular position from which it is possible and practical to select and appoint a competent person or persons.

- *Selection* is a process which involves the application of appropriate techniques and methods with the aim of selecting, appointing and inducting a competent person or persons.

Recruitment and selection are components of the same system or process and can be considered separately, but they are not mutually exclusive functions. A systems approach to recruitment and selection (Figure 6.1) is based on the idea that a system has inputs, a processing unit and outputs. The processing unit contains the recruitment and selection sub-systems. The inputs are the candidates, the processing unit consists of various methods and techniques, and the outputs are either effective employees or candidates who return to the labour market. The candidates who return to the labour market are either rejected by the organisation or choose to exit from the recruitment and selection process. The system is subject to considerable external influence – the legal framework, the economic situation, social and demographic change, competitor activity and labour market characteristics. The systems approach provides a convenient analytical framework and permits the penetration of the recruitment and selection sub-systems.

Figure 6.1 The systems approach to recruitment and selection

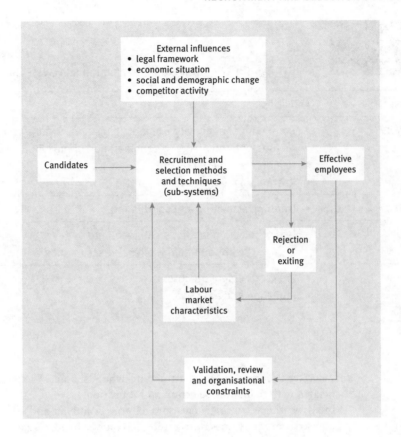

It is also possible to recognise the interdependence of the sub-systems with the changes in one sub-system having implications for another and also for the quality of the outputs. For example, the most sophisticated selection methods will be rendered impotent by recruitment activity which fails to attract qualified candidates, and highly effective recruitment activity which generates appropriate candidates will be neutered by selection methods which fail to predict performance in the job.

RECRUITMENT AND SELECTION SUB-SYSTEMS

The sub-systems can be categorised as:

1 *Attraction*: attracting suitable candidates.
2 *Reduction*: eliminating unsuitable candidates.
3 *Selection*: assessing, choosing and appointing a suitable candidate.
4 *Transition*: converting the successful candidate to an effective employee.

The components and activities of each sub-system are exposed in Exhibit 6.1.

The activities within each sub-system can be scrutinised to assess the contribution that each makes to the overall recruitment and selection process. The remainder of

EXHIBIT 6.1 The recruitment and selection sub-systems

Sub-systems	Activities
1 *Attraction*	• Pre-recruitment activity – establishing a *prima facie* case for recruitment; job analysis; consideration of the labour market • Use of recruitment methods • Responding to enquiries
2 *Reduction*	• Filtering, screening and shortlisting
3 *Selection*	• Use of selection methods and techniques • Making the appointment – offer and acceptance
4 *Transition*	• Pre-engagement process • Induction and appraisal

this chapter is concerned with **attraction**, while Chapter 7 focuses on the activities associated with **reduction, selection** and **transition**.

In advocating a contingency approach to recruitment and selection activities it is recognised that rarely does the recruiter have a free hand. Organisational constraints and influences on choice in recruitment and selection activities, methods and techniques include the:

- degree of flexibility within organisational recruitment and selection procedures and the potential for conflict with procedural standardisation perceived to be necessary to achieve diversity objectives
- previous experience of organisational recruiters, and whether it is positive or negative, in relation to different methods and techniques
- physical and human resources available, together with time scale and time constraints
- skill and expertise of the recruiters
- relative costs of recruitment and selection techniques and methods
- nature of the employment contract, hours of work and relative importance of the vacancy.

Some commentators argue that the recruitment and selection philosophy should be 'select for attitude and train for skill'. What this means is focusing the recruitment and selection process on behavioural competencies such as customer focus, teamworking skills, responsiveness to change, willingness to conform with dominant corporate values and so on. Any deficiencies in technical skill can then be remedied through training needs analysis and the provision of learning opportunities. This philosophy in no way undermines the validity of a systematic recruitment and selection process; it merely refocuses it.

Figure 6.2 Pre-recruitment activity

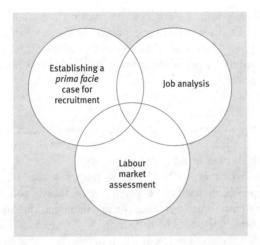

PRE-RECRUITMENT

The pre-recruitment process combines the three interdependent elements of establishing a *prima facie* case for recruitment, job analysis and labour market assessment (Figure 6.2).

Establishing a *prima facie* case for recruitment

When a vacancy occurs, whether through resignation, dismissal, increased workload or reorganisation, there is only the **opportunity** for recruitment and a *prima facie* case should be established before proceeding (ACAS, 2006). Each vacancy presents management with an opportunity to rethink the structure of the organisation and the allocation of duties. There are alternatives to recruitment when a vacancy occurs, and several questions can usefully be addressed.

- Is there actually a job to be done or can elements be distributed, eliminated or achieved through alternative means, for example by utilising technology or contracting it out?
- Do the workload predictions justify recruitment?
- Does the filling of the vacancy integrate with the human resource plan?
- How does the recruitment proposal fit with diversity objectives?

Job analysis

Once a *prima facie* case for recruitment has been established, job analysis provides the opportunity for assessing whether the job has changed and for reviewing the knowledge, skills and competencies required; for a newly created position the job analysis is a predictive activity. Job analysis is the systematic **process** of collecting information about the tasks, responsibilities and contexts of a job. The **outputs** of the job analysis process are job descriptions and person specifications. In addition to recruitment and selection, job analysis information is fundamental to many other HR management activities, including establishing the job requirements for appraising performance and identifying development needs; making reward comparisons between jobs; considering the implications of legislation relating to health and safety, unfair discrimination and the Working Time Directive; and contributing to a common understanding of the job in grievances, disciplinary matters or the negotiation of job changes.

Job analysis is an information-gathering process and decisions need to be made about who does the job analysis, what information-collection methods are appropriate and which sources of information are the most useful. The job analysis can be undertaken solely or jointly by the line manager or the HR specialist depending upon the techniques being used, the expertise of the analyst and the complexity of the job. The sources of information include the line manager, the supervisor, the existing job-holder and other members of the team. A triangulation of these sources will generate the most balanced data, as different perspectives will be provided by each of the contributors. Informal and formal job analysis methods are available and include questionnaires, interviews, observation, critical incident techniques, the use of standard checklists and the keeping of work logs and diaries. The information to be collected includes:

- data which identifies the job and locates it within the organisational structure
- job objectives and performance measures
- accountabilities, responsibilities and organisational relationships
- job duties and content
- terms of employment and work conditions
- skills, knowledge and competencies required
- other distinctive job characteristics.

The job analysis process generates information which is converted into the tangible outputs of a job description and a person specification and it is important to distinguish between these two outputs. A job description specifies the purpose, the task and the scope of the job (Exhibit 6.2), and the person specification profiles the people characteristics required to do the job effectively – the job description is the '**what**' (has to be done) and the person specification is the '**who**' (does it).

EXHIBIT 6.2 **Template headings for a job description**

1 Job title, department, location
2 Job level and pay rate
3 Responsible to . . .
4 Key relationships, responsibilities and accountabilities
5 Job purpose and objectives
6 Specific tasks and responsibilities
7 Key performance indicators
8 Any special circumstances relating to the job

The job description and person specification may be combined in one document and the complexity will vary according to the nature of the job. It is not possible to be prescriptive about format or content, but the objectives of the job description and the person specification in recruitment and selection include, first, to provide an objective focus for the matching of applicants to the job requirements; second, to communicate a clear idea of the job to the applicant – a realistic job preview (RJP); and, third, to provide a basis for appraising performance and identifying training needs during the transition from candidate to effective employee. Without wishing to undermine the contributions made by the well known Rodger's seven-point plan and Munro's five-fold grading system in providing systematic templates for the design of person specifications, a death knell has effectively been sounded by the evolving framework for unlawful discrimination, intrusion into private life, labour market changes and changing patterns of work and also increasing concern over workforce diversity. This raises questions about the appropriateness of using, for example, assessment categories relating to 'bearing', 'interests', 'disposition' and 'circumstances'.

> Although the broad framework may still be valid, it is now unethical, inappropriate and potentially discriminatory to probe too deeply into some of these areas (of the person specification).   (Marchington and Wilkinson, 2008)

This does not eliminate the need for a systematic approach in determining person specifications, but the approach needs to be founded on two concepts – *job relevance* and *measurability*. There are two fundamental questions. First, am I satisfied that the specified skills, knowledge and characteristics are necessary for the effective performance of the job? Second, can I systematically measure, or assess, them as part of the recruitment and selection process? The six-factor formula is offered as an alternative model for a person specification (Exhibit 6.3).

EXHIBIT 6.3 A six-factor formula for a person specification

The **'relevance and measurability'** of the following six factors in relation to a specific job.

1   Skills, knowledge and competencies
2   Personality characteristics
3   Level of experience
4   Certificated qualifications
5   Physical characteristics
6   Development potential of the candidate

Job requirements may need to exceed those which are essential for a particular job when candidates are assessed on the basis of potential and career development in line with the human resource plan. Further guidance on compiling person specifications includes:

1 Skills and knowledge should be specifically related to job needs, and preconditions on length and type of experience should be restricted to what is necessary for effective job performance.

2 Education and training preconditions should not exceed the minimum requirements for satisfactory job performance, and training to enable candidates to achieve satisfactory job performance should be identified.

3 Criteria covering personal qualities and circumstances should be directly related to the job and applied equally to all groups regardless of age, sex, race, ethnic origin or disability.

Person specifications provide fertile ground for the introduction of personal prejudices, subjectivity and arbitrary criteria and this is not in the interests of the organisation or the applicants. There is also a tendency to over-specify in person specifications by seeking the super-human candidate or demanding characteristics which disbar perfectly competent people. There needs to be a balance between idealism and reality in person specifications. Characteristics can be divided into those which are **essential** and those which are **desirable** or, in the case of competencies, the threshold level of competence and a superior level of competence. This will introduce a necessary degree of person specification flexibility and enable some desirable matching of the job to the person. It is salutary to test each element of the person specification against whether it can be measured or assessed in a consistent, valid and reliable way; if it cannot, it probably needs to be discarded. Despite these 'health warnings', the job description and person specification have invaluable parts to play in creating a systematic approach to recruitment and selection and in focusing the minds of the participants. It is fundamental to effective recruitment and selection activity to begin with a current job description and person specification.

Attention is drawn to four contemporary and interrelated issues which justify reflection. First, there is a debate about the value of comprehensive and detailed job descriptions in rapidly changing organisations, which increasingly emphasise flexibility. Conventional job descriptions are criticised for focusing too heavily on tasks and processes and for being inflexible. It is suggested by some commentators that accountability profiles which concentrate on outputs, such as the results, purposes and added-value dimensions of the job, rather than job inputs are more versatile and complementary to HR strategies relating to empowerment, worker flexibility and autonomy in job design. This has implications for the design, rather than the concept, of job descriptions and person specifications. It also raises the question of the extent to which the person fits the job or the job is fitted to the person – perhaps there needs to be a bit of both with the achievement of business objectives as the primary concern. Second, the job analysis information only provides a snapshot of a job at one point in time. Job descriptions and person specifications decay from inception and they need regular review to ensure currency and relevance. Third, there is a tension between the need for record-keeping and evidence of job descriptions and person specifications for organisational purposes or as a requirement of validating and auditing bodies, such as Learning and Skills Councils (LSCs) or Investor in People (IiP) assessors, and the need for the job description and person specification to be organic documents, with a rate of change which is at least equal to the rate of change of the organisation. Fourth, the issue of corporate culture is difficult to address in formal job descriptions and person specifications. If the organisation is highly organic and having to adapt continuously to turbulent environments, a candidate with a career to date in a more mechanistic or steady-state organisation may not represent the best fit. But how is culture measured and how is cultural fit objectively and fairly assessed? Is cultural fit essential at recruitment or is it 'acquired' during the transition phase? Is cultural fit merely the cloning of conformity of behaviour? Is there any conflict between cultural fit and diversity objectives? Chapter 8 argues that the pursuit of equal opportunities is a social responsibility and a legal requirement and makes sound business sense, and it is in the interests of every organisation to ensure that it does not reduce the pool of talent from which it can draw employees by allowing unfounded prejudices to influence the decision. How legitimate is it, therefore, to reduce the pool of talent through applying corporate culture criteria?

Analysing the labour market

The third element of pre-recruitment activity is labour market assessment. This is fundamentally about establishing the availability of candidates who meet the person specification and the ease or difficulty with which they can be attracted. It also involves consideration of the appropriateness of the terms, conditions and rewards being offered, as incongruence with candidate expectations will have adverse implications for the recruitment and selection process.

It is necessary to consider the specific labour market and its characteristics as a prerequisite to designing and applying recruitment and selection methods. As a working definition, 'a labour market is the identified pool of potential employees from which it is possible to attract candidates of the required calibre for a specified job'. The organisation has access to the internal labour market (ILM) and the external labour market (ELM). The ILM describes arrangements whereby existing staff can apply and be considered for organisational vacancies which occur, resulting in the promotion or transfer of current employees. The ILM has positive potential in terms of motivation, continuity and retention, but the organisation is effectively constraining access to a wider pool of talent. In addition, it may be more difficult to orchestrate a managerially desired change in culture if relying on ILMs. The ILM cannot be relied upon indefinitely unless the rate of staff turnover exactly equals any planned or necessary adjustments in head count. Reasons for accessing the ILM include:

- the provision of opportunities for training and development to existing employees
- enabling employees to pursue reward through internal promotion
- the retention of the investment in the organisation's human capital
- lower costs of recruitment
- scarcity in the ELM
- the reinforcement of corporate culture and values.

The external labour market is segmented and stratified by occupation, industry, geography, gender, race and age *inter alia*. It is dynamic in nature and subject to many influences including demographic change; for example, the ageing UK population and a smaller pool of young people, emerging and declining skills, changing patterns of work and increasing female participation. The ELM can also be considered in terms of primary, secondary and tertiary sectors, reflecting the flexible firm divisions (*see* Chapter 4).

A critical factor in recruitment and selection is the establishment of whether there is likely to be a shortage or surplus of candidates.

A shortage labour market is characterised by demand exceeding labour supply, giving more power to potential candidates and highlighting the two-way nature of the recruitment relationship. A surplus labour market is characterised by labour supply exceeding demand, giving more power and control to the employing organisation. In terms of strategy, a shortage labour market needs a more **nurturing** recruitment and selection system, and a surplus labour market needs a more **targeted** approach.

The job-seeking habits of the applicants in the identified labour market also need consideration. For example, and at the risk of being stereotypical, a chief executive candidate may expect the employing organisation to adopt the role of suitor within a sophisticated and considerate recruitment and selection process, while a casual kitchen porter may expect a minimum of bureaucracy and form filling, an interview with a very realistic job preview and an immediate start. The task for the recruiter is to anticipate the expectations of potential candidates in relation to the methods of application and treatment during the selection process.

In summary, the analysis of the labour market needs to take account of:

- the factors associated with ILM and ELM recruitment
- the stratification, segmentation and characteristics of ELMs
- the implications of recruiting and selecting within primary, secondary and tertiary labour markets
- whether the identified labour market reflects a shortage or surplus of labour in relation to demand
- the job-seeking habits and expectations of potential candidates.

Labour market assessment also involves the critical evaluation of the recruitment and selection process for each vacancy; record-keeping of numbers, quality and expectations of applicants; market research through accessing the employment service, employment agencies and advertising media; and networking with other employers. Labour market intelligence is essential to determining appropriate recruitment and selection methods. Labour market analysis will also be influential in determining the nature of the contract, the pattern of work and the terms and conditions of employment.

RECRUITMENT METHODS – ATTRACTING APPLICATIONS

Once pre-recruitment activity is complete it is necessary to consider recruitment methods. This section introduces a range of recruitment methods, identifies the characteristics of each method and discusses potential advantages and disadvantages.

The objective of a recruitment method is to attract an appropriate number of suitable candidates, at a reasonable cost. There is no ideal number of applications and there is no intrinsic value in attracting a high volume of candidates. Is the epitome of recruitment effectiveness the attraction of one well-qualified candidate for each vacancy? This would clearly have advantages in terms of time, effort and cost, but it is unrealistic. It does, however, provoke a useful mental discipline by focusing attention on attracting quality candidates rather than quantity of applications. There is a tension between a desire to ensure that sufficient applications are attracted and a sharp 'targeting' of the relevant labour market; this tension is reconciled by a knowledge of alternative recruitment methods and the exercise of informed judgement. There are many ways of attracting applications. They are listed in Exhibit 6.4 to demonstrate the range and to emphasise that advertising, often the first managerial response, is only one approach within a battery of potential methods. They can be used exclusively or in combination.

EXHIBIT 6.4 **Recruitment methods**

- Press advertising including:
  - local, regional and national newspapers
  - professional and trade journals, and other specialist publications
- Internet and Web 2.0 recruitment
- Other advertising:
  - television and radio
  - vacancy boards – internal and external
  - leaflet drops, posters and recruitment caravans
- Talent banks – applicant waiting lists
- Employment agencies and recruitment consultants
- Job centres
- Direct access to schools and colleges
- University milkround
- Open days, recruitment fairs and careers conventions
- Employee referrals

Press advertising

Scanning job vacancy advertisements will inevitably reveal wide ranges of style, opinion and skill in recruitment advertising. Although there is no one best way, and prescriptions are ill-advised, professional guidance is available from bodies such as the CIPD, the EHRC, the CRE and ACAS (Exhibit 6.5).

Effectiveness in recruitment advertising involves considering the following elements:

- the budget freedom or constraint
- media choice
- the compilation of advertising copy
- the opportunity to give a realistic job preview
- achieving the diversity objectives
- the resource requirements to deal with the anticipated response.

EXHIBIT 6.5 Recruitment advertising – professional guidance

- Recruitment advertising should be genuine in that either a vacant job actually exists or recruiters seriously intend to consider applicants for employment.
- A person specification should be the basis for outlining the job requirements.
- The description of the employing organisation should be realistic, factual and clear.
- Job location, pay and allowances should normally be specified.
- Clear application procedure instructions should be given – whether a CV should be sent or whether to request an application form.
- Advertisements should not discriminate on the grounds of sex, race, disability, age and membership or non-membership of a trade union, except in specific statutory circumstances.

Most of these elements can be applied to other recruitment methods as well as press advertising. The recruiting organisation may elect to undertake these activities independently or with the advice and support of an advertising agency. Where used, an advertising agency can advise on labour markets, media choice and copy design. The compilation and production of the advert and also the purchasing of the advertising space will normally be undertaken by the agency. The agency covers its costs and makes a profit from the revenue received from the media in which the advertisements are placed, and the larger and more expensive the advertisement, the greater the revenue for the advertising agency. Multi-site or national organisations with a house style will find the services of an advertising agency of value in ensuring consistency and the construction of a recruitment brand.

The budget constraints will need to be applied in the context of a cost–benefit analysis, but ultimately the advertisement has to achieve the objective of attracting candidates of a suitable calibre. The professional recruiter should develop a portfolio of advertisement costs in relation to size, style and media location to inform decision-making.

The choice of media should be determined by labour market characteristics of the job being advertised. The local, regional and national press segment the labour market by geography, travel to work considerations and the practicality of relocation. Professional and trade journals and other specialist publications segment the labour market by skills and occupation, and newspapers segment the labour market by socio-economic group.

The compilation of the advertising copy needs to take account of the type of advertisement. The three types are, in descending order of size and potential impact, full display, semi-display and lineage. Big, bold and beautiful is the conventional wisdom, but the budget available and the expectations of the likely applicants will temper this. Clearly, the bigger the advertisement, the greater the cost. Three principal components of an advertisement provide a structure for copy design.

1 A strategy for gaining attention – headings, messages and illustrations.
2 Information about the position – to develop applicant interest and to enable the application decision.
3 The action message – how and when to apply and what information to supply.

An important consideration is the balance between the volume of wording and the 'white space'. There is a temptation to seek the greatest value from the advertisement by packing it with words and information, whereas in terms of impact the 'white space' provides a powerful window for the message. The astute recruiter will come to terms with paying for the correct amount of white space in order to enhance visual appeal.

A realistic job preview opportunity is presented by the advertisement. The greater the information which is communicated effectively and the more realistically the job is previewed, the greater the probability that an informed application decision can be made by the applicant. The advertisement is potentially a filter for the recruitment and selection system by allowing unsuitable applicants to self-select out, and all advertisements should be overviewed from the perspective of potential applicants.

Achieving diversity objectives can be pursued through recruitment advertising. This should go beyond the rhetorical statements of being an equal opportunities employer. The absence of criteria which constitute direct or indirect discrimination will send a more powerful message. Gender-neutral job titles, although giving succour to politically correct sceptics, provide one means of seeking to redress gender segregation in employment. The CIPD endorses the positive use of advertising in order to re-balance situations where particular groups may be under-represented, and the use of appropriate visual images can contribute to the reinforcement of non-discriminatory practices. The overt welcoming of applications from disadvantaged groups sends a firm equal opportunities message.

The resource requirements necessary to deal with applicant response also need consideration. The choice is between a 'mail box' approach, which just receives applications, and the personal contact approach, where applicants respond by calling in or telephoning. The personal contact approach is more resource intensive, but it is an opportunity to filter applications through objective and predetermined pre-selection criteria.

Internet recruitment

The Internet provides increasing access to labour markets and relies on the positive efforts of the individual to visit the job vacancy and initiate the job search, but increasing use of Internet recruitment by employers, recruitment consultants and job-seekers is evident. Seventy-five per cent of employers use their own websites to advertise vacancies, with 25 per cent of all employers using commercial websites (CIPD, 2009a). The use of the Internet for advertising jobs needs to be based on the likelihood of Internet surfers being within the target labour market. Internet job search is broadening its base in terms of the job-seeking habits of applicants. As the incidence of broadband Internet access increases and as familiarity with online job search has grown, Internet recruitment is becoming mainstream recruitment practice. Advertising on the Internet for six months costs approximately the same as one full display advertisement in a broadsheet newspaper.

The basic differences between traditional advertising and using the Internet for recruitment are that job details are viewed electronically and the application form can be completed and sent online, or a CV can be sent as an attachment to an email. There are three principal ways an employer can use the Internet for recruitment (CIPD, 2009a). First, a recruitment zone may be added to an existing organisational website. This may be a good starting point because it is relatively quick and inexpensive, but it has limitations, because other than for well-known or high-profile organisations there is little reason for the job-seeker to visit the site. The extent to which visitors to the corporate website will migrate to the recruitment pages will be influenced by the clarity of the signposting and the user-friendliness of the hyperlinks. The second way is to design a separate recruitment website. This is more expensive than the first option, but it can be actively promoted and is likely to reach more job-seekers. It can provide a direct access point for all vacancies and project a strong corporate identity through incorporating information about the company and the training and career opportunities. The third method is by advertising jobs on a specialist media site. Used like traditional press advertising, this may feature just a job advertisement or it could incorporate an extended description of the vacancy and have a link to a company website. Key players, among 300+ providers, include Monster, Top Jobs, Total Jobs, Net Jobs and Guardian Jobs Unlimited. It continues to be difficult for the HR professional to verify the claims of these service providers in terms of the size of their databases, the volume of job-search hits and the relative costs and success rates. The potential advantages of using the Internet include a shortening of the recruitment cycle, accommodating the job-seeking habits of an increasing proportion of the labour market, reducing the volume of paperwork associated with recruitment, projecting a technologically progressive corporate image and providing job-search availability 24 hours a day. The potential disadvantages are associated with the possibility of generating high volume but not necessarily high quality or genuine job-seekers (termed 'electronic time-wasters') and limiting access to some labour markets.

The Internet can also be used as a pre-selection technique and a preliminary stage in the matching of applicants to the job. Banks of curricula vitae (CVs) and personal profile questionnaires are constructed on the system by specialist providers and can be accessed by employers. The level of sophistication is developing rapidly and job-seekers can enter CVs directly on to the system; the CVs are scanned and artificial intelligence software recognises skills, knowledge and qualifications regardless of how they are presented within the CV. The candidate profile is appraised against the employer's selection criteria and a candidate shortlist. Candidate confidentiality can be maintained through the use of identity numbers. These developments would appear to herald the age of the multimedia curriculum vitae. The 1998 Data Protection Act gives applicants a limited right to access the criteria and method of selection.

Web 2.0 and recruitment

Web 2.0 is the label for second generation web activity where individuals interact and contribute rather than be passive receivers of information. This interaction manifests itself through blogs and through social networking sites such as LinkedIn, MySpace and Facebook. There are two principal opportunities for employers. First, through

EXHIBIT 6.6 e-recruitment at Xerox and Nike

Xerox Europe employs 6000 sales and support staff working in 600 individual businesses and receives 100 000 applications per year for 2000 positions as telesales specialists, product specialists and sales managers. An e-recruitment programme provides all businesses with access to self-service recruitment and this enables managers to manage the entire recruitment process. Each business has Internet access to an e-HR portal which is divided into a 'Xerox-manager gateway' and a 'job-applicant gateway'. This enables Xerox recruiters to post job offers online, receive applications and automate the follow-up. Database-search features, a scoring engine, screening criteria and a job-posting engine maximise candidate sources and generate shortlists. The benefits include:

- delivering a stronger and more consistent employer brand to the talent market
- more targeted and focused recruitment campaigns with greater control over internal and external processes, agencies and individuals
- reducing errors through continuous performance monitoring and reporting.

Nike's Europe, Middle East and Asia (EMEA) headquarters in the Netherlands receives 800 job applications a month for around 100 vacancies. Concerns about maintaining standards and keeping track of CVs, together with a need to reduce the cost per recruit and improve applicant quality, resulted in Nike implementing e-recruitment which handles the application process from the receipt to the job offer. External applicants apply for positions via the Nike website. Links with recruitment websites, such as Monsterboard, provide further opportunities to attract candidates. Applicants attach a CV, the system matches the competencies and experience of the candidate to the job requirements and Nike managers access the shortlisted candidates. The system retains a talent bank of CVs and searches the database when positions arise. There was decreased reliance on external recruitment agencies, savings of 50 per cent on recruitment costs and the average time to fill vacancies reduced from 62 to 42 days.

For further information see:

Pollitt, D. (2004) 'E-recruitment helps Xerox pick the cream of the crop', *Human Resource Management International Digest*, 12(5) 33–5.

Pollitt, D. (2005) 'E-recruitment gets Nike seal of approval', *Human Resource Management International Digest*, 13(2) 33–5.

exploiting social networking sites to engage with potential job-seekers and to promote the employer brand and, second, through seeking information about potential job-seekers through their social networking presence and activity. Clearly there are inherent dangers in seeking out information on individuals in relation to reliability and validity, and also ethical issues in relation to respect to privacy (the same may be said of 'googling' potential recruits). However, the growing pervasiveness of social networking activity warrants consideration in relation to recruitment opportunities. Attraction of graduates appears to offer rich opportunities and this is illustrated by T-Mobile, which used a social networking dimension in the 2007 graduate recruitment process. T-Mobile created a Facebook site and invited potential graduate recruits to join. The site provided information on selection procedure and assessment centre programmes, and enabled potential recruits to interact with each other. This provided a vehicle to project T-Mobile values, to provide information to candidates and to garner information on the potential recruits. This information became part of the selection process, which also involved extensive interviews and psychometric assessment. A DWP survey (2009) highlighted the benefits of social networking sites, such as Facebook, LinkedIn and Twitter, for those seeking employment. A third of employers utilised such sites to connect with potential employees and to reach out to a wider pool of talent and a half of the employers said that if candidates invested time in developing a strong online site with links to career networks, a 'personal brand', they were more likely to be hired. The use of these networks looks set to surge as organisations continue to improve corporate social networking tools and promote employee–employer links. These networks are potentially the 'new frontier' in talent spotting.

Other advertising

Vacancy boards may be either internal, and only seen by current employees, or external – located in a public place. They are a low-cost way of advertising jobs, but will only access a limited pool of applicants. Internal vacancy boards enable existing employees to apply for a job change, personal development or promotion. Employees may also bring vacancies to the attention of family members and friends. External vacancy boards are often used by restaurants and retail shops and are effectively utilising the customer base as the labour market. These window boards need to be professionally designed and strategically positioned to maximise the impact on the flow of customers and other members of the public. Some retailers take the concept further by advertising jobs on shelf labels and at checkouts. Employers should be aware of the possibility of unlawful indirect discrimination if access to the noticeboard makes it more difficult for one sex or for members of ethnic groups to apply for the advertised job. Vacancy boards may need to be used as a supplementary rather than the only method of recruitment.

Television and radio offer innovative ways of attracting applicants. The use of television is confined to teletext services or used by government to promote particular professions, careers in the armed services or in teaching, for example. Local radio advertising is relatively low cost and functions by listener intrusion and message repetition. A limited amount of job and organisational information can be communicated by radio, but it can spark interest.

Leaflet drops, posters and recruitment caravans, as well as being recruitment methods, can function as promotional activities to raise the organisation's profile. Leaflets are relatively cheap to produce and deliver, but are poor at targeting a particular labour market. Leaflet drops may be a useful supplementary method within a recruitment campaign aimed at filling a substantial number of vacancies. They are often associated with the opening of new businesses, particularly retail or personal services outlets, where the need is for a high volume of low-skilled or semi-skilled applicants. The public suffer from unsolicited mail fatigue and leaflets may not trigger interest or action. Posters are another adjunct to wider recruitment activity; the issues are, first, deciding on and accessing appropriate locations and, second, how to stimulate applicant attention. A recruitment caravan is a mobile recruiting centre. The mobile unit can be located in a public place for a specified period of time and is more suited to multi-site national recruitment. The investment and maintenance cost is considerable, but this method has been used effectively by the armed services and by retailers looking to staff new supermarkets.

Talent banks

A talent bank consists of speculative enquiries and also applications retained from previous recruitment activity, and provides a pool of potential candidates that can be accessed when a vacancy occurs. The advantages are lower costs, resource efficiency and a shortened recruitment time scale, but talent banks are problematic to manage and demand efficient and effective recording, filing and retrieval systems. An HR information system can target the search of a talent bank in relation to a person specification. Three factors militate against talent banks. First, they have a tendency to decay quickly. Applications have a limited life as candidate interest may wane over time or personal and occupational circumstances may change. Second, the resurrection of an application and the contacting of a candidate by the employer has implications for the psychological contract. The approach to the applicant by the employer, a reversal of normal roles, raises expectations about the likelihood of job success, with subsequent employer rejection being less acceptable to the candidate. This role reversal may also increase candidate perceptions of strength in negotiating the contract of employment and heighten the expectations of the successful candidate in respect of more positive or favourable treatment during the employment itself. Third, the exclusive use of talent banks may not help the pursuit of diversity objectives, because they may restrict access to jobs and may potentially constitute unlawful indirect discrimination. Twelve of Hampshire's local authorities have developed a recruitment website advertising all of their jobs in one place. Candidates submit application details and they are stored in the Hampshire Talent Bank, which then allows authorities to match skills against job roles. Candidates choose which authority can access their details and are effectively applying for a number of jobs although only submitting their application once. This enables the authorities to save on advertising costs, matches applicants to job skills and offers an opportunity for positive employer branding. At Xerox the e-recruitment system retains a talent bank of CVs and each registered applicant is automatically asked to update the CV every six months in order to remain active. The system searches the database when positions arise.

Employment agencies and recruitment consultants

Employment agencies and recruitment consultancies have a profit motive and provide a wide range of services in return for fees. Their services include:

- supplying temporary workers (agency staff) to accommodate peaks and troughs in work or to cover employee absence

- attracting, pre-selecting and referring candidates for 'permanent' positions
- seeking out candidates (head-hunting) and maintaining a register for specialist, professional, management, executive or technical positions
- providing training and development opportunities for individuals to make them more attractive to employers, for example updating on current business software packages.

The use of employment agencies constitutes the externalisation of elements of the recruitment and selection system. These elements include some administrative tasks, candidate attraction and applying pre-selection criteria. Success depends on a precise specification of requirements by the employer and the professionalism and ability of the agency. Since 1995, employment agencies have not required a licence, but the Secretary of State can prohibit individuals from running employment agencies. New regulations governing the private recruitment industry were drafted in 2001 and these regulate activities in areas such as constraints on work-seekers' future employment, the payments demanded when a work-seeker supplied by an agency is offered permanent employment, the payment of wages direct to the worker by the hirer and not by the agency, the advertising of work only where a genuine job exists, and ensuring that adverts contain details of pay rates and also the qualifications required. The Employment Consultants Institute provides a code of professional conduct, membership services, and professional training and accreditation for employment consultants.

The costs of services to employers can be high in relation to other recruitment methods. Where the agency can meet recruitment needs more quickly, efficiently or effectively through the availability of resources, contacts or recruitment expertise, this is a desirable option. Head-hunting of senior executives is frequently undertaken by executive search agencies or consultants through a network of contacts. Using executive search is rather like recourse to a dating agency, 'selling the job to the potential candidate and then trying to sell the candidate to the employer' (Taylor, 2002). The advantage to the employer is the opportunity to instigate confidential dialogue with talented executives from competitor organisations. It also enables approaches to be made to candidates who may not be actively seeking employment and would therefore be unlikely to respond to press advertisements. In this executive labour market many individuals may not have realised they were in the labour market until they were contacted by an executive search agency. Although executive search is initially expensive, the benefit of securing an influential executive can make it worthwhile. There are clearly ethical, confidential and professional boundaries that should not be breached. Employment agencies and recruitment consultancies, by having greater access to persons in employment, have certain advantages over job centres.

Job centres

Job centre applicants are more likely to be unemployed, although job centres offer services to employed people seeking a job change. Databases of candidates are maintained which facilitate a speedy search on the basis of employer requirements. A professional and executive recruitment service is also provided and, in addition to local services, job centres can access national and European Union labour markets. A proactive and cooperative job centre can respond quickly and effectively and may also advise on the development of the job description, the person specification and the terms and conditions of employment. The provision of a job description and a person specification will enable job centre staff to match candidates with employer requirements more objectively, in effect offering a screening service. However, a job centre refusal to refer a candidate to an employer may be perceived by the candidate as an inappropriate role for the job centre and raises questions about the responsibilities of job centre staff as agents of the employer or as agents of job-seekers, although clearly it is not in the interest of any of the parties to refer to employers those candidates who do not match the job criteria. Job centres may be able to provide promotional and marketing opportunities, interviewing arrangements, form-filling facilities and interview rooms. Job centres represent a responsive and economical recruitment opportunity. The extent of cooperation and the range of services will be influenced by local factors, and employers wishing to maximise the recruitment potential of a job centre should seek a positive and mutually beneficial relationship with job centre staff. The profit motive may be absent in job centres, but efficiency measures and performance targets increasingly drive job centre activity.

Direct access to schools and colleges

This recruitment method requires the organisation to establish mutually beneficial relationships with schools and colleges with the aim of encouraging a flow of suitable applicants. The employer can establish professional networks with teachers, lecturers and careers advisers, attend careers fairs, make careers presentations, advise on job search and provide work experience. In return the school or college will distribute and make available the employer's careers literature and will be in a position to give knowledgeable advice to students about specific job opportunities. This requires a balancing of the school or college responsibility to the student and the responsibility to the employer, and, as with the careers service, there is a potential tension between the student, or parent, expectation of the promotion of career choice and the reality of exposure to 'jobs of work'. The advantages to the employer are relatively low cost and also access to careers advisers, who will have some knowledge of the potential applicants. Restricting the development of school or college relationships to one or two institutions may, depending on institutional characteristics and location, be perceived as elitist.

University milkround

The 'milkround' is the process of promoting employment opportunities through employer attendance at careers and other recruitment events at universities. This may involve the employer in responding to student enquiries, the initial screening of candidates and the formal presentation of organisational information. It is clearly targeted at the graduate and postgraduate labour market. Facilities are provided by the institution, but the milkround is resource-intensive in terms of organisational representatives, travel, accommodation and the quality of display stands and supporting literature. The degree of milkround participation by an employer depends on the number of graduate vacancies and the need to maintain or increase the profile of the organisation. It is useful to involve previous trainees, who have been converted into successful employees, not only to provide evidence of progression, but also to exemplify the desired characteristics of the graduate recruit. It is difficult to measure directly the effectiveness of the milkround, and employers should be prepared for student enquiries which seek to gather information rather than demonstrate suitability for employment. The milkround is also used by undergraduates to search out 'sandwich' placements and employers should be ready for these enquiries as well. The milkround is probably best viewed as a component of overall graduate recruitment strategy. It is also an opportunity to find out what other employers are offering.

Open days, recruitment fairs and careers conventions

Attracting applicants through open days, recruitment fairs and careers conventions is a proactive response to competitive labour markets or recruitment difficulties. The employer effectively takes its value proposition, namely the employer brand, jobs available and the rewards package, to the potential employee rather than wait for the candidates to come to them. The open day format may range from informal drop-in sessions to highly structured events which incorporate presentations, guided tours, sophisticated hospitality and work sampling. Recruitment fairs and careers conventions are normally organised by educational institutions, training providers, SFAs or Chambers of Commerce. They require employer participation in what is effectively 'a shop window of opportunities'. In common with the university milkround, quality representation and supporting material is essential. Open days, recruitment fairs and careers conventions can be labour-intensive and fatiguing for representatives and demand professional organisation. Careful planning and effective resourcing are necessary to ensure that a positive message is communicated. These promotional activities offer opportunities for potential applicants to find out more about the organisation and the job without necessarily making a commitment to apply.

Offering incentives to employees for referrals

Organisations can use employee incentives to recruit qualified applicants – an employee referral scheme. An employee recommending a candidate who is offered employment, and achieves a satisfactory performance level, can be extrinsically or intrinsically rewarded for the introduction. This is not a new idea, with the *John Lewis Partnership Gazette* reporting in 1918 that 'We will pay an employee who introduces us to someone who we do actually employ a fee of one guinea.' In the 1990s, because of recruitment difficulties in the army, soldiers were being paid £250 for every successful recruit introduced. Not only is this a way of utilising employees as search consultants, but also the applicant is likely to receive a more realistic job preview than would be the case with less personal recruitment sources. The previously introduced caveat about the potential for indirect discrimination applies. Nearly a half of respondents in the CIPD recruitment survey (2008) reported using an employee referral scheme.

CASE STUDY   A-B-Zee: Human resource planning and recruitment for new superstores

This case explores the HRM implications of a business decision to launch a new chain of superstores. It enables a comparison to be made between two strategies for recruiting sales assistants, one in a shortage labour market for a London superstore and one in a surplus labour market in the north of England. A well established leading UK retailer, Goodwins, has decided to set up an independent subsidiary, A-B-Zee, to launch two superstores specialising in children's products and based on edge-of-town sites. Responsibility for human resource planning and recruitment fell to the HR Director, based at A-B-Zee headquarters in the west of England. As the first stores were to be located in both the south-east and the north of England, the HR Director had to contend with local labour markets characterised by either a shortage or a surplus of suitable people. Locations for the new superstores are chosen primarily for commercial reasons, with less consideration being given to the availability of labour. As a member of A-B-Zee's executive board the HR Director does have a strong input in the choice of new sites, but the criteria of customer affluence and site access weigh far more heavily than the ease of getting the best staff.

Background to the case

The HRM challenge

The HRM objectives for the new superstores were:

- A-B-Zee will recruit only those who meet its minimum standards.
- Each store should recruit a balanced workforce across gender, age and ethnic group to reflect the company's policy of equal opportunity.
- Recruitment and resourcing must be cost-effective.
- Recruitment and resourcing must serve the company's public relations interests.

Recruitment of sales assistants

A store manager's position is filled from the national labour market and well before the recruitment of sales assistants. Each store manager has responsibility for the HR function in-store. The HR Director decided to coordinate the recruitment campaigns centrally. Her HR expertise would be invaluable in setting A-B-Zee policy and procedures, and her involvement would take pressure off newly appointed store managers. She recognised that store managers would need to have 'ownership' of the recruitment and selection process. They would need to take responsibility for their staff. Consequently store managers were heavily involved in the process. Each store's human resource structure is planned for mainly part-time workers, able to cover extended trading hours. While minimum standards of literacy and numeracy are essential, A-B-Zee's preference is for staff with a mature outlook and good communication skills rather than experience of the product range. Furthermore, parental experience or a responsibility for children is considered an advantage. The nature of the work, A-B-Zee's product range and the part-time hours generate far more applications from women than men.

(Box continued)

HRM constraints

1 The rates of pay still follow those of the parent company. This causes few problems in areas of labour surplus, but rules out any pay improvements that might help combat problems of serious labour shortage.
2 Not only is A-B-Zee new to each labour market, it is also a new company with an unfamiliar name. As such it has no reputation to call upon in its search for quality employees.
3 It is company policy to refuse to employ second-best. The company expects to adhere to the minimum standards outlined above.
4 Each recruitment campaign is faced with a demanding timetable for store opening. 'You've got to hold your nerve; as it gets closer to opening the pressure increases. Operations management will be pressing you to get people by a certain date, in time for training and ready for trading' (HR Director).

HRM in shortage and surplus labour markets

In London the company has difficulty in meeting its employee targets for new stores, where a 'sellers' market' has prevailed and competition for talented labour is strong. The strategy here has been to develop a variety of innovative recruitment approaches. In the north of England a surplus labour market characterised by higher unemployment undoubtedly favours the 'buyer', but A-B-Zee soon found that this brought problems of a different kind.

The London store

Experience in London earlier in the year had confirmed that the traditional process of a newspaper advertisement inviting requests for application forms, followed by an interview for those shortlisted, was inadequate in meeting the human resource target of 60 part-time sales assistants who fully met A-B-Zee's criteria. Although the full-page display advertisements were imaginative and attracted attention, the recruitment process as a whole was found to be relatively slow in terms of (1) sustaining a candidate's interest in the vacancy and (2) the store opening date. This shortage labour market focused the HR Director's attention on supplementing the existing recruitment practices with more innovative methods. In order to obtain enough applicants of the right quality A-B-Zee had to take more of the initiative and be more accessible to potential employees. In other words it was obliged to adopt a more proactive strategy in this competitive job market.

Newspaper advertisements now invited candidates to telephone a 'hot line' number. This method provides immediate contact with the company and encouragement to those who might not otherwise request an application form. The phone-in enabled A-B-Zee to arrange immediate interviews for those evaluated as suitable on the evidence of the telephone interview. In addition, the application form was simplified to make its completion more convenient and acceptable to candidates. An alternative to the 'phone-in' was the 'walk-in', where candidates where invited to call at a local hotel and meet company staff. Where parents seemed likely to cancel the visit because they were unable to arrange for someone to look after the children, they were invited to bring their children with them. A-B-Zee staff were there to provide children with appropriate care and activities, while the candidate had an interview. A-B-Zee successfully used the 'walk-in' to increase the number of applicants and then to influence those suitable to join the company. The speed of the company's response to candidates is crucial, and so application forms and letters of offer were readily available. This also met the company's needs, since speed was of the essence. The HR Director soon appreciated that the attraction of applicants is limited by the readership of the newspaper. Consequently, A-B-Zee produced leaflets which were distributed to every house in those areas which (1) were relatively close to the new store and (2) would assist towards the objective of employing a 'balanced workforce' in terms of the ethnic composition of the locality. The 'leaflet drop' would not only act as a recruitment channel but would also publicise A-B-Zee's new store opening.

These supplementary recruitment methods were making life more convenient for applicants. Things were certainly not as convenient for the team of recruiters, who were required to be available to applicants during the evenings and at weekends. A-B-Zee also had to consider making its working hours more convenient for its prospective employees. Its pattern of working hours needed to be modified to accommodate individuals' requirements. In a sellers' market applicants felt able to ask, for example, for term-time contracts and school-time hours. Some applicants did not meet the minimum standards for skills and knowledge. This required a more intensive training programme, which increased the strain on the training resources.

The northern store

After the resourcing challenges of London the HR Director was more relaxed about recruiting for A-B-Zee's new store in the north of England. The closure of several manufacturing companies had contributed to a higher level of unemployment, and the local Job Centre was keen to help with the distribution of application forms and the organisation of interviews. The HR Director was confident that an advertisement inviting requests for application forms would provide enough good applicants to meet the target of 60 part-time sales assistants. She also looked forward to employing a workforce that reflected the composition of the locality, including people from the ethnic minority community. The display advertisement announced the forthcoming launch of A-B-Zee's new store and invited applications for positions as sales assistants. Application forms were available from the town's Job Centre, where staff were ready to respond to written, telephone and personal requests.

On the morning after the appearance of the advertisement, Job Centre staff arrived to find a queue outside the building. A couple of hundred people had called for A-B-Zee application forms. Bristol headquarters received a total of 600 applications for the 60 vacancies. Over 1000 forms were eventually received. Disappointingly, only a handful appeared to be from applicants from ethnic minorities. The interest generated now created severe problems for the HR Director. First, the task of shortlisting for interview was huge: how to identify accurately and quickly applicants for interview from the first wave of 600? It became evident that few applicants could be rejected on the basis of the essential job requirements and there was often little to choose between people. The size of the task can clearly influence the quality of shortlisting decisions.

A second issue related to the time, effort and resources that had to be directed to the screening process. The layout of the application form, for example, slowed the process down considerably. The most relevant information ought to have been grouped together on the front page. Considerable resources had to be devoted to responding to all the applicants. The HR Director accepted that it is vital to any company to initiate and retain goodwill among its potential customers. It was just as important to respond quickly and courteously to unsuccessful as well as shortlisted applicants. The satisfaction created by the huge

(Box continued)

response was replaced by acceptance that the recruitment exercise had been very resource-intensive. There was also disappointment in attracting so few applicants from the town's ethnic minority community.

Getting it right

A company setting up a business in a new area usually has only the one chance to establish its reputation as an employer; A-B-Zee, however, will be continuing to establish its new stores in other locations. It has the opportunity to learn from and improve upon the recruitment experiences outlined above. Future strategy is to devolve responsibility for recruitment and selection to each store manager, who will benefit from the handbooks, training and advice to be provided by the small, centralised HR function.

Source: With acknowledgements to the author, David Walsh, Nottingham Trent University.
This material is taken from *Case Studies in Personnel* by Winstanley, D. and Woodall, J. (1992), with the permission of the publisher, the Chartered Institute of Personnel and Development, London.

Questions

1 What does the case tell us about the link between business strategic decision-making and human resource planning at A-B-Zee?

2 On the basis of the A-B-Zee experience in London, outline the characteristic features of a shortage labour market, and explain why the traditional recruitment process, a newspaper advertisement inviting requests for application forms and followed by shortlisting for interview, was inadequate for a shortage labour market.

3 Explore the two-way nature of the relationship between A-B-Zee and its potential employees in a shortage labour market, and the evidence that the balance of 'power' to some extent favours the candidates.

4 What action can A-B-Zee take to ensure that it retains the best employees in a shortage labour market?

5 Identify some of the advantages of the 'phone-in' as a recruitment method, and the measures that need to be taken to ensure its success.

6 Recommend how the company's next campaign in a surplus labour market might (a) be made more cost-effective and (b) ensure a greater response from members of the ethnic minority community.

7 Which selection techniques would be appropriate for the selection of sales assistants with customer service, merchandising and IT competencies? How would you evaluate the predictive validity of your chosen techniques?

RECRUITMENT METHODS – ANALYSIS AND TRENDS

It is essential for employers to analyse and evaluate the recruitment process and the methods of recruitment. First, this may be done through the capture of data relating to the number of responses, the number of applications received, the number of candidates interviewed and the number of candidates appointed and relating this data to the direct and indirect costs of the recruitment process. Second, it may be achieved by asking applicants to state on the application form the particular recruitment source that initially attracted their attention. Third, the coding of each recruitment method will identify the sources of successful candidates.

There is a trend away from traditional announcement advertisements towards job advertisements which are creative in nature and visually striking because the quality of applicant response can be positively influenced by the appropriate use of humour, a more conversational style and a people-friendly approach and the most effective advertisements are informative, enticing, persuasive and include a clear and distinct proposition to the target audience. Exhibit 6.7 summarises the frequency of use of recruitment methods (CIPD, 2009b).

EXHIBIT 6.7 Percentage of organisations using different recruitment methods (sample = approx. 750)

- Own website   –   78 per cent
- Employment agencies   –   76 per cent
- Local press adverts   –   70 per cent
- Professional journals   –   55 per cent
- Employee referral scheme   –   46 per cent
- Job Centre Plus   –   43 per cent
- School/college links   –   34 per cent
- National press adverts   –   31 per cent
- Search consultants   –   31 per cent
- Commercial website   –   29 per cent
- Placements/secondments   –   23 per cent
- Posters   –   8 per cent
- Social networking sites   –   7 per cent
- Radio and/or TV   –   6 per cent

RESPONDING TO ENQUIRIES AND THE CANDIDATE'S VIEW

In recruitment the element of choice applies to the recruiter and the applicant. The discerning candidate is more likely to choose an employer that applies a professional approach to recruitment. Recruitment and selection is therefore a two-way process and **applicants have considerable control because they can, at any stage, decide to exit from the process.** They are empowered not to respond to advertisements, not to return application forms, to decline the invitation of an interview, to reject an offer of employment, not to turn up on the first day, and ultimately to resign from a position which fails to meet their expectations. A comparison of the number of enquiries with the number of applications received, the conversion rate, will quickly reveal the exercise of choice by applicants. The recruiter needs to recognise these multiple opportunities for the candidate to exit. The objective in responding to enquiries is to influence positively the conversion rate from enquiry to application by inhibiting the exiting of suitably qualified candidates. Professionalism in responding to enquiries includes, first, the speed and the courtesy of the employer response; second, the provision and style of information about the job, the organisation and how to apply – a recruitment pack (Exhibit 6.8); third, the reasonableness of the effort and time expected from the applicant; and, fourth, the availability of informed and skilled staff to deal with job enquiries.

Enquiries and applications should be recorded to ensure that good candidates are not lost, that applications are acknowledged and that unsuccessful applicants are informed of the outcome of their application. A computerised HR information system with a recruitment database will facilitate the tracking of applications, the generation of correspondence and the provision of data for analysis and evaluation of the recruitment and selection process.

EXHIBIT 6.8 The recruitment pack

The style and content of the recruitment pack depend on the nature of the position and the culture and resources of the employing organisation. It may include the following:

- a letter of thanks and instructions on what happens next
- an application form or a request for a CV or a request to contact the employing organisation to arrange an interview
- a job description and a person specification
- an information booklet which includes wider organisational information
- reference to appropriate HR policies of interest to the candidate, for example equal opportunities, training, promotion and reward systems.

The objective is to create the right impression and solicit appropriate applications. The recruitment pack is an opportunity to offer a realistic job preview and to project the employer brand.

CRIMINAL CERTIFICATES – POLICE ACT 1997

Recruiters may need to check the criminal record of an applicant. Three types of certificate are available from the Criminal Records Bureau:

1 A Criminal Conviction Certificate (CCC) – details convictions which are not legally spent, is issued to individuals at a small cost and needs to be produced on application for employment, if requested.

2 A Criminal Record Certificate (CRC) – details spent and unspent convictions and police cautions and is issued to individuals and registered employers at a

small cost in excepted occupations, for example the teaching, health, legal and caring professions.

3 An Enhanced Criminal Record Certificate (ECRC) – comprises a full criminal check of convictions, cautions, acquittals and police intelligence and is available to individuals and registered employers (exceptionally to the employer only) in special occupations, for example judges and magistrates, those working unsupervised with children and where a betting or gaming licence is required.

UK IMMIGRATION SYSTEM AND THE UK BORDER AGENCY

A new immigration system for skilled migrants came into effect in 2008 and as a consequence employers can no longer legally employ migrants who need a work permit without holding a sponsorship licence from the UK Border Agency (UKBA) (www.ukba.homeoffice.gov.uk). Employers now have to apply to the UKBA to become licensed sponsors of skilled workers from outside the EEA and Switzerland. The sponsor can then award a certificate to each migrant who gets enough points. Points are awarded for skills, experience, age and, where appropriate, skill-sector needs. Migrants must be able to speak English and support themselves financially. A licence is issued only if the employer is able to demonstrate that the necessary HR monitoring and record-keeping systems are in place. If the UKBA decides that an employer is in breach of its sponsorship duties, it can issue a written warning, send in a UKBA compliance team, downgrade the employer to a B rating, cancel the licence, serve an on-the-spot fine of up to £10 000 for each illegal worker, or prosecute the employer, which carries a possible two-year prison sentence. The names of employers that are fined are published on the UKBA website. In addition, employers need to report an employee to the UKBA if they have 'suspicions that a migrant is breaching conditions of leave'. They also have to report to the police if they suspect a migrant may be 'engaged in terrorism or other criminal activities'.

The five tiers are:

1 Highly skilled migrants such as scientists and entrepreneurs; these do not need a sponsor.

2 Skilled workers with a job offer or who are intra-company transfers. It is the route of most use to employers. Migrants apply for leave to remain in the UK once they receive sponsorship.

3 Limited numbers of low-skilled workers.

4 Students, who will need a UK academic institution to sponsor them.

5 Those on the 'youth mobility scheme' and cultural and religious temporary workers, such as visiting musicians.

Organisations wishing to use Tier 2 migrants must prove that a post cannot be filled by a resident worker before recruiting a migrant, unless the job is on a shortage-occupation list. To appear on a shortage list a job must require skills in short supply and it must be 'sensible to recruit those skills from outside the European Economic Area'. The lists are compiled by the Migration Advisory Committee (MAC).

SUMMARY LEARNING POINTS

1 While organisations need agreed, written and communicated policies and procedures for recruitment and selection, a contingent and flexible approach to recruitment and selection processes and methods is advocated.

2 Recruitment and selection can be viewed as a system with interrelated sub-systems. The first sub-system is **attraction** and this involves pre-recruitment activity, the use of recruitment methods and responding effectively to enquiries.

3 Pre-recruitment activity includes establishing a *prima facie* case for recruitment, undertaking job analysis as a prerequisite to undertaking business-focused recruitment and an assessment of the labour market.

4 A wide range of recruitment methods can be used exclusively or in combination and the professional recruiter should be able to evaluate each method critically and thereby exercise informed choice.

5 Responding effectively to employment enquiries requires an acknowledgement that the potential applicant can exit from the recruitment and selection process at any time.

REFERENCES AND FURTHER READING

Advisory, Conciliation and Arbitration Service (2006) *Recruitment and Induction.* London: ACAS.

Aikin, O. (2001) 'The new seekers', *People Management*, 22 February, 18–19.

Anderson, N. and Shackleton, V. (1993) *Successful Selection Interviewing.* Oxford: Blackwell.

'Annual Review of the Advertising Industry' (1996) published with *People Management*, June. IPD.

CIPD (2001) *Labour Turnover Survey.* London: CIPD.

CIPD (2009a) *E-recruitment – Factsheet.* London: CIPD.

CIPD (2009b) *Recruitment, Retention and Turnover – Annual Survey Report.* London: CIPD.

Courtis, J. (1994) *Recruitment Advertising: Right first time.* London: IPD.

Curnow, B. (1989) 'Recruit, retrain, retain: personnel management and the three Rs', *Personnel Management*, November, 40–7.

DWP (2009) *Online Social Networks Boost Opportunities for Job Seekers*, www.harveynash.com/oam_iphone/articles/online_social_networks_boost_o.htm

Herriot, P. (1989) *Recruitment in the 90s.* London: IPM.

IPD (1995) *The IPM Code on Recruitment.* London: IPD.

IRS (2003) 'Spinning the recruitment web', *IRS Employment Review 767*, 34–40.

Kiceluk, A. (1996) 'The net that helps you fill vacancies', *People Management*, May, 34–6.

Longmore-Etheridge, A. (1995) 'Personnel purgatory', *Security Management*, 39(7), 19–20.

Marchington, M. and Wilkinson, A. (2008) *Human Resource Management at Work* (4th edn). London: CIPD.

Overell, S. (1995) 'Agency woos big firms to recruit on the Internet', *People Management*, October, 18.

Paddison, L. (1990) 'The targeted approach to recruitment', *Personnel Management*, November, 54–8.

Pearn, M. and Kandola, R. (1993) *Job Analysis: A manager's guide*. London: IPD.

Plumbley, P. (1991) *Recruitment and Selection*. London: IPD.

Reed, J. (2000) 'The scatter-gun approach', *People Management*, 26 October, 69.

Taylor, C. (2001) 'Windows of opportunity', *People Management*, 8 March, 32–6.

Taylor, S. (2002) *People Resourcing*. London: CIPD.

Theaker, M. (1995) 'Entering the era of the electronic CVs', *People Management*, August, 34–7.

Walsh, D. (1992) 'ABZee' in Winstanley, D. and Woodall, J. (eds) *Case Studies in Personnel*. London: IPD.

Warner, J. (2002) 'All change as on-line recruitment gets real', *IRS Employment Review* 747, 37–9.

ASSIGNMENTS AND DISCUSSION TOPICS

1 Describe and explain the distribution of recruitment and selection activities between the HR specialist and the line manager in your organisation. Is the distribution appropriate? In addition, argue the case for and against the devolution of recruitment and selection responsibilities to line managers.

2 Identify and discuss the elements and activities of the recruitment and selection system within your organisation in relation to Exhibit 6.1. Comment critically on how the system might be improved, taking account of organisational constraints.

3 Why is it valuable to undertake job analysis activity? What organisational purposes can it serve? For a specified job decide how job analysis information can be collected.

4 Obtain a job description (or an accountability profile) and a person specification for a job in your organisation and examine how effective they are in achieving each of the following:
- providing a focus for recruitment and selection
- communicating a realistic job preview
- providing a basis for appraising performance and identifying training needs during the transition phase of the recruitment and selection process.

5 Identify shortage and surplus labour markets and consider the reasons for them.

6 Scan recruitment advertisements in the local or regional press. Select and critically evaluate three advertisements and prepare a checklist of learning points, both positive and negative, to share with colleagues at work or in class.

7 Which **recruitment** methods are appropriate for these vacancies?
- A university lecturer
- Fifty seasonal fruit pickers
- Twenty retail management graduate trainees
- A secretary to a managing director
- Maternity cover for a word processing operator
- An electrician
- A head chef
- Eighty part-time sales assistants for a new supermarket
- The manager of a security services firm
- One hundred call centre workers.

8 Evaluate critically the potential of the Internet to contribute to more effective recruitment.

Chapter 7

Selection: choosing the right people

LEARNING OUTCOMES: TO BE ABLE TO

- Distinguish between the elimination of applicants and the selection of candidates

- Contrast the concepts of validity, reliability and popularity in selection methods

- Critically evaluate a range of selection techniques

- Advise on the effective transition of the applicant to performing employee

INTRODUCTION

The attraction of job applications is succeeded by efforts to eliminate and reject unsuitable applicants, the aim being to reduce the number of candidates to that which can be managed effectively in the selection stage of the process. Many selection methods are available and managers who select employees need to be aware of the strengths and limitations of the various techniques. The selection decision is not the end of the process, as the transition from successful candidate to successful employee requires further effort, skill and attention.

SUBJECTIVITY, DISCRIMINATION, PROFESSIONALISM AND ETHICS

Although the recruitment and selection process can be made more methodical and systematic, it will inevitably remain subjective. A structured recruitment and selection system with rigour and consistency in the application of selection methods is desirable, but the appointment decision remains a matter of human judgement. It is important not to be beguiled by pseudo-scientific selection techniques. The selection decision is a discrimination decision, as the employer discriminates between applicants on the basis of ability and suitability. This discrimination should be based on criteria which are valid and related to the requirements of the job. Unlawful direct or indirect discrimination needs to be avoided and all candidates should be able to demonstrate abilities for the job regardless of race, ethnic origin, gender, marital or family circumstances, sexual preference, age, spent convictions and disability, except in exempted statutory circumstances. This fair approach to discrimination is professional and ethical and also makes sound business sense (*see* Chapter 8). A contract of employment includes an implied duty of mutual respect. As every candidate for a job is a potential employee, and while recognising that the contract of employment is not legally formed until there is offer, acceptance and consideration, it is a simple ethical principle to:

> incorporate the duty of mutual respect into the recruitment and selection process.

A psychological contract is developed during recruitment and selection, and the transition from candidate to employee is the realisation of the psychological contract. The recruitment and selection process, whether through the advertising material, a job description, the application form or personal contact, creates expectations for employers and for employees. The creation of these expectations and the development of the employment relationship should be based on mutual trust and should ensure that both parties have realistic expectations, if a firm foundation for the psychological contract is to be established. Mutual respect and mutual trust are therefore desirable aims in recruitment and selection (Exhibit 7.1). This is not a one-way street because applicants have ethical responsibilities as well, although these are difficult for the employer to enforce.

EXHIBIT 7.1 Employer ethics in recruitment and selection

- Advertising only genuine jobs
- Not abusing the power position
- Soliciting only the information that is necessary
- Not asking loaded questions or seeking to entrap candidates
- Assessing suitability on the basis of ability
- Maintaining confidentiality in the use and storage of candidate information
- Informing candidates appropriately of the selection decision.

ELIMINATION AND REDUCTION

As identified in the previous chapter, the second recruitment and selection sub-system is **reduction**. This has the objective of reducing the pool of applicants to a manageable number by eliminating and rejecting unsuitable candidates. This can be done indirectly, through the characteristics of the recruitment activity, and directly, through using predetermined job criteria. The processes involved are filtering, screening and short-listing. Recruitment activity filters applications not only through specifying job requirements, but also, indirectly, through factors such as whether a realistic preview of the job is communicated, the ease or difficulty of application, the time scale for applicant response and the quality of the recruitment pack information. These factors need critical evaluation as they contribute to ensuring that suitable candidates are retained within the recruitment and selection system and unsuitable applicants are eliminated.

Surplus labour markets can generate a high volume of applicants and candidates are often screened through the written information they provide, and sometimes through telephone or personal contact. Effective screening involves using job criteria which are predetermined and applied consistently. For example, to enable more effective candidate and job comparisons to be made, and also prevent the use of unlawful criteria, telephone screening can consist of a set of structured questions asked of each candidate and the systematic recording of responses. Simple grading or scoring sheets are easy to develop and will contribute to a methodical approach. For example, candidates can be graded high, medium or low in relation to the essential and desirable criteria in the person specification. A grid can be created using the six-factor formula (Exhibit 7.2). Further sophistication may be needed in order to develop and weight the different factors according to their importance. The removal of personal information, such as age, gender, ethnic origin and family or marital circumstances, from the application form prior to screening will reduce the opportunity for personal prejudice, perceptual error and unwarranted assumptions.

Once applicants have been screened and unsuitable candidates eliminated, a shorter list remains. There are a number of simple principles to guide the construction of the final shortlist. First, only candidates who match the person specification should be considered for the shortlist, as making up the number with unsuitable candidates will be unproductive. The shortlisting of candidates will raise their individual expectations

EXHIBIT 7.2 Shortlisting and the six-factor formula

Factor – where *relevant* and *measurable*	High 3 points	Medium 2 points	Low 1 point
Skills, knowledge and competencies			
Personality characteristics			
Level of experience			
Certificated qualifications			
Physical characteristics			
Development potential of the candidate			
Overall rating and recommendation:			

and create time, effort and stress demands; and in keeping with the mutual respect ethic, only candidates who are genuinely going to be considered should be shortlisted. Second, the time spent on screening and shortlisting presents an opportunity for applicants to exit from the recruitment and selection process. Employers should not only be mindful of this, but also have a contingency arrangement to compensate for withdrawals. Third, a shortlist should be manageable in number in relation to the resources of the organisation and the selection methods being used.

The point was made previously that each element of each sub-system is interdependent and effectively the recruitment and selection system is only as strong as the weakest link. The screening and shortlisting 'link' is another example of this, as insufficient attention at this stage will undermine the overall effectiveness of the recruitment and selection activity. As Napoleon said, 'time spent on reconnaissance is rarely, if ever, wasted', and this is particularly true in the context of shortlisting and screening.

The reduction and selection sub-systems merge at this point, but before discussing selection methods the concepts of validity, reliability and popularity are introduced.

VALIDITY, RELIABILITY AND POPULARITY OF SELECTION METHODS

The important concepts of validity, reliability and popularity provide dimensions for probing the potential and the limitations of different selection methods. The validity of a selection method is the extent to which it measures what it intends to measure. The main concern of recruiters is the predictive validity of selection methods – how effective is an interview, a test or an assessment centre in predicting the eventual job performance of a candidate? Predicting job performance through the selection process is a challenging task and cannot be underestimated. The predictive validity of selection methods can be compared by using a correlation coefficient to measure the

EXHIBIT 7.3 Predictive validity of selection methods: a summary of correlations

1.0 Certain prediction
0.9
0.8
0.7 Assessment centres for development
0.6 Skilful and structured interviews
     Ability tests, including numerical and verbal reasoning
0.5 Work sampling
0.4 Assessment centres for job performance
     Biographical data
     Personality assessment
0.3 Unstructured interviews
0.2
0.1 References
     Interests
     Years of job experience
0.0 Graphology
     Astrology
     Age

probability that a selection method will predict performance in a job. A correlation coefficient of 1.0 represents certain prediction, a correlation coefficient of 0.5 approximates to a 50 per cent chance that the selection method will predict performance, and a correlation coefficient of 0.0 indicates no connection between the selection method rating and job performance. There can also be negative correlations, meaning that positive candidate performance in a selection process correlates with poor job performance! A number of studies have attempted to provide a comparison of predictive validities in selection methods. Exhibit 7.3 contains a summary of rounded figures (Smith and Robertson, 1993; Shackleton and Newell, 1991; Smith, 1994; Arnold *et al.*, 1998; Conway *et al.*, 1995; Fowler, 1997, 1998; CIPD, 2004a, 2005; Barclay, 2001; Robertson and Smith, 2001; Harel *et al.*, 2003; Bertua, Anderson and Salgado, 2005).

The predictive validity correlations listed are of limited value because they cannot be generalised to particular organisational situations, as any validity study will be constrained by, first, the people sample chosen; second, the job performance measures used to establish validity which may be single criterion or multiple criteria based on appraisal ratings, manager's judgement, and performance measures, *inter alia*; and, third, the way in which the selection methods were applied. The summary of predictive validities in Exhibit 7.3 therefore needs to be treated with caution, but important messages remain. First, faith in the ability of selection methods to predict job performance should be circumscribed and, second, some methods may be better than others. The search for appropriate methods can proceed accordingly. It is generally accepted that an appropriate combination of selection techniques improves predictive validity.

Figure 7.1 Validating
the selection process
and decision

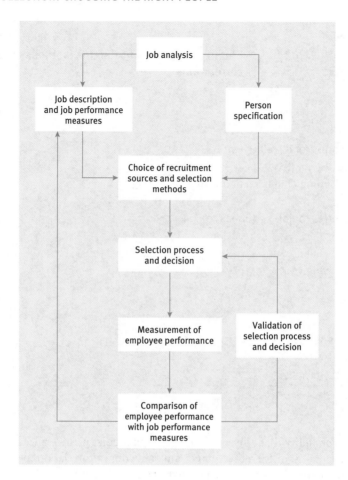

Of particular note is the evidence to suggest that the interview, although almost universal in use, is frequently a poor performer in the selection process.

In an ideal world each organisation should attempt to validate its own selection methods for each type of job. This would involve comparing the information used in selection, for example test results or interview scores, with work performance criteria, for example output measurement or appraisal grading, of the candidates appointed, perhaps over variable time periods. Figure 7.1 identifies the elements in validating selection methods.

There is a significant problem with the validation of selection methods, because candidates who fail the selection process, usually because good performance is not predicted, are denied the opportunity to attempt the job to demonstrate that they are not good performers. It would therefore be necessary to appoint candidates with both high and low ratings in the selection process and conduct a validation study, as only then could it be determined that poor performers in the selection process are also poor performers at work. These issues are discussed, not because it is expected that organisations will be prepared, or able, to commit resources to the routine and rigorous validation of the selection methods used, but to expose the difficulties of predicting performance.

Other types of validity include face validity and construct validity. A selection method has face validity if, on the 'face of it', there appears to be a connection between the method and the job. For example, a word-processing test for a secretarial job has high face validity. An assessment centre activity which involves making a raft out of planks and oil drums, may appear to have much less face validity. A selection technique with low face validity can still have high predictive validity, but it is important to be aware of the potential impact on the candidate if low face validity is perceived. As Fowler (1997) usefully put it, 'Will it be acceptable to candidates who may lack confidence in, or resent, a test that seems to ask irrelevant or intrusive questions?' Construct validity refers to whether or not a selection technique is based on sound evidence or underpinning theory. This is particularly important in psychometric assessment. It is frequently easier to demonstrate low construct validity than the reverse.

Reliability in selection methods is a consistency measure. To be considered reliable a method, such as an interview or a test, should be able to produce the same candidate result regardless of the interviewer or who is administering or scoring the test. A further reliability measure would be the extent to which a selection method consistently produced the same outcome when used for the same candidate at different times. It is interesting to reflect on whether a consistent judgement would emerge if the same candidate group was interviewed by different interviewers – the inter-individual reliability of the interview as a selection method. There are also intra-individual reliability issues – the extent to which the same interviewer will be consistent in judgement at different points in time.

The popularity of selection methods in UK organisations provides another comparative dimension, with three broad groupings identifiable. Interviews, references and application forms, termed *the classic trio*, have almost universal popularity despite evidence of low predictive validity and lack of reliability in practice. Ability tests, personality assessment, use of biographical data and assessment centres have medium, but increasing, popularity, and graphology and astrology have low popularity (Shackleton and Newell, 1991; CIPD 2004b; CIPD, 2008b). The most predictive methods are therefore not the most popular and it would appear that preferences prevail over utility.

SELECTION METHODS

HR specialists and line managers should be aware of the main selection techniques and recognise the extent and limits of their professional expertise. In this section selection methods are described, relevant issues and debates exposed and the fit within the overall recruitment and selection system discussed. The pursuit of a perfect selection method is perhaps unrealistic as there exists only a variety of less than perfect techniques. A critical perspective, which recognises that selectors need to exercise informed choice between and within selection methods, is suggested as the most constructive approach and understanding the potential and the limitations of selection methods is essential to using them effectively and appropriately.

The application form

The application form has an important part to play in recruitment and selection, and attention to form design and use is warranted. Attention is drawn to three interrelated application form issues – duality of purpose, ease or difficulty of completion, and standard or flexible design.

Duality of purpose

Typically, the application form is designed to capture personal information which becomes part of the personnel record, should the applicant become an employee. The application form also has the purpose of providing job-related information which is used for shortlisting decisions and to structure the interview. There may be a tension between these two purposes, and application forms should be evaluated critically for usefulness in employee selection. Personal information which is not relevant to a selection decision can be extracted from the selection process or can be collected later, and only for those candidates who are offered employment.

The collection of personal information has become significantly constrained by law, and as the application form is the first collection point it is useful at this stage to consider some of the constraints on the employer. The Data Protection Act 1998 places an obligation on employers to ensure that the information asked for on an application form, and throughout the recruitment and selection process, is 'adequate, relevant and not excessive'. The application form should not therefore seek information which is irrelevant to the applicant's ability to do the job. Particular care must be taken in the collection of sensitive personal data, such as ethnic origin, political opinions, religious beliefs, health, sexuality, family or marital circumstances, and trade union affiliation. Basically, such data can only be collected if relevant to the entering into of an employment contract and with the applicant's consent. The application form will also need to make it clear that the information may be used as a basis for the personnel record and that it may also be used for monitoring purposes. The application form may need to incorporate a phrase such as: 'By signing this application form you are giving permission for your personal information to be stored and processed for the purpose of arriving at a selection decision, for it to be used as a basis for a personnel record and for sensitive data to be used for the purpose of equal opportunities monitoring'. Anti-discrimination legislation has promoted the withdrawal of questions on marital status and children, and questions on nationality or ethnic origins or sexual orientation or religious belief have been similarly affected, or are asked only for monitoring purposes. The Disability Discrimination Act 1995 has increased sensitivity to questions about health and sick absence (Leighton, 2000). Key clauses in the Human Rights Act 1998 guarantee the right to privacy in family life and beliefs and the right to freedom of expression. The latter potentially has implications for requiring employees to conform with organisational rules and corporate values. The implementation of EU Directives on equal treatment outlawed discrimination based on age from 2006. Clearly, the principles relating to data protection, equal treatment and human rights need to be borne in mind throughout the recruitment and selection process, but they are introduced here to raise awareness in application form design.

Application forms can be developed to generate more useful data by asking applicants to respond to extended questions or statements. For example, where a particular competency is required, an applicant could be asked to describe an instance where a competency was developed or exhibited. Exhibit 7.4 provides one example of how this approach is used in graduate recruitment. Used in this way, the application form becomes 'a correspondence interview'. An application form which contains this type of extended statement is much more difficult to complete and will not be suitable for all types of job.

EXHIBIT 7.4 **Extended application form statements for behavioural competencies**

1 Provide an example of where you had to persuade others to accept an unpopular course of action.
2 Describe how you provided leadership for a team and how you set about achieving the team's objectives.
3 Evaluate an occasion when you needed to assert yourself.
4 Describe the most difficult non-academic problem you have solved, indicating why it was difficult.
5 Evaluate a piece of your own work, which may be practical, academic or artistic, to demonstrate your personal creativity.
6 Describe a situation where your planning skills made a significant contribution to the successful achievement of individual or team objectives.
7 Identify three personal standards which you consider are important for a manager to have.

Ease or difficulty of completion

The desire to collect useful candidate information needs to be balanced against the deterrent effect on the applicant of a lengthy and complex application form. In a surplus labour market the deterrent effect may be a useful way of eliminating less strong applicants. In a shortage labour market, or where the job-seeking habits of applicants do not expect a difficult application form, the deterrent effect may cause a low rate of return and the exclusion of good candidates because applicants exercise their right to deselect the employer.

Standard or flexible design

A standard application form is administratively attractive and less expensive, but there is a case for flexibility in design. Flexibility may not extend to individual forms for each job, but could reflect the varying requirements of different job categories. A range of form styles will improve the contribution of application form information to the recruitment and selection process. Application form information can be compared systematically to the job description and person specification to reduce personal bias and to avoid the use of arbitrary criteria. There are arguments for and against the acceptance of CVs in place of, or to supplement, the application form. Information presented in a standard format on an application form facilitates candidate and job comparison and contributes to a common interview structure. Conversely a CV is an opportunity for candidates to demonstrate individual capacity for providing evidence of achievement and suitability for the job (or demonstrating they have been coached in preparing CVs).

References

Despite low validity and reliability, and the reluctance of referees to express negative views, many organisations continue to seek references. Choices exist over the use of references in recruitment and selection and it is not possible to be prescriptive about which is the correct choice – it depends on the organisational context. The first choice relates to the **stage** at which references are obtained and used – before shortlisting, before the interview or after the offer of employment. Sensitivity to the impact on the applicant's existing employment relationship is a factor because the receipt of a reference enquiry for a current employee may provoke an employer judgement that the employee is disloyal or lacking in commitment. The second choice is whether it is **opinions** or **facts** that are sought. Valid opinions are highly dependent on a sound knowledge of the applicant and also the specific job for which the individual has applied. The third choice relates to the **weight** given to reference information, bearing in mind that applicants choose their own personal referees and that employers of the applicant are bound by the duty of care in providing references. The duty, both in contract, through an implied term of mutual trust and confidence, and in tort, is to provide a true, fair and accurate reference. The duty extends to current employees and also to former employees. The employer is not obliged in law to give a comprehensive reference, except when not giving a comprehensive reference results in unlawful discrimination or victimisation. However, it is not enough that the reference is accurate; the overall impression given must be fair and reasonable. This duty of care has been reasserted several times, in *Spring* v *Guardian Assurance* [1994] IRLR 460; *Bartholomew* v *London Borough of Hackney* [1999] IRLR 246; *Coote* v *Granada Hospitality* [1999] IRLR 452; and *TSB* v *Harris* [2000] IRLR 157. All of this is making employers more cautious about expressing opinions, and many are instigating 'no talk' reference policies or confining a response to information about the position held and employment dates – a tombstone reference. There appears to be a growing gap between the information employers would like to receive and what they are willing to give. A sensible guideline for completing reference enquiries may be to restrict the response to facts, or where opinions are to be given they should be based on facts.

In the context of the provisions of the Data Protection Act 1998 it can remain difficult for employees to see their references. The recipient of a confidential reference can disclose it only if the Act's confidentiality rules are complied with, basically meaning that the permission of the referee is required, and the referee can withhold a reference from disclosure where it is given in confidence. Where the reference is 'in confidence' the employer will need to have separate filing arrangements or will have to remove the reference from the employee's file each time subject access is requested.

The speed of return and the usefulness of a written reference can be improved by using the job description and person specification as the basis for reference questions; giving sufficient background information; clearly indicating the nature of the response required; user-friendliness and ease of completion, plus enclosing a stamped and addressed envelope; specifying a response time which is reasonable; and sending the enquiry to a named individual.

Oral references are an alternative and are arguably more likely to elicit a 'truthful' response. Providers of telephone references should be aware of the ease with which the conversations can be recorded, although reputable suppliers of telephone equipment include a warning signal to inform you that a recording is taking place, and there are ethical issues involved in seeking 'off the record' references. A further reference decision is whether the completion of reference enquiries should be devolved to line managers or administered by an HR function. There is a legal, ethical and business need for care, fairness, accuracy and consistency, and each organisation needs to have a policy to achieve this in practice.

The interview

An interview is a social encounter between an applicant and a representative, or representatives, of an employer and personalises the recruitment and selection process. It is subject to all the problems associated with social interaction, individual personality and perceptual processes. Locate this within a ritualistic framework, and a context which may be emotionally charged, and a cauldron of tensions is created, often inhibiting appropriate selection decisions. This raises the question of why organisations continue to bother with the selection interview. There are a number of reasons. First, it is almost inconceivable that employment would be offered without the employer actually seeing the prospective employee, and potential employees would be unlikely to feel comfortable about joining an organisation without meeting some of the organisational members. Second, interviewers frequently feel that they do it well and are insulated against healthy self-doubt about their ability to make good selection decisions. Third, despite being subject to considerable criticism, the interview can be improved through planning, structuring and the development of interviewing skills.

The interview is more than a selection device. It is a mechanism which is capable of communicating information about the job and the organisation to the candidate, with the aim of giving a realistic job preview (RJP). The RJP enables the applicant to make a more informed judgement. The interview also provides a forum for agreeing a course of action with the applicant. The structure of an interview is subject to many variations, but it contains four basic elements. There will be oscillation between points 2 and 3 and variations in emphasis and time allowed for each of the elements.

1 Initial contact and explanation of the interview programme.
2 The interviewer asks questions and the interviewee responds with answers, and other information.
3 The interviewee asks questions and the interviewer responds, and supplies additional information.
4 Closing the interview and agreement on what happens next.

Interviewers have a tendency to make up their minds within the first few minutes of the interview, and the remainder of the time is spent confirming these first impressions. This is referred to as 'confirmatory information seeking bias' and describes the situation where an interviewer asks questions to actively seek information in confirmation of the initial judgement. Other perceptual problems frequently occur in interviews, including:

- the halo or horns effect – a single good or bad characteristic or piece of information carries disproportionate weight in the selection decision
- the projection of the interviewer's characteristics or preferences – treating candidates more favourably or unfavourably on the basis of either similarity or dissimilarity to the interviewer
- positive or negative expectancy – created prior to the interview through access to partial candidate information
- stereotypical assumptions – about behaviour, preferences and probable work performance
- the recency effect – the influence and contrast of previous candidates distorting the proper assessment of current candidate information

- personal liking bias – the interviewer is influenced by whether or not the candidate is likeable
- risk aversion – the interviewer guards against making a wrong decision, resulting in greater weight being given to negative indicators at the expense of focusing on the positive areas of candidate suitability.

This potential for perceptual distortion can be compounded by other problems relating to the subjectivity and lack of skills of the interviewer. These problems include having inaccurate information about the vacancy, having too much faith in the interview as a fair discriminator, unwarranted confidence in interviewing skills, and variations in interview structure. Interviewers should recognise that it is easy for them to spend too much time talking, and the figure of only 20 per cent of the time is suggested by some commentators as a good target. Behavioural variations of the interviewer, caused by mood, time constraints or the importance or urgency of other work demands, should not be overlooked. Poorly structured interviews and a lack of interviewing skills will neuter the validity and reliability of the interview as a predictor. Recognising the fallibility of the interview is a prerequisite to enhancing the contribution it can make to the selection decision. The interview should normally be structured to ensure a focus on job-relevant information, sufficient time should be allocated to prepare for each candidate, and interviewers need to develop and exhibit sound interview skills (Exhibit 7.5). Training and practice in interviewing can improve effectiveness and increase predictive validity and reliability. Interviewer judgements based on structured interviews are more predictive of job performance than those from unstructured interviews.

Interviews take different forms. These include the one-to-one, the panel and the group interview.

The one-to-one interview relies on the interface between the candidate and the individual representative of the organisation. It is often less oppressive than a situation where a candidate is faced with several organisational representatives at the same

EXHIBIT 7.5 Selection interviewing skills

- Awareness of perceptual distortions
- Practice in multi-sensory perception – listening, observing, evaluating, thinking, speaking (sequentially and simultaneously)
- The ability to probe and gather relevant information through the use of appropriate questioning techniques, particularly open and probing questions
- The confidence and ability to control the interview structure
- Positive use of body language and facial expression
- Finely tuned listening skills and the ability to recall elicited information accurately
- Stamina and sensitivity
- The use of appropriate strategies, including formality or informality, information gathering or problem-centred, real-life or hypothetical issues and so on.

time. It can take place on its own, which raises questions about the appropriateness of locating the responsibility for the appointment decision in one person alone, or as part of a sequential process where the candidate may meet organisational representatives successively. The sequential process of one-to-one interviews allows cross-referencing of information before the decision is made, but unless the roles of each interviewer are clearly defined the result can be a duplication of questions.

Panel interviews may be more time-efficient than one-to-one interviews unless, of course, there is a sequence of panel interviews. They enable more members of the organisation to be involved, but there is a consequent proliferation of opinions and agendas, and also variable expertise. The panel interview may be perceived as more oppressive by the interviewee and this needs to be taken into account. In a panel interview the roles and contributions of the participants need to be agreed and precisely defined, and unless there is a clear locus of decision-making there is potential for either internal disputes or consensus-seeking and 'group thinking'. Properly structured and conducted, panel interviews are considered appropriate by many organisations, particularly in the public sector, and are a defence against accusations of the personal bias which may be associated with a dependence on a single interviewer in a one-to-one interview.

A group interview enables a number of applicants to be interviewed simultaneously by one or more interviewers. Such interviews are probably more eliminative than selective, and purport to measure characteristics such as sociability, self-confidence, leadership, teamworking and competitiveness. Group interviews can be time-efficient and a significant advantage is the opportunity to present organisational information to a number of applicants, rather than having to repeat it for each individual, and questions raised by one candidate may be of interest and value to other candidates. Group interviews need sensitive and skilled facilitation to ensure equity of treatment and should probably not be used as the sole basis for decision-making. Displaying personal characteristics in front of interviewers and competing candidates is a stressful and uncomfortable experience for the interviewee and may impact negatively on the quality of the information generated. Group interviews presuppose a relatively large pool of applicants and will need to be acceptable in the context of the job-seeking expectations of the labour market from which the applicants are being drawn, for example in graduate recruitment where there may be a small number of vacancies and a large number of applicants.

Buckley *et al.* (2000) usefully sum up 100 years of research into selection interviewing:

> Negative findings about the predictive power, reliability, or validity of the interview have little meaning to the employers and interviewers that depend on the interview as their primary selection tool. The interview provides the personal, face-to-face contact that humans seek and desire. Until another method is developed that allows employers the same benefits and freedoms as the interview, the interview will continue to be used as a primary hiring tool. After almost 100 years of research on the interview, few strides have been taken toward creating a new and better selection tool to replace the interview. Many scholars, including a number of recent meta-analytic researchers, have attempted to encourage the use of the structured interview, citing its higher validity and inter-rater agreement. Others have taken an opposite stance, promoting the group interview, with little or no structure or interviewer involvement. The answer lies, perhaps, in a combination of the two methods.

Research by Barclay (1999) found increased interest in structured interviews which used job and competence analysis to make questions relevant to the job, asked the same questions of all candidates, used systematic scoring procedures and deployed questioning strategies such as behavioural or situational questions. She attributes this to three reasons. First, there are the social aspects of interviewing – it is flexible, it provides the opportunity to meet the 'whole' person face to face, it involves line managers and it allows some bargaining and influencing to take place. Second, other methods have limitations, such as the time and costs and specialist training required, the potentially adverse effects on candidates, and the monopoly of techniques by HR specialists, leading to marginalisation of line management. Third, there are benefits of structure in interviewing – more focus on relevant criteria and candidates' competencies, hence an increased likelihood of better selection decisions, and more consistency and fairness in treatment of candidates.

There are three principal types of structured interview – biographical, situational and behavioural. Biographical interviews consist of structured probing of the areas identified in the application form and the application form design is therefore critical to the effectiveness of the process. In situational interviews applicants are asked how they would respond to hypothetical job situations – a form of scenario setting. In behavioural interviews applicants are asked to describe past job, or job-related, behaviours – these are very much like the behavioural questions exposed in Exhibit 7.4 and are based on the assumption that behaviour patterns are consistent over time. Barclay (2001) suggests that behavioural and situational interviews are likely to have greater predictive validity than 'standard' biographical interviews because 'situational questions may predict future behaviour because of the relationship between intentions and future behaviour . . . past behaviour questions may predict future behaviour because of the old adage that "the best prophet of the future is the past" (Byron).' Interviews do not have to be one type and may consist of biographical, situational and behavioural questions. The essential factor is that the interview is structured so that all candidates are asked the same questions in the same sequence, facilitating the comparison of candidate information with the predetermined person specification criteria. HR research (Robertson and Smith, 2001; Salgado, 1999, for example) consistently reports that the predictive validity of interviews is doubled through structuring. Structure can therefore enhance the reliability and validity of interviewer evaluations and although there is no agreed definition of what constitutes a structured interview it will incorporate elements of standardisation in terms of the questions asked, the relevance of those questions to the vacant position and to the method of assessing the quality of candidate responses to the standard questions (Macan, 2009). Robertson and Smith (2001) suggest that situational interviews have higher predictive validity at 0.5 compared with behavioural interviews at 0.4. It would seem that the popularity of interviews as a selection technique is undiminished and it will continue to be universally deployed in parallel with strenuous efforts to improve its reliability and validity.

Psychometric testing

Expert and professional advice is a prerequisite to the design, choice, administration and interpretation of psychometric tests. **The aim in this section is not to instruct in the use of psychometric tests, but to stimulate awareness of some of the main issues and themes.** Psychometric testing is generally used as a term which encompasses all forms of psychological assessment. Psychometric tests are tests that can be systematically scored and administered, which are used to measure individual differences – for example in personality, aptitude, ability, attainment or intelligence. They are normally supported by a body of evidence and statistical data which demonstrates their validity and are used in an occupational setting. There are five broad categories:

- *Attainment tests* measure current levels of knowledge or skill, for example word-processing tests or examinations.
- *General intelligence tests* measure overall intellectual capacity for thinking and reasoning.
- *Specific cognitive ability tests* measure verbal reasoning or numerical reasoning or manual dexterity or spatial ability.

EXHIBIT 7.6 Verbal reasoning – test question examples

This test assesses verbal and written skills and is designed to measure vocabulary and word usage. It is commonly used for recruitment in commercial and managerial roles which require the preparation of contracts, service-level agreements and other written documents.

Choose the combination of words which best fit the blank spaces for each question. Your answers should be grammatical and make the most sense. The time allowance for 6 questions is three minutes.

1   The _____ of the venture might have been predicted if _____ attention had been paid to the report which pinpointed several fundamental problems.
   a.   Failure / no
   b.   Failure / less
   c.   Failure / more
   d.   Success / more
   e.   Success / greater

2   The problem is not so _____ the total amount of funding assigned to the department, but rather that this funding has been _____ too thinly amongst individual managers.
   a.   Much / given
   b.   Much / spread
   c.   Much / focused
   d.   Uniquely / assigned
   e.   Uniquely / distributed

3   The company will provide _____ clothing and equipment where it is required. However, it is up to the _____ to take reasonable care of their own safety by using equipment that is provided.
   a.   Protection / employed
   b.   Protective / employment
   c.   Protective / employers
   d.   Protective / employees
   e.   Precautionary / employees

(Box continued)

4   The decision was _____ by the workforce as an important move towards providing a _____ defined career structure.
   a.   Applauded / radically
   b.   Greeted / poorly
   c.   Criticized / poorly
   d.   Dismissed / well
   e.   Welcomed / well

5   Her first step in _____ the problem was to _____ the opinions of those who would actually be involved in the day to day running of the scheme.
   a.   Creating / define
   b.   Generating / imitate
   c.   Solving / seek
   d.   Enhancing / discredit
   e.   Identifying / divulge

6   The job losses came despite _____ pressure to reverse the demand for _____ cuts.
   a.   Growing / tax
   b.   Decreasing / job
   c.   Increasing / sales
   d.   Weakening / spending
   e.   Mounting / expenditure

7   _____ are reminded that all expense _____ should be authorised by their _____ and sent to Accounts with the relevant VAT receipt.
   a.   Staff / forms / clients
   b.   Staff / allowances / supervisors
   c.   Staff / claims / supervisors
   d.   Managers / claims / subordinates
   e.   Managers / bills / subordinates

8   _____ recent industrial relations _____, the company hopes that profits will _____ a dividend to be paid to the shareholders.
   a.   Despite / conflicts / allow
   b.   Because of / set backs / prevent
   c.   In view of / acrimonies / permit
   d.   In line with / improvements / deter
   e.   Due to / difficulties / preclude

Answers: 1c 2b 3d 4e 5c 6e 7c 8a

- *Trainability tests* measure responsiveness to instruction or training and seek to assess learning potential and rate of response in relation to specific tasks or activities.
- *Personality questionnaires* aim to infer relatively enduring individual characteristics and traits as a basis for predicting behaviour.

In the case of properly validated attainment, general intelligence, cognitive ability and trainability tests, there is a general acceptance that the measurement outputs can be related to specific jobs and, appropriately chosen and used, there is little contention that they are able to provide useful information for selection decisions. The assessment of personality provides much more fertile ground for controversy.

Psychometric tests proliferated in the 1980s and 1990s, with hundreds now being available. The use of psychometric tests increased from around 30 per cent of organisations in 1985 to 50 per cent of organisations in 2000 (Baker and Cooper, 2000) and the CIPD (2008) put the figure at a similar level. The increased availability and use of psychometric tests gives rise to concern about the huge potential for poor test design, indiscriminate use and inappropriate interpretation of outcomes. Shackleton is quoted as saying that 'some of the stuff on the market is rubbish, I wouldn't use it to select a toothbrush' (Pickard, 1996). The dangers to potential users lie in two beguiling features. First, the 'scientific' nature of psychometric devices can create an exaggerated impression of their value and accuracy. Second, design features in the test may generate information which effectively takes responsibility for a selection decision by indicating a pass or fail outcome, satisfying the risk aversion needs of the selector. It is beyond the scope of this generalist text to advise on the specific application of tests, but it is essential that organisations are professional and discriminating in their use of psychometric instruments. The British Psychological Society and the CIPD provide a framework for regulating the use of psychometric tests through a voluntary 'licensing' mechanism based on codes of practice and the certification of user competence.

Personality questionnaires are the most contentious form of psychometric assessment and therefore it is useful to focus on these. Personality questionnaires produce either a profile or a descriptive narrative of an individual. This raises the question of which profile or description is the 'best type' for the job. It is the identification of this 'best type' that is elusive. The individual personality information is compared to the profile of a representative sample of an appropriate population, either produced by the questionnaire supplier or generated by the user on the basis of the personality characteristics of successful and less successful organisational performers. Popular examples of personality assessment include the Myers Briggs Type Indicator (MBTI), Cattell's Sixteen Personality Factors (16PF) and the Saville and Holdsworth Occupational Personality Questionnaire (OPQ). The MBTI reports individual preferences on four scales of two opposite preferences. The opposite scales are extroversion and introversion, sensing and intuition, thinking and feeling, and judging and perceiving. They respectively deal with where the individual likes to focus attention, the way the individual looks at things, the way that the individual makes decisions and how the individual relates to the outer world. The MBTI outcome is one of 16 personality types, and Myers Briggs publish a description of the characteristics and work preferences frequently associated with each 'type' for the purpose of helping either the individual or the organisation to make more informed choices about the appropriateness of different types of work. The 16PF profile infers personality using Cattell's 16 primary traits and produces a line profile for each individual which can be used for comparison with the perceived 'best type' for a job. The OPQ is based on 30 personality dimensions and has scoring norms derived from 4000 British managers who took part in development trials. These OPQ dimensions are used to construct a desired personality profile against which the profiles of job applicants are matched. These examples of personality assessment are introduced to illustrate different approaches and because of widespread use – any criticisms of personality assessment in selection are not directed specifically at these reputable psychometric instruments.

Personality assessment has its advocates and accusers. Among the accusers are Blinkhorn and Johnson, who many years ago asked the question:

> Are personality tests serious measures of personal qualities which predict behaviour, or are they the stage-managed bits of flummery intended to lend an air of scientific rigour to personnel practice? We fear the flummers are winning. (1991: 38)

Personality assessment which seeks to identify 'the one best personality type' can be charged with being 'Tayloristic' by not fully taking into account contingency factors and also being at odds with concepts of promoting and managing diversity. As Goss points out:

> Selecting only particular types of personality may, eventually, lead to an incestuous organisational profile where, weakened by inbreeding, the ability to think innovatively and challengingly is eroded in favour of slavish conformity to established norms. (1994: 47)

Goss also raises the question of whether selection on the basis of personality profiling is an ethically acceptable form of social engineering in pursuit of corporate conformity. There are also issues about the acceptability of the intrusive nature of some of the instruments used to assess personality. The arguments are similar to those being used to debate the acceptability of using genetic profiling in employment decisions. Finally, there is the fairly obvious, but often overlooked, factor that personality assessment tends to measure stated preferences rather than behaviour. Although it is generally accepted that preferences shape individual behaviour, the correlation between these two factors is not necessarily going to be strong and will certainly be moderated by other factors in the workplace.

Despite these accusations it is important not to discard a potentially useful selection device.

> CIPD broadly supports the use of psychological testing and believes that, used appropriately, testing can enhance decision-making, thus enabling managers to develop more informed and accurate perceptions about the ability and potential of individuals. To achieve this it is essential to integrate testing into the decision-making process. As well as selecting the right test, it is crucial to implement it properly. The best tests on the market are only as good as the process of which they form a part, and flawed decisions can be made based on sound and verifiable data. A well designed policy on testing is therefore essential to ensure good practice and that the maximum benefits accrue from its use. Particular care should also be taken to ensure that tests themselves do not indirectly discriminate unfairly between certain groups. Test use alone is no guarantee of objectivity despite their scientific background. (CIPD, 2008)

The arguments in favour of personality assessment are threefold. First, there is evidence to suggest that personality assessment, used appropriately, has fairly good predictive validity. Second, there are factors which enhance the potential contribution of personality assessment, including using only properly validated tests, the appropriate training of administrators of the tests and the interpreters of the information generated, the carrying out of tests in standard conditions, proper confidentiality, sensitivity in giving feedback on test and profile results, and validating the match between individual personality characteristics and job requirements and performance. Third, personality assessment should be restricted to providing additional information for the selection process and should not constitute the sole method or principal basis for decision-making.

> The CIPD is fully aware of limitations of personality assessment generally and does not support its use as the sole basis of decision-making. It can be useful as an added dimension to decision-making but only when practitioners generally use those instruments that have been rigorously developed and for which thoroughly researched validation evidence and norms are available. (CIPD, 2005)

Although most of this section has focused on personality assessment, there are some general guidelines which are applicable to all psychometric measurement – Fowler (1997), Sternberg (1998), Fletcher (1998), Stairs *et al.* (2000) and CIPD (2008). These are as follows.

- Psychometric assessment may have a useful role in selection provided it is used properly and in conjunction with other methods.

- Careful consideration should be given to the costs of psychometric testing, in terms of purchase and the time and effort required to administer and interpret the tests, in relation to the added value to the selection decision.

- The limitations of psychometric testing and the limits of individual professional expertise should be recognised.

- Only reputable suppliers should be used and all assessors need to be trained to approved professional standards.

- Psychometric testing should respect the dignity of the individual.

EXHIBIT 7.7 Examples of personality assessment

The Myers-Briggs Type Indicator (MBTI) is based on the teachings of Jung and identifies four behavioural preference dimensions: extroversion/introversion, sensing/intuition, thinking/feeling and judgement/perception. Combining the four produces a personality type, such as ESTJ. Each personality type has identified characteristics and it is useful principally for developing interpersonal skills, self-awareness, career counselling and team-building.

Cattells 16 PF (Personality Factors) profiles relatively enduring personality characteristics with each characteristic measured on a scale. The factors are grouped into the themes of extroversion, anxiety, will, self-control and independence.

(Box continued)

The Occupational Personality Questionnaire (OPQ) generates insights in relation to three dimensions: people relationships, thinking styles and emotions. OPQ can be used in selection and in development by providing insights into behavioural predisposition at work.

Belbin's team roles identify patterns of behaviour that may characterise individual contributions to a team. The team roles are grouped into action oriented, people oriented and cerebral, and the potential for self-awareness facilitates greater flexibility in adopting different roles by individual team members. It may also provide insights into team make-up and team-building.

Fundamental Interpersonal Relations Orientation-Behaviour (FIRO-B) assesses interpersonal needs and the impact on the individual's behaviour towards others. The dimensions include: giving and receiving; desire to form new relationships; control, influence and structure; need for dominance and/or power; and emotionality and warmth. It can identify similarities between team members and also potential for conflict.

Work sampling and job simulation

Work sampling as an employee selection technique provides opportunities for candidates to experience or simulate job tasks and for the employing organisation to observe and assess candidate competencies and performance. Work sampling is an ability test which is organisation and job specific in design. There are clearly links with more generic tests of ability. Work sampling opportunities may be real, where the candidate actually does the job under supervision for a limited period, or simulated, where the job tasks are performed through role play or management games. Work sampling is valuable in giving the candidate a realistic job preview. The technique is illustrated by providing examples:

- car mechanic – diagnosing and repairing vehicle faults
- NVQ assessor – the assessment of the assessor assessing a candidate
- chef – preparing a meal
- telephone sales – following up leads by telephone
- sales assistant – selling a product and demonstrating ability to make add-on sales
- chauffeur or chauffeuse – driving a vehicle and interacting with the passenger
- HR practitioner – interviewing a job applicant, advising line managers or conducting a training session
- store detective – identifying suspicious behaviour, detecting a 'planted' shoplifter or, as a role reversal, simulated shoplifting by the store detective applicant without being detected!

The success or otherwise of this selection method will depend on appropriate design and use. It has the potential for relatively high predictive validity and to be acceptable to candidates through good face validity. The design principles include:

1 Determine the essential abilities for the job in question through discussion with job-holders and line managers – competency analysis.

2 Construct a work sampling activity which provides a genuine opportunity for the demonstration of the critical abilities required.

3 Determine the performance standards and assessment criteria, together with a mechanism for rating or scoring individual candidate performance.

4 Train assessors, pilot the work sample, evaluate and refine.

5 Develop clear, fair and consistent instructions for work sample candidates which include common advance information and a briefing immediately prior to the work sampling activity.

6 Locate the work sample appropriately within the recruitment and selection system, either to supplement other selection techniques or integrated within an assessment centre approach.

This systematic approach to work sampling in selection can be a disincentive, because it presents design challenges, is demanding in terms of time, people and other resources and, being organisation and job specific, will need to be regularly updated. It is therefore underused. A useful caveat provided by Fowler is still relevant today (1998): 'Work simulations provide valuable indications of actual or potential expertise, not precise measurements.' Work sampling can also include job-related outputs that a candidate 'may have prepared earlier', for example (and subject to authenticity) a fashion design portfolio, a piece of French polishing or photographic evidence.

Assessment centres

An assessment centre is a process rather than a place. Assessment centres attempt to improve validity and reliability through the integration of multiple selection techniques. They are founded on the identification and assessment of dimensions which are judged to be indicative of future job performance. They exhibit certain characteristics, including a variety of assessment methods to form a total assessment system, the bringing together of a number of candidates, multi-dimensional evaluation of candidate competencies, behaviours, motivation and personality, and the training and use of organisational members to perform the roles of facilitators, observers and assessors. Thornton and Gibbons (2009) define assessment centres as consisting of:

> a unique combination of essential elements where multiple, trained assessors observe overt behaviour displayed by candidates in organisational simulations and make ratings of performance on dimensions deemed important for effective performance in target positions. The dimensions of performance are identified through job analysis and/or competency modelling. Any dimension that can be defined in terms of observable behaviours has the potential for assessment and methods of integrating the information collected typically include consensus seeking amongst assessors.

The cost of an assessment centre, financially and in terms of time, effort and other resources, is considerable, and it is only a practical proposition where there are a number of candidates for critical positions. Assessment centres are frequently associated with managerial jobs and selection to graduate training schemes. Assessment centres which are properly developed, applied and validated will improve the effectiveness and credibility of the selection process. They are used not only for the selection of employees, but also for internal promotion decisions, the identification of individual development needs and, somewhat controversially, in redundancy selection. It is not possible to be prescriptive about how to develop assessment centres because they are tailored to the specific needs of an organisation. The potential pitfalls are considerable, and those considering developing an assessment centre should seek experienced advice and assistance, but it is possible to outline a design process, to identify a range of selection techniques and to draw attention to some key issues.

Assessment centre design will include job and competency analysis, choosing and combining assessment techniques, assembling an integrated programme, choosing and training assessors, selecting and preparing candidates, and post-event review. Proper job analysis is necessary to identify the principal competencies and characteristics required for successful job performance. The outputs of the job analysis are job descriptions (or accountability profiles) and person specifications which provide the criteria for assessment centre design and facilitate the choice of assessment techniques to reflect the competencies and characteristics identified. Assessment centres are useful in excavating behaviours relating to interpersonal relationships, leadership, influencing ability, sociability, competitiveness, self-motivation, tolerance, persuasiveness, problem analysis and decisiveness, *inter alia*. In addition to the collection of behavioural information it is possible and practical to make assessments of skill and gather biographical data. The key issue is to be clear about what is being assessed and to exercise informed judgement about the choice of assessment techniques. The range of techniques is wide and they can either be purchased from reputable suppliers or designed by the organisation. They include:

- group discussions
- group activities – with leaders or leaderless
- presentations
- in-tray exercises and analytical activities
- role plays
- work simulations
- interviews – individual and/or group
- personality questionnaires
- other forms of psychometric assessment.

The assessment techniques need to be used in appropriate combinations, requiring a specific focus on analysing the extent to which they are complementary or in conflict, and whether they are scheduled at suitable times within the assessment centre programme. Assessment centres lasting one day are typical and a duration of two or three days is not uncommon. A typical assessment centre may assess 8–12 candidates. However, increasingly selection methods are being combined in a mini-assessment centre of perhaps half a day's duration for non-managerial positions such as sales assistants and administrators because of the increased predictive validity.

The assessment process needs to be structured to enable the identification of candidate behaviours and performance. This involves the development and provision of assessment criteria for the assessors and the design of forms which can be used to capture information accurately on individual candidates, and which also provide a means of summarising each activity to contribute to the overall judgement. There is research evidence which questions whether it is necessary to assess candidates at a detailed level. The alternative to seeking summative information under a range of competence or behaviour dimensions is to require assessors to make an overall judgement. Clearly this is less complex for the assessor and more intuitive, but it acts against the provision of detailed information for participants and makes it more difficult to justify decisions. Assessors need to be appointed and trained and require skills in the observation, recording and evaluation of behaviour and performance. The application of these skills can be focused by, first, the clear definition of the objectives of the assessment centre; second, a specification of the assessment criteria; and, third, active assessor participation in, and reflection upon, the assessment activities prior to the assessment centre. The ratio of assessors to candidates is typically 1:2, demonstrating the labour-intensive nature of this selection method. A useful by-product of assessor training can be the development and transfer of appraising skills back to the workplace, together with a sharpened awareness of behaviour and its relationship to performance. There are clearly some ethical issues about the treatment of the candidates and these are briefly articulated in Exhibit 7.8.

EXHIBIT 7.8 Ethics and assessment centres

- Candidates are entitled to know what to expect in order to exercise their right to withdraw.
- Unreasonable surprises should be avoided, although assessor intervention in some activities may be positive and appropriate.
- Observation of behaviour at informal times, for example over dinner or in the bar, is questionable practice.
- The assessment centre should not be designed as a tortuous event or incorporate features of physiological or psychological deprivation, for example by depriving candidates of sleep through requiring all-night preparation for a presentation.
- Sensitivity, professionalism and care should be exercised in giving feedback on behaviour or performance.
- Facilitators of activities should be skilled, to reduce the probability of causing psychological 'damage' to the participants.

The assessment centre arrangements are an important feature and although, like Herzberg's hygiene factors (1959), they may not improve candidate assessment, unsatisfactory arrangements will significantly inhibit the quality of assessment. Equal time and attention therefore need to be given to the factors of location, date, travel, coordination of material, administrative support, refreshments and accommodation. A post-event review of the assessment centre is necessary to validate the process, to check for racial, sex, disability or other bias, as a reflective activity in order to improve future events, to identify any assessor development needs, and to conduct a cost–benefit analysis. There is value in piloting or having a trial run of a new assessment centre.

Assessment centres, because they are capable of combining selection methods in a structured way, represent a powerful diagnostic device. Their predictive validity is comparatively high, but there is a positive correlation between investment costs and benefits achieved.

> Assessment centres have been shown to be the most comprehensive and predictive assessment device. And so they are – when they conform to certain principles. Unfortunately, this does not mean that sundry exercises cobbled together and called an assessment centre will automatically confer on the user the same level of effectiveness.
> (Fletcher and Anderson, 1998)

CASE STUDY   Recruitment and selection of graduate trainees

Garland Hotels is an expanding UK upmarket hotel chain of 95 hotels with an average bedroom capacity of 400. All of the hotels are located out of town in parkland settings, have fine restaurants and extensive indoor and outdoor leisure facilities. The board of directors is considering controlled expansion of the business through the selective acquisition of hotels in the UK and also in the European Union. The HR director sits on the board and has a strategic role in human resource planning and managing organisational change in a competitive hospitality market. Four regional HR business partners provide advice and consultancy to hotel managers who have devolved responsibility for operational HR matters. The total number of employees is 18 000.

Historically Garland Hotels has not recruited many graduate trainee managers and did not have a systematic process for doing so. Graduates were recruited at the discretion of individual hotel managers who devised individual training programmes. Success rates, judged by graduate trainees moving into general management positions, were poor and attrition was high. Three years ago the board decided that high-quality graduate recruits would be needed to support future business development and a more systematic, but small-scale, graduate recruitment has taken place. Graduate recruitment has been supported by a two-year training scheme of six four-month secondments to customer-facing and to support service departments. The training scheme involves the trainee working in at least three different hotels and the general manager of the hotel in which the trainee is working acts as a coach and mentor. The objectives of the graduate management trainee include delivering high customer service standards, working as part of the team for each area, contributing to staffing decisions, budgetary control and developing an all-round understanding of the hotel business. The onus is on the graduate trainee to apply for management positions as they become available. Hours of work are 'unsociable' but compensated for by free meals, access to leisure facilities and a reasonable (for the hotel industry) total working week averaging 45 hours. The total reward strategy for the graduate trainees encompasses pay rates in the top market quartile, six weeks' holiday, profit share, a defined benefit pension scheme (currently under review) and subsidised private medical insurance.

The board of directors, following the advice of the HR director, has decided that the business requires 100 graduates to be recruited and trained in a three-year period. This is clearly a significant increase in the small-scale intake of the past three years and will involve significant investment. The graduate management trainees are to provide the future lifeblood of the organisation at hotel manager level. The board is convinced that graduates with a good honours degree in a business-related discipline, who are well rewarded and receive good training, will make a significant contribution to the future success of the organisation.

Questions

You are one of the four regional HR business partners and you have been tasked by the HR director to develop the graduate recruitment **and** selection process to ensure that the right numbers and quality of graduates are recruited to meet medium- and long-term business needs. The other HR business partners are focusing on the development of the graduate training programme, performance management and future reward strategy for graduate trainees. Your task is to prepare a written report for your HR director to deliver at the next board of directors' meeting and you are required to address the following issues:

1 The preparation of a job description and person specification for a graduate trainee.

2 The critical review of graduate recruitment sources and an outline recruitment strategy.

3 A method for reducing the number of graduate applications to a number that can effectively be put through an assessment centre.

4 A pilot design for a systematic assessment centre process for the selection of 30–35 graduates a year, which can be tested for predictive and face validity on existing managers.

5 Recommendations for an induction programme for graduate trainees to ensure their swift and effective transition to the organisation and also reduce early attrition through an induction crisis.

Prepare a report based on points 1–5 above in which you justify your recommendations and also include costings and resource implications.

Graphology

Graphology consists of the analysis of handwriting features such as size, slope, space, connection and pressure in order to generate a graphological profile. The profile is used to infer personality, cognitive and social characteristics in order to contribute to a judgement about job suitability. The use of graphology for selection decisions in Britain is estimated to be very low, but it is much more popular in continental European countries, particularly France and Switzerland where a significant number of organisations use it. Advocates of graphology argue that it is relatively cheap and easy to use and provides a vehicle for the projection of personal characteristics and the garnering of insights into the applicant. These insights can focus subsequent discussions and thereby make a useful contribution as an additional, but not as a stand-alone, selection technique.

The absence of empirical research data to underpin the credibility or validity of graphology makes it difficult to create a supportive case for it as a useful predictor of job performance, and considerable scepticism is evident:

> In many respects . . . graphology raises similar issues to those associated with biodata, in terms of an intuitive appeal mixed with an all too easy potential for confirming social stereotypes and superficial judgements . . . the potential dangers are probably greater [than biodata] as the mysteries of interpretation tend to be more esoteric and less directly derived from work place experience.   (Goss, 1994: 51)

The CIPD (2004a) was assertive about the non-efficacy of graphology:

> Employers considering the use of graphology should be aware of the limitations of the technique, its unreliability and the potential harm this could cause to their business. At present we can find no viable argument why graphology should be seen as a real alternative to properly validated personality assessments. The low predictive validity of graphology may not be attributable to an inability of the technique to measure personality, but may indicate that personality characteristics themselves are actually poor indicators of performance.

SELECTION TRENDS

A systematic approach to recruitment and selection has been presented because this provides the basis for understanding the process. However, it is important to recognise that this systematic paradigm can be affected, first, by power in the employment relationship with shortage labour markets influencing employers to be more image aware and also malleable in matching the job to the person, and, second, by the dynamic nature of many job roles which influences employers to seek candidates who are not just competent for the advertised job but who also demonstrate behavioural and technical competencies which will enable them to adapt to changes in the job role in the future. Fundamentally, it cannot be taken for granted that organisations will have a wide choice provided by an abundant labour market from which good applicants can be harvested; nor is it sufficient to just recruit for the 'here and now'. Several selection trends are evident.

Focus on employer brand

Competition for talent resulted in a greater concern with organisational image and its implications for the ability to recruit good employees resulting in marketing principles being integrated with many HR activities; this extends to the treatment of applicants during the selection process. Turban *et al.* (1998) found that an organisation's public image, the characteristics of the recruitment and selection process and the characteristics of the recruiter were related to organisation attractiveness. Applicants are more likely to want to work at organisations which they find attractive: 'The science of marketing may be relevant here, because attracting and retaining employees have a lot of parallels with attracting and retaining customers to buy products or brands' (Lievens *et al.*, 2002). Therefore an important dimension of recruitment and selection strategy becomes projecting a desirable image and hence the use of phrases and techniques, such as 'the employer of choice', 'brand equity' and the 'the value proposition'. This need for positive branding does not just apply to successful applicants because organisations need to ensure that rejected applicants are also left with a positive orientation in order to protect the brand profile. Although the Stansfield and Day (1998) research, in which they identified the main ingredients of a positive applicant orientation, focused specifically on assessment centres, the ingredients can be utilised as general selection principles; these are:

a professional and effective selection procedure management, effective pre-briefing, fair treatment, respect, the creation of a genuine and supportive atmosphere and the provision of quality feedback facilities.

The CIPD (2008) reported that over two-thirds of organisations are using employer brand as a recruitment tool.

Exploitation of information technology and the Internet

IT and the Internet can be used to promote the vacancy (enabling self-selection), for processing the application and contributing to the selection decision through testing, scoring and assessment. At a basic level, technology is utilised as a substitute for paper testing. Sophistication in online testing may include multimedia enhancements to present work-related scenarios to applicants with either post-scenario questioning and/or stoppages at appropriate points for candidates to indicate what they would do next. Kwiatkowski (2003) expresses this as:

Computer simulations of complex organisational factors will rapidly become more possible. Advances in virtual reality will mean that people can walk and talk through organisational environments and, for example, meet the sort of people that they are likely to come across in the organisation itself and interact with them in real time. This obviously offers up a much richer and potentially much more realistic environment within which to assess people.

This all sounds like one big video game in a virtual world, but indications are of high predictive validity of around 0.5 (Salgado and Lado, 2000). Clearly there are issues around applicants wanting to provide the right answers and as with all tests *candidate fidelity* is a factor. Development and maintenance costs of sophisticated online testing are likely to be substantial and a cost–benefit analysis is required in relation to other selection techniques.

Online testing as a selection method is increasing in popularity, particularly in graduate recruitment or where an employer anticipates a large number of applicants. It is useful to recognise three online testing variations because this enables consideration of important issues relating to standards of administration, security of the tests and test data, and control over the testing process. First, **uncontrolled and unsupervised**: the applicant takes the test on the open Internet. Second, **controlled but unsupervised**: the organisation making use of the test registers the applicant and ensures their identity, but takes no other action to supervise the timing of the test or the test environment. Third, **controlled and supervised**: a qualified test user is required to log in the applicant and ensure that timing and other test requirements are met. Kwiatkowski (2003) expresses some concerns: 'The Internet has already had an impact on selection, making it easier to test people at a distance. There are all sorts of issues associated with this technology however, including security, identity, confidentiality, technical issues of equivalence, equality of access, and fairness.'

EXHIBIT 7.9 Online testing at Toyota Manufacturing UK

In 2006 Toyota made significant cost, time and resource savings after introducing online numerical and logical reasoning tests as part of its graduate selection process. After receiving over 1000 applications per year for its graduate training schemes and typically recruiting around 20 graduates, 300 candidates were invited to take paper-based psychometric tests. This was logistically complicated with high staff costs and also the candidates' travelling. With online testing, candidates sit the tests at home or at college, making it much more accessible for them and assessment is just as effective. Also, the graduate market is familiar with online testing as a selection process. Candidates submit an online application and answer competency-based questions in areas such as planning, analysis and problem solving. Those meeting the initial screening criteria are emailed a web link for the psychometric tests. The tests feature randomised selections from a large question bank, so each candidate sits a unique test. Toyota invites the successful candidates to an assessment centre and a final panel interview is then held.

Power in the labour market and applicant perceptions

It has already been argued that selection is a two-way process with multiple opportunities for the applicant to self-select out. The social dimension of the selection process consists of both parties accumulating information about each other and deciding on whether to develop a relationship through a psychological contract. Therefore, employers may need to cultivate favourable applicant perceptions to secure the working relationship through successful selection. Stansfield and Day (1998) draw attention to the Robertson and Smith notion of *impact validity*, defined as 'the extent to which a measuring instrument has an effect on a subject's psychological characteristics'. Ryan and Ployhart (2000), Anderson (2001) and Robertson and Smith (2001) report applicant perceptions being influenced by the following factors: the acceptability of the selection techniques being used including the perceived relevance of any questions, the characteristics and interpersonal skills of the recruiter/s, the speed, perceived fairness and user-friendliness of the recruitment and selection process, the extent of the opportunity to demonstrate suitability for the job, the nature of the job itself and the extent of the information provided by the organisation. Each of these factors may need to be tested for its impact on applicant perceptions of the desirability of working for the organisation. As well as having an affective impact on applicant decision-making the nature of the recruitment and selection process is a pre-entry socialisation device and has implications for the development of a healthy psychological contract. Seeing things from the applicant's perspective is therefore an important dimension in determining the utility of selection methods.

Utility over preference

As HR processes become more sophisticated and business driven, the philosophy of recruitment and selection processes being designed primarily for fairness, consistency and historical preferences is being challenged. Contemporary employment climates generate a questioning of the traditional employer preferences in selection and require reconsideration of what is the most effective way of selecting employees. Ultimately this involves subjecting recruitment and selection processes to robust scrutiny in pursuit of business-focused continuous improvement – don't just carry on doing it the way you have always done it.

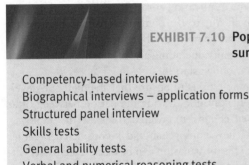

EXHIBIT 7.10   Popularity of selection methods (percentage of surveyed organisations: CIPD, 2009b)

Competency-based interviews	69 per cent
Biographical interviews – application forms/CVs	68 per cent
Structured panel interview	59 per cent
Skills tests	50 per cent
General ability tests	44 per cent
Verbal and numerical reasoning tests	39 per cent
Telephone interview	38 per cent
Personality questionnaires	35 per cent
Assessment centres	35 per cent
Group interview and exercises	26 per cent
Employment reference: pre-interview	19 per cent
Online tests	17 per cent

SUCCESSFUL TRANSITION THROUGH PRE-ENGAGEMENT AND INDUCTION

Transition, from applicant to employee, is the fourth and final sub-system in the recruitment and selection process and the beginning of successful retention. **Transition** warrants equal attention to the first three sub-systems of **attraction, reduction** and **selection**. The employer–employee relationship begins to be formalised through job offer and acceptance and through pre-engagement communication. The contract of employment is enacted through the employee being ready, willing and able to work on the agreed date and the employer having work and wages available. The psychological contract, consisting of the preconceptions and expectations created during recruitment and selection, is realised or not realised when the employee starts work and employee induction is therefore the final stage in the recruitment and selection process.

The pre-engagement process

An offer of employment should normally be in writing and include the main features of employment, for example job, hours, start date, pay and benefits and so on. The offer letter specifies any conditions to which the offer is subject and states a method and a time scale for candidate acceptance or rejection. The pre-engagement process is also important in providing necessary information to both parties and can usefully be viewed as a communication activity which further develops the employment relationship. Pre-engagement checklists can be designed to collect and provide information necessary to integrate the candidate as an employee. A health check may be a part of the pre-engagement process; this may consist of the completion of a medical questionnaire or a consultation with a general practitioner appointed by the employer or through seeking to access medical records held by the employee's medical practitioner. The requirements of the Access to Medical Records Act 1988 need to be observed and employee consent is required prior to the application for medical information. Any medical requirements should relate specifically to the demands of the particular job being offered and should be compatible with employer obligations under legislation relating to equality of employment opportunity, including any reasonable adjustments expected under the disability discrimination legislation.

The objective of the pre-engagement activity is to ensure that the dialogue developed up to the selection decision actively continues during the period between offer and employment, as the potential employee remains empowered to deselect the employer. Information expected of or required by the new employee should be considered, together with the best way of communicating it. This information can be discovered by reflecting on several empathetic questions – What would I like to know if I was coming to work here? Are there particular characteristics of the job or organisation that ought to be communicated? Does the employee know where to come on the first day, what to bring, what to wear and what to expect?

Induction

Induction is activated during the pre-engagement process and is not complete until the employer and the employee are reasonably satisfied with the employment relationship – distancing induction from the common misconception that it consists of a first-day induction course with a programme of 'information overload'. This holistic approach to induction recognises that the transition from candidate to employee may commence several months prior to starting work and continue for 6, 12 or even 24 months into employment. An event known as an induction crisis frequently occurs during employee transition. The induction crisis occurs when an employee questions and then reasserts or rejects the initial decision to accept the employment. The reassertion of the decision is achieved through a reconciliation of any doubts, but the rejection of the initial decision will typically result in the employee seeking alternative employment. The induction crisis is often triggered by a relatively small incident, but will result in consideration being given by the employee to an accumulation of concerns. The message for the manager seeking successful transition is to be alert to this potential for an induction crisis and to respond to it in an empathetic and conflict-resolving manner. It is not practical to prescribe an induction programme or package, but it is possible to identify the potential elements as a basis for formal and informal managerial interventions. Induction is a multifaceted and continuous activity and the elements include:

- the provision of organisational information, including sources of rules and regulations
- the provision of job and department information
- the communication of organisational values and beliefs

- the encouragement of effective organisational relationships
- the provision of opportunities for concern resolution
- the analysis of training needs and the consideration of short-, medium- and long-term development responses
- the formal and informal review of performance
- access to a mentoring system.

Induction demands compete with operational demands and there is considerable scope for employers to revisit pre-engagement and induction arrangements, as time and effort invested in sound recruitment and selection practices can be squandered by poor transition.

THE CONTRACT OF EMPLOYMENT AND THE WRITTEN PARTICULARS OF EMPLOYMENT

The Employment Rights Act 1996 provides for employees to receive a written statement of the main terms and conditions of employment, but it is essential to recognise that this constitutes only one element of the contract of employment. Other constituent elements of the contract are, typically, common law duties and obligations, statutory rights, expressed terms, implied terms, collective agreements, and custom and practice, *inter alia*. The written statement of particulars has no direct legal force. It is only a written record of what the employer believes to be the main terms and conditions of employment, although it can be used as evidence by an employment tribunal in deciding upon contractual terms. The recruitment and selection process may also generate terms which can be implied or incorporated into the contract; examples include job advertisements, the recruitment pack, the job description, the person specification, agreements entered into at interview, and letters of offer and acceptance. It is therefore important to seek accuracy, consistency and good faith in recruitment and selection because of the potential implications for the contract. The Data Protection Act 1998 gives employees access to their records whether manual or computerised, including information and interview notes retained from the recruitment and selection process.

Employees are entitled to a written statement of the particulars of employment within two months of starting work (Employment Rights Act 1996), if they are employed for over eight hours a week and for a period of more than one month. The issuing of a written statement to all employees as soon as practicable after starting work also provides the basis for resolving any contractual misunderstandings or disagreements. Core employment information is given in a single written statement, termed the 'principal statement'. The information to be given is detailed in Exhibit 7.11. Within the statement reference can be made to other sources of information such as organisational rules or policies on, for example, sickness, pensions or discipline. Reference can also be made to procedural agreements and general reference material incorporated into an employee handbook. Changes to written particulars must be notified to employees individually and in writing, as early as possible and at the latest within one month of the change. The written notification can refer the employee to updated reference documents, collective agreements or the employee handbook. Prior to working overseas for more than one month an employee must be given additional written particulars

EXHIBIT 7.11 **The written particulars of employment required by law**

The written particulars required by law include:

- names of the employer and employee
- the date the employment started
- the date when continuous employment began
- place of work, or the required places of work, and the employer's address
- where the employment is not intended to be permanent, the expected length, or the end date if fixed term
- the particulars of collective agreements directly affecting individual terms and conditions
- rate of pay, method of calculation and payment interval
- hours of work and normal working hours
- holiday entitlement and holiday pay
- arrangements for sickness and sick pay
- pension arrangements
- length of notice periods, on both sides
- job title or brief description of the job
- disciplinary and grievance – rules, arrangements and procedures.

relating to the length of the posting, the currency for payment, any additional benefits and the terms and conditions of employment on return to the UK.

EXIT INTERVIEWS – THE INITIAL STAGE OF THE RECRUITMENT AND SELECTION PROCESS?

This may seem a strange place to introduce exit interviews. Exit interviews are an important aspect of employee release, but they can also generate useful information and be revealing about the nature of the job and the desirability of the terms and conditions from the perspective of the employee. It can be argued, therefore, that *the exit interview is the initial stage in the recruitment and selection process*.

An exit interview is an information-gathering exercise that attempts to excavate the reasons why an employee is leaving the organisation with a view to preventing or reducing dysfunctional attrition. It should normally be conducted at some point between the employee resigning and the employee's last day of work, although some organisations attempt to collect information retrospectively. There are two perspectives on how the information collected might be useful. First, in the case of a valued employee it may enable the employer to prevent the employee leaving. This may at its simplest be the removal of a barrier to continued employment, for example a minor adjustment to working hours, the provision of a particular type of training or reassurance about opportunities for advancement. In these cases it would clearly have been preferable if the line manager had detected employee concerns earlier. Where the reason for leaving is better financial rewards, the employer may be able to match what the departing employee is being offered, but this has implications in terms of the potential impact on the reward perceptions of other employees and also the integrity of the employer's reward strategies and practices. Making an increased offer also impacts on the balance of the psychological contract by implicitly bestowing more power on the employee, and the employer would have to live with the consequences of this. An alternative employer philosophy is to recognise that once an employee has reached the decision to leave, and communicated formally that they wish to end the contract, the cause is a lost one and the best the employer can hope for is a professional parting of the ways that maintains the dignity of the employer and the employee. The second, and perhaps more realistic perspective on exit interviews is the collection and analysis of information on why employees leave in general. The information collected in this way can be used to evaluate HR practices such as financial and non-financial rewards, training and development opportunities, advancement and career prospects, style of supervision and performance management, job design and degree of empowerment, socialisation opportunities and teamworking. The exit interview information then becomes part of the process of refining HR strategy, particularly in relation to the retention of talented employees.

The practical issues relating to exit interviews are who should do them and what questions should be asked. There is a strong argument for exit interviews being conducted by the line manager, who is closest to the employee and to the nature of the work. It is interesting to note that some studies indicate that employees leave managers and not organisations, and the underlying causes of attrition may therefore be in managerial behaviour rather than the organisation's HR practices. The line manager would therefore need to be objective and detached about the information being collected. However, even this may not reassure the employee who may be unwilling to confront the line manager with information that the line manager may find unpalatable – after all, what is in it for the employee (apart perhaps from revenge) who is moving on to pastures new? The employee may also harbour fears about critical comments at the exit interview having a negative impact on the reference being provided to the new, or subsequent, employers. This interface of employee and employer perspectives raises an important issue and that is the potential difference between 'a reason for leaving' and 'the result of a reason for leaving'. Although these two concepts can be synonymous, this is not necessarily the case. For example, the result of a reason for leaving might be that the departing employee has secured a job with a higher rate of pay, but the real reason for leaving might be dissatisfaction with the style of supervision. It is the latter that has prompted the employee to seek alternative employment, but the employee will only resign once they have obtained a job which offers not only an escape from the supervisory style, but also the prospect of increased financial rewards. In this scenario it would be quite natural for the employee to propose that the increased financial rewards are the reason for leaving and for the line manager to accept this, leaving the real reason for leaving submerged. There is also the potential for an embittered employee to exaggerate scenarios or make unfounded accusations. The aim of the employer is therefore to excavate the underlying reasons for leaving rather than the *prima facie* reasons. For this reason, some organisations prefer the exit interview data to be collected by HR specialists. There may also be advantages in terms of consistency in the exit interview activity, but conversely it may cast the HR specialist in the role of 'big brother' to the line manager.

Exit interviews require particular skills. These include providing a non-threatening environment, establishing rapport and the professional use of probing questions. Kransdorff (1995) observes that:

> While an exit interview appears little more than a conversation between two people, its effective utility necessitates it being professionally researched, scripted and edited to ensure its content, clarity, continuity and readability. Alongside the employment of professional oral research techniques, this requires the skills of an expert interviewer with a keen understanding of management issues, human resource management and corporate culture.

It is essential to create a climate where departing employees can feel relaxed about providing information on their reasons for leaving. The aim of the employer is to collect genuine information in a potentially rich arena for spurious data; for example, an employee may inflate the financial rewards being offered by their new employer in order to maintain face and overtly rationalise their reason for leaving. Not only is successful exit interviewing about providing the right environment, it is also about asking the right questions. As Kransdorff (1995) puts it, 'an exiting individual is a teeming repository of all the experiences over his/her period of tenure'. Baumruk (1999) recommends addressing seven key issues at exit interviews:

1 Compensation: Was the employee fairly paid? Were the benefits satisfactory? Was he/she recognised for the work he/she did?
2 Quality of the workplace: Is it safe and secure? Is there a realistic work–life balance?
3 Relationships: Were there problems with managers, co-workers or customers?
4 Opportunities: Were there opportunities for advancement, training and career development?
5 Culture: How well did the employee fit in? Was the work environment too conservative or too radical?
6 Job description: Does it fit the position? Could it be modified?
7 Leadership: Were there doubts about the company's goals or direction?

Exhibit 7.12 provides an example of a pro-forma for an exit interview and there are two key issues with which to finish this section. First, strenuous efforts to collect genuine data will be fruitless unless something is done with the data. It therefore needs to be analysed, disseminated, discussed and actioned. This leads to the second issue, which is that appropriate degrees of confidentiality will need to be maintained. As Pont and Pont (1998) put it, 'once the information has been collated, it may be necessary to make further enquiries elsewhere, which then raises the issue of confidentiality – a factor which may contribute to the success, or not, of receiving candid answers from the leaver'. It is in reconciling this potential tension between employer action and confidentiality that exit interview information can be used by the organisation to gain valuable insights into how HR practices are perceived and, as a consequence, potentially critical problems can be identified and addressed.

EXHIBIT 7.12 Example of an exit interview pro-forma

The individual
Name
Department
Position
Job title
Length of service

The job
Best aspects
Worst aspects
Satisfaction with the type of work
Adequacy of training
Provision of equipment
Working conditions
Levels of responsibilities
Workload
Promotion opportunities

Work environment
Appropriateness of supervision
Relationships with colleagues
Inter-departmental relationships
Morale
Communication
HR policies and procedures
Would the employee consider returning?
Overall comments on company

Rewards in the new position
Pay
Benefits
Recognition
Hours of work
Other contractual terms

Reasons for leaving
What prompted the employee to consider leaving?
Could anything have been done to retain the employee?
Was internal redeployment offered?

Interviewer's observations and points for further action

SUMMARY LEARNING POINTS

1 Mutual trust and mutual respect in the recruitment and selection process are desirable ethical and business-related aims for the employer and the potential employee.

2 The **reduction** sub-system consists of filtering out and rejecting unsuitable candidates on the basis of pre-determined job criteria. In this way the pool of applicants is fairly and systematically reduced to a manageable number.

3 Candidates are empowered to deselect the employer at any stage of the recruitment and selection process, and process design should take account of this factor.

4 Validity, reliability and popularity are important concepts in understanding the potential, the limitations and the use of the various selection methods.

5 A range of **selection** techniques is available and a critical perspective is essential to the exercise of informed choice in deciding which methods to use.

6 The **transition** from applicant to employee is a vital element of the recruitment and selection process and is the beginning of successful retention. Effective transition consists of giving proper weight of attention to the pre-engagement process, to holistic induction and to the legal, economic and psychological contracts of employment.

7 Current trends in selection include a focus on employer brand, exploitation of information technology and the Internet, power in the labour market and the associated applicant perceptions, and utility over preference in selection technique choices.

8 An exit interview can be considered the *initial* stage of recruitment and selection activity, because it is potentially revealing about the nature of the job and the desirability of the terms and conditions from the perspective of the employee. Exit interviews can generate useful information on a range of HR practices, but obtaining good-quality data from departing employees is a challenging activity.

REFERENCES AND FURTHER READING

Adam-Smith, D. and Peacock, A. (eds) (1994) *Cases in Organisational Behaviour: Case 22*. London: Pitman Publishing.

Advisory, Conciliation and Arbitration Service (2000) *Employing People: Advisory Booklet* (periodically revised). London: ACAS.

Aikin, O. (1996) 'Be prepared for a data remember', *People Management*, May, 38–40.

Anderson, N. (2001) 'Towards a theory of socialization impact: selection as pre-entry socialization', *International Journal of Selection and Assessment*, 9, 84–91.

Anderson, N. and Ostroff, C. (1997) 'Selection as socialization', in Anderson, N. and Herriott, P. *International Handbook of Selection and Assessment*, 413–40, London: Wiley.

Anderson, N. and Shackleton, V. (1993) *Successful Selection Interviewing*. Oxford: Blackwell.

Anderson, N. and Shackleton, V. (1994) 'Informed choices', *Personnel Today*, November, 33–4.

Arnold, J., Cooper, C. and Robertson, I. (1998) *Work Psychology: Understanding human behaviour in the workplace* (3rd edn). London: Pitman Publishing.

Baker, B. and Cooper, J. (2000) 'Occupational testing and psychometric instruments: an ethical perspective', in Winstanley, D. and Woodall, J. (eds) *Ethical Issues in Contemporary HRM*. Basingstoke: Macmillan Business.

Barclay, J. (1999) 'Employee selection: a question of structure', *Personnel Review*, 28(1/2), 134–51.

Barclay, J. (2001) 'Improving selection interviews with structure: organisations' use of behavioural interviews', *Personnel Review*, 30(1), 81–101.

Baumruk, R. (1999) 'Questions for exiting employees', *Training*, 36(10), 28.

Bertua, C., Anderson, N. and Salgado, J. (2005) 'The predictive validity of cognitive ability tests: A UK meta-analysis', *Journal of Occupational and Organizational Psychology*, 78(3), 387–409.

Blinkhorn, S. and Johnson, C. (1991) 'Personality tests: the great debate', *Personnel Management*, September, 38–43.

Brotherton, P. (1996) 'Exit interviews can provide a reality check', *HR Magazine*, Spring, 45–50.

Buckley, M., Norris, A. and Wiese, D. (2000) 'A brief history of the selection interview: may the next 100 years be more fruitful', *Journal of Management History*, 6(3), 113–26.

CIPD (2004a) *Factsheets: Graphology. Induction*. London: CIPD.

CIPD (2004b) *Recruitment, retention and turnover survey*. London: CIPD.

CIPD (2005) *Factsheets: Psychological Testing*. London: CIPD.

CIPD (2008) *Factsheets: Recruitment, Psychological Testing*. London: CIPD.

CIPD (2009a) *Factsheet: Assessment Centres*. London: CIPD.

CIPD (2009b) *Recruitment, retention and turnover. Annual Survey Report*. London: CIPD.

Conway, J., Jako, R. and Goodman, D. (1995) 'A meta-analysis of inter-rater internal consistency and reliability of selection interviews', *Journal of Applied Psychology*, 80(5), 565–79.

Courtis, J. (1995) 'When it's incompetent not to discriminate', *People Management*, May, 23.

Farnham, D. and Pimlott, J. (1995) *Understanding Industrial Relations*. London: Cassell. Chapter 9.

Farnham, D. and Stevens, A. (2000) 'Developing and implementing competence-based recruitment and selection in a social services department', *International Journal of Public Sector Management*, 13(4), 369–82.

Fletcher, C. (1992) 'Ethics and the job interview', *Personnel Management*, March, 36–9.

Fletcher, C. (1993) 'Testing time for the world of psychometrics', *Personnel Management*, December, 46–50.

Fletcher, C. (1998) 'A deciding factor', *People Management*, 26 November, 38–40.

Fletcher, C. and Anderson, N. (1998) 'A superficial assessment', *People Management*, 14 May, 44–6.

Fowler, A. (1991) 'An even handed approach to graphology', *Personnel Management*, March, 40–2.

Fowler, A. (1996) 'How to: use games and choose winners', *People Management*, June, 42–3.

Fowler, A. (1997) 'How to select and use psychometric tests', *People Management*, 25 September, 45–6.

Fowler, A. (1998) 'Role rehearsal', *People Management*, 11 June, 52–5.

Goss, D. (1994) *Principles of HRM*. London: Routledge.

Gunter, B., Furnham, A. and Drakely, R. (1993) *Biodata: Biographical indicators of business performance*. London: Routledge.

Hackney, M. and Kleiner, B. (1994) 'Conducting an effective selection interview', *Work Study*, 43(2), 8–13.

Harel, G., Arditi-Vogel, A. and Janz, T. (2003) 'Comparing validity and utility of behaviour description interview versus assessment centre ratings', *Journal of Managerial Psychology*, 18(2), 94–104.

Harvey-Cook, J. and Taffler, R. (2000) 'Biodata in professional entry-level selection: statistical scoring of common format applications', *Journal of Occupational and Organizational Psychology*, 73, 103–18.

Herzberg, F. (1959) *The Motivation to Work*. New York: John Wiley.

Incomes Data Services (2002) 'Assessment Centres', *IDS Study 735*. London: IDS.

Incomes Data Services (2003) 'Recruitment Practices', *IDS Study 751*. London: IDS.

Incomes Data Services (2004) 'Psychometrics – a guide to suppliers', *HR Studies plus*. London: IDS.

IRS (2003) 'Psyching out tests', *Employment Review 787*, 43–8.

IRS (2003) 'Sharpening up recruitment and selection with competencies', *Employment Review 782*, 42–8.

IRS (2003) 'Testing times for selectors', *Employment Review 769*, 32–8.

Kransdorff, A. (1995) 'Exit interviews as an induction tool', *Management Development Review*, 8(2), 37–40.

Kwiatkowski, R. (2003) 'Trends in organisations and selection: an introduction', *Journal of Managerial Psychology*, 18(5), 382–94.

Leighton, P. (2000) 'Don't ask don't tell', *People Management*, 8 May, 42–4.

Lievens, F., van Dam, K. and Anderson, N. (2002) 'Recent trends and challenges in personnel selection', *Personnel Review*, 31(5), 580–601.

Lord, W. (1994) 'The evolution of a revolution', *Personnel Management*, February, 65.

Macan, T. (2009) 'The employment interview: A review of current studies and directions for future research', *Human Resource Management Review*. Doi: 10.1016/j.hrmr.2009.03.006.

McHenry, R. (1997) 'Tried and tested', *People Management*, January, 32–7.

McHenry, R. (2003) 'How to make use of psychometrics', *People Management*, 17 April, 52–3.

Pickard, J. (1996) 'The wrong turns to avoid with tests', *People Management*, August, 20–5.

Pickard, J. (2004) 'Testing times', *People Management*, 29 January, 43–4.

Pont, T. and Pont, G. (1998) *Interviewing Skills for Managers*. London: Piatkus.

Robertson, I. and Smith, M. (2001) 'Personnel selection', *Journal of Occupational and Organizational Psychology*, 74, 441–72.

Ryan, A.M. and Ployhart, R.E. (2000) 'Applicants' perceptions of selection procedures and decisions: a critical review and agenda for the future', *Journal of Management*, 26, 565–606.

Salgado, J. (1999) 'Personnel selection methods', in Cooper, C. and Robertson, I. *International Review of Industrial and Organizational Psychology*. London: Wiley.

Salgado, J. and Lado, M. (2000) 'Validity generalization of video tests for predicting job performance ratings', *Annual Conference of the Society for Industrial and Organizational Psychology*, New Orleans, LA.

Shackleton, V.J. and Newell, S. (1991) 'Management selection: a comparative survey of methods used in top British and French companies', *Journal of Occupational Psychology*, 64, 23–36.

Sisson, K. (1994) *Personnel Management*. Oxford: Blackwell.

Smith, M. (1994) 'A theory of the validity of predictors in selection', *Journal of Occupational and Organizational Psychology*, 67, 13–31.

Smith, M., Gregg, M. and Andrews, D. (1989) *Selection and Assessment*. London: Pitman Publishing.

Smith, M. and Robertson, I.T. (1993) *The Theory and Practice of Systematic Staff Selection*. Basingstoke: Macmillan.

Stairs, M., Kandola, B. and Sandford-Smith, R. (2000) 'Slim picking', *People Management*, 28 December, 28–30.

Stansfield, M. and Day, J. (1998) 'A rewarding experience or just sheer torture? A study of participant experience of advanced selection techniques', *Career Development International*, 3(6), 252–9.

Sternberg, R. (1998) 'Survival of the fit test', *People Management*, 10 December, 29–33.

Thornton, G, and Gibbons, A. (2009) 'Validity of assessment centres for personnel selection', *Human Resource Management Review*. Doi: 10.1016/j.hrmr.2009.02.002.

Toplis, J., Dulewicz, V. and Fletcher, C. (2005) *Psychological testing: A manager's guide*. London: CIPD.

Turban, D.B., Forret, M.L. and Hendrickson, C.L. (1998) 'Applicant attraction to firms: influences of organization reputation, job and organizational attributes, and recruiter behaviors', *Journal of Vocational Behavior*, 52(1), 24–44.

Welch, J. (1996) 'Recruiters face up to the moral imperative', *People Management*, June, 16.

Wood, R. and Baron, H. (1992) 'Psychological testing free from prejudice', *Personnel Management*, April, 34–9.

ASSIGNMENTS AND DISCUSSION TOPICS

1 Argue the case for and against the removal of personal information, such as age, gender, ethnic origin and family or marital circumstances, prior to the screening and shortlisting of applicants for employment.

2 Consider the extent to which your organisation validates the selection methods used and make recommendations on improving the validation process.

3 Review the extended application form statements illustrated in Exhibit 7.4. Consider jobs in your organisation and comment on the extent to which this type of approach could be used in the application form. Give examples of specific questions for a particular job.

4 Critically evaluate each of the components of the recruitment and selection system in your organisation with reference to Exhibit 6.1 and either justify their use or make recommendations for improvement.

5 Design, develop and pilot a work sampling selection technique for a job of your choice.

6 Here are examples of statements used in food retailing to test the suitability of applicants for employment as retail assistants. The work involves serving customers and replenishing stock, and employees are expected to be flexible about the areas in which they work and the hours that they do. Applicants are required to respond to each statement with a yes or a no.
    (a) I find it easy to change from one routine to another.
    (b) People say I am a very sociable person.
    (c) I do not enjoy lots of detail in my work.
    (d) People say I am organised.
    (e) When I join a company, I like to stay for quite a few years.
    (f) I sometimes find it hard to cope with new things.
    (g) People say I have quite a temper.
    (h) I give myself plenty of time to get to work, so there's never any chance of being late.
    (i) Untidy rooms bother me.
    (j) I would rather do the same things in a job than swap around.
    (k) If the money is good, I would take just about any job.
    (l) When I am with bosses, I don't mind saying how I feel about something.
    (m) Sometimes I find it hard to keep smiling.
    (n) When I start something I always see it through to the end.
    (o) People have sometimes said I live in a world of my own.
    (p) I spend a lot of time going out with friends.
    (q) I enjoy work for its own sake, not just for the wages.

(r)   Quite often I leave things unfinished and move on to something else.

(s)   People have told me I'm thorough in my work.

(t)   I would prefer to work the same hours every day.

What qualities are being assessed and how legitimate and effective is the test? Critically evaluate this battery of test questions using the dimensions of face validity, construct validity, concurrent validity, predictive validity, reliability, the motivation to give the right answers and methods of assessing the results.

7   *Impact validity* in relation to the selection process is defined as 'the extent to which a measuring instrument has an effect on a subject's psychological characteristics'. Applicant perceptions are influenced by the following factors: the acceptability of the selection techniques being used including the perceived relevance of any questions, the characteristics and interpersonal skills of the recruiter/s, the speed, perceived fairness and user-friendliness of the recruitment and selection process, the extent of the opportunity to demonstrate suitability for the job, the nature of the job itself and the extent of the information provided by the organisation. Test each of these factors for their impact on applicant perceptions of the desirability of working for your organisation.

8   Review the pre-engagement process in your organisation through brainstorming, first, information which needs to be collected from employees and, second, information which needs to be given to prospective employees. How should this be communicated?

9   Consider the elements of induction outlined in this chapter. To what extent are they present in your organisation? How can your induction processes be improved?

10 Who should conduct exit interviews, what questions should be asked and what should be done with the information collected?

Chapter 8

Managing Diversity

LEARNING OUTCOMES: TO BE ABLE TO

- Examine and critically review the concept of diversity
- Critically review the business benefits of diversity in the workplace
- Explain the nature of discrimination and the way in which the UK law affords protection against unlawful discrimination in the workplace
- Evaluate the framework of equal pay legislation and develop processes for the review of equal pay practice within the workplace

THE MANAGING DIVERSITY CONCEPT

The managing diversity concept challenges the traditional equal opportunities approach by focusing on the individual rather than on disadvantaged or under-represented groups. The primary managerial concern, therefore, is on harnessing the advantages to be gained from a diverse workforce through maximising the achievement of all employees and not just those covered by discrimination legislation. Traditional equality of opportunity initiatives have focused on disadvantaged groups, on target setting, on positive action and on seeking to remedy past discrimination. It can be argued that this fosters the development of a compliance-based approach rather than an added-value, business approach and may indeed hinder rather than facilitate the achievements associated with managing a diverse workforce. While the law may be an important lever and enabler in changing practice when it comes to discrimination, it has not delivered on its objective of eliminating discrimination in the workplace.

Defining diversity

The CIPD (2005b) identifies the differences between the traditional equal opportunities and managing diversity approaches with:

> Equal opportunities being externally driven [by legislation], is viewed as operational, costing money, group focused, process focused, with an ethical, moral and social basis. Whilst diversity is internally driven, strategic, providing pay back to the business, individual focused, outcome focused, with a clear business basis.

Workforce diversity, and its benefits to organisations, has been under significant scrutiny within the business world for many years (Cox and Blake, 1991; Ross and Schneider, 1992; Harung and Harung, 1995; Kandola and Fullerton, 1994 and 1998; Cornelius and Gagnon, 2000; The European Commission, 2003; Anderson and Metcalf, 2003) and according to the CIPD (2005a) 'managing diversity is central to good people management'. The CIPD (2008) define diversity as 'valuing everyone as an individual – valuing people as employees, customers and clients'. Managing diversity includes recognising the value of all employees and making employment decisions based on objective, job-related criteria rather than on the personal characteristics of the individual.

The inclusive philosophy of managing diversity is not a collection of management initiatives, it is a driving force for change. The war for talent continues to test organisations that are seeking to maintain or improve their competitive position in the market and that recognise that recruiting and retaining talent is the key to success. Diversity is about inclusion, not exclusion, it is about valuing the contribution of everyone, not about seeking protection for those groups identified by legislation as having 'protected characteristics'. All people are different; it is the capturing of that difference, and creating an environment where diverse talent can flourish that will enable organisations to maximise their human resources, and enhance their competitive position. Managing diversity is a way that an organisation expresses its values and beliefs and it needs to permeate the behaviour of all employees.

Many organisations have moved from having equal opportunities policies focused on remedying past discrimination to having diversity statements which say something about organisational values. However, these statements need to be converted from rhetoric into action, and herein lies the challenge. Examples of value statements in

Exhibit 8.1 demonstrate that some organisations retain remnants of their equal opportunities approach. According to CIPD (2008):

> In order for the management of diversity to have a higher profile in the UK, raising public awareness is vital. It should not marginalise people who cannot be labelled according to the law. Rather it is about everybody because everyone is different; it should be based on making information about the business case coherent and robust. And, through the provision of easily accessible practical guidance to remove the fear and paralysis that the focus on compliance feeds on.

EXHIBIT 8.1 Diversity statements

Royal Mail – Our values

At Royal Mail, our aspiration is to create an inclusive culture where everyone feels valued and respected, and where discrimination, harassment, bullying and prejudice will not be tolerated. We recognise that all employees have a responsibility to treat each other fairly and with respect, no matter what their race, gender, sexuality, disability or religious beliefs. Only if all our people feel valued and respected will they be motivated and committed to help us achieve our goal. We believe that recognising and celebrating the diversity in our workforce is key to delivering an inclusive culture where everyone feels valued and respected. We promote values, behaviours and working practices which recognise and value the difference between people, releasing their potential, enhancing performance and delivering improved services to customers. We recognise that different people have different needs, and are able to contribute in different ways. Diversity is about understanding and influencing workplace attitudes and culture, and focuses on individual skills, contributions and potential. (www.royalmail.co.uk)

Microsoft Corporation – Diversity Mission Statement

At Microsoft, we think of the business case for diversity as having three components: talent, customers and innovation.

Talent: Microsoft seeks to attract and retain the best and brightest employees. This enables us to gain a competitive advantage in the new emerging markets.

Customers: If we truly want to have a compelling value proposition for our customers, we must understand the rich diversity of our customer base.

Innovation: We work to build innovative products for an increasingly diverse customer base by using the diverse talents, ideas and perspectives of our employees.

Microsoft strives to understand, value and incorporate the differences each employee brings to the company so that we can build the greatest multicultural workplace in the technology industry and reflect the growing diversity and inclusion of our communities and the global market. (www.microsoft.com)

The business case for managing diversity

The CIPD (2005a) indicates that:

> The jury is still out on the business case for diversity – we are on the nursery slopes regarding the management of diversity and the ways in which it can improve business performance. The challenges in managing diversity are great.

Anderson and Metcalf (2003) examined the evidence and analysed a range of academic studies on the business benefits of diversity and their conclusions indicate that narrow interpretation, and differences in definition, organisational goals and operational contexts make it difficult to draw reliable conclusions from these studies. They point to the complexity of the evidence of business benefits, contending that there are many types of diversity such as social category; age, race, and gender; the informational; education, function and contract type; and value diversity including personality and attitudes; and they argue that more work is needed to identify causal links between the management of diversity and the outcomes for the business. The external business environment is constantly changing and organisations need to maximise the contribution of everyone in the workforce to achieve competitive advantage. The state of the psychological contract is a key factor in encouraging employee engagement and well-being and a positive approach to diversity, where employees feel valued and respected, is an important aspect of a healthy psychological contract (Guest and Conway, 2004).

The EU report (2003) prepared by the European Commission concluded that 'the evidence of business benefit was substantial'. An interesting finding from this study is the identification of a link between organisational commitment and *perceptions* of business improvements which include stronger cultural values within the organisation, the enhancement of corporate reputation, the recruitment and retention of highly talented people, increased levels of motivation and efficiency among the existing workforce and enhanced customer satisfaction. The Commission also point to the importance of measurement and action, stating that 'what gets measured gets done'. However, they also concede that 'hard evidence' to really enhance the argument for the business case and return on investment for diversity is 'yet to be proven'.

The CIPD (2005b) discussed the way in which the Kaplan and Norton balanced scorecard can provide a framework for the management and measurement of diversity and suggests eight propositions for a *diversity balanced scorecard*.

1 Diversity in employment promotes cost-effective employment relations
2 Diversity enhances customer relations
3 Diversity enhances creativity, flexibility and innovation in organisations
4 Diversity promotes sustainable development and business advantage
5 Diversity diminishes 'cultural relatedness'
6 Flexibility, which managing diversity fosters, needs to be financially supported
7 Diversity may jeopardise workplace harmony
8 Organisational slack and tight fit may conflict.

Propositions 1 to 4 are positive forces of diversity and 5 to 8 are negative forces. The development of this diversity balanced scorecard framework may help an organisation to determine the particular business drivers and also to identify suitable organisational measures. The CIPD (2005b) examined the three business inputs of *customer focus*, *business process improvements* and *innovation and learning*. These business inputs lead to a finance output which, the CIPD argues, contributes to building a sustainable business case for managing diversity.

Customer focus

Age-neutral policies at Aberdeen City Council encouraged applications from all age groups, leading to more positive perceptions from their customers. The partnership of Marks & Spencer and Disabled Go provided employment opportunities for more than 100 disabled people, resulting in disability training for employees and improved store access and product ranges to engage with the needs of disabled people, thus extending the Marks & Spencer customer base.

Business process improvements

Barclays Bank changed their approach to retain older workers by removing age-related barriers, by changing their practices on flexible working and retirement, and supporting staff through awareness and increased development opportunities, resulting in an increase in the over 60s who choose to remain in work to 61 per cent of that age group.

Innovation and learning

BP implemented a Mutual Mentoring Programme which paired senior executives with junior executives who are different to them. Murray (2004) explained: 'The pairings are designed to foster understanding between people of different genders and backgrounds so, for example, a junior woman might be mentoring a senior man, and executives of different national origins or ethnic backgrounds are often put together.' She goes on to state that 'BP reports that not only has the programme proved very motivating for both junior and senior staff but the sharing of understanding is leading to improved communications and decision making.'

Given the difficulties associated with developing a credible business case for diversity, the balanced scorecard framework may provide the way to move forward. Research by CIPD (2006, 2007, 2008) challenges previous thinking on managing diversity, saying, 'a new approach to the agenda of managing diversity is needed to support the new thinking or mindset about diversity and inclusion'. UK legislation has outlawed *positive discrimination* (except in clearly prescribed situations), with limited *positive action* being allowed in order to solicit increased applications from a more diverse population or to provide training to prepare under-represented groups for increased participation. There is a growing opinion that there may be a place for positive discrimination in the workplace: the CIPD (2008) assert that:

> new ways of thinking are urgently needed about what personal forms of individual differences, abilities and traits, constitute 'merit' because 'merit' is rightly the cornerstone of fairness regarding equality, diversity and inclusion. Personal characteristics are being considered not as 'irrelevant' but as factors that should be taken into account if we want to move forward on diversity and inclusion.

The CBI and the TUC (2008) report that 'promoting diversity need not be expensive, complex or a legal minefield for business' and it identifies some key ingredients for bringing about change, including leadership from senior management and employee involvement, especially through unions and other workforce representatives. TUC General Secretary Brendan Barber said at the launch of the report in June 2008 that 'The need to unlock the talents of all – to create a truly representative workforce – is even more crucial at a time of economic uncertainty. The issue is not whether business can afford to diversify the workplace, but whether it can afford not to.' The report identifies several examples of how small and large companies, through focusing on what employees and potential employees can do, rather than classifying people by their personal characteristics, have helped in addressing skills shortages in tight labour markets. Examples of the impact of diversity management on businesses were included in the report as an indication that positive outcomes ensue for organisations of any size and in any sector – *see* Exhibit 8.2.

EXHIBIT 8.2 Managing diversity in practice

RBS works with staff who become disabled to keep them in their jobs, believing that acquiring a disability doesn't remove the talent that led the bank to employ them in the first place. And hotel group IHG has found disabled staff are less likely to be off sick than their non-disabled counterparts.

Hospitality company Botanic Inns has taken the rare step in its sector to provide employees with a wide range of flexible working options, and a 24-hour advice service as well as enhanced maternity and paternity pay, resulting in lower staff turnover.

Smaller firms Beacon Foods, Oakwood Builders and Joinery, and mouse mat manufacturer Listawood believe that age, ethnicity, gender and the need for flexibility to look after children are less important than whether someone can do the job, while pharmaceutical and consumer healthcare giant GSK has worked with trade unions to end age bias in recruitment processes and retain workers with key skills beyond normal retirement age. (www.cbi.org.uk)

The discussions about diversity and its impact on business, both positive and negative, will continue to challenge many organisations, but to remain competitive, organisations need to look for contributions from the entire workforce. Rather than equal opportunities and diversity being driven by legislation and compliance they need to become embedded in what is done within the business in order to contribute to organisations where everyone feels valued, treated with respect and more likely to be engaged with the objectives of the organisation.

UK DISCRIMINATION AND EQUALITY LEGISLATION

UK discrimination legislation was enacted in a piecemeal way over a period of more than 40 years and the thrust of legislation has been aimed at protecting identified groups from discrimination. The legislation covers sex, marital status, race, ethnic origin, disability, religion or belief, sexual orientation, ex-offenders where a conviction is legally spent, and age. According to the Equal Opportunities Review (2009), employers in the UK paid out more than £6.5 million in compensation for sex, race and disability discrimination in 2008, with average awards being just over £17 000 and awards for injury to feelings being just over £6500. A summary of discrimination legislation follows, but this is to be superseded by an Equality Act, which reforms and consolidates this legislation.

Sex Discrimination Act 1975 (SDA)

The SDA made it unlawful to discriminate in employment on the basis of sex, pregnancy or marital status, except in the few cases where sex is a genuine occupational qualification (EOQ). Both women and men are afforded protection against less favourable treatment.

Race Relations Act 1976 (RRA)

The RRA has a similar framework to the SDA and made it unlawful to discriminate unfairly on the grounds of race, colour, nationality or ethnic origin. As with the SDA, there is scope for exemption when a genuine occupational requirement (GOR) exists.

Disability Discrimination Act 1995 (DDA)

The DDA conferred statutory rights and some limited protection against discrimination to people with disabilities. The DDA applies to all employment matters including selection, training, pay, promotion and dismissal. The Act defines disability as 'a physical or mental impairment which has a substantial and long-term adverse effect on a person's ability to carry out normal day-to-day activities', and requires employers to make 'reasonable adjustments' to the work to accommodate a disability. The Equality Bill maintains the disability definition.

Sex Discrimination (Gender Reassignment) Regulations 1999

The regulations amended the SDA to provide protection against discrimination on the grounds of gender reassignment. Gender reassignment is defined in the regulations as 'a process which is taken under medical supervision for the purpose of reassigning a person's sex by changing physiological or other characteristics of sex, and includes any part of such process'.

Employment Equality (Sexual Orientation) Regulations 2003

The Sexual Orientation Regulations made discrimination on the grounds of sexual orientation unlawful. Sexual orientation is defined as 'having a sexual orientation towards persons of the same sex, persons of the opposite sex or persons of the same sex and the opposite sex and includes perceptions of sexual orientation'.

Employment Equality (Religion or Belief) Regulations 2003

The regulations made it unlawful for employers to discriminate, harass or victimise on the grounds of religion or belief. Employees, applicants for jobs, contract workers and former employees are afforded protection. The regulations define religion or belief as, 'Any religion, religious belief or similar philosophical belief'. Employment tribunals will consider collective worship, a clearly defined belief system or a profound belief which affects the individual's way of life as indications of a religion or belief. In 2007 a minor change to the regulations was made to remove the requirement for 'philosophical belief' to be 'similar to' a religious belief. Concerns were expressed about a 'lack of clarity' about what would be seen as a 'philosophical belief'. However, a preliminary hearing of a case for discrimination on the basis of a profound belief in climate change which affected how the claimant lived his life was allowed to proceed (*Nicholson* v *Grainger Plc*) as it was considered that he was protected by this legislation.

Employment Equality (Age) Regulations 2006

The Age Regulations made it unlawful to discriminate in employment and access to vocational training on the grounds of age. This continues to be a complex and challenging area for employers and therefore some further explanation is provided here. Employers, training and education providers, trade unions, professional associations and the trustees of occupational pension schemes are required to avoid discrimination based on age. Employers are not able to use age as a criterion for selection for employment or promotion, except where different treatment can be objectively justified to fulfil a legitimate aim, or that the particular circumstances make it appropriate to have someone of a particular age. Compelling supporting evidence is needed to demonstrate that the age requirement is necessary. As with other discrimination legislation there will be circumstances where age is a genuine occupational requirement; for example, a person serving in a bar selling alcohol must be over 18 years of age.

EXHIBIT 8.3 Age discrimination is expensive

In 2009, a female 56-year-old NHS manager, having been encouraged by the head of department to apply for a job running breast-screening services, was rejected in favour of a colleague who was 13 years younger. When she indicated at interview that she less than four years from retirement the head of department said he did not realise she was 'so old'. The NHS manager had 38 years' experience compared to the three years' experience of the appointed colleague. Not only did she not get the job, but her grievances were not dealt with properly. She was off sick with stress, was sacked, later reinstated and then immediately made redundant. The tribunal chair said that the injury to feelings was 'as bad as it gets' and awarded compensation for injury to feelings of £33 500, and a further £5700 in aggravated damages.

Also in 2009, another case concerned the redundancy of an electronic engineer aged 59. The engineer had been employed for eight years when, following an initial redundancy consultation meeting, he was immediately excluded from the premises. Objective selection criteria were not applied, and although a suitable alternative position was available, he was not even considered for it. In deciding the compensation the Tribunal commented that 'the reality is that age discrimination exists and is likely to be highly influential in limiting his opportunities', thus identifying that older workers continue to be disadvantaged in the labour market. Consequently, the engineer was awarded £90 000.

Recruitment, selection and promotion decisions cannot normally be based on the ages of the applicant, requiring employers to ensure that procedures such as job advertisements do not contain reference to age or other wording which may imply age, such as 'young', 'energetic' or other similar descriptions. Service-related pay and benefits are used to reward loyalty, motivate and recognise experience and the regulations accommodate this, but only to a limited extent. The upper age limit for unfair dismissal protection was removed, giving those employees who are 65 years old and above, and who have continued working, the right to claim unfair dismissal. Lower and upper ages for calculating redundancy payments were removed. However, age-banded calculations were retained and service-related redundancy criteria, and therefore putatively age related, may be still be lawful where length of service is used in a measured-factors-in-combination approach when selecting for redundancy – *see* Chapter 19. The default retirement age is set at 65 years and retirement ages below this are unlawful, unless a lower age can be objectively justified by the employer. This default retirement age has been challenged in the European Courts, which referred the issue back to the High Court to decide whether the compulsory retirement age of 65 is 'objectively and reasonably justified'. However, there was to be a government review of the default retirement age in 2011, but this has been brought forward to 2010 in response to changing demographic conditions. The CIPD (2009b) welcomed this decision: 'The economic situation and panic about pension income means maintaining the default retirement age is unsustainable. In these tough times, the government has no choice but to bring this review forward to help organisations to make better use of talent, skills and knowledge of experienced older employees, but also help to supplement their diminishing pensions.' The default retirement age is likely be abolished or raised.

CASE STUDY   Review of age discrimination at Family Fitness

Family Fitness Plc is a company providing gym and fitness services in England. It has five fitness centres located throughout England which operate on a seven-days-a-week basis from 0600 to 2230 364 days a year – they close only on Christmas Day. The company employs 250 staff in total from fitness instructors and personal trainers to service and centre managers. Most of the fitness instructors, which includes swimming instructors and health and fitness instructors, are employed on a full-time basis, as are the service and centre managers. The personal trainers, bar and restaurant staff and some of the fitness instructors are employed on a part-time basis and there are some people who offer fitness classes such as Pilates and Keep Fit who are on a contract for services to provide a certain number of classes in a given period.

Family Fitness is aware of its responsibilities under the Employment Equality (Age) Regulations 2006 and has in place a small working group which reviews its diversity responsibilities holistically. The management team has tasked this group:

- to review its progress on age diversity
- to assess the business case of a more diverse age profile
- to recommend any changes to HR policies, procedures and practices that may have a positive impact.

The working group has asked for and received the following age profile of the organisation which shows that the average age of the employees in the organisation is just over 33 years with an average length of service of three years.

Post title	Age 18–20	21–25	26–30	31–35	36–40	41–45	Over 45	Vacancy	Total
Director					1	2			3
Centre manager				1	2	2			5
Section managers –									0
swimming		1	1	2	1				5
fitness classes			2	2				1	5
gymnasium			2	1	2				5
food and beverage					1	3		1	5
Fitness trainers		62	78	41	5			15	201
Administration and finance			2	4	1	2	1		10
Maintenance and cleaning				1	5	4	4		14
Total staff	0	63	85	52	18	13	5	17	253

Questions

1 Consider the data as presented and, as members of the working group, outline the issues related to the three objectives above that you feel should be addressed by the directors on the position of the organisation with respect to working towards a more age diverse workforce.

2 What factors would you consider in building the business case for a more age diverse workforce?

3 What HR policies and procedures would you review to take into account this legislation and why?

THE EQUALITY BILL 2009

The Equality and Human Rights Commission (EHRC) took over the roles of the Equal Opportunities Commission, Commission for Racial Equality and Disability Rights Commission in October 2007. The EHRC assumed the powers of the previous commissions as well as taking on the additional responsibility for policing discrimination on the grounds of sexual orientation, religion or belief, and age. In addition, the EHRC has the responsibility to promote increased understanding of equality and human rights, to challenge unlawful discrimination, to promote human rights and to encourage good relations between communities and provide advice, information and guidance across all areas of discrimination. The establishment of a single commission paved the way for an extensive overhaul of discrimination legislation, which resulted in the Equality Bill 2009. The Government Equalities Office (2008) sets out the reasons for decluttering the discrimination laws in an Equality Bill by explaining that:

> **The development of the discrimination legislation over a period of 40 years has led to legal complexity with nine major pieces of discrimination legislation, around 100 statutory instruments setting out the connecting rules and regulations and more than 2500 pages of guidance and statutory codes of practice.**

The Bill establishes the concept of **'protected characteristics'** and these are identified as: *age, disability, gender reassignment, marriage and civil partnership, pregnancy and maternity, race, religion or belief, sex*, and *sexual orientation* and protection is provided against unreasonable or unfavourable treatment through direct and indirect discrimination on the basis of a protected characteristic. It also aims to strengthen the law to enable greater equality progress. Some of its measures are familiar to UK employers, whereas others impose new and challenging duties.

Gender pay gap: Public sector employers will be required to publish information about the differences in pay between male and female employees. This obligation may also apply to private sector employers from 2013.

Secrecy clauses: These restrict employees from discussing pay with colleagues on pain of disciplinary action. This will be outlawed to promote greater openness and understanding of equality in the workplace (*see* equal pay section below).

Equality duties: Public bodies will be obligated to eliminate discrimination, harassment and victimisation in contractual relationships. This includes choice of suppliers and business partners. Private sector organisations tendering for public sector contracts will need to demonstrate transparency in achieving workplace equality.

Positive discrimination: Positive discrimination in selection is permitted in 'a genuine tiebreak situation'. If two candidates are equal in all material respects, the employer may have regard to the personal characteristics of one candidate if he or she is from a group that is under-represented in the organisation.

Discrimination by association: Unlawful discrimination or harassment will take place not only when related to the protected characteristic of the employee, but also of someone with whom the employee is connected. For example, if an employee is dismissed due to excessive absence for looking after a disabled dependent this could constitute disability discrimination against the employee even though he or she is not disabled.

Harassment by third parties: The scope of protection against harassment is extended to oblige employers to protect staff against harassment, not just from their colleagues, but also third parties such as customers and suppliers.

It will be unlawful for an employer to discriminate on the basis of a protected characteristic:

- in deciding to whom to offer employment
- in the terms on which employment is offered
- by not offering employment
- by not affording access to opportunities for promotion, transfer or training or for receiving any other benefit, facility or service
- by dismissing the employee
- by subjecting the employee to any other detriment.

Definitions of discrimination

The Equality Bill defines discrimination as potentially being direct or indirect in relation to the protected characteristics.

The Bill defines *direct discrimination* as occurring when:

13 (1)   A person (A) discriminates against another (B) if, because of a protected characteristic, A treats B less favourably than A treats or would treat others.

Examples of direct discrimination include:

- If an employer recruits a man rather than a woman because she assumes that women do not have the strength to do the job, this would be direct sex discrimination.
- If a Muslim shopkeeper refuses to serve a Muslim woman because she is married to a Christian, this would be direct religious or belief-related discrimination on the basis of her association with her husband.
- If an employer rejects a job application form from a white man, whom he wrongly thinks is black, because the applicant has an African-sounding name, this would constitute direct race discrimination based on the employer's mistaken perception.
- If an employer advertising a vacancy makes it clear in the advert that Roma need not apply, this would amount to direct race discrimination against a Roma who might reasonably have considered applying for the job but was deterred from doing so because of the advertisement.

It would appear that direct discrimination cannot be objectively justified as 'a proportionate means of achieving a legitimate aim', except in the case of age discrimination. There is special treatment of disability discrimination – see below. This replaces the definition of discrimination in previous legislation and is considered sufficiently broad to include discrimination by association, as it does not require the person being discriminated against to personally have the protected characteristic. For example, in *Coleman* v *Attridge Law*, Mrs Coleman who had a disabled child had to go to the ECJ to get a ruling that she experienced discrimination, not because she had a disability but because her child did. The Equality Bill definition will now encompass that situation, as well as *perceptions* that a person has a protected characteristic.

The Bill defines *indirect discrimination* as occurring when:

18 (1)   A person (A) discriminates against another person (B) if A applies to B a provision, criterion or practice which is discriminatory in relation to a relevant protected characteristic of B's.

18 (2)   For the purposes (of 18.1) a provision, criterion or practice is discriminatory in relation to a relevant protected characteristic if:

a)   A applies, or would apply, it to persons with whom B does not share the characteristic,

b)   it puts, or would put, persons with whom B shares the characteristic at a particular disadvantage when compared with persons with whom B does not share it,

c)   it puts, or would put, B at that disadvantage, and

d)   A cannot show it to be a proportionate means of achieving a legitimate aim.

This definition permits indirect discrimination to be objectively justified by the employer as 'a proportionate means of achieving a legitimate aim'. Exhibit 8.4 provides further

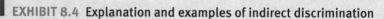

EXHIBIT 8.4 Explanation and examples of indirect discrimination

Indirect discrimination applies to all the protected characteristics, apart from pregnancy and maternity.

Indirect discrimination occurs when a provision, criterion or practice (PCP) which applies in the same way for everybody has an effect which particularly disadvantages people with a protected characteristic because they have that characteristic. Where a particular group is disadvantaged in this way, a person in that group is indirectly discriminated against if he or she is put at that disadvantage, unless the person applying the PCP can justify it. Indirect discrimination can also occur when a PCP would put a person at a disadvantage if it were applied. This means, for example, that where a person is deterred from doing something, such as applying for a job or taking up an offer of service, because a PCP which would be applied would result in his or her disadvantage, this may also be indirect discrimination. This definition replaces similar provisions in previous legislation. It applies the EU definition of indirect discrimination, replacing pre-existing domestic definitions in the Sex Discrimination Act 1975 and the Race Relations Act 1976, to ensure uniformity of protection across all the protected characteristics in all areas where it applies.

Examples

A woman is forced to leave her job because her employer operates a practice that staff must work in a shift pattern which she is unable to comply with because she needs to look after her children at particular times of day, and no allowances are made because of those needs. This would put women (who are shown to be more likely to be responsible for childcare) at a disadvantage, and the employer will have indirectly discriminated against the woman unless the practice can be justified.

An observant Jewish engineer who is seeking an advanced diploma decides (even though he is sufficiently qualified to do so) not to apply to a specialist training company because it invariably undertakes the selection exercises for the relevant course on Saturdays. The company will have indirectly discriminated against the engineer unless the practice can be justified.

explanation of this definition of indirect discrimination. It is anticipated that it will have a significant impact on disability discrimination, as it introduces the concept of indirect discrimination to disability for the first time; there remains a duty to make reasonable adjustments. However, indirect discrimination will not apply to pregnancy and maternity, because discrimination on these grounds will normally constitute direct discrimination.

The Bill singles out *disability discrimination* for special treatment by creating a new prohibition on discrimination arising from a disability. Defined as:

14 (1)   A person (A) discriminates against a disabled person (B) if:
  a)   A treats B in a particular way,
  b)   because of B's disability, the treatment amounts to a detriment, and
  c)   A cannot show that the treatment is a proportionate means of achieving a legitimate aim.

14 (2)   (This) does not apply if A shows that A did not know, and could not reasonably have been expected to know, that B had the disability.

14 (3)   It does not matter whether A had complied with a duty to make reasonable adjustments in relation to B.

In defining harassment, which was treated differently under the previous legislation, the Bill seeks simplicity and consistency:

24 (1)   A person (A) harasses another (B) if:
  a)   A engages in unwanted conduct related to a relevant protected characteristic which has the purpose or the effect in 24 (2)
  b)   A engages in any form of unwanted verbal, non-verbal or physical conduct of a sexual nature that has that purpose or effect, or
  c)   because of B's rejection of or submission to conduct (whether or not of A), A treats B less favourably than A would treat B if B had not rejected or submitted to the conduct.

24 (2)   The purpose or effect is:
  a)   violating B's dignity, or
  b)   creating an intimidating, hostile, degrading, humiliating or offensive environment for B.

24 (3)   In deciding whether conduct has that effect, each of the following must be taken into account:
  a)   the perception of B
  b)   the other circumstances of the case
  c)   whether it is reasonable for the conduct to have that effect

There are three types of harassment. The first type, which applies to all the protected characteristics, apart from pregnancy and maternity, and marriage and civil partnership, involves unwanted conduct that has the purpose or effect of creating an intimidating, hostile, degrading, humiliating or offensive environment for the complainant or violating the complainant's dignity. The second type, sexual harassment, is unwanted conduct of a sexual nature where this has the same purpose or effect as the first type of harassment. The third type is treating someone less favourably than another because they have either submitted or failed to submit to sexual harassment, or harassment related to sex or gender reassignment. The Bill extends employer liability to third-party harassment.

Victimisation is also defined in order to protect employees when asserting a statutory employment right.

25 (1)   A person (A) victimises another person (B) if A subjects B to a detriment because:
a)   B does a protected act, or
b)   A believes that B has done, or may do, a protected act.
25 (2)   Each of the following is a protected act:
a)   bringing proceedings under this Act;
b)   giving evidence or information in connection with proceedings under this Act;
c)   doing any other thing for the purposes of or in connection with this Act;
d)   making an allegation (whether or not express) that A or another person has contravened this Act.
25 (3)   Giving false evidence or information, or making a false allegation, is not a protected act if the evidence or information is given, or the allegation is made, in bad faith.

The Bill will provide protection in cases of *multiple discrimination*. The disparate nature of previous legislation meant that it was problematic to get a satisfactory legal outcome where a person with more than one protected characteristic experienced discrimination where it was difficult to determine whether the discrimination was related to, for example, race, age or sex. The Equality Bill will enable claims for multiple discrimination and this will enable direct discrimination claims to be brought in relation to a combination of any two of the following protected characteristics: age, disability, gender reassignment, race, religion or belief, sex and sexual orientation. For example, when an older woman applies for a job as a driving instructor she is told that she is unsuccessful and when she asks why, she is told it is because they do not think it is a suitable job for an older woman. They do not think she has sufficient strength to deal with a potential emergency or that she could brake quickly. She has clearly experienced discrimination, but is it because she is a woman or because she is older? Under previous legislation, she would have had to select one of the relevant Acts to bring her case.

EQUAL PAY

The Equal Pay Act 1970, as amended by 1983 Equal Value Regulations, implied a pay equality clause into the contract of employment. This position is being maintained in the Equality Bill. Men and women are entitled to the same pay for the same work, and it is unlawful to differentiate between them in terms and conditions of employment where they are employed on:

- like work (work which is the same or broadly similar)
- work rated as equivalent under a non-discriminatory job evaluation scheme
- work of equal value even where the jobs are of a totally different nature (the equal value amendment).

Therefore, in addition to similar work and jobs rated as equivalent, an employee is entitled to equal pay where a higher paid job being done by a member of the opposite sex is of equal value. Equal value is assessed using criteria such as job demands, skill, effort, responsibility and decision-making. Equal pay legislation and subsequent case law define pay very broadly and include all contractual terms. It may include base pay, occupational pension, performance- and profit-related pay, sick pay, overtime and holiday pay. For an equal pay claim to be legitimate, there must be a job comparator of the opposite sex, and the comparator must be employed by the same employer at the same place of work or at another place of work of the same or an associated employer where common terms and conditions are observed. The comparator can be a current employee or a predecessor or a successor. If the employer fails to respond to an equal pay claim, the employee has recourse to an employment tribunal.

An equal pay claim

The EHRC has produced a strategic approach to equal pay which it says 'involves a mix of legislative and non-legislative interventions'. Since the Equal Pay Act came into force the gap between average hourly rates for men and women in full-time employment has reduced from 31 per cent in 1970 to 17.1 per cent in 2008 (ONS, 2008) – see Exhibit 8.5. The EHRC paper (2009b), states that the main reasons for the gap are:

- Women's propensity to work part time, which often means a shift to lower paid work with highly qualified women often working well below their potential: 'A decade of working part-time rather than full-time will reduce women's relative hourly wages by a third' (Woodroffe, 2009).

- Occupational segregation, with women concentrated in the 5 Cs, catering, cleaning, caring, clerical and cashiering and few holding senior management positions. They quote PWC as saying that the proportion of women in senior management jobs in FTSE 350 companies fell from 38 per cent in 2002 to 22 per cent in 2008.

- Persistent undervaluing of women's work, commenting that according to the ONS (2006) 'we pay more to look after our cars (£9.72 per hour) than we do to look after our children (£7.64 per hour)'.

- Discrimination in pay systems, with a variety of factors mitigating against objectivity and transparency in pay, including the UK's unusually wide pay dispersion, low levels of TU penetration and haphazard growth in pay determination.

Educational attainment also plays a part in the lifetime earnings of women – see Exhibit 8.6.

The EHRC acknowledge that there is not full agreement on the causes of pay inequality with a recognition that it is not about overt discrimination but more about the jobs that people do. While national figures give an indication of what is happening across the country it cannot tell us what is happening within an organisation. The Equal Opportunities Commission developed the Equal Pay Review Kit and this has been retained by the EHRC. This provides employers with a structured approach to reviewing equal

EXHIBIT 8.5 Gender pay gaps, 2008: mean average of hourly pay (ONS)

Full-time pay for men	Full-time pay for women	Full-time gender pay gap
£15.54	£12.88	17.1 per cent

EXHIBIT 8.6 Gross lifetime earnings

Level of education	Man	Woman with no children	Woman with 2 children
No qualifications	731 000	534 000	249 000
GCSE	891 000	650 000	510 000
Graduates	1 333 000	1 190 000	1 171 000

Source: Rake, Davies and Joshi (2000).

pay within the organisation. Within the organisation, it is important to analyse and understand the reasons for pay differences in order to ensure that fair, lawful and business-focused organisational policies and practices exist. An employee can take a claim to an employment tribunal. If the tribunal decides that the work is 'like work', 'equivalent work' or 'work of equal value', and the employer does not have a genuine material defence, the claim will succeed. The claimant will be entitled to equal pay and to compensation. Under the Equal Pay Act 1970 Amendment Regulations 2003, compensation was increased to six years' back pay in England and Wales and five years' in Scotland, and the time limits for bringing a claim were increased to 6 months from termination of employment. Unlike sex discrimination cases, the case of the *Council of the City of Newcastle upon Tyne* v *Allen and others* (14 April 2005, Case No. EAT 0845/04) makes it clear that in equal pay claims there is no entitlement to compensation for 'hurt feelings'.

In an 'equal value' claim an employer will need to demonstrate that the work is not of equal value because of job differences that are of 'practical importance'. A tribunal will consider the size and nature of any differences as well as the frequency with which the differences occur. For example, in the case of physical strength being required for a particular job, the tribunal will take account of the degree of physical strength required and the frequency with which that strength is exercised. In reaching a judgement, the tribunal can elect to rely on the documentary evidence provided by the parties or to visit the workplace and observe the work or to appoint an independent expert to evaluate the jobs of the claimant and the comparator. An appointed independent expert does not make the decision about whether or not the jobs warrant equal pay; this is a matter of fact to be established by the tribunal. If the tribunal decides that the jobs are not equal, the claim will fail. If a tribunal finds that the claimant is employed on like work or work rated as equivalent or on work of equal value, it does not necessarily end there, as the employer can resist the claim through providing a genuine material defence (GMD), which acknowledges that the jobs are equal but justifies the inequality in pay by a reason which is not related to sex. Indicative, but not necessarily reliable, GMD factors include:

- geographical or cost of living differences
- labour market forces
- separate collective bargaining arrangements
- differences in qualifications
- the value of other contractual terms.

Red circling, where an individual employee is on protected terms, was generally considered to be a GMD until Court of Appeal decisions in 2008 – *Redcar and Cleveland Borough Council* v *Bainbridge and others*; *Surtees and others* v *Middlesbrough*. Following a job evaluation exercise the jobs of male workers were 'red circled' to give the men time to adjust to the lower pay. The female workers successfully argued that if they had been paid the same rate as men, they too would have been entitled to this protection. Consequently, red circling can no longer be relied upon and employers will have to demonstrate that their actions are 'an appropriate and proportionate means of achieving the objective'.

Achieving equal pay in practice

In addition to meeting the legal requirement, there are sound economic reasons for ensuring equal pay:

> While the pay gap matters to women – the EOC calculated that an average woman working full time would lose an estimated £330 000 over the course of her working life, as compared to an average male – it has wider economic consequences. At a macro-economic level, the Women and Work commission estimated that closing the gender pay gap would result in an increase in GDP of £23bn.
>
> (EHRC (2009b) Equal Pay Position Paper)

In order to achieve equal pay, the Equal Pay Task Force (2001) made recommendations to the EOC. The Task Force recommendations still have resonance today. They suggest a two-stage review process to enable organisations to assess where they are in relation to pay equality. The first stage of the review focuses on the policy and asks the following questions:

1 Do you have an equal pay policy?
2 Is that policy communicated to all employees?
3 Is senior level responsibility for equal pay assigned?

4 Have your pay systems been reviewed to identify any gender gap?

5 Do you have a single job evaluation system?

If the answer is 'Yes' to all of these questions, the organisation is making progress towards achieving equal pay. If the answer to questions 4 and 5 is 'No', the organisation can have no confidence that it is complying with equal pay legislation. The second stage of the process looks for more detailed and specific analysis such as:

* Comparisons of male and female average pay in each job within your organisation.
* A clear statement of objective justification of any substantial difference in pay between men and women.
* Need for targets to be set and regular monitoring to take place.

The EHRC is tasked to work with organisations to develop measures of the pay gap between male and female pay. The EHRC (2009) is seeking to 'secure radical reform in the future and to maximise the effectiveness of the Equality Bill' through:

* bringing claims on behalf of workers
* using of hypothetical comparators where no comparator is available
* urging tribunals to use the power to make general recommendations in equal pay claims
* persuading organisations to publish figures showing the numbers of men and women in each pay band.

The Equality Bill will put in place a government power to require employers, with more than 250 employees, to report on the *gender pay gap*. However, there is a commitment not to use this power until 2013 and it will only be used if there is insufficient progress in equal pay reporting. The CIPD annual reward management survey (2009a) shows that more than half of employers surveyed had undertaken or were planning to undertake an equal pay review. However, this survey also reports that many employers do not acknowledge that they are at risk from equal pay claims, with some continuing to asserting that, despite not having done a review, they have no problems with gender pay disparity. The Equality Bill also addresses the issue of **pay secrecy**. Pay details will not have to be published, but it will be unlawful to restrict pay discussions between employees. The aim is to enable those working together to discuss pay and to ascertain whether there any differences in pay that are attributable to a protected characteristic. Any action taken against an employee for discussing pay will be *victimisation*. Equal pay is a significant equal opportunities and managing diversity issue and will continue to feature prominently on the HR agenda.

CASE STUDY Equal pay review at Greenacres College of Further Education

The Principal and the HR Director of Greenacres College of Further Education have been discussing the issue of equal pay and they are concerned that they may find it difficult to defend an equal pay claim if one were to be brought. They have never undertaken an audit of pay and nor can they say with confidence that they fully comply with the requirements of the equal pay legislation. The HR Director has been looking at the Equal Pay Review Kit, which was developed by the Equal Opportunities Commission in 2002, and is available from the EHRC, and they would like this to be used as the basis for a full investigation into the pay arrangements at the college.

The Equal Pay Review Kit

This exercise provides an introduction to the Equal Pay Review Kit (www.equalityhumanrights.com), and gives advice to employers on good equal pay practice. Legal information is provided for guidance only and should not be regarded as an authoritative statement of the law, which can only be given by the courts. While employers are not required by statute to carry out an equal pay review, only an equal pay review can ensure that an organisation is providing equal pay. Pay is one of the key factors affecting motivation and relationships at work. It is therefore important to develop pay arrangements that are right for the organisation and which reward employees fairly. Providing equal pay for equal work is central to the concept of rewarding people fairly for what they do. Employers are responsible for providing equal pay and for ensuring that pay systems are transparent, or easy to understand. A structured pay system is more likely to provide equal pay and is easier to check than a system that relies primarily on managerial discretion. It is important that employees know how their pay is arrived at. This is more likely to be achieved if the pay system is accepted both by the employees and by the managers who operate the system. Employers should therefore aim to secure the involvement of employees and, where appropriate, their representatives, and all levels of management, when carrying out an equal pay review.

An equal pay review

An equal pay review involves comparing the pay of women and men doing equal work, investigating the causes of any gender pay gaps and closing any gaps that cannot be satisfactorily explained on grounds other than sex. An equal pay review is concerned with an important, but narrow, aspect of sex discrimination in employment – unequal pay for equal work. It does not directly address other aspects of inequality, such as the glass ceiling, but such aspects – which may well contribute to the overall gender pay gap – may be highlighted by the review. An equal pay review is not simply a data collection exercise. It entails a commitment to put right any gender pay inequalities and this means that the review must have the involvement and support of managers with the authority to deliver the necessary changes. It is also important to involve the workforce to maximise the validity of the review and success of subsequent action taken.

The essential features of an equal pay review

Whatever kind of equal pay review process is used, the essential features are the same whatever the size of the organisation and involve comparing the pay of men and women doing equal work, explaining any equal pay gaps and closing those pay gaps that cannot satisfactorily be explained on grounds other than sex. A step-by-step guide is illustrated in Figure 8.1.

(Box continued)

Figure 8.1
A step-by-step guide
to equal pay

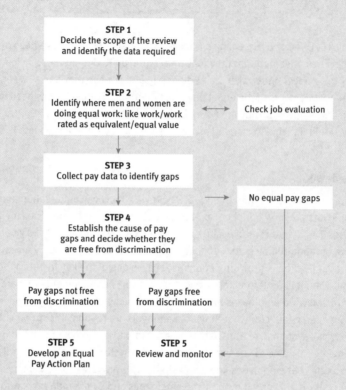

Source: The Equal Pay Review Kit is reproduced by permission of the Equal Opportunities Commission.

Questions

Consider the issue of equal pay within Greenacres College of Further Education and, based on the requirements of the Equal Pay Review Kit, address the following questions.

1   Should an equal pay review be solely limited to gender differences in pay?

2   Who would you include in an equal pay review team?

3   What indicators would you look for to determine:
    • employees doing 'like work'?
    • employees undertaking work rated as equivalent?
    • employees doing work of 'equal value'?

4   Identify the data requirements to undertake an equal pay review.

5   What factors would you include in calculating pay?

6   How might you establish the causes of pay differences between men and women and justify the reasons for them?

7   What might you include in an Equal Pay Action Plan?

WORK–LIFE BALANCE

Work–life balance has become a key issue for employers, driven by the changes in the world of work associated with 24/7 societies and increased customer expectations of service at a time and place that suits them. These changes increase the pressures on employees to work unsocial hours as well as balancing caring responsibilities for either children or adults. Retaining talented employees may also mean that employers need to recognise that employees, even those without caring responsibilities, may wish to pursue interests outside the working environment and have a good work–life balance. The CIPD (2009c) quote Clutterbuck as defining work–life balance as 'being aware of different demands on time and energy, having the ability to make choices in the allocation of time and energy, knowing what values to apply to choices and making choices'.

The CIPD factsheet (2009c) indicates that three out of four people say they are working very hard; many say they are working as hard as they can and could not imagine being able to work any harder. Changes in technology have allowed some work to be done anywhere and at any time and while there are benefits to be derived from remote working, it has also made the worker more accessible. This increased accessibility may increase work-related stress, absenteeism and labour turnover. Work–life balance issues are not only concerned with legal compliance, but also encompass the added-value dimension of recruiting and retaining talented employees who exercise discretionary effort. Much of the focus has been on women with caring responsibilities and 'family friendly' working arrangements but the issue of work–life balance is wider. Employees without children and caring responsibilities want a good work–life balance. According to the CIPD (2009c), potential benefits to the business in addressing work–life balance include: increased productivity; reduced absence due to work-related stress; improved commitment and motivation; attracting talent by becoming an employer of choice. The legal requirements to protect those with caring responsibilities include:

The right to request flexible working. The Employment Act 2002 gave parents with caring responsibilities for children under 6 years of age (18 years of age for disabled children) the right to request flexible working, provided they are an employee and have the qualifying length of service of 26 weeks. From 6 April 2009, the right to request flexible working has been extended to employees with parental responsibility for children aged 16 and under. With this extension more than 4 million more parents will have the legal right to ask their employer for the right to work flexibly. The employer has a statutory duty to consider the employee's request for flexible working arrangements. The statutory procedure to be followed requires the employee to make the request, in writing, providing they have not made a request in the previous 12 months. The change requested is a permanent change and the employee does not revert to the previous working arrangements when the child reaches the age of 16 (or 18). The employer is obliged to consider the request and meet with the employee within 28 days of receiving the request. Within 14 days of the meeting, the employer must notify the employee in writing of the decision. The employee has a right of appeal if the decision goes against the request. This right in law is a *right to request flexible working*; it is not *a right to work flexibly*. Employers are increasingly recognising that there may be benefits in extending this right to request flexible working to all employees.

Maternity and paternity leave. Women giving birth are entitled to 26 weeks' maternity leave, plus an additional 26 weeks' maternity leave, making a year in total. Fathers are entitled to two weeks' paid leave, which can be taken as a single block of leave within 56 days of the birth of the child.

Adoption leave. Employees adopting a child are entitled to 26 weeks' ordinary adoption leave and 26 weeks' additional adoption leave. Only one parent can take adoption leave.

Parental leave. All employees (women and men) have the right to 13 weeks' unpaid parental leave at any time up to the child's fifth birthday, giving 21 days' notice to the employer.

Time off for dependant care. Employees have the right to take reasonable and unpaid time off to deal with family emergencies.

However, work–life balance and flexible working can be complex. There may be as many reasons why employees wish to work flexibly as there are employees, so circumstances are often different and need to be considered on an individual basis. Janman (2002) identifies the questions to be asked when looking at implementing work–life balance initiatives. First, why is flexible working being considered? It is important to look at the business outcomes and whether these can be achieved through different work patterns. Second, are there specific roles that are suitable for flexible working? This requires a systematic approach to reviewing work roles and not just automatically ruling out the possibility of working in a more flexible way. Third, is there any way you can tell if an employee is suitable for flexible working? This requires frank and honest reflection on the realities of a more flexible way of working and ensuring that employees have looked at all aspects of changing work practices. Fourth, what is the manager's role? The line manager's role is critical in making sure that the flexible working arrangements work well in practice. Fifth, is work–life balance a strategic issue? It is often seen as an operational issue in response to a request but the strategic impact is seen in the influence on the culture of the organisation. Sixth, the push from the employee and pull from the organisation are both increasing. These factors need to be identified and translated into a package of benefits for employee and employer that address the issues raised by work–life balance initiatives.

According to Hayward *et al.* (2007), the availability of flexible working has increased by 88 per cent since 2003 and although the law gives rights to parents to seek flexible working arrangements 92 per cent of employers in this survey said that they consider a request for flexible working from any employee. Attitudes to flexible working appear to be very positive with 92 per cent agreeing that 'people work best when they can balance their work and the other aspects of their life' and half stating that 'providing flexible working practices improved customer service'. According to the CIPD (2009c):

> Flexible working policies and other work–life balance practices are now becoming the norm in our workplaces, spreading out from larger organisations and the public sector. The key issue is how to implement and operate those policies in practice, to create a positive and supportive culture, and to deliver the potential benefits they offer, both in terms of competitive performance and employee well-being.

SUMMARY LEARNING POINTS

1 The business case for diversity is complex and difficult to quantify. Legal arguments appear persuasive but these often fail to deliver change within the organisation.

2 The diversity balanced scorecard may facilitate the identification and measurement of factors which enable a business case to be developed.

3 UK discrimination legislation is extensive and knowledge of the law can guide principled managerial action. However, the law has had variable impact and may result in a compliance approach to the management of diversity.

4 The Equality Bill 2009 promises to simplify and consolidate discrimination legislation and is based on the notions of direct and indirect discrimination in relation to 'protected characteristics'.

5 Discrimination can be direct or indirect or occur because of harassment or victimisation. Unlawful discrimination can be reduced through focusing only on objective and job-related criteria when making pay, selection or other people resourcing decisions.

6 Equal pay for equal work regardless of sex has the force of UK and European law. The number of variables in the pay and job equation make this a complex area and make employers vulnerable to employee claims.

7 Despite legislation dating back 40 years there continues to be a gender pay gap and equal pay at work for men and women is not yet a reality. The Equality Bill may stimulate further progress.

8 Work–life balance initiatives, supported by legislation, enable parents of children to request flexible working and employers have a duty to consider the request seriously.

REFERENCES AND FURTHER READING

Advisory, Conciliation and Arbitration Service (2006) *Age and the workplace*. London: ACAS.

Advisory, Conciliation and Arbitration Service (2009a) *Religion or belief and the workplace*. London: ACAS.

Advisory, Conciliation and Arbitration Service (2009b) *Sexual Orientation and the workplace*. London: ACAS.

Anderson, T. and Metcalf, H. (2003) *Diversity: stacking up the evidence: a review of knowledge*, Executive Briefing. London: CIPD.

Anon (2005) 'Prison Service loses equal pay appeal', *People Management*, 11 August, 11.

Arkin, A. (2005) 'Chip off the old block', *People Management*, 21 April, 32–3.

CBI and TUC (2008) *Talent not tokenism, the business benefits of workforce diversity*, CBI Human Resources Policy Directorate, www.ukcae.co.uk/pdfs/TUC-CBI-EHRC-Talent_not_Tokenism.pdf.

CIPD (2005a) *Diversity: stacking up the evidence.* London: CIPD. www.cipd.co.uk/subjects/dvsequl/general/diversity.htm.

CIPD (2005b) *Managing diversity: linking theory and practice to business performance.* London: CIPD.

CIPD (2005c) *Managing diversity: learning by doing.* London: CIPD.

CIPD (2005d) 'Discrimination and the Law: Does the system suit the purpose?' *Executive Briefing.* London: CIPD.

CIPD (2006) *Diversity in business: how much progress have employers made?* London: CIPD.

CIPD (2007) *Diversity in business: a focus for progress.* London: CIPD.

CIPD (2008) *Managing diversity and the business case.* London: CIPD.

CIPD (2009a) *Reward Management: annual survey report.* London: CIPD.

CIPD (2009b) 'Review of default retirement age', *People Management*, PM On-line, www.peoplemanagement.co.uk/pm/articles/2009/07/review-of-default-retirement-age-brought-forward.htm.

CIPD (2009c) *Work–life balance: Factsheet.* London: CIPD.

CIPD and CMI (2005) *Tackling age discrimination in the workplace.* London: CIPD.

Cornelius, N. and Gagnon, S. (2000) *Exploring diversity from an ethical perspective.* Conference paper presented at the 'Towards a Human Centred Human Resource Management' Conference, Imperial College, London.

Cox, T. and Blake, S. (1991) 'Managing cultural diversity: implications for organizational competitiveness', *Academy of Management Executive*, 5(3), 45–56.

Czerny, A. (2005) 'Age proofing will take time', *People Management*, 28 July, 13.

Davidson, M.J. and Cooper, C.L. (1992) *Shattering the Glass Ceiling.* London: Paul Chapman Publishing.

DfEE (1996) *DL70 – Disability Discrimination Act – Employment.* London: The Stationery Office.

DfEE (2000) *Towards Equal Pay for Women.* Consultation paper. London: The Stationery Office.

EOC (1997) *Code of Practice on Equal Pay.* London: Equal Opportunities Commission.

EOC (2000) *Research Findings: Attitudes to equal pay.* London: Equal Opportunities Commission.

Equality Bill (2009) London: HMSO. www.publications.parliament.uk/pa/cm200809/cmbills/085/09085_iw/09085_iw_en_1.htm.

Equal Opportunities Commission (2003) *Code of Practice on Equal Pay.* www.eoc.org.uk/PDF/law_code_of_practice.pdf.

Equal Opportunities Commission (2007) *Closing the Gender Pay Gap.* www.eoc.org.uk/.

Equal Opportunities Review (2009) *Compensation awards 2008, Parts 1 and 2.* Michael Rubenstein Publications.

Equal Pay Task Force (2001) *Just Pay.* London: Equal Opportunities Commission. The Stationery Office (TSO). www.tsoshop.co.uk.

Equality and Human Rights Commission (2009a) *Equality Bill: Parliamentary briefing*. The Stationery Office (TSO). www.tsoshop.co.uk.

Equality and Human Rights Commission (2009b) *Equal pay position paper*. The Stationery Office (TSO). www.tsoshop.co.uk.

European Commission (2003) *The costs and benefits of diversity: a study on methods and indicators to measure the cost effectiveness of diversity policies in enterprises*. Brussels: European Commission.

Government Equalities Office (2008) *Framework for a fairer future*. The Stationery Office (TSO). www.tsoshop.co.uk.

Government Equalities Office (2009) *A fairer future: The Equality Bill and other action to make equality a reality*. The Stationery Office (TSO). www.tsoshop.co.uk.

Government Equalities Office (2009) *Equality Bill – Equality Impact Assessment*. The Stationery Office (TSO). www.tsoshop.co.uk.

Government Equalities Office (2009) *Equality Bill: Assessing the impact of a multiple discrimination provision*. The Stationery Office (TSO). www.tsoshop.co.uk.

Guest, D.E. and Conway, N. (2004) *Employee well-being and the psychological contract: a report for the CIPD*. Research Report. London: CIPD.

Harper, D. (2002) 'Balancing the pay scales', *People Management*, 10 January, 17.

Harung, H.S. and Harung, L.M. (1995) 'Enhancing organizational performance by strengthening diversity and unity', *The Learning Organisation*, 2(3), 9–21.

Hayward, B., Fong, B. and Thornton, A. (2007) 'The third work-life balance employer survey', *Employment relations research series, No 86*. London: BERR. www.berr.gov.uk/files/files42220.pdf.

Hope, K. (2005) 'Holding back the years', *People Management*, 21 April, 23–30.

IDS (2004a) *Pay Report 917*. London: IDS.

IDS (2004b) *Pay Report 918*. London: IDS.

IDS (2005) *Pay Report 923*. London: IDS.

IPD (1996) *Managing Diversity – A position paper*. London: IPD.

Janman, K. (2002) 'How to improve work life balance in your organisation', *People Management*, 28 September.

Kandola, R. and Fullerton, J. (1994) 'Diversity: more than just a slogan', *People Management*, November.

Kandola, R. and Fullerton, J. (1998) *Managing the Mosaic: Diversity in action*. London: CIPD.

Meager, N., Doyle, B., Evans, C., Kersley, B., Williams, M., O'Regan, S. and Tackey, N. (1999) 'Monitoring the DDA'. *DfEE Brief 119*, May. London: The Stationery Office.

Murray, S. (2004) 'Different strokes for different folks: a case study of BP', *Financial Times, FT Report on Business and Diversity*, 10 May.

ONS (2001) *Labour Force Survey*. London: The Stationery Office.

ONS (2008) *Annual Survey of Hours and Earnings*, Office for National Statistics, November, www.statistics.gov.uk/pdfdir/ashe1108.pdf.

Pitt, G. (2000) *Employment Law*. London: Sweet & Maxwell.

Rake, K., Davies, H. and Joshi, H. (2000) *Women's incomes over the lifetime*. London: Cabinet Office.

Ross, R. and Schneider, R. (1992) *From Equality to Diversity*. London: Pitman Publishing.

Selwyn, N. (2000) *Selwyn's Law of Employment*. London: Butterworth.

Taylor, C. (2005) 'Time for an equality check', *People Management*, 11 August, 20–1.

Welch, J. (1996) 'The invisible minority', *People Management*, September, 32–4.

Woodroffe, J. (2009) *Not having it all: How motherhood reduces women's pay and employment prospects*. The Fawcett Society. www.fawcettsociety.org.uk/documents/NotHavingItAll.pdf.

ASSIGNMENTS AND DISCUSSION TOPICS

1 Critically review the diversity (or equal opportunities) policy in your organisation. Comment on its coverage and on any guidelines for implementation.

2 Design a one-day training session for managers on their responsibilities under anti-discrimination legislation. What will you include in this training session and why?

3 Critically review the diversity balanced scorecard factors proposed in the CIPD (2005b) *Managing diversity: linking theory and practice to business performance*. In small groups, identify the detailed measures which you may be able to quantify under the three inputs and the impact which they may have on the finance output.

4 Critically examine the procedures within your organisation for the response to requests to work flexibly which may be made by a parent with a child under 16 (or a disabled child under 18 years old). If you do not have a formal procedure, design one which meets legal and organisational requirements.

5 What action would you take to reduce the chance of a successful equal pay claim in your organisation?

6 Identify occupationally segregated jobs in your organisation. Compare them with regard to pay, and comment on whether any differences in pay are due to job demands or are objectively justifiable in terms of a genuine material defence.

Chapter 9

Pay, Reward and Resourcing

- Distinguish between the concepts of 'old pay' and 'new pay'

- Explain the nature of reward strategy and the total reward concept

- Evaluate the principal characteristics of graded pay, market-related pay and performance-related pay strategies

- Contingently advise management on the development of a best-fit reward strategy

INTRODUCTION

A prime objective of effective people resourcing is to have 'the right people, in the right place, at the right time, doing the right thing'. This cannot be achieved without integrated reward strategies. It is therefore appropriate to address some of the fundamentals of pay and reward, in this chapter and the next, while recognising that it is a turbulent area characterised by contextual complexity and tension. Pay and benefits, and also non-financial, intrinsic rewards, can directly influence recruitment and retention of employees and employee performance, flexibility and identification with business goals.

The broader political and economic context is important when trying to understand the strategic choices made by management in reward policies and practices. In the 1980s and 1990s Conservative governments' free-market economic policies and the promotion of enterprise cultures contributed to an ideological shift towards paying employees for performance rather than attendance and time served and in recent years lower levels of price inflation have reduced the significance of pay determination based principally on cost of living pay increases and provided greater scope for the individualisation of pay. Lower levels of unemployment up to 2009 created conditions whereby employers often had to compete for available labour and this stimulated greater interest in pay strategies which seek to ensure that employers can recruit and retain talented individuals from the available labour market supply. The recession of 2009 focused activity on constraining costs while at the same time continuing to achieve the HR and business objectives in relation to the recruitment, retention and motivation of talented employees.

Universal reward solutions remain elusive and at best the choice is one of compromise between sometimes competing reward alternatives. For contingency theorists there is no such thing as best practice in reward, only best fit.

> **Research findings have squashed once and for all any idea that there is such a thing as best practice when applied to pay systems. It is best fit that matters, and a contingency approach is the one usually adopted.** (Armstrong, 2000b)

REWARD

The approach to paying people in the UK has undergone considerable change, and the term 'reward' is increasingly being applied to contemporary pay and remuneration strategies. Reward encompasses pay, remuneration and compensation and it represents a portfolio of managerial practices where financial and non-financial elements are flexibly directed at enabling and rewarding employees who add value in the interests of competitive advantage. Reward is used as a holistic term to reflect a more dynamic and a more flexible approach. Reward is the old total remuneration concept of pay and benefits combined with non-financial recognition and motivation and applied in a contemporary HRM context.

NEW PAY AND OLD PAY

In addition to reward, the term 'new pay', originating in the USA, is in use in the UK (Lawler, 1995; Lewis, 1998; Armstrong and Brown, 2001; Armstrong and Murlis,

2004). 'New pay' and its juxtaposed stereotypical opposite of 'old pay' are concepts which are used to distinguish between contemporary and traditional reward practices. Old pay is characterised by bureaucratic salary administration, organisational hierarchy, rigid job evaluation and grading systems, incremental progression, the lack of horizontal integration with other HR activities and the detachment of pay from the strategic objectives of the organisation. The primary concerns of old pay are fairness, consistency, equity and transparency. This is arguably more compatible with the traditional organisation structures and employment relationships of the 1970s and the 1980s. In the twenty-first century old pay, it is alleged, inhibits organisational responsiveness and development in more turbulent organisational environments. New pay can be viewed as a functional adaptation to changes in the external context and increasing competitive pressures. These external influences are demanding flatter, leaner and more flexible organisational forms, and this includes new forms of reward. The prime characteristics of new pay are, first, the pursuit of the integration of pay with corporate strategy in order to achieve organisational objectives and commercial imperatives and, second, the use of pay and reward as a sophisticated lever to apply pressure to employee performance. New pay fits well with the 'people make the difference' doctrine by seeking to reward individuals in line with managerial perceptions of their worth to the organisation. Also at the heart of new pay and reward strategies is the need for the horizontal integration of reward practices with resourcing, development and employee relations strategies. This horizontal integration (joined-up HR) is necessary to increase the potency of the HR bundle and to avoid stimulating contradictory employee responses through conflicts in HR policies and practices.

New pay is focused on managing financial reward in order to 'send the right messages' about performance and corporate values to employees. The emphasis is on rewarding contribution rather than seniority or status. New pay incorporates several reward themes:

- a connection between employee pay and employee performance as a variable incentive linked to corporate objectives through a performance management process
- a market-related approach to pay and benefits to reflect the commercial worth of employees
- pay structures which are broadbanded to encourage flexibility at work and flexible deployment, and which increase line manager discretion
- a flexible benefit approach which aims to promote individual choice within a diverse workforce.

Employees are rewarded for assuming roles, displaying values, exhibiting behaviours (for example, in relation to customer orientation and quality initiatives) and pursuing performance objectives which are determined by management. An alternative title for new pay might therefore be 'business driven pay' (Armstrong and Brown, 2001). New pay is overtly managerialistic and in the absence of any regulation through employee representation promotes a unitary employment relationship. This approach has to be squared with the possibility that employees and employers have different, and sometimes competing, objectives in terms of reward. A process of listing respective employer and employee expectations of a pay strategy will reveal that the overlap of objectives is never total, raising the ethical question about the extent to which managers are obligated to acknowledge the pay and reward expectations of employees (Heery, 1996).

In the twenty-first century, managerial concern for equity and fairness in differentials and relativities may be subordinated to the flexibility and uncertainty of new pay, with 'nimble reward systems' required for corporate survival. However, in contrast to managerially-driven new pay, skills or labour market shortages empower employees to determine reward arrangements and this contextual factor clearly undermines any prescription in reward approaches. Conversely difficult economic conditions and higher levels of unemployment generate greater scrutiny of cost effectiveness and return on investment in reward strategies. There is no escape from the contingencies of the reward context (*see* Chapter 10 on reward trends).

These dichotomised concepts of old and new pay are introduced here to provide a framework for analysis and investigation, rather than to prescribe new pay as the dominant or prevalent model, although the trend does seem to be towards new pay. As with all contemporary HRM developments, new pay will have its critics and its champions, and this is best illustrated by two quotations from the 1990s which still resonate today:

> The year 2000 . . . will see the beginning of relationships between employees and organisations that help us forget the labels of disenfranchised, adversarial and 'we versus them' that are presently too common. Although new pay is not likely to be the only factor that will help us move towards a more positive future, it is clearly the only way to make employee pay a constructive catalyst for this change.
>
> (Schuster and Zingheim, 1992)

> Literature on this subject [of new pay] seems riddled with imprecise clichés, generalisations, byzantine methodological accounts and evangelical reports using the latest buzz words. (Roberts, 1997)

Research by Poole and Jenkins, reported in Taylor (2000: 14), found substantial endorsement of new pay and human resource management approaches in a survey of 909 senior managers, but less evidence of their translation into reward practices, with the researchers concluding that 'in contrast with the policies of companies, many elements of new pay do not appear to have been widely adopted in practice in British companies'. While there is clearly a momentum to the strategic integration of reward and the pursuit of a 'new pay' philosophy, rather than having reached the final pay destination organisations are on a journey towards what may become the dominant reward approach.

PAY DETERMINATION

Pay determination in essence means how pay is determined within a particular organisation – basically is it by employers or by employees or through a process of co-determination? Pay determination is increasingly unilaterally determined by management and the UK trend is towards pay for performance. Where trade unions are recognised for collective bargaining purposes then co-determination can be said to exist and this will constrain managerial prerogative to unilaterally decide pay and other terms and conditions of employment. However, this co-determination, which reflects a pluralistic approach to the employment relationship, only occurs in around one-fifth of organisations. However, it needs to be recognised that the decline in pay bargaining is largely confined to the private sector, where pay bargaining exists in only around 10 per cent of organisations. In the public sector, and reflecting higher levels of trade union membership, pay is co-determined in over three-quarters of organisations (Kersley *et al.*, 2006: 182). However, evidence from the *Workplace Employment Relations Survey* (2004) indicates that:

> By far the most common form of pay determination was unilateral pay setting by management, either at workplace or a higher level in the organisation. Seventy per cent of workplaces set pay for at least some of their employees in this way.

This reflects the growing trend, associated with contemporary HRM practices and the rise of 'new pay', where managers unilaterally assert the right to manage the pay relationship – a unitary approach to the employment relationship. In the public sector there remains a higher incidence of 'old pay' approaches with emphasis on job grades, incremental pay progression and equity, and where trade unions generally seek to retain an emphasis on transparency, equal pay and pay fairness and consequently resist attempts by management to strengthen managerial prerogative through the introduction of pay for performance strategies.

In the private sector, pay for performance is the managerial mantra and reflects this increased unilateralism in pay, because performance judgements and the selective allocation of pay are principally managerially determined. Performance pay is often referred to as variable pay because worker pay varies according to a managerial judgement of performance or contribution. Basically employee performance is rewarded through increased pay and rewards. Thus, although fairness is a feature in employers' decisions to deploy variable pay, it is used primarily to 'extract greater effort from employees and to increase employees' motivation and commitment to organisational goals' (Kersley *et al.*, 2006: 189). It is apparent that pay, in being related to employee performance, seeks to achieve the strategic alignment of employee effort and performance with managerially determined organisational objectives. Marsden (2004: 130–31) argues that the employer interest in variable performance-related pay, in preference to co-determination in pay, is motivated by the managerial desire:

> to make their organisations more responsive to more competitive and faster changing markets by devolving decision-making and relying more heavily on employee initiative.

REWARD STRATEGY

In essence, reward strategy involves the organisation in thinking ahead to set a strategic course which aligns the reward practices with the business direction, expressed by Armstrong and Brown (2001) as:

> a business focussed statement of the intentions of the organisation concerning the development of future reward processes and practices which are aligned to the business and human resource strategies of the organisation, its culture and the environment in which it operates.

Armstrong (2005) defines reward strategy as 'the alignment of the reward policies and practices with the business and HR strategies of the organisation, its culture and its environment, providing a set of goals and a declaration of intent as to what the organisation wants to reward, and how critical reward issues will be addressed'. Mercer (2004) draws attention to the need to balance three perspectives – the employer, employee and cost perspectives. The employer perspective involves achieving a reward strategy which fosters the knowledge, competence and behaviours necessary for business success; the employee perspective involves ensuring that the reward strategy offers a compelling value proposition; and the cost perspective is to deliver a reward strategy which incurs costs that are affordable and sustainable. Clearly one of these perspectives may be the initial driver of a reward strategy review, but ultimately it is achieving the right balance of these three perspectives that will enable the organisation to drive competitive advantage. According to Lewis (2001), 'the reward orthodoxy which has arisen in recent years argues that business strategy . . . determines the behaviours employees need to demonstrate for that business strategy to be implemented effectively. These behaviours may, in part, be delivered by the reward strategy.' In this context the purpose of reward strategy is clear: it is an HR tool to be used to generate desired employee performance and behaviours in the pursuit of business goals and therefore the key objective is one of alignment with the business strategy – *see* Figure 9.1. Indeed the top reward strategy priority in each of the CIPD's annual reward surveys from 2002 to 2009 was to use reward to support the achievement of business goals (CIPD, 2009b).

This sequential approach to reward strategy assumes the rational development of business strategy and is quite deterministic. It fits with a unitary employment relations perspective which extends managerial prerogative in reward decisions. Collective representation and the extent to which employees are to be partners in determining the reward strategy, through some form of co-determination, will influence the reward outcomes, articulated by White and Druker (2000) as:

> The 'good for business case' should be questioned for the same reasons that a unitarist approach to HRM is challenged – namely that there are different interests at play within the business and they cannot all be subsumed so easily in the pursuit of business goals.

This existence of different interests at play and different levels of managerial prerogative is demonstrated by different responses to the question asked at a CIPD Reward Conference – *What are you doing about aligning your reward strategy with business*

Figure 9.1 Reward strategy – vertically integrated, deterministic and unitarist

objectives? The answers are revealing. First, from a train operating company: *What, with ASLEF and RMT, we wouldn't even try.* Second, from the NHS: *We are revising our reward strategy but it is important that we work in partnership with the trade unions, we want them on board and if it takes more time then so be it.* Third, from a British telecommunications company: *We will invite the trade unions to meetings and explain what we are going to do and we hope they will agree, but if they don't we will impose it anyway.*

The CIPD reward management survey (2009b) reports that nearly one-half of organisations have developed, or are in the process of developing, a reward strategy aligned to business needs, with this figure increasing to nearly two-thirds for large employers. The principal reward strategy objective, identified in the survey, is business related with the primary aim being to ensure that the reward strategy supports the achievement of business goals. This is achieved through the alignment of the reward strategy and the business strategy so that they are mutually reinforcing and vertically integrated. This CIPD survey evidence supports the trend of reward strategy within a contemporary HRM approach being increasingly directed at encouraging employee behaviours and performance which promote and enable the achievement of organisational objectives. This is illustrated by an increasingly typical reward strategy statement, in this case from a multinational organisation:

> **The reward strategy aims to use the full range of rewards – pay, bonus, shares, benefits and recognition – to recruit and retain the best people and to encourage and reward achievement where actions and behaviours are consistent with corporate values.**

A reward strategy therefore aims to, first, ensure that employee rewards are driven by organisation needs and not historical practices; second, articulate core principles in relation to what is valued, recognised and rewarded by management; third, ensure a coherent direction for reward and other HR practices to prevent mixed messages for employees; and, fourth, establish responsibilities and accountabilities for reward management. The managerial rationale for having a reward strategy is therefore to clarify organisational values, to provide a coherent sense of purpose and to promote a consistency between employee results and behaviour and key organisational goals. The Royal Bank of Scotland usefully articulates the impact of strategic reward as:

- Expressing what the organisation values and being prepared to pay for what it gets from employees.
- Providing a sense of purpose and direction.
- Integrating with business and HR strategy.
- Valuing people according to their contribution.
- Being driven by a total reward philosophy.

By way of further examples, Glaxo-Wellcome, as a world leader in pharmaceutical research and knowing that long-term investment is needed for survival at the top, has a reward strategy of paying salaries at the upper quartile level to attract, develop, motivate and retain quality research staff. Dow Chemicals has a strategy to recognise the quality of performance of both employees and the business. Textron uses rewards to support a strategy of employee flexibility through skills-based pay while Whitbread Beer Company and Vauxhall both use rewards to encourage initiative and innovations.

TOTAL REWARD PHILOSOPHY

Having established that reward is a holistic term and that organisations are in pursuit of the integration of reward practices with business objectives through having reward strategies, it is appropriate now to explore the concept of total reward because this is exerting considerable influence on approaches to contemporary reward. Total reward consists not only of pay (discussed in this chapter) and financial benefits (discussed in the next chapter) but also encompasses non-financial benefits. This is best illustrated in diagrammatic form, and Figure 9.2 exposes three non-financial reward clusters: work–life balance; recognition, development and self-actualisation; and the work environment and the work itself. Non-financial benefits are also described as intangibles, in contrast to the tangible rewards of pay and financial benefits, and are principally intrinsic. These intrinsic and intangible benefits are referred to as non-financial because there is not necessarily a direct and quantifiable cost to the organisation, as there is with pay and financial benefits.

Wright (2004) defines total reward as viewing 'pay and benefits as only one part of the reward picture, bringing in other aspects that affect the quality of an individual's working life – for example, learning and development opportunities, work environment, leadership styles and employee involvement'. Armstrong and Stephens (2005) define 'the conceptual basis for total reward as that of configuration or bundling, so that different reward processes are interrelated, complementary and mutually reinforcing'. As a consequence total reward strategies are vertically integrated with the business objectives and complementary to other contemporary HR practices. The CIPD reward management survey (2008) reported that 25 per cent of organisations had adopted, or were in the process of adopting, a total reward approach, with higher proportions in private sector organisations and larger employers. Armstrong's total reward components (2005) are the financial rewards of base pay, contingent pay and benefits and the non-financial rewards of learning and development, the work experience, achievement, recognition, responsibility, autonomy and growth. The application of non-financial reward includes:

- Redesigning work to provide greater variety, identity, significance, autonomy, discretion and feedback, together with concern with the health of the physical and psychological work environment.

- Providing symbolic rewards where appropriate; for example, the recognition aspects of 'employee of the month' designation, badges, citations; and creating a managerial culture of positive feedback, praise and recognition.

Figure 9.2 Total reward dimensions

Financial rewards = pay and benefits (tangible)	Work–life balance
Recognition, development and self-actualisation	The work environment and the work itself

- Investing in people as a reward through facilitating access to training and development and opportunities to engage in new learning and experiences in the workplace.
- Providing flexible work patterns, greater time sovereignty for individuals and wellness activities.

Why total reward?

The principal reason for adopting a total reward approach is the opportunity to recognise that employees come to work for more than money. Armstrong and Stephens (2005) put this in unequivocal terms: 'the notion of total reward says that there is more to rewarding people than throwing money at them'. The employer goals of recruiting and retaining talented employees who engage in high performance and exercise discretionary effort are therefore facilitated through recognising the needs of the whole person. Thompson (2002) states that the benefits accruing 'from a total reward scheme are easier recruitment of better quality staff, reduced wastage from staff turnover, better business performance and the enhanced reputation of the organisation as an employer of choice'. Armstrong and Brown (2005) argue that:

> the significance of pay as a means of attracting, retaining and providing tangible rewards to people is not to be underestimated. It is important to get it right – much harm can be done by getting it wrong. But as a means of generating long-term commitment and motivation, pay has to be regarded as only part of the whole. It is the non-financial rewards that will ultimately make the difference.

All of this makes it sound like 'a magic bullet' – solve all your HR problems with total reward! It is, of course, not quite like that, as all of the above writers recognise, and as a consequence total reward is best viewed as a contemporary approach to managing employee reward rather than the final solution. It all comes down to using reward strategically, being responsive to the consumerist world of employment, through employer branding and the pursuit of becoming an employer of choice, and enhancing the attractiveness of the 'value proposition' to employees. In other words, recognising that individuals have differing needs and that rewards need to be customised for 'reward consumers'. Ultimately it is a question of how organisations best package their total reward offer to achieve the strategic reward objectives, and what total reward does is to expose a range of options and the potential for a holistic approach. An employer of choice will exploit the potential of non-financial rewards, as well as the pay and benefits.

Organisations can achieve success with a total reward approach to make up for an inability to offer the highest salaries. The Eden Trust has pioneered a range of innovative benefits, including on-site yoga, podiatry and massages. High-performing employees are nominated for one-off bonuses, vouchers for the Eden Project shop, or a one-to-one lunch with Eden's chief executive. Workers are also entered into a draw to take an extra week's annual leave. Total reward makes working for Eden rewarding but not only through the pay packet. Organisations should perhaps not be afraid to try new things when it comes to total reward, and consider a range of intrinsic and extrinsic rewards. Cambridgeshire County Council has adopted a total reward strategy. It overhauled every aspect of pay and benefits including terms and conditions, childcare vouchers, training and flexible working. It also communicates the range of rewards on offer, both financial and non-financial, to all employees. The HR director states that 'reward and recognition are part of our strategic approach to managing people and the move has reaped considerable benefits. For example, average sick absence rates amongst the 18 000 employees fell from 10 days to 6 days, employee satisfaction improved considerably, staff turnover for key roles also fell and recruitment for difficult posts has been easier.' At Land's End, the mail-order clothing retailer, total reward covers the whole of the employment relationship from financial rewards through to to pride, appreciation, challenging work and fun, leader relations and involvement. A further example is provided in Exhibit 9.1. This broad definition of total reward resembles much of contemporary HR management but places an emphasis on the delivery of rewards, with a key role for front-line managers.

EXHIBIT 9.1 Total reward and talent management at Yahoo!

Everyone at Yahoo! is talent but there are three types of special talent. Special talent is identified through the consideration of 'winning behaviours', 'competencies' and 'engagement' and allocated to one of three categories, which in turn influence their pay.

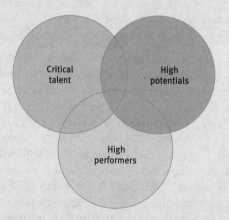

- Critical talent represents the organisation's **'winners'** and they are paid in the upper quartile
- High performers are the **'stars'** and are paid in quartiles three and four.
- High potentials (HIPOs) are the **'future'** and defined as those who are likely to perform in the top 25 per cent when promoted, and are paid in quartile three.

In addition to competitive pay at the top end of the market and stock options, flexible benefits and non-financial rewards are deployed to manage talent effectively. Non-financial rewards include superior development opportunities, work–life balance considerations, opportunities for excitement and innovation in the job, recognition awards and organisational 'fame'.

Source: CIPD Reward Conference 2008.

PAY STRATEGIES

This section of the chapter focuses on specific **pay** strategies and an awareness of the principal pay strategies is a prerequisite to informed organisational choice. The three principal pay strategies are:

1 Graded pay based on job evaluation and incremental progression
2 Market-related pay
3 Performance-related pay.

Each of these pay strategies is exposed but the extent to which each is implemented will be constrained by, first, the existing pay arrangements; second, the desired reward strategy values; third, the extent of any co-determination of pay; and, fourth, affordability. It is acknowledged that there are few pure reward strategies of each type and that in reality pay strategies are hybridised to get the best fit. However, it is useful to identify and explore the characteristics of each of the three pay strategies in order to promote understanding and the exercise of informed choice. In essence graded pay reflects *the relative worth* of an employee, relative to the importance of the job that an employee does; market-related pay reflects *the commercial worth* of an employee, in relation to the value of the employee in the labour market; and performance-related pay reflects the *individual worth* of an employee, in relation to the perceived desirability of an individual's performance and behaviours from a managerial perspective. Each of these pay strategies is addressed in turn, but it is useful to recognise that each of the three strategies, in having different but desirable objectives, leads to some tensions and to hybridisation of pay strategies. Can you attribute each of the three pay strategies in 1, 2 and 3, above, to the circles in Figure 9.3?

Figure 9.3 Multiple employer pay objectives lead to the hybridisation of pay strategies

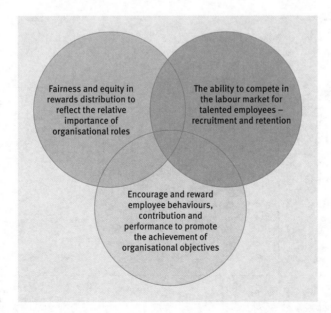

GRADED PAY AND JOB EVALUATION

Graded pay and incremental progression

Graded pay structures are developed following a process of formal or informal job evaluation – see below. The output from this job evaluation process is a distribution of jobs based on their ranking or points rating (Figure 9.4) and decisions need to be taken about how these jobs will be clustered. Traditional graded structures cluster jobs in narrow pay bands with some overlapping of the grades. The number of grades will depend on the organisational structure, with a tall organisational structure generating more grades, while a flatter structure will require fewer grades.

Each job grade will have an associated pay band and the width of the band needs to be sufficient to allow for adequate incremental increases. It is typical for the percentage width of the pay band to be larger for more senior jobs to reflect the greater range of responsibilities. The bandwidth of each grade can vary from 20 per cent in the lower grades, for example pay ranging from £15 000 to £18 000, to up to 50 per cent at the top of the structure, for example pay ranging from £40 000 to £60 000. Where the pay is to be market related the midpoint of the band can represent the median positioning in the labour market. A narrow banded graded pay structure produces a high number of grades and this can reduce organisational flexibility because of the reduced scope for pay enhancement, and as a consequence less scope for individual progression and development. A narrow graded pay structure is therefore less likely to integrate with a reward strategy of flexibility and continuous employee development. Graded pay structures enable employees to progress incrementally through the steps within the grade band based on length of service. Each year the employee receives an annual increment until the top of the scale is reached. The underlying premise is

Figure 9.4 Graded pay structure

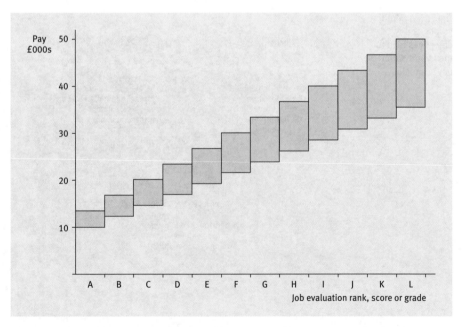

that the longer an employee spends in a job, the greater the acquisition of skills and knowledge – incremental progression therefore rewards experience. If the job does not change or the job-holder does not move to a higher grade job there is no scope for further pay increases above the annual award. Incremental pay progression within a graded pay structure is therefore consistent with a strategy that rewards loyalty and commitment to the organisation, but is less consistent with a strategy which focuses on flexibility and rewarding performance. Traditionally, graded pay is the structure deployed in the public sector, although increasingly public sector organisations are using a hybrid model that has elements of graded incrementalism, but also includes elements of performance measurement and market-related supplements in order to achieve multiple pay strategy aims.

Graded pay structures have the advantage of being transparent; everyone knows the grades and the monetary values assigned to the grades and in principle everyone on that grade will receive the same salary if they have been with the organisation for the same length of time. In the twenty-first century there continues to be a freeing up of traditional structures to allow more managerial discretion and consequently new employees may start part-way up the grade. However, this can lead to problems because the new employee reaches the top of the scale sooner and may become demotivated by the lack of opportunity for pay progression. Control of the total pay bill is more straightforward in graded structures with incremental progression because the numbers in each grade are determined by the organisational structure and therefore the costs are known. Financial control is based on the assumption that employees join the organisation and natural wastage or internal promotion will move employees out of grades before they reach the top of the grade, or shortly afterwards. This movement up and out of the grade provides a mechanism for controlling costs on or about the midpoint of the grade. This may happen in a dynamic labour market, but in a static labour market with lower staff turnover, costs increase as more employees reach the top of the grade. An example of this was the devolving of school budgets from Local Education Authorities. Staff budgets were devolved and funded on the basis of the midpoints of the approved grade distribution for the school, and not on the basis of actual staff costs. A school with a high number of long-service staff, who were at or near the top of the grade, immediately had a funding problem as the devolved staff budget would not meet the actual pay bill. As a consequence newly qualified teachers became a financially attractive proposition at the expense of more experienced teachers.

Graded pay structures with incremental progression provide managerial challenges. First, grade boundaries may be rather arbitrary and it can be difficult to accurately grade jobs on the grade boundaries. Second, incremental progression based on time served lacks direct motivational potency because each employee receives the annual increment, although individuals are motivated to achieve their objectives for a variety of reasons. Third, the potential rigidity of narrowly banded structures constrains an organisation seeking structural change, a greater emphasis on teamworking or greater work flexibility.

The pursuit of reward strategies aligned to business objectives is contributing to some decline in narrow banded grade structures based on incremental progression. In addition, the privatisation of public utilities, the change to agency status of many public sector organisations and 'best value' is generating greater managerial freedom to make changes to existing graded pay structures. One change that enables greater flexibility is broadbanding.

Broadbanding

Broadbanding means taking several job grades and forming them into one band with the result that graded pay structures feature fewer grades, perhaps 4 or 5 instead of 10 to 15, and broader bands. The CIPD (2005b) defines broadbanding as:

> the compression of a hierarchy of pay grades or salary ranges into a small number of wide bands, typically four or five. Each of the pay bands therefore spans the pay opportunities previously covered by several separate pay ranges. The focus is on lateral career movement within the bands and on competence growth and continuous development.

Broadbanding emerged in the USA in the 1990s and although its application may be increasing it may remain inappropriate for some organisational structures. Organisations most suited to the introduction of broadbanding are those that have delayered, and become leaner and flatter. Organisations where promotion opportunities have declined and the need for flexibility and multi-skilling have increased are more likely to benefit from the flexibility and managerial discretion which is inherent in broader bands. Limited opportunities for promotion may mean that employees are resistant to lateral development opportunities if the consequence is a detrimental effect on pay. Broadbanding aligns the reward strategy with other HR strategies which encourage lateral career movement. Broadbanding gives the manager greater freedom to reward the willingness to move and to acquire new skills; as Reissman (1995) puts it, 'broadbanding helps to eliminate the obsession with grades and instead encourages employees to move to jobs where they can develop their career and add value to the organisation'. Armstrong and Brown (2001) summarise the potential benefits of broadbanded pay structures as:

- increasing flexibility in pay management
- reducing bureaucracy
- rewarding lateral development and continuous improvement
- clarifying career paths
- responding to the changing nature of work and employee expectations
- enabling greater line management involvement in pay determination.

A move from narrow bands to broad bands presents challenges because employees in lower grades may be concerned that promotion opportunities have disappeared, while those in the higher grades may perceive that their job has been devalued. Broadbanding enables lateral job moves to be viewed by the employee as an opportunity for self-development and by the employer as an opportunity to enhance workforce skills. Broadbanded pay is therefore concerned with more than just pay:

> Broadbanded and job family structures are no longer treated simply as vehicles for delivering pay and are often seen as being complementary to competence and career development policies. The main aim is to provide information on development opportunities and career paths that, as part of a performance management process, can contribute to personal development planning.   (Armstrong, 2000b)

Job evaluation and graded pay

Job evaluation is a systematic, but not scientific, way of determining the relative worth of jobs within a graded pay structure by ranking jobs in a hierarchy. Fundamental to this process is the fact that it is the job and not the job-holder that is being evaluated.

The job-holder is then paid at the rate for the job. A formal system of job evaluation provides transparency and increases the likelihood that pay decisions will be understood and generally accepted. An analytical job evaluation scheme can also provide a defence in an equal pay claim. However, job evaluation is not without criticism. First, job evaluation assesses jobs at one point in time and if organisational change is rapid then the rank order of jobs produced may soon become outdated. Rigid job definitions may also deter employee flexibility because the job-holder may focus on the job that is described and evaluated, reducing the potential for job development. Second, the concentration on internal equity largely ignores market rates. Market supplements can be introduced to offset this market problem, but this may distort the grade structure. Third, job evaluation is time-consuming and costly to introduce and to maintain and formal systems of appeal are needed for employee regrading claims. Finally, the formality of the process and the apparent 'accuracy' of the outcome belies the fact that job evaluation relies heavily on individual judgement and the associated managerial preconceptions of the value of particular jobs, leaving the process open to charges of distortion and subjectivity.

Job evaluation schemes can be categorised as non-analytical or analytical. Non-analytical schemes make *whole job comparisons* without breaking jobs down into constituent parts. Non-analytical schemes include job ranking and job classification. Analytical schemes define or analyse the jobs using a number of factors and each job is scored against these factors. Analytical schemes include points rating and also competency-based schemes, which define, analyse and evaluate the jobs in terms of the competencies that are needed. However, this can shift the emphasis from the job to the person doing the job and therefore potentially conflicts with the fundamental precept of job evaluation, that it is the job which is evaluated and not the person doing the job.

Job ranking

This is the most simple job evaluation method. Whole jobs are compared with one another and ranked on the basis of whether one job is considered to be of more value than another. Job descriptions, or accountability profiles, are produced for all jobs within the organisation. Benchmark jobs, which are representative of the range of jobs in the organisation, are identified and ranked; other jobs are compared to the benchmark jobs and are inserted into the hierarchy based on the perceived value of the job. The process is subjective and subject to stereotyping, preconceptions and misconceptions, lacks transparency and would not provide a defence in an equal pay claim. It may be relatively easy to decide between jobs where there is a significant difference in value, but it becomes increasingly difficult to deal with subtle or small differences and the rank order produced gives no indication of the size of the differences between the jobs. However, it is a low-cost scheme which can be undertaken quickly.

Paired comparisons

A refinement of job ranking, this is an attempt to overcome some of the subjectivity of job ranking by systematically comparing each job with every other job and scoring 2, 1, or 0 in terms of whether the job is more, the same or less demanding. The output is a paired comparison score chart (Figure 9.5) which produces total scores and a ranking of the jobs.

Figure 9.5
Example of a paired
comparison score
chart

Job	A	B	C	D	E	F	G	Total	Rank
A	–	2	2	1	0	2	1	8	4
B	0	–	2	0	0	1	0	3	5
C	0	0	–	0	0	1	0	1	7
D	1	2	2	–	1	2	1	9	2
E	2	2	2	1	–	2	1	10	1
F	0	1	1	0	0	–	0	2	6
G	1	2	2	1	1	2	–	9	2

Paired comparison reduces bias and inconsistency through scrutinising every job in the organisation. However, this increases the size of the job evaluation task and is clearly only appropriate for small organisations because, for example, the calculations needed for an organisation with 100 jobs would be 4950 (X squared minus X divided by 2, where X equals the number of jobs to be evaluated). A spreadsheet can be used to speed up the process of calculation, but the task of making the judgement on the scoring remains onerous.

Job classification

This is a job evaluation method which measures jobs against predetermined classifications, grade definitions or role profiles. This in effect works in the reverse way to the job ranking and points rating in that the first task is to define the jobs or roles within the group of employees that are to be evaluated. This method is most commonly used in large bureaucratic organisations with a fairly rigid hierarchy and where there are many jobs of a particular type – for example, nurses, teachers and civil servants. A significant problem with job classification is that it is difficult to devise meaningful definitions appropriate for diverse jobs. For example, how easy is it to formulate a definition to meet the job requirements of an HR officer, a lecturer in higher education and an IT systems support manager, all of which might fall within the same grade in a single pay spine? A classic example of job classification is the nurse grading system used in the National Health Service and it works because it is restricted to one occupational group, there is a logic to it and there is a clear hierarchy of responsibility. The three stages in developing and implementing a job classification scheme are:

1 The grade definitions or role profiles have to be drawn up and agreed.
2 A job description must be produced for each job to be evaluated.
3 Each of the job descriptions is matched to the definition that most closely reflects the duties and responsibilities of the job and the appropriate grade is assigned.

This sounds relatively simple but the process is fraught with tensions, the most notable being the agreement of the grade definition. As jobs become more complex, the grading definitions become more generalised and the matching process more difficult. The 2004 NHS Agenda for Change initiative has resulted in a massive job evaluation exercise requiring all NHS jobs to be re-graded and, with appeals and salary protection arrangements for downgraded jobs, it is likely to extend beyond 2010. Higher Education Role Analysis (HERA) provided the same degree of challenge with increased pay costs, grading appeals, 'red circling' and implications for the state of the psychological contract, but it has increased managerial prerogative.

A points rating scheme

This is more complex to devise and operate, but being analytical it will potentially provide a defence in an equal pay claim, provided that the factors chosen are free from gender bias. A points rating scheme starts with the definition of a number of factors that are common to all jobs. For example, responsibility for resources, skill and knowledge, decision-making, level of education and job complexity. The factors are weighted to reflect their importance to the job and each factor is divided into a number of factor levels. Not all of the factors need the same number of levels; for example, responsibility for resources could be divided into several levels indicating responsibility for people, responsibility for budgets and responsibility for physical resources. Each job factor is scored using the factor level, adjusted by the weighting, and the scores for each factor are totalled to produce a points score for the job and to position the job relative to the other jobs. Exhibit 9.2 represents an example of a points rating job evaluation scheme. It shows the factors and their respective weightings. Each job can be judged against these factors, with the resultant score out of 1000 establishing the rank position (*see* assignment 5). Points rating is a complex process to design, implement and maintain, and consequently a disadvantage of the points rating scheme is higher administrative cost. The generation of a numerical job score also gives the impression of accuracy, but job evaluation is neither scientific nor completely accurate as subjective (human) decisions are taken at several stages of the process – at the factor stage, at the factor level stage and at the weighting stage. There are therefore several opportunities for bias and stereotyping to occur.

Competency-related job evaluation is a contemporary method which analyses job roles and the competencies required to undertake the role. In operation it is similar to the points rating method except that it is competence-related factors that are identified, levels defined and weightings allocated.

The rank ordering of jobs through job evaluation is fundamental to the development of a graded pay structure. The death knell of formal job evaluation systems predicated on the rise of performance-related pay strategies may be premature. Although job evaluation has been a declining trend in reward strategies, the link between analytical job evaluation schemes and the ability to mount an equal pay defence means that employers are reluctant to disengage from them altogether (Brown and Dive, 2009).

MARKET-RELATED PAY

Market-related pay describes a reward approach where pay and benefits policy and practice is responsive to the external labour market. It incorporates the philosophy of a particular job being 'worth' what the labour market commands at any one time – the concept of the market rate of pay. Market-related pay is based on classical economic theory, where pay decisions are influenced by market supply and demand for

EXHIBIT 9.2 Job evaluation through the points rating of job factors – an illustration of a typical public sector approach

Each job is evaluated and scored against the job factors, with the maximum points figure indicating the relative weight given to each job factor. The resultant score out of 1000 establishes the rank position, and determines the pay grade and the pay band for the job.

Job factor	Maximum points available
Communication and relationship skills	60
Knowledge, training and experience	240
Analytical skills	60
Planning and organisation skills	60
Physical skills	60
Responsibility for patient care	60
Responsibility for policy and service development	60
Responsibility for financial and physical resources	60
Responsibility for staff	60
Responsibility for information services	60
Responsibility for research and development	60
Freedom to act	60
Physical effort	25
Mental effort	25
Emotional effort	25
Working conditions	25

Points score for a job	Pay grade	Pay band – £ per annum
0–160	1	11 782 to 12 853
161–215	2	12 177 to 15 107
216–270	3	14 037 to 16 799
271–325	4	16 405 to 19 730
326–395	5	19 166 to 24 803
396–465	6	22 886 to 31 004
466–539	7	27 622 to 36 416
540–584	8a	35 232 to 42 278
585–629	8b	41 038 to 50 733
630–674	8c	49 381 to 60 880
675–720	8d	59 189 to 72 281
721 and over	9	69 899 to 88 397

Source: www.nhscareers.nhs.uk.

labour. Buyers and sellers of labour, employers and employees respectively, engage in an employment and contractual relationship through the price mechanism of pay. Where supply of labour exceeds demand this will tend to suppress levels of pay; conversely, where the demand for work or skills of a particular kind exceeds supply there will be a tendency for upward pressure on pay. In order to secure the quality and quantity of employees required, employers, as the buyers of labour, adjust pay and reward packages to reflect the 'going rate'. Market-related pay therefore focuses primarily on external relativities and is more concerned with 'commercial worth' than with establishing the 'relative worth' of jobs within an organisation. In a pure form, market-related pay gives primacy to the recruitment and retention objectives of reward strategy and implicitly subordinates concepts of fairness, equity and relative job worth.

A market-related approach enables an employer to compete more effectively for the workers it requires and it is therefore an important consideration in developing reward strategy. However, as with other types of market there is not a perfect labour market and employers cannot simplistically rely on market-related pay to deliver all pay strategy objectives. Factors to be considered include the impact on equity and fairness in the psychological and motivational equation, variations in individual performance which may need to be rewarded, the external labour market (ELM) relativities will affect internal labour market (ILM) relativities and, finally, the extent to which the organisation is able to pay the going rate. Market-related pay is therefore a question of emphasis rather than the sole basis for making reward decisions. Establishing the market rate is probably best viewed as the identification of a range of pay for a particular type of work, within which decisions can be made about organisational positioning within the range. Identifying the market rate or range therefore serves to inform wider reward decisions within a market-related approach.

Establishing and interpreting market rates

The identification of market rates for specified jobs is not an exact science because collecting labour market information (market intelligence) does not produce a single pay figure which can be mechanistically relied upon as 'the market rate'. Market intelligence provides information which can be incorporated into reward decisions – market rates are more a question of judgement than a matter of fact. However, the tracking of labour market rates of pay is a fundamental activity where the objective is to recognise the external labour market in reward policy. The collection of comparative pay data depends on comparing jobs on a like-for-like basis. The method of data collection is through surveys of like jobs in the external labour markets. In order to match jobs for survey purposes, a job title is inadequate and it is advisable to have a job description which summarises the main elements of the job, specifies the job context and also contains details of the reward package, including allowances, bonuses and other benefits. An individual market rate job profile can be produced prior to a survey (Exhibit 9.3) and it is against this organisational job profile that other jobs in the external labour market can be benchmarked for similarity, and hence give meaning to any pay comparison.

Comprehensive and accurate information will be difficult to acquire even with a job profile, but there are a number of sources which can be used for survey purposes. A survey form will capture external data more systematically (Exhibit 9.4). Survey sources include:

EXHIBIT 9.3 Market rate survey: organisational job profile (internal)

1   Job title
2   Relative position in the organisation
3   Organisational context
4   Tasks, responsibilities and accountabilities
5   Competencies, qualifications and experience
6   Pay range
    Bonuses
    Benefits
7   Date of last review

EXHIBIT 9.4 Outline survey form for collecting market rate data (external)

Organisation:
Job title: *(underpinned by a market rate survey job profile)*
Pay rate or range:
Incremental points and basis for progression:
Median pay rate:
Benefits:
• Performance-related pay
• Bonuses
• Allowances
• Weighting (e.g. London)
• Holidays
• Pensions
• Life/health insurance
• Discounts/employee purchase plan
• Car
• Other benefits

Next pay review date:
Date of survey:
Contact name, address, telephone no:

- Telephone or postal surveys of other organisations that compete in the same labour market – many organisations will be prepared to exchange pay data for mutual advantage.

- Subscription to proprietary sources of data – produced either by specialist reward consultancies or by government, for example the Annual New Earnings Survey.

- Participation in local 'salary clubs' – professional networking with HR practitioners with the aim of sharing market intelligence.

- Monitoring and analysing the pay information in job advertisements – although clearly the extent to which the advertisement data can be relied upon to reflect reality is uncertain.

- Surveying employment agencies and Job Centres – as these organisations are likely to have a finger on the pulse of local and regional labour market rates.

- Collecting pay data at exit interviews – this can be problematic to analyse because, first, obtaining accurate data may be difficult because of either employee reluctance to disclose the new pay package or employee tendency to inflate it and, second, employees frequently only change employment when a better reward package is secured, which may skew this source of data.

Market rate information sources are complementary rather than mutually exclusive and can be triangulated to generate a more reliable labour market picture.

When the raw market data has been collected it needs to be analysed and presented in meaningful ways. The main analytical techniques include determining the range of pay for a particular job, calculating the mean average, the median or mid-point to compensate for extremes in the data set, establishing upper and lower quartiles to define the market rate of the job in terms of the top 25 per cent and the bottom 25 per cent of the organisations in the survey, and generating deciles which graduate the market rate in tenths. These statistical measures, as well as making comparison easier, will also enable decisions to be made about organisation positioning within the market rate range. For example, choices need to be made about whether rewards will reflect median rates, the upper or lower quartiles or, in the case of an organisation wishing to pay the best, the top decile. Market range positioning decisions will be based on beliefs about whether or not paying more for employees buys better performance and also, and often more pragmatically, about direct financial affordability. The market rate therefore provides an important external dimension to reward and resourcing strategies.

PERFORMANCE-RELATED PAY

Although associated with 'new pay', performance-related pay (PRP) is not a new phenomenon, although in recent years PRP has received increased emphasis within reward strategies that seek alignment with corporate strategies. As long ago as 1996 Hall and Torrington stated that, 'Some attempt to relate pay to performance is the dominant feature of current reward strategies.' The CIPD reward management survey (2009) reported that around two-thirds of employers link individual progression to an assessment of employee performance and the competencies they apply in the job. PRP remains more common in the private sector, while the public and voluntary sectors are more likely to use service-related progression. As an emerging, some would say the dominant, feature in reward strategies, PRP is given comprehensive treatment in this section which examines the motivational basis for PRP, places PRP within a wider context, explores some of PRP themes, conflicts and ambiguities and discusses the role of PRP within a performance management system. Individual PRP provides the principal focus, but there is increasing organisational interest in team-based PRP, team reward, and this is also given attention. PRP is defined as follows:

> Individual PRP is the direct linkage of payment within the contract of employment to an assessment of performance based on the perceived contribution or value of the individual employee to the organisation at one point in time.

PRP has three sequential stages:

Stage 1 – the establishment of individual **performance criteria** by imposition, discussion or agreement.
Stage 2 – an **assessment of performance** against performance criteria, normally by the line manager.
Stage 3 – the **selective allocation of pay** to the assessment of performance, usually through the exercise of managerial prerogative.

First, a form of measurement needs to be established and while this may be relatively easy in some jobs such as sales or factory production, it clearly becomes more challenging for jobs with less tangible outputs – how, for example, would you measure the outputs of a police officer, a surgeon or an HR manager? In order to address this measurement challenge many organisations use one of four measures which may be combined:

- performance indicators
- acquisition or utilisation of competencies
- achievement of job objectives
- appraisal rating.

Second, having established the performance measures there needs to be a system of measuring individual employee performance against those measures. This is normally done by the employee's manager, providing the opportunity to direct employee performance so that it aligns with organisational objectives. This does of course make the performance measurement subject to the manager's judgement and hence it is a subjective measurement. This subjectivity issue, which may result in inaccurate or misdirected assessments of performance, can be addressed through articulating employee performance measurement criteria and also having a regulatory system of PRP allocation which is not only subject to parameters but also scrutiny by the manager's manager, or an HR specialist. Third, having measured employee performance a variable pay amount needs to be allocated (*see* Exhibit 9.5).

The aims of PRP include:

- linking the efforts of individuals to the needs and objectives of the organisation
- encouraging and rewarding behaviour consistent with the values of the organisation
- stimulating a performance-conscious culture through putting a performance message in the pay packet
- improving recruitment and retention capability
- increasing managerial control.

The theoretical basis for PRP

The underlying theoretical basis for PRP is motivation theory. Content theories, such as those of Maslow (1943, 1987) and Herzberg (1959), draw attention to pay as one

EXHIBIT 9.5 Performance descriptions and PRP: an illustration of performance descriptions used by a blue chip company in the IT sector for determining PRP

Rating	Description	Definition
1	A top performer	Achieves exceptional results and as a top performer clearly stands out from the rest in making a distinctive contribution linked to business objectives and is a role model for the organisation's values.
2*	Above average performer	Exceeds job responsibilities in achieving business objectives and in doing so outperforms most peers, and is constantly seeking ways to grow in scope and impact.
2	Consistently solid performer	Consistently achieves business objectives and meets job expectations; is fully reliable and demonstrates a good level of knowledge, skill, effectiveness and initiative.
3	A lower performer and needs improvement	When compared to solid performers, a lower performer: Does not fully execute all job responsibilities or executes with lower degree of results *and/or* Does not demonstrate as high a level of knowledge, skill, effectiveness or initiative. Consecutive ratings at this level are unacceptable in a high-performance culture and will require improvement to be demonstrated within a 3-month improvement plan period, after which a new rating will be determined.
4	Unsatisfactory performer	Does not demonstrate or utilise knowledge and skill required to execute against job responsibilities. Shows no improvement after consecutive level 3 ratings. Immediate, significant and sustained improvement to a solid performance level is to be demonstrated to prevent employment being terminated, subject to local legal requirements.

Performance-related pay is an annual bonus in addition to the annual review of salaries
Managerial discretion to make awards in the following ranges, subject to an overall Business Unit budget:

Rating 1 = 7 to 9 per cent
Rating 2* = 4 to 6 per cent
Rating 2 = 1 to 3 per cent
Ratings 3 and 4 = zero PRP

of many sources of human need. The satisfaction of this need can contribute to motivation at work, but the relative importance of pay as a motivator will vary with individual circumstances. More specific to PRP are the process theories of equity (Adams, 1965) and expectancy (Porter and Lawler, 1968; Lawler, 1973; Vroom, 1964) and it is useful to have an understanding of these. Equity theory is founded on the psychological concept that humans have a need to be treated fairly at work in relation to other employees. Fairness is calculated by employees, primarily subconsciously, making comparisons of the ratio of job inputs to job outputs. Inputs (*by the employee*) are effort, knowledge, skills, loyalty and flexibility, and outputs (*from the work*) are financial and non-financial rewards. Where rewards are perceived to be fair and equitable in relation to job inputs *in comparison* with other workers a state of equity exists, and according to equity theory this will contribute to and maintain motivation. Where inequity is perceived it has the potential to be demotivational. PRP in this equity context provides a mechanism for relating job outputs, in this case financial rewards, to inputs, thereby securing equity and employee motivation. Equity theory gives contemporary credence to the old concept of 'a fair day's pay for a fair day's work'.

Expectancy theory has many forms but all relate to the notion that employees will be motivated if direct relationships exist between effort, performance and reward (Kessler and Purcell, 1992). The summary expectancy model in Exhibit 9.6 is indicative of these relationships.

EXHIBIT 9.6 Expectancy theory of motivation

MOTIVATION

=

Effort to Performance relationship (E to P)

×

Performance to desired Rewards linkage (P to R)

×

The Valence – personal perceived value of the desired rewards (V)

As with equity theory some form of individual cognitive calculus (subconscious mental calculation) is assumed. First, the individual will make judgements about the probability (an expectancy) that increased effort, or decreased effort, will impact on performance levels (E to P relationship). Second, an assessment will be made of the likelihood (another expectancy) of certain levels of performance attracting a desirable reward outcome (P to R linkage). The third element is a measure of the perceived value and desirability of the rewards, termed the valence or value to the individual (V). The theoretical connection with PRP is made through an assumption that pay is a desired reward outcome, thereby creating a case for expressly linking pay to performance, in order to maintain or improve motivation. Implicit in this is the need to ensure that the reward has a high valence, which means that the PRP element of reward needs to be of sufficient value to the individual employee to be desirable. In short, if pay depends on performance then employees will apply effort in pursuit of performance in order to secure the desired outcome of more pay.

There are several obvious problems with this pay and motivation equation. First, expectancy theory assumes that pay is a desired outcome, but other desired outcomes, both intrinsic and extrinsic, in a particular situation for a given individual, need to be identified in order to determine the weight of the pay element as a motivator. Second, expectancy theory suggests that the PRP element has to be meaningful and substantive in order to acquire a high valence, but organisations may not be able to afford meaningful amounts. If the PRP element is not significant or meaningful then, according to expectancy theory, it is unlikely to make a significant contribution to the motivation equation. Third, expectancy theory is silent on what amount of money motivates. Despite these difficulties expectancy theory does provide additional insights into the relationship between pay, performance and motivation.

The emergence of PRP

As discussed elsewhere, the competitive pressure in the external environments has intensified interest in ensuring that employees add value through increased effort and focused performance. PRP is therefore a central tenet of 'new pay'. The aim is to 'put a performance message in the pay packet' and thereby induce a more performance-conscious culture. There are a number of drivers which have contributed to the emergence of PRP. First, the strategic (vertical) integration of reward is increasingly seen as an essential prerequisite for optimising organisational performance and, when explicitly linked to the achievement of organisational objectives, acts as a lever to direct individual performance to the pursuit of corporate goals. Second, the weakening of collectivism in the employment relationship, and a reduction in collective bargaining, have created a climate where it has been possible for organisations to individualise employment arrangements further through extending PRP. Third, the Conservative government in the 1980s and 1990s was concerned with injecting enterprise values into the public sector, resulting in PRP being used as a mechanism for championing values associated with flexibility, efficiency and customer orientation. This approach continued with New Labour governments. The factors contributing to the emergence of PRP are summarised in Figure 9.6.

PRP themes, conflicts and ambiguities

> Much of the HR profession has leapt on to performance related pay as the solution to the challenge of tailored reward. Two thirds of firms now have some kind of PRP scheme. Attempts to link pay to performance are fraught with difficulty – how to measure individual output in a team based environment, ensuring objective standards are applied across diverse jobs and the administrative effort of managing the scheme.
> (Reeves and Knell, 2001)

It is through an awareness of PRP themes, conflicts and ambiguities that attention can be paid to PRP design and practice; these include:

- doubts about PRP as a motivator
- PRP and teamworking – facilitator or inhibitor?
- the challenges of measuring and assessing performance

Figure 9.6 Factors contributing to the emergence of PRP

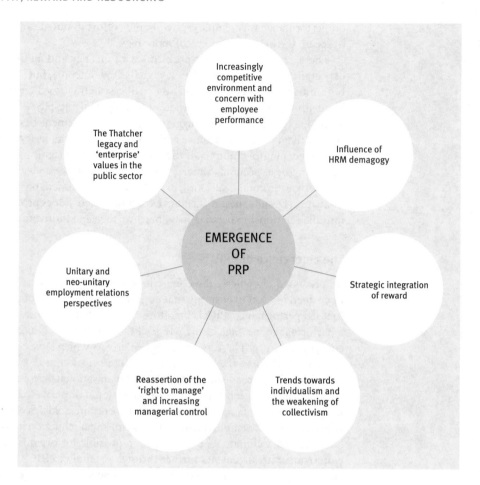

- PRP and the potential for unfair discrimination
- compatibility of PRP with a professional ethos
- the perceptions of PRP recipients.

Although in theory PRP has motivational potential, considerable research evidence reveals doubts about the motivational effects in practice. The contrary argument was summarised some time ago by Kohn (1994): 'pay is not a motivator and all that money buys is temporary compliance'. Many managers, as well as researchers, are sceptical and have low expectations about the motivational abilities of pay and PRP may actually demotivate average performers because they receive small amounts of PRP (IDS, 1993). There appears to be some disparity between what it might be necessary to pay for PRP to be motivational and the actual amount of PRP awards. Evidence from the USA suggests that PRP payments need to be set at 30 per cent of basic pay in order to improve performance. Lawson (2000) is more modest, but still suggests that a merit-based increase of the order of 10 to 15 per cent is needed to have any impact on motivation. Average pay awards in single figures, the norm in low inflation economies, do not compare favourably with these research findings. Marsden *et al.* (2001) report that while there is:

evidence of a clear incentive for those gaining above average PRP, it is likely that it is offset by a more widespread de-motivating effect arising from the difficulties of measuring and evaluating performance fairly. These motivational outcomes are found to affect workplace performance.

Another aspect of the motivational properties of PRP relates to the potential for the displacement of objectives. The process of reducing a whole job into a relatively easy to quantify collection of appraisal objectives may create an employee focus on achieving the objectives as determined, but not result in getting the whole job done effectively. The individual may focus on the specified objectives to secure enhanced payments, but may neglect other important features of the job. The motivational integrity of PRP may be more a matter of faith than fact, but Armstrong and Murlis (2005) argue that it is essential to distinguish between using PRP to manage performance (motivation) and using PRP to recognise performance (reward). If the PRP element is relatively small, it is unrealistic for managers to expect PRP to offer much incentive and to motivate.

The individual performance focus of PRP has potential to inhibit teamworking and fragment team behaviour and may conflict with team cultures. Not only is there potential for individual performance and teamwork objectives to come into conflict, but also the greater the individual dependency on other team members, the less strong is the motivational potency of PRP because much of the achievement of performance is not within the control of the individual.

These concerns are prompting increasing interest in PRP based on team or group performance, although this practice is not yet widespread. Team- or group-based pay may solve some of the problems of individual PRP, but it does throw up some new ones. An alternative strategy to team-based pay is to seek to reward individuals for demonstrating teamwork behaviours and thereby reinforce the attitudes of individuals towards teamworking.

There are fundamental challenges associated with Stages 1 and 2 of the PRP framework – establishing performance criteria and assessing performance effectively. It may be possible to do this where there is a direct and overt measurement available, as might be the case in some manual production work, but it is problematic for work which has less tangible and quantifiable outputs, as is likely in non-manual, managerial and professional occupations. In establishing and assessing performance against performance criteria there can be a tendency to measure what is easy to measure rather than what ought to be measured. An illustration of this is police effectiveness being assessed by the criteria of the incidence of crimes and of detection rates. In reality the ability of individual police officers to influence these measures is minimal, as levels of crime are attributable to much wider reasons than police performance. In any case, much police work is symbolic and therefore intangible – how is this element of performance assessed and measured (Savage, 1996)? Should teachers' and lecturers' performance be assessed on the basis of student results? – intuitively attractive, but a pause for thought will recognise that multiple factors impact on student achievement and teaching performance is only one factor. The Church of England set up a professional HR department – what performance indicators are suitable for the clergy and how should they influence pay? In addition to the difficulty of establishing meaningful performance indicators, subjectivity is an inherent feature of PRP assessment, because the interactive process between assessor and assessee is vulnerable to a whole range of perceptual errors, including recency, the halo or horns effect, projection and other forms of distortion. Workplace pressures will almost inevitably impact on the assessment process. The pressures facing managers and the perceived intrusion of formal assessments, with associated form filling, may militate against managers taking the time and trouble to compensate for subjectivity.

The linkage of PRP decisions to an appraisal system produces a tension, because the dual managerial roles of *coach* and *judge* are potentially incompatible. On the one hand employees are being asked to expose weaknesses and areas for development so that they can be coached, and on the other hand a judgement of performance, with pay implications, will take place – hardly a scenario for a full and frank discussion about how an employee can develop in order to produce an even better performance. The solution is the separation of appraisal interviews from pay discussions, but although it is possible to seek to dissolve the link between performance appraisal and pay reviews to achieve more meaningful development discussions, it is probable that total divorce is not realistic as some connection may remain in the minds of the assessor and the assessee.

PRP may discriminate unfairly against women because, in practice, it is primarily male managers who measure performance and they may tend to reward performance characterised by male values, with equal pay implications. There is concrete, if limited, evidence that the qualities associated with female workers tend to be downgraded in establishing performance criteria for PRP. The Equal Opportunities Commission (2005) suggested that discrimination may be occurring and recommends the monitoring of performance-related payments by gender. Some time ago McColgan, from the Institute of Employment Rights (1994), attributed some inequalities in pay for men and women to PRP and presents a radical view by suggesting that if employers:

> wish to avoid such tiresome and expensive [equal value] litigation [they] would do well to place performance related pay on the scrapheap of unacceptable pay practices!

It is anathema to many public servants, and others in professional occupations, to suggest that they might be motivated by pay linked to a judgement of their performance, but PRP has penetrated the health service, local authorities, the civil service, the police and education. The injection of enterprise values and governmental concern with organisational performance indicators is being translated into individual performance indicators and PRP. There is tension between the professional ethos of self-management and the managerialistic approach of PRP. Performance-related pay may fail to recognise that for professionals and public servants the psychological contract may have primacy over the economic contract – professionalism and ethics may matter more than money (Pilbeam, 1998).

Lawson (2000: 312) summarises recent research on employee perspectives towards PRP which indicate that employees are negative, or at best neutral, about PRP because they are not convinced that it motivates or that it is applied fairly. Whether or not PRP is fair is a recurring theme and employees often suspect that some form of quota operates and that 'favouritism and unfairness is endemic' (Richardson and Marsden, 1991). Although PRP is rooted in equity theory, PRP practice may be different – PRP being rhetorically fair but unfair in reality. Table 9.1 reflects the outcomes of the Marsden *et al.* (2001) 'study of large numbers of ordinary employees', and suggests that all may not be well with PRP strategies.

A number of these PRP conflicts and ambiguities are presented as dichotomies in Exhibit 9.7 in order to stimulate a debate about the right balance between PRP belief and PRP scepticism.

Table 9.1 Believing particular effects of PRP (rounded percentages)

	Agree %	Disagree/no view %
PRP is a good principle	52	49
PRP means good work is recognised and rewarded	33	66
PRP has given me an incentive to work beyond my job requirements	17	83
PRP has given me an incentive to show more initiative	18	82
PRP has made me more aware of the organisation's objectives	36	64
PRP causes jealousies among staff	67	33
PRP is bad for teamworking	46	54
Management operate a quota	61	39
PRP has made me less willing to cooperate with management	17	83

EXHIBIT 9.7 **Conflicts and ambiguities in PRP**

Cautious PRP believer – the rhetoric?	**Confirmed PRP sceptic – the reality?**
<ul><li>rewards performance at work</li><li>allows individuals to be paid according to contribution</li><li>complements performance management, empowerment and flexible working</li><li>is intrinsically fair – in theory</li><li>motivates employees</li><li>management view – performance improved</li><li>focuses effort on organisational goals</li><li>amounts are meaningful</li><li>is based on fair and objective performance measurement</li><li>should be integrated with appraisal systems</li><li>is central to the management of performance</li><li>enables managers to reward employees</li></ul>	<ul><li>pays for conformity to organisational norms</li><li>divides teams and encourages individuals to pursue selfish goals</li><li>complements rhetorical trickery and fads</li><li>creates feelings of unfairness and inequity – in practice</li><li>demotivates more employees than it motivates</li><li>recipients' view – performance not improved</li><li>has confused objectives which are difficult to evaluate</li><li>amounts are not worth the effort</li><li>performance is assessed subjectively and only on what is easy to measure</li><li>transforms the appraiser from a development coach to a judge and jury</li><li>is marginal to the management of performance</li><li>significantly strengthens the right to manage/manipulate</li></ul>

Making PRP work and PRP within a wider performance management system

Although there are conflicts and ambiguities in PRP there is also widespread application of PRP schemes and it is useful to examine opportunities to contribute to success in PRP through the dismantling of some 'myths and legends'. First, that the bad press and the executive reward debate contribute to negative PRP attitudes and need to be kept in perspective – don't throw the baby out with the bathwater. Second, assumptions that PRP can manage performance on its own are misguided because PRP is only one dimension of performance management. Third, there is potential for PRP to be used as a search and punish tool, particularly in a low-trust environment, but it is an abuse of PRP to punish failure. Fourth, the perception that PRP needs quantifiable objectives is a management by objectives hangover and should be replaced by focusing on what constitutes good performance. In relation to this, Armstrong and Brown (2001) prefer the term contribution-based pay – rewarding people for their outputs (results) *and* their inputs (competence); in other words, not only what they do but how they do it. Fifth, it is problematic to prove that PRP contributes to the bottom line, but PRP clarifies perceptions about performance and supports a performance culture. Sixth, the inflationary potential of PRP can be constrained by limiting overall budgets and although rating drift and central tendency are endemic, they can be compensated for by regularly revising rating schemes. In summary, the following are some of the conditions necessary for PRP to be an effective reward strategy:

- PRP to be integrated with holistic performance management by managers who have the willingness and the skill to manage.
- High levels of trust between the appraising manager and the employee.
- Work activity which can be measured, together with validity and reliability in the measurement of differences in individual job performance.
- A systematic assessment of performance which is not only fair in practice but is perceived to be fair by managers and employees.
- PRP amounts which are meaningful.
- Overall reward structures which are competitive so that PRP is genuinely in addition to 'normal' pay.

Exhibit 9.8 provides another illustration of the PRP decision-making process.

Team-based PRP

Interest in team-based PRP is a reaction to the potential for individual PRP to prejudice teamworking and also reflects the significance being given to teamworking in contemporary organisations. Often referred to as 'team reward' (CIPD, 2009), team-based PRP incorporates the principle of linking the pay and non-financial benefits of the individual to the performance of a working group or team. The aim is to focus effort, encourage cooperative behaviour and send the cultural message that the organisation values teamworking. While team-based PRP addresses some of the concerns about individual PRP, a number of different issues need to be appreciated and these include:

- the difficulty of identifying teams, particularly where they are transient
- the feasibility of establishing and measuring team performance through transparent criteria

EXHIBIT 9.8 Illustration of PRP decision-making process in the professional services sector

Managers make a judgement on the two dimensions of 'values, skills and behaviours' and 'achievement of business objectives'. This results in a rating which is aligned with a percentage increase in pay. Managers are guided by a forced distribution of employees in each rating category.

	Values, skills and behaviours High --------------------------------------Low		
Achievement of business objectives Low------------------------------------High	Exceptional Performance EP 1	Exceptional Performance EP 3	Strong Performance SP 6
	Exceptional Performance EP 2	Strong Performance SP 5	Needs Development ND 8
	Strong Performance SP 4	Needs Development ND 7	Needs Improvement NI 9

Rating	*Forced distribution of ratings*	*Maximum PRP percentage if standard is 3 per cent*
EP 1	10%	6.0
EP 2 and 3	20%	4.5
SP 5	40%	3.0
SP 4 and 6	20%	1.5
ND 7 and 8	7%	0.5
N 19	3%	zero

- the frequency of team PRP, whether by time period or project, and the amount of payment in relation to other elements in the reward package
- the reliance of one team on another and whether this inhibits or facilitates team performance
- the potential for dysfunctional inter-team competition, 'groupthink' and resistance to change
- the possibility of stifling individual creativity and motivation through pressure to conform to group norms
- contributions to the process of teamworking may need recognition as well as recognising team results.

It can be seen from this list that many of the issues relate to disadvantages associated with very cohesive groups and therefore some theoretical appreciation of group development and the factors which influence group effectiveness is a necessary pre-requisite to developing team reward systems.

The CIPD reward management survey (2004b) put the figure for team-based PRP at 10 to 20 per cent of organisations. Team-based PRP is an opportunity, rather than a solution, and it is probably best suited to mature, stable and well-defined working groups. Other prerequisites for team reward include scope for team autonomy, the interdependency of individual team members and teams composed of individuals who are flexible, multi-skilled and good team players. Team reward is unlikely to create a team culture on its own and requires underpinning with other teamworking initiatives. Team reward is another element in the search for perfect pay and probably needs to be applied uniquely and in appropriate conditions. There is no reason why it cannot be integrated within a reward strategy which includes other forms of individual and market-related rewards – a blended or hybrid strategy.

COMPETENCE-BASED PAY

If competencies are used in other contemporary HR areas it is logical to include them in the reward strategy. Competence-based pay systems may focus on:

- the acquisition of competencies, *or*
- the demonstration of competencies, *or*
- the extent to which competencies are used in the performance of the job.

The reward strategy needs to be explicit about which of these is being rewarded. Payment for competence acquisition may be part of a strategy to increase flexibility and multi-skilling, whereas rewarding the application of competence may stimulate better performance. A job described and evaluated in competencies offers the opportunity to use this framework for the appraisal and assessment of the job-holder, but it raises issues about the extent to which the job or the person is being evaluated. The trend in performance-related pay strategies is from a measure of inputs (how hard employees work) to a measure of outputs (how well employees have achieved their agreed objectives). Competence-based pay may be a return to the measurement of inputs, and the question then is what contribution does this make to achieving the objectives of the organisation? Competence is a fashionable concept, but should be applied discriminately, and competence-based pay needs to be complementary to the organisation's overall reward strategy (*see* Chapter 3).

PROFIT SHARING

Profit-related pay and employee share schemes are arrangements which enable employees to have a stake in the ups and downs of an enterprise; they represent financial participation by the employee. Profit-related pay involves the linkage of a proportion of employee reward to organisational profitability, while share ownership is a separate concept and involves financial investment by the employee with the prospect of dividend payment and increased share value. The aim of profit-sharing arrangements is to encourage employees to identify with and pursue the objectives of the organisation, and in return for this commitment employees share in corporate success. The effectiveness of profit sharing is difficult to evaluate because of the distance that exists between the effort of each individual employee and total corporate performance. The links between effort, performance and corporate outcomes, to use expectancy theory terms, may be too uncertain to be motivational for the individual. However, profit sharing may engender a sense of commitment, ownership and esteem and contribute to corporate cohesiveness.

Although the idea that employees should have a financial stake in their employing organisation involves potential gain and potential loss, inevitably there is employee reluctance to jeopardise a portion of pay. In practice, profit-related pay schemes have tended either to reduce the risk of loss associated with salary substitution (sacrifice) arrangements or to guarantee to make up any loss. The 'employee stakeholder investing in the business' through profit sharing is the reciprocal concept of the 'business investing in people'; both are desirable in theory but more difficult to achieve in practice.

> Employees have complex sets of attitudes and desires, and financial participation schemes have to recognise these if they are to be successful. It is probably unrealistic to expect that any one participation scheme can have a transformational effect on employees or upon the firm in which it was introduced. They have to be used in conjunction with other human resource management instruments and, if well designed, may have mildly positive effects on firm performance. (Pendleton, 2000)

Profit sharing is another imaginative reward opportunity rather than a universal solution.

CASE STUDY   Reward systems at City in the Woods City Council

City in the Woods is a unitary authority providing the full range of public services to a population of 200 000 residents in central England. The authority received unitary status with the local government reorganisation in 1997 and provides education, social services, planning, environmental and other services and employs around 2500 staff. The council's reward system is based on the traditional graded structure with the grade defining the salary range. Progression within the grade is on an incremental basis related to length of service with some discretion for the award of merit increments or one-off payments for special achievements. The one-off payments are not consolidated into pay. Employees may only progress to a different grade if they apply for and are appointed to a new job at a higher grade or if their existing job is re-graded to a higher grade. The reward structure has been simplified into one pay scale, which covers all employees on a single pay spine. The pay levels and grades are indicated in Table 9.2, overleaf. The total pay bill for the City Council is around £50 million per annum and this budget cannot be increased by more than 3 per cent.

Questions

In groups of four or five assign the following roles: department manager responsible for a staffing budget, HR business partner to advise on internal HR issues, employee representative and reward consultants and select one of the following reward strategies.

(Box continued)

1 Individual performance (appraisal-related) pay.
2 Team-based pay.
3 Broadbanding.

You are a working group and you have been asked to:

- critically review the current reward strategy of City in the Woods City Council
- review your selected reward strategy and fully investigate its appropriateness for the council
- prepare a strategy paper to present to the cabinet of the council, making recommendations for changes to the current reward strategy
- assess costs of implementation as far as practicable.

Table 9.2 Grades, scale points and salaries for City in the Woods City Council

Grades and scale point	Salary	Grades and scale point	Salary	Grades and scale point	Salary
Grades 1–3		18	£16 929	Grades 10–14	
4	£11 742	19	£17 561	33	£27 472
5	£12 017	20	£18 202	34	£26 157
6	£12 189	21	£18 867	35	£28 839
7	£12 581	22	£19 356	36	£29 604
8	£12 979	23	£19 926	37	£30 433
9	£13 371	24	£20 577	38	£31 324
10	£13 653	25	£21 228	39	£32 355
11	£14 535	26	£21 919	40	£33 207
12	£14 836	27	£22 648	41	£34 082
13	£15 234	28	£23 386	42	£34 950
				43	£35 821
Grades 4–7		Grades 8–9		44	£36 703
14	£15 513	29	£24 313	45	£37 526
15	£15 837	30	£25 126	46	£38 433
16	£16 216	31	£25 920	47	£39 314
17	£16 602	32	£26 685	48	£40 189
				49	£41 051

SUMMARY LEARNING POINTS

1 'New pay' is a label for contemporary reward practices which are strategically aligned with business strategy and which use pay as an HR lever on employee performance and behaviour.

2 A total reward approach utilises financial and non-financial rewards such as work–life balance opportunities, recognition, opportunities for development

and interesting work to enhance the value proposition to employees with the aim of achieving higher quality recruitment, motivation, performance and retention.

3   Graded pay reflects the relative worth of an employee, market-related pay reflects the commercial worth of an employee and performance-related pay reflects individual worth. These are sometimes competing reward strategies and often hybridised in pursuit of the best of all worlds.

4   The basis for a graded pay structure is job evaluation which provides a systematic method for the rank ordering of jobs within an organisation. Non-analytical schemes consider whole jobs and analytical schemes factorise jobs. Only analytical schemes have the potential to provide a defence in an equal pay claim.

5   The market rate of pay is the 'going rate' for a job in the labour market and is a measurement of the commercial worth of employees. Market rate surveys gather labour market intelligence which informs reward decisions.

6   An increasingly dominant feature of current reward strategies is to seek to relate pay to employee performance. While performance-related pay is an attractive concept there are conflicts and ambiguities which need to be addressed in practice.

REFERENCES AND FURTHER READING

ACAS (1994) *Job Evaluation: An introduction.* Advisory Handbook. London: ACAS.

Adams, J.S. (1965) 'Injustice in social exchange', *Advances in Experimental Social Psychology*, vol. 2. New York: Academic Press.

Applebaum, S. and Shapiro, B. (1991) 'Pay for performance', *Journal of Management Development*, 10(8).

Armstrong, M. (1999) *Employee Reward.* London: CIPD.

Armstrong, M. (2000a) 'Feel the width', *People Management*, 3 February, 34–8.

Armstrong, M. (2000b) *Employee Reward.* London: CIPD.

Armstrong, M. (2005) *Employee Reward.* London: CIPD.

Armstrong, M. and Baron, A. (1995) *The Job Evaluation Handbook.* London: IPD.

Armstrong, M. and Brown, D. (2001) *New Dimensions in Pay Management.* London: CIPD.

Armstrong, M. and Brown, D. (2005) 'Reward strategies and trends in the United Kingdom: The land of diverse and pragmatic dreams', *Compensation Benefits Review*, 37, 41–53.

Armstrong, M. and Murlis, H. (2004) *Reward Management.* London: Kogan Page.

Armstrong, M. and Murlis, H. (2005) *Reward Management: A handbook of remuneration strategy and practice.* London: Kogan Page.

Armstrong, M. and Ryden, O. (1997) *The IPD Guide to Broadbanding.* London: IPD.

Armstrong, M. and Stephens, T. (2005) *Employee Reward Management and Practice.* London: Kogan Page.

Beaumont, P.B. (1993) *HRM: Key concepts and skills.* London: Sage.

Bradley-Hill, R. (1993) 'A two component approach to compensation', *Personnel Journal*, May.

Brown, D. (1996) 'Team rewards: lessons from the coal face', *Team Performance Management: An International Journal*, 2(2), 6–12.

Brown, D. (2005) *How to develop a reward strategy.* London: CIPD.

Brown, D. and Dive, B. (2009) 'Level pegging', *People Management*, January, 26–29.

CIPD Survey Report (2000) *Performance Pay Trends in the UK.* London: CIPD.

CIPD (2004a) *Total Reward Factsheet.* London: CIPD.

CIPD (2004b) *Reward Management Survey of Policy and Practice.* London: CIPD.

CIPD (2008) *Reward Management: annual survey report.* London: CIPD.

CIPD (2009a) *Team Reward Factsheet.* London: CIPD.

CIPD (2009b) *Reward Management: annual survey report.* London: CIPD.

Equal Opportunities Commission (2005) *Equal Pay Toolkit*, www.eoc.org.uk.

Fowler, A. (1992) 'How to design a salary structure', *Personnel Management Plus*.

Fowler, A. (1996a) 'How to design and run salary surveys', *People Management*, September.

Fowler, A. (1996b) 'How to pick a job evaluation system', *People Management*, February.

Goss, D. (1994) *Principles of Human Resource Management.* London: Routledge.

Hall, L. and Torrington, D. (1996) Paper on *Developments in the Personnel Management Function – summary of research results.* CIPD Conference.

Haslett, S. (1995) 'Broadbanding: a second generation approach', *Compensation and Benefits Review*, November/December, 27(6).

Heery, E. (1996) 'Risk, representation and the new pay', *Personnel Review*, 25(6). MCB University Press.

Herzberg, F. (1959) *The Motivation to Work.* New York: John Wiley.

IDS Study 518 (1992) *Performance Management.* November. London: IDS.

IDS Report 654 (1993) *Study Questions the Effectiveness of Performance-Related Pay.* December. London: IDS.

IDS Management Pay Review 156: Policy and Analysis (1994) *More Doubts about Performance Pay.* February. London: IDS.

IDS Management Pay Review (1996) *New Evidence on Broadbanding.* London: IDS.

Industrial Relations Services (1998) 'Pay prospects survey', *Pay and Benefits Bulletin 458*, 10–13.

IPD (1997) *Guide to Broadbanding of Pay.* London: IPD.

Johnson, D. and Johnson, F. (1997) *Joining Together: Group theory and group skills.* Boston, MA: Allyn & Bacon.

Kersley, B. *et al.* (2006) *Inside the workplace: Findings from the 2004 Workplace Employment Relations Survey*, Routledge.

Kessler, I. and Purcell, J. (1992) 'Performance-related pay: objectives and applications', *Human Resource Management Journal*, 2(3), 16–33.

Kohn, H. (1994) 'PRP does not work', *Personnel Management Plus*, May, 3.

Lawler, E. (1973) *Motivation in Work Organisations*. Maidenhead: Brooks/Cole.

Lawler, E. (1995) 'The new pay: a strategic approach', *Compensation and Benefits Review*, July/August.

Lawson, P. (2000) 'Performance-related pay', in Thorpe, R. and Homan, G. (eds) *Strategic Reward Systems*. Harlow: FT Prentice Hall.

Ledford, G. (1995) 'Designing nimble reward systems', *Compensation and Benefits Review*, July/August.

Lewis, P. (1998) 'Exploring Lawler's new pay theory through the case of Finbank's reward strategy for managers', *Personnel Review*, 29(1), 10–31.

Lewis, P. (2001) 'Reward management', in Redman, T. and Wilkinson, A. *Contemporary Human Resource Management*. Harlow: FT Prentice Hall.

Marsden, D. (2004) 'Unions and procedural justice: an alternative to the "common rule"', in Verma, A. and Kochan, T. (eds) *Unions on the 21st Century: An International Perspective*. London: Palgrave Macmillan.

Marsden, D., French, S. and Kubo, K. (2001) 'Does performance pay de-motivate, and does it matter? *LSE Centre for Economic Performance Paper 0503*. London: LSE.

Maslow, A.H. (1943) 'A theory of human motivation', *Psychological Review*, 50, 370–96.

Maslow, A.H. (1987) *Motivation and Personality*. New York: Harper & Row.

McColgan, A. (1994) 'Time for equal merit', *Personnel Today*, March.

Mercer HR Consulting (2004) *Striking the right balance: Total rewards at work*, http:www.mercerhr.co.uk/mediacenterarchive.jhtml.

Murlis, H. (1994) 'The myth about performance pay', *Personnel Management*, August, 18.

Murlis, H. (ed.) (1996) *Pay at the Crossroads*. London: IPD.

Pay and Benefits Bulletin 306 (1992) 'Merit pay in the nineties', June, 3–7.

Pendleton, A. (2000) 'Profit sharing and employee share ownership', in Thorpe, R. and Homan, G. (eds) *Strategic Reward Systems*. Harlow: FT Prentice Hall.

Pilbeam, S. (1998) 'Individual performance related pay: believers and sceptics', *Employee Relations Review*. Croners.

Porter, L. and Lawler, E. (1968) *Managerial Attitudes and Performance*. New York: Irwin.

Reeves, R. and Knell, J. (2001) 'All of the futures are yours', *The Future of Reward*. London: CIPD, 39–46.

Reissman, L. (1995) 'Nine common myths about broadbands', *HR Magazine*, 40(8), 79–86.

Richardson, R. and Marsden, D. (1991) 'Does performance pay motivate?' *A Study of Inland Revenue Staff*. London: LSE.

Roberts, I. (1997) 'Remuneration and reward', in Beardwell, I. and Holden, L. (eds) *HRM: A contemporary perspective*. London: Pitman Publishing.

Robinson, S. (1992) 'The trouble with PRP', *Human Resources*, Spring.

Savage, S. (1996) in Farnham, D. and Horton, S. (eds) *Managing the New Public Services*. London: Macmillan.

Schuster, J. and Zingheim, P. (1992). *The New Pay: Linking employee and organisational performance*. New York: Lexington.

Sparrow, P. (1996) 'Too good to be true?' *People Management*, December.

Taylor, S. (2000) 'Debates in reward management', in Thorpe, R. and Homan, G. (eds) *Strategic Reward Systems*. Harlow: FT Prentice Hall.

Thompson, P. (2002) *Total Reward: Executive Briefing*. London: CIPD.

Thorpe, R. and Homan, G. (2000) *Strategic Reward Systems*. Harlow: FT Prentice Hall.

Vroom, V.H. (1964) *Work and Motivation*. New York: John Wiley.

White, G. and Druker, J. (2000) *Reward Management: A critical text*. London: Routledge.

Workplace Employment Relations Survey (2004) DTI.

Wright, A. (2004) *Reward Management in Context*. London: CIPD.

ASSIGNMENTS AND DISCUSSION TOPICS

1 What are the characteristics of 'old pay' and 'new pay' and which characteristics can you identify in your organisation or an organisation with which you are familiar?

2 In an organisation with which you are familiar, identify and discuss the reward strategy in relation to what it is seeking to achieve and the extent to which it is aligned with the business strategy.

3 Focus on the three intangible/non-financial segments of total reward and generate a range of reward practices that could be deployed under each of the three segments. Select one example from the range you have generated and discuss how it could be implemented, what challenges managers might face and how the effectiveness of your chosen practice could be measured.

4 Assess the extent to which your organisation relates reward strategy to external labour market rates and discuss how it gathers market intelligence.

5 Using Exhibit 9.2, discuss the benefits that may accrue from the illustrated points rating scheme and identify the challenges that will need to be addressed in operationalising it. To what extent are the benefits and challenges indicative of points rating job evaluation schemes in general?

6 You have a problem in recruiting and retaining good calibre secretaries in your organisation and you are concerned that your rates of pay are less than fully competitive. What issues would you need to consider in planning to collect market rate intelligence, what would be your sources of information and how would you be able to decide if your rates of pay were competitive or not?

7 Your managing director wishes to establish closer integration between business strategy and reward strategy and she wants you to prepare a concise briefing paper in which you articulate the organisational conditions necessary for performance-related pay to be effective. What would be the content of your briefing?

8 Based on your *own personal experience and perceptions* of individual performance-related pay (PRP), complete the activity below, by circling a number for each statement. If practical, aggregate the results with a sample of students or work colleagues. In any event discuss your responses and findings in small groups – does a consensus emerge?

PLEASE CIRCLE A NUMBER FOR EACH STATEMENT

Scoring System

Strongly disagree	= 1
Disagree	= 2
Neither disagree nor agree	= 3
Agree	= 4
Strongly agree	= 5

	Strongly disagree				Strongly agree
PRP is motivational	1	2	3	4	5
PRP is effective in rewarding good performance	1	2	3	4	5
PRP helps in recruitment	1	2	3	4	5
PRP assists in the retention of valuable people	1	2	3	4	5
PRP increases management control over individuals	1	2	3	4	5
PRP encourages a performance-conscious culture	1	2	3	4	5
PRP is fair in principle	1	2	3	4	5
PRP is fair in practice	1	2	3	4	5
PRP incorporates valid and reliable measures of job performance	1	2	3	4	5
PRP inhibits teamworking	1	2	3	4	5
PRP only measures what is easy to measure	1	2	3	4	5
PRP is a good thing	1	2	3	4	5
PRP improves flexibility	1	2	3	4	5
PRP is inherently subjective	1	2	3	4	5
PRP makes financial control easier for organisations	1	2	3	4	5
PRP encourages common behaviours among employees	1	2	3	4	5
PRP enables employees to share in organisation success	1	2	3	4	5
PRP amounts are/have been meaningful to me	1	2	3	4	5
PRP improved my performance	1	2	3	4	5
PRP demotivates those who do not receive any	1	2	3	4	5
PRP performance measures were appropriate for me	1	2	3	4	5

Chapter 10

Reward, Financial Benefits and Pensions

LEARNING OUTCOMES: TO BE ABLE TO

- Evaluate the role of financial benefits within total reward strategies
- Contribute to the development of a flexible benefits approach
- Appreciate the complexity of pensions and explain the principal characteristics of state, occupational and personal pensions
- Analyse emerging and declining reward trends

INTRODUCTION

This chapter continues to explore the concept of total reward by examining financial benefits, including flexible benefits and pensions. Current reward trends are exposed because the search for perfect pay continues enthusiastically. The external context, internal organisational contingencies and the pursuit of competitive advantage are driving this search for perfection in reward strategies.

EMPLOYEE FINANCIAL BENEFITS

Armstrong (2002, originally 1996) states that the main aims of financial benefits are:

> To contribute to the provision of a competitive total reward package, to provide for the needs of employees in terms of their security, and, sometimes, their requirements for special financial help, thus demonstrating to them that they are members of a caring organisation, to increase the commitment of employees to the organisation and to provide a tax-efficient method of remuneration.

While Armstrong's definition of 15 years ago is helpful in setting the scene, in order to further distinguish business-focused HR practices from the paternalistic past it is perhaps appropriate to substitute the phrase 'members of an organisation which values its employees' for 'members of a caring organisation'. Concerns for employee welfare formed the basis of benefit package development but in contemporary organisations the focus is shifting from paternalism to the role that financial benefits can play within a total reward approach. The HR objective becomes one of integrating financial benefits with pay and with non-financial rewards to form a coherent reward strategy which stimulates employee performance and engagement. The reasons for offering financial benefits are, first, to increase the potency of the total reward package in terms of recruitment, retention and motivation, although the impact of financial benefits remains more a matter of faith than proven correlation. Second, the provision of financial benefits enhances the value proposition and contributes to the employer brand in the pursuit of becoming the employer of choice. Third, because employees in the labour market from which the employer recruits may expect a certain range of benefit provision. In examining the impact that benefits can have in employee attraction, retention and motivation, Leopold (2002) identifies the three main types of employee benefits as welfare benefits, family-friendly/work–life balance benefits and job-related benefits. Welfare benefits include pensions, life insurance and health insurance; family-friendly/work–life balance benefits include holiday entitlement, maternity, paternity, parental and other family leave, and childcare vouchers, sports, social and holiday facilities; and job-related benefits include company car provision or car allowance, loans and financial assistance, product discounts and subsidised canteens. Organisations need to appreciate what other employers are doing in order to remain competitive, and market intelligence (*see* Chapter 9) needs to generate information about competitors' financial benefit provision to inform decisions on labour market positioning.

With the cost of employee financial benefits averaging 10 to 20 per cent of total pay costs, and being as much as 30 to 40 per cent in some cases (Wright, 2004), there is a compelling argument for the active management of the benefits package to ensure that reward strategy objectives are met and value for money is achieved. Each employee benefit should be costed and assessed for the contribution it makes to specific reward strategy objectives to ensure that this element of reward is horizontally integrated with other HR strategies. A significant challenge is that the provision of a standard benefits package for all employees makes the *de facto* assumption that the valence, or perceived personal value, of the benefits package is the same for all employees, and this is clearly not the case. This suggests that an element of employee choice in financial benefits will not only recognise diverse needs but also increase the ability of the reward strategy to achieve HR objectives. It is not possible to propose an ideal benefits package but the fundamental questions for management in making benefit decisions are:

- Which financial benefits are to feature as part of total reward?
- What are the objectives of offering the selected benefits?
- What degree of choice will be available to employees?
- What is the cost to the organisation of the benefits package?
- How is the effectiveness of the benefits offer measured?

The top ten employee benefits (CIPD, 2008) in descending order are 25+ days' holiday leave, training and career development, free tea/coffee/cold drinks, Christmas party, childcare vouchers, life insurance, car allowances, health and well-being benefits, mobile phones, and enhanced maternity and paternity leave. This is quite a catholic list and it is evident that *popularity* of benefits provision is only one dimension because the potential strength of each of these in meeting reward strategy objectives is differentiated in terms of cost to employer and value to the employee. Clearly employees will become suspicious if management start messing with the benefits provisions and as a result changes in provision are constrained by the *status quo* and also the extent of co-determination.

The range of financial benefits

Employee benefits are many and varied and there is no intention to review all of the options here. A focus on the most commonly provided benefits is adopted.

The occupational pension is one of the most significant benefits provided by the organisation and valued by the employee and as a consequence this is given more comprehensive treatment later in this chapter.

Private healthcare has increased in provision and importance. It has advantages for the employer by potentially reducing the amount of sick leave taken through enabling health issues to be addressed earlier and thereby enabling the employee to return to work earlier than may have been the case. It has advantages for the employee who has access to medical provision when it is required and has greater control of treatment. It may also be valued by the employee in providing access to care that may otherwise be out of reach.

Life insurance cover may be provided as an element of the pension scheme or provided outside the scheme. Levels of cover may vary from four times annual salary for senior staff to just annual salary for less senior positions.

Severance payments are valued by employees at a time of insecurity in employment. Enhanced payments, in addition to statutory redundancy pay, are supported by the tax system to a level of £30 000.

Financial assistance can range from low interest loans to mortgage benefits. These benefits are commonly associated with the finance sector and are in effect employee product discounts. A mortgage benefit is a good retention tool, but it can present a dilemma for employees in making it difficult to leave an employer because it will impact on housing costs.

Company cars play an important role in benefit provision in the UK. A company car may be provided as a business necessity or as a perk with no job use requirement and little business mileage undertaken. The income tax implications have changed in recent years to reduce the value of the car benefit to the employee. This tax disincentive appears to be having little impact on the desirability of the car benefit perhaps because a company car is also important in defining status.

Childcare provision through nurseries and crèches will be important in the retention of women workers, although access to childcare solely by female employees is likely to be unlawfully discriminatory. Other childcare options include vouchers or enhanced payments to fund childcare for a period of time on return to work following maternity leave.

Leave entitlement is also a benefit and ranges from emergency leave to annual holiday entitlement. Entitlement to these may be affected by length of service or level within the organisation.

Additional benefits, ranging from staff discounts and luncheon vouchers to subsidised meals and sports and social facilities are available for evaluation in the context of the total reward package.

FLEXIBLE BENEFITS

Flexible, cafeteria or 'pick and mix' benefits are terms given to benefit arrangements which allow the exercise of employee choice within a total reward package. Adding flexibility to traditional benefits packages can mean anything from allowing some choice in company car value to having different levels of pension contributions, but a full-blown flexible benefits scheme will allocate a benefits allowance to each employee and allow employees to choose benefits according to preferences and lifestyle needs.

> In essence flexible benefits involve the presentation of a menu or portfolio of benefits from which employees can select according to their needs, within manageable guidelines.

Exhibit 10.1 illustrates a flexible benefits menu and within each of the elements there will be further choices available to employees. For example, pensions could be enhanced through increased contributions and a reduction elsewhere in the selected benefits, life cover could be extended to dependants, extra holidays could be bought, a car benefit could be cashed in or a better model selected. The menu provides a quasi-market where employees spend their benefits allowance. The flexible benefit approach acknowledges diversity of workforce need and circumstances and therefore has managing diversity as well as reward strategy objectives. Other potential advantages to the employer are, first, through targeting the cost and value of employee benefits (and avoiding paying for what individuals do not want) and, second, through linking available benefits with particular reward objectives. Reward objectives include, among others, recruitment, retention, motivation, offering incentives, recognising performance, equity and cost reduction. A paired comparison exercise which rates elements of the benefits package as high, medium or low against the various pay and reward objectives will be revealing about the extent to which each benefit contributes to the achievement of particular objectives (*see* end of chapter assignments). The key reasons for introducing flexible benefits are staff retention, staff motivation, enhancing recruitment, competitive pressures in the labour market, not paying for benefits that employees do not want, and the ability to recognise diverse individual needs. Flexible benefits therefore provide an imaginative opportunity to integrate reward strategy with other HR strategies, and also with corporate strategy.

EXHIBIT 10.1 Illustration of a flexible benefits menu – which would you choose?

Enhanced pension benefits	Income protection	Health assessments	Travel insurance	Learning account
Critical illness cover	Personal accident cover	Childcare vouchers	Partner life insurance	Concierge services
Personal computers	Health screening	Enhanced life insurance	Extra holiday purchase	Private medical cover
Hospital cash plan	Retail vouchers	Dental cover	Sports club subsidy	Car upgrades

Flexible benefits empower employees by enabling them to recognise the value of their benefits and to exercise some control over their own rewards. This fits with a general shift in the UK towards individual citizens accepting greater responsibility for life management, not only in employment, but also in education, health and provision for old age. Taxation and other fiscal changes have also impacted on the value and cost of providing certain benefits, for example the increasing taxation liability of company cars. Flexible benefits are also compatible with moves to individualise the employment relationship, and with personal contracts. Employees have diverse economic, security and social needs, and several demographic trends have contributed to this. These trends include an increase in female participation in the labour market, an increase in single parents, those with caring responsibilities and others in the sandwich generation, an ageing workforce with increasing post-employment life expectancies, new career patterns, and dual-career families. It is evident that flexible benefits potentially enable organisations to be responsive to the lifestyle needs of a more diverse workforce.

EXHIBIT 10.2 Flexible benefits at EON, BAE and Scottish Widows

Energy firm EON introduced a new flexible benefits scheme in 2008 giving employees more power over their own finances and holiday options. A 'one size fits all' approach to benefits packages was not cost-effective and did not recognise individual interests. Employees have the opportunity to buy and sell a week's holiday and to choose between options such as travel and life insurance, discounted bicycles for getting to work and childcare vouchers. Benefits such as insurance and private health cover are also extended to an employee's family. The extensive choice made the process complex, but a communication scheme had helped staff make decisions and volunteer employee champions acted as a first line of enquiry. The HR team held enrolment surgeries to answer any questions.

BAE systems offers an á la carte style benefits programme where benefits are customised to meet individual needs under a Value Benefits plan. Employees choose from a range of options:

- Flexible health benefits
- Dental/vision
- Short- and long-term disability
- Life insurance
- Long-term care
- Dependant care
- Paid time off
- Pension plan
- Flexible working

At Scottish Widows employees have a percentage of salary awarded either to buy additional benefits or take in cash. It is paid in 12 monthly instalments along with the basic salary. The choices are:

- *Living life to the full*: bicycles, buy or sell up to five days' holiday entitlement, matched learning fund, retail vouchers, childcare vouchers.
- *Cash lump sum*: some or all of the flex cash as a lump sum just before Christmas.
- *Keeping fit and healthy*: private medical benefits, health screening, dental plan.
- *Protecting the future*: pension fund top-up, personal accident insurance, critical illness cover, life insurance.

While intrinsically attractive, flexible benefits present a number of complications and challenges, particularly in relation to the costs, time and effort associated with set-up, implementation and ongoing administration. The start of the process involves deciding on which reward strategy objectives are to be actively pursued. A benefits audit is needed to establish the relative costs to the organisation and the value to employees, or in expectancy theory terms the valence, of particular benefits. Assessing employee benefit valence needs to be based on consultation and the surveying of preferences. The balance between core (for everyone) and flexible (choice) benefits also needs to be considered, along with the extent to which benefits can be exchanged for cash.

Although paternalistic in tone, the employer clearly has an ethical responsibility to ensure that employees do not deny themselves, for example, sufficient holiday to prevent overwork and burnout, or sufficient provision for old age, which may receive less priority of attention from younger workers. The scope for benefit decision either *between* benefits or *within* benefits is also an important factor. For example, can life assurance cover be traded for extra holiday? Can different levels of healthcare provision be selected according to need, thereby releasing benefit credit for other benefits or for cash?

The organisation needs to determine a method of allocating benefit credit to employees. Is it a percentage of pay? Is it a fixed amount? Is it harmonised for every employee? Is it influenced by length of service or performance? One illustrative method is to calculate the total reward figure for each employee, combining the value of pay and benefits, and stipulate that at least 85 per cent must be retained as pay, 8 per cent must be used to buy core benefits and 7 per cent is available for enhancing core benefits, selecting flexible benefits or exchanging for cash. It is apparent that a system of flexible benefits involves considerable administrative complexity, but web-based systems are well equipped to deal with this and, increasingly, the management of flexible benefits can be outsourced. The extent to which employees can change their benefit decision also needs to be addressed; too short a review time will intensify administrative complexity, while too long a time between review may reduce the positive impact of flexible benefits that the employer is seeking. An annual review may therefore be an appropriate arrangement, although to meet employee needs it may be necessary to allow benefit adjustment in response to significant lifestyle changes such as getting married or divorced or having children. The advent of e-HR can potentially exploit the power of intranets to facilitate the self-management of flexible benefits through enabling employees to go online to find out the value of their benefits package and model the impact of trading one benefit for another. The French-owned telecommunications manufacturer Alcatel Telecom introduced flexible benefits for its 600 employees and installed electronic kiosks in the workplace to enable staff to monitor and modify their benefits. Objective benefit advice also needs to be available for employees as choice for some may represent dilemmas for others. A change to flexible benefit arrangements may be viewed suspiciously by employees if the arrangements are not fully transparent and communicated effectively, as altering reward benefits goes to the heart of the employment relationship and employer motives may be questioned.

There are three final issues which need to be exposed. First, it is likely that professional taxation and actuarial advice will be necessary and this will have an associated cost. Second, statutory provision, for example in relation to maternity, parental and holiday entitlements, will provide constraints in scheme design and range of employee choice. Third, an organisation can elect either an incremental or a big bang approach to flexible benefit introduction. Ultimately the decision to pursue flexible benefit arrangements depends on a judgement about whether the advantages of recognising diversity, providing choice and focusing reward objectives outweigh the costs of complexity and administration – do flexible benefits gain competitive advantage? In 1997 there were fewer than 100 genuine flexible benefits schemes in the UK, but the number was increasing (Arkin, 1997). The CIPD reward management survey (2008) reports that 1 in 10 employers were using a flexible benefits approach and typically these were private sector organisations with over 5000 employees. The 2008 survey predicted that a further 12 per cent of employers would be considering flexible benefits within the next

EXHIBIT 10.3 Illustration of a flexible benefits approach

1 Base Pay	85 per cent	Salary	Cash
2 Core benefits – for everyone	8 per cent	A basic core, but with enhancement options through using the flex value	Minimum holidays Pension contribution Life insurance
3 Flexible benefits – lifestyle choice	Flex value of 7 per cent	The flex value in cash or as a points value is used to enhance core benefits or purchase additional benefits	*Flexible options:* Extra holiday Medical insurance Private health screening Dental cover Disability insurance Critical illness cover Childcare vouchers Travel insurance Car upgrade Mobile phone Concierge services Retail vouchers Gym membership Cash

In this illustration, employees would have 7 per cent of salary to enhance core benefits, purchase flexible benefits or to take as cash. Evaluate the core and flexible benefits and discuss the optimum range of choice within each. Also, discuss how the cost of each benefit option can be calculated.

year. A Towers Perrin survey (2008) reported that that employers with flexible benefits considered them effective in improving retention, aiding recruitment and enhancing employee perceptions of the value of benefits (http://www.employeebenefits.co.uk/benefits/flexible-benefits.html – accessed 1 June 2009). While there is interest in flexible benefits as an innovative and business-focused reward initiative, the anticipated cost of implementation and administration, together with 'benefit inertia', are significant barriers to progress.

PENSIONS

Employee pension arrangements and occupational pension schemes present a considerable challenge in terms of provision, administration and adherence to statutory and HM Revenue & Customs requirements. Specialist actuarial and financial advice is normally needed for this complex benefit. In order to understand the advice, to be able to contribute to the development of pensions policy and to provide accurate information to employees, it is necessary to be familiar with broad pensions types and the specialist language that is used. Pension types can be categorised as follows:

- state pension arrangements
- occupational pensions – final salary (defined benefit), money purchase (defined contribution) and mixed benefit schemes
- personal pensions – group and individual.

Although addressed again later in this section, it is useful at this stage to distinguish between **final salary** and **money purchase** arrangements. Final salary schemes pay benefits which are determined by taking the number of years of employee service and applying them to final salary on retirement to produce a pensions entitlement.

Final salary arrangements therefore provide defined benefits (DB).

In contrast, money purchase schemes pay benefits which are determined by the value of a pot of money which is accumulated through employee and/or employer contributions and investment decisions. The pot of money is ring-fenced to purchase a pension for the employee.

Money purchase arrangements therefore provide defined contributions (DC), but do not provide defined or predictable benefits.

State pension arrangements

A broad outline of state pension arrangements follows, but this is a dynamic area because of increasing life expectancies and the consequent increased costs associated with providing state pensions.

Subject to the payment, or the receiving of credit, for national insurance contributions (NICs) and age, pensioner citizens are entitled to a basic retirement pension. It has become apparent that this cannot be relied on by individuals to guarantee a continuation of their normal lifestyle in retirement. The uprating of basic state pension has for some time been linked to a general index of increases in prices rather than increases in pay. This has had the effect, because pay increases normally exceed price increases, of eroding the value of state pensions in relation to average earnings. Basic state pension stands at around 15 per cent of male median earnings. The basic state pension can be topped up through the state second pension (S2P) which provides an additional pension (AP) based on individual earnings and consequent national insurance contributions above the lower earnings limit. In effect higher earners pay higher national insurance contributions, currently subject to an upper limit, and therefore become entitled to additional state pension.

Certain types of occupational pension schemes allow employees and employers to contract out of S2P, but not the basic state pension. It is necessary for a contracted-out occupational pension scheme to provide benefits in place of S2P and in return the employee and the employer will pay lower NICs. In order to draw state pension it is necessary to be of state pension age. This is being equalised at 65 years for men and women. Women born before 6 April 1950 will continue to be of state pension age at 60 years and women born between 6 April 1950 and 5 April 1955 will be of state pension age between 60 and 65 years depending upon their date of birth within this period.

The state pensions element of NICs is not invested in a fund for future pensioners, but is used to pay the pensions of current pensioners, and therefore NICs need to equal or exceed state pension payments at any one point in time, in a 'pay as you go' arrangement. There is considerable concern in the UK, and in the European Union generally, that the ageing population and increasing life expectancy post-employment effectively means that those in work will not be able or willing to finance the pensions of those in retirement. Effectively, as the dependency ratio, as it is known, increases, so will the financial demands on those in active employment, pushing up the required levels of national insurance contribution. The current state pension arrangements are not sustainable and this 'pensions crisis' has demanded radical revision, including an increase in state pension age and a shifting of pensions responsibility to employers and employees.

In 2002, Adair Turner was appointed Chairman of the Pensions Commission to consider the case for increasing compulsory saving for pension provision. The main recommendations of the Commission were:

- to encourage more saving for retirement through a national pension savings scheme
- to index increases in basic state pension to earnings, instead of inflation
- to increase the state pension age to 68 by 2050.

This resulted in the Pensions Acts of 2007 and 2008. From 2010 the number of years needed to qualify for the basic state pension will be reduced to 30. Between 2012 and 2015, the basic state pension will be re-linked to average earnings and contracting out for defined contribution schemes will be abolished at the same time. From 2030 SP2 will become a simple, flat-rate weekly top to the basic state pension. The state pension age for everyone born after 5 April 1959 will increase from 65 to 68 between 2024 and 2046. A new national savings scheme, called National Employment Savings Trust (NEST), is to be introduced from 2012 with a minimum contribution of 8 per cent of earnings (within certain limits):

- employees will contribute 4 per cent of earnings between the lower and upper earning limits
- employers will make matching contributions of 3 per cent on the same earnings band
- a further 1 per cent will be contributed through tax relief.

There will be automatic enrolment for employees, aged 22 to state pension age, into either the new national savings scheme or the employer's occupational pension arrangement, provided it meets a minimum standard.

Occupational pension schemes

An occupational pension scheme normally exhibits certain characteristics, including the following.

- Pensions, or a lump sum to purchase a pension, are paid by the employing organisation to employees on retirement.

- Deferred pensions, or pension transfers, are provided for employees who leave the organisation early.

- Pension benefits accrue to employee dependants.

- Pension funds are financed, first, through a combination of employer contributions, tax relief and (usually) employee contributions and, second, through investment by the pensions fund trustees.

In order to attract employee and employer tax relief on contributions, an occupational pension scheme must meet approved status criteria as determined by the HM Revenue & Customs. The tax advantages are considerable and make it attractive for organisations to conform to the criteria. Briefly, the criteria include the setting up of the pension scheme as a trust, limiting maximum employee pension to two-thirds of final salary, allowing employees to commute a proportion of pension as a tax-free lump sum, conforming to rules governing the provision of life insurance and dependants' pensions benefits, and observing maxima for employee and employer contributions.

Typically many occupational pension schemes have required employee contributions and employer contributions of the order of 5–6 per cent and 6–9 per cent of pay respectively. Where the scheme is non-contributory for the employee, a less frequent arrangement but an attractive employee benefit, an employer may need to contribute around 11 to 15 per cent of pay. These figures are only indicative, as clearly the level of employee and employer contributions will be determined actuarially through analysis of expected benefits in relation to the contributions and anticipated investment returns necessary to fund them. In effect it is the required 'funding rate' which determines scheme contributions. Stock market fluctuations and increasing life expectancies are generating upward pressure on these contribution figures.

A final salary scheme (defined benefits)

This uses employee length of service and final salary in the calculation of pension entitlement. Typically, for each year of service final salary schemes accrue an employee entitlement to either 1/60 or 1/80 of final pay – this is termed the accrual rate. Final pay may be defined as the salary on retirement, an average of the final three years' pay, the highest rate of pay during pensionable service or increasingly on career average pay adjusted for *retail* price inflation. Forty years' service in a 1/60 scheme will produce a pension of two-thirds of final pay, the maximum allowable under HM Revenue & Customs rules, and in a 1/80 scheme the same 40 years' service will produce a pension of one-half of final pay, plus a lump sum benefit, which taken together approximates to two-thirds of final pay. The scheme may allow employees to purchase extra years of pensionable service (past added years is the term used in the public sector) to compensate for service below a total of 40 years. The purchase of extra years will not benefit from employer contributions, but the employee contributions will qualify for income tax relief up to the lifetime cap on contributions (Finance Act, 2004). Commutation of a proportion of salary, in order to release a tax-free lump sum for the employee, will normally be available in a 1/60 final salary scheme. Early leavers from the scheme will normally qualify for a deferred pension, based on the number of years of pensionable service and salary on leaving, which is subject to statutory increases. Alternatively the early leaver may request a transfer of the value of the pension fund to the new employer, but actuarial assumptions will often mean that the number of years of entitlement in the new scheme is less than the number of years in the old scheme. Therefore, the early leaver will need to make predictions and judgements about expected pay increases, rates of inflation, value of the transfer and so on. If pensionable service on leaving is short, say under two years, the leaver may only receive a return of employee contributions. There are therefore potential disadvantages to early leavers and final salary schemes present portability problems.

Final salary schemes are attractive to employees because the higher the salary and the longer the pensionable service, the greater the pension on retirement. In addition, the pension benefits have high predictability and reliability. Final salary schemes are less certain for the employer, because contributions will need to be made at whatever level is necessary to meet and sustain final salary pension commitments and therefore the investment risk is primarily with the employer. The cost of a final salary scheme rises as the number of pensioners and deferred pensioners increases. The number of final salary occupational pension schemes is declining as employers seek less open-ended and more predictable contribution arrangements.

The money purchase scheme (defined contributions)

This is an alternative to final salary arrangements and although it involves employee and/or employer contributions it has an entirely different basis for the calculation of employee benefits. The money purchase scheme has defined contributions and the investment risk is effectively transferred from the employer to the employee. The employee and employer contributions are paid into an investment fund to create a pot of money. The pension entitlement on retirement will be the value of the fund and this is used to purchase a pension. The money purchase pension benefits depend, first, on investment growth and, second, on the pension conversion, or annuity, rates at the time the pension is purchased (which continue to worsen in line with longer life expectancies and lower stock market returns). The rules governing the time at which the pension has to be purchased have been relaxed to give the individual some flexibility in deciding precisely when to purchase the pensions product. Money purchase schemes may also present the employee with investment choices which may attract lower or higher returns in relation to the degree of investment risk. Money purchase schemes therefore give relative contribution certainty to the employer, but introduce great unpredictability for the employee in terms of both making investment decisions, and in not having guaranteed pension benefits. Money purchase schemes have portability advantages over final salary arrangements, because the individual's fund can more easily be transferred to a new employer. There is no reason why with sufficient contributions and sound investment decisions a money purchase scheme cannot provide an adequate pension, but this relies on the employee entering a scheme relatively early in working life and having sufficient disposable income to sustain adequate contributions. In order to expect a pension of one-half of final salary an employee may need to invest at least 15 per cent of salary for 40 years.

Money purchase schemes effectively enable a financial disengagement of the retiring employee, because the employer will not be paying the pension itself and not be responsible for any uprating. Therefore, predictability in funding rate and relatively clean break payment arrangements can make money purchase schemes more attractive to employers. Money purchase arrangements also provide employers with an

EXHIBIT 10.4 **The death knell of final salary (defined benefit) pension schemes?**

Two-thirds of private sector final salary pension schemes are closed to new employees. Increasing numbers of schemes are being closed to all employees and/or increasing the employer and/or employee contribution requirements.

Final salary pension schemes	Manufacturing and production	Private sector services	Public sector
Open to all	18 per cent	19 per cent	83 per cent
Closed to new employees	68 per cent	64 per cent	10 per cent
Closed to all employees	15 per cent	14 per cent	6 per cent

Source: CIPD, *Reward Management Survey*, 2008.

opportunity to reduce the overall level of contribution made to pension benefits, but the likely effect will be that, on average, employees will retire with smaller pensions than if a final salary pension scheme had been maintained.

Decline in final salary schemes

Back in 2001, British Telecom notably closed its final salary scheme to new employees and offered money purchase arrangements instead. Other high-profile companies such as the Cooperative Group, Marks & Spencer and British Airways followed. The closing of final salary schemes continues at a pace (*see* Exhibit 10.4). The abolition by the Treasury in 1997 of the advanced corporation tax credit for pension fund dividends effectively reduced the dividend income of a fund by around 20 per cent. This increased costs for employers and/or employees and this, together with stock market uncertainty and longer life expectancy predictions, is contributing to a trend away from defined benefit schemes linked to final salary towards money purchase schemes where contributions are defined. Alternatives to closing final salary schemes, while still responding to funding challenges, include raising employer and/or employee contribution rates so that the historical norm of 15 per cent is exceeded, increasing the age at which occupational pensions can be taken and basing the final salary calculation on average earnings.

A mixed benefit scheme is effectively a hybrid of final salary and money purchase principles and seeks to spread the investment risk between the employer and the employee, providing some predictability and allocating some risk to both parties. A minimum pension linked to final salary is guaranteed, while some pension entitlement will depend on investment returns. A mixed benefit scheme therefore contains elements of defined benefits and defined contributions. See Exhibit 10.5 for a comparison of final salary and money purchase arrangements.

EXHIBIT 10.5 Comparison of final salary and money purchase pension schemes

Final salary	Money purchase
• Benefits are defined as a fraction of final pensionable pay, depending on length of service	• Benefits are purchased by the accumulation of contributions invested in a fund
• Benefits are not dependent on investment returns or annuity rates	• Benefits are dependent on contributions, investment returns and the cost of annuities
• Employer contributions are variable and made in excess of employee contributions	• Employer contributions are fixed
• Employer takes the financial risk	• Employee takes the financial risk
• Certainty for the employee	• Certainty for the employer
• Early leavers' benefits are eroded because increases in deferred pension increases are linked to prices rather than earnings	• Early leavers do not lose because they effectively take their pensions fund with them
• Designed for long-serving employees with expectations of progressive increases in pensionable pay	• Designed for short-serving employees or those whose pensionable pay fluctuates
• Low portability	• High portability

Occupational pension schemes – rules and regulations

An occupational pension scheme needs rules which determine the type of scheme, eligibility for membership, contributions rate, range and type of benefits, method of calculating pensionable service and the normal pensionable age. In order to qualify as an HM Revenue & Customs approved scheme the pension arrangements must be separated from the employing organisation and be set up as a trust. Trustees of the scheme are appointed to manage the investments, to ensure that employees receive proper entitlements and to ensure compliance with statutory obligations. The management of investments is normally achieved through the delegation of this role to investment and financial professionals. Trustees are obligated in law to act in the best financial interests of the scheme members and seek to maximise 'prudently' the investment returns.

Occupational pensions are subject to the provisions of the Pensions Act 1995 and also to the Pensions Act 2004 which replaced the Occupational Pensions Regulatory Authority (OPRA) with the Pensions Regulator and also set up the Pensions Protection Fund. The Pensions Protection Fund pays benefits where an employer becomes insolvent and as a result its pension fund is unable to meet its obligations. The Pensions Protection Fund and the Pensions Regulator are funded by a levy on occupational schemes and the Pensions Regulator has powers which can be likened to those of the Health and Safety Executive. The powers include prohibition or suspension of trustees, disqualification of auditors or trustees, and fines on individuals and corporate bodies for malpractice, with imprisonment for serious acts. Actuaries and auditors are statutorily obliged to report malpractice to the Pensions Regulator. Trustees, and employees, may also complain to the Pensions Regulator and are provided with some protection against legal action for alleged breach of confidence.

Pension earned after April 1997 is subject to a minimum annual increase in payment of either the increase in the retail price index or capped at 25 per cent; deferred pensions have been protected by limited indexation for some time. However, if the inflation rate exceeds 2.5 per cent for several years, the relative value of the pension will be eroded. Some schemes provide for additional triennial or quinquennial reviews which take account of higher inflation rates, but action of this kind is voluntary. Pension entitlement is normally considered as pay and is therefore subject to European Directives on equality of treatment and equal pay, the consequence being that all occupational pension schemes must avoid direct and indirect discrimination, and scheme rules will need to ensure that men and women are treated equally. Since July 2000 employers have been obliged to provide access to their pension schemes to part-time employees unless there is a genuine and objective reason for not doing so.

Why have an occupational pension scheme?

It is evident that associated with offering occupational pensions is complexity, regulation, administration and risk. Why is it that employers offer pensions arrangements? The answer lies in analysing the extent to which pension provision achieves reward and other corporate objectives. Employer reasons for having a pension scheme may include:

- contributing to a competitive position in the labour market and enhancing recruitment and retention
- a genuine belief in the value of investing in people
- contributing to a positive employer brand
- because employees expect it and by sending signals that employee expectations are important there is potential for impact on motivation, commitment and performance
- providing management with the facility of flexing staff numbers through early retirement arrangements.

It needs to be recognised that whether or not these objectives are realisable, and also the extent to which employee behaviour is affected by pension arrangements, is dependent on labour market characteristics and this has implications for employers, and indeed for public policy. Research by Taylor (1999) identified groups of workers that appeared to value occupational pensions more highly – older employees, professional and higher paid staff, staff protected by trade unions and employees working in the financial sector. His research concludes that:

> Most firms perceive pensions to have a significant effect on the attraction and retention of some staff groups. It is questionable to assert that pension schemes continue to have a general effect on the attraction and retention of staff or that they are primarily provided to fulfil such objectives. Their significance in fact seems to vary considerably from labour market to labour market. Appropriately designed and

communicated schemes continue to have an effect on the labour market behaviour of specific employee groups. Furthermore, there is evidence to suggest that this effect remains significant in spite of legislation designed to reduce the retentive power of occupational pensions.

Personal pensions

Personal pensions, whether individual or group, are not occupational pensions. A personal pension plan offers a defined contributions arrangement with the contributions being invested in a fund which is used to buy a pension in retirement. Personal pension benefits are therefore not guaranteed. As a general guide an investment fund of around £150 000 to £200 000 will need to be available to an individual on retirement to purchase an inflation-protected pension of £5000 per year. Contributions attract income tax relief and are subject to the statutory maxima. Employers can contribute to an employee's personal pension, and although there is an organisational cost there is no involvement in risk or in benefit determination and the administrative burden is limited. Government concern for the substantial minority of people without adequate occupational or personal pension arrangements is focusing attention on improving private sector provision and also public/private partnering arrangements. 'Stakeholder' and 'citizen' pensions are available for the lower paid and carers respectively.

CASE STUDY Pensions change at Goodwins

Goodwins was formed out of a parent company demerger, and is one of the UK's largest general retailers. It employs 32 000 permanent staff, with a turnover of around 10 000 each year. Approximately 10 000 of its staff are aged 16–20. However, beyond the high turnover rate and young staff it has a high degree of loyalty within the organisation. The company inherited control of the parent company pension scheme, and committed to maintaining it without making any changes for two years. During this time it undertook a major review exercise of its pension scheme and introduced a redesigned scheme for new staff and changes to the scheme for existing members.

Scheme design

When the parent company demerged, Goodwins carried over around 8500 members from the existing 1/60 defined benefit (DB) scheme. Employee contributions to the scheme, as at parent company, were set at 5 per cent with a commitment not to change the scheme for two years. At the time of the demerger, all existing pensioners remained in the parent company scheme, so that at the outset there were no deferred members and no members actually drawing a pension from the Goodwins scheme. Goodwins believed that it could not sustain the scheme in the form it had been inherited from parent company, as the costs and risks to the employer were simply too high. However, it also felt that if a way could be found to manage these risks, maintaining some form of DB scheme even for new entrants, *it would mark them out as an 'employer of choice' and result in significant recruitment and retention benefits within the current pensions climate.*

(Box continued)

It was therefore reluctant to move to a defined contribution (DC) scheme. The company carried out a six-month research and review exercise, during which time it did extensive research into the demographic make-up of its workforce and the implications of the various pension options available to them. It was particularly keen to strike a balance between issues of loyalty and staff turnover on the one hand, with those of profitability and responsibility to shareholders on the other. The approach it took was to strip down its pension scheme and to view it in pieces, looking for opportunities to reduce the risks to the company while retaining a DB scheme. These pension scheme pieces were:

- retirement age;
- accrual rate;
- contribution level;
- early retirement terms;
- provision for spouses on death after retirement;
- administration costs as a result of members joining the scheme and then leaving the company within a short space of time; and
- whether the scheme is contracted into the state second pension (S2P).

Goodwins believed it could produce a sustainable final salary scheme by adjusting these variables. So for new entrants, it raised the retirement age to 65 and changed employee contributions to 6 per cent. It also contracted back into the state second pension, used cost-neutral early retirement terms, removed the automatic provision for a spouse's pension on death after retirement and imposed a one-year minimum service requirement for new staff wishing to join the scheme. At the same time, existing scheme members were given the option to raise their contributions to 7 per cent and maintain their 1/60 accrual rate, or to maintain their contributions at 5 per cent but reduce to a 1/80 accrual rate. These new terms came into place once the two-year commitment not to change the scheme for existing members had expired. The scheme for new entrants has been contracted back into the S2P. This is in light of the view that it is important for state pension provision and occupational schemes to interact. Contracting in recognises the greater generosity of the S2P for people on lower incomes. Similar logic drove the decision to raise the company's pension age to 65 – lower-income employees struggle to afford to retire without the state portion of their benefits, so it made sense to bring the company retirement age into line with the state pension age. Goodwins did not seriously consider either a hybrid or a career average scheme for new entrants. It believes that such schemes are over-complicated, making them difficult to communicate to employees and therefore reducing any recruitment and retention benefits of a pension scheme. It was also concerned that over-complicated scheme design could impact on trust in pensions, which is already at a low level.

Communication

When employees became aware that a review of the pension scheme was being undertaken, they were understandably nervous about the likely outcome. To counter this, a steering group was formed to ensure that all areas of the Group would receive a consistent message. Goodwins undertook a two-week cascade exercise, explaining the changes to all levels of management before any general announcement was made. When the announcement did come, management were careful to explain the problems facing pension schemes in general, to draw comparisons with other companies' (generally DC) schemes, and to highlight that the company was increasing its financial commitment to the scheme too. Against this background, the eventual announcement that the final salary scheme was being retained, and that the negative impact on employees was effectively restricted to a 2 per cent increase in contributions, was well received. All scheme members received a letter at home outlining the choices available to them. The letters came with a grid outlining how the changes would affect members, non-members and new joiners. This was followed up with an annual benefit statement including a personalised analysis of what the impact would be on each employee if they chose to raise their contributions or to accept the reduced accrual rate. A tear-off form was attached and a pre-paid envelope provided for members to return their decision: 92 per cent responded (of which 90 per cent opted to raise their contributions) with the remainder defaulting on to the lower accrual rate.

Participation

The Goodwins pension scheme has around 8500 members (of which about 3000 are based in offices and large distribution centres, with the rest based on the shop floor). This is out of a total of 32 000 employees. The company provides branded pensions literature to all new joiners, and then a reminder about their right to join is automatically triggered after 10 months. There are also posters advertising a helpline number at its various sites. Goodwins operated automatic enrolment in the past, but has since moved away from this mechanism. This was based on an awareness that membership of the scheme wasn't going to be appropriate for all employees, as well as on the fact that automatically enrolling employees in a sector with such high turnover generated a substantial additional administrative burden on the company.

Questions

1 Why did Goodwins decide to change the pension scheme arrangements?

2 What are the main changes in the pension scheme and why were these selected?

3 Assess the extent to which the following declared HR objective will be achieved – *Marking Goodwins out as an 'employer of choice' and thereby result in significant recruitment and retention benefits within the current pensions climate.*

Group personal pensions are effectively a collection of individual personal pensions with the documentation and contributions being administered by the employer, or the employer's agent, on behalf of the employees. The employer will need to be clear about the distinction between the provision of pension information and the giving of financial advice, not only because of the financial services regulation, but also in the context of public disquiet about the quality of pension advice in recent years. In flexible and deregulated labour markets group personal pensions may be an appropriate employer provision for employees on non-standard contracts.

Employees in occupational pension schemes can top up their pension by paying additional voluntary contributions (AVCs) to an approved provider. The AVC arrangements may be linked to the occupational pension scheme and administered by the employer, or the individual may elect free-standing additional voluntary contributions (FSAVCs) with a provider who is not connected with the employing organisation. Tax relief is currently available on AVC/FSAVC contributions, subject to the lifetime maximum for all pension contributions.

From 2006, rather than the investment of personal pension contributions being confined to a mix of shares, property and bonds purchased through an insurance company, it became possible to use a self-invested personal pension (SIPP) to choose where the contributions are invested. While personal pensions were previously confined to those workers not in occupational schemes, SIPPs are available to all, subject to (substantial) annual and lifetime limits. The intention was to give greater freedom and control to individual investors in managing their personal pension provision. The other principal change was that the flexibility to purchase an annuity during retirement was increased. In effect individuals remain free to take the 25 per cent tax-free lump sum, but can leave the remaining fund to accumulate until it is needed to provide an income, while at the same time drawing income from the fund to live on to a figure which is broadly equivalent to what would be received if an annuity had been purchased. The annuity is therefore not necessarily purchased on retirement, but at a subsequent benefit crystallisation event (BCE).

CONTEMPORARY TRENDS IN REWARD

Internal and external 'shapers' influence reward strategy (Figure 10.1) and these contextual factors give rise to emerging and declining trends.

Internal shapers include the culture of the organisation, including managerial beliefs about what motivates employees; integrated and strategic reward approaches associated with HRM; the reward expectations of the employee; employee consultation or negotiation arrangements; and the nature of the task.

External shapers include the economic climate; labour market shortages or surpluses; public policy on employment; pay legislation, for example tax breaks or the statutory minimum wage; the influence of EU Directives; the changing structure of work and sectoral changes in types of work; and technological developments.

Figure 10.1 Internal and external shapers of reward trends

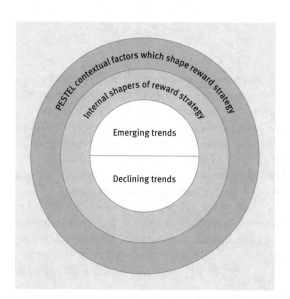

EXHIBIT 10.6 Emerging and declining reward trends

Declining reward trends

'Best practice' in reward	Is there such a thing?
Incremental pay systems	Viewed as not responsive to the strategic integration of reward or to market pricing
Inflation-linked increases	A low inflation climate is loosening the link between inflation and employee pay expectations
Annual pay reviews	Longer-term pay deals are not uncommon
Collective pay bargaining	Not only because of a hostile political environment in the 1980s and 1990s, but also because of structural changes in employment
Final salary pensions	Escalating costs and the financial risk to the employer
Allowances and add-ons	Reflecting movement to consolidate and simplify reward arrangements through 'clean pay'
Traditional job evaluation	Inflexibility concerns when nimble reward strategies are needed in organic organisations

Emerging reward trends

Total reward	Pay plus financial and non-financial benefits deployed in pursuit of competitive advantage
'Best fit' in reward	Acknowledgement of the contextual and contingent nature of reward – 'horses for courses'
New pay	The strategic alignment of rewards with business objectives and the use of pay as a lever on employee performance
Market-driven pay	Labour market responsiveness in tight labour markets to meet local conditions
Performance-related pay	Widespread application of individual PRP to reward the exhibition of desired performance, behaviours and competencies and increasing interest in team reward
Broadbanding	For increased flexibility in delayered organisation structures
Equal pay and equal value	Increasing employee, trade union and governmental pressure for equal pay audits
Money purchase pensions	The escalating costs of final salary schemes and a transfer of the risk to employees; the pursuit of pensions portability in flexible labour markets
Flexible benefits	To reflect the needs of a diverse workforce, to increase the potency of the reward strategy and to target benefits cost

The internal and external shapers of reward strategy give rise to general, but not universal, trends and an illustrative snapshot is provided in Exhibit 10.6 as the basis for discussion and further development. Stredwick (2000) recognises the changing nature of pay through identifying the characteristics associated with treating pay as 'an expense' and treating pay as 'a means to competitive advantage'. In this context, his model identifies the characteristics of the 'new pay' trend as encompassing:

- rewards for achieving desired results
- pay for performance, skills or competence
- flexibility within a broadbanded structure
- flexible benefit programmes
- pay determined to meet local conditions
- paying for employees' ideas, initiative and innovation
- incentives based on broad measures of organisational success.

Emerging and declining trends reflect the contextual and contingent nature of reward and in no way dampen enthusiasm for pursuing 'perfection' in reward systems. The search continues vigorously with reward systems increasingly characterised by sophistication and complexity. Figure 10.2 exposes for analysis a summary of the potential elements of contemporary reward strategies. Clearly, 'there are no quick fixes in reward, no perfect solutions, but there are genuine gains to be had' (Brown, 2000).

Figure 10.2 Towards a more sophisticated and complex reward strategy integrated horizontally with HR policies and vertically with corporate strategy

6	Reinforcement through non-financial rewards	Total reward strategy to include recognition, opportunities for self-actualisation, responsibility, job design and work–life balance
5	A share in organisational success	A variable pay element which is effectively a profit share in the private sector and an efficiency share in the public sector
4	Team- or group-based PRP	A variable pay element to reflect the perceived contribution of a team or unit
3	Individual PRP	A variable pay element related to a judgement about individual performance and/or contribution
2	Flexible benefits	A benefits package which allows choice and targets benefit cost in order to reflect diverse individual and organisational needs
1	Base pay	Market driven to reflect the commercial worth of employees; including incremental progression within broadbanded job grades or job families

SUMMARY LEARNING POINTS

1 Financial benefits are an important component of the total reward strategy. Benefits are costly to provide and need to be linked to reward objectives to ensure value for money. Market comparisons are valuable and benefits should be surveyed and benchmarked.

2 A diverse workforce has diverse benefit needs. Flexible benefits provide an opportunity to respond to this diversity in the workforce, to target benefit cost and to increase the potency of the benefits offer within the total reward value proposition.

3 Employee pension types consist of state, occupational and personal arrangements. Pensions are characterised by complexity, and knowledge of the specialist language is essential to understanding pensions legislation and options for provision. Defined contribution schemes are growing at the expense of defined benefit schemes.

4 Internal and external factors shape reward strategies, and emerging and declining trends in reward can be tracked through scanning external organisational environments. The elusive search for 'perfect pay' continues unabated.

REFERENCES AND FURTHER READING

Allen, S. (1994) 'Sea change for pensions industry', *Personnel Management*, March, 44–8.

Arkin, A. (1997) 'Mutually inclusive', *People Management*, March.

Armstrong, M. (2002) *Employee Reward*. London: CIPD.

Armstrong, M. and Brown, D. (2001) *New Dimensions in Pay Management*. London: CIPD.

Armstrong, M. and Stephens, T. (2005) *Employee Reward Management and Practice*. London: Kogan Page.

Blackman, T. (1999) 'Trading in options', *People Management*, 6 May, 45–9.

Brown, D. (2000) 'Pay per view', *People Management*, 3 February, 41–2.

CIPD (2004a) *Reward Management Survey of Policy and Practice*. London: CIPD.

CIPD (2004b) *Occupational Pensions: strategic issues*. London: CIPD.

CIPD Annual Reward Conference (2005a) *Reward Management Handbook*. London: CIPD.

CIPD Annual Survey Report (2005b) *Reward Management*. London: CIPD.

CIPD (2005c) *Flexible Benefits – executive briefing*. London: CIPD.

CIPD (2008) *Reward Management: annual survey report*. London: CIPD.

Conoley, M. (1995) 'Executive share options: a new dilemma for HR', *People Management*, August.

Cooper, D. (2000) 'A tale of two pension systems', *Employee Relations*, 22(3).

Department for Work and Pensions (2005) *The Employer Task Force on Pensions*. London: The Stationery Office.

Farnham, D. and Pimlott, J. (1995) *Understanding Industrial Relations*. London: Cassell.

Fowler, A. (1997) 'Let's shed a tier', *People Management*, March.

Gee Reward and Remuneration Strategies Survey (1998) London: Gee Publishing.

Hackman, J. and Oldham, G. (1980) *Work Redesign*. Reading, MA: Addison-Wesley.

Herzberg, F. (1959) *The Motivation to Work*. New York: John Wiley.

Industrial Society (2000) *Managing Best Practice No. 75: Flexible Benefits*. London: Industrial Society.

Leopold, J. (2002) *Human Resources in Organisations*. Harlow: FT Prentice Hall.

Littlefield, D. (1995) 'Personnel looks to pay role after Greenbury hint', *People Management*, August, 1(16), 15.

Merrick, N. (1994) 'Benefits to suit all tastes and lifestyles', *Personnel Management*, December.

Mullen, J. (1998) 'Booth opportunities', *People Management*, 16 April, 50–1.

National Association of Pension Funds (2004) *30th Annual Survey*, www.napf.co.uk.

Oldfield, M. (1994) *Understanding Occupational Pensions*. Croydon: Tolley.

Pensions Act (1995) London: HMSO.

Pensions Act (2004) London: HMSO.

Pensions Act – changes affecting occupational pensions contracted-out of SERPS (1996) Leaflet PECS-9/96. London: DSS.

Redman, T. and Wilkinson, A. (2001) *Contemporary Human Resource Management*. Harlow: FT Prentice Hall.

Report of the Committee on the Financial Aspects of Corporate Governance (1992) London: The Committee and Gee Publishing.

Roberts, C. (1985) *Harmonization: Whys and wherefores*. London: IPM.

Self, R. (1995) 'Changing roles for company pensions', *People Management*, October, 24–9.

Stredwick, J. (2000) 'Aligning rewards to organisational goals: a multinational's experience', *European Business Review*, 12(1). Bradford: MCB University Press.

Study Group on Directors' Remuneration (1995) Directors' remuneration: report of a study group chaired by Sir Richard Greenbury. London: Gee Publishing.

Taylor, S. (1999) 'Occupational pensions and the labour market', *Employee Relations Review*, 10, 25–32.

Taylor, S. and Earnshaw, J. (1995) 'The provision of occupational pensions in the 1990s: an exploration of employer objectives', *Employee Relations*, 17(2), 38–53.

The Guardian (1997) 'Shareholder power plan on top pay', 8 November, 26.

The Guardian (1997) 'Beckett hints at beefing up corporate governance', 12 November, 23.

Thompson, P. (2000) 'How to implement stakeholder pensions', *People Management*, 11 May, 46–8.

Wright, A. (2004) *Reward Management in Context*. London: CIPD.

ASSIGNMENTS AND DISCUSSION TOPICS

1 List a range of employer reward strategy objectives and list the range of financial benefits potentially available to employees. Undertake a paired comparison exercise in which you classify each benefit as high, medium or low in terms of the likelihood it will contribute to each reward strategy objective. Aggregate your results and discuss your findings in small groups. How can this activity inform reward and benefit decisions?

2 Which benefits ought to be core (fixed and non-negotiable) and which benefits should be flexible (involving employee choice) within a flexible benefits package? Use Exhibit 10.3 in your discussion. Justify your decisions.

3 The directorate of your organisation is considering the introduction of flexible benefits for all employees and is seeking your advice. What advice would you give, first, about the added-value business advantages of flexible benefits and, second, about the feasibility, design and implementation of an appropriate flexible benefits scheme?

4 Discuss the relative advantages and disadvantages of final salary (defined benefits) and money purchase (defined contributions) pension schemes from employer and employee perspectives.

5 Which internal and external shapers of reward are currently influential and which emerging and declining trends are evident?

Chapter 11

Managing and Appraising Performance

LEARNING OUTCOMES: TO BE ABLE TO

- Explain the relationship between organisational objectives and performance management

- Critically review the performance management process

- Examine the various approaches to appraisal and the role of appraisal in the management of performance

- Evaluate the reasons for employee absence and identify a range of managerial interventions

- Contribute to the management of absence and recommend action at corporate and individual levels

INTRODUCTION

Effective people resourcing includes not only the acquisition of the appropriate quantity and quality of people but also the management of employees to ensure that skills and competencies are developed and that performance levels are consistent with the achievement of organisational objectives. Employees need to know what is expected, not just in terms of duties and responsibilities but also in terms of standards of performance. Performance management does not consist solely of the appraisal of performance. It is a holistic process which encompasses the definition of organisational aims, the development of team and individual objectives, effective processes for measurement and assessment, the integration of reward strategies, constructive feedback and support for employees to develop and acquire the skills needed to contribute to organisational success. Performance management is a process, not an event, and operates in a continuous cycle. Managing employee absence is an important part of managing performance and is also addressed in this chapter.

PERFORMANCE MANAGEMENT AND CORPORATE STRATEGY

Much is written and spoken about performance management and to understand this more fully it is important to be clear about what is meant by the term. Definitions include:

> a process which contributes to the effective management of individuals and teams in order to achieve high levels of organisational performance. As such, it establishes shared understanding about what is to be achieved and an approach to leading and developing people which will ensure that it is achieved.
>
> (Armstrong and Baron, 2005)

> a systematic approach to improving individual and team performance in order to achieve organisational goals . . . the approach you take should depend on your organisation: its culture, its relationship with employees and the types of job that they do. (Hendry *et al.*, 1997)

However, Bones (1996) made an interesting observation that 'Performance does not need managing. It needs encouraging, developing, supporting and sustaining.' These definitions recognise that performance management should be a strategic and integrated activity with processes designed to facilitate improvements through personal development while encouraging and rewarding appropriate employee behaviours. The People and Performance model of Purcell *et al.* (2003) emphasises the role of individual behaviour in delivering high performance by explaining that *performance* is a function of *ability*, having the necessary knowledge and skills; *motivation*, having the willingness to use the skills; and *opportunity*, having the chance to perform to a high level. This also relies on having a supportive context in terms of the organisational structure and culture while acknowledging the need 'to gain employee commitment which is central to the achievement of positive organisational outcomes such as high quality goods and services which are at the heart of organisational performance' (Guest, 2000). Armstrong and Baron (2005) stress the importance of strategic fit and integration and consequently performance management needs to include broad issues and long-term goals as well as bringing together all the aspects of the business. To be successful performance management needs to focus on both continuous improvement and the development of people. Holbeche (2008), in launching the CIPD research project examining high performance working 'Shaping the Future', asserts that 'great performance occurs when people know what is expected and why that matters'. She explains how 'recent global events show how fast the context is moving and how interconnected our fortunes are as individuals, organisations and society as a whole'. Consequently organisations that cannot lever up performance and build change into the heart of the organisation will find the business climate challenging. When asked about the essential components of high performing organisations Holbeche stressed the need for 'the right people, delivering the right results'. However, she acknowledged that:

> even the right people may not produce great results if they are not engaged with what they do or do not identify with the organisation's aims . . . The capabilities that underpin the speed and agility of (organisational) response are delivered through process, technology and the way people are managed and led, but most of all they are delivered through people's skills, mindsets and strategic anticipation.

The development of an appropriate performance management process is just one element in the development of a performance culture because it will require employees to continuously examine their business processes in order to maximise the quality of their outputs and regularly review their competencies to determine their personal development needs. However, performance management is not an annual event, it is a continuous process and the elements and linkages of a performance management process are identified in Figure 11.1. The performance management concept may be readily understood and be seen as a suitable way of successfully managing people, but the challenges lie in developing a performance management process that works.

Figure 11.1
The performance management process

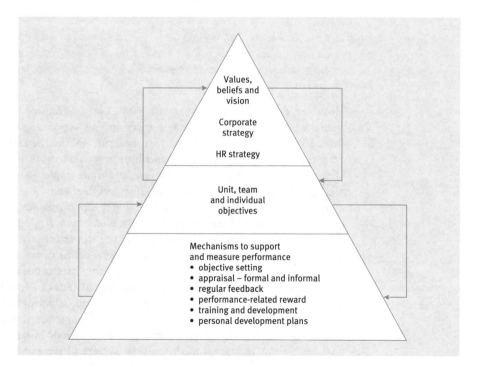

There are stages to be followed to ensure an effective, systematic performance management process.

THE PERFORMANCE MANAGEMENT PROCESS

Performance management is a flexible process and consists of sequential stages. First, clearly define organisational goals to support the setting of unit, team and individual objectives (or performance indicators). Second, the agreement of training and development plans to ensure that learning needs are met and objectives can be achieved. Third, an appraisal process to encourage an open exchange of views and discussion on whether objectives have been achieved, exceeded or not achieved. Fourth, regular feedback is necessary to enable the individual or the team to assess the extent to which their objectives are being achieved. Fifth, financial and non-financial rewards need to be allocated to encourage people to continue to perform. Finally, the process can come full circle by encouraging the individual to develop individual career plans which take into account the long-term vision of the organisation and the strengths, weaknesses and aspirations of employees.

Organisational values, beliefs and vision

Performance management starts with a clear exposition of the organisation's values and beliefs to support the definition of the organisational vision and provide a framework for the corporate culture necessary to achieve business objectives. The organisation vision is an important component of corporate strategy in communicating consistently and succinctly to employees and customers the underpinning values and beliefs which drive the business. The publication of a vision is not an end in itself. Effective communication and enactment of the vision and the associated values is critical because employee acceptance is fundamental to the development of involvement and commitment. Success through people is often espoused and claimed, but it can only be achieved if the people buy in to the vision and cooperate in working towards achieving it. A vision that consists merely of fine words will fail.

Developing corporate strategy

Corporate strategy needs to reflect the vision and focus on both where the organisation is going and how it will get there. It is not a one-off activity, but a continuous process which is reviewed and adjusted in line with changes in the internal and external contexts. Consideration should be given to factors such as global changes, the stage in the economic cycle, product and labour markets and changing technology, *inter alia* (*see* Chapter 1). To be workable the strategy needs to be simple and focused and identify the critical success factors, including the part played by the management of employee performance in realising the corporate vision.

Developing HR strategy

In recognising the critical workforce role in achieving organisational goals and the need for integration of the business with the talent management activities, an effective HR strategy can contribute to an environment where employees understand the culture of the organisation, the standards expected and the support available to achieve high levels of performance. A communication strategy is needed to engage the 'hearts and minds' of employees. This somewhat evangelical perspective can attract the criticism that performance management is merely a mechanism for managerial control. This criticism can be exacerbated if employees neither understand nor accept the basis of the process. Warm words can sound like empty words in the absence of a genuine managerial acknowledgement of the employees' contribution to corporate success or a failure to appreciate employee concerns about the operation of the performance management process. Research supported by the Institute of Employment Studies (Strebler *et al.*, 2001) questions the relevance and effectiveness of traditional performance management processes in flatter and more flexible organisations, and also raises doubts about whether the performance management process supports the needs of the business in practice. This research demonstrates that the performance management process can lack strategic focus and also give conflicting messages about employee encouragement and control while having limited impact on business performance. In addition, performance review can provide a challenge to managers who often lack the skills and motivation to operate it effectively. Nonetheless, participation in the performance review process, rather than the outcomes, appear to matter most to employees and evidence suggests that performance review participation can increase employee commitment. This research highlights the importance of continuously reviewing the performance management processes to ensure that they continue to fit with the business needs.

Setting unit, team and individual objectives

Objectives, or performance indicators, can be defined at business unit, team or individual levels. At business unit level they are closely aligned to organisational goals and will specifically define the targets that the unit is expected to achieve in order to maximise its contribution. At team or individual level the objectives need to relate specifically to the role of the team or individual and the contribution that they are expected to make to the achievement of business unit objectives. Management normally set objectives, but legitimacy will be increased if the objectives are agreed with the team or individual. Setting objectives requires managers to be familiar with the skills and competencies of the employees and with business unit objectives. Managers need to be able to describe the objectives in terms of tasks and behaviours and to allocate these tasks to the most appropriate individuals or teams. In order to maximise the business impact of the performance management process the description and allocation of objectives should be done within a framework of equity and fairness and aim to provide motivating jobs which utilise skills and competencies while offering personal development opportunities. There is value in objectives being SMART, but this approach may be seen as lacking flexibility in the modern fast moving business environment:

S   **Specific:** Define precisely what is required in clear language, so that it is clearly understood by both employee and employer.

M   **Measurable:** Normally include both quantitative targets and qualitative outputs which can be objectively assessed.

A   **Agreed/Achievable:** Managers define objectives, but they are agreed with the employee. Management-imposed objectives that are not owned or accepted by the employee have less chance of being achieved.

R   **Realistic:** Objectives must be achievable and fairly allocated. Setting objectives which are easy to achieve for one employee while giving another objectives that are unlikely to be met is not only unfair but it may also be de-motivational for both of these individuals.

T   **Time-related:** Incorporate clear target dates or time scales which are not open ended.

Hall (2009) usefully expands the SMART acronym:

S   specific, significant, stretching
M   measureable, meaningful, motivational
A   attainable, agreed upon, achievable, action orientated
R   realistic, relevant, reasonable, rewarding, results orientated
T   time-based, timely, tangible

Exhibit 11.1 provides examples of a quantitative objective or target (1), a qualitative objective described in behavioural terms but measured quantitatively (2), and also what is best described as a performance standard (3). Armstrong and Baron (2000) describe performance standards as 'a statement of the condition that exists when a job is being performed effectively'. These are more focused on the level of service provision and are a fundamental part of the job; although the detail of the objective may change, for example from two to three days if resources change, the task still has to be done to an agreed standard.

EXHIBIT 11.1 Examples of individual objectives

No.	Objective	Measure	Date	Rating
1	Make sales of £20 000 each quarter	Sales value	Year end	
2	Deal with customers promptly and politely, resolving problems quickly, ensuring that any delay is communicated to the customer	Customer complaints	Six monthly	
3	Respond to requests for recruitment details within two working days	Monitoring of records	Ongoing	

Two principal criticisms of objective setting are, first, *the difficulty of setting objectives*, which results in the setting of objectives that can easily be measured, at the expense of the less tangible elements of the job – the intangibles may be fundamental to the achievement of a high level of performance and therefore not all parts of the job will be covered; and, second, *a loss of flexibility* because organisational changes need to be incorporated into the objectives and if objectives are not continuously reviewed to retain currency, the individual may put effort into out-of-date objectives because they remain the basis for performance measurement and reward. Rigid performance objectives therefore decay in rapidly changing environments. Rose (2000) examined the continuing role of SMART objectives and contends that:

> SMART objectives assume that organisations operate within a stable environment, but changes in technology and increased globalisation create a world in which winning organisations are those that can lead change, or can at least respond rapidly to market changes. The losers are those that are still driven by year-old objectives.

Consequently, it is important that the performance management process is able to recognise and respond to the external and internal environments, and managers need to guard against the danger that rather than being a force for change the performance management process can become an inhibitor of change. Rose examined the extent to which a process of continuous improvement would be more suited to organisations. The basis of continuous improvement is to identify key performance indicators and to strive to enhance these rather than setting targets which are based on past performance. This moves the organisation from being backward-looking to becoming more forward-looking and increases the flexibility in the performance management process. Rather than the rigidity of SMART objectives, CASE objectives may provide a more appropriate framework. CASE objectives are:

C **Conditions:** reviews the environments within which the organisation operates, if these change then the performance objectives should be reviewed.

A **Action:** describes what the employee or team should do.

S **Standards:** defines the level of achievement expected.

E **Evaluation:** develops a process of regular review and adjustment.

Training and development plans

The setting and agreement of objectives will require an assessment of the individual's competence to achieve them because lack of skill is a major impediment to effective performance. Training and development needs can be analysed within the framework of the objectives, and learning plans put in place for the acquisition of the skills needed to achieve the required performance. It is unrealistic to expect improved performance without continuously updating skills. Performance management can act as a catalyst in identifying and securing the most appropriate training and development activity for the organisation and for the individual. The performance management process promotes training which is aligned to organisational objectives, as well as training that employees value for personal development. Coaching and mentoring have an increasing role in promoting learning and performance improvement and this is evident in the CIPD (2005) definition of coaching, 'developing a person's skills and knowledge so that their job performance improves, leading to the achievement of organisational objectives; it targets high performance and improvement at work'.

Performance appraisal

Performance appraisal is a critical element in the performance management process but it is not the performance management process itself. Performance appraisal is a sub-set of performance management and relates to the formal process of assessing and measuring employee performance against agreed objectives. Formal appraisal takes place regularly, usually annually, although it can occur more often. Performance appraisal invokes a variety of employee responses, from a feeling that it is 'a waste of time' to feelings that 'I want to know how well I am doing'. An observation by Neale (1991) continues to be insightful:

> Appraisal is a compulsively fascinating subject, full of paradoxes and love–hate relationships. And appraisal schemes are really controversial . . . Some schemes are popular, with overtones of evangelical fervour, while others are at least equally detested and derided as 'the annual rain dance', 'the end of term report', etc.

A primary aim of the performance appraisal dimension of performance management is to assess or measure the achievement of the individual or the team against the agreed objectives. This requires the exercise of managerial judgement in the review of quantitative and qualitative objectives, and with judgement comes the potential for subjectivity and bias. Performance measurement presents challenges, and the performance appraisal process needs to recognise the limitations of the process and endeavour to address these in the design of the process. Armstrong and Baron (2005) indicate that performance measures should relate to strategic goals, focus on outputs, indicate the evidence that is available as the basis for measurement and provide a sound basis for feedback. It follows, therefore, that in agreeing objectives the employee needs to fully understand what evidence will be required as the basis for measuring the achievement of the performance objectives. Appraisal schemes take different forms and include top-down, self, peer, upward and multi-rater/360 degree.

Top-down schemes are common, with the immediate line manager normally undertaking the formal appraisal of the employee. Criticisms of this include allegations about favouritism and lack of impartiality. Managers may be less than open and honest and respond differently to employees with whom they are friendly and employees whom they dislike. To offset this tendency a grandparent appraiser (another manager or the HR specialist) can be involved to act as moderator in the appraisal process by examining the reports and ratings and being an arbiter if there is disagreement between the appraising manager and the appraisee. However, there is no doubt that the immediate manager is often in the best position to appraise employee performance.

Self-appraisal can be incorporated in top-down schemes as a mechanism for encouraging openness and employee self-reflection. Self-appraisal is a logical dimension to formal appraisal processes and the views of the individual can be integrated into the assessment.

Peer appraisal involves peers and colleagues in the assessment of performance. This introduces logistical difficulties, as it is impractical to have one-to-one interviews with each member of the relevant peer group. One option is an assessment questionnaire circulated to key work colleagues of the employee being appraised. Peer appraisal can be challenging because, first, it may be difficult to identify the appropriate peer group and, second, peer appraisers will need sufficient skill and knowledge of the individual objectives and performance of the appraisee to be able to undertake a meaningful assessment. Organisations structured in teams may be more able to introduce effective peer assessment and this can be formalised through an open discussion forum.

Upward appraisal includes the views of those employees who report to the appraisee and can be an important dimension of management development. It operates by inviting assessment by the manager's employees as part of the performance management process. The assessment can relate to managerial style and effectiveness, rather than the achievement of organisational objectives and is most commonly undertaken through the completion and submission of appraisal process documents or, alternatively, as part of an employee attitude survey. These results are analysed and returned to the manager and can provide a forum for discussion as well as encourage a problem-solving approach to management development. Upward appraisal may be threatening for a manager and uncomfortable for subordinate appraisers. Although comments may or may not be individually identifiable, upward appraisal may be effective in an organisation which has an open and supportive culture and which encourages participation as a legitimate element in employee and management development.

Multi-rater appraisal or 360-degree feedback is a way of limiting the effect of the one-dimensional approach of the top-down schemes and building on the positive aspects of peer and upward appraisal. Multi-rater appraisers include peers, subordinates, internal and external customers and the manager. The aim is to achieve a broader view of employee performance. It can dilute subjectivity, increase customer focus, support team initiatives, decrease the hierarchical approach and provide greater employee involvement. The use of 360-degree feedback may be more suited to contemporary organisational structures, especially flatter structures, where the span of control may be such that it is difficult for managers to appraise the increased number of employees reporting directly to them. An important dimension of 360-degree feedback is it can improve validity and encourage self-awareness, thereby providing the basis for improved performance (Leopold, 2002; Fletcher, 2004; Marchington and Wilkinson, 2008).

CASE STUDY   Objective setting and appraisal

Administrative assistant

The appraisee is the administrative assistant in the marketing department of a large university business school. The marketing department is responsible for the preparation of marketing plans, production of marketing information and materials and the arrangement of open days and 'drop in' events for potential students. In order to keep informed of what is happening in the sector there is a need to amass a variety of information from a range of sources to ensure that they can keep the business school on track in filling its courses.

The administrative assistant is responsible for collecting articles and press comments on the particular business school, as well as relevant business education articles and information from competitors in the

HE sector. Therefore, she keeps an eye on everything that could be of interest to senior management of the school. The appraisee has to check local and national press as well as keeping a watchful eye on relevant international press. She has to collect these articles and circulate them to senior managers, compile statistics in response to queries from the dean and heads of departments and compile a pack of information for the monthly executive board meeting.

The appraisee, who has been in post for 9 months, began well but recently her manager has the feeling that she is not progressing as expected. The initial enthusiasm that she showed when she joined the department from university is no longer apparent, although her work rate and the hours she puts into the job are generally above average. She has missed some important articles in the past three months and she has required help from others in the department twice in the past three months, to ensure that the pack was not late for the executive board. However, she has received increasing praise from the dean and the heads of departments who are impressed with the accuracy and timeliness of the statistical reports she produces for them.

Assess the performance of the administrative assistant using for following ratings:

1 **Outstanding** – significantly exceeds the requirements for the job

2 **Very Good** – above the requirements for the job in all key areas

3 **Acceptable** – performance in key areas in an acceptable range

4 **Improvement needed** – performance in some key areas below the acceptable range and needs to improve to meet the job requirements

5 **Poor** – significantly below the job requirements.

Questions

1 Record your rating and justify your decision by providing supporting evidence. You may make assumptions that are reasonable within the context of this case and your assumptions must also be recorded.

2 What actions must the administrative assistant take to improve her rating? Translate these actions into SMART or CASE objectives.

Performance appraisal challenges

Challenges associated with the implementation and management of performance appraisal schemes include:

- Increased bureaucracy – systems can be time-consuming, not just in the time needed for the appraisal discussion, but also in the time needed to complete the appraisal documentation. Poorly designed systems are an additional management burden that interferes with achievement. The process can be seen to impede the development of high performing staff. However, well-designed systems where processes are embedded in the day-to-day management activities are more likely to be accepted and successful. More complex systems, such as

360-degree feedback, generate a substantial amount of information to be analysed and acted upon.

- Lack of commitment – a system has to deliver the objective of identifying, promoting and rewarding performance; if it is not seen to do this in practice it will fall into disrepute and both employees and managers will reduce their commitment.

- The tension between identifying development needs and allocating fair rewards can undermine the system.

- Subjectivity and bias are inherent in one individual's assessment of another and there are difficulties in developing objective measures. Managers require training to be able to identify and reduce personal bias.

- The recency effect – it is a human perceptual characteristic to be influenced by recent events, and employee achievement or lack of achievement close to the appraisal interview may distort the assessment. Skilled appraisees may capitalise on this by 'saving' achievements until just before the appraisal discussion.

- Employees may perceive the appraisal process as a tool for managerial control used to reinforce managerially desired behaviours and to subdue the expression of dissatisfaction. In these circumstances the level of trust may be insufficient for the process to work effectively.

Regular feedback

Effective performance management is more than a once-a-year formal appraisal event. Continuous review of employee performance is needed together with effective feedback. Giving feedback can be challenging and managers need good communication skills to ensure that feedback is constructive and helpful. Feedback primarily focused on allocating blame damages employee self-confidence and acts as a negative influence on performance. Gillan (2002) identifies two key management skills required to give effective feedback. First, the manager needs the ability to assess the situation, so that a clear picture of the performance problem can be described. Managers who can assess the situation are more likely to be able to identify the cause of the problem and then work with the employee towards a successful outcome. Second, the manager needs good communication skills to be able to explain fully to the employee any change that may be required. Good communication requires both critical and positive feedback. Critical feedback means being able to describe the observed employee behaviours and also articulate the standards expected. Positive feedback means being able to describe the behaviours being praised, discussing what enabled the employee to achieve those behaviours and motivating the employee to continue. Feedback is therefore a critical element in the performance management process as it is the vehicle for reinforcing appropriate behaviour or for bringing about change. Objective setting and ensuring 'the right thing is done' is only one aspect; ensuring that 'it is done right' can be achieved through open dialogue. One of the main purposes of feedback is to promote development and enable employees to achieve their potential. Success in improving performance reinforces constructive feedback and can also increase employee confidence.

Relating rewards to performance

Within a performance management process the linkage between employee performance and rewards is self-evident and often necessary, but there is an argument for separating the formal appraisal process from pay decisions. The argument for separation is that the linkage with pay may affect the honesty of self-appraisal and interfere with the development objectives of the appraisal process by effectively transforming the manager from a coach to a judge. The employee is less likely to be self-critical and expose weaknesses and development needs if it is going to impact on the allocation of monetary reward. However, in practice it is difficult to divorce the formal appraisal process from pay decisions (*see* Chapter 9 on performance-related pay). Intrinsic and non-financial rewards, such as the provision of opportunities for self-development and the reinforcement of a sense of achievement through positive feedback from the manager, have an important role in relating rewards to performance.

Personal development plans

Outputs from performance appraisal can be the construction of individual performance development plans and organisational succession plans. The performance management process can encourage individuals to reflect on their personal development and to identify internal and external development priorities and opportunities. Knowledge of individual strengths and weaknesses will facilitate this self-reflection. The manager can gain an improved understanding of the aspirations and ambitions of the employee in order to contribute to succession planning (*see* Chapter 4). With openness and honesty these aspirations and their feasibility can be explored and plans developed which take into account individual aspirations, performance and potential and the fit with the future needs of the organisation.

THE BALANCED SCORECARD AND PERFORMANCE MANAGEMENT

The balanced scorecard was developed by Kaplan and Norton (1992) as a response to the primary measure of performance at that time, namely the achievement of financial targets, which they argued did not always give a 'balanced' picture of how well an organisation was doing. The balanced scorecard, which continues to grow in application and use (Kennerley and Bourne, 2003) seeks to redress the balance by focusing on four perspectives – learning and growth, business processes, customer and financial perspectives (Figure 11.2).

The learning and growth perspective examines employee capabilities and the core competencies that employees need to do their jobs effectively, the employee tools required and the motivation employees have to use their capabilities and tools most effectively. Learning and growth is the foundation perspective in achieving high levels of performance.

The business process perspective has three key aspects: the underpinning values which drive the business, the support processes which deliver the values, and the good citizenship processes which seek to maintain good relationships with stakeholders.

Figure 11.2
The balanced
scorecard: four
perspectives

The learning and growth perspective	**The business process perspective**
Focuses on the contribution made by the people in the organisation, their competencies, their capabilities and their motivation.	Focuses on the values that drive the business, the support to deliver the values and the 'good citizen' process.
The customer perspective	**The financial perspective**
Focuses on the customer value proposition and includes: cost, quality and service.	Includes profitability, growth, risk, assets and value creation.

The customer perspective defines the customer value proposition and articulates how the organisation will be distinctive from others. The customer value proposition will include cost, quality, service, time and innovation. The customer value proposition may be based on operational excellence, product leadership or customer relationships.

The financial perspective supports the development of the measures in the other three perspectives and includes profitability, growth, risk, intellectual assets and value creation.

In practice, a small number of interrelated measures are identified against each of the four perspectives and are able to be displayed on a single sheet – hence the balanced scorecard. The four perspectives can be tailored and even weighted to reflect the factors which are key success factors for the business. This approach enables managers and employees to see at a glance the key targets and performance indicators. Measuring performance against the key targets informs judgement on which areas are doing well and which are doing less well. As with employee performance management processes, the success, or failure, of the balanced scorecard is significantly affected by the precision with which objectives are set and valid and reliable measurements are taken. The balanced scorecard can also be used in specific areas of the business and can become a useful tool by allowing the key performance factors to be identified and measurements to be taken. Regular analysis of the details will allow trends to be identified, areas of high or low performance more easily seen and intervention to be taken in a timely way. Expertise developed in using the tool will enable greater fine-tuning of the factors to provide ever more useful information.

The example of the balanced scorecard methodology in Exhibit 11.2 illustrates that the organisation has identified the key indicators against each dimension and it has an articulated rationale for each measure. Targets enable an assessment to be made against each measure. The organisation has developed a highly visual mechanism for regular reporting to the executive management team based on colour coding performance against target – red, amber or green. The information is produced and presented on a single sheet 'a dashboard summary' which enables the team to see clearly where they are exceeding target or failing to meet target. The benefits of the balanced scorecard methodology are in the framework it provides to focus on more than just financial targets and to facilitate the identification of interrelated measures which, when they come together, provide a clear indication of where the organisation is succeeding and where it is failing.

EXHIBIT 11.2 **A balanced scorecard used in HR in an NHS Trust**

Portsmouth Hospitals Trust is applying the balanced scorecard methodology to workforce planning to produce a 'workforce scorecard'; this scorecard has three key aims:

- To enable workforce strategies and HR interventions to be aligned with the Trust's goals.
- To measure the contribution of these strategies and interventions to improved organisational performance.
- To support efficiency improvements by linking increases in productivity to financial improvements.

The four dimensions are:

Workforce capacity Optimise workforce costs and deliver workforce plan to support the maintenance of the Trust's financial health. **Measures:** Substantive workforce Temporary workforce usage Overtime rate Workforce controls	**Workforce resourcing** Maintain efficient and effective HR interventions to supply and develop future workforce and retain best staff **Measures:** Recruitment attractiveness Workforce stability Essential skills training Diversity profile
Workforce efficiency Improve quality of patient care by increasing workforce efficiency and productivity. **Measures:** Staff sickness absence rate Staff turnover rate Unit staff costs Workforce productivity	**Workforce skill mix** Adapt the skill mix of the organisation to maintain a more capable and cost-effective workforce **Measures:** % staff at career framework level 6+ % staff at career framework level 5 % staff at career framework level 1–4 % professionally qualified clinical workforce

MANAGING UNDERPERFORMANCE

A critical part of performance management is the effective management of the employee whose performance is not meeting the required standard. The key questions to be answered are: Is the underperformance because of capability or is the underperformance because of conduct? Until the cause of the gap between expected performance and actual performance is fully understood effective remedial action cannot be put in place. Prior to managerial action it is necessary to have specified the performance

Figure 11.3 A systematic diagnosis of under-performance

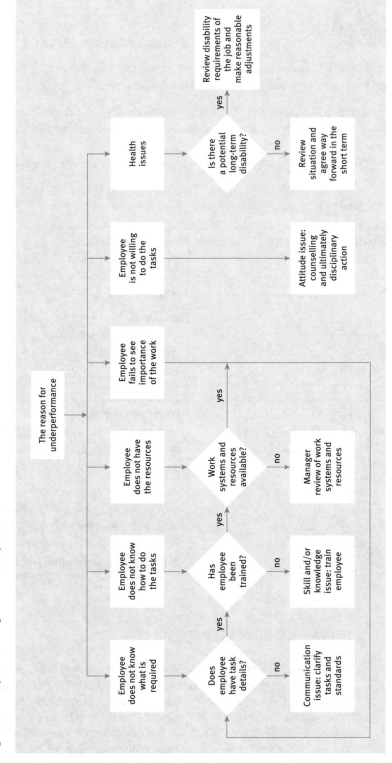

standard, assessed the employee's current performance level and identified and communicated the performance gap. A systematic approach to identification of the underlying cause of underperformance is required if appropriate managerial action is to be taken and a positive outcome achieved.

Gillan (2002) asserts that there are four main reasons why staff underperform and careful identification of the reason will assist in determining the managerial response. First, the employee may not know what the manager wants them to achieve. This is a communication problem and the manager needs to clarify the nature of the tasks and the performance standards, agree objectives and criteria for assessment. Second, the employee knows what is required but does not have the knowledge and skill to do the task. This is a learning problem and the manager needs to ensure that staff receive the necessary training to ensure that they develop the skill to do the task. If, following training, the employee still cannot perform to the standard required then this may be a capability issue. Assessment will have to be made on whether the employee is unable to reach the required standard because of a lack of ability which cannot be remedied through training in which case it is a capability issue. Alternatively, the employee may not be achieving the required standard due to an unwillingness to use the skills acquired through training in which case it may be a conduct issue (Chapter 17). Third, the employee knows what is required and can deliver to the standard expected but they do not have the resources required to fulfil the task and lack influence to access these resources. Consequently they fall below the required standard because of this lack of access to resources and their lack of ability to influence effective access to resources. In this case the manager needs to ensure that effective work systems are in place to support the employee in delivering to the required standard and that suitable resources are available to enable the employee to achieve the standard. Fourth, the employee knows what is required and how to do it but they do not want to do it. This may be because they do not see the importance of the task, in which case this may be rectified through effective communication, or they may not agree with the task, in which case it may be an attitude problem, or there may be an unwillingness to perform to the standard required and as a conduct issue this would need to be resolved through the disciplinary procedure (Chapter 17). In addition the manager should investigate whether there is an underlying health problem which is impacting on the employee's ability to perform the duties required by the job (Chapter 18, Exhibit 18.4) and consider reasonable adjustments if a disability is involved. Figure 11.3 exposes a systematic diagnosis of underperformance.

MANAGING EMPLOYEE ABSENCE

If the purpose of employing people is to get work done in the pursuit of organisational objectives, it is a truism that employee absences, through impacting upon overall individual performance, have considerable potential to impede efficient and effective organisational performance. Absence from work cannot be eliminated, nor would this be a desirable aim, but employee absence can be proactively managed in the context of the needs of the organisation and the needs of the individual employees. Proactive absence management requires an understanding of the types of absence, a knowledge of the consequences of absence and skill in applying techniques for monitoring and controlling absence. Employee absence which is sanctioned in advance, holiday leave for example, is less disruptive than absence which is unplanned, and a primary focus on the management of sick absence is therefore adopted in this section.

Types of absence

It is useful to identify the types of employee absence to illustrate the many reasons that employees have for not being present at work. Broad absence categories include:

- normal days off and flexitime
- annual leave and holidays
- other sanctioned leave, such as jury duty or reserve forces leave
- unauthorised absence which includes failure to attend when expected at work
- sick absence.

The contract of employment will specify normal working hours, days off and any flexitime arrangements and it is through the determination of the contract, and through making any justifiable contractual changes, that management can seek to control the impact of normal employee absence by specifying when employees should be present at work. Therefore, effective human resource planning provides a means for managing normal days off and flexitime. Holiday leave can also be managed through advance planning and through holiday controls which take account of patterns of organisational activity. These controls include the extent of individual holiday entitlement, subject to statutory minima, the determination of 'holiday-free time zones', the specification of compulsory holiday periods and limitations on the number and type of employees permitted to take leave at various times in the holiday year. These managerial controls are subject to legal, contractual and employee consent constraints, but the underlying principle is that holiday absence can be effectively managed through planning.

Other sanctioned employee leave can include maternity, parental, carers, time off for dependants, jury service, public duties, domestic emergencies, sabbaticals, trade union duties, training and development, religious observance and so on. It is evident that the potential for employee absence is huge and the development, definition and expression of the employer's attitude towards each of these types of sanctioned leave will achieve a balance between the needs of the individual and the needs of the business, and provide a means of reconciling the short-term disadvantages and long-term benefits to the organisation of these forms of employee absence. Formal written policies in these areas will articulate organisational values and provide line managers with guidelines for sanctioning leave other than normal days off and holidays. These sanctioned leave policies should address issues of payment, or non-payment, in the context of any statutory requirements, the extent of the leave available and the process for sanctioning it. Written, agreed policies will promote business-focused equity and transparency in dealing with these inescapable leave issues.

Unauthorised absence, or absenteeism, can be defined as an occasion when an employee fails to report for work when contractually obliged to do so and without prior agreement for absence. Employee failure to notify the employer in line with sick absence procedures or sanctioned leave arrangements may also constitute unauthorised absence. Unauthorised absence threatens to breach the contract of employment because the employee is not ready, willing and able for work and would normally be treated as a disciplinary matter, being subject to proper investigation, the opportunity for the employee to explain, and a considered decision by a reasonable employer (*see*

Chapters 17 and 18). The volume of this type of absenteeism is normally relatively small in comparison to other reasons for employee absence, and managerial control of absenteeism is available through the application of disciplinary procedures and the enforcement of the contract of employment. It is inevitable that some employees will conceal absenteeism as short-term sick absence and claims of being ill in these instances are difficult to disprove. However, if an employee exploits or abuses the sick absence rules or arrangements, there is the potential for gross misconduct leading to dismissal; for example, the dishonest claiming of sick pay or the wilful deceit of the employer will significantly undermine the mutual trust and confidence necessary to sustain the contract.

The management of sick absence not only presents a more complex set of issues and difficulties, but also sick absence normally causes greater disruption to organisational activity. The management of sick absence therefore requires particular attention.

THE MANAGEMENT OF SICK ABSENCE

The principal reason for focusing on the management of sick absence is because of the cost to work organisations, and its impact on the organisation's ability to achieve the level of performance expected. Attempts are regularly made to measure and quantify sick absence volumes and costs, and surveys consistently reveal figures which provoke managerial concern (IDS, 1998; CIPD, 2004; CBI, 2004; CIPD, 2008a; NICE, 2009; ACAS, 2009). Illustrative examples of these figures follow; however, in monitoring these measures of the costs of sick absence within organisations, it is evident that there has been little change in the last decade despite attempts at more proactive management of absence.

- NICE (2009) indicate that the estimated annual costs of sickness absence and 'worklessness' (those unemployed or economically inactive because of ill-health who may be receiving incapacity benefits) is around £100 billion – greater than the NHS budget.
- In the UK approximately 1 million people are absent from work each day because of sickness or other unanticipated cause (ACAS, CBI).
- Each employee averages eight to nine days' sick absence per year (CBI, CIPD).
- An average of 3.5 to 4 per cent of the potential working days available are lost because of sick absence, representing around 175–200 million days per year in the UK (IS, CIPD).
- Around two-thirds of absence is accounted for by spells of seven days or less and 16 per cent by spells of eight days to four weeks (CIPD).
- The annual direct financial cost is around £600 to £700 per employee (CIPD, ACAS).

Financial figures are crude because they are predicated on the assumption that the calculation of sick absence payments equates to direct financial costs. Clearly this is not necessarily the case, but the figures serve to illustrate that sick absence justifies managerial intervention. In addition to any direct financial costs of covering the work of the absent employee, through temporary replacement or overtime working, there may be implications for productivity levels or the quality of customer service, the absence may be disruptive to the planning and organisation of work, and absent colleagues place extra demands on those who remain at work. High levels of sick absence may impact negatively on overall job satisfaction and morale.

> Absence is often unplanned, so you need to be prepared to manage the employees you have at work to cushion the impact on customers and the overall flow of the work. High absence levels affect everyone in the organisation and cannot be regarded purely as a management problem. Employers, workers and their representatives should work together to monitor and control absence. This will help to maintain job satisfaction, increase productivity and control costs. (ACAS, 2009)

General sick absence patterns suggested by the research include the following.

- Workers in manual jobs tend to have higher levels of sick absence than non-manual employees; absence most commonly related to musculo-skeletal conditions.
- Public sector workers experience higher levels of sick absence than their private sector counterparts, by about 2 days a year.
- Lack of job satisfaction and stress-related sickness are cited as significant causes of absence.
- Younger employees tend to have more frequent, short-term sick absence, while older employees tend to have less frequent but longer-term sick absence.
- Sick absence tends to be greater in larger working groups than in small groups where there is a heightened perception of interdependence.

Why does the management of sick absence continue to be on the organisational agenda? Bevan and Hayday (1998) indicate that drivers for more active absence management include:

Maintaining competitiveness: as organisations reduce the number of staff they employ, the value of each remaining employee rises. Employers recognise that each day lost through absence represents lost production, disruption, reduced efficiency, compromised quality and lost opportunities.

Employee expectations: employees have generally higher levels of health awareness and higher expectations of what a 'good' employer should provide in terms of working conditions and benefits. There is a growing body of case law where employees have sought, and obtained, legal redress for damage to their physical and mental health at work.

Announcements by government: signalling that reducing sickness absence in the public sector is a high priority.

Although it is possible and practical to manage sick absence more actively in the pursuit of equity and organisational effectiveness, there is a danger of adopting a punitive managerial paradigm – the sending of a message to employees that management suspect that much of the sick absence lacks authenticity and validity. An over-zealous managerial approach may make genuinely committed employees feel guilty or at risk of retribution for being unwell and this is potentially detrimental to the employment relationship. There is a balance to be struck between the identification and resolution of employee attendance problems and the potential for the development of a destructive or dysfunctional organisational climate in relation to sick absence.

Causation

The root cause of sick absence is the fact that an employee is unwell, and where the employee is incapacitated there exists a state of being unfit for work. However, being unwell and being unfit for work are not necessarily synonymous. Research into causation (Steers and Porter, 1991) identifies scope for the exercise of employee judgement in deciding at which point 'being unwell' corresponds with 'being unfit for work' (*see* Exhibit 11.3). In effect, employee perceptions and decision-making impact on levels of workplace sick absence. There are a number of influences on employee perceptions and decisions – first, the individual employee's attitudes and values; second, the level of job satisfaction and whether absence is considered as legitimate in remedying a perceived imbalance in the employee effort to reward relationship; third, discomfort or tensions at work may predispose an unwell individual to engage in pain-avoidance behaviour, inducing a state of unfitness for work; fourth, the prevailing absence or attendance culture within the organisation; and, fifth, the nature of organisational policies, procedures and practices relating to sick absence. These causation influences, which need to be considered at individual, group and organisational levels, are introduced to demonstrate that a holistic approach to the management of sick absence is necessary and to suggest that the health of the psychological contract will be a factor in sick absence levels.

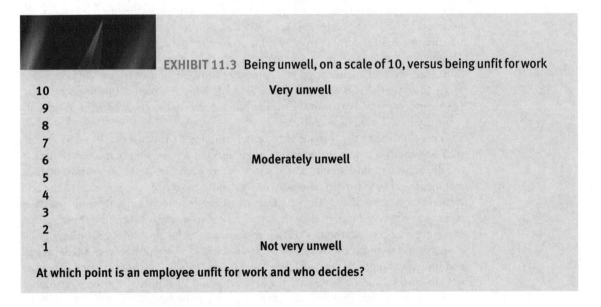

EXHIBIT 11.3 Being unwell, on a scale of 10, versus being unfit for work

10	**Very unwell**
9	
8	
7	
6	**Moderately unwell**
5	
4	
3	
2	
1	**Not very unwell**

At which point is an employee unfit for work and who decides?

Monitoring, measurement and control of sick absence

A systems approach to sick absence provides a useful framework for analysing the entry points for managerial intervention. The sick absence system (Figure 11.4) consists of candidates for employment (the inputs), the managing of sick absence (the processing unit) and either a return to acceptable attendance levels or the exit of employees with unacceptable absence levels (the outputs or outcomes).

Controlling entry to the organisation is part of managing sick absence. Candidates for employment can be given pre-engagement screening through health questionnaires

Figure 11.4 A systems
approach to managing
sick absence

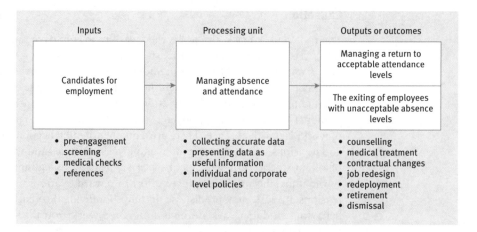

in the recruitment process. Checks by medical practitioners involve greater cost, and are subject to statutory restrictions (Access to Medical Records Act 1988), but provide a more informed opinion on fitness for employment. References relating to previous employment can include questions which solicit factual information about absence and attendance records. The objective of these activities is to establish capability for a particular job and to determine whether any reasonable adjustments to the work are necessary. The Data Protection Act 1998 classes information on health as sensitive information requiring more overt employee consent to its collection, security and use. The employer also needs to be able to demonstrate that the health information is going to be used for a legitimate purpose. This poses some challenges for the employer, but it would appear that a distinction can be made between 'medical information' and 'attendance records', with only the former being subject to employee consent constraints (Information Commission, 2002).

A prerequisite to the management of sick absence is the collection of good-quality data and managerial attention needs to be directed at ensuring that absence data is timely, accurate and reliable. The distinction between 'medical information', which includes the reason for any absence, and 'attendance records' also applies to the collection and storage of sick absence data for current employees and therefore medical records and absence records may need to be kept separately. Without tight reporting and recording systems there is considerable potential for the under-reporting of sick absence, and without hard facts impressionistic and unsupported views will prevail and limit meaningful action. The employer needs to establish and communicate how sick absence should be reported, to whom it should be reported and when it should be reported. This involves consideration of whether absence should be reported to the line manager or to an HR function. The argument for the former is not only that line managers should take responsibility for the effective management of their human resources, but also that employee absence raises immediate operational issues. The argument for the direct reporting of sick absence to an HR function is that the central collection of data is necessary for accurate adjustments to pay and for the coordination and analysis of organisation-wide sick absence data. Clearly, whichever arrangement applies, there needs to be reliable communication between HR and line managers.

When should employees report absence from work? From an employer's perspective the sooner the better, and it may be reasonable to require employees to make contact before the contractual starting time, or soon after, so that operational decisions can be made expediently. The legitimate requirement for an employee to report sick within a constrained time period is dependent upon the employee's ability to make contact, either through being physically able and having a telephone or through having contact with someone who can call instead, and therefore any time requirement needs to be interpreted reasonably. Certification requirements need to be effectively communicated to employees and statutory obligations for the administration of statutory sick pay need to be observed. Certification is the subject of debate with some employers claiming that self-certification is open to abuse by employees and also that GPs are inadequately trained for, and often indisposed to, making a fitness for work judgement. Black (2008), in addressing the issue of 'fitness or work' at the request of government, argued that 'Any improvement in work-related support for those who develop health conditions will need to be underpinned by a fundamental change in the widespread perception around fitness for work; namely that it is inappropriate to be at work unless 100 per cent fit and that being at work normally impedes recovery.' Black recommended a change from a 'sick note' to a 'well note', both in name and in philosophy, arguing that the concept of sick note dates from a time when 'an employer expected an employee to do a specific job rather than today's more flexible workplace'. Reforming the Medical Statement (2009) proposed a 'change to the format and content of the medical statement to include additional information from the doctor to help in discussions between the employer and the employee in achieving a return to work', with the aim of changing the focus from what the employee cannot do, to what they can do. The doctor can indicate that the person *'may be fit for some work now'* and suggest some common types of workplace or job role changes, subject to employer agreement, such as a phased return to work, altered hours of work, amended duties and workplace adaptations. The proposal is not seeking to take the decision away from the employer on whether an employee is fit to do the job. The employer, having considered all the circumstances of the case, still determines whether the employee is capable, or not, to undertake the work they are contracted to do. The changes to the medical statements also empower individuals to a greater extent to make informed decisions, through a 'personal capability assessment', about when they judge themselves fit to return to work, without necessarily having to be 'signed off' by the GP. This overall approach to intervention in sickness absence is based on the biopsychosocial model which simultaneously considers the biological (the medical condition), the psychological (the impact of the medical condition on the well-being of the individual) and the social (the impact on work and family), and the links between these three factors. All of this does raise the question about the extent to which GPs are capable of and comfortable in providing what is effectively occupational health advice, particularly when the GP's primary allegiance is to the patient and not to the employer.

Certificated raw sick absence data needs to be converted into managerial information and presented in a usable format. Basic absence measures such as the number of days for each employee and the total number of days in a given period are relatively easily available. A comparative measure known as the lost time rate or the potential working days lost (PWL) rate is calculated by taking the number of days lost due to sick absence, for an individual or for a group of workers, as a percentage of the potential working days available in a period, of a month or a year.

$$\text{PWL} = \frac{\textbf{Number of days absence}}{\textbf{Potential working days available}} \times \textbf{100}$$

For example, if a month (four weeks) is the given period, a department with 10 employees who work five days a week will have 200 potential working days ($4 \times 10 \times 5$). If during that period eight days are lost, the PWL rate is 4 per cent – the UK average in 2009 was 3.3 per cent, made up of private sector services, manufacturing and public services at 2.8, 2.9 and 4.3 per cent respectively (CIPD, 2009). The PWL calculation can be refined by using hours lost through sick absence, rather than whole days lost, to reflect more accurately the absence of part-time workers and the part-day absence of full-time workers. As long as a consistent measure is used, comparative information is generated (*see* Exhibit 11.4).

The PWL is a volume measure and does not reveal whether the sick absence in a period consists of the long-term absence of a small number of employees or whether it is made up of a high frequency of short-term sick absence. The frequency rate, sometimes called the inception rate, measures the number of instances or episodes of sick absence that occur in a given period.

$$\text{Frequency rate} = \frac{\text{Number of instances of sick absences}}{\text{Average number of employees}} \times 100$$

If, for example, a month is the given period, the average number of employees is 194 and the number of separate instances of sick absence, regardless of whether the same employee was absent more than once, is 35, the frequency rate is 18 per cent.

These measures provide valuable comparative information in terms of volume and frequency. Comparisons can be made between individuals, between departments or teams, on the basis of age, gender, job or working hours, and comparisons can be made over time. The measures can be benchmarked against those of other organisations. The objective is to determine the scale of any problem, to highlight any fluctuations and to focus attention on identified problems. The use of a computerised HR information system will be invaluable in generating comparative reports (*see* Chapter 5).

The frequency rate measure can be incorporated into an absence or attendance policy to provide 'triggers' for concern. This involves determining the frequency of individual employee absence which automatically stimulates managerial intervention and identifies an employee as an irregular attender. For example, concern may be triggered if an employee has four or more absences in a 12-month rolling period. Although attention may be drawn to a particular problem, the trigger point is a reason for scrutiny and **not** a reason for automatic warnings or other sanctions, as each case should be fairly and equitably considered on its merits. These triggers for concern send a powerful message to employees about what levels of absence are considered acceptable and also provide a consistent framework for managerial intervention. A disadvantage of these trigger points is that absence up to the trigger point level may be interpreted as an acceptable employee entitlement – the trigger point may legitimise a certain employee absence level. The Bradford Index (Exhibit 11.5) is a sick absence measuring tool which takes account of both volume and frequency of absence. The higher rating of frequency of absence produces a weighted comparative index and management can determine a points score to trigger scrutiny.

In addition to considering volume and frequency, the proactive management of absence should seek to detect dysfunctional patterns of employee absence, perhaps relating to weekends, bank holidays, busy or slack periods, significant sporting events and so on. Detecting these patterns, exposing them to employees and having sufficient

EXHIBIT 11.4 Absence management: costing sick absence

Organisations are increasingly recognising the significant costs associated with high levels of employee absence. At the same time, managers are often unsure about the level and nature of the problems they may be facing, or about how these problems are most effectively addressed. Most managers would accept, for example, that some level of absence is inevitable (and that it is generally desirable for employees to be absent from work if they are genuinely ill). Equally, most managers recognise that handling individual absence issues is often complex and potentially sensitive.

(CIPD, ACAS and HSE, 2006).

While acknowledging the *caveat* that financial figures are crude, because they are predicated on the assumption that a calculation of sick absence payments equates to direct financial cost, a simple costing mechanism to use is *direct* wage costs – the cost of paying employees who are absent through sickness.

Direct cost calculation

Number of employees		a
Average annual pay	£	b
Total annual pay bill = a × b	£	c
Total absence – days per year		d
Total potential working days per year		e
Potential working days lost (PWL) rate = d/e × 100		f
Direct cost per year = c × f	£	

Using the above method of calculation for a business unit of 200 employees, average pay of £22 500 per year, potential working days of 220 days per employee and an average absence level of 9.9 days per employee per year, the annual direct cost of absence is over £200 000 – equivalent to more than eight employees. A reduction in the absence level to eight days would reduce the direct cost figure by nearly £40 000 a year – equivalent to the work of almost two employees.

Questions

1 Work through the example above and calculate the direct cost of sick absence.

2 Calculate the direct cost of sick absence in your organisation – for a team, department or business unit.

3 Identify and justify three managerial sick absence interventions to reduce sick absence.

4 How realistic is it for any organisation to reduce the PWL rate by 0.5 per cent?

reasonable belief to take action are in fact based on concerns about the authenticity of any sick absence and raise issues about the mutual trust and confidence necessary to sustain a contract of employment rather than raising questions about the health and capability of the employee.

EXHIBIT 11.5 Bradford Index

Frequent episodes of absence are disruptive. The Bradford Index is a mechanism for weighting frequency of sick absence.

$$\text{Bradford Index} = S^2 \times D$$
where S = spells of absence in the period
and D = total number of days absence in the period

For example, three employees, all with a total of 10 days' absence in a year, but with different spells, have a very different index:

Employee 1 with 1 spell – $1^2 \times 10$ days = 10
Employee 2 with 2 spells – $2^2 \times 10$ days = 40
Employee 3 with 10 spells – $10^2 \times 10$ days = 1000

The higher rating of frequency of absence produces a weighted comparative index and management can determine a points score to trigger scrutiny.

Corporate level action on sick absence

Although most employee sick absence is not within managerial control, action can be taken to reduce overall corporate absence. Corporate level action includes the improvement of working conditions, the provision of health services, attention to the motivation and satisfaction of employees, and having fair and consistent procedures for dealing with individual employees with sick absence problems. Ten specific areas are identified for possible managerial attention.

1 Examine the health of the psychological contract, measured by employee morale, perceptions of equity in treatment, intrinsic and extrinsic job satisfaction, levels of stress and the extent of reciprocal loyalty relationships.

2 Evaluate the prevailing corporate culture, sick absence custom and practice, organisational attendance norms and any perceptions of sick leave as an entitlement to identify whether the reorientation of employee values and beliefs is appropriate.

3 Audit organisational contributions, physical and psychological, to sick absence to reveal potential for work environment improvement, the redesign of jobs, the genuine empowerment of employees and the encouragement of team responsibility.

4 Review the provision of occupational health services and positive health programmes and design policies which address wellness at work (*see* Chapter 14).

5 Provide good absence information and increase the skill of line managers to deal fairly and consistently with sick absence problems.

6 Use return to work interviews to establish the fitness of the employee to return and to express concern where appropriate – on a cautionary note there is potential for causing detriment to the employment relationship if the employee perceives that the purpose of the interview is to reach a verdict about whether or not the sick absence was genuine.

7 Consider the application of waiting days before the employee is entitled to company sick pay – in the short term this may act as a deterrent and can have a dramatic impact on absence levels, but there is the potential for it to be seen as a punitive measure with consequential harm to the employment relationship.

8 In contrast to point 7, consider offering incentives for attendance through rewarding, with extra payments or other rewards, employees who have little or no sick absence in a period. Clearly there are cost implications and employees are being paid again for what they are contractually required to do. In addition, once a qualification for an attendance bonus is lost through an episode of sick absence, the incentive value is also lost for the remainder of the period. An attendance reward may convert sick absence into 'sickness presence' which may be detrimental to the employee, to other employees and to the organisation.

9 Review organisational policies critically in relation to flexibility in working times and the authorisation of reasonable absence for significant life events or emergencies. Flexibility in these areas can reduce sick absence.

10 Communicate corporate sick absence values. Transparent policies reassure employees that genuinely sick employees will be treated with fairness and consistency and that there are procedures in place to deal with excessive sick absence (because it increases the workload of others).

The CIPD survey (2008a) of over 800 organisations, employing more than 2.3 million employees, reports on the percentage of those organisations using the following absence management practices to address short-term absence:

83 per cent Return-to-work interviews for all absences
76 per cent Disciplinary procedure for unacceptable absences
76 per cent Providing sickness absence information to line managers
74 per cent Use of trigger mechanisms to review attendance
64 per cent Leave for family circumstances
63 per cent Line managers taking primary responsibility for absence management
53 per cent Managers trained in absence handling
47 per cent Occupational health professional involvement
46 per cent Restricting sick pay
44 per cent Providing flexible working opportunities
38 per cent Changes in work patterns or environment
38 per cent Absence rate is a key performance indicator
36 per cent Capability procedure
33 per cent Attendance record as recruitment criteria
32 per cent Stress counselling
31 per cent Health promotion
30 per cent Employee assistance programme
27 per cent Absence considered in promotion decisions
21 per cent Tailored support for line managers

15 per cent   Physiotherapy services
15 per cent   Rehabilitation programme
14 per cent   Attendance bonus incentives

When asked to rate the effectiveness of these practices in managing short-term absence the users considered the most effective to be return-to-work interviews (70 per cent), trigger mechanisms to review attendance (32 per cent), the use of disciplinary procedures (24 per cent) and line managers taking primary responsibility for managing absence (18 per cent). Restricting sick pay seems to be increasing in perceived effectiveness with 18 per cent citing this in the top three most effective approaches for the management of short-term absence. In respect of long-term absence, the most effective practices were considered to be the involvement of the occupational health professional (53 per cent), rehabilitation programmes (20 per cent) and flexible working (16 per cent) with return-to-work interviews (14 per cent) and restricting sick pay at (13 per cent). Interestingly, rehabilitation programmes for long-term sick absence which were way down the list in 2004 are now seen as the second most effective tool for managing long-term absence with the use of disciplinary procedures not featuring at all, and line managers taking responsibility and being trained way down at 7 per cent. These figures and employer perceptions are introduced here not as some sort of definitive guide for managerial action but in order to stimulate debate about which practices might be most effective in particular organisational circumstances; there is no escape from contingency in HR practice.

CASE STUDY   Managing absence and attendance: comparative strategies

Reducing unplanned leave of absence at a major supermarket

Each employee is to be given three extra days of paid leave each year, but sick pay will not be paid for the first three days of any illness, regardless of whether the illness is genuine or not. Shopping voucher incentives will be given to employees who have zero unplanned absence in a year. The HR manager has stated that 'the aim of the scheme is to reduce absence which affects the level of customer service and increases the pressure on the employees who have to cover extra work. The aim is to encourage employees to plan absence and although we do not want to penalise genuinely ill employees, we do want to discourage employees from taking regular days off.' The HR manager provides reassurance that the organisation will be sympathetic to reasonable employee requests for time off for family or domestic matters to avoid employees feeling they have to claim to be sick to attend to pressing personal matters. The scheme has the tentative support of USDAW, although they are less happy about the lack of sick pay for the first three days of sick absence.

Managing absence at a UK train operator

Managers are reluctant to appear heavy-handed and want to maintain good relations with the recognised trade union. It was recognised that there were deficits in accurate sick absence data and in management capability to manage sick absence. In particular there was a lack of understanding of the purpose of return-to-work interviews and therefore they were rarely undertaken. Absence management was perceived by line managers, who were intensely financially focused, as not their problem and expected HR to deal with it. The response of the organisation was to ensure the accuracy and reliability of the data, to produce a league table which was made available to managers and employees and to introduce a 'One of our team is missing' training programme to raise individual awareness of the impact of sick absence on the rest of the team. Other initiatives included enabling easier access to occupational health professionals, setting up a joint management and trade union 'Sickness and release group' to focus on preventive measures and setting targets of a reduction in sick absence from 9 to 7 per cent for on-train employees and from 5 to 4 per cent for station-based employees.

Questions

1 Discuss these two approaches to managing absence and attendance and identify the management challenges associated with them.

2 Evaluate the extent to which each approach is likely to reduce the frequency and/or volume of sick absence.

Individual level action on sick absence

Managerial action in relation to an individual with an unacceptable absence record is problematic to prescribe, but there are a number of issues to consider. First, it is important to distinguish between frequent short-term absence and long-term ill health. The latter may best be pursued as ill-health termination of contract or retirement, depending on organisational provision and the characteristics, circumstances and service of the employee concerned. Ill-health which results in incapability is a potentially fair reason for dismissal (*see* Chapter 18). 'It is a commonly held view that to dismiss an employee because of ill health is unfair if the person is genuinely sick; this is not the case' (Stevens and Fitzgibbons, 2001). Where frequency of absence is the problem the employer may consider whether the validity of absence is in doubt. Where there are validity concerns it may be more appropriate to deal with the absence as a disciplinary issue. If there appears to be an underlying medical problem, a prognosis should be obtained from a medical practitioner, or comments from the GP asserting 'may be fit for some work now' may initiate discussions on whether and when the employee will be able to undertake some or all of their contracted duties. A prognosis may also provide an opportunity for an employee to receive counselling or medical advice. The outcome of the prognosis will inform managerial action, but deciding on how to proceed remains a managerial and not a medical decision. It is not sensible or practical to define a point at which sick absence levels become unacceptable, as this depends on many factors such as the nature of the work, the consequences of the absence, the size and resources of the organisation, the length and quality of the employee's service and any mitigating circumstances. The employee has a duty to be ready, willing and able for work and it is for the employer to decide reasonably and fairly at which point 'enough is enough' and to take action against the employee. An interview or hearing with the

EXHIBIT 11.6 The sick absence encounter between manager and employee

- The encounter is potentially emotionally charged and there can be a clash of perspectives, with the employer, while being sympathetic, having a primary concern with organisational attendance needs and employees perceiving that they are being criticised for being sick.
- The facts from earlier discussions and the sick absence record are needed.
- The employee should receive notice of any interview together with the reason for the interview, have the right to be accompanied and have the matter conducted in privacy and with confidentiality.
- The objective is to convey managerial concern and listen to and consider any employee response; this may involve an adjournment.
- Based on the information available, the managerial decision should be made and communicated in writing, ensuring that the employee is clear on what is expected and on the consequences of an inability to meet the specified standard.
- It is normally appropriate to monitor attendance, provide support and instigate reviews.
- Even-handedness in the treatment of employees is an important principle of natural justice – employees with similar sick absence records should normally be treated similarly.

individual employee will form part of any decision-making process, and factors relating to the sick absence encounter between the employee and the employer are exposed in Exhibit 11.6.

Alternative courses of action are available to managers following full consideration of the sick absence facts in relation to the individual employee. These include managing a return to acceptable attendance levels through counselling, medical treatment, job redesign, redeployment (although there is no obligation on the employer to create a job) or contractual changes to accommodate the 'problem'. If these fail, or are inappropriate, then the employee may need to be released through either retirement or dismissal. In summary, three principles emerge for the management of long-term individual sick absence. First, the decision is not a medical decision but a managerial decision with a medical input; second, even-handedness of managerial action is desirable; third, being prepared to recognise the 'enough is enough' principle, the point at which all alternatives have been exhausted and dismissal becomes a reasonable employer action in the circumstances.

The management of sick absence in relation to pregnancy, disability and stress requires particularly careful handling. Pregnancy sick absence is probably a no-go area for managerial action, although in certain circumstances it can trigger the start of maternity leave. For employees with a disability who qualify for protection under the Disability Discrimination Act (1995) the employer has a duty to consider reasonable adjustments to the work and may need to discount any absences related to the particular disability. Case law suggests that the application of an attendance policy to disability-related absences may be discriminatory and therefore dismissal for disability-related absence may be unfair. The 'stress paradox' describes a situation in which a distressed employee may be fit for work as long as he or she is not at work, but the return to work, and the associated stress, provokes a recurrence of absence.

In an investigation into managing absence in retail, financial services and manufacturing organisations Dunn and Wilkinson (2002) found that:

> Policies and procedures, whilst an important influence on the management of absence, are not a panacea. Instead, the responsibility of everyday cases, which make up the bulk of the problem, rests with line managers. Whilst HR played an important and integral role in ensuring that line management recognise their responsibilities in absence management, in some cases the position was left unclear. In some companies, the somewhat ad hoc approach to managing absence on the part of HR and line management, coupled with a clear lack of distinction in responsibility, resulted in a case of muddling through. As such, absence problems were not identified and dealt with at an early stage. This lack of accountability often resulted in inconsistencies in approach, which had the effect of discrediting the system as a whole. Many managers did not find out they were presiding over a problem until it was too late. Finally, the unclear distinction of accountability was also a result of inadequate training in basic counselling techniques.

Some gains can be made in managing sick absence, but there is limited potential to reduce it and there is no quick fix. Indeed, the CIPD (2008a) absence survey shows that the level of absence has declined only slowly in the past 10 years from 4.1 per cent in 2000, peaking at 4.4 per cent in 2002 and falling to 3.5 per cent in 2008. There is potential to create a punitive managerial paradigm which can be dysfunctional to the organisation. Perhaps there needs to be a shift away from the more punitive philosophy of absence control in favour of more enlightened 'attendance management' strategies which aim to provide a working environment which maximises and motivates employee attendance. McHugh (2001), although specific to local government in Northern Ireland, raises issues which have wider currency for the management of sick absence. In particular, she identifies a failure 'to acknowledge the interdependence of individual and organisational well-being' and comments that 'high levels of ill health are indicative of ill health on the part of the organisation'. There is therefore a need for managers to recognise that absence levels will not be reduced purely by tightening controls on employees or setting targets (CIPD, 2001); the organisation needs to be introspective about the contribution it makes to absence levels.

SUMMARY LEARNING POINTS

1 Performance management is a holistic process which aligns corporate, unit, team and individual objectives. It is supported by HR strategies and processes which encourage a performance culture with the aim of improving overall corporate performance.

2 SMART objectives may lead to rigidity in the performance management process and organisations may need to consider the process of continuous improvement or CASE objectives.

3 Performance appraisal is a sub-set of performance management and includes the processes and procedures for the assessment of employee performance, the identification of training and development needs and the allocation of rewards.

4 Types of appraisal systems include top-down, self, peer, upward and 360-degree or multi-rater appraisal. The choice of appraisal system is influenced by the nature of the organisation and the external context.

5 The balanced scorecard may be a useful tool by enabling a number of balanced and interrelated objectives related to people, tools, processes and finance to be identified and monitored on a regular basis and the balanced scorecard methodology can be customised to measure the performance of different functions within the organisation.

6 Mechanisms for managing underperformance include training and development, redeployment, counselling and disciplinary action. Diagnosis of the cause determines the managerial response.

7 Normal days off, holidays and other sanctioned leave can be managed through careful planning and through the application of clear organisational policies. Unauthorised absence (absenteeism) is effectively a disciplinary matter. Managing sick absence presents a more complex set of issues and difficulties.

8 Sick absence has a financial and an operational cost to the organisation and warrants managerial attention. However, an over-zealous approach to managing sick absence may lead to a punitive paradigm which is detrimental to the employment relationship.

9 Corporate sick absence levels are influenced by an array of individual and organisational factors. A systems approach to managing sick absence provides a framework for identifying entry points for managerial intervention.

10 Prerequisites to the effective management of sick absence are the collection, analysis and presentation of accurate and timely information. Managerial action needs to adopt a corporate approach as well as having firm and consistent policies for dealing with individuals.

REFERENCES AND FURTHER READING

Advisory, Conciliation and Arbitration Service (2009) *Managing Attendance and Labour Turnover: Advisory Booklet*. London: ACAS.

Armstrong, M. (2002) *The Performance Management Audit*. Cambridge: Cambridge Strategy Publications.

Armstrong, M. (2002) *Employee Reward*. London: CIPD.

Armstrong, M. and Baron, A. (2005) *Managing Performance: Performance management in action*. London: CIPD.

Bevan, S. *et al.* (2004) 'How employers manage absence', *DTI Employment Relations Research Series*, 25.

Bevan, S. and Hayday, S. (1998) *Attendance Management: A review of good practice* (IES Report 353). Brighton: Institute for Employment Studies.

Black, C. (2008) *Working for a healthier tomorrow*. London: TSO.

Bones, C. (1996) 'Performance Management: The HR contribution'. Paper delivered at the Annual Conference of the Institute of Personnel and Development, Harrogate, October.

CBI (2003) *Absence and Labour Turnover Survey: The lost billions: addressing the costs of absence.* London: CBI.

CBI (2004) *Absence and Labour Turnover Survey: Focus on absence.* London: CBI.

CIPD (2005) *Coaching and Mentoring Factsheet.* London: CIPD.

CIPD (2008a) *Absence Management: Annual Survey Report.* London: CIPD.

CIPD (2008b) *Shaping the future – a vision for sustainable high performing organisations.* CIPD: London.

CIPD (2009) *Absence Management: Annual Survey Report.* London: CIPD.

CIPD, ACAS and HSE (2006) *Absence Management – how do you develop an absence strategy?* CIPD: London.

Dibben, P., Philip, J. and Cunningham, I. (2001) 'Absence management in the public services: recent evidence from the UK', HRM Discussion Paper Series: No. 7. April. Middlesex University.

Dunn, C. and Wilkinson, A. (2002) 'Wish you were here: managing absence', *Personnel Review*, 31(2), 228–46.

Fletcher, C. (2004) *Appraisal and feedback: making performance review work.* London: CIPD.

Gillan, T. (2002) *Leadership skills for boosting performance.* London: CIPD.

Gilmore, S. and Williams, S. (2009) *Human Resource Management.* Oxford: Oxford University Press.

Guest, D. (2000) 'Human resource management, employee well-being and organizational performance', Paper presented at the CIPD Professional Standards Conference, 11 July 2000.

Guest, D. *et al.* (2003) 'Human Resource management and corporate performance in the UK', *British Journal of Industrial Relations*, 41(2), 291–314.

Hall, D. (2009) in Gilmore, S. and Williams, S. (2009) *Human Resource Management.* Oxford: OUP. Chapter 7.

Harris, L. (2001) 'Rewarding employee performance – line managers' values, beliefs and perspectives', *International Journal of Human Resource Management*, 12(7), 1182–92.

Hendry, C., Bradley, P. and Perkins, S. (1997) 'Missed a motivator', *People Management*, May.

Holbeche, L. (2006) 'Building high performance – the key role for HR', *Impact*. Iss: 20. August.

Holbeche, L. (2008) 'High Performance Working', *People Management*. 30 October, 24–27.

Hope, K. (2005) 'Sick-note strategy planned', *People Management*, 10 February, 7.

IDS (1998) *Managing Absence.* Incomes Data Services Study 556. London: IDS.

IDS (2003) *Performance Management.* Incomes Data Services Study 748. London: IDS.

IDS (2003) *Sick pay schemes.* Incomes Data Services Study 766. London: IDS.

Information Commission (2002) *Data Protection Code of Practice: Employment Records.* Wilmslow: Information Commissioner's Office.

IRS Employment Review (2003) *Performance Management: Policy and Practice* 781, August, 12–19. London: IRS.

IRS Employment Review (2003) *Time to Talk: How and why employers conduct appraisals* 769a, February, 8–14. London: IRS.

Kaplan, R.S. and Norton, D.P. (1992) 'The Balanced Scorecard: measures that drive performance', *Harvard Business Review*, Jan–Feb, 71–9.

Kaplan, R.S. and Norton, D.P. (1993) 'Putting the balanced scorecard to work', *Harvard Business Review*, September–October, 134–42.

Kennerley, M. and Bourne, M. (2003) *Assessing and maximizing the impact of business performance*. Cranfield Centre for Business Performance. Cranfield School of Management.

Leopold, J. (2002) *Human Resources in Organisations*. Harlow: FT Prentice Hall.

Leopold, J. and Harris, L. (2009) *The Strategic Managing of Human Resources*. Harlow: FT Prentice Hall.

Marchington, M. and Wilkinson, A. (2008) *Human Resource Management at Work*. London: CIPD.

McHugh, M. (2001) 'Employee absence: an impediment to organisational health in local government', *The International Journal of Public Sector Management*, 14(1), 43–58.

Neale, F. (1991) *The Handbook of Performance Management*. London: IPM.

NICE (2009) *Managing sickness absence and incapacity for work*. London: NICE Publications.

Pollitt, D. (2004) 'Tesco pilots scheme to cut unplanned leave of absence', *Human Resource Management*, 12(6), 21–3.

Pollitt, D. (2006) 'Performance Management in practice: a comparative study of executive agencies', *Journal of Public Administration Research and Theory*, 16(1), 25–44.

Power, M. (2007) 'Workforce scorecard metrics for business-focused HR performance reporting', *HR Bulletin: Research and Practice*. CIPD: Portsmouth Group.

Purcell, J., Kinnie, N., Hutchinson, S., Rayton, B. and Swart, J. (2003) *Understanding the People Performance Link: Unlocking the black box*. London: CIPD.

Purcell, J., Hutchinson, S., Kinnie, N., Swart, J. and Rayton, B. (2004) *Vision and values: organizational culture and values as a source of competitive advantage*. Executive briefing. London: CIPD.

Reforming the Medical Statement (2009) 'Draft Medical Statement Regulations'. Health, Work and Well-being Directorate, Department for Work and Pensions, www.dwp.gov.uk.

Rose, M. (2000) 'Target practice', *People Management*, 23 November.

Silcox, S. (2003) 'Adopting a risk management approach to manage absence', *IRS Employment Review* 786, 21–4.

Steers, R. and Porter, L. (1991) *Motivation and Work Behaviour*. New York: McGraw-Hill.

Stevens, P. and Fitzgibbons, E. (2001) 'How to tackle long term sick leave', *People Management*, 12 July, 42–3.

Strebler, M. (2004) *Tackling Poor Performance*. IES Report 406. Brighton: Institute for Employment Studies.

Strebler, M.T., Robinson, D. and Bevan, S. (2001) *Performance Review: Balancing objectives and content*. IES Report 370. Brighton: Institute for Employment Studies.

Torrington, D., Hall, L. and Taylor, S. (2008) *Human Resource Management*. Harlow: FT Prentice Hall.

Work Foundation (2002) 'Maximising attendance', *Managing Best Practice*, 96.

ASSIGNMENTS AND DISCUSSION TOPICS

1 Identify and then critically examine a performance management process. Discuss the extent to which it meets the requirements of the organisation for improved performance and the needs of the individual for recognition and reward.

2 In small groups critically review examples of individual performance objectives; what objective measures would you use to assess performance against these objectives?

3 Critically examine the process for collecting sick absence information in your organisation. How effective is it in capturing accurate, timely and reliable data?

4 Find out the potential working-days lost (PWL) rate and the frequency rate in relation to sick absence, in percentage terms, in your organisation and benchmark it against those of other organisations. Comment on similarities and differences.

5 Examine the 10 specific areas for managing sick absence at a corporate level, listed in this chapter, and comment on the effectiveness of each in relation to your own organisation.

6 The CIPD survey (2008a) of management practice in dealing with employee absence reported the finding that around 27 per cent cite 'other absences not due to genuine ill health' as a cause of short-term absence. Clearly, this is a perception and the reality is difficult to verify, but the implication is that a substantial proportion of sick absence is not genuine. Make your own assessment of this finding – is it the case that 27 per cent of absence involves dishonest intent? What does this mean? What can be done about it?

7 High levels of sick absence are costly and disruptive to an employer. How would you, as the HR professional, respond to a demand from a line manager (your internal customer) to terminate the employment of an employee who has been absent from work with a legitimate illness for three months? How differently, if at all, would you respond to the demand if the employee in question had been absent from work for a total of two months in the past year, but this was made up of 10 incidents of sick absence which averaged four days each?

Chapter 12

Human Resource Development

by Valerie Anderson

LEARNING OUTCOMES: TO BE ABLE TO

- Assess the significance of human resource development (HRD) for individual and organisational performance and change

- Evaluate the systematic approach for identifying and responding to learning and development needs

- Assess different approaches to HRD strategy formulation

- Review the management development requirements of effective HRD

- Consider the contribution of knowledge management and human capital management processes to organisational effectiveness

- Discuss the influence of national skills development processes on HRD in organisations

INTRODUCTION

This chapter is concerned with training, development and learning processes at individual and organisational levels. It introduces the broad topic area of human resource development (HRD) as a way of ensuring that individuals and organisations can improve their performance and adapt to change through learning, training and development processes. HRD links with all other features of people resourcing, in particular HR planning, performance management, employee reward and the management of the employment relationship.

HRD is grounded and based in the practices and principles of training and development so these are considered first. The organisational features of strategic HRD, knowledge management and human capital management are then outlined before a final discussion about the influence that wider government-sponsored features of education and skill development have on individual and organisational performance.

HUMAN RESOURCE DEVELOPMENT

HRD is a broad and continuously evolving area of activity concerned with the training and development of individuals but also wider learning processes at an organisational and at a national level. There is no consensus on the extent to which HRD should be seen as a 'sub-set' of HRM or whether it should form an organisational function and a profession in its own right (Garavan *et al.*, 2004; Gold *et al.*, 2003: 437). Some organisations have a training function or department and some do not. In some organisations, there is an HRD function that forms part of the HRM department and in other organisations HRD is linked with an organisation development (OD) function and operates separately from the HRM function. In this chapter HRD is defined as **the activities involved in organising individual and collective learning processes aimed at the development of both employees and the organisation as a whole.** The workplace is a vital context for HRD as it is here that learning is achieved and applied. Effective HRD can lead to sustainable competitive advantage if employees are encouraged to engage in personal and professional development in ways that are appropriate for them as individuals and for the work-based context in which they operate (Poell, 2007). HRD involves training, development and learning; definitions of these terms are provided in Exhibit 12.1.

EXHIBIT 12.1 **Key activities in HRD**

- Training – activities that are 'instructor-led' and focused on acquiring skills and performing tasks in the required way.
- Development – a process of growth associated with realising individual potential and ability.
- Learning – a process leading to increased adaptive capacity associated with skills, knowledge and understanding, values and attitudes.

As ideas about the nature and purpose of HRM have developed (*see* Chapters 1 and 2) so also have ideas about the activities that are required to enable learning to occur in the workplace. Instructor-led training and development processes remain important to HRD but the importance of work-based learning activities (both formal and informal) has become increasingly accepted through, for example, teamworking processes or coaching and mentoring activities. A key issue for HRD, therefore, is the recognition that learning and development are integrated with a wide range of other organisational processes and systems, particularly those related to performance management, reward and employment relations.

THE SYSTEMATIC APPROACH TO TRAINING AND LEARNING

A key feature for effective HRD (McCracken and Wallace, 2000; Gibb, 2008) is a systematic and business-focused approach to planning and delivering training and learning rather than relying on fragmented or '*ad hoc*' approaches to coping with skills shortages. The systematic approach to training and learning has developed over many decades and involves a planned, cyclical process, as illustrated in Figure 12.1. The systematic approach can be relevant to the provision of training activities for groups of employees but it can also be applied to learning processes for individuals and to a 'whole organisation' level. The four stages that comprise the systematic approach are outlined in the following sections.

Identifying and analysing learning needs

The process of training needs analysis (TNA) or learning needs analysis works from the assumption that effective organisational performance requires clear organisational goals and attractive and relevant learning opportunities (Bee and Bee, 2003). The TNA

Figure 12.1 The systematic training model

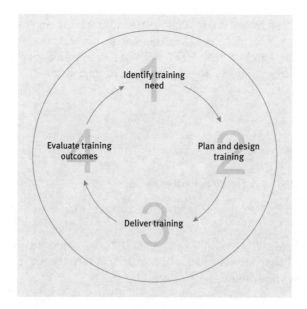

process can be broken down into three main stages (Harrison, 2009); collect data, identify the 'capability and performance gap' and then make recommendations to close the gap.

- Collect data. This involves finding out what the capability and performance 'needs' (of the organisation, team or individual) are as well as finding out about current capability and performance levels.

- Assess the capability and performance gap. This is the process of analysis that clarifies the extent of the gap between desired and actual capability and performance and the extent to which the gap can be closed by some form of learning, training or development intervention(s).

- Make recommendations to learners, managers and other stakeholders that will be feasible and relevant to the context in which the individual, team or organisation is operating.

Data for TNA processes can come from a range of different sources. Much of the 'written down' information will already be available within the organisation. Other information may need to be gathered at the time, through interviews with job-holders or their managers, for example. Much of the data, particularly data generated from management information systems, can demonstrate trends over time and any variation from expected or required levels of performance. Some ideas about sources of information are listed in Exhibit 12.2.

EXHIBIT 12.2 Learning needs analysis: examples of sources of information

Current capability and performance	Future issues: capability and performance 'needs'
Measures • Productivity • Quality • Financial contribution • HR issues (e.g. absence)	*Performance and capability information* • Strategic targets • Market/client base data • Technological developments • Legislative changes • Planned organisational change initiatives
Feedback information • Appraisal/competence assessment • Customer surveys • Benchmarking data • Managers' assessments	*Methods of articulating future issues* • SWOT or PESTLE analyses • Brainstorming • Force field analysis • Scenario planning
Self-assessment information • Job-holders' opinions • Personal development plans • Professional development plans	

Analysis of the **capability and performance gap** may be differently undertaken depending on the purpose or the trigger for the TNA process as follows:

- A **trainer-led** approach. This approach is likely where some form of training is the expected outcome. The analysis focuses on job tasks and behaviours and identifies the 'gap' in knowledge, skills and attitudes (KSA) or competencies which will be addressed through some form of training intervention designed by a specialist trainer.

- An **individual-led** approach. This will involve self-analysis and self-development. A range of development and learning processes may result from this process which often integrates problem identification, learning and problem-solving processes together. The result of this analysis may be some 'trainer-led' intervention but it is also likely to lead to other less formal forms of self-development process.

- An **organisation-wide** approach. This will focus on the continuous development and learning of **all** employees. A range of different learning outcomes may well be expected and an integrated approach to their achievement can be formulated.

Learning needs analysis does not have to lie wholly within the province of specialist trainers or HRD practitioners and may involve a range of different stakeholders, as indicated in Exhibit 12.3.

EXHIBIT 12.3 Roles and responsibilities in learning needs analysis

Stakeholders	Key skills needed to undertake a learning needs analysis
• Learners	• Managing expectations
• Colleagues	• Relationship skills
• Line managers	• Information gathering
• Senior managers	• Analytic skills
• Clients/customers	
• Suppliers	**Roles for HRD specialists**
• Change agents	• Information gathering
• Budget holders	• Information analysis
• HRD practitioners	• Facilitation to help people and managers collect and analyse information for themselves

Recommendations that might emerge from an analysis of learning needs should take into account the extent to which the capability and performance gap is attributable to an HRD issue. It may be that the root cause of the gap is a lack of resources, inappropriate physical working conditions, or the break-down of team or management relationships etc. In such circumstances non-HRD actions are appropriate. Effective recommendations from a TNA process will have the following characteristics:

- Include positive as well as negative feedback.
- Have regard for the feelings of job-holders and their managers in the way the feedback and recommendations are offered.
- Present evidence-based (rather than opinion-based) information.
- Present a business case for the proposals that are made.

Design of learning activities

This second stage of the systematic approach, that of the design of learning events or activities, also has three main stages:

- Formulate training objectives or learning outcomes.
- Select an appropriate learning or training strategy.
- Design and plan the activity in detail to ensure participants can achieve the training objectives or learning outcomes.

Gibb (2008) provides a useful description of the relationship between learning aims, goals and objectives:

- Aims – these are not directly measurable but are statements of intent, purpose, focus and boundaries.
- Goals – these relate to general outcomes and should provide clarity for the designers of the learning activities and the potential participants.
- Objectives – these should be measurable and are statements of specific outcomes against which the learning activities will be developed.

If the learning activity is focused on specific job skills and behaviours then specific objectives should be established that relate to the **knowledge** that the learner should acquire, the **skills** that the learner should be able to demonstrate (be they tactile, manual, interpersonal etc.) and the **attitude** or **behaviour** that is appropriate. Opinion varies about the extent to which learning objectives or outcomes for all forms of training and learning can be measurable. It is possible to assess whether someone can use a new piece of software with a given proficiency level, for example, but it is less easy to measure the extent to which 'customer service attitudes' have been demonstrated and might be sustained.

Once training objectives or learning outcomes have been defined it is possible to consider which learning and training strategies are most appropriate in order to achieve them. Learning strategies vary extensively. At one extreme is the option of a pre-programmed, course-based strategy where a predetermined body of knowledge and skills are delivered by specialist trainers. At the other extreme is the strategic option of a flexible, informal, experiential approach where learning is facilitated rather than delivered, not necessarily by training specialists or experts. Strategic choices to be made when deciding on the learning strategy are shown in Figure 12.2.

Delivery of learning interventions

Once the broad strategy has been determined the final planning and design of the learning activities can commence. There is an extensive range of learning and training

Figure 12.2 Learning
strategy decisions

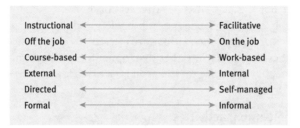

methods from which to choose. The CIPD *Learning and Development Survey* (CIPD, 2008a), which is completed by HRD/HRM specialists, provides an indication of the most popular methods in UK organisations. Data taken from the 2008 survey is shown in Exhibit 12.4 which suggests the most popular methods at that time.

The 2009 survey (CIPD, 2009a) examined which learning and training methods had been used to a greater extent over the previous two years, with over 40 per cent of respondents highlighting an increased use of in-house development programmes, coaching by line managers, e-learning and internal knowledge-sharing events.

EXHIBIT 12.4 Percentage of survey respondents using different learning and training methods

Method	%	Method	%
On-the-job training	92	Instructor-led training delivered off the job	75
In-house development programmes	88	Mentoring and buddying system	75
Coaching by line managers	88	Job rotation, secondment, shadowing	72
Formal education courses	83	Coaching by external practitioners	68
External conferences, workshops, events	81	E-learning	67
Internal knowledge-sharing events	75	Audio-tapes, videos, learning resources	53

Learning styles

To ensure that learning outcomes or training objectives are achieved and that appropriate methods are used it is important to take account of the different ways in which people learn. One of the most influential explanatory frameworks for 'how people learn', which has underpinned the practice of almost all HRD professionals, comes from the work of Kolb (1996), who conceptualised learning as a cyclical process with four main stages (*see* Figure 12.3) grounded in action, observation, reflection, and application in practice.

Figure 12.3 The
experiential learning
model

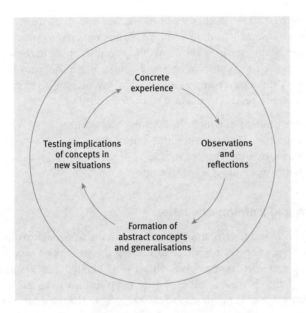

Source: Kolb *et al.* (© 1974) *Organizational Psychology: Book of Readings*, 2nd edn. Reprinted by
permission of Prentice-Hall, Inc. Upper Saddle River, NJ.

Kolb suggests that individuals may have a preference for different 'stages' in the
experiential learning cycle and Honey and Mumford's (1982) learning style preferences categorise these as:

- Activists – learn best when actively involved in tasks.
- Reflectors – prefer to learn through observation and reflection on activities.
- Theorists – learn best through linking their experiences with concepts and
  theories.
- Pragmatists – prefer to apply new information in practical 'real-life' situations.

From a learning design and delivery perspective it is important to take into account
the learning style preferences of those who will participate in the activities when
choosing which methods to adopt. The expectations of adult learners, who bring a
great deal of experience to the learning environment, should also be taken into account.
Adult learners expect to have a high degree of influence on what they are to learn,
how they are to learn and how it is to be evaluated. Race (1993) highlights, in addition, the importance of taking into account the motivation of learners (what they
need or want). He argues that training design and delivery should incorporate four
considerations:

- learner motivation(s);
- opportunities for 'doing' (through practice, trial and error);
- provision of feedback for learners (seeing the results and other people's
  reactions);
- the opportunity to 'digest' or to make sense of what has been learned, thus giving
  ownership to the learners.

Active participation of learners in the design and implementation of learning interventions is important and, in addition, adults who have invested time in training and learning expect to see how they can apply their learning in their work. Adult learners also expect their responses to be acted upon when and if they are asked for feedback (Knowles, 1990; Pogson and Tennant, 1995). When choosing methods of learning and training, therefore, it is important to take account of:

- the environment in which the learning will occur;
- opportunities for experience and reflection;
- learner motivation and emotions;
- different ways and styles of learning.

Training and learning evaluation

Evaluation is the fourth stage of the systematic approach to learning and training. Evaluation is concerned with: 'establishing the success or otherwise of development activities, and with assessing whether the associated benefits justify the investment' (Stewart, 1999: 178). A number of different frameworks to guide evaluation processes have been proposed and Simmonds (2003) argues that evaluation may relate to a range of different questions (*see* Exhibit 12.5).

EXHIBIT 12.5 Different evaluation questions

- How effective was the learning or training needs analysis?
- How effective were the training or learning strategies and methods?
- What were the reactions of learners and trainers to the learning or training activities?
- To what extent were intended knowledge, skills and attitudes acquired by those who participated in the learning or training activities?
- What changes in workplace performance are attributable to learning or training activities?
- To what extent have learning activities contributed to the achievement of organisational goals?

Evaluation is a key activity for learning, training and HRD specialists, and the literature reflects a professional search for the 'best way' to answer these questions. However, there is no consensus and Anderson (2007) argues that a 'one size fits all' approach to evaluation is inappropriate. Two very different philosophical approaches can be taken to evaluation. The 'scientific/quantitative approach' (see, for example, Phillips, 1991) seeks to develop evaluation techniques that focus on objective measurement carried out by experts whereby the costs and benefits of any learning and training activities can be measured and so a 'return on investment' can be calculated. Evaluation frameworks that focus on 'levels of measurement' are popular within this approach. Kirkpatrick (1975) offers a four-level framework and Hamblin (1974) suggests five levels are appropriate, as illustrated in Exhibit 12.6.

EXHIBIT 12.6 **Levels and evaluation**

Level of evaluation	Evaluation questions
Reaction	What do learners feel about the learning activity and the learning process they have undertaken?
Learning	What have learners actually learned as a result of the activity they have participated in (knowledge, skills, attitudes etc.)?
Job behaviour	What impact has the learning activity had on job performance; to what extent has 'learning transfer' occurred?
Team/department	What impact has the learning activity had on team or departmental performance?
Organisational/ ultimate benefit	To what extent has value for money been achieved? How cost-effective was the learning/training activity? What business contribution has been achieved?

This approach to evaluation, therefore, seeks to quantify the economic benefits of training (Phillips, 1991), which may include:

- Cost savings – doing more and/or better for less money; decreasing unit costs and/or overheads etc.
- Time savings – doing more and/or better work more quickly, achieving improved order response times etc.
- Work habits – improving productivity, reducing absenteeism, diminishing levels of rule violations.
- New skills – improved quality of work, fewer defects, reduced accident rates, increased capability levels within the organisation.
- Work climate – reduced staff turnover, fewer grievances, increased commitment or job satisfaction.
- Initiative – more and better new ideas and work accomplishments.

This approach has been criticised as being limited in scope. Talbot (1992) suggests that learners should be the main stakeholders involved in evaluation and that intangible benefits should be included such that the long-term consequences of learning can be evaluated. A key issue here is the enhancement of learning processes rather than a focus on 'proving' the worth or value of training activities. Thompson (2007) suggests that focusing too much on return on investment and 'whether training works' may distract energy from finding out **why and how** training works so that the most appropriate approaches can be harnessed. These issues are particularly relevant where management training and development is being evaluated and, in this context. Easterby-Smith *et al.* (1994) suggest a broader framework of evaluation to consider:

- Evaluation of the context in which the activities were organised (the organisational culture, values, support etc.).
- Evaluation of the administration supporting the event (publicity, joining instructions, venue etc.).
- Evaluation of the 'inputs' (learning content and methods etc.).
- Evaluation of learning process (responses/feelings of learners during as well as after the activities).
- Evaluation of outcomes/change (what changes to knowledge, skills and attitudes have resulted, in what ways has performance changed at organisational and individual levels?).

Although evaluation is a vital part of the systematic approach to learning there is evidence that it rarely takes place as thoroughly as these models would imply. UK survey data (CIPD, 2006a) has suggested that only one-third of UK organisations seek to capture the effect of learning at the organisational/ultimate benefit level as indicated by the Kirkpatrick and Hamblin frameworks. A CIPD poll undertaken in 2007 (CIPD, 2007) to examine the difficulties experienced by practitioners relating to evaluation suggested that 'serious' evaluation was considered to be too time consuming and costly to undertake; the benefits of learning and training were too complex to measure and line managers were not interested in the evaluation data.

A number of factors may explain why, in practice, there are problems with implementing traditional approaches to evaluation. One problem concerns time-orientation. Traditional approaches to evaluation look backwards at what has been achieved to determine the effectiveness of programmes that have taken place (Russ-Eft and Preskill, 2001). While useful, the focus of attention of most managers is on a more forward-looking assessment of the contribution learning is currently making and might make in the future to improve the productivity of individuals or the organisation as a whole. A further difficulty is with the nature of the data that are collected for traditional evaluation purposes. Detailed attempts to collect data that are directly relevant to specific learning activities and the attribution of cause and effect to any one aspect of organisational performance is time consuming and often inaccurate as individual or organisational performance occurs as a result of a wide-ranging context of which training forms only one part.

CASE STUDY LSC Clothing: four stages of the training cycle

LSC Clothing is a manufacturer of leading brand casual wear employing almost 4000 people across 25 countries with products that can be found in retail outlets across the world. In 2005 concerns were raised by senior managers about inconsistent sales performance within the sales division. It was recognised and accepted within the division that a step change in effectiveness was needed but opinions differed about the nature of the current performance problems. The learning and development team set out to undertake a detailed learning needs analysis process relating to the sales process which incorporated a range of different forms of information from different stakeholders. The use of a systematic diagnostic process meant that the organisation could get a consistent view of the current capability gap.

The learning needs analysis process provided the foundation for the learning and development team to develop a tailored training and development programme for the salesforce focused on the basic principles of good selling within the LSC Clothing business model. Four 'Sales in LSC' training modules were developed in partnership with sales executives over a period of 12 months. Each module focused on one 'phase' of the LSC sales cycle. The initial courses were delivered by a specialist sales training organisation in collaboration with local sales directors from the different country groups. Those who had participated were then responsible for cascading the modules in their own locations. Each of the different modules was scheduled to occur at times when they would be most relevant to the LSC sales cycle to ensure that what had been learned could be applied directly and so become embedded into ongoing sales practices.

Effective learning programmes rely on the involvement and support of top managers at all stages of the systematic learning cycle and the learning and development team ensured top level management involvement by asking sales directors to devise and introduce a 'dashboard of key metrics'; figures that would assess sales effectiveness and sales skills and would feed directly into the training evaluation process. In addition senior managers (not learning and development specialists) conducted a series of telephone interviews with a sample of the sales staff to find out what participants had found useful about the training, which of the tools they were using and how the training process might be improved.

Questions

1 Critically comment on the effectiveness of the LSC Clothing approach.

2 How could the effectiveness of the sales training be evaluated?

STRATEGIC HRD

Although the training and development of individuals is important, developing collective organisational 'people capabilities' that are hard for competitors to copy and so can be a source of competitive advantage is the focus of strategic HRD and this part of the chapter focuses on what this may involve.

Early attempts to define the remit and activities of strategic HRD identified nine key characteristics (Garavan, 1991):

- Integration of HRD activities with the organisation's mission and goals.
- Top management support for HRD activities.
- Environmental scanning to ensure HRD activities take account of opportunities and threats for the organisation from the external environment.
- HRD policies and plans that are integrated with wider organisational plans and policies.
- Line manager commitment and involvement in HRD processes.
- Horizontal and vertical 'fit' with wider HRM activities.
- HRD practitioners who act as innovators and consultants rather than 'merely' training providers or managers.

Figure 12.4 From training to strategic HRD: a developmental model

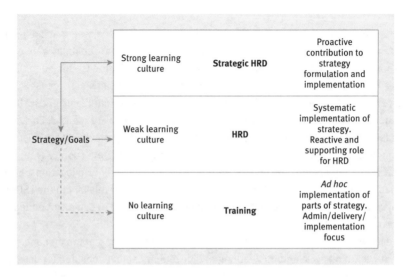

Source: McCracken and Wallace (2000).

- Recognition of, and alignment with, corporate culture and strategy.
- Emphasis on strategic evaluation of the HRD contribution.

McCracken and Wallace (2000) set out to build on this model and suggested that strategic HRD should do more that 'merely' **respond** to organisational priorities. They argue that HRD should also be engaged in **shaping** the context within which strategic discussion and strategy formulation occurs within the organisation. They propose a framework whereby they distinguish between training, HRD and strategic HRD, as shown in Figure 12.4.

This approach makes the case that strategic HRD is characterised by:

- Activities that shape and contribute to the formulation of organisational mission and goals.
- Top management leadership of HRD agenda.
- Environmental scanning involving top management.
- HRD strategies, plans and policies.
- Strategic partnerships with line management.
- Strategic partnerships with HRM.
- HRD practitioners as organisational change consultants.
- Ability to influence corporate culture.
- Emphasis on cost-effectiveness evaluation.

Walton (1999) also argues that organisations may move towards strategic HRD in a staged way and he identifies four stages characterised by:

- A piecemeal approach to HRD.
- The development and implementation of a coherent **training** strategy.
- The development and implementation of a coherent **training and development** strategy.

- Strategic HRD (where an HRD strategy is formulated and implemented with 'full strategic intent'). This involves ensuring a 'fit' with an explicit learning philosophy which is part of the organisation's mission or values.

Although there is no shortage of calls for HRD to have a strategic remit there is scant evidence that strategic HRD is actually achieved in practice; for example, survey data from USA (Accenture, 2004) has indicated that less than 20 per cent of chief executive officers (CEOs) are very satisfied with the level of alignment of learning, training and development with business goals. Interview-based research with senior HRD executives and chief executive officers in the USA also found 'significant opportunities for the HRD function to align more closely with executive-level expectations and aspirations, to make learning more strategic and central to the ongoing success of the enterprise' (O'Driscoll *et al.*, 2005: 70). Data from the IBM 2008 Global Human Capital Study (IBM, 2007) found that, while HRM/D contributes to business strategy in some organisations, it does not provide input to strategic issues in many others. Other UK-based HR practitioner survey data from 2007 (Wolff, 2007) also suggest that UK HRD managers see their greatest challenge as achieving greater support from their organisations' leaders and the necessity of aligning LTD with forthcoming or current organisational change.

HRD strategy

Although there is a strong case for an HRD strategy in organisations, therefore, there are difficulties in formulating and implementing such an approach and this section considers what may be involved. Whittington's (2001) seminal work about different 'idealised perspectives' concerning strategy and strategic management more generally is discussed in Chapter 2 and Harrison (2009) offers an outline of the approach that would be taken to HRD strategy from within the deliberate, rational and outcome-focused 'classical' approach (*see* Exhibit 12.7, adapted from Harrison, 2009), which Whittington outlines.

Mayo (2004) takes a similarly rational and staged approach, suggesting that an appropriate HRD strategy should be both proactive and reactive as it is important to meet the long-term needs of the organisation, foster commitment to the values of learning and development and maintain the organisation's core competencies. **Proactive** drivers for an organisation's HRD strategy are: business strategies and goals, the organisation's HR plan and organisational change initiatives. At the same time the HRD strategy should take account of **reactive drivers** which are: operational issues, individual and team needs and external changes. HRD strategy, understood in this way, will have three points of focus: the first point may be termed 'remedial', being focused on capability enhancement; the second supports short-term development and operational goals; and the third level is relevant to the achievement of the organisation's medium to long-term objectives. In bringing these points of focus together it is important that any HRD strategy should develop and articulate a set of beliefs or values about learning which underpin organisational policies and practices as well as HRD choices relating to learning processes and methods, resources, HRD marketing and communication, and 'success measures'.

Such staged and planned approaches to HRD strategy are attractive but research evidence suggests that they rarely occur. Research in the Netherlands (Wognum, 2001),

EXHIBIT 12.7 Staged approach to HRD strategy formulation

Take responsibility for HRD strategy development	Formulate a strategy development group – involve managers as well as HRD/HRM specialists
Clarify organisational mission and strategy	Gather and interpret information from key individuals in the organisation as well as published documents
Conduct internal and external stakeholder analysis	Diagnose key performance issues from the perspective of employees and external stakeholders (e.g. customers and suppliers); key issues relating to strategic barriers and enablers; learning culture and climate etc.
Identify strategic challenges and opportunities for the organisation	Include issues with a longer-term perspective; issues where operational effectiveness is imperative; issues with clear learning and development implications
Generate strategic alternatives for HRD and get commitment for the most appropriate way forward	Focus on HRD goals that add value to the organisation. Identify how individuals may benefit; incorporate immediate and long-term priorities
Agree a strategic HRD plan	For each area identified in the strategy agree what actions are required; the resources required to achieve them; and who will be accountable for them

USA (Kuchinke, 2003) and UK (Anderson, 2007) identified a number of difficulties faced by organisations in their attempts to formulate and implement a formal and planned approach to HRD strategy. First, the extent to which organisational strategies are clear and unambiguous is often questionable. Organisations have to react fast in a turbulent and dynamic environment so strategic clarity may be rare and short-lived. This means that there is no lasting point of reference for any HRD strategy formulation. Second, there is often a fragmentation of HRD activities as different aspects of training and development are funded through a variety of different budgets that may be the responsibility of different people; some budgets are managed by the HRD or training function but other sources of funding are the responsibility of other stakeholders who may or may not be positive towards learning.

Given these sorts of difficulties there may well be merit for HRD strategy to be considered in line with Whittington's (2001) 'processual' characterisation where it is seen as something which is 'emergent and pluralistic' as it has to incorporate a range of different stakeholder interests and organisational priorities. This position is preferred by Harrison (2009) who argues that HRD strategy is more of a process than an output and should take into account the need for continuous adjustments, sometimes of a radical nature, to take account of changes to individual and organisational learning priorities and in response to emergent opportunities and challenges that are faced by the organisation.

This 'processual' approach to HRD strategy requires a continuous and pragmatic approach to the analysis and diagnosis of HRD priorities in collaboration with line managers at all levels to ensure proposals that are acceptable to key strategic stakeholders. Anderson (2007) highlights a number of key processes that this will involve:

- Proactive activity by HRD practitioners in regular business planning processes.
- Informal dialogue with other stakeholders to ensure that budgets with implications for learning which may be dispersed throughout the organisation take account of organisational HRD priorities.
- Developing and communicating a 'business case' for investment in additional learning opportunities that may emerge outside the formal business planning process and are needed to address specific organisational priorities.
- Ensuring a cost-effective use of resources used for HRD purposes, particularly where 'year-on-year' budgeting for HRD has become established. In such cases it is also important that HRD practitioners guard against a 'drift' of learning and development processes away from emerging organisational priorities.
- Assessment and evaluation of the strategic level contribution that HRD processes are making in line with the characteristics shown in Exhibit 12.8 (Anderson, 2007).

EXHIBIT 12.8 Characteristics for HRD strategy evaluation

Focus on:	Strategic organisational learning processes rather than individual learning interventions
Purpose:	To improve HRD contribution to the organisation's strategic goals rather than to 'prove' the value of individual training and development activities
Perspective:	Organisational perspective rather than learner and trainer perspective
Data:	Aggregate organisational data rather than specific learning measures
Measures:	Assessment of the effectiveness of learning processes rather than trainer effectiveness only

The evaluation characteristics shown in Exhibit 12.8 are unlikely to be achieved through traditional approaches to training evaluation and a variety of alternative approaches have been advocated (*see*, for example, Fitz-Enz, 2000; Phillips, 1991). UK research undertaken on behalf of the CIPD (Anderson, 2007) argues that a combination of four different approaches to evaluation of strategic HRD is required:

- Learning function efficiency measures – to assess the efficiency and effectiveness of the work of the HRD function.

- Return on investment measures – to assess the benefits of specific and appropriate HRD interventions compared with the costs incurred.
- Key performance indicators and benchmark measures – to provide an overall evaluation of HRD processes and performance through a comparison with key performance indicators for the organisation or with external standards of 'good practice' or 'excellence'.
- Return on expectation – to assess the extent to which the anticipated benefits of strategic level stakeholders about HRD processes have been realised.

As this overview of strategic HRD shows, it is not wholly the province of a specialist HRD or training and development function but requires the involvement of a range of different organisational groups (stakeholders), some of which are indicated in Exhibit 12.9 (*see*, for example, CIPD, 2005; McCracken and Wallace, 2000).

EXHIBIT 12.9 Stakeholders in strategic HRD

Stakeholder group	Expectations of HRD	Contribution to HRD
Top managers	• Alignment of learning with business strategy • Cost-effective learning processes • Contribution to organisational change and adaptation	• Clear commitment to learning, risk-taking and career development • Resources for learning activities • Role modelling of learning behaviours
Line managers	• Improved performance by individuals • Improved performance by department/business unit	• Provide formal and informal opportunities for individuals to develop and learn • Enable people to apply what they have learned
Individual employees	• Improved job performance • Development of skills, knowledge and attitudes • Career development opportunities	• Take ownership and responsibility for learning • Seek out appropriate learning opportunities • Apply learning where possible
HRD practitioners	• Provision of effective and timely learning interventions • Develop appropriate and flexible learning resources	• Direct learning interventions to meet organisational needs • Provide learning interventions that are appropriate to individual contexts and learners.

CASE STUDY   SPS Research: HRD strategy of 'build not buy'

SPS Research is a leading provider of independent credit ratings, indices, risk evaluation, investment research, data and valuations services. As part of an organisational refocusing process a 'people strategy' was launched that gave more responsibility to line managers for HRM and HRD processes. The HR strategy comprised three main strands: a 'build not buy' approach to recruitment and development; performance management, and rewards; all of which were linked to the wider business strategy and to a number of organisational performance outcome targets.

A number of interrelated policies were needed to achieve these requirements. First, the HR strategy targeted inexperienced yet skilled staff in recruitment and selection processes. Line managers were then encouraged to be actively involved in providing opportunities for their 'fast track' development through work-based learning opportunities such as job placement, job design and job rotation of team members and identifying where attendance at formal training courses was necessary. Individual employees were also expected to be responsible for the self-management of their own development and to ensure that they gained maximum benefit from the work-based development opportunities that were provided for them. In this way a 'build not buy' HRD approach was adopted. Training, learning and development throughout the organisation was also seen as a fundamental part of HR strategy. A highly experienced HR director led the functional team with the remit of ensuring that line managers' development was prioritised as a key feature of the support of HRD processes.

The incentive for everyone involved in the HR strategy was success in a highly competitive business environment; the perpetuation of an enviable reputation for excellence and the development of hard to copy 'people capabilities' able to sustain the competitive advantage that SPS had built up over the years.

Questions

Discuss the extent to which the 'build not buy' approach would be effective in your organisation. What HRD resources would need to be in place?

Exhibit 12.9 and the SPS Research Case Study indicate how line managers, at all levels in the organisation, are vital to the achievement of HRD in any organisation. Without effective management and leadership individuals are unlikely to benefit from formal and informal learning opportunities and to apply what they have learned. The achievement of strategic HRD, therefore, is often interrelated with appropriate management development processes within the organisation (Purcell and Hutchinson, 2007) and these issues are considered now.

MANAGEMENT DEVELOPMENT

Management development is a concept which is almost impossible to define. In part this is a result of the difficulties experienced in trying to 'pin down' what is involved in the work of being a manager. Current debates about the relationship between leadership and management have also served to complicate the issue and make effective definitions even more difficult. However, it can be said with some certainty that management development embraces some or all of the following features:

- Manager or management training – which focuses on the skills managers as individuals or throughout the organisation need to perform management tasks (for example, time management, presentation skills, dealing with conflict etc.).

- Manager development – which focuses on enhancing the potential performance of individual managers (for example, by participating in specific developmental opportunities, undertaking some form of management education etc.).

- Management development – which focuses on enhancing the capability of 'management as a whole' throughout the organisation.

Some of the different definitions of management development that have been offered are shown in Exhibit 12.10.

EXHIBIT 12.10 Definitions of management development

The process by which individuals gain the skills and abilities to manage themselves and others	Margerison, 1991
The system of corporate activities with the espoused goal of improving the managerial stock in the context of organisational and environmental change	Lees, 1992
The management of managerial careers in an organisational context	Burgoyne, 1989
Developing the ability of people to manage in their own organisational environment	Sadler, 1998
An attempt to improve managerial effectiveness through a learning process	Mumford and Gold, 2004
The entire structured process by which managers learn and improve their skills for the benefit of their employing organisations and themselves	CIPD, 2008b

Exhibit 12.10 indicates the lack of consensus about what is (and is not) to be counted as management development and this arises from the variety of different ideas about the purpose of management development and how it should be undertaken. For some organisations management development is focused on a requirement to support and ensure that organisational change and development is achieved. For others the focus is on manager self-development and career development. In other cases it may be focused on the need to reinforce organisational values or attitudes. There is also no consensus about the methods or approaches through which management development should occur and these are illustrated in Figure 12.5.

Although there is little agreement about what constitutes management development and the most appropriate way for it to occur there is no doubt that management

Figure 12.5 Different approaches to management development

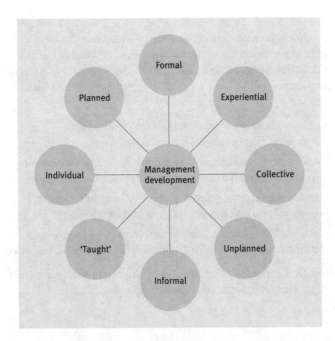

development is strategically significant if HRD is to be effective in organisations. Line managers are expected to be fully involved in facilitating and encouraging the development of members of their teams in both formal and informal ways but very few managers receive any development or support for this part of their role. In many cases managers may feel that their responsibility for people development is an additional and unsought extra burden for which they lack the appropriate knowledge, skills and attitudes (Hutchinson and Purcell, 2007).

As Figure 12.5 indicates, there are a range of different approaches that may be appropriate to the development of management capability and these include:

- Management development or management training programmes either 'in-house' or through the use of an external provider; undertaken on-site or off-site or through some form of e-learning or blended learning.

- Work-based learning methods, such as coaching, counselling, mentoring, action learning, project working and secondments.

- Organisational systems such as performance and development reviews, development centres, career planning workshops, 360-degree feedback and succession planning.

- Education and training processes, including formal courses, educational programmes, outdoor development and so on.

Strategic management development

Just as the achievement of effective HRD in organisations requires the support of line managers, so the achievement of strategic HRD, characterised by a strong learning culture as well as by an alignment of HRD activities with the organisation's strategy and plans, is more likely to be achieved where strategic management development occurs.

Brown (2003: 292) defines strategic management development as: 'management development interventions which are intended to enhance the strategic capability and corporate performance of an organisation'. Mumford and Gold (2004) point out that delivering interventions to enhance strategic capability is not something that all organisations will achieve and they suggest that a four-staged process is likely which comprises:

- Unplanned experiential management development – where there is the assumption that managers will 'emerge' from experience.

- Unplanned reactive management development – where interventions occur in response to immediate pressures or problems.

- Planned management development – where some structures, procedures and provision for management training and development are introduced.

- Planned strategic management development – focusing on longer-term issues and identifying and developing key management capabilities or competencies.

Figure 12.6 provides an indication of the organisational basis from which effective strategic management development might occur.

Figure 12.6
Requirements for successful strategic management development

- High organisational commitment to strategic management

- Strategic goals for management development championed by CEO

- Strategic basis for management competency model or framework

- Management development integrated with real management work

KNOWLEDGE MANAGEMENT AND HUMAN CAPITAL MANAGEMENT

Interest in strategic HRD forms part of a wider interest in organisations to harness the knowledge, behaviours and values of individuals to develop and exploit organisational 'intellectual capital' assets. Two currently prominent approaches, knowledge management and human capital management, are briefly outlined in the remainder of this section (Baron and Armstrong, 2007; Collins and Smith, 2006).

Ideas about knowledge management and human capital management are grounded in concepts that are drawn from two very different HRD traditions. First, humanist ideas about HRD that highlight the social features of formal and informal learning and emphasise individual learning as much as organisational learning as part of a long-term view of the development process. Second, economic concepts that emphasise the potential return on investment and 'added value' of knowledge, skills and experience through the development and delivery of products and services that have market value.

Humanist ideas about HRD formed the basis for ideas developed in the 1990s about the learning organisation, defined as an organisation which facilitates the learning of all its members, and continuously transforms itself (Pedler *et al.*, 1990). Ideas about organisational learning are underpinned by a 'systems thinking' approach (Senge, 1990), which focuses on the integrated nature of any enterprise and an acceptance that the 'whole' is greater than the sum of the individual parts. Key issues for learning organisations are: the need for a shared vision and a close link between learning and organisational strategy; effective team relationships; a commitment to personal learning; and a learning approach that values attempts to challenge assumptions about the 'organisational world' so that things can be improved.

The learning organisation idea is attractive but a key inhibiting factor is the extent to which individual learning is able to be 'transformed' into organisational learning; there is always a danger that individual learning will dissipate if what has been learned is not shared at group level and embedded at an organisational level in systems, structures, strategies and routines. Therefore, those who have promoted the learning organisation idea (*see*, for example, Senge, 1990; Pedler *et al.*, 1997; Pearn, 1994) highlight the importance of knowledge acquisition, distribution and interpretation throughout the organisation resulting in changes to 'collective thinking' that can influence approaches to problem solving and organisation development (Nonaka and Takeuchi, 1995).

Although attractive, no consensus has emerged since the 1990s on what a learning organisation would 'look like' (Rowley, 2000) and critics of the approach argue that the learning organisation idea has been more of a metaphor and a 'Holy Grail' that has to be taken on trust rather than a practical and measurable way forward for learning, training and organisational performance in most organisations (Garavan, 1997).

Knowledge management

The development of interest in knowledge management can be understood in part as an attempt to overcome some of the difficulties with the learning organisation idea. Advances in data storage and data sharing technology and an appreciation of the growing importance of 'knowledge work' were also contextually important. The term 'knowledge worker' was first used by Drucker (1993) to describe those who add value to the organisation by processing existing information and generating new knowledge to define and solve problems. Knowledge workers (for example lawyers, doctors, marketing experts, managers, software engineers and so on) increasingly have to use their intellects to convert ideas into products, services or business processes.

Skapinker (2002) defines knowledge management as all the processes that make use of the experience and ideas of employees, customers and suppliers in order to enhance organisational performance. However, experience and ideas have to be applied in practice if organisational performance is to be enhanced and, drawing on a hierarchy proposed by Ackoff (1989), those who advocate knowledge management indicate that knowledge must be seen as more than 'just' information and must be 'transformed' into 'organisational wisdom', as illustrated in Figure 12.7.

This hierarchy has been criticised (*see*, for example, Rowley, 2007) for a lack of clarity about **how** data is transformed into knowledge and wisdom and the potential

Figure 12.7 The DIKW hierarchy

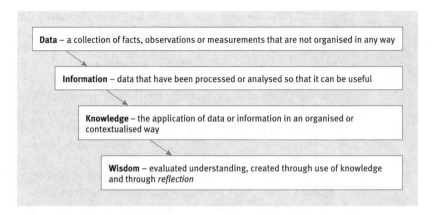

Source: Ackoff (1989).

for overlap between the categories is a problem. The evidential basis for the concept of 'wisdom' is also very scant. However, the hierarchy does suggest that knowledge (not simply information) is a key asset for organisations, particularly those that operate in the 'knowledge economy' and Swan *et al.* (1999) highlight the vital role of the creation, acquisition, capture, sharing and use of knowledge skills and expertise in order to maximise the intellectual capital of the organisation. Those who advocate knowledge management highlight two very different types of knowledge: explicit knowledge and tacit knowledge. Explicit knowledge ('know-what') is knowledge that can be articulated, captured and exchanged. This type of knowledge is often written down in the form of procedures, manuals, books, web pages and so on and is easily copied. Tacit knowledge ('know-how'), by contrast, is embedded in the experience of individuals and underpins their actions and decisions although it is rarely articulated or 'written out' and so is not easily replicated. A comparison of the two different types of knowledge is shown as Exhibit 12.11 (*see*, for example, Nonaka and Takeuchi, 1995) and both types of knowledge are important components of an organisation's intellectual assets.

Although there are many similarities between ideas underpinning the learning organisation and the knowledge-sharing ideas that form part of knowledge management there are also important differences of focus. In contrast to the humanist and developmental principles underpinning the learning organisation, knowledge management ideas are economically oriented and treat knowledge as a commodity to be managed in order to derive economic benefit from the organisation's collective 'intellectual assets' which should be codified and stored and then disseminated and applied through networks and relationships. The aim is that knowledge (both tacit and explicit) becomes embedded in organisational rules and routines in order to achieve competitive advantage.

These aspirations seem simple enough but a number of problems can occur. First, not everyone in an organisation may want to share their knowledge with others. An implicit assumption that 'knowledge is power' can be a powerful disincentive to sharing what is known within a team or organisation. Micro-political processes that affect behaviour in organisations may also act as powerful inhibiters or blockers of knowledge sharing. Developments in technology, with increasing attention on the tools and techniques available, can also deflect attention from the people aspects of knowledge management. This can lead to a situation where, in spite of expensive investments in knowledge capture and sharing technology, knowledge is not actually shared or used

EXHIBIT 12.11 Explicit and tacit knowledge

Explicit knowledge	Tacit knowledge
Transmissible	Hard to transmit
Codified/patented	Subconscious
Generic in application	Individually situational/organisationally distinctive
Objective	Subjective
Can be taught and copied	Intuitive
Valued as part of organisational systems and practices	Taken for granted
Acquired through study and applied procedurally	Acquired through practice and revealed through application
Accessible (therefore vulnerable to copying)	Hard to get at

in a relevant way. Indeed, Hislop (2002) argues that knowledge management relies on the motivation of workers in organisations who must be willing to share their knowledge. Organisational commitment and a 'healthy' psychological contract are key variables, therefore, for any organisation committed to knowledge management.

Although the argument for knowledge management is made using an economic justification, these problems highlight the importance of social and developmental features of organisations more in line with the ideas underpinning the learning organisation approach. Taking this into account, Lank and Windle (2003) advocate four 'building blocks' to achieve what they refer to as a 'knowledge productive organisation'.

- Make knowledge visible – encourage as much sharing and recording of data as is possible.
- Increase 'knowledge intensity' by cross-boundary, department or function knowledge sharing.
- Create a knowledge infrastructure where groups of people who are interested in the same issues can come together to share information and learn from each other.
- Develop a knowledge culture through encouraging knowledge-sharing behaviour using company value statements and so on that are reinforced in organisational training and development processes.

Human capital management

The idea of using knowledge to enhance the intellectual assets of the organisation also forms a major part of interest in human capital management (HCM). This approach works on the basis that the value of any organisation is made up of both tangible assets (such as equipment and money) and intangible assets (such as 'brand', reputation and 'knowledge'). Like knowledge management approaches, therefore, those who advocate human capital management argue for a strategic approach to people management that focuses on the knowledge, experience, relationships and skills that provide an organisation with competitive advantage (Edvinsson and Malone, 1997; Scarborough and Elias, 2002).

However, 'human capital' in the form of skills, experience and expertise resides in individuals who make their own decisions about how much effort and skill they will contribute to their work organisation; decisions that will be affected by a range of factors within their employment relationship with the organisation. Therefore, in addition to encouraging investment in learning and training processes, those who advocate human capital management highlight the important contribution of HRD in fostering an appropriate culture and set of values that encourage a 'conversion process' such that individually held human capital assets are deployed and shared as part of the organisation's collective 'intellectual capital' (CIPD, 2006b). Another important contribution made by those who advocate HCM is an emphasis on measuring the 'return on investment' in human capital as a way of managing and enhancing the contribution to organisational performance that has been made.

Although attractive, there are some problems with the HCM approach. First, the contribution of knowledge, skills and experiences is difficult to isolate from other contextual factors and this presents problems with measurement as quantitative (financial) measures, which are most often used to assess organisational performance, are often inappropriate. Second, most HR data in organisations serve an administrative rather than a strategic evaluative purpose and HRD practitioners do not always have the skills to analyse data in a way that is relevant to assessing the contribution of people's knowledge, skills and experience to business performance. Third, and more significantly, just as some approaches to knowledge management assume that knowledge and skills should be treated as a commodity, so the focus in HCM on measurement and data resembles a 'Taylorist' approach to management that might be associated with commodification, standardisation and cost-reduction which might inhibit the innovation and creativity that are important for strategic differentiation.

SKILLS AND HUMAN CAPITAL DEVELOPMENT: A NATIONAL PERSPECTIVE

HCM approaches, which seek to maximise the value of skills within the internal labour market, have much in common with concern about the skill levels in the external labour market as the performance and productivity of any organisation will depend on the quality and skills of the people that are recruited (*see* Chapter 4 on HR planning). In a globally competitive market where 'added value' and 'knowledge work' is increasingly important, national policy relating to skills, education and learning is vital and this last section of the chapter provides a short discussion about these issues.

Interest in national skill levels, like much of the debate about human capital and knowledge management, is underpinned by an economic perspective about investment in learning. Individuals who have higher skills are able to earn more money and enjoy a better standard of life. Organisations that invest in 'upskilling' their employees also report improved productivity and performance rates. This, in turn, leads to improvements in gross domestic product and other national measures of growth and economic productivity (CIPD, 2009b).

A 'skill' is a specific ability held by an individual to perform some type of activity. Within any country there are two ways in which skills are developed; through the education system and through the provision of 'post-education' work-related training and education. Within the UK three different levels of skill are often referred to:

- Basic skills – such as literacy, numeracy and information and communication technology (ICT) activities. In the UK these are expected to have been developed by the time any individual leaves the school-based education system.
- Intermediate skills – technical or craft skills often gained as a result of further education or advanced apprenticeship schemes.
- Higher skills – 'knowledge-intensive' skills, often the result of university level degree or postgraduate level study.

Any government has three broad policy options with regard to skills and education. One option is to insist that employers and individuals undertake prescribed skill-related activities and to manage this system through a process of regulation. A second policy option is to provide centralised funding for training and education to ensure that what is seen to be essential is delivered. The third policy option is of 'voluntarism' where individuals and organisations choose for themselves whether to invest in training and skills within a market mechanism. In reality, many governments, the UK included, make use of elements of all of these policy options as the subsequent overview of developments in England demonstrates.

The Leitch Report and UK skills development

Since the end of the Second World War in the UK successive governments have formulated a range of different policies and strategies relating to vocational education and training such that very little remains the same for very long. This chapter focuses on the situation since the publication of the influential Leitch Report (2006), which proved to be something of a catalyst to significant development of national education and training policy in the UK. Some areas of vocational training and education, such as the National Vocational Qualifications (NVQs) and Investors in People (IiP) systems, which have been in place since the 1990s, are not covered here but information about them can be found through the further reading section. The devolution of legislative power to Northern Ireland, Scotland and Wales has also meant that different approaches have developed in different parts of the UK. There are many similarities as well as some differences (and these can be pursued through the further reading section) but this chapter relates to policy developments in England.

When the Leitch Report was published in 2006 the UK economy had experienced 14 years of unbroken growth and had the highest employment rate in the G7 group of leading industrial nations. However, even at this point, before the onset of the economic downturn and subsequent recession in the UK, the analysis underpinning the Leitch Report projected the prospect of long-term economic decline for UK organisations in global markets due to a lack of skills.

Leitch highlighted a number of important challenges relating to the 'national skills agenda'. First, there were fundamental weaknesses in the UK skills base at all levels (basic, intermediate and higher) which were seen to lead to poor productivity levels and a restriction on economic growth. The Leitch analysis predicted that by 2020 UK economic growth and productivity would slip to near the bottom of the league of European economies and would be well below the economic growth rates achieved by emerging economies such as China and India.

In its recommendations to improve the supply of skills to the labour market the Leitch Report argued for a demand-led rather than a 'supply side'-led system so that the skills identified as necessary by employers would be given priority in decisions about what courses should be provided.

Key themes that have dominated UK skills policy since the Leitch Report have been:

- The need for employers and individuals to be more willing to undertake training and education (increasing 'informed demand').
- The need for an effective employer-led demand system to underpin more appropriate skills development and delivery processes.
- The need for a more effective delivery of training and education through better coordination between schools, colleges, universities, employers and other training providers.

Following the Leitch Report the UK government initiated a range of interventions to try to stimulate the 'step change' in skills development that was seen to be necessary. As Chancellor of the Exchequer, Gordon Brown had commissioned the Leitch Report and when he became Prime Minister in 2007 the work of two government departments – Education and Skills (DfES) and Trade and Industry (DTI) – were reallocated between three new departments:

- Department for Innovation, Universities and Skills (revised in 2009 to become the Department for Business, Innovation and Skills).
- Department for Children, Schools and Families.
- Department for Business, Enterprise and Regulatory Reform.

In addition, a UK Commission for Employment and Skills (UKCES) was established to become a single employer-driven body with the aim of integrating employment and skills services: 'depoliticising' the skills agenda and raising employer engagement through a (reorganised) network of Sector Skills Councils.

Education, education, education

When the UK Labour government was elected in May 1997 a key part of their manifesto and election commitment was summed up by the slogan 'education, education, education'. Over their ensuing terms of government this resulted in different policy initiatives, beginning with an emphasis on basic level skills development through funding and regulation of the curriculum for early years and secondary level school-based education. Ten years later, following the Leitch Report, concern about basic skills remained but attention shifted to basic and intermediate skill levels of the 14–19 years age group.

Part of the concern about basic skill levels has been consistent attention on young people (those between the ages of 16 and 24) who were 'not in employment, education or training' (NEETs). By the time of the Leitch Report this group was steadily increasing in size with a particularly large rise in those aged 16–17, a trend which was exacerbated by the economic recession from 2009 onwards. Four main initiatives were developed in response to the Leitch Report that sought to increase 'informed demand', stimulate the delivery of employer-led demands for skills, and coordinate better between different agencies involved in skills development and education and so tackle the 'NEETs problem'.

1 New diploma courses for 14–19s age groups

Traditional school-based qualification-based courses (GCSEs usually taken at the age of 16 and A levels usually taken at the age of 18) have long been criticised by employ-ers as lacking vocational relevance. Policy-makers have also argued that traditional qualifications are inappropriate for less academic individuals (who may go on to join the group known as NEETs) and National Vocational Qualifications (NVQs) are difficult to operate where people are not in employment. In response, the Department for Children, Schools and Families introduced new types of diploma courses to run alongside the GCSE and A level system which are explicitly vocationally oriented and involve a mix of classroom-based learning and work experience. There are three levels of diploma course, all of which take two years to complete:

- Foundation level (equivalent to 5 GCSEs at grades D to G)
- Higher level (equivalent to 7 'good' GCSEs at Grades A* to C)
- Advanced level (equivalent to 3.5 A levels)

2 Introduction of a compulsory learning age

The school leaving age was established as 16 years in 1972 but the 'education leaving age' will rise to 17 from 2013 and to 18 from 2015. From that time those aged 16–18 will be required to undertake either full-time education, an apprenticeship or part-time training if they are working or volunteering for more than 20 hours per week, thus providing a further opportunity for those aged 16–18, who might otherwise have joined the 'NEETs group', to be offered some form of education or vocational training.

3 Management and funding of further education

In the early part of the twenty-first century funding for the 16–19 years age groups was the responsibility of Local Skills Councils, which were established in 2001 and took over the roles of the previous Further Education Funding Council and Training and Enterprise Councils. Most secondary schools were funded by Local Education Authorities. As part of the objective to provide a more coherent basis for planning and funding training and education for the 14–19 years age group a post-Leitch develop-ment is to phase out Local Skills Councils and give local authorities responsibility for schools and further education from 2010.

4 Widening participation in higher education

The policy initiatives described so far relate to the development of basic and inter-mediate level skills but a further area of concern has been the low level of 'higher skills' in the labour market. The Labour government has been committed to achieving a wider participation in higher education with a target that 50 per cent of those aged between 18 and 30 years should access higher education courses. The Leitch Report, however, recommended that 'high skills' courses provided through higher education institutions should be available to those already over the age of 30 and in employment. The development of foundation degrees is a policy initiative that can be understood in these terms, requiring collaboration between higher education and further education institutions and employing organisations. Foundation degrees are designed to be equivalent to the first two years of an undergraduate (bachelor's) degree and focus on work-related subjects. They take around two years to complete on a full-time basis or three to four years on a part-time basis.

At the time of writing (2009) a lengthy consultation process is being undertaken about further change within the higher education sector. Key issues that are likely to require action are:

- Closer collaboration between higher education institutions and employers (to achieve a demand-led system).
- Greater willingness by employers to fund higher education level study for current or future employees.
- Better coordination between further and higher education institutions to ensure an easier transition from intermediate level to higher level qualifications.
- Requirements for work experience where possible as part of degree level study.

'Post-education' vocational training

As noted, a key part of current government policy for skills is to increase 'informed demand' for training by employers as well as individuals and the Department for Business, Innovation and Skills responded to the Leitch Report with a set of new initiatives and a revision to older schemes.

1 Skills Pledge and Train to Gain

The Skills Pledge was launched in 2007 and aims to encourage employers to better appreciate the value of training and to invest in it. The Skills Pledge is a public commitment that an employer can make to develop the level of achievement of basic skills through the achievement of 'level 2' vocational qualifications (the equivalent of five good GCSEs, grades A* to C). Linked with this, a further initiative is the Train to Gain system which replaced the previous 'Business Link' system as a national 'skills service' where employers can receive advice on basic skills (the primary focus) and more latterly for level three and four leadership and management skills. Organisations that participate are advised by a 'skills broker' whose remit is to identify the skills needed by the organisation and then recommend training providers and sources of government funding to subsidise the costs. Like the Skills Pledge, the Train to Gain process focuses mostly on training geared to basic level skills and almost all funding available is linked to qualification-bearing courses. In the first three years of the Train to Gain scheme 359 500 level two qualifications were achieved as well as 34 000 at level three. Level four qualifications (mostly in management and leadership) were permitted from August 2008 and by July 2009 they had been achieved by 1800 people. In the context of the economic recession the government has consistently expressed the view that organisations should invest in training as part of the recovery process but this has led to funding problems for the Train to Gain scheme (Shappard, 2009; Phillips, 2009; Blyth, 2008; CIPD, 2008c).

2 Apprenticeships

A further long-standing policy commitment by the Labour government has been the development of an improved apprenticeship system to enable people to work and gain intermediate level skills and qualifications as a complement to formal school- and college-based education. Most apprenticeships last between one and two years, although some take up to five and employers can receive funding support to subsidise parts of the training and learning process. In 2008 the government made a public commitment to apprenticeships with the aim that they would be offered as a 'mainstream option' for every 16 to 18-year-old person. However, apprenticeships rely on employment opportunities, so the government commitment can only be realised by employers, something that does not look likely by 2010 as employers impose recruitment limits in order to cope with economic recession.

3 Management and leadership skills

This brief overview of vocational training initiatives organised through the Department for Business, Innovation and Skills shows that government attention is primarily focused on the achievement of basic and intermediate level skills. Critics have argued, however, that this overlooks the important issue of higher level skill development and the need to include wider management and leadership skills within the 'skills agenda' (CIPD, 2008c). Indeed, the Leitch Report (2006) indicated that over 40 per cent of UK managers held lower level qualifications than those held by most school leavers. International comparative data indicate that the UK lags well behind other competitor nations in management development. In response to these criticisms some funds from the Train to Gain budget have been made available for management development, although the amount of funding is small and the overall thrust of Train to Gain remains targeted at basic level skills.

4 Welfare to work

Another long-standing commitment of the Labour government which is relevant to concern about skill levels in the labour market is the New Deal system managed by the Department for Work and Pensions. Those on unemployment benefit are four times less likely to have any qualifications than those in work. The New Deal system forms part of a 'welfare to work' process whereby claimants are compelled to seek work and/or undertake training to increase their employability so that they become 'job ready'. In the period since the launch of the New Deal programme specific schemes have been initiated for young people, those aged over 25, those aged over 50, disabled people, lone parents and musicians. While the New Deal has clearly had an effect on basic level skills, government data suggest that its success relies heavily on local labour market conditions; it is less effective in inner-urban or depressed industrial labour markets where 'recycling and churning' of participants through the schemes is evident (Sunley *et al.*, 2001).

Implications for HRD practitioners

Most managers in most organisations remain blissfully unaware of the wider issues relating to national skills strategies, beyond bemoaning the poor levels of basic skill levels they may come across when they recruit young workers and the difficulties they experience finding people with the 'right' skills. However, HRD professionals are well advised to monitor changing developments and opportunities presented by the external labour market and skills environment. Although government policy overlooks the important features of informal and non-qualification-based learning and focuses excessively on basic level skills at the expense of intermediate and higher level skills, four key tasks relevant to the national skills strategy can be identified for HRD practitioners:

- Remain fully informed about funding streams and vocational education and training provision locally or within the organisation's sector. In times of limited budgets it is important that all appropriate available funding is secured to support learning and development within the organisation.

- Work with line managers to identify current and anticipated skill or capability gaps for the organisation and then use local or sector-based networks to find ways of closing those gaps.

- Where internally sponsored management development is unavailable, the opportunities presented by the Train to Gain process for management and leadership training should be explored.

- Ensure that senior managers in the organisation lobby the UK Commission for Employment and Skills, Local Skills Councils (before they are phased out), Sector Skills Councils and any other government body about the importance of broadening the national skills agenda, particularly to embrace management and leadership development and higher level skills which will be vital if organisations are to compete in a global knowledge-based economy.

SUMMARY LEARNING POINTS

1 HRD is concerned with the activities involved in organising individual and collective learning processes aimed at the development of both employees and the organisation as a whole.

2 The systematic approach to training and learning involves a planned, cyclical process of: identifying and analysing learning needs; design of learning interventions; delivery of learning activities; and evaluation of learning processes and outcomes.

3 The training needs analysis or learning needs analysis process involves: collecting data; identifying the capability and performance gap; and making recommendations to close the gap.

4 The design of learning processes involves: formulating training objectives or learning outcomes; selecting an appropriate learning or training strategy; and design and planning of the activity to ensure participants can achieve the training objectives or learning outcomes.

5 Evaluation of training or learning activities involves establishing the success or otherwise of development activities and assessing whether the associated benefits justify the investment.

6 Although the development of individuals is important, harnessing their knowledge, skills and experience for organisational learning or organisation development offers the potential to develop collective people capabilities that can be a source of competitive advantage for the organisation.

7 Strategic HRD involves integrating HRD activities with strategy formulation and implementation leading to both vertical and horizontal alignment with other HR and organisational processes in partnership with line managers.

8 Effective strategic HRD in organisations relies on the involvement of line managers at all levels. Management development processes are an important part of building organisational HRD capability. Strategic management development is concerned with all the learning interventions designed to enhance the strategic capability and corporate performance of the organisation.

9 Knowledge management involves making use of the experience and ideas of employees, customers and suppliers in order to enhance organisational performance. Both explicit knowledge ('know-what') and tacit knowledge ('know-how') are important components of an organisation's intellectual assets.

10 Human capital management is a strategic approach to people management that focuses on managing and measuring the knowledge, experience, relationships and skills that provide an organisation with a competitive edge in its market.

11 The Leitch Report (2006) highlighted the poor skills base of the UK and the detrimental effect this has on national and organisational competitiveness. National policy initiatives taken in response to the Leitch Report focus on: increasing 'informed demand' by employers and individuals for training; the development of an 'employer-led' demand system to underpin skills development in the UK; and better coordination between different stakeholders to ensure more effective delivery of vocational training and education.

12 HRD practitioners should remain aware of channels through which they may be able to obtain government funding to support skills development in their own organisations. Where capability gaps are identified they should make use of local and sectoral networks to find out how to close those gaps. As part of the 'employer-led' demand system they should encourage top managers to articulate the need for funding to support the development of higher level and management-oriented skill development as a national priority.

REFERENCES AND FURTHER READING

Accenture (2004) *High-performance workforce study*. Retrieved on 28 May 2007 from: www.cpp.com/pr/accenture.pdf.

Ackoff, R.L. (1989) 'From Data to Wisdom', *Journal of Applied Systems Analysis*, 16, 3–9.

Alberga, T., Tyson, S. and Parsons, D. (1997) 'An evaluation of the Investors in People standard', *Human Resource Management Journal*, 7(2), 47–59.

Anderson, V. (2007) *The value of learning: from return on investment to return on expectation*. London: CIPD.

Argyris, C. (1990) *Overcoming Organisational Differences: Facilitating Organisational Learning*. Boston, MA: Allyn & Bacon.

Argyris, C. and Schon, D. (1978) *Organisational Learning*. Reading, MA: Addison-Wesley.

Baron, A. and Armstrong, M. (2007) *Human capital management: Achieving added value through people*. London: Kogan Page.

Bass, B.M. and Vaughan, J.A. (1967) *Training in industry: the management of learning*. London: Tavistock Publications.

Bell, E., Taylor, S. and Thorpe, R. (2002) 'A step in the right direction? Investors in People and the learning organization', *British Journal of Management*, 13, 161–71.

Bee, R. and Bee, F. (2003) *Learning needs analysis and evaluation*. London: CIPD.

Blyth, A. (2008) 'Skills pledge: view to a skill', *Personnel Today*, 22 April. Retrieved on 22 April from: www.personneltoday.com/articles/2008/04/22/45199/skills-pledge-view-to-a-skill.html.

Brown, P. (2003) 'Seeking success through strategic management development', *Journal of European Industrial Training*, 27(6), 292–303.

Burgoyne, J. (1989) *Management development: context and strategies*. Aldershot: Gower.

CIPD (2005) *Training to Learning*, Change Agenda. London: CIPD. Retrieved on 15 February 2007 from: www.cipd.co.uk/subjects/lrnanddev/general/train2lrn0405.htm.

CIPD (2006a) *Learning and Development Annual Survey Report 2006*. Retrieved on 18 May 2007 from: www.cipd.co.uk/NR/rdonlyres/97BE272C-8859-4DB1-BD99-17F38E4B4484/0/lrnandevsurv0406.pdf.

CIPD (2006b) *What's the Future for Human Capital?* London: CIPD.

CIPD (2007) 'The value of learning: first poll and debate'. Retrieved on 23 July 2009 from: www.cipd.co.uk/helpingpeoplelearn/_vllrngpll1.htm.

CIPD (2008a) *Learning and development: annual survey report 2008*. London: CIPD. Retrieved on 23 July 2009 from: www.cipd.co.uk/subjects/lrnanddev/general/_lrngdevsvy.htm.

CIPD (2008b) *Management Development: Factsheet*. Retrieved on 24 July 2009 from: www.cipd.co.uk/subjects/lrnanddev/mmtdevelop/mngmntdevt.htm.

CIPD (2008c) *The skills agenda in the UK: Factsheet*. Retrieved on 24 July 2009 from: www.cipd.co.uk/subjects/lrnanddev/general/ukskillsagenda.htm.

CIPD (2008d) *Investors in People*, CIPD Factsheet. Retrieved on 24 July 2009 from: www.cipd.co.uk/subjects/lrnanddev/general/iip.htm.

CIPD (2009a) *Learning and development: annual survey report*. London: CIPD. Retrieved on 23 July 2009 from: www.cipd.co.uk/subjects/lrnanddev/general/_lrngdevsvy.htm.

CIPD (2009b) *Understanding the economy and labour market: Factsheet*. Retrieved on 24 July 2009 from: www.cipd.co.uk/subjects/recruitmen/labourmarket/econlabmrkt.htm?IsSrchRes=1.

Collins, C.J. and Smith, K.G. (2006) 'Knowledge exchange and combination: The role of human resource practices in the performance of high-technology firms', *Academy of Management Journal*, 49(3), 544–560.

Department for Employment and Learning (2008) *A statement of skills in Northern Ireland*. Belfast: DEL.

Drucker, P. (1993) *Post-capitalist society*. Oxford: Butterworth-Heinemann.

Easterby-Smith, M. *et al.* (1994) *Evaluating Management Development, Training and Education*. Aldershot: Gower.

Edvinsson, L. and Malone, M. (1997) *Intellectual Capital: Realising Your Company's True Value by Finding its Hidden Brainpower*. New York: HarperCollins.

Fitz-Enz, J. (2000) *ROI of Human Capital: Measuring the Economic Value of Employee Performance*, NY: Amacon.

Garavan, T.N. (1991) 'Strategic human resource development', *Journal of European Industrial Training*, 15(1), 17–30.

Garavan, T. (1997) 'The learning organisation: a review and evaluation', *The Learning Organisation*, 4(1), 18–29.

Garavan, T.N., McGuire, D. and O'Donnell, D. (2004) 'Exploring human resource development: A levels of analysis approach', *Human Resource Development Review*, 3(4), 417–41.

Gibb, S. (2008) *Human resource development: process, practices and perspectives*. Basingstoke: Palgrave Macmillan.

Gold, J., Rodgers, H. and Smith, V. (2003) 'What is the future for the human resource development professional? A UK perspective', *Human Resource Development International*, 6(4), 437–56.

Hamblin, A.C. (1974) *Evaluation and control of training*. Maidenhead: McGraw-Hill.

Harrison, R. (2009) *Learning and Development*. London: CIPD.

Hislop, D. (2002) 'Linking human resource management and knowledge management via commitment: a review and research agenda', *Employee Relations*, 25(2), 182–202.

Honey, P. and Mumford, A. (1982) *Manual of Learning Styles*. London: Peter Honey.

Hutchinson, S. and Purcell, J. (2007) *Line managers in reward, learning and development*. London: CIPD.

IBM Global Business Services (2007) *Unlocking the DNA of the Adaptable Workforce: The global human capital study: 2008*. Presentation on 15 October 2007, CIPD, Wessex Branch. Retrieved on 31 March 2008 from: www.cipd.co.uk/NR/rdonlyres/8BB4CFC5-CD7E-424A-9241-3A40DDD6308C/0/Hewit_AM.pdf.

Kirkpatrick, D.L. (1975) *Evaluating training programs*. Madison, Wisconsin: American Society for Training and Development.

Kuchinke, K.P. (2003) 'Contingent HRD: Toward a theory of variation and differentiation in formal human resource development', *Human Resource Development Review*, 2(3), 294–309.

Kolb, D.A. (1996) *Management and the learning process*, in Starkey, K. (ed.) *How Organisations Learn*. London: ITP.

Knowles, M.S. (1990) *The Adult Learner: A Neglected Species*. Houston: Gulf Publishing Company.

Lank, E. and Windle, I. (2003) 'Catch me if you can', *People Management*, 6 February, 40–42.

Lees, S. (1992) 'The ten faces of management development', *Management Learning*, 23, 89–105.

Leitch, S. (2006) *Review of skills: prosperity for all in the global economy – World-class skills. Final report*. Norwich: HMSO.

Lessem, R. (1991) *Total Quality Learning: Building a Learning Organisation*. Oxford: Blackwell.

Margerison, C. (1991) 'Management development policies and practices', *Journal of European Industrial Training*, 15(4), 29–31.

Mayo, A. (2004) *Creating a learning and development strategy: the HR partner's guide to developing people*. London: CIPD.

Mayo, A. (2006) *Supporting knowledge management*, CIPD Factsheet. Retrieved on 30 April 2008 from: www.cipd.co.uk/subjects/corpstrtgy/knowman/supknowman. htm?IsSrchRes=1.

McCracken, M. and Wallace, M. (2000) 'Exploring strategic maturity in HRD: Rhetoric, aspiration or reality?' *Journal of European Industrial Training*, 24(8), 425–62.

Mumford, A. and Gold, J. (2004) *Management development: strategies for action*. London: CIPD.

Nonaka, I. and Takeuchi, H. (1995) *The knowledge-creating company*. Oxford: Oxford University Press.

O'Driscoll, T., Sugrue, B. and Vona, M.K. (2005) 'The C level and the value of learning', *Training and Development*, October, 70–75.

Pearn, M. (1994) 'Tools for a learning organisation', *Management Development Review*, 7(4), 9–13.

Pedler, M., Burgoyne, J. and Boydell, T. (1997) *The learning company: a strategy for sustainable developmen*. London: McGraw-Hill.

Pedler, M., Burgoyne, J., Boydell, T. and Welshman, G. (1990) *Self Development in Organisations*. Maidenhead: McGraw-Hill.

Phillips, J. (1991) *Handbook of Training Evaluation and Measurement Methods*. Houston: Gulf Publishing Company.

Phillips, L. (2009) 'Train to gain fails to deliver value for money says audit office', *PM online*, 22 July. Retrieved on 23 July from: www.peoplemanagement.co.uk/pm/ articles/2009/07/train-to-gain-fails-to-deliver-value-for-money-says-audit-office.htm.

Poell, R.F. (2007) 'W(h)ither HRD? Towards a self-conscious, self-critical, and open-minded discipline,' *Human Resource Development International*, 10(4), 361–3.

Pogson, P. and Tennant, M. (1995). *Understanding Adults*, in G. Foley (ed.) *Understanding adult education and training*. St Leonards: Allen & Unwin, 20–30.

Purcell, J. and Hutchinson, S. (2007) 'Front-line managers as agents in the HRM-performance causal chain: theory, analysis and evidence', *Human Resource Management Journal*, 17(1), 3–20.

Qualifications and Curriculum Authority (2009) *National Vocational Qualifications.* Retrieved on 24 July 2009 from: www.qcda.gov.uk/6640.aspx.

Race, P. (1993). 'Never mind the teaching, feel the learning', *SEDA Paper 80.* Retrieved 28 October 2008 from: www.londonmet.ac.uk/deliberations/seda-publications/race.cfm.

Ram, M. (2000) 'Investors in People in small firms: case study evidence from the business services sector', *Personnel Review*, 29(1), 69–91.

Rowley, J. (2000) 'From learning organisation to knowledge entrepreneur', *Journal of Knowledge Management*, 4(1), 7–15.

Rowley, J. (2007) 'The wisdom hierarchy: representations of the DIKW hierarchy', *Journal of Information Science*, 33(2), 163–80.

Russ-Eft, D. and Preskill, H. (2001) *Evaluation in Organisations*, Cambridge MA: Perseus.

Sadler, P. (1998) *Concepts and components of management development*, in J. Propokenko (ed.) *Management development: a guide for the profession*, 35–58. Geneva: International Labour Office.

Scarbrough, H. and Elias, J. (2002) *Evaluating Human Capital*. London: CIPD.

Scottish Government (2007) *Skills for Scotland: a life-long skills strategy*. Edinburgh: Scottish Government.

Senge, P.M. (1990) *The Fifth Discipline: The Art and Practice of the Learning Organization*. London: Century.

Shappard, G. (2009) 'Train to Gain: what's the real story?' *Training Zone*, 22 July. Retrieved on 22 July 2009 from: www.trainingzone.co.uk/topic/train-gain-real-story.

Simmonds, D. (2003) *Designing and delivering training*. London: CIPD.

Skapinker, M. (2002) *Knowledge Management: the change agenda*. London: CIPD.

Stewart, J. (1999) *Employee development practice*. London: Pitman Publishing.

Sunley, P., Martin, R. and Nativel, C. (2001) 'Mapping the New Deal: Local disparities in the performance of Welfare-to-Work', *Transactions of the Institute of British Geographers*, 26(4), 484–512.

Swan, J., Newell, S., Scarbrough, H. and Hislop, D. (1999) 'Knowledge management and innovation: networks and networking', *Journal of Knowledge Management*, 3(4), 262–75.

Talbot, C. (1992) 'Evaluation and validation – a mixed approach', *Journal of European Industrial Training*, 16(5), 26–32.

Thomson, I. (2007) *Evaluation of training*, CIPD Factsheet. Retrieved on 18 May 2007 from: www.cipd.co.uk/subjects/training/trneval/evatrain.htm.

Walton, J. (1999) *Strategic human resource development*. Harlow: Pearson.

Whittington, R. (2001) *What is strategy – and does it matter?* London: Thomson Learning.

Wilson, J.P. and Beard, C. (2003) 'The learning combination lock: an experiential approach to learning design', *Journal of European Industrial Training*, 27(2/3/4), 88–97.

Wognum, A.A. (2001) 'Vertical integration of HRD policy within companies', *Human Resource Development International*, 4(3), 407–21.

Wolff, C. (2007) 'Workplace training – budgets and challenges', *IRS Employment Review*. Retrieved on 31 March 2008 from: www.xperthr.co.uk/article/79809/survey —workplace-training—budgets-and-challenges-2007.aspx.

ASSIGNMENTS AND DISCUSSION TOPICS

1 Critically discuss the extent to which the processes in the systematic training cycle are carried out in your organisation. Which stages in the cycle receive most attention and which receive least? What are the limitations of the systematic training cycle as a framework for practice?

2 What is strategic HRD? In what ways is strategic HRD distinct from knowledge management and human capital management?

3 Identify and critically discuss the ways in which HRD is aligned with organisational strategy in your organisation. How can HRD professionals ensure that ongoing alignment is achieved?

4 How can the impact of strategic HRD be evaluated? Giving organisational examples explain what information is required and how data should be analysed and findings communicated.

5 Compare and contrast knowledge management and human capital management. What are the similarities and what are the differences?

6 What is the distinction between manager training, manager development and management development? What are the challenges of integrating work-based and off-the-job forms of management development and what can be done to meet the challenges?

7 Critically evaluate the impact of the following national initiatives as a way of redressing the UK's skills gap: Train to Gain, Skills Pledge, apprenticeships, raising of the education leaving age.

Chapter 13

Managing Health and Safety at Work

LEARNING OUTCOMES: TO BE ABLE TO

- Explain the perceived tension between the performance imperative and employee health and safety at work

- Recognise that prescriptive legislative approaches have been found wanting and the health and safety focus has shifted to ascribing employee and employer duties and responsibilities

- Apply the legislative framework, and in particular the Health and Safety at Work Act 1974 and the Health and Safety Regulations 1992 (consolidated in ERA 1996 and MHSW Regulations 1999), which implemented EU Directives

- Contribute to the creation of an active and positive health and safety culture

INTRODUCTION

Each year approximately 2 million people suffer ill health caused or aggravated by work activities (HSE, 2008). This affects their quality of life, impairs work performance and gives rise to the loss of millions of working days. Effective people resourcing demands that managerial attention be given to health and safety and employee well-being at work, but despite the importance of health and safety matters they can be subordinated to immediate operational demands. There are three principal themes to this chapter. The first is the identification of a perceived tension between good health and safety practice and operational demands. The second is a practical overview of the legislative framework which informs health and safety practice and which is of relevance to the managers of people. The third is the promotion of the view that the effective management of health and safety is dependent not only on the legislative framework, but also on creating a positive health and safety culture. The strategic management of wellness is addressed in the next chapter.

HEALTH AND SAFETY AT WORK AND THE PERFORMANCE IMPERATIVE

A concern in principle for the health and safety of employees and the encouragement of employee self-interest in health and safety are obvious prerequisites to the effective resourcing, management and well-being of people at work. Workplace reality can be different because of perceptions that health and safety constrains operational freedom and inhibits productivity. These perceptions may relegate health and safety attitudes and actions to a reluctant compliance to good practice and the law, or even result in the avoidance of employee and employer obligations. The potential for conflict between the unfettered pursuit of operational efficiency and the protection of employees from hazards needs to be recognised in planning to manage health and safety successfully. The tension between the performance imperative of organisations seeking survival in competitive environments, and health and safety responsibilities towards employees, is sometimes difficult for line management to reconcile. The reconciliation is dependent on the belief that good health and safety equals good business. Organisations do, of course, have an ethical and social responsibility to give priority to workplace health and safety, but there are compelling business reasons why health and safety should be of significant interest to managers seeking quality employee performance. These include the following.

- Injuries, absence and ill health directly and seriously impact on organisational efficiency and effectiveness (Exhibit 13.1).
- Mutual employer and employee interest in health and safety contributes to a healthy psychological contract.
- Health and safety concerns distract employees from quality concerns.
- Health and safety at work provides fertile ground for disciplinary breaches and grievance expression.
- Considerable obligations are placed on employers by an extensive legal framework and increasing European influence through Directives and decisions.

EXHIBIT 13.1 **The facts on work-related ill health and injury, 2008**

Ill-health

- 2.1 million people were suffering from an illness caused or made worse by their current or past work.
- Over half of these were suffered within in the last 12 months.

Injuries

- 229 workers were killed at work, a rate of 0.8 per 100 000 workers.
- 136 771 other injuries to employees were reported under RIDDOR, a rate of 518 per 100 000 employees.
- 299 000 reportable injuries occurred, according to the Labour Force Survey, a rate of 1000 per 100 000 workers.

Working days lost

- 34 million days were lost overall (1.4 days per worker), 28 million due to work-related ill health and 6 million due to workplace injury.
- Highest rates of work-related illness were in public administration, health and social work.

Principal causes

- Musculo-skeletal disorders are the most common type of work-related illness, but mental health, mainly stress related, gives rise to more working days lost.

Enforcement

- Enforcement notices totalled 13 750.
- 565 cases prosecuted by HSE and 156 by local authorities with a conviction rates of 95 per cent and 97 per cent respectively.
- Excluding 'exceptional cases' of fines in excess of £100 000, of which there were 37, the average fine is still around £20 000.

The development of an active health and safety culture requires attitudinal and behavioural change, with key roles for training, supervision and managerial standard setting.

High performance HR strategies recognise, first, that people are a major source of competitive advantage and, second, that to contribute fully to organisational performance people need to feel valued. Creating an environment where people feel physically and psychologically safe seems to be a fairly fundamental demonstration that workers are valued. Effective health and safety therefore does make good business sense, and contributes to gaining the trust, commitment and involvement of employees, but health and safety will only receive priority of attention with top management commitment and an acceptance of responsibility throughout the organisation.

FROM PRESCRIPTION TO RESPONSIBILITY – STATUTORY REGULATION TO SELF-REGULATION

Contemporary health and safety concerns within the employment relationship have become more complex and include psychological as well as physical well-being. Health and safety legislation, until the Robens Report of 1972 and the Health and Safety at Work Act (HASAWA) 1974, was primarily focused on statutory regulation and on 'prescribing actions, behaviour and work processes'. This prescriptive approach was being defeated by accelerating technological development and the creative talents of employees who were finding new and innovative ways to damage themselves at work. The prescriptive legislation was onerous for employers, lacked clarity in wording and did not address the need to influence attitudes as well as constraining unsafe behaviour. Prescriptive legislation and statutory regulation are also difficult to police and enforce. HASAWA heralded a new approach to health and safety by shifting the emphasis from buildings, machinery and prescribed employer actions to the establishment of the rights, responsibilities and duties of people at work. There remains a role for unambiguous guidance in many safety areas, but the philosophy of ascribing employer and employee responsibility and the promotion of self-regulation was maintained in the important Health and Safety Regulations 1992 (*see* below). This was articulated by the HSE (2002) as 'much of modern health and safety law is goal setting – setting out what must be achieved, but not how it must be done'. Statutory provision therefore aims:

> to encourage the exercise of employer and employee judgement and responsibility, with decreased faith in legal prescription.

This approach is more likely to engage the commitment of employers and employees than the alternative of always being directed what to do. The development of an active and positive health and safety culture replaces a reliance on the legislation to predict and regulate every health and safety eventuality. Paradoxically, the 'responsibility and judgement approach' produces a tension between human desire for certainty, in this case the desire to know what is required in a particular health and safety situation, and the freedom to exercise discretion and judgement in a particular organisational context. To illustrate this point, the Display Screen Equipment Regulations (*see* below) allow employer discretion by not prescribing time threshold criteria for defining a display screen user. This discretion can make it uncomfortable for managers who have to decide on the designation of users for the purposes of the regulations, with the result that prescriptive internal criteria are often applied, for example the imposition of fixed time thresholds to define a display screen user. With discretion goes uncertainty.

> Effectively there is a displacement of the tension between prescription and the exercise of judgement from the legislation to managerial decision-makers.

RECONCILING THE TENSIONS

The tension between the performance imperative and health and safety concerns, on the one hand, and *the balance between legislative prescription and the exercise of managerial judgement,* on the other, both need to be reconciled if the management of health and safety at work is to be effective. A starting point for reconciliation is knowledge of health and safety law, codes of practice and Health and Safety Executive guidance, as these represent the body of knowledge associated with effective health and safety practice. Health and safety is a detailed legislative area and the aim here is to provide sufficient information for managers and others responsible for health and safety to appreciate key principles and to know when expert advice is required. A basic understanding of health and safety law is useful regardless of whether specific organisational responsibility for health and safety is located with an HR specialist, a health and safety officer or another 'competent person'. While compliance with the law is an important concern, effective practice in health and safety can add value to organisational performance. All managers and employees have responsibility for health and safety at work, and a cascading of legislative knowledge will contribute to the development of an active and positive health and safety culture.

COMMON LAW DUTIES OF CARE

Employers have a common law duty **to take reasonable care** of each employee and are expected to safeguard employees against hazards which are reasonably foreseeable. The standard of care required is that of a 'prudent' employer. The duty of care includes operating safe premises, safe work systems and safe equipment, and ensuring that, through selection, training and supervision, employees are able to work safely and competently. Employees have common law duties **to cooperate** with the employer and **to exercise reasonable care** in the performance of work. These duties oblige an employee to make every effort to work safely, to abide by health and safety instructions and to contribute to achieving a safe working environment. Health and safety is therefore firmly rooted in the contract of employment through common law, making health and safety an employment issue. Statutory health and safety provision supports and extends these common law rights and duties.

THE HEALTH AND SAFETY AT WORK ACT (HASAWA) 1974

Prior to HASAWA the guiding statutes for employers were the Factories Act (FA) 1961 and the Offices, Shops and Railway Premises Act (OSRPA) 1963. These Acts applied to the premises indicated in the title of the Act, determined statutory employer and employee duties and set minimum standards in the working environment. FA and OSRPA regulated lighting, ventilation, working space, cleanliness, hygiene facilities, temperature and first aid arrangements. These Acts remain in force but their provisions continue to be replaced by health and safety regulations and codes of practice, and particularly by the Workplace Health, Safety and Welfare Regulations 1992 and the health and safety provisions of the Employment Rights Act 1996. HASAWA represented a sea-change in the UK approach to health and safety legislation and was aimed at combating the endemic apathy towards health and safety provision, attributed to excessive, prescriptive and unintelligible law and compounded by ineffective policing and enforcement. HASAWA incorporated fundamental shifts in the approach to health and safety at work by:

1 Promoting a self-regulatory system in recognition that it is those who work with the risks who are most effective at recognising and responding to them.
2 Encouraging voluntary effort and personal responsibility for health and safety, rather than a reliance on prescriptive regulation.
3 Directing the statutory provision to cover people rather than just machinery and premises.
4 Extending the legislative scope to cover most employed persons, rather than specific places of work.
5 Enforcing the law through strengthened criminal sanctions.
6 Unifying the administration and enforcement through creating the Health and Safety Commission (HSC) and the Health and Safety Executive (HSE).

The provisions of health and safety law can be examined from the perspectives of *duties* (general duties and duties relating to safety policies, committees and representatives) and *enforcement*.

HASAWA – general duties

General statutory duties placed on the employer include providing:

- safe equipment, a safe workplace and a safe system of work
- safe arrangements for the use, handling, transport and storage of all articles and materials
- the information, training and supervision necessary for effective health and safety
- an adequate and safe means of entering and exiting the workplace
- adequate welfare – although welfare is not defined it is taken to mean the work environment features associated with FA and OSRPA, reflected more recently in the Workplace Health, Safety and Welfare Regulations (*see* below).

There are clearly similarities between the statutory and the common law duties, but HASAWA duties are more explicit and breaches of HASAWA duties are subject to criminal enforcement and sanction. A schedule of criminal penalties incorporates un-limited fines and imprisonment for employer failure to discharge a duty or failure to remedy a breach. Employers are not expected to exercise their duties without regard for the cost, difficulty and commercial implications, nor are they expected to predict unforeseen circumstances. The phrase which defines the extent and scope of the employer's duties is **as far as is reasonably practicable** (HASAWA, 1974). This per-mits employer judgement which weighs the health and safety risk against the burden of reducing or removing it. The employers' statutory duty of care also applies in respect of non-employees legitimately on the premises and people outside the organisation who may be affected by employer or employee acts or omissions. Further important duties placed on employers include:

- to prepare and update a written health and safety policy and to communicate it effectively and comprehensively to employees

- to recognise the appointment of safety representatives from recognised trade unions or where a trade union is not recognised to consult directly with employees or with employee representatives
- to form a safety committee, where requested to do so in writing by at least two union safety representatives.

Employees also have HASAWA duties: first, 'to take reasonable care of their own safety', implying that a failure to do so will be a breach of duty punishable under HASAWA and therefore subject to legitimate managerial discipline, and also potentially subject to criminal proceedings; and, second, 'to take reasonable care in respect of other people who may be affected by the employee's actions or omissions'. Employees are therefore mutually responsible to each other for health and safety at work. Employees are also obligated 'to cooperate and not to interfere, whether by design or carelessness, with the employer, other people or any workplace provision which seeks to secure health and safety at work'. These employee duties are made even more explicit in the Management of Health and Safety at Work Regulations and seek to engender the personal values and responsibility essential to achieving a positive safety culture.

Designers, manufacturers, suppliers and installers of articles, equipment and substances do not escape duties and responsibilities under HASAWA. The responsibilities include, as far as is reasonably practicable, incorporating safety features in the design stage, testing for risks to health and seeking to minimise or eliminate them, and providing information, training and instruction for installation and use. HASAWA, along with more specific environmental legislation (the Environmental Protection Act 1990, for example), makes reference to the emission of noxious and offensive substances and a higher standard of care is specified. Those responsible for premises are obligated to prevent noxious or offensive emissions by **the best practicable means**, which does not permit the costs and difficulty of eliminating pollution being weighed against the nature of the risk to health and safety, although a judgement about what constitutes the best practicable means still remains. This provides a contrast with the standard of care implied by 'as far as is reasonably practicable'.

The health and safety policy

A health and safety policy should include three sections – a positive statement of management attitude and commitment to health and safety, a specification of responsibilities and accountabilities for health and safety, and operational arrangements for health and safety. The content of the policy is not prescribed beyond these general sections, but guidance is available from the HSE (*Writing a Safety Policy Statement*: periodically revised), the intention being that management should reflect on their own particular hazards and risks and design an appropriate policy. Risk assessment outcomes, the designation of the safety competent persons (1992 and 1999 Regulations) and emergency procedures should be included in the policy.

Safety representatives and safety committees

HASAWA requires employers to recognise safety representatives appointed by trade unions, where trade unions are recognised. Union safety representatives have a right to be consulted about the full range of health and safety matters, including the appointment of the competent persons required by the 1992 and 1999 Regulations, and have a wide range of functions which include:

- being consulted and making representations to employers
- investigating hazards and risks
- making safety inspections, having given reasonable notice
- considering employee complaints
- accessing and consulting with HSE inspectors
- being a member of the safety committee.

The Health and Safety (Consultation with Employees) Regulations 1996 corrected the inconsistent position where only employers who recognised trade unions were required to recognise safety representatives. The 1996 Regulations require employers to consult with employees where there is no appointed union representative. The consultation can either be directly with employees or through elected representatives of employment safety (ROES), and there is a duty to consult about:

- the introduction of measures substantially affecting health and safety
- the appointment of representatives
- the supply of statutory health and safety information
- health and safety training
- the health and safety consequences of introducing new technology.

There are similarities between the role of union safety representatives and ROES, but the investigatory functions are less evident in the latter. In order to perform their function adequately, all safety representatives are entitled to the information and training necessary to fulfil their duties, to reasonable time off work with pay during normal working hours, and to appropriate facilities. All safety representatives should be included in the updating and the communication of the safety policy. Union safety representatives and ROES have strengthened statutory protection against dismissal or action short of dismissal for duties associated with their legitimate role.

The statutory duty to create a safety committee relies on the appointment of union safety representatives, and consequently the duty is circumscribed, but where at least two safety representatives request it the employer is required to establish a safety committee. Apart from specifying a requirement for the committee to keep under review the measures taken to ensure the health and safety at work of employees, the composition and terms of reference of the committee are left to the discretion of the employer after consultation with employee representatives (Safety Representatives and Safety Committees Regulations, 1977).

Enforcement of health and safety law

The Health and Safety Commission (HSC) and the Health and Safety Executive (HSE) were established by HASAWA. The HSC was primarily an advisory body and the HSE was primarily the enforcement agency. The HSC consisted of a chairperson, appointed by the Secretary of State, and other members chosen from employers' organisations, employee representatives' organisations and local authorities. The HSC was responsible for providing direction for national health and safety policy and proposing new or updated law to secure the health, safety and welfare of the public and people at work. The HSC role incorporated research, approving codes of practice and providing information, training and advice, while the HSE assisted the HSC through being responsible for policing and enforcing health and safety law. In 2008 a single regulatory body was formed, and called the Health and Safety Executive, with the aim of strengthening links between health and safety strategy and the delivery of better health and safety at work. However, there was no change in practice to the statutory functions of either of the previous bodies, or to the enforcement of health and safety at work. Local authorities retain significant responsibility for enforcement (Enforcing Authority Regulations, 1989) and, along with the HSE, appoint safety inspectors. Safety inspectors have wide-ranging powers, including the authority to:

- enter premises at any reasonable time
- be accompanied by authorised persons and a police officer, if obstructed
- use any equipment or materials necessary for investigation
- take samples, measurements and photographs
- direct that work areas be left undisturbed
- take possession of articles, substances or equipment, if reasonable cause is established
- take statements from appropriate persons
- examine organisational documents.

Safety inspectors have a range of tools at their disposal in order to achieve compliance with the law. Inspectors may offer advice and guidance, serve improvement or prohibition notices, vary licence conditions, issue formal cautions or prosecute. An improvement notice is used where the inspector is satisfied that there is a contravention of a statutory provision. An improvement notice identifies the statutory provision being contravened and requires that the contravention is remedied by a prescribed date. Where the inspector is of the opinion that an activity involves a risk of serious personal injury a prohibition notice, ordering the immediate or deferred cessation of the activity, can be issued. Failure to comply with an improvement or a prohibition notice is an offence. Appeals against these notices can be made to an employment tribunal (ET). In the case of an improvement notice, the appeal has the effect of suspending the notice until the appeal is determined. In the case of a prohibition notice the appeal does not suspend the notice. Approximately 15 000 improvement or prohibition notices are issued each year (HSE, 2008) and they can be entered in a public register for at least three years, exposing 'transgressors' to public scrutiny and increasing the deterrent value of the notices (Environment and Safety Information Act, 1988). A record of successful prosecutions also appears on the HSE website (www.hse.gov.uk).

The use of these notices and the willingness of inspectors to prosecute under the statutory provisions are circumscribed by three factors. First, there are insufficient numbers of inspectors to police all employers and all employees; second, prosecution is time-consuming for inspectors; and, third, there are difficulties in achieving successful prosecutions and therefore prosecutions only proceed where there is a real prospect of conviction. The HSE aims to secure compliance with the law through an educative and persuasive approach to discourage the displacement of health and safety responsibility to the inspectors. This is also intended to engender a view of the inspecting role as supportive and cooperative. The inspectorate is reasonably tolerant of employers who need time to respond to new health and safety regulations, and formal enforcement measures are unlikely unless risks to health and safety are obvious and imminent.

Regulations and approved codes of practice (ACOP)

HASAWA is an 'enabling Act'. It enables the Secretary of State to lay down legal standards in respect of health and safety through the simpler and more flexible process of making health and safety regulations. This regulation-making power is used widely, and regulations can be made in respect of almost anything related to health and safety at work. Examples include the Control of Substances Hazardous to Health Regulations (COSHH, 1988), which protect people at work from exposure to potentially hazardous substances through a process of risk assessment and responsible employer action; the Reporting of Injuries, Diseases and Dangerous Occurrences Regulations (RIDDOR, 1995) which impose reporting requirements for accidents and industrial diseases; and the 'six-pack' of 1992 Regulations which implemented European Directives. The Secretary of State is empowered to approve codes of practice drawn up by the HSC, the HSE or any other appropriate organisation. The purpose of the codes of practice is to provide practical guidance in interpreting and applying statutory provision. There is not a strict legal obligation on employers to observe the provisions of an approved health and safety code of practice, but a failure to do so may be taken into account by the courts. If an employer does not adhere to a code of practice, it is open to them to demonstrate that a statutory health and safety obligation has been observed in some other way. It is sensible to follow the guidance in the codes as not only do they reflect effective safety practice, but they also afford some protection against successful prosecution.

A PRACTICAL GUIDE TO THE HEALTH AND SAFETY REGULATIONS 1992 (CONSOLIDATED IN ERA 1996 AND AMENDMENT REGULATIONS 1999 AND 2003)

The 1992 Regulations, known as the 'six-pack' (Figure 13.1), are representative of contemporary thinking in health and safety at work, and managers will benefit from an appreciation of the content and approach of these regulations. The concept that employers are normally only obligated 'as far as is reasonably practicable' remains a core principle. Most of the requirements of the 1992 Regulations were already covered by existing UK legislation, but they expressed and make explicit a European standard for health and safety. Compliance with a more specific regulation, for example COSHH, is sufficient to comply with a corresponding duty in the 1992 Regulations, but where the 1992 Regulations go further than existing legislation it is necessary to consider additional health and safety measures. The Management of Health and Safety at Work Regulations are largely a reflection of HASAWA, but incorporating risk assessment. The Manual Handling Operations, the Display Screen Equipment and the Personal Protective Equipment Regulations were mostly new areas of regulation. The Provision and Use of Work Equipment Regulations were a combination of existing and new legislation. The Workplace Health, Safety and Welfare Regulations represent a contemporary version of the FA and OSRPA.

The Management of Health and Safety at Work Regulations emanated from the 'European Framework Directive' and provide a context for the other five sets of regulations. Health and safety remains high on the European Union agenda for two reasons: first, because it is integral to the social dimension of the Single European Market

Figure 13.1
The 1992 Regulations (consolidated in ERA 1996): a European standard located in a UK health and safety philosophy

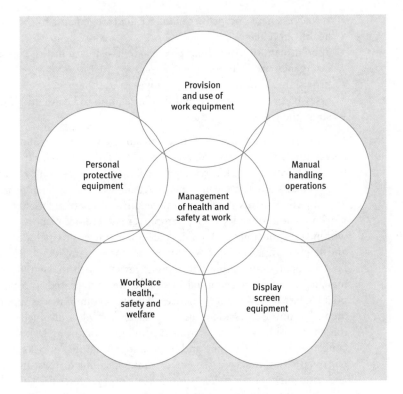

and, second, because of the desire to contribute to a level (competitive) playing field through the harmonisation of health and safety standards across the member states. The Single European Act (SEA, 1987) designated health and safety as an area of competence for qualified majority voting (QMV). This effectively removes the power of any one member state to veto health and safety proposals; and there has at times been contention between the UK and the European Commission over what should be included in health and safety QMV, for example in the case of the Working Time Directive which was designated as a health and safety measure.

The emphasis in the 1992 Regulations, maintained by the HSE, and in line with HASAWA, is away from prescription towards responsibility. The regulations were published to include approved codes of practice and guidance on regulations.

> The underpinning philosophy is one of suitable and sufficient risk assessment, the exercise of informed judgement and a response that is reasonable in the circumstances.

This philosophy recognises that different workplaces have different levels of risk, but enables all organisations to engage in meaningful health and safety activity based on effective risk assessment.

Management of Health and Safety at Work (MHSW) Regulations

These regulations provide a wide context for health and safety at work. The principal obligations include:

- risk assessment and proper managerial arrangements for health and safety
- health surveillance
- appointment of 'competent persons' to assist with health and safety
- emergency procedures
- provision of information to employees and others
- assessment of employee capability in relation to health and safety
- strengthened employee duties.

Risk assessment which is 'suitable and sufficient' is a critical requirement of MHSW and is simply a careful examination of the hazards in the workplace and their potential to cause harm. The risk assessment facilitates scrutiny and evaluation of risks which leads to managerial action in terms of elimination, reduction or protection (HSE, 2006). The objective is to assess the risks to health and safety of employees and others, in the workplace and outside, and the employer is therefore responsible for assessing risks within 'a responsibility zone'. Risk assessment needs to include a check on the health and safety competence of contractors and the self-employed. Risk assessment should be documented and subject to regular review, with the significant findings and the managerial response recorded in writing and integrated into the health and safety policy. The MHSW code of practice advocates a common-sense approach to risk assessment. The initial assessment can be quick and simple and aimed at identifying whether there is a problem which warrants further investigation. Risk assessment is therefore concerned with recognising and responding to significant risks, not with bureaucracy or trivial risks. Risk assessment can take account of existing preventive measures and assessments undertaken for other purposes, under the COSHH Regulations for example, need not be repeated if they are considered to be 'suitable and sufficient'. Employers are required to undertake a systematic examination of work activity, and a five-step example of the process is provided in Exhibit 13.2.

A risk assessment is an important step in protecting workers and the business, as well as complying with the law. It helps focus attention on the risks that really matter in the workplace – the ones with the potential to cause real harm. In many instances straightforward measures can readily control risks. The law does not expect

EXHIBIT 13.2 **A systematic approach to risk assessment**

1. Identify the hazards – a hazard is the *potential* of a process, substance or activity to cause harm.
2. Assess and rank the risks associated with each hazard using three dimensions:
   - potential severity of harm
   - likelihood of harm
   - proportion of people at risk.
3. Identify the significant risks through the points rating of each hazard (Exhibit 13.3).
4. Prioritise the measures that need to be taken, obtaining expert assistance if necessary, to promote a safe and healthy working environment and to comply with statutory provision.
5. Plan and implement preventive and protective responses; monitor, evaluate, review and feed back into the risk assessment process.

employers to eliminate all risk, but requires workers to be protected as far as
is reasonably practicable. (HSE, 2006)

An illustrative points-rating framework for the ranking of risks is provided in Exhibit 13.3, but each organisation should design an appropriate model to reflect their particular work environment and health and safety concerns. Risk assessment can be made more systematic, but a scoring framework only informs decision-making – it is no substitute for the exercise of responsible judgement. For each identified hazard the risk assessment rating model incorporates three dimensions and a total hazard score.

Potential severity of harm – the seriousness of injury or illness that may occur, the length of the recovery time and the possibility and length of any absence.

Likelihood of harm – the probability that harm from a particular hazard will be realised, ranging from unlikely to inevitable.

Proportion of population at risk – the number of employees and others who may be exposed to the risk, ranging from several individuals to the total population of a responsibility zone.

Total hazard score – this is produced by multiplying the points ratings from which a total hazard score can be generated. The higher the score, the more significant the risk. Finer graduations of four-, five- or six-point scales can be used.

The aim of risk assessment is to identify significant risks and not obscure those risks with an excess of information or by concentrating on trivial risks. The level of detail in the risk assessment should be broadly proportionate to risk. The risk assessment response should recognise the hierarchy of measures which focuses attention on eliminating risks rather than just compensating for them; the hierarchy is: avoid the risks altogether; combat the risks at source; reorganise the work or redesign the job; reduce the risk by training; and finally, protect against the risk.

Extensive case study examples of risk assessment are available on: http://www.hse.gov.uk/risk/casestudies/

EXHIBIT 13.3 **Systematic risk assessment through points rating
of each hazard**

Hazard description:			
	Low	**Medium**	**High**
Potential severity of harm	1	2	3
Likelihood of harm	1	2	3
Proportion of population at risk	1	2	3

For a total hazard score from 1 to 27 circle a number for each of the three dimensions and multiply the three numbers.

Total Hazard Score (THS) =

Health surveillance has the objective of detecting adverse health effects. Surveillance is necessary where there is a known adverse health condition and in other circumstances identified by risk assessment. Surveillance includes monitoring the workplace and the individual, and requires suitable equipment to measure physiological and psychological effects. Employers are required *to appoint one or more competent persons who are able to assist . . . in undertaking the measures [necessary] to comply with* the regulations. Competent persons need training, experience and knowledge to be able to assist effectively. The key word is *assist*, because the responsibility for health and safety remains with all managers and employees; it is not abdicated to the competent health and safety person. What constitutes competence is contingent on the organisational situation and at its simplest might include a basic knowledge of the work involved, an appreciation of the principles of risk assessment and an understanding of current health and safety applications. Complex and high risk activities will require specialist technical expertise. To be effective the competent person will need autonomy and authority.

Employers are required to establish *procedures to be followed in the event of serious and imminent danger*. The assessment of emergency procedures should focus on the adequacy of warning procedures, routes to places of safety, evacuation and mustering arrangements and first aid. Procedures for preventing or limiting access to dangerous areas are also necessary. Employers have a responsibility to *provide comprehensible and relevant information* about the risks identified by the assessment, the preventive and protective measures being taken and the procedures for serious or imminent danger. Information can be provided on a need-to-know basis, but it must be comprehensible to those who do need to know. Information must also be made available to contractors and the self-employed, and the risk assessment should take account of specific risks to these groups. Employers are required to assess *the health and safety capability* of employees as a continuous process and respond with adequate training. Health and safety training needs will be greatest on recruitment, job transfer, change of hours, new methods of working and the introduction of new technology.

Duties on employees are imposed by the MHSW Regulations and these extend HASAWA obligations. Employee duties are:

- to use and respect equipment, machinery and safety devices
- to cooperate with the employer and inform either the employer, or an employee with responsibility for health and safety, of any risk or threat to health and safety
- to inform the employer if health and safety arrangements, including training, are inadequate.

Manual Handling Operations (MHO) Regulations

Little manual handling regulation existed prior to the MHO Regulations. The rationale for a focus on manual handling in the workplace is the comparatively high risk of injury. More than a quarter of all reported accidents are associated with manual handling, the vast majority of manual handling injuries result in absences of three days or more, and almost one-half of all manual handling injuries are sprains and strains of the back (HSE, 2008). Many injuries could be avoided through an *ergonomic* approach to lifting and handling which takes account of the nature of the task, the characteristics of the load, constraints in the working environment and the capability of the individual. The MHO Regulations establish a hierarchy of safety measures:

1 *AVOID* hazardous manual handling as far as is reasonably practicable through eliminating the need to move the load or through automating the process.

2 *ASSESS* the risks to health and safety where manual handling cannot be avoided.

3 *REDUCE* the risk of injury by considering the size, shape and location of the load, the working environment, the need for further instruction and training in handling techniques, and the potential for provision of mechanical assistance.

An illustrative manual handling risk assessment checklist is provided in Exhibit 13.4 and the risk profile informs managerial intervention.

EXHIBIT 13.4 **An illustrative manual handling checklist**

Is there a risk associated with	Please tick		
	Low	Medium	High
The task?			
– turning and twisting			
– bending			
– stretching			
– pushing or pulling			
– repetition			
– distance			
– handling equipment			
The environment?			
– space			
– lighting			
– temperature			
– obstacles			
The load?			
– shape			
– size			
– weight			
– special hazards			
The ability requirements?			
– skills and knowledge			
– information and training			
– physical or psychological capabilities			
Options for preventive and protective measures (avoid – assess – reduce):			

Display Screen Equipment (DSE) Regulations

The DSE Regulations cover three key areas. First, defining display screen users; second, risk assessment of display screen workstations; and, third, eye test provision. There is no clear-cut definition of a display screen user, as it depends on whether an employee 'habitually uses a display screen as a significant part of normal work' (HSE, 1996; see also HSE, 1992a). The definition of a 'user' is therefore dependent on the frequency, continuity, pacing and intensity of display screen use and whether an employee habitually uses a display screen as a significant part of normal work.

Workstation risk assessment focuses on ergonomic factors and the potential for visual or musculo-skeletal fatigue (including RSI), but other display screen concerns include stress through pacing of work, epilepsy, facial dermatitis, radiation and threat to pregnancy. There are three ways of responding to workstation risks: first, examine workstation design; second, consider the daily routine of users; and, third, provide training. Workstation design requires consideration of posture, lighting, adjustability of equipment, space, heat, noise and software ergonomics. The daily routine of users should be planned to include periodic interruptions of display screen work, through breaks or changes of activity which reduce the intensity of the display screen workload. Training of users should include recognising hazards and risks, the need for rest or other activity breaks, the importance of posture, the use of equipment adjustment mechanisms and general ergonomics.

A user can request an eye and eyesight test and the employer has a duty to make arrangements for an appropriate test, at the time of the initial request and at regular intervals. There is no conclusive evidence that display screen work causes permanent damage to eyes or eyesight, but uncorrected vision defects contribute to visual fatigue. The rationale for testing and correcting vision is therefore to improve comfort and performance. The employer is responsible for financing corrective appliances, but this liability only extends to providing adequate corrective appliances, normally spectacles, which correct vision at display screen viewing distance, normally measured by a keystone machine.

Workplace Health, Safety and Welfare (WHSW) Regulations

The WHSW Regulations replaced 38 pieces of existing legislation, including large parts of the Factories Act and the Offices, Shops and Railway Premises Act, and the standards are principally those of these Acts. General requirements can be categorised into four broad areas – the working environment, safety of movement, workplace facilities and housekeeping.

The working environment – should have a 'reasonable' indoor temperature; the code of practice recommends 16°C for sedentary work and 13°C for more active work. Ventilation should ensure a sufficient quantity of fresh or purified air, and lighting is required to be suitable, sufficient and, as far as is reasonably practicable, natural light. Personal space should be sufficient for health, safety and welfare purposes; the guideline is 11 cubic metres per person.

Safety of movement – focuses on safe traffic routes for people, including surfaces, slopes, obstructions, flooring construction, crossings, sensible speeds and signs. The safety and construction of doors, gates, stairways, lifts and escalators warrant special attention. The particular hazards associated with glazing require employers to assess glazing material and the arrangements for opening, cleaning and marking. Falls from heights, falls into substances and risks from falling objects also merit specific assessment.

Workplace facilities – include toilet, washing, changing, eating and resting arrangements; these are required to be 'suitable and sufficient'. Drinking water should be 'wholesome, accessible and marked'. Pregnant women and nursing mothers need to be provided with rest facilities near to sanitary facilities. People are entitled to protection from tobacco smoke discomfort.

Housekeeping – obligations require the efficient maintenance of the workplace, the equipment and the facilities, and emphasise the importance of cleanliness and the removal of waste material.

Provision and Use of Work Equipment (PUWE) Regulations

The PUWE Regulations reinforce the obligations of designers, manufacturers, suppliers, installers and employers specified in HASAWA. They consolidate the extensive legislation relating to work equipment, espouse general duties and list minimum requirements for work equipment. The principal obligations are that:

- selection of work equipment should consider safety integrity and maintenance should be routine, preventive and logged
- information and instruction on the use of the equipment or machinery should be adequate, available in writing and comprehensible
- special protective measures are necessary for dangerous machine parts and where there is a risk of discharge, rupture, explosion, ejection and extreme temperatures
- the safety role of controls, control systems and isolation from power sources should receive special consideration.

Risk assessment is the key in deciding the level and complexity of the hazards, and frequently specialist and technical knowledge will be necessary in considering the safe provision and use of workplace equipment.

Personal Protective Equipment (PPE) Regulations

Personal protective equipment includes clothing and is defined as 'all equipment . . . worn or held . . . at work which protects against risks to . . . [personal] health and safety' (HSE, 1992d). Detailed guidance and a specimen risk survey table are available in the PPE booklet (L25). The HSE also provides specific guidelines covering the head, the eyes, the arms and hands, the feet and the body. Hearing and respiratory protective equipment is covered under separate regulations. Employers have a duty to assess the need for personal protective equipment and provide equipment which is suitable for the purpose. This means ensuring that it offers adequate protection, it fits the employee, it is adequately maintained, storage is available and employees are appropriately trained and instructed. Employees have a duty to make full and proper use of PPE, to take care of it and report any defects or loss. PPE should be used as a 'last resort', as the hierarchy of responses principle demands that other health and safety measures should receive prior consideration.

THE HEALTH AND SAFETY (OFFENCES) ACT 2008 AND THE CORPORATE MANSLAUGHTER AND CORPORATE HOMICIDE ACT 2008

Under the Health and Safety (Offences) Act 2008 anyone convicted of a health and safety offence can be imprisoned and not just fined. Directors and senior managers face up to two years in prison if they fail to look after the safety of employees or members of the public. The aim of the Act is to ensure that the penalties for health and safety offences are sufficiently robust to deter individuals from breaking the law. Magistrates' courts can impose a sentence of up to 12 months' imprisonment and a fine not exceeding £20 000, while crown courts can sentence offenders for up to two years, with no limits on fines. The Act increased the financial penalties for regulatory offences, such as not making a suitable or sufficient risk assessment, from £5000 to £20 000. If senior employees agree to, or cooperate with, an offence being committed or if the offence is attributable to their neglect, they will be liable to up to two years in prison. The new penalties also cover individual employees who commit an offence by not taking reasonable care of fellow employees. Employees who cause an injury to a fellow employee by failing to follow their training or engaging in horseplay face a prison sentence or a large fine. Prior to this 2008 Act, a custodial sentence for health and safety failings was generally available only following a death in the workplace and if the person charged had been grossly negligent.

The Corporate Manslaughter and Corporate Homicide Act 2008 sets out a new offence for convicting an organisation where 'gross failure' results in death. Under this new approach courts are able to look at management systems and practices across the organisation, rather than simply the actions of individuals. This is a remedy to the previous position where convicting individuals, because of diffused responsibility, was particularly problematic. There are no new health and safety duties or obligations under the Act, nor is the new offence part of health and safety law. It is, however, specifically linked to existing health and safety requirements. Under the Act, health and safety legislation means 'any statutory provision dealing with health and safety matters' so it includes transport (road, rail, river, sea, air), food safety and workplace safety as enforced by the HSE and local authorities. Juries are required to consider breaches of health and safety legislation in determining liability for corporate manslaughter or homicide. Juries also consider the extent to which an organisation has taken account of any health and safety guidance and the extent to which there were 'attitudes, policies, systems or accepted practices' within the organisation that encouraged any serious management failure.

PROTECTION AGAINST DISMISSAL – HEALTH AND SAFETY DUTIES AND CONCERNS

The influence of Europe in health and safety at work is also apparent in the Employment Rights Act (ERA) 1996, which consolidated health and safety measures stimulated by EU Directives. Employers are not lawfully able to dismiss, select for redundancy or subject employees to any other detriment for carrying out designated health and safety duties, alerting the employer to a reasonable health and safety concern, taking steps to protect themselves from danger which is reasonably believed to be serious and imminent, or leaving the workplace because of a reasonable fear of unavoidable danger. There is no service requirement for claims of unfair dismissal in relation to these actions.

SPECIAL GROUPS – YOUNG PEOPLE AND PREGNANT WOMEN

The Health and Safety (Young Persons) Regulations 1997 implemented the health and safety provisions of the European Directive on the Protection of Young People at Work and complement the risk assessment and information requirements of the 1992 Regulations. Employers are required to:

- take particular account of young workers' lack of experience, absence of awareness of existing or potential risks and maturity when assessing risks to health and safety
- take account of the risk assessment in deciding whether a young person is prohibited from engaging in certain work
- inform parents (or those with parental responsibility) of school-age children of the outcome of the risk assessment and the health and safety measures introduced.

Pregnant employees, regardless of length of service, are also afforded greater protection (ERA 1996). Risks to the health of the pregnant employee and the unborn child need to be assessed. This risk assessment needs to be undertaken by all organisations that employ, or potentially employ, women of childbearing age (which needs to be defined widely). The risk assessment cannot be left until pregnancy is declared, because damage to health may have already occurred. If risks are present, employers are obligated to redesign the work to make it safe or to transfer the employee to suitable alternative work, or if neither of these options is available to give paid leave.

THE WORKING TIME DIRECTIVE 1993

As a health and safety measure the Working Time Directive (WTD) was adopted by qualified majority voting. In the UK the Directive was implemented through the Working Time Regulations 1998. The implications for organisations have been significant, because prior to this there was no generally applicable statutory provision which limited weekly working hours, regulated rest periods or gave entitlement to paid holiday. Exemptions, derogations and exclusions from the provisions of the WTD and the UK statutory response make this a complex area, and further legislation and case law will no doubt continue to be needed to clarify the position, but the main provisions, which apply to workers and not just employees, include:

- a maximum 48-hour working week, on average, together with protection for workers against suffering a detriment for a refusal to work more than 48 hours

- a minimum of four weeks' paid annual leave
- a minimum of 11 consecutive hours' rest each working day and a minimum of 35 hours' uninterrupted rest each week
- night work restricted to eight hours' maximum in certain circumstances and health assessments are required for night workers
- in-work rest breaks of 20 minutes when working time is more than six hours.

The paid leave entitlement is relatively easy to implement, but the calculation of the 48-hour working week maximum, and the other provisions relating to working times, are more problematic, particularly as there is so much scope for individuals to opt out and for exemptions. The administration associated with monitoring and record-keeping is perceived as burdensome by employer representative organisations. The Working Time Directive articulated an employer responsibility to adapt work to the worker and to seek ways to alleviate monotonous or repetitive work, but this was not given a high profile in the 1998 Regulations.

CASE STUDY   Health and safety in Cobras department store

A year ago you were appointed by the store director as the competent person responsible for assisting with health and safety in the Cobras department store. The store has a turnover of £30 million per annum and a staffing establishment of around 400. This case relates to the general services, warehousing and maintenance (GSWM) department. There are 50 staff in the GSWM department who undertake work associated with cleaning, general maintenance and repairs, transport and storage of goods and store security. The GSWM working environment contains many hazards and is characterised by significant risks to health and safety.

The GSWM department has traditionally had a poor health and safety record. The demands of supporting customer-focused sales departments have resulted in health and safety concerns being subordinated to operational demands. There is a carefree and fatalistic attitude towards health and safety among the staff, which is evident from high accident, injury and absence rates. Other problems include:

- unsafe manual handling
- irregular use of personal protective equipment
- untidy working areas
- poor storage of goods.

In a cooperative and supportive way you pointed out these health and safety problems to the GSWM department manager some months ago. Although being a bit 'put out' by what he perceived as something of an encroachment on his responsibilities, he reluctantly agreed to do something about your concerns. He stated, however, that his primary focus was on operational efficiency in a climate of tight resources and incessant demands from sales departments where the 'customer was king'. The GSWM manager prided himself on his direct management style and his ability to 'knock problems on the head' first time round. In his view it would be pointless to try to train and educate his staff and he had no time for presentations from occupational health professionals, video tapes or poster initiatives. He decided on a strategy of dealing immediately and severely with any incidents of unsafe practice, as he believed in the 'red hot stove' approach to the punishment of undesirable behaviour. He briefed his supervisors accordingly and they began a campaign of warnings and punishments in relation to unsafe practices, injuries and accidents. The punishments and sanctions included giving out unpleasant jobs, restricting access to desirable overtime, and causing embarrassment to health and safety transgressors by dressing them down in front of their co-workers.

A monitoring of accident and injury statistics revealed a downward trend in the first few months. This had to be offset by some deterioration in the relationship between GSWM and the sales departments. Sales department managers reported that GSWM staff were more concerned with health and comfort than they were with keeping the business competitive. It also became apparent that the decrease in accidents and injuries was illusory, as informal discussion with GSWM staff revealed that accidents and injuries were being under-reported because of a fear of being punished. It was also clear that the staff and the supervisors were uncomfortable about the adversarial relationship that was being created by the GSWM manager's policy on health and safety.

You had little alternative but to discuss this unsatisfactory picture with the GSWM manager. He was distressed by his apparent failure to resolve the problem and admitted that he appeared to have made things worse. You agreed that you would work together to put things right.

Questions

1 Comment on the style and approach of the GSWM manager in attempting to resolve the health and safety problems in his department. Why did his approach fail?

2 What strategy would you adopt to resolve the problems?

3 How can an active and positive health and safety culture be developed and what organisational processes or mechanisms will be required?

CREATING AN ACTIVE HEALTH AND SAFETY CULTURE

Health and safety legislation and regulation can only provide a framework, and it is the approach and actions of employers and employees that determine whether a safe and healthy work environment is a reality. In many low- or medium-risk environments compliance with the law is a rather blunt tool, and it is a belief in the added-value dimension of health and safety which is more likely to encourage an active and positive health and safety culture:

> The avoidance, prevention and reduction of risks at work needs to be an accepted part of the approach and attitudes at all levels of the organisation and apply to all of its activities. The existence of an active health and safety culture affecting the organisation as a whole needs to be ensured. (HSE, 2000)

The commitment of top management, both articulated and enacted, is essential, as without this health and safety efforts will be undermined. A specific policy designed to reflect the risks in the organisation provides a health and safety infrastructure. The policy should be a working document which not only makes a statement of intent, but also clearly allocates health and safety resources and responsibility. Line managers have a critical role as standard setters. They need to be empowered and made responsible for health and safety in specific work areas, but this will not be sufficient if time and resources for health and safety are not made available. In addition, if managers are not judged on their health and safety performance, there is less chance of health and safety being given a business priority, and there is a case for appraising managers, or even offering them incentives, in relation to health and safety performance indicators. The appointment of competent persons with the expertise, status and influence to foster a positive health and safety culture will underpin managerial responsibility.

Those working with the risks, the employees, need to be involved in assessing and responding to the risks through effective communication processes and active consultation. One imaginative way of consulting with employees and engaging commitment is through creating safety focus groups as a channel for the expression of concerns and the examination of health and safety solutions. Disciplinary procedures should constructively reinforce health and safety rules, values and behaviours, and grievance procedures should encourage the expression of employee dissatisfaction with health and safety. The commitment of employees can be encouraged through appraising individuals on safe performance of the job and through safety training needs analysis. There may be advantages in integrating the reward strategy with the health and safety policy in the pursuit of complementarity in the bundle of HR practices. A quality management approach of continuous improvement, individual responsibility and 'right first time' (TQM) can be adapted to health and safety management to create a 'total safety culture' (TSC), with safety values integrated with other organisational values.

The HSE (2005) differentiate between safety culture and safety climate. Safety culture refers to the behavioural aspects of 'what people do' and the situational aspects of the organisation. Safety climate refers to psychological characteristics of employees and 'how people feel', reflecting the values, attitudes, and perceptions of employees with regard to safety. According to the HSE key influences on safety culture and climate include:

Leadership: Performance and safety priorities should have equal merit and senior managers should visibly demonstrate a commitment to safety in order to create a shared vision. Organisations should have effective systems in place for the management and coordination of safety, led by a strategic safety management team.

Two-way communication: A positive safety culture requires effective channels for top-down, bottom-up and horizontal communication. Feedback mechanisms should be in place to respond to any health and safety concerns expressed by employees.

Involvement of employees: Employee ownership of safety can be increased through effective training, through opportunities for employees to be personally responsible for safety and through having channels to report concerns about decisions that are likely to affect them, particularly during organisational change.

A learning culture: Encouragement to employees to proactively contribute ideas for improvement enables organisations to identify, learn and change unsafe conditions. In-depth analysis of incidents together with good communications, with provisions for feedback and sharing of information, also contribute to a learning culture.

A just culture: According to Whittingham (2004), organisations with a blame culture 'over-emphasise individual blame for the human error, at the expense of correcting defective systems'. Organisations should move from a blame culture to a just culture, but one of accountability. Employees should feel that they are able to report issues or concerns without fear that they will be blamed or disciplined as a result of coming forward.

HEALTH AND SAFETY – PRINCIPLE AND REALITY

The principle that good health and safety at work adds value to the business can be promoted, but some employment trends may contribute to a contrasting operational perspective.

- The devolution of greater HR responsibility to line managers may intensify the tension between the performance imperative and concern with health and safety at work.
- There is increasing incidence of peripheral or atypical workers and this group may not attract the same health and safety attention as core workers.
- Job security concerns may inhibit the employee expression of genuine health and safety concerns.
- Managers continue to experience a renewed confidence in the right to manage and unless they are appraised on health and safety performance indicators it may not receive priority of attention.
- The legislative framework may come under challenge from the deregulatory pressures associated with creating freer competitive markets and more flexible labour markets.

There is a conundrum associated with the HR role in connection with health and safety at work. The HR profession is seeking to demonstrate a sharper business focus and become engage in business partnership with front line managers and senior managers. This requires a detachment from welfare origins and a dumping of 'the caring personnel role'. However, embracing an active health and safety role may result in HR practitioners straddling a tension between the operational preoccupation of some line managers and the added-value concern of creating an environment which enhances employee well-being and demonstrates that employees are valued.

A FRAMEWORK FOR ANALYSIS

This chapter provides opportunities for knowledge and understanding in the complex field of health and safety at work. The treatment of the subject is necessarily restricted, but tensions are exposed and managerial guidance is provided. Prescriptive assertions have been avoided, because an assertive approach will founder on organisational contingencies. A framework for analysis is proposed in Figure 13.2 and this will help the critically evaluative student or HR practitioner to examine and respond to the health and safety issues at work.

Figure 13.2 Health
and safety at work: a
framework for analysis

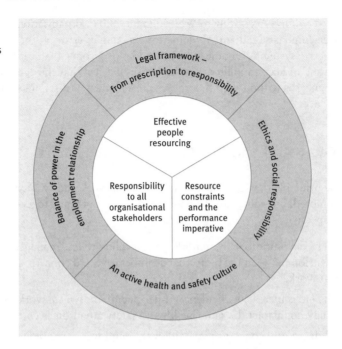

Competitive and economic pressures raise questions about the effectiveness of a self-regulatory approach to health and safety. Where responsibility for health and safety is primarily allocated to employers and employees, the continued strengthening of the right to manage allows managers who are anxious about maximising performance to subordinate health and safety concerns. Delayered, lean organisations, the intensification of work and employee feelings of insecurity do not provide a conducive environment for health and safety at work, but good health and safety remains good business and personal well-being remains a prime concern of individuals at work. In any case, if managers do not convincingly appear to value the safety and health of employees, how can any claims that 'we value our people' be believed? This may then undermine the whole HR strategy.

SUMMARY LEARNING POINTS

1 There is a tension between the performance imperative and a concern for the health and safety of employees. Although this tension is perceived rather than real, it needs to be reconciled as good health and safety is good business.

2 The legislative emphasis since 1974 has shifted from prescription and statutory regulation to employer responsibility and self-regulation. There is no escape from health and safety as employers and employees have extensive duties of care under common law, HASAWA and specific health and safety regulations.

3 A general knowledge of the law, particularly HASAWA and the 1992 Regulations (consolidated in ERA 1996), is a prerequisite to effective health

and safety management, but the law is insufficient on its own, as it is the development of an active and positive health and safety culture which creates a safe and healthy working environment.

4 The European Union has been driving the health and safety agenda, but the semi-prescriptive tone of the European approach is contrary to the self-regulatory philosophy of the UK. Some employment trends, including the balance of power in the employment relationship, may also threaten the effectiveness of a self-regulatory approach.

5 The focus needs to be away from reluctant compliance with the law to extracting the benefits potentially accruing from an active and positive health and safety culture – a belief that effective health and safety can add value to the business.

6 If managers do not convincingly appear to value the safety and health of employees, how can any claims that 'we value our people' be believed? This may then undermine the whole HR strategy.

REFERENCES AND FURTHER READING

Aikin, O. (1995) 'Taking care of pregnant workers', *People Management*, February.

CIPD (2009) *Health and Safety at Work Factsheet*. London: CIPD.

DTI (1998) *A Guide to the Working Time Regulations*. London: DTI.

Eves, D. (1995) 'Health and safety beyond the millennium', *Safety and Health Practitioner*, 13(4), 13–17.

Fairman, R. (1994) 'Robens: 20 years on', *Industrial Relations Review and Report 559*, May.

Goss, D. (1994) *Principles of Human Resource Management*. London: Routledge.

Health and Safety at Work etc. Act 1974 (1975). Chapter 37. London: HMSO.

HSC (1977) *Safety Representatives and Safety Committees*. London: HMSO.

HSC (1989) *Writing a Safety Policy Statement*. London: HMSO.

HSC (1992) *Management of Health and Safety at Work: Approved Code of Practice*. L21. London: HMSO.

HSC (1992) *Workplace Health, Safety and Welfare: Approved Code of Practice and Guidance*. L24. London: HMSO.

HSE (1988) *Introduction to COSHH*. London: HMSO.

HSE (1991) *Successful Health and Safety Management*. London: HMSO.

HSE (1992a) *Manual Handling: Guidance on Regulations*. L23. London: HMSO.

HSE (1992b) *Display Screen Equipment Work: Guidance on Regulations*. L26. London: HMSO.

HSE (1992c) *Work Equipment: Guidance on Regulations*. L22. London: HMSO.

HSE (1992d) *Personal Protective Equipment at Work: Guidance on Regulations*. L25. London: HMSO.

HSE (1996) *Good Health is Good Business*. Published in association with Works Management.

HSE (2000) *Management of Health and Safety at Work Regulations (MHSW) 1999: Approved Code of Practice and Guidance*. L21. London: HSE Books.

HSE (2002) Enforcement Policy Statement, www.hse.gov.uk.

HSE (2003) *Five steps to risk assessment*, www.hse.gov.uk.

HSE (2004) *Occupational Health Statistics Bulletin 2003/2004*, www.hse.gov.uk.

HSE (2005) *A review of safety culture and safety climate literature for the development of the safety culture inspection toolkit. Research Report 367*. London: HMSO.

HSE (2006) *Five steps to risk assessment*, www.hse.gov.uk/risk/fivesteps.

HSE (2008) *Health and Safety Statistics 2007/2008*, www.hse.gov.uk/statistics.

IPD (1995) *Personnel and Europe: Executive brief*. London: IPD.

IPD (1999) *Key Facts: The Working Time Regulations*. London: IPD.

IRS Employment Review 581 (1995) *Employers Back TUC Safety Strategy*, April.

James, P. (1990) 'Holding managers to account for health and safety', *Personnel Management*, April.

James, P. (1994) 'Worker representation and consultation: the impact of European requirements', *Employee Relations*, 16(7), 33–42.

Kloss, D. (2005) *Occupational Health Law*. Oxford: Blackwell.

Management of Health and Safety at Work and Fire Precautions (Amendment) Regulations (2003) SI2003/2457.

Management of Health and Safety at Work Regulations (1999) SI1999/3242.

Robens Report (1972) *Safety and Health at Work*. Cmnd 5034. London: HMSO.

Stranks, J. (2008) *Health and Safety at work: an essential guide for managers*. London: Kogan Page.

Thatcher, M. (1998) 'Clock wise', *People Management*, 3 September, 34–41.

Whittingham, R. (2004) *The Blame Machine: why human error causes accidents*. Elsevier.

Wright, M. (1998) 'Why do we manage health and safety?' *Occupational Health and Safety*, October, 34–7.

ASSIGNMENTS AND DISCUSSION TOPICS

1 Make suggestions on how the tension between health and safety at work and the performance imperative can be addressed within your organisation. How would you convince business-focused managers that the tension needs to be reconciled?

2 How can you quantify the economic and social costs of accidents and injuries at work?

3 Regulation and a legal framework are unlikely to be sufficient to create a healthy and safe working environment; this will require the commitment and cooperation of all those who manage the risks and of all those who create the risks. Make practical and convincing proposals on how an organisation can seek to create and maintain an active health and safety culture. What added value is there in creating and sustaining such a culture?

4 Health and safety policies are often written to meet legislative requirements rather than encourage an active health and safety culture. Defend your organisation's policy against this charge and make recommendations on how it can contribute more effectively to an active health and safety culture.

5 Discuss the distinction between a hazard and a risk. Illustrate your discussion with examples of hazards and risks in your own organisation.

6 Present an argument to your managing director that line managers and employees ought to be appraised and rewarded on health and safety performance indicators.

Chapter 14

The Strategic Management of Employee Well-being

LEARNING OUTCOMES: TO BE ABLE TO

- Develop the case for a strategic approach to employee well-being and recognise the importance of managing this to the benefit of the employer and the employee

- Evaluate the causes of dysfunctional pressure at work and recommend primary, secondary and tertiary stress management interventions (SMIs)

- Explore the potential impact of harassment and bullying at work

- Analyse the policy implications for effective management of alcohol misuse and drug abuse in the workplace

- Analyse the nature and extent of violence at work and recommend managerial interventions

INTRODUCTION

UK organisations are recognising the importance of employee well-being in enabling and encouraging employees to attend work regularly and productively. The importance of well-being issues is not driven solely by compliance with legislation, but by the recognition that a fit and healthy workforce positively impacts on business performance through low levels of absence and through better performance. Stress, harassment and bullying, alcohol misuse and drug abuse and violence are important aspects of employee well-being and it could be argued that they are of no concern to the employer, but government policy, demographic changes and increased competition for talent place employee well-being firmly on the organisational agenda. In 2000, the UK government together with the HSC/HSE launched a 10-year occupational health strategy for Britain built on the premise that there are:

> sound moral, legal and economic reasons for employers and others in positions of responsibility to . . . work together to reach the following common goals: to reduce ill-health both in workers and the public caused, or made worse, by work; to help people who have been ill, whether caused by work or not, to return to work; to improve work opportunities for people currently not in employment due to ill-health or disability; and to use the work environment to help people maintain or improve their health.

Organisations that accept that these issues are of concern and have well-developed initiatives to manage workplace well-being can anticipate higher levels of performance. This chapter addresses a range of issues within the area of the strategic management of employee well-being and provides practical guidance on policy formulation and development.

A STRATEGY FOR EMPLOYEE WELL-BEING

Organisations seeking to achieve a competitive edge recognise that investment in the health and well-being of the workforce can have a positive payback. The law requires the employer to provide a safe and a *healthy* work environment (*see* Chapter 13), but it is not only the legal framework that levers up employer concern for well-being, it is also changing social attitudes and increasing employee expectations. Employee well-being is defined by the CIPD (2007) as:

> creating an environment to promote a state of contentment which allows employees to flourish and achieve their full potential for the benefit of themselves and their organisation.

Juniper (2009a) constructs a new definition of employee well-being as:

> that part of an employee's overall well-being that they perceive to be determined primarily by work and which can be influenced by workplace interventions.

Juniper considers the key factors of this definition to be the recognition of employee perceptions of the impact of work on their own well-being and the definition also focuses on aspects that can be affected by action of the employer. Juniper (2009b) deploys a work and well-being assessment (WWBA) diagnostic tool which measures well-being in 10 domains: *psychological, direction and understanding, workload, physical, control, engagement, workplace environment, relationships at work, impact outside of work, and advancement.* Measuring employee well-being in these 10 domains identifies areas of concern and can lead to more informed managerial interventions. For example, in one study of a Primary Care trust it was the domains of *impact of work on mental health (psychological)* and *the impact of organisational change on staff (direction)* that generated most concerns, while *opportunities for training and development (advancement)* were positively perceived and *how work interfered with home life (impact outside of work)* was considered by respondents to be minimal. Effectively the domain analysis provides diagnostic opportunities.

Looking for ways to measure employee well-being looks an attractive option in the search for added-value in the management and development of employees. Macdonald (2005) suggests that employee well-being programmes are set to overtake flexible working as a key focus of employer action on staff morale, levels of productivity and employee retention. The UK Government White Paper *Choosing Health: Making healthy choices easier* (DoH, 2004) also identifies the need for a new approach to public health and the importance of working with employers to address issues of smoking, diet and nutrition, sensible levels of alcohol consumption and improved mental health, including the reduction of stress levels within the workplace. The DWP and PwC report (2008) calls for employers to be proactive rather than reactive in relation to employee health issues, focusing on preventative measures to avoid injuries and illnesses, rather than on strictly rehabilitative measures once an event has occurred. Jack (2004) suggests that 'the smart ones [organisations] will recognise the added-value of well-being and its capacity to enhance corporate success at a relatively low cost'. This increased awareness together with a more educated and informed workforce will increase expectations that the employer takes note of emerging evidence on health-related issues and changing lifestyles and reflects these in the workplace. Employee expectations place increasing pressure on organisations to accept their social responsibility across a range of personal and environmental matters.

This chapter will consider a multi-dimensional approach to the management of employee well-being (see Figure 14.1). Many areas can be identified under the broad heading of well-being, but special consideration is given here to the issues of stress, bullying and harassment, alcohol and drugs, and violence. These specific issues, together with the effective management of absence, increased flexibility in working arrangements and planned retention strategies, dealt with elsewhere in this text, provide employers with the basis for a well-being strategy.

Developing a well-being strategy

Organisations wishing to give increased priority to employee well-being need to reflect this by, first, placing well-being issues within their HR strategy, second, developing an appropriate strategy that provides a vision of what is important to the organisation and, third, constructing messages that convey this to the workforce. Jack (2004) describes a six-step approach to developing and implementing this strategy:

1 *Clarify your vision.* This involves revisiting the strategic objectives of the organisation to identify the aims regarding people management. Are you wishing to promote a healthy way of life within your organisation or are you looking at a holistic well-being management regime? What are the key factors in the business case for well-being strategy? Demographic changes and employees working into

Figure 14.1
A multi-dimensional
perspective of
employee well-being

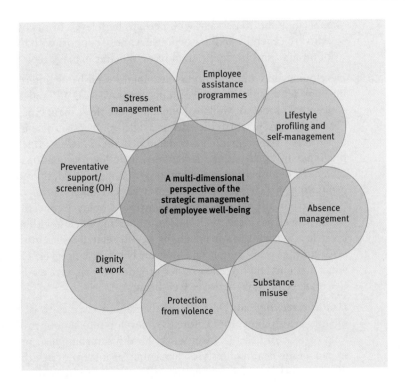

their 70s will present different challenges. There is a belief that a healthier workforce is a more productive workforce – is increased profitability a driving force?

2 *Gain top-level commitment.* Buy-in from the senior management is essential. A clear vision, together with carefully defined costs and benefits, well-developed tools to assess employee and organisational well-being and a sound business case will increase the commitment from the senior managers.

3 *Involve your employees.* Jack (2004) observes that 'staff are the best critics of what will or will not work in an organisation. If the strategy is genuinely one of empowerment, then involve employees from the outset.'

4 *Pilot well-being tools.* A variety of well-being tools are on the market including online, self-administered, diagnostic, lifestyle questionnaires. Decide on an appropriate tool and pilot this with different employee groups across different organisational levels to ensure it meets the organisation's needs.

5 *Create HR performance indicators.* The vision and business case should enable the employer to identify the important areas for measurement. This needs to include qualitative and quantitative measures to identify the organisational added-value of the well-being strategy. Measures may include staff turnover, levels of sickness absence, levels of employee satisfaction or success in recruiting and retaining talent.

6 *Be realistic.* Jack (2004) emphasises the need to be realistic in terms of the likely achievements: 'In developing and implementing a wellness strategy we are looking at culture change. We are switching the focus from concentrating on

managing the 20 per cent with perhaps high levels of sickness to the 80 per cent who are generally well but who we want to support with the provision of a range of mechanisms to enable employees to better manage their level of well-being.'

Developing and implementing meaningful well-being interventions is both good business sense and a way of valuing employees. DWP and PwC (2008) provide a conceptual model for wellness which includes three main types of intervention. First, *health and safety*, which they define as 'driven by government initiatives and shaped by statutory requirements'. Second, *managing ill-health,* which they suggest 'focuses predominantly on reactive interventions, including, occupational health, return to work schemes and absence management programmes'. Third, they identify *prevention and promotion,* which include a range of well-being interventions.

Positive health policies can demonstrate employer concern with health and well-being, as well as safety. Well-developed health policies, within a well-being strategy, provide a mechanism for managing health-related issues in the workplace, and are evidence that well-being is taken seriously by the employer. Health screening, health education and employee assistance programmes all have a role to play in the proactive management of employee well-being.

Health screening can be provided to monitor the health of the workforce and to identify health difficulties before they develop into serious problems, which result in long periods of absence from work. Health screening also presents an opportunity to encourage healthy lifestyles. Screening, as a form of health observation, can also identify workplace factors that contribute to ill-health and put in place mechanisms to address them.

Health education on specific topics, such as smoking, diet and nutrition, sensible levels of alcohol consumption and improved mental health, can be provided to inform the workforce about health issues and the associated benefits and risks. This identifies the organisation as an employer that values its employees and can enhance its reputation as an employer of choice, which may have a positive impact on recruitment and retention.

Employee assistance programmes (EAP) are confidential counselling services, often provided by an external supplier, which support employees in difficult personal circumstances. EAPs provide access to counsellors trained in handling potentially sensitive issues such as alcohol misuse, bereavement, financial difficulties, ill-health and job loss. The advantage of an external EAP is that contact with the counsellor is seen as outside the organisation and the employee may feel more reassured about confidentiality. The employer can be provided with an aggregated statistical return by the EAP provider which analyses service use; this information can help in identifying workplace issues to be addressed. This secures anonymity for the employee at an individual level, but provides the employer with useful information about the issues that are challenging employees.

STRESS AND DISTRESS

What is the extent of the stress problem? According to the HSE (2007) approximately 13.5 million working days were lost in 2007/8 due to work-related stress, depression and anxiety. Midgely (1997) estimated that inefficiencies arising from stress can cost up to 10 per cent of a country's gross national product. The HSE and CIPD (2009a) state that 'stress is likely to become the most dangerous risk to business in the early part of the 21st century'. About one in six people find their work either very or extremely stressful (CIPD, 2009), in excess of 5 million workers in the UK. There is no consensus on the precise cost of stress, because of the difficulty of defining and measuring it accurately, but there appears to be a general agreement that the potential costs are substantial. All of this highlights the business imperative for managing employee well-being effectively. Briner (1999) urges a note of caution in the interpretation of findings like those above and questions whether stress is the modern epidemic that some people claim it is:

> A survey conducted by the Industrial Society in 1996 revealed that, while 53 per cent of respondents agreed that stress had increased, 76 per cent admitted that it had never been measured in their organisation. Similarly, 76 per cent thought that absenteeism was the most damaging effect of stress, while only 7 per cent measured the amount of absence caused by stress. It seems that many of us, HR managers and employees alike, simply assume that stress levels are high and having detrimental effects on people's well being and performance.

While warning us against the 'stress bandwagon', Briner acknowledges that identifying and acting upon dysfunctional stress warrants further research and managerial attention. Acting knowledgeably on employee stress with the incentive of reducing costs, avoiding litigation, valuing people and protecting the investment in human capital would seem to be a prime area for managerial intervention, but effective intervention is not easy and the search for magic solutions is likely to be frustrating.

The power of the employer and the employee to act on stress effectively is constrained, because common reasons for stress are at least partially attributable to a conjunction of social, political, economic and global factors. These factors include the intensification of work, feelings of job insecurity, and employer demand for 'emotional labour'. The intensification of work, where employees are required to work harder, smarter and more flexibly, is a product of increasingly competitive organisational environments. Levels of unemployment, a strengthening of the right to manage, deregulated and 'flexible' labour markets, right-sizing and process re-engineering programmes, together with a proliferation of non-standard contracts of employment, contribute to feelings of insecurity at work. Customer-focused cultures require 'emotional labour', as well as physical and intellectual labour, from employees, and HRM practices which seek to engage the hearts and minds of employees through increased employee involvement and through seeking behavioural commitment invite a psychological relationship between employer and employee which is more stressful than a simple wage for work bargain. Add to this the disappearance of a job for life, continuous organisational change and an emphasis on taking personal responsibility for lifetime learning, and the turbulence and potential stress of the job context become even more evident.

Simplistic stress solutions, often individually focused, fail to recognise the complex interplay of these contextual factors. As an example, assertiveness, including the ability to say 'No', and the effective management of time often feature in stress management programmes and are valuable management skills, but the contribution of these individual coping strategies to stress reduction is circumscribed by the wider societal and organisational context. Briner (1999) also challenges the efficacy of stress management courses:

> Does this [stress] training work? We need only to consider what is required in any course for it to have a reasonable chance of success. As a minimum the criteria would include an initial assessment of training needs; training design that can change behaviour that is linked to the outcomes of interest; an environment which allows the transfer of the newly learnt skill; and, evaluation. With stress management training it is often the case that none of these elements is in place. So, even in principle it is unlikely that stress management training can achieve its aims.

The effective management of stress at work therefore requires a corporate approach as well as the promotion of individual coping strategies.

The nature and sources of stress

In order to seek stress solutions it is important to understand the nature of stress, the potential sources of stress, the potential implications for the individual and for the organisation and the range of responses available. A stress audit and a stress policy help to target individual and organisational action. A framework for analysing stress is exposed in Figure 14.2 but, before discussing the elements of the framework, two general points need to be made. First, an appropriate level of stress or pressure can be stimulating, healthy and desirable. It is when the perceived level of pressure becomes sub-optimal that human dysfunctionality can occur. Second, textbooks and articles on stress often expose a large menu of potential stressors and a huge range of negative implications, and this text is no different, but this gives the impression that stress is super-endemic and will inevitably produce all of the undesirable consequences. This encourages an exaggerated perception of the stress problems, which is unhelpful either by giving succour to stress sceptics or in inhibiting the development of focused and targeted managerial action.

Figure 14.2
A framework for
analysing stress at
work

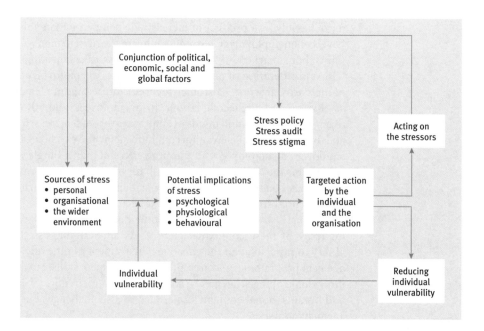

Figure 14.3 Eustress and distress

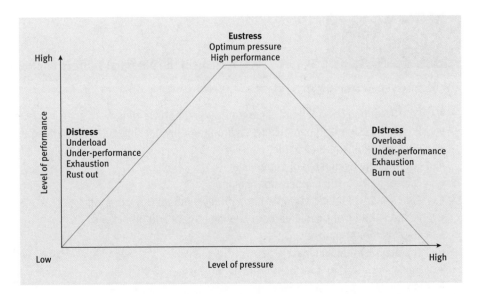

Stress is about pressure on the individual and may be physical, intellectual, emotional or social. Pressure becomes distressing when the individual perceives it to be either excessive and beyond their ability to cope or, alternatively, insufficient to provide stimulation. It is therefore *distress* which is potentially harmful and *distress* that ought to be the focus of attention. Using the term *distress* distinguishes it from positive pressure at work – termed eustress. Whereas *distress* is about an imbalance between the level of pressure and individual ability to cope, eustress represents the 'goldilocks' pressure point, where the level of pressure on an individual is neither too much nor too little, but just right.

Figure 14.3 illustrates a general relationship between pressure and performance and incorporates the idea that insufficient pressure as well as too much pressure causes distress. Identifying the eustress point for an individual is problematic. It will vary over time because the whole individual needs to be considered, and the level of pressure will be determined by a combination of work stress, life stress and event stress. Work stress includes workload, deadlines, work relationships, the nature and extent of change, the degree of control, working conditions and levels of security. Life stress describes the pressures of day-to-day living and will include personal finance, emotional relationships, family responsibilities and personal health. Event stress describes significant events such as getting married, buying a house, the birth of a child or coping with bereavement. Organisational, personal and wider environmental stressors are exposed in Exhibit 14.1.

Individual vulnerability to distress is influenced by many factors, including: individual personality differences, for example whether type A or type B (*see* below); internal or external locus of control – the extent to which individuals feel able to influence their own destiny; the extent of personal support networks; the capacity of personal coping strategies; the ability to act on own perceptions of stress; and the compatibility of job experience, knowledge and skills with current job demands. Type A behaviour is characterised by 'an aggressive involvement in a chronic, incessant struggle to achieve more and more in less and less time and, if necessary, against the opposing efforts of other things or other people'; and Type B behaviour is characterised by being 'rarely

EXHIBIT 14.1 A menu of the potential sources of stress

Organisational stressors

- Work overload or underload – repetitive work, unrewarding work
- Poor job design – ergonomically, environmentally, lacking autonomy or variety
- Role ambiguity or role conflict
- Poor-quality leadership or supervision
- Lack of participation in decision-making
- Poor quality of relationships – horizontally, vertically or externally
- Responsibility for people or for achieving targets and objectives
- Organisational change
- The organisational climate
- Being subjected to bullying or harassment
- Pay, conditions and job insecurity

Personal stressors

- Unhealthy eating, sleeping or exercise
- General health and whether it is abused
- Family and social relationships
- Significant life events
- Conflicting personal and organisational demands

Wider environmental stressors

- The general economic situation
- Political uncertainty
- Social change and threats to personal values and standards
- Concern with the natural environment
- The pace of technological change
- Changing male and female role perceptions

harried by the desire to obtain a widely increasing number of things or to participate in an endlessly growing series of events in an ever decreasing amount of time' (Robbins, 1993). Type A people may be more vulnerable to stress and more susceptible to ill-health because of feelings of mistrust, hostility and anger generated by personality characteristics.

The general adaptation syndrome consists of the phases of alarm, resistance and exhaustion and maps the human response to stressful situations. The initial phase of 'alarm' produces physiological reactions, referred to as the 'fight or flight' response. This prepares the individual either to confront the challenge or to run away. The physiological reactions include increased heart rate, decreased blood flow to the digestive system and increased flow to the brain and muscles, release of adrenalin, rapid breathing and a sharpening of the senses. Unless the individual takes flight, the second general adaptation phase will be a heightening of the individual's 'resistance' to confront the stressful situation and to deal with it. Where the stressful situation persists without being resolved, individual resistance may be worn down, ultimately resulting in the third phase of 'exhaustion' and breakdown. There is therefore a limited human capacity to resist or adapt to stressful situations.

The potential implications of distress and a range of responses

Harmful pressure, or distress, can manifest itself in a wide range of psychological, physiological and behavioural consequences. Psychological implications include: anxiety, irritability, frustration, depression; inability to concentrate, procrastination, decision paralysis, inaccurate recall, feelings of unreality; job dissatisfaction, suppressed motivation; and disturbed sleep patterns. Physiological implications include: muscular tension, headaches, palpitations; heart disease, high blood pressure; digestive problems, irritable bowel; and increased susceptibility to colds, influenza and respiratory infection. Behavioural implications include: sub-optimum performance and productivity; higher levels of absence, labour turnover and accident rates, and poor timekeeping; tobacco, alcohol, caffeine and other substance abuse; negative personal appearance and hygiene changes, weight loss or gain; and less effective personal and professional relationships. These three areas are not mutually exclusive as some of the consequences overlap and feed each other. An important caveat that needs to be borne in mind is the fact that it is unlikely that one individual will suffer all of these potential implications of stress. They are reproduced here to highlight the range and extent of possible consequences and to enable recognition and targeted action.

A major hurdle to the effective management of distress at work is the social and professional stigma often associated with an admission of being a stress sufferer and not coping. It may be acceptable to admit to being pressurised, but less acceptable to admit to an inability to cope with work pressure. Macho cultures will label a stress admission as a sign of weakness and inadequacy. Addressing the stress stigma is fundamental to the encouragement of 'coming out' by stress sufferers. An awareness of this stigma can help direct the organisation towards creating a climate, or at least a mechanism, where it is relatively safe for an employee to declare distress. Only through accessing stress information can employers begin to measure and assess the existence and the extent of the problem.

The three ways to manage stress are through a hierarchy of *primary, secondary and tertiary stress management interventions* (SMIs). A primary intervention is characterised by a stress risk assessment process and then acting to eliminate or reduce the stressors. A secondary intervention is concerned with the training of employees to raise stress awareness and increase individual coping skills, thereby reducing individual vulnerability. At a tertiary level the SMI focus is on providing support and rehabilitation opportunities for stressed employees.

Primary strategies for acting on the stressors include workload rebalancing, role clarification, job redesign; critical evaluation of communication and change processes; critical evaluation of the quality of leadership, management and supervision; critical evaluation of intrinsic and extrinsic rewards; provision of training and development opportunities to enhance job skills; evaluating the physical work environment; and educating managers to recognise and respond to distress.

Secondary strategies to reduce individual vulnerability include the encouragement of healthy habits such as diet, sleep and exercise; the development of coping techniques such as assertiveness, time management, the creation of safety zones and allowing time for leisure; the use of relaxation techniques such as massage, aromatherapy and yoga; the displacement or ventilation of negative feelings through legitimate means such as rigorous physical exercise, catharsis and a 'bug' list; and the development of skills, knowledge and competencies in line with job demands.

Tertiary strategies include counselling services, referral systems and the development of support networks together with a rehabilitation plan which may also include individual primary and secondary level interventions.

The HSE (2004) identified good practice procedures for managing stress-related absence as 'early intervention, accurate medical assessment, clarification of roles and responsibilities and return to work interviews together with a flexible return and a supportive working environment'.

The strategies for reducing individual vulnerability normally receive priority of attention in stress management programmes at the expense of acting on the stressors. This risks a focus on the symptoms of stress rather than on the underlying causes, and tends to shift the stress burden and responsibility from the organisation to the individual.

> The role of the organisation in producing unhealthy systems and conditions of work is in danger of being ignored. In its place we get systems reinforcing the self-attribution of stress and anxiety as personal problems to be coped with rather than structural issues to be contested.
>
> (Thompson and McHugh, in Clark *et al.*, 1997)

Briner (1999) provides a framework for a more strategic and targeted approach to managing stress based on a healthy scepticism about the extent of the problem, a search for specific problems, an evidence-based assessment of the nature of the problem, focused SMIs which integrate with other HR practices and an evaluation of the effectiveness of the SMIs. In short, effective diagnosis is a prerequisite to focused stress solutions. A further individual strategy for dealing with stress is the self-management of beliefs and the reframing of perceptions (Honey, 1993). There are three necessary beliefs. The first belief is that 'stress is not instinctive, but a learned reaction to stimuli', the second belief is that 'external stimuli do not automatically cause distress, it is the individual who chooses to be stressed' and the third belief is that 'it is preferable to "prevent" unwanted stress rather than suppressing it or expressing it'. The individual preventive response, based on these three beliefs, is to reframe the perceptions of pressure by challenging the thoughts themselves. This is done through making the thoughts more reliable, more rational, less exaggerated and less dogmatic, thus preventing 'feelings' of distress.

Stress management policy

There are a number of reasons for having a stress policy, while recognising that stress issues may be subsumed within general health or well-being policies (CIPD, 2001). The reasons for a policy include focusing managerial attention on reducing the direct and indirect costs of stress, employer responsibility for the physical and mental health and safety of employees, the increasing threat of expensive litigation from distressed

EXHIBIT 14.2 Indicative content of a formal stress policy

1 A positive statement about the organisational attitude towards harmful stress.
2 A recognition of the need to de-stigmatise an admission of stress by an employee and the provision of stress-reporting channels.
3 Confidential counselling and referral services.
4 Stress education and awareness training.
5 Stress audit arrangements, risk assessment, use of well-being indicators and a commitment to act upon the stressors as well as support individual coping strategies.
6 A process of stress monitoring and policy review and integration with other HR practices.

employees (*see Walker* v *Northumberland County Council* [1995] IRLR 35 and *Cross* v *Highlands and Islands Enterprise* [2001] IRLR 336), protecting the organisational image in relation to the customer base and the labour market, and underpinning a belief that people are a source of competitive advantage. Indicative stress policy content is listed in Exhibit 14.2.

The HSE produced stress management standards in 2004 and this framework was refined in 2008 with the publication of management competencies for preventing and reducing stress at work (HSE and CIPD, 2008a). The standards do not constitute law but following them will assist employers in meeting their legal duties. The standards are effectively a tailored risk assessment framework which enables organisations to diagnose employee workplace pressures in relation to six areas.

1 Demands – appropriate workload, work patterns and work environment.
2 Control – sufficient say in the way work is done.
3 Support – adequate information, support and encouragement from colleagues and line managers.
4 Relationships – positive working relationships are promoted and unacceptable behaviours are dealt with.
5 Role – clear understanding of the role and responsibilities.
6 Change – employee involvement in the management and communication of change.

These standards are deployed to elicit employee opinion with positive responses indicating that stress is not a problem, and negative employee responses suggesting that there is potential for management intervention. Employers can utilise an HSE 35-item stress questionnaire indicator tool to automatically analyse the results of an employee survey. Three scores are given for each of the management standards; first, an overall percentage score; second, a suggested target; and, third, the scores of the 'best' 20 organisations for comparative purposes. All of this reinforces the principle that risk assessment and diagnosis precede targeted SMIs – data collection and analysis are prerequisites to an action plan (see Figure 14.4). While the HSE can provide guidance and support, it can also issue improvement notices to employers in relation to stress and the first of these was issued to an NHS Trust in 2004.

CASE STUDY   Stress management policy and responsibilities at Goodwins department stores

Goodwins are committed to protecting the health, safety and welfare of employees; the company recognises that workplace stress is a health and safety issue and acknowledges the importance of identifying and reducing workplace stressors. Managers are responsible for implementation and the company is responsible for providing the necessary resources. This policy will apply to everyone. The Health and Safety Executive define stress as 'the adverse reaction people have to excessive pressure or other types of demand placed on them'. This makes an important distinction between pressure, which can be a positive state if managed correctly, and stress which can be detrimental to health.

Policy: Goodwins will identify all workplace stressors and conduct risk assessments to eliminate stress or control the risks from stress. These risk assessments will be regularly reviewed. Goodwins will consult with Trade Union Safety Representatives on all proposed action relating to the prevention of workplace stress. Goodwins will provide training for all managers and supervisory staff in good management practices. Goodwins will provide confidential counselling for staff affected by stress caused by either work or external factors. Goodwins will provide adequate resources to enable managers to implement Goodwins agreed stress management strategy.

Responsibilities of managers: Conduct and implement recommendations of risks assessments within their jurisdiction. Ensure good communication between management and staff, particularly where there are organisational and procedural changes. Ensure staff are fully trained to discharge their duties. Ensure staff are provided with meaningful developmental opportunities. Monitor workloads to ensure that people are not overloaded. Monitor working hours and overtime to ensure that staff are not overworking. Monitor holidays to ensure that staff are taking their full entitlement. Attend training as requested in good management practice and health and safety. Ensure that bullying and harassment is not tolerated within their jurisdiction. Be vigilant and offer additional support to a member of staff who is experiencing stress outside work e.g. bereavement or separation.

Responsibilities of occupational health and safety staff: Provide specialist advice and awareness training on stress. Train and support managers in implementing stress risk assessments. Support individuals who have been off sick with stress and advise them and their management on a planned return to work. Refer to workplace counsellors or specialist agencies as required. Monitor and review the effectiveness of measures to reduce stress. Inform the employer and the Health and Safety Committee of any changes and developments in the field of stress at work.

Responsibilities of HR: Give guidance to managers on the stress management policy. Assist in monitoring the effectiveness of measures to address stress by collating sickness absence statistics. Advise managers and individuals on training requirements. Provide continuing support to managers and individuals in a changing environment and encourage referral to occupational workplace counsellors where appropriate.

Responsibilities of employees: Raise issues of concern with your Safety Representative, line manager or occupational health. Accept opportunities for counselling when recommended.

Function of Safety Representatives: Safety Representatives must be meaningfully consulted on any changes to work practices or work design that could precipitate stress. Safety Representatives must be able to consult with members on the issue of stress including conducting any workplace surveys. Safety

Representatives must be meaningfully involved in the risk assessment process. Safety Representatives should be allowed access to collective and anonymous data from HR. Safety Representatives should be provided with paid time away from normal duties to attend any Trade Union training relating to workplace stress. Safety Representatives should conduct joint inspections of the workplace at least every 3 months to ensure that environmental stressors are properly controlled.

Role of the Safety Committee: The Safety Committee will perform a pivotal role in ensuring policy implementation. The Safety Committee will oversee monitoring of the efficacy of the policy and other measures to reduce stress and promote workplace health and safety.

Questions

1 Critically evaluate the Goodwins stress management policy and allocation of responsibilities to identify strengths and weaknesses.

2 Recommend specific ways in which the policy can be translated into effective action.

Hartmann v *South Essex Mental Health and Community Care NHS Trust* [2005] EWCA Civ 6 (CA) clarified some important principles in relation to stress claims by employees (Aikin, 2005). The Court of Appeal reiterated that the rules for stress-related psychiatric injury are the same as those for physical injury – the employer has a duty to prevent *foreseeable* injury, and the employer is only liable if it fails to take steps to prevent foreseeable injury and the employee suffers injury as a consequence. In addition, employers are entitled to assume that an employee is robust enough to do the contracted job particularly if the employee has not articulated that their job is proving stressful. It is therefore the employee's responsibility to inform the employer that they are not coping with the pressure of work. In seeking to demonstrate an employer's responsibility for stress-related ill-health, the employee will need to demonstrate that the risk and the ill-health were *reasonably foreseeable* by the employer. However, once alerted to a stress-related risk, for example by medical advice or the occurrence of a stressful event or being informed by an employee (or fellow employees), then the employer becomes obligated to be proactive in eliminating or reducing the stress risk. Exhibit 14.3 highlights the importance of employers taking the issue of workplace stress seriously, listening to staff when they say they are unable to cope with their job, taking appropriate action to relieve the employee of aspects of the job which may be contributing to the stress, and planning a way forward.

Why do organisations find it difficult to manage stress effectively? The answer may lie in where this section on stress started. The conjunction of external factors may

Figure 14.4 Diagnosis precedes targeted SMIs

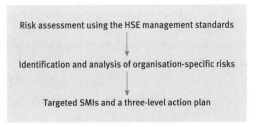

Risk assessment using the HSE management standards

Identification and analysis of organisation-specific risks

Targeted SMIs and a three-level action plan

EXHIBIT 14.3 Foreseeable risks, duty of care and causal links

In 2008 O_2 lost an appeal against a 2007 decision which awarded nearly £110 000 to Mrs Dickins for psychiatric injury negligently caused by excessive stress in the course of her employment. Mrs Dickins had worked at O_2 since 1991, for the first 9 years as a secretary. In 2000 she was promoted to the position of Regulatory Finance Manager and it was the performance of this role that caused Mrs Dickins to take increasing time off work, and in 2002 she informed her manager that she was 'stressed out' and asked for a 6-month sabbatical. She was refused and referred to the counselling service provided by O_2.

The appeal decision indicated four key issues in the Appeal Court's findings:

1   Given the discussion that took place it was *foreseeable* that Mrs Dickins' health was deteriorating and that the stress of her employment was a contributory factor, and that her employer should have taken action.
2   The actions taken by O_2 were inadequate and they were *in breach of their duty of care* to their employee. Counselling services are not a panacea by which employers can discharge their duty of care.
3   The court decided that there was a '*sufficient causal link*' between the employer's breach of duty of care and Mrs Dickins' illness. O_2 had failed to take account of Mrs Dickins' situation; she asked for a less stressful job and was asked to hold on for 3 months; she was referred to occupational health but not as a matter of urgency. This was not considered to be sufficient action.
4   The calculation of damages suggests that the employer is responsible for all the employee's loss; it regards the employer as having caused damage to which they have materially contributed.

Employers therefore need to be vigilant in dealing with workplace stress claims. In particular they should:

•   Watch for signs of workplace stress.
•   Not rely solely on providing counselling; it is not likely to be a sufficient response.
•   Moniter the situation closely, because active management intervention is a duty.

inevitably produce levels of employee distress which are beyond managerial capacity to resolve. In this scenario, a stress management policy may merely be the key to a 'Pandora's box', a box which the organisation may pragmatically prefer to keep closed; but this does not resolve the fundamental issue that harmful stress is bad for the employee and bad for the organisation because it threatens to burn out the workforce.

> Humans are not robots . . . Most cannot sustain the pace required by ever-more demanding performance targets in the long term, particularly if they have inadequate rest periods and work long hours. People must feel that they are sharing in the gains of lean organisational systems, not paying for it with their health.
>
> (Baron, in Littlefield, 1996)

The UK does not yet have a word for death from overwork, but Japan does – *karoshi*!

CASE STUDY   United Biscuits and the stress management standards

United Biscuits decided to manage stress using the management standards in order:

- To address the increase in reported 'stress' cases during the period 2003–2005.
- To introduce preventive measures to tackle work-related stress with a view to reducing litigation.
- To take responsibility and care for the well-being of employees.

The United Biscuits Management Board developed and promoted a stress policy within their organisation, requiring annual risk assessments to measure stress levels within United Biscuits. They also introduced an internal system to identify and distinguish work-related disorders (e.g. mental health and asthma) from non-work-related issues. HR and Occupational Health teams gathered data on staff turnover, claims, absenteeism and 'stress' cases to identify 'hot spots' which may be the result of stress. Procedures for managing individual cases of stress were introduced for line managers, HR and Occupational Health professionals. The main challenges were gaining acceptance that stress was an important business issue, and training all line managers. Measures of success included an increased awareness among line managers who received training; a decrease in 'stress cases for which work was the most significant cause'; better defence in claims/tribunals; and reduced stress absence costs. Each time absence was prevented, 4 weeks' wages and other associated costs were saved. In three years this represented about 40 weeks of absence.

Reported stress cases 2004–2007 – United Biscuits

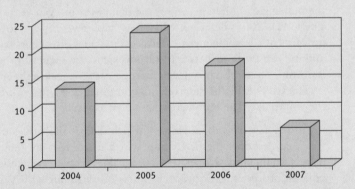

Source: Extract from http://www.hse.gov.uk/stress/casestudies/unitedbiscuits.htm.

Questions

1 Critically evaluate the United Biscuits approach to stress management.

2 A major challenge was 'getting all managers trained to manage stress'. Discuss the design of a training course for managers in managing stress in terms of content, delivery method and evaluation, giving reasons for your choices.

HARASSMENT AND BULLYING AT WORK

Bullying is characterised by ACAS (2009) as:

> . . . offensive, intimidating, malicious or insulting behaviour, an abuse or misuse of power through means intended to undermine, humiliate, denigrate or injure the recipient.

The CIPD (2005) is similar, but more expansive, in describing bullying as:

> . . . involving repeated negative actions and practices that are directed at one or more workers. The behaviours are unwelcome to the victims and are undertaken in circumstances where the victims have difficulty defending themselves . . . These behaviours cause humiliation, offence and distress to the victims. The outcomes of bullying cause psychological distress which affects social and work behaviour.

The Human Rights Act 1998 introduced into UK legislation the right not to be 'subjected to degrading treatment or punishment' and this covers behaviour which constitutes bullying and harassment. The CIPD survey (2004) *Managing conflict at work* identified that 83 per cent of organisations have policies on bullying and harassment with most policies defining behaviour in negative terms rather that defining positive behaviour which demonstrates respect. The negative behaviour they identified included: personal insults; intimidation; work-related harassment, which included having responsibility withdrawn and misrepresenting your work as theirs and social exclusion. As suggested by ACAS, above, bullying is often based on the power relationship, namely, when there is unequal balance of power. The power can be the power of position, the power of number, the power of knowledge or psychological power and the bullying can often go on for many months or even years before it is recognised. The CIPD (2005) describe bullying as 'bad news for employers . . . costing the UK upwards of £2 billion a year'. This cost includes direct costs such as sickness absence and indirect costs such as staff turnover and the reduced productivity of the victim. Bullying is therefore damaging to the organisation, against the law and financially costly.

The CIPD (2007b) describes a good practice framework for tackling bullying in the workplace. The framework has seven aspects:

A positive organisational culture, which defines the values of the organisation in a way that describes the behaviours which employees are required to exhibit such as respect, truth, fairness, openness. These values should be operationalised through robust policies, procedures and practices and ways of dealing with negative behaviour should be agreed.

Dealing with everyday conflict through positive communication can mean that minor conflicts and disagreements are dealt with and this can stop these escalating into major problems which require the use of formal procedures. One of the perceived difficulties of handling bullying is the potential problem of identifying the difference between strong or robust management and bullying, which may make managers concerned about tackling a problem with a member of staff for fear of being accused of bullying. The CIPD (2005) includes a format for looking at the differences between strong management and bullying behaviour when tackling poorly performing teams, which may help managers in identifying appropriate behaviour in dealing with a difficult situation (*see* Exhibit 14.4).

EXHIBIT 14.4 The contrast between strong management and bullying in tackling poor team performance

Assessing poor performance in teams	Strong Management	Bullying
Identifying the performance issue	Involves looking at all the potential reasons for poor performance, e.g. people, systems, training and equipment	No attempt to identify the nature or source of the performance problem
Seeking the views of the team or individual to identify the cause of the unacceptable level of performance	The team takes part in looking for the source of the problems in performance and helps the manager to identify solutions for the whole team	No discussion of the cause of the performance deficit, or opportunities for the team members to discuss their difficulties
Agreeing new standards of performance with all team members	Involves setting and agreeing standards of performance and behaviours for each team member and the manager	Imposing new standards without team discussion on appropriate standards of performance or behaviour
Agreeing the method and timing of monitoring/auditing team performance	Wherever possible the team or team member takes part in the monitoring process. The outcome of the monitoring is openly discussed	Without agreeing standards the monitoring can occur at any time and can involve areas that are unexpected by team members
Failure to achieve the standards of performance is dealt with as a performance improvement issue	Opportunities are taken to identify individuals who are struggling, and support is provided. Where individuals are unwilling to comply with the agreed performance improvement process, disciplinary action may be taken	Individuals who fail to achieve the standards of performance are put under pressure to conform. This may include ridicule, criticism, shouting, withholding of benefits, demotion, teasing or sarcasm
Recognising positive contribution	Recognises and rewards improvements in performance, attitudes and behaviours	With no monitoring, it is impossible to recognise where there have been positive contributions. Rewards and recognition are therefore arbitrary and open to acts of favouritism

Regular monitoring of the organisational culture and climate through a range of options, including positive behaviour questions in an employee survey, focus groups, teambuilding or graffiti boards, can help to identify the positive features of the organisational culture and support management action in finding ways to reinforce these.

Informal mechanisms for addressing claims or complaints of bullying or harassment, such as talking to the person using listeners or buddies, or mediation may help to clarify the situation for all parties and bring about changes in behaviour.

Formal procedures including grievance procedures, to bring about a timely resolution of the situation and make sure that the organisation stays within the law.

Training of managers, mediators, line managers, listeners and buddies; this will send a strong message that it is an issue that the organisation takes seriously.

Counselling and other support mechanisms for employees as an indicator of how harassment and bullying are perceived by the organisation.

Harassment at work

Harassment should be eliminated from the workplace, not only because of legal and ethical requirements, but also because of the negative impact on the organisation. Harassment based on sex, race, colour, disability, religious belief and sexuality is unlawful in the UK. Harassment causes misery, increases absenteeism and staff turnover, and affects individual and team performance – it makes no business sense. ACAS (2009) defines harassment as:

> unwanted conduct affecting the dignity of men and women in the workplace. It may be related to age, sex, race, disability, religion, sexual orientation, nationality or any personal characteristic of the individual, and may be persistent or an isolated incident.

The Sex Discrimination Act was amended in 2008 to change the definition of sex harassment and to include employer liability for third party harassment. The Government Equalities Office (2008) defines *sex harassment* as 'when someone behaves in an offensive way to another on the grounds of their gender', while by way of contrast *sexual harassment* 'occurs when a person subjects another to unwanted attention of a sexual nature'. There is no objective test of what constitutes harassment because the recipient of the behaviour defines it. The conduct of an individual may be deemed harassment by one person, but not by another. Harassment may include offensive posters, jokes, obscene gestures, physical contact, coercion for sexual favours and social isolation or exclusion. It is important, therefore, that, like bullying, organisations encourage positive behaviour which respects the dignity of all people at work. Respecting the dignity of people at work means acknowledging that people can be subjected to humiliating behaviour on a number of grounds and that this is unacceptable in the workplace. The Sex Discrimination Act 1975 (Amendment) Regulations 2008 allow an employee to bring a claim against an employer that does not take 'reasonable steps' to protect the employee from harassment by a third party where the employer knows that harassment has occurred against that employee on at least two other occasions. The previous instances of harassment do not need to have been carried out by the same person. This presents a particular challenge in customer-facing organisations such as pubs, clubs and restaurants and means that employers will need to take positive steps to protect employees from third party harassment.

Dignity at work policy

A dignity at work policy can cover all types of harassment and bullying. The potential benefits are that it demonstrates managerial commitment, sets boundaries for employee behaviour and engenders a climate in which employees feel safe and not distracted from their work. The policy should have the public support of senior management, and an opening statement which asserts the importance of a work environment where everyone feels valued, where they can expect to be treated with respect and where harassment and bullying will not be tolerated. This approach is central to the development of a well-being culture, the creation of an open, transparent environment where people expect to be treated with respect, and when this does not occur they expect appropriate management intervention. By undermining the dignity of people at work and affecting performance, both bullying and harassment are detrimental to the individual and to the organisation, and this managerial standpoint should be explicit in the policy. The policy should be positive, encourage victims to handle or report incidents and deter potential bullies and harassers. It should focus on describing positive behaviour expected of all employees and outline the benefit to the organisation and the people working within it of having a place of work where everyone is treated with respect.

The policy needs to specify the procedure to be followed in cases of bullying and harassment. The procedures should be fair and consistent and provide formal and informal mechanisms for resolving problems quickly and effectively. Access to a confidential counselling, advice or support service, either internal or external, should be available. Each allegation should be quickly and thoroughly investigated, and effective solutions implemented. The investigation process should be fair and objective and respect the confidentiality needs of all parties. The procedure should include informal as well as formal processes and the victim should have options for action at each stage. The policy should make clear that both employers and employees have responsibilities with regard to bullying and harassment at work. Employers have a duty of care under health and safety legislation and responsibilities under discrimination law to put in place systems and procedures which encourage incidents of bullying and harassment to be reported and ensure that appropriate action is taken to resolve the issues. Behaviour at work is also an individual responsibility and if an individual harasses a colleague they could be in breach of criminal law as well as civil law and be personally responsible for compensation payments.

The development of a positive, well-being culture should help individuals to behave in a way that supports positive behaviour and encourages them to challenge any bullying or harassing behaviour which they may observe. Grievance and disciplinary procedures need to reflect the principles of the dignity at work policy, to refer to investigatory processes when allegations are made and to detail the disciplinary sanctions available. According to the CIPD (2005):

> Building a culture of dignity and respect at work means creating a workplace where appropriate ways of behaving are clearly communicated, promoted and supported. It also means individuals being supported in accepting responsibility for their behaviour and actions, and working towards solutions when problems occur.

ALCOHOL AND DRUG MISUSE

Alcohol misuse is an employment issue because of the effect it can have on safety and performance at work. The employer has an explicit duty under the Health and Safety at Work Act 1974 to ensure the health, safety and welfare of employees and employees are required to take reasonable care of themselves and others at work. Failure to do this, by allowing those that the employer knows are unfit to work to continue working, or the employees themselves choosing to continue working, would make the employer and the employee liable to charges of breaking the law. In addition, those working within the transport industry are covered by specific legislation, the Transport and Work Act 1992, which makes it a criminal offence to work on railways, tramways and other guided systems while unfit through alcohol- or drug-related impairment.

The cost of alcohol misuse relates to sick absence, accidents at work, labour turnover, disruptions to working relationships and the adverse impact on the organisation's image. The HSE (2009) estimated alcohol to be a contributory cause of 3 to 5 per cent of all absences from work, a total of between 8 million and 14 million working days. These levels of absence and the costs of absence, together with the associated productivity costs, make alcohol misuse an employer concern. It is difficult, if not impossible, to measure the extent of drug abuse with any degree of accuracy, although it is recognised that the global incidence of drug dependency and abuse are a feature of modern society. According to Ghodse (2005), 'about 70 per cent of people with alcohol related problems and more than 60 per cent of drug users hold some form of employment'; therefore, many people with alcohol problems or drug users are in work and when drug use or abuse affects workplace safety, employee performance or the reputation of the employer, drugs become an employment issue. For the purposes of policy-making, it is sensible to include *any* substance taken by the employee which adversely affects the ability to perform the job to the required standard. This may include prescribed as well as controlled drugs and alcohol. There are two related issues associated with controlled drugs: it is illegal knowingly to have controlled drugs on the premises and take no action (Misuse of Drugs Act 1971), and the organisation will need a stance on police involvement.

Alcohol-related employment problems fall broadly into two categories: first, the employee who *occasionally* drinks inappropriately and may be unable to work for the odd day; and, second, the employee who *often* drinks inappropriately, who may have an alcohol dependency and whose ability to attend work regularly or to perform effectively is severely affected. The first category can be treated as misconduct and dealt with through counselling and through the disciplinary procedure (*see* Chapters 17 and 18). The second category may indicate alcohol dependency and require treatment as an ill-health issue (*see also* Chapters 11 and 18). Employment tribunals classify addiction as an illness and as such would expect a reasonable employer to treat employees with an alcohol addiction fairly and reasonably and in the same way as employees with other health concerns.

The possession or taking of controlled drugs at work, as well as the likely impact on workplace performance, potentially places the employer in an unlawful situation. The possession of controlled drugs should normally constitute gross misconduct and be dealt with under the disciplinary procedure. An employee who takes controlled drugs outside the workplace and whose performance is not affected is unlikely to come to the attention of the employer, but where employees are convicted for drug taking or possession the employer is legitimately entitled to consider the consequences for employment. Publicity, which damages organisational reputation, or convictions, which damage employer confidence in the employee, may warrant disciplinary action.

Prescribed drugs present a different scenario – the drugs may be legitimate and necessary for the health of the employee, but employee work performance may be adversely affected. Policy development should recognise this problem, and prescribed drug taking which adversely affects performance should normally be dealt with under the sickness procedures. Action should be taken to:

- obtain a prognosis which includes the length of time for which the employee will need to take the prescribed drug and the work performance consequences of continued prescription;
- identify and discuss with the employee the performance issues giving concern;
- consider reasonable adjustments to the work, such as changing the contractual arrangements, allowing more flexible working or revising the job to accommodate the time needed for the employee to return to full health.

Increasingly, employers are developing a single policy to cover both alcohol and drugs, with the focus being on the effect on work performance and the emphasis on health and safety, confidentiality and training (Pawsey, 2000). Whether the employer implements a single policy or two specific policies will depend on the nature of the organisation and the approach to be taken. However, the employer should be seeking a fair and consistent managerial response to those employees who declare an addiction to drugs and whose ability to attend regularly or perform satisfactorily is affected. Positive employee attempts to eliminate dependence on drugs can be supported through counselling, treatment and occupational sick pay, with the aim of enabling a return to effective working.

Alcohol and drug policy considerations

The policy needs to focus on establishing and articulating the managerial attitude towards alcohol use and drug misuse. A precise statement of the rules is required to govern alcohol consumption in the workplace and attendance at work when unfit due to the effects of alcohol. Work arrangements which encourage alcohol consumption, such as access to lunchtime drinking, customer hospitality and availability of alcohol on the premises, are powerful influences on employee 'norms' of behaviour, and the implementation of an alcohol policy without addressing these arrangements is less likely to succeed. An effective policy can lead to a safer, healthier and more motivated workforce through early identification of problems, dealing fairly with employees and offering assistance to treat and rehabilitate where appropriate. Whether the organisation chooses to involve the police is a managerial decision, but the organisational attitude to the involvement of the police should be known by employees and action should be consistent.

Screening of employees for alcohol and drugs is a sensitive issue and may contravene Article 8 of the Human Rights Act 1998. The Information Commissioner's Office (2005) has issued useful guidelines to help employers to comply with the law if they undertake any testing for alcohol and drugs within the workplace. The advice includes making sure that the benefits justify any adverse impact: unless it is required by law, it is unlikely to be justified unless it is for health and safety reasons, or, for post-incident testing, unless there is a reasonable suspicion that alcohol or drugs are a factor; make sure that employees know that alcohol or drug testing is taking place and also the possible consequences of the testing, for example is there a blood-alcohol level that would lead to disciplinary action? The introduction of an alcohol and drug-testing programme should therefore be treated with extreme caution. The culture of the organisation and the nature of the work will clearly influence whether testing is a reasonable option. The Joseph Rowntree Foundation (2004) in an enquiry into workplace drug testing found that employers had a legitimate interest in alcohol and drug use in a specific set of circumstances, that is:

- where employees were engaged in illegal activities in the workplace
- where employees were under the influence of alcohol in the workplace
- in a high risk workplace, where there was a higher than normal risk of accident
- in areas of work where there was contact with the public, where certain standards of behaviour were expected.

In addition, Snashall and Patel (2005) add that employer interest is legitimised where safety-critical work is inherent in the job (for example, the nuclear industry) or where there is statutory regulation (for example, transport), where professional regulation imposes standards of behaviour and where employees may be open to blackmail.

Alcohol and drug policy content

The policy should be designed to reassure those with an alcohol or drug problem that they will be treated fairly and therefore increase the likelihood that they will be encouraged to look for help. Policies will differ in their form and structure but Snashall and Patel (2005) identify 15 generic headings which featured in a survey of large British companies in 2004 and which can form the basis of an alcohol and drug policy:

1 *Policy aims and objectives.* The statement of the policy objectives, which may include: the promotion of good health among staff, the need to deal fairly and equitably with staff who have alcohol- and drug-related problems, the need to ensure safety at work and the image of the employer.

2 *The applicability or coverage of the policy.* This should be clearly stated and may include all employees, contractors and non-employees, customers and other visitors; be clear about exemptions which may include business entertaining or work parties.

3 *The scope of the policy.* Does it cover all times and all locations (e.g. how does it relate to home workers)? Does it apply to consumption of alcohol or drugs on and off the premises, intoxication or possession of drugs? What are the rules governing the sale or availability of alcohol at work?

4 *Responsibilities.* The responsibilities of all should be clear. This includes: managers, employees, contractors and occupational health services and the issue of rights and confidentiality should be included.

5 *Statutory regulations and standards.* Mention should be made to the legal requirements of the different parties including the employer and the employee. In addition, reference to the specific laws governing the health and safety

within the workplace should be included; this may include HASAWA 1974, Management of Health and Safety Regulations 1992, Misuse of Drugs Act 1971, Misuse of Drugs Regulations 2001 and the Transport and Works Act 1992, as well as anything specific to the industry you are working in.

6 *Definitions*. The terms drug misuse, alcohol and dependency should be defined. Drug misuse is defined in the Misuse of Drugs Act 1971 and should probably form the basis of the definition, but does it also include solvent abuse? Alcohol may be named as a separate substance and treated differently; if so, this should be clear. Reference needs to be made to what is meant by dependency. Snashall and Patel (2005) defined this as 'any drug misuse which interferes with an employee's health, social functioning, performance or behaviour either physically or mentally'.

7 *Identification of problems*. This is a tricky area as problems may be identified by the employee, identified by the manager as a result of performance or behavioural issues or raised by peers concerned about changes in work outputs or behaviour.

8 *Management protocols*. This relates to how issues will be handled. As mentioned previously, is this a one-off or occasional occurrence, which may be handled through the disciplinary procedures, or is it a long-term issue which needs support? Explicit reference to addiction being treated similarly to other long-term health issues will put the issue into an ill-health context. Reference should be made to the support available for treatment and to other forms of employee assistance that can be accessed. Where possible, sick pay entitlement should be maintained for the duration of agreed treatment and reassurance given that employment will not be in jeopardy if treatment is successful.

9 *Employee rights*. Reference can be made to employee rights including the right to confidentiality and the right to be accompanied at any disciplinary procedure. Also, reference to any appeals procedure related to management action should be identified.

10 *Potential role of an occupational health department*. If appropriate, the occupational health department will have a role in the management of alcohol- and drug-related issues; this will include: assessment of the individual, monitoring and, if included, the screening of employees, the ongoing monitoring, including dealing with staff who are refusing help, counselling and dealing with staff taking prescribed drugs, liaison with GPs or treatment facilities and education for staff, managers and others in recognising addiction and how to handle it.

11 *Advice to managers*. This will cover different aspects such as returning to work, support to attend work regularly and the management of staff with a dependency problem.

12 *Other disciplinary issues*. Issues mentioned here include reference to violence in the workplace, controlled drugs in the workplace, drug dealing at work and stealing drugs from the workplace. Many aspects of this will be organisation-specific and require the organisation to look carefully at the nature of the industry that they are in and to identify the risks associated with that industry.

13 *Implementation of the policy.* Details will be given here about the individual and departmental responsibilities for implementing the policy; relevant dates of the policy including the issue date and the review date.

14 *Communication.* As with any policy designed to guide employee and employer action, it is important that the policy is effectively communicated. This will normally happen when it is given to new employees when they start, or to contractors and visitors when they first visit the organisation. In addition, it should be available with other HR policies either on the company intranet or in the handbook, in line with normal practice.

15 *Source of help and advice.* It is helpful for staff to have names and addresses of local and national support organisations, including the EAP details if relevant.

This is an extensive framework for an alcohol and drug policy but it provides practical guidance to policy developers to select the areas that are most appropriate and to work with employee representatives in developing, agreeing and implementing a policy. This will promote a focus on support rather than punishment and, with the commitment of managers and employees, will act as a framework for managing a sensitive and challenging HR area.

VIOLENCE AT WORK

Violence appears to be a part of the modern environment and also impacts on working life. The 2006/07 *British Crime Survey* figures (HSE, 2008a) show that there were an estimated 397 000 threats of violence at work and 288 000 physical assaults by members of the public on workers in a 12-month period. This total of 685 000 incidents has fallen from a peak of 1.3 million in 1995. Those most at risk are the police, followed by health and social welfare professionals, while science and technology professionals were least at risk. Employers have a duty to look after the safety, health and welfare needs of their employees as well as customers and visitors to their premises. In order to meet this obligation, employers have to acknowledge the presence of violence within their workplace, undertake a comprehensive risk assessment and put in place policies and procedures to deal with it. Violence is not just limited to physical attacks but is defined more widely to reflect the role that verbal attacks and threats can have on the health and welfare of employees. The HSE (2006) define work-related violence as:

> any incident in which the person is abused, threatened or assaulted in circumstances relating to their work.

The 1997 revision of the 1995 Reporting of Injuries, Diseases and Dangerous Occurrences Regulations requires incidents of non-consensual workplace violence to be recorded and, in some cases, reported to the HSE. This is limited to acts of physical violence and has been criticised by the TUC and by public service unions as being limited in scope through excluding physical threats and verbal assaults. This change in reporting does, however, enable a more complete picture of the nature and extent of physical violence in the workplace to be established. Surveys related to the incidents of violence in specific employment sectors are revealing; for example, the BMA survey of 3000 doctors (2008) found that 'violence was a problem' for almost half of respondents with one-third experiencing 'some form of violence', with 33 per cent reporting threats and 20 per cent reporting physical assault. It is not only a legal requirement to provide a safe work environment; the protection of employees from violence at work can contribute to effectiveness and productivity. Investment in recruitment and training, which is undermined by a lack of managerial action to protect employees from exposure to violence, is wasted and likely to be repaid with low performance, high labour turnover and recruitment difficulties. Violence between employees normally constitutes serious or gross misconduct and is a disciplinary matter (*see* Chapters 17 and 18). The review of workplace violence in this section is primarily focused on violence against employees from sources external to the organisation.

There are a number of issues to be taken into consideration when reviewing the broader work environment where violence is likely to occur. These include the following.

The work environment – Both internal and external factors contribute to the risk of violence at work. The internal environment needs to be assessed for the availability of 'weapons', such as handy items of equipment, and also the need for protective devices such as screens and alarms. The assessment of the external environment includes the geographical location of the employer's premises and the incidence of local crime. If the geographical location of the place of work is a problem then systems for the safety of employees entering and leaving the building may be required, together with building security itself to combat unauthorised access.

The nature of the work – As discussed above, there are types of employment which have an increased risk from external violence. Those who provide services to the public, by the very nature of their work, come into contact with the clients and customers in sometimes frustrating and confrontational situations. The combination of frustration, anger and an inability of the employee to meet the customer demands can lead to 'customer rage' and increase the likelihood of a violent incident. Jobs that involve cash handling also carry increased risks, with bank staff, post office staff and retail staff being at higher risk from theft and associated violence.

The work situation itself – The high profile case of Suzy Lamplugh, the estate agent who was abducted when showing a client around a vacant property, highlights the risks to staff of working alone. Occupations where staff necessarily work alone, such as community nurses, some transport workers and social workers, present particular challenges and therefore need special consideration. An employee who works outside normal hours and after others have left the premises may be at greater risk, and work systems should ensure that employees are not permitted to work alone without adequate security arrangements in place.

The personal characteristics of the individual – All people are different and some employees are better equipped to deal with confrontational and potentially violent situations, but all staff should be trained to recognise potentially difficult situations and to respond accordingly. A survey of interactions between staff and customers can indicate triggers for frustration and anger and causes of violent exchanges. An analysis of these incidents informs managerial action, which may include changes in systems of work, the reduction of waiting time or the provision of a more amenable customer environment. Employees who are adequately trained to assess and control violent situations are less likely to be the victims of attack than employees who are unable to manage emotional exchanges, or cannot provide relevant information, or lack skills and confidence in difficult encounters with customers.

Causes of violence

It is difficult to be prescriptive about the causes of violence, but it is useful to recognise the range of situations and circumstances to be considered. Examples are as follows.

- Waiting and delays can increase customer frustration, lead to anger and increase the potential for violence.
- The HSE (2006) suggest that alcohol consumption can increase aggressive behaviour and contribute to a more threatening environment; in a quarter of violent incidents the offender was under the influence of alcohol.
- Criminal intent, such as theft, may lead to violence against the worker.

Record-keeping and careful analysis of reported incidents will enable the causes of workplace violence to be identified and assessed.

The effective management of violence

The Health and Safety Executive publication *Violence at Work: a guide for employers* (2006) sets out a four-stage process for the effective management of violence in the workplace:

1 Identify whether there is a problem.
2 Decide on appropriate action to be taken.
3 Take action.
4 Evaluate what you have done.

This is an iterative process because the evaluation will indicate which problems remain and the process will need to be worked through again.

1 Identify whether there is a problem

This is the first step in risk assessment and the advice to the employer is to talk to employees and register their concerns. All incidents of violence need to be recorded, including verbal abuse and threatening behaviour as well as physical attacks, in order that the triggers for violence can be identified. Employees may be reluctant to report everything as they may see the acceptance of aggressive behaviour as part of the job. Employees should be encouraged to report everything and to recognise the role this plays in the development of safe systems of work. Complete reporting and accurate records will enable appropriate procedures to be developed and appropriate action to be taken. Coding and classifying incidents, including place, time, trigger situation, nature of injury and the experiences of staff, will allow for useful reporting and analysis.

2 Decide on appropriate action to be taken

Following the consultation and the analysis, the employer will identify the extent of violence and the nature of the risk. It is useful also to examine existing security arrangements, systems of work and procedures and whether these are working effectively.

Consideration can be given to job redesign to make jobs safer and provide a safer environment, for example better lighting or a more customer-friendly waiting area. Roberts (2001) identifies open plan offices and an appointment system as factors which reduced violent incidents from 5 per cent to 1 per cent in Australia. The UK Department for Work and Pensions is examining the impact of making changes to office layout and systems in an effort to reduce violent incidents. This has not met with an entirely positive reaction from employee representatives, highlighting the need to talk to staff and take on board their concerns. It is important to record the results of assessments and the subsequent decisions and to provide, first, clear frameworks for action and, second, the information for evaluation and review.

3 Take action

This involves developing a detailed and precise policy for dealing with violence in the particular place of work based on the views of staff, the evidence of incidents and the work situation. The policy should include:

- the legal responsibilities of both the employer in providing a safe working environment and the employees in taking reasonable care of themselves and following safe procedures;
- details of specific risks emanating from the risk assessment together with the organisational response, precautions and procedures;
- what constitutes an incident, how it is reported and to whom;
- education and training arrangements;
- the availability of counselling services either through in-house trained counsellors or through an employee assistance programme.

A clear policy will help employees to understand what the employer is trying to achieve, and to support them in achieving it and to follow the correct procedures.

4 Evaluate what you have done

This policy, like all HR policies, should be regularly reviewed. A system of regular reporting of incidents, either through the health and safety committee or through some other appropriate forum, will enable the continuous assessment of workplace violence and ensure that the action being taken is appropriate.

The HSE funded the development of national occupational standards in managing work-related violence which were launched in September 2002 to support organisations in developing policies and management skills to deal effectively with the assessment of risk, the implementation of policy and to reduce the number of incidents of workplace violence. The national standards are included in Exhibit 14.5.

The legal requirement for risk assessment means that employers cannot ignore the intrusion of violence into the workplace. Open discussion of the issues, recruitment of staff who understand the nature of the work and the risks attached to it, and a well-designed and well-communicated policy will enable violence at work to be managed more effectively. Provided that employers know the causes of violence, assess the hazards to staff and seek to minimise the risk, they are fulfilling the statutory obligation and giving credence to the dictum of people being their most valuable resource.

EXHIBIT 14.5 Employment National Training Organisation (ENTO) national standards in managing work-related violence

The national occupational standards for tackling workplace violence include:

- Assess the risk of violence to workers
- The formation of a basis for national qualifications
- Develop effective policy and procedures for minimising the risk of violence to your workers
- Implement policy and procedures to reduce the risk of violence at work
- Develop and maintain an effective management information system
- Promote a safe and positive working environment
- Ensure that your actions contribute to a positive and safe working environment
- Protect yourself from the risk of violence at work
- Respond to work-related violent incidents
- Support individuals involved in violent incidents at work
- Investigate and evaluate incidents of violence at work
- Ensure effective communications following an incident of violence at work

CASE STUDY   Central Bar: workplace violence

Central Bar is an independent bar located in the centre of a large university city in the UK. It is a popular bar with students and is always full and very busy on Friday, Saturday and Sunday nights. Isabella has been working there for three months and despite always being very busy she generally enjoys the work. A couple of weeks ago she felt very threatened when a male customer started to shout abuse at her because he had to wait to get his drinks. She reported this to her manager and told him that she felt frightened by the incident. A few days later another incident happened when a customer pulled her around when she was walking back to the bar, to complain because he had been waiting a long time. Again, she reported this to her manager, expressing her concerns about the situation. The manager said that this was bound to happen in a busy bar and that she should learn to deal with it.

Isabella has had little training except on the range of drinks sold, taking and handling money and issues such as time-keeping and general duties. She speaks to her manager and at this meeting she asks to see the risk assessment and the procedures which are in place for the protection of the employees. The manager brings out a health and safety policy which was written two years previously and he talks this through with her. There has been no risk assessment done for over a year and there is no mention of harassment by customers.

The manager agrees to review the policy and to meet with employees within two weeks. Two weeks later he shows employees the actions he recommends. These include:

- A policy on barring customers who threaten employees
- Clear employee guidelines on refusing drinks to customers who are considered to be a threat

- The introduction of door staff at certain times of the year when they are very busy
- CCTV cameras will be installed to allow better visibility of all areas of the bar

Questions

1 Do these actions fulfil the legal requirements of the bar owner?

2 Analyse the actions recommended by the Health and Safety Executive in *Managing work-related violence in licensed and retail premises* (2008b, www.hse.gov.uk/pubns/indg423.pdf) to manage work-related violence and detail the further actions you recommend should be taken to provide a safe and healthy workplace for the Central Bar employees.

SUMMARY LEARNING POINTS

1 Investment in well-being initiatives can benefit the employer through higher levels of performance, lower levels of absence and improved recruitment and retention of staff.

2 Pressure is stimulating and motivating and a state of 'eustress' is a desirable aim, but inappropriate levels of pressure result in 'distress', which is harmful to the individual and to the organisation. The costs of distress are potentially substantial and warrant managerial attention. Managing harmful pressure involves engaging in risk assessment, acting upon the stressors and promoting individual coping and rehabilitation strategies. A stress management policy needs to address the stigma associated with admitting distress and also provide for a stress audit against the HSE stress management standards, an action plan, monitoring and review. Managerial efforts to combat stress are circumscribed by the conjunction of social, political, economic and global factors which tend to increase pressure at work.

3 Harassment and bullying at work deny dignity to the individual and are dysfunctional to the organisation. A dignity at work policy and associated procedures are needed to deal with problems, to demonstrate that harassment and bullying are unacceptable and to create an environment where employees can feel secure and can be productive.

4 Alcohol misuse and drug abuse may impact on employee attendance and work performance. As a consequence the organisational attitude towards alcohol and drugs, the counselling and support available to employees and the training and backing available to managers should be articulated in clear policies.

5 The nature of the work determines the likelihood of violence at work. Violence may be threatened or actual, and verbal or physical, but whatever form it takes the employer has a statutory duty to assess the risks and implement strategies to reduce or eliminate the risk. As well as adversely impacting on employee performance and effectiveness, employer failure to address violence at work can result in the constructive dismissal of employees.

REFERENCES AND FURTHER READING

Advisory, Conciliation and Arbitration Service (2008) *Advisory Booklet: Stress at Work*. London: ACAS.

Advisory, Conciliation and Arbitration Service (2008) *Advisory Booklet: Health Work and Well-being*. London: ACAS.

Advisory, Conciliation and Arbitration Service (2009) *Advisory Booklet: Bullying and Harassment*. London: ACAS.

Aikin, O. (2005) 'The pressure zone', *People Management*, 24 February, 18.

Anonymous (2003) *Alcohol and the workplace*. St Ives: Institute of Alcohol Studies.

BMA (2008) *Violence at work: the experience of UK doctors*, Health Policy and Economic Research Unit, www.bma.org.uk/images/violenceatwork_tcm41-37871.pdf.

Briner, R. (1999) 'Against the grain: stress', *People Management*, 30 September, 32–41.

CIPD (2004) *Managing conflict at work: a survey of the UK and Ireland*. London: CIPD.

CIPD (2005) *Bullying at Work: beyond policies to a culture of respect*. London: CIPD.

CIPD (2007a) *What's happening with well-being at work?* London: CIPD.

CIPD (2007b) *Tackling bullying at work: a good practice framework*. London: CIPD.

CIPD (2007c) *Harassment and bullying at work*. London: CIPD.

CIPD (2007d) *Managing drug and alcohol misuse at work*. London CIPD.

CIPD (2008) *People Management guide to wellness at work*, October. London: CIPD.

CIPD (2009) *Stress: Factsheet*. London: CIPD.

Clark, H., Chandler, J. and Barry, J. (1997) 'Gender and work stress: experience, accommodation and resistance', Occasional Papers in Organisational Analysis, University of Portsmouth.

Croft, P. (2005) 'Legal action: stress', *People Management*, 10 March, 56.

Department of Health (2004) *Choosing Health: Making healthy choices easier*. www.dh.gov.uk/assetRoot/04/09/47/51/04094751.pdf.

DWP and PwC (2008) *Building the case for wellness*, PricewaterhouseCoopers, www.workingforhealth.gov.uk/documents/dwp-wellness-report-public.pdf.

Einarson, S., Hoel, H., Zapf, D. and Cooper, C.L. (2003) *Bullying and emotional abuse in the workplace*. London: Taylor & Francis.

Ghodse, H. (2005) 'Drugs and alcohol in the workplace', in Ghodse, H. (ed.) *Addiction at Work: tackling drug use and misuse in the workplace*. Aldershot: Gower.

Government Equalities Office (2008) *Changes to the definition of sex harassment and employer liability for third party harassment under the Sex Discrimination Act 1975*, www.equalities.gov.uk/legislation/index.htm.

HSE (2000) *Securing health together: a long term occupational health strategy for England Scotland and Wales*. Sudbury HSE.

HSE (2004) *Work-related stress – a short guide*. London: HSE Books.

HSE (2006) *Violence at work: a guide for employers*. London: HSE Books.

HSE (2007) *Why Tackle Work-Related Stress?* www.hse.gov.uk.

HSE (2008a) *Violence at Work: Findings from the British Crime Survey 2006/07*. London: HSE Books, www.hse.gov.uk/statistics/causdis/violence/.

HSE (2008b) *Managing work-related violence in licensed and retail premises*, www.hse.gov.uk/pubns/indg423.pdf.

HSE (2009) *Don't mix it: A guide for employers on alcohol at work*, www.hse.gov.uk/pubns/indg240.pdf.

HSE and CIPD (2008a) *Line Management Behaviour and Stress at Work: refined framework for managers*. CIPD: London.

HSE and CIPD (2008b) *Managing work-related stress in licensed and retail premises*. London: HSE Books.

Home Office, Research, Development and Statistics Directorate and BMRB. Social Research, *British Crime Survey 2006–2007*. Colchester, Essex: UK Data Archive.

Honey, P. (1993) 'Managing unwanted stress', Seminar Paper. London: IPD.

Incomes Data Services (2004) *Managing stress*, HR Studies. London: IDS.

Incomes Data Services (2005) *Alcohol, drugs and employment law*, IDS Brief No. 778, April, 10–17. London: IDS.

Information Commissioner's Office (2005) *The Employment Practices*. Wilmslow: ICO.

IPD (1996) *Occupational Health and Organisational Effectiveness – key facts*. London: IPD.

IRS Employment Review (2008) *How well-being schemes cut absence at the City of London Police*, No. 892, February.

Jack, R. (2004) 'How to implement a wellness strategy', *People Management guide to wellness at work*. October. London: CIPD.

Joseph Rowntree Foundation (2004) *Drug Testing in the Workplace: The Report of the Independent Inquiry into Drug Testing at Work*. York: York Publishing Services.

Juniper, B. (2009a) 'Measuring employee well-being: you can only manage what you can measure', *HR Bulletin: research and practice*. CIPD Portsmouth, June.

Juniper, B. (2009b) 'Measuring employee well-being at Portsmouth Teaching Primary Care Trust', *HR Bulletin: research and practice*. CIPD Portsmouth, September.

Littlefield, D. (1996) 'Stress epidemic hits modern workforces', *People Management*, October.

Lovewell, D. (2004) 'Run rings around stress', *Employee Benefits*, October, 35–40.

Macdonald, L. (2005) *Wellness at work: protecting and promoting employee well-being*. London: CIPD.

Manocha, R. (2004) 'Well adjusted', *People Management guide to wellness at work*, October. London: CIPD.

Midgely, S. (1997) 'Pressure', *People Management*, 10 July, 36–9.

Pawsey, V. (2000) 'High time for action', *People Management*, 11 May, 24–32.

Prime Minister's Strategy Unit (2003) *Alcohol Harm Reduction Project: Interim analytical report*, www.strategy.gov.uk/publications/.

Rayner, C., Hoel, H. and Cooper, C.L. (2002) *Workplace bullying: what we know, who is to blame and what can we do about it?* London: Taylor & Francis.

Robbins, S. (1993) *Organizational Behavior*. Upper Saddle River, NJ: Prentice-Hall.

Roberts, Z. (2001) 'A rough guide to harmony', *People Management*, December.

Smith, A., Johal, S. and Wadsworth, E. (2000) *Bristol Stress and Health at Work Study*. London: HSE Books.

Smith, A., Wadsworth, E., Moss, S. and Simpson, S. (2004) *The scale and impact of illegal drug use by workers*. London: HSE Books.

Snashall, D. and Patel, D. (2005) 'Drug and alcohol policies – a review', in Ghodse, H. (ed.) *Addiction at Work: tackling drug use and misuse in the workplace*. Aldershot: Gower.

Stephens, T. (1999) *Bullying and Sexual Harassment*. London: CIPD.

Stuart, L. (2001) 'All stressed up and no place to go', *The Guardian*, 17 March.

Tehrani, N. (2001) *Building a culture of respect: managing bullying at work*. London: Taylor & Francis.

Tehrani, N. (2004) *Recovery, rehabilitation and retention: maintaining a productive workforce*. London: CIPD.

Terrence Higgins Trust (2001) 'Prejudice, discrimination and HIV: a report', *Policy Campaigns and Research Division*, November, 1–26.

Wells, S.J. (2008) 'Finding wellness's return on investment', *HR Magazine*, 53(6), 75–84, June.

White, P. and Hamer, C. (2001) 'No time for relaxing over stress at work', *Personnel Today*, 30 October, 13.

ASSIGNMENTS AND DISCUSSION TOPICS

1 What would you look for in your organisation (or one with which you are familiar) to identify whether it has a well-being strategy? How might this strategy be operationalised and how might its effectiveness be monitored?

2 Using the HSE stress management standards, discuss the main sources of stress for particular jobs in your organisation. What are the implications of these organisational stressors for the individual and for organisational effectiveness and how can management respond effectively?

3 What should be done in your organisation to address the potential for violence against employees? Assess and respond to the training needs of a group of staff who may face violence in the workplace.

4 For your organisation (or an organisation where you are able to get access) use the HSE four-stage process to critically review the management of violence in the workplace. What conclusions can you draw from your review and what recommendations would you make to ensure compliance with the legislative responsibilities?

Chapter 15

Employment Relations in Context

by Derek Adam-Smith

LEARNING OUTCOMES: TO BE ABLE TO

- Appreciate the roles played by the key actors in employment relations

- Explain the implications for employers of statutory union recognition and the National Minimum Wage

- Evaluate the principal characteristics of management style in employment relations

- Identify and assess the ways in which trade unions are seeking to respond to declining membership and their influence on the employment relationship.

INTRODUCTION

Effective people resourcing is not achieved without an understanding and appreciation of the employment relationship. This chapter and the next expose the contextual nature of the employment relationship and the associated processes. Over the past 30 years, the subject area of employment relations has undergone significant change. Conservative governments between 1979 and 1997 initiated a series of policies designed to weaken the power of trade unions, and the post-1997 Labour governments have introduced legislation which provides for a National Minimum Wage, places restrictions on working hours and introduced a statutory right for union recognition. In response to increased competition for goods and services, many organisations introduced employment strategies devised to produce a closer fit with their business objectives. Such strategies are often accompanied by an emphasis on individualising the employment relationship. As a result of these developments, the reliance on collective bargaining between employers and trade unions to determine employees' terms and conditions of employment has declined, significantly so in much of the private sector. Consequently, trade unions themselves have been forced to re-examine the way in which they express their traditional role as the formal representative of employees.

EMPLOYMENT RELATIONS AND PEOPLE RESOURCING

An understanding of the field of employment relations (or employee relations or industrial relations, as the subject may be titled) remains an important one for those concerned with the management of people at work. Blyton and Turnbull (2004) maintain that its relevance is fourfold. First, the world of work remains central to the lives of most people, provoking interest in the settlement of terms and conditions of employment and the way in which people are treated at work. Second, employees are vital to an organisation's ability to achieve its business strategy, whether in the manufacturing or service sectors of the economy or in the public and voluntary sectors. Unless employees deliver the required skill and attention to their work, an organisation's potential for success will not be realised. Third, while managers and employees may share a common interest in ensuring a continuing successful enterprise, a tension exists between an employer's need for profit (or, in the case of the public sector, to remain within budget) and the workers' needs for wages and employment security. Fourth, the decline in the collective dimension to employment and the emergence of the individualism associated with contemporary HRM practices do not signal the end of the need to study collective employment relationships. Blyton and Turnbull argue that:

> At first sight these 'position' statements, reflecting the basic importance, problematic nature and contemporary significance of employee relations, may appear almost too simple to warrant re-stating . . . [however] the tendency for them to be discarded or overlooked in some of the recent management literature may have led to a misconception about the continuing significance of collective employee relations in contemporary work organisations. (Blyton and Turnbull, 2004: 5)

Thus decisions over the wage–work bargain between employers and employees remain central to the achievement of effective resourcing of organisations. This will necessitate managers formulating answers to the following sorts of questions. If the employment relationship is conducted on an individualised basis, how will terms and conditions of employment be determined? Is a representative role for trade unions acceptable to the organisation and required by the employees? If so, how will this collective relationship be structured? What knowledge and skills are needed by managers and HR professionals involved in dealing with trade unions? To what extent is it important for employees, individually or collectively, to be involved in wider decisions outside their immediate work requirements? How do economic and political changes influence these relationships? There is no one best way to structure the employment relationship. Providing answers to these questions will involve making decisions that take account of the contexts and sector within which the organisation operates, the preferred style of key managers, and the organisation's size, ownership, product market and business objectives. This chapter aims to provide an initial opportunity to examine those factors which have a bearing on the answers to these questions through a consideration of some key contextual changes in employment relations.

THE CHANGING NATURE OF EMPLOYMENT

Chapter 4 explored the way in which labour markets and patterns of work have changed in recent years. These changes have particular significance for the structuring of the employment relationship and the interests of the key parties in employment relations – employers, employees, trade unions and the state. A number of key trends can be discerned from a consideration of statistics drawn from official publications.

First, the level of unemployment has risen and fallen dramatically since the late 1970s when it stood at around 5 per cent. It rose to over 10 per cent in 1987 before declining to below 7 per cent in 1990. During the recession of the early 1990s unemployment climbed to almost 10 per cent again before falling to just over 4 per cent in the mid-2000s. These wide swings in the unemployment rate suggest that workers are more likely to move in and out of employment, leading to feelings of job insecurity. As Gregg *et al.* (2000: 54) point out, 'For nearly three-quarters of the workforce, job instability as measured by job tenure has increased in the last ten years or so.' The economic recession that began in 2008 has led to a further upturn in unemployment levels with the number of workers seeking employment rising to over 2 million by mid-2009. Given the severity of this downturn in economic activity, workers' feelings of insecurity are likely to increase markedly.

Second, as shown by data revealed by the *Labour Force Survey*, there has been a gradual increase in the number of people working under what may be described as 'atypical' contracts. Part-time employment grew from around 20 per cent of the working population in 1980 to a little over 25 per cent in 2008. Temporary employment grew from around 5 per cent in 1980 to peak at a little over 7 per cent in the 1990s before falling back to its 1980 level in 2008. There has been a significant growth in the number of workers who are self-employed: over a million between 1984 and 2008. While some view these developments as being a positive choice for workers (Barley and Kunda 2004; Leadbeater 1999), others are more sceptical arguing that many of those in such employment have little choice, and often work in low-paid jobs with little scope for advancement (see, for example, Bradley *et al.*, 2000). As Beatson (1995:57) points out, this has little to do with workers' choice; rather:

the most important reason is the fit between these types of work and specific business needs (such as part-time jobs which cover extended opening hours).

Third, the UK has witnessed a process of de-industrialisation that has seen the decline of traditional, staple industries such as mining and shipbuilding, and a similar decline in manufacturing capacity. While millions of jobs were lost in these sectors, as far as overall employment was concerned, there was a rapid expansion in private sector services, including finance and leisure which limited the impact on unemployment and offered new opportunities for employment. However, the 2009 recession has not only continued to affect what remains of the UK manufacturing sector, it has also had a major impact on banks and other financial services with consequential job losses.

The combination of these trends suggests that the nature of employment has undergone, and continues to undergo, significant changes in a relatively short period of time. There has been a shift away from full-time, male employment in the manufacturing sector. There are substantially more women in employment, often working on a part-time or temporary basis. The use of subcontracting by employers, utilising the growing numbers of the self-employed, provides greater flexibility because the employer enters into a contract for services rather than a contract of employment, with its attendant legal protection. As a result of these trends in the nature of employment, some commentators have suggested that 'employment relations' provides a more adequate description of the subject area (Sisson, 1991; Blyton and Turnbull, 2004). For many, the term 'industrial relations' is characteristic of a previous era of high trade union membership among predominately manual workers in extraction, heavy engineering and manufacturing industries. Even the more 'modern' employee relations does not always reflect the fact that many of those working in organisations are not employees but self-employed, and the nature of temporary work means that many employees know that they will spend little time employed in a particular organisation.

These developments pose particular challenges for those concerned with the management of human resources. Worker insecurity, whether caused by worries over unemployment or by a contractual relationship that provides less legal protection, has potential to negatively affect their commitment to their work and employer.

THE ROLE OF THE STATE

Employment relations does not exist in a vacuum but is affected by, and in turn affects, the political, economic and social contexts within which it operates. In order to understand the changes that have taken place, it is therefore necessary to examine the way in which governments have sought to influence British employment relations, since 'it is the only actor in the situation which can change the rules of the system' (Crouch, 1982: 146).

To aid this analysis it is possible to identify four interrelated roles that the state plays. First, as its elected custodian, governments develop a range of policies aimed at developing a stable and competitive economy, controlling inflationary pressures and seeking to maintain a healthy balance of payments. Second, to support some of its policy objectives the government can introduce legislation to Parliament. Of particular interest here is the law governing employment and trade unions. Third, where conflict between employers and employees, or their representative trade unions, is viewed as having a detrimental impact on economic performance or the achievement of social objectives, the government can, either through its own ministers or through specially created agencies, intervene in industrial disputes. Finally, since a substantial number of people are employed in the public sector, actions by the government in its role as an employer (either directly in the case of the civil service or indirectly in local authorities, for example) will have significant consequences for employment relations. Each of these roles – policy-maker, legislator, intervenor and employer – will be considered in turn.

Policy-maker

In order to understand the contemporary relevance of the interrelationship between employment relations and economic policy, it is helpful to briefly review the way in which public policy has developed since 1945. The period from 1945 to 1979 is generally characterised as one of consensus between the two main political parties in the management of the economy and in the role trade unions and collective bargaining were to play in employment. According to Farnham and Pimlott (1995: 214), this consensus involved:

> the maintenance of full employment and the welfare state; continuing state ownership of industries nationalised between 1945 and 1951; high levels of public expenditure; the continuation of the legal-abstentionist or voluntarist tradition of industrial relations; and the involvement of the Trades Union Congress (TUC) in government decisions affecting the welfare state and the management of the national economy.

Of these, 'a commitment to the maintenance of full employment had been the centre-piece of the . . . consensus' (Kessler and Bayliss, 1998: 54). This policy was philosophically underpinned by an adherence to Keynesian demand management economics which offered a strategy for managing the economy so that full employment could be maintained. However, this commitment, combined with a reliance on 'free' collective bargaining as the preferred method for determining pay and terms and conditions for employees, began to produce significant difficulties for employers. In the private sector powerful trade unions were able to bargain for increased earnings (over and above the market rate) and, with limited alternative labour available, employers were forced to raise pay rates to attract and retain employees, particularly where there were skill shortages. Employers in the public sector were unable to attract sufficient staff unless they were able to offer comparable pay rates, which led to increased demands on the public borrowing requirement to fund these pay awards. The result of these pressures in the economy was an increase in inflation. Faced with this problem, governments throughout the 1960s and 1970s searched repeatedly for an incomes policy which would limit the increase in earnings levels without abandoning the commitment to full employment. Despite some limited success, the search for an effective incomes policy came to an end in the 'winter of discontent' in 1978–79. However, it has been observed that the policy of full employment also hindered any fundamental adjustment of the economy to the increasingly competitive international pressures:

> So, not only did governments find it increasingly difficult to prevent unemployment rising but productivity, unit labour costs, investment and profitability were getting

> increasingly out of line with Britain's major competitors in Europe and the rising
> economies of the Far East.   (Kessler and Bayliss, 1998: 55)

The election of the Conservative government led by Margaret Thatcher in 1979 marked a 'sea-change' in economic policy and fundamental changes in the relationship between government and trade unions, in part driven by the need to make the economy more competitive. The tenets of the incoming administration are succinctly summed up by Crouch (1995) thus:

> The post-1979 Conservative governments have had a strong neo-liberal ideology. This has predisposed them: to reject Keynesian demand management and the search for full employment; to oppose policy deals with trade unions that would involve taking action incompatible with neo-liberal principles; and to reject relations with organisations of interests – on both sides of business but especially on the labour side – that interfered with neo-liberal policy priorities.   (Crouch, 1995: 238)

Demand management strategies pursued under Keynesian economics, complemented by incomes policies, were replaced by an adherence to monetarist policies. The control of inflation was to be achieved through tight control of the money supply and use of interest rates, leaving the market mechanism to prevail. Not only did this mean that ailing industries and organisations would not receive public subsidies (if there was no market for its products at the price demanded, the organisation would have to rationalise its operations or close), but also that the labour market should be subject to these same disciplines. If unemployment rose, the cause was that the cost of labour (wages) was too high. As employees adjusted their expectations in this new economic reality, jobs would be accepted for lower pay. The resultant profitability of companies would encourage them to take on more staff (assuming demand remained) and lead to a consequent fall in unemployment. Since trade unions were a major factor in distorting the working of the labour market through their ability to bargain collectively on behalf of employees, the achievement of this policy required that the pervasiveness of collective bargaining would need to be tackled. Primarily this objective was achieved through the use of legal measures designed to curtail what was seen as the excessive power of the trade unions (Howell, 2005). In addition, as Crouch (1995) has noted, government policy between 1979 and 1997 also removed the elements of tripartism (cooperation between government, unions and employers) which had become a key element of public policy. In part this was achieved through *ad hoc* measures such as the exclusion of union leaders from government inquiries, commissions and the like, and a reduction in meetings between ministers and unions. In particular, tripartite channels such as the National Economic Development Council (NEDC) (a regular forum bringing together representatives of unions, employers and government to discuss economic issues) and the Manpower Services Commission (MSC) (which involved employers and workers' organisations in discussions concerning the working of the labour market and industrial relations) were gradually marginalised and eventually abolished (Crouch, 1995). Thus, public policy on employment relations under these Conservative governments can be seen to be one seeking to remove barriers to the working of the free labour market and, in particular, reducing the power and influence of trade unions both in their negotiations with employers and in the management of the economy.

The election of a Labour government in 1997 (and its subsequent re-election in 2001 and 2005) heralded a further change in public policy. The approach of New Labour to employment policy has been characterised as the Third Way. Although its precise meaning remains elusive and open to debate, it is perhaps best understood to involve a rejection of both the voluntarist, consensus period from 1945 to 1979 and the monetarist, free-market policies of Conservative governments up to 1997, hence the *Third Way*. As Tony Blair has defined it: 'not *laissez-faire* nor state control and rigidity; but an active Government role linked to improving the employability of the workforce' (Blair, 1998, cited in Undy, 1999: 316).

Four main components of Labour's employment policy can be identified. The first is a more active labour market policy. This can be seen, for example, in the development of the New Deal, the broad aim of which is to improve the skill base of the workforce. Initially targeted at young people without jobs and initially funded by a windfall tax on the privatised utilities, the scheme was extended to include older people who have difficulty finding employment where jobs require increasing levels of skill. As the 2009 recession continued to affect employment, the government sought to introduce further measures aimed at 'helping people back to work'. A further example is the government's commitment to 50 per cent of all young people experiencing university education. Second, it sought to provide greater fairness in the employment relationship through the provision of minimum employment rights. The practical application of this component can be seen in the introduction of the National Minimum Wage in 1999, which provided for a statutorily backed minimum hourly pay for all workers in the country. Third, as part of its attempt to build social partnership with trade unions it passed legislation which provides trade unions with a legal route to gain recognition where an employer has refused to grant it voluntarily. Fourth, the Labour government has taken a more pro-European stance than that of its immediate predecessors, including the signing of the Social Chapter of the Maastricht Treaty. Each of these last three components is dealt with in later sections of this chapter.

Important as these changes are to the landscape of employment relations, it is important to note that there is considerable continuity between the employment policy of the Labour governments and those of their Conservative predecessors. For example, most of the anti-union legislation passed in the previous two decades has been retained since workforce flexibility remains a central concern. Thus:

> ... interventions ostensibly designed to improve employment rights and ease the position of trade unions were pursued only in so far as they did not challenge the prevailing neo-liberal assumption that deregulation is the most effective means of generating improvements in economic competitiveness ...
>
> (Williams and Adam-Smith, 2005: 89–90)

Legislator

The law that applies to employment can be divided broadly into two parts: that concerned with an individual employee's contract of employment with the employer, and the law governing the relationship between employers and trade unions. The position of individual employment rights, in relation to health and safety, job protection and discrimination, is discussed elsewhere in this book. This section will concentrate on the development of collective labour law and, in addition, will outline the provisions related to statutory union recognition and the National Minimum Wage.

Collective labour law

Turning first to the changes in collective labour law, significant changes were made to the legal status of action taken by trade unions in pursuit of their objectives by the Conservative governments between 1979 and 1997 and, as noted above, the overwhelming majority of the legislation remains in place. In order to meet its policy objectives of deregulating the labour market, Conservative governments in the 1980s and 1990s abandoned the 'abstentionist role' that the law played in employment relations. British industrial relations up to this time had been characterised as a voluntary process in which the law 'stood apart' from the determination of terms and conditions of employment. This, it was believed, was best left to employers and trade unions to decide through the medium of free collective bargaining. Legislation that was enacted had the aim of supporting and complementing collective bargaining (in areas such as health and safety, and employment protection) and of providing trade unions with the ability to call for industrial action without being subject to legal claims by employers for common law liabilities. Although some commentators have noted that the voluntary system was under pressure through the 1960s and 1970s (Hyman, 1995; Crouch, 1995), it was the election of the Thatcher government which initiated a series of Acts of Parliament which have made far-reaching changes to the collective labour law framework. 'The period has seen the final death of voluntarism, under which law was essentially an adjunct to an autonomous self-regulated system of industrial relations' (Dickens and Hall, 1995: 256). The aims of this legislation have been characterised as follows:

> The major thrust of the legislation since 1979 is clear: to weaken trade union power, to assert individualist rather than collective values and reassert employer prerogative.
> (Dickens and Hall, 1995)

As the previous section indicated, the bargaining strategies of trade unions were seen to distort the operation of the labour market, and thus the immunities granted to trade unions in relation to industrial action became the prime focus of the legal measures adopted by the government.

In Britain, there is no 'right to strike' – employees who do so are in breach of their contracts of employment and thus liable to dismissal by their employer. Although legislation passed in the 1970s prevented selective dismissal of strikers, these provisions were amended to give employers greater freedom to lawfully dismiss those on strike. However, since coming to power the Labour government has passed legislation so that workers undertaking official industrial action cannot be dismissed during the first 12 weeks of the dispute. For trade unions the freedom to take industrial action is derived from the granting of statutory immunities from claims under common law where such action would be judged otherwise to be 'in restraint of trade'. Trade union power was weakened through a series of Acts of Parliament designed to limit these immunities.

According to Auerbach (1990), the approach of successive Conservative governments can be seen as a 'dual track' policy – a policy of restriction and a policy of regulation. The former concentrated on the immunities enjoyed by unions. The circumstances under which these immunities were applicable were substantially narrowed, making industrial action outside the employees' workplace generally unlawful. Sympathy strikes (where employees not in dispute with their employer go on strike to support others, as was seen in the dispute in 2005 at Gate Gourmet, see Exhibit 15.1), picketing not at the employees' own place of work and industrial action for political purposes were all made unlawful.

EXHIBIT 15.1 The Gate Gourmet dispute

Gate Gourmet is the company that supplies in-flight meals to British Airways' (BA) Heathrow-based services: the service having been contracted out of BA in 1997. In August 2005 the company sought redundancies from its workforce at the same time as attempting to recruit lower-paid staff from employment agencies. Some 700 union members of staff went on strike, without a ballot, and were sacked by the company. The following day around 1000 BA ground staff went on strike in sympathy with the Gate Gourmet workers.

The strike by BA employees was unlawful since there was no dispute between them and their employer, but BA did not sack them as it was legally entitled to, but persuaded them to return to work within 48 hours. Why did the BA staff go on strike, and why did BA not sack them? Many of the BA staff saw the Gate Gourmet workers as colleagues closely linked to, if not employed by, the airline company. Also, there were strong family ties between the two groups of workers, and many lived in the same local area. For British Airways, despite the damage to their operations, sacking their staff would have probably led to further action by other employees. Besides, dismissing them would have caused further disruption since finding sufficient replacement workers quickly would have been difficult, if not impossible.

The policy of regulation sought to place specific legal requirements on trade unions engaged in industrial action. Complex, detailed requirements on secret postal ballots needed before lawful action can be embarked upon were put in place. In addition, unions that are found to be involved in unlawful industrial action can be sued. In the case of employers that suffer as a result of unlawful action, limited damages to be paid by the union are available. Legislation passed under successive Conservative governments has reduced the power of trade unions in their bargaining relationship with employers and their ability to pursue political objectives. How employers and unions have responded to these new circumstances will be considered later in the chapter. It is clear, however, that as a result of these changes, the balance of power has swung in favour of employers. Labour governments have been at pains to point out that there is no intention to significantly alter this body of law beyond those relatively minor changes made already.

Statutory union recognition

Although maintaining much of the legislation passed under its Conservative predecessors, in June 2000, as part of the Employment Relations Act 1999, the Labour government introduced a statutory right for trade unions to gain recognition from a reluctant employer. Although the procedures are designed to encourage voluntary agreement between the trade union and an employer, they are supported by mandatory provisions which can be activated if no agreement is reached. Although subsequent evidence has proved otherwise, in the view of one commentator, writing at the time the legislation was enacted, the measure 'could change the face of employee relations in the UK' (Younson, 2000: 44). The Employment Relations Act 2004 made amendments to these provisions which are designed to prevent unions and employers from using 'unfair practices' to influence workers to vote either for or against recognition. Such practices would include threats or incentives. While apparently highly favourable to unions, the legislation was introduced in such a way as to limit the impact on employers' discretion (Smith and Morton, 2001). For example, the legislation does not apply to firms with fewer than 21 employees, and the union must be able to show that it has at least 10 per cent of employees already in membership if it is to be able to use the mandatory provisions. Where voluntary agreement is not reached the union is required to apply to the Central Arbitration Committee (CAC), a long-standing body in UK employment relations. The CAC will oversee the operation of the statutory procedure, including the conduct of a ballot of all workers for whom the union is claiming recognition. Where a union is granted recognition under these provisions, the employer is required to negotiate with it on, at least, matters concerned with pay, hours of work and holidays.

The first decision that the CAC needs to make is the 'bargaining unit'. This is a definable group of employees, for example hourly paid staff or clerical workers, for which the union will be recognised as the negotiating body. Since it is a majority of these employees that will need to vote in favour, employers may be tempted to argue that the unit should be as large as possible as this may dilute the union's influence. Similarly, the union is likely to seek a small unit where it believes it has strong support. Thus the definition of the bargaining unit is a key step in the procedure. Under the legislation, the CAC is required to take account of a number of factors in addition to employer and union views when determining the size of the unit. These include the compatibility of the unit with effective management, the avoidance of small, fragmented bargaining units, the physical location of the employees, and any existing bargaining arrangements.

Once the bargaining unit is defined, if at least 50 per cent of the employees in the unit are union members then the CAC will declare that the union should be recognised. If membership is less than this figure, the CAC will call a secret ballot of employees. However, even if the 50 per cent threshold is achieved, the CAC may require a ballot in two circumstances: first, if it believes that this would be in the interests of good employment relations and, second, if it feels that membership evidence, for example a snap recruitment campaign by the union, suggests that employees may not wish union representation. Where a secret ballot is undertaken, recognition will be granted if it is supported by a majority of those voting *and* this majority amounts to at least 40 per cent of those in the bargaining unit. Exhibit 15.2 provides an example of these requirements.

EXHIBIT 15.2 Union recognition and bargaining unit ballot

As an example of how the majority requirements apply, suppose that there are 100 employees in the bargaining unit and 45 take part in the vote, with 36 voting in favour of union recognition. While a majority of those voting want the union to be recognised (36 out of 45 means that 80 per cent are in favour), this result does not meet the threshold under the second test since fewer than 40 per cent of those in the unit voted in favour.

This second condition appears to have been included to ensure that a small number of union members, voting in a ballot with a small turnout, cannot impose recognition on the rest of the members of the bargaining unit. The questionable assumption behind this provision is that employees not voting were against union recognition. It is equally valid to suggest that those not voting had no strong views either way, and were not against a union being recognised.

There was an initial rush of claims between 2000 and 2002 under the procedure; over 700 according to one estimate (TUC, 2003), but the number has subsequently declined. Gall (2007) suggests two factors may account for the reduction. First, initially, unions were able to target firms where employees already displayed support for unions, and second that unions were able to secure recognition in industries where they already had a strong presence. However, unions have not been able to make much headway in expanding sectors such as the service sector.

The overwhelming majority of claims have been settled voluntarily, and without recourse to the full procedure. According to the CAC, the statutory procedure has produced 184 new recognition agreements from 630 applications: 84 of these without recourse to a ballot of workers (CAC, 2008). This perhaps suggests that employers view a protracted battle over union recognition where there is support from the workforce is unlikely to engender good employment relations in the longer term. As Brown *et al.* (2001: 192) comment: 'Statutory intervention to enforce the enhancement of that [employment] relationship may have as little likelihood of success as compulsory marriage has of achieving domestic stability.'

CASE STUDY   Union recognition at Key Bits Ltd

Key Bits Ltd is a medium-sized engineering company, manufacturing components for the electronics and defence industries. It has developed specific expertise in design and production, and has been able to prosper even in periods where customers were facing falls in sales. The company is privately owned and, from relatively small beginnings in the 1970s, has grown to employ just over 300 workers. However, in times of peak demand, the company supplements its staffing with agency workers, for up to three months at a time.

The company employs 310 staff in total. The majority of the workforce, 210 employees, are production staff engaged in semi-automated assembly work. Of these production staff, 140 are semi-skilled whose in-company training period lasts up to three weeks. The remaining 70 are unskilled, and are mainly employed in packaging, warehousing and distribution work. The 210 manual employees are split into two rotating double-day shifts (Shift A and Shift B) that work from 06.00 to 14.00 and 14.00 to 22.00. The other 100 members of staff are engaged in the following work: 20 are skilled maintenance staff and toolsetters; 30 are in design, quality control and estimating functions; 10 are sales personnel; and the remaining 40 are in a variety of clerical and administrative posts. The company outsources its deliveries and cleaning work.

The company describes employment relations as 'good'. Members of the original founding family are in senior positions in the firm, and pride themselves at 'looking after' their employees. A team briefing is held monthly, and the company has tried, but failed, to give production workers responsibility for their own quality control matters. The HR manager carries out regular benchmarking exercises with colleagues in

(Box continued)

other firms, and believes that the company pays the 'going rate' in the local labour market. This survey forms the basis for annual pay rates, and there is, at the directors' discretion, an annual bonus which pays around 3 to 5 per cent of annual salary. Labour turnover among production workers exceeds 15 per cent, and the company often has difficulty filling these vacancies quickly.

The managing director has received a letter from the engineering union asking for a meeting to negotiate a recognition agreement with the company. The union officer writing the letter claims that 'well over' half of the employees on Shift A are in membership of the union. She adds that 'virtually all' the maintenance staff are union members. The letter asks the company to formally recognise the union for these two groups of workers. The union official concludes by expressing the wish to make a voluntary agreement with the company, but adds that she is confident in securing recognition through Central Arbitration Committee (CAC) procedures if the company resists the claim.

Question

The managing director has asked you, the HR manager, to draft a briefing paper in order that the board of directors can decide how to respond. In producing this paper you should include the options available to the company, outline the legal position with respect to union recognition and indicate the relative merits of each course of action. Your paper should end with a set of justified recommendations.

The National Minimum Wage

The second major legislative change introduced by the Labour government has been the establishment of a National Minimum Wage (NMW). Soon after its 1997 election victory the government established a Low Pay Commission (LPC) comprised of employer, trade union and independent members to consider the scope and level of the potential minimum wage. The LPC recommended that the hourly rates for the NMW should be defined for three different groups: a full adult rate; a development rate for adults in receipt of formal accredited training; and a young person's rate. The government accepted these principles, although with some amendments to the rates proposed by the LPC. The NMW was introduced in April 1999, giving the UK, for the first time, a legally enforceable minimum hourly rate of pay for all workers with no sector or regional variations. The original rates set in 1999 were: an adult rate of £3.60 per hour and a youth rate for those between 18 and 21 years of age of £3.00 per hour. Minimum rates are reviewed each year, and have normally been increased. In October 2008 the adult rate stood at £5.73 (rising to £5.80 in October 2009), and the youth rate £4.77 per hour (£4.83 from October). A new rate for 16- and 17-year-olds, introduced in 2004, was increased to £3.57 in October 2009.

The introduction of the NMW attracted a significant amount of criticism, mainly from employers and their representatives who argued that it would cause significant job losses, as employers in low-paying industries would not be able to afford the increases. However, the evidence available suggests that this has not been the case in general, although some small businesses found the impact on their wage bills difficult to manage (LPC, 2001; Adam-Smith et al., 2001). The relative ease with which the NMW has been accommodated by most firms can be attributed to four main, interrelated reasons (Adam-Smith *et al.*, 2003; Williams and Adam-Smith, 2005). First, the NMW was introduced at a comparatively low level, which meant many firms were unaffected, and those that were could relatively easily afford the increases in pay. Second, firms were given lengthy notice of subsequent upratings. For example, the increases in the rates for October 2009 were announced in May that year. Third, the NMW was introduced in a period of relative economic prosperity. This allowed many businesses to recover increased cost through raising prices. Wage rates were often forced up anyway, often beyond that required by minimum wage requirements, in order that firms could continue to attract and retain staff. Fourth, the informality characteristic of wage determination in small firms allows managers to 'juggle' the work and pay of staff in order to respond to external changes.

In terms of its impact, the National Minimum Wage has increased the rates of pay for more than 2 million workers; over a million saw their wages increase following its introduction in 1999. In terms of enforcement, this rests primarily with officers employed by HM Revenue and Customs who make visits to employers to inspect wage payments. Individual workers can also bring claims for failure to pay the legal minimum rate to an employment tribunal. However, visits by Revenue and Customs Officers are infrequent and workers may be reluctant to pursue a tribunal claim for fear of victimisation or being sacked. The government has sought to strengthen enforcement by targeting Revenue and Customs visits to sectors where underpayment is more likely, and, under the Employment Act 2008, employers who do not pay the minimum wage can face civil penalties.

Intervenor

That industrial action, particularly strikes, can have a damaging impact on the economy and society has long been recognised by governments. Similarly, individual complaints and grievances, if not resolved promptly can also damage an organisation's efficiency. This leads to the identification of a third role of the state in employment relations, that of 'industrial peacekeeper' or intervenor. Here the government accepts some responsibility for seeking a speedy and satisfactory resolution to the dispute. This aim can be achieved by both formal and informal mechanisms. In the former case it involves the establishment of either permanent or *ad hoc* agencies or bodies to intervene in the dispute. Informal means include the direct involvement of government ministers in the dispute – an approach which has declined in significance in recent years.

Although formal mechanisms for the settlement of industrial disputes can be traced back to the passing of the Conciliation Act in 1896 and the Industrial Courts Act 1919, the current publicly-funded agency primarily having these responsibilities is the Advisory, Conciliation and Arbitration Service (ACAS). Established in 1974, ACAS has four main functions related to its overall aim of improving industrial relations:

- conciliation between an employer and an individual employee in cases which may lead to a claim at an employment tribunal, including unfair dismissal and unlawful deductions from pay
- collective conciliation between employers and trade unions where an employment dispute exists
- making arrangements for arbitration where conciliation has proved unsuccessful
- providing free advice and guidance to employers, trade unions and employees on a range of employment matters.

The nature of conciliation and arbitration is elaborated upon in the next chapter.

The development of ACAS's policy and operational matters are determined by a nine-member council (plus chair) which includes equal representatives of trade unions and employers, and three independent members. It is one of the few tripartite organisations which have survived the changes to British employment relations since the 1970s. The emphasis that is attached to each of these functions reflects changes in the landscape for employment relations. For example, the decline in collective bargaining and collective relations between employers and trade unions has seen a shift in ACAS's focus towards the provision of advisory services (Towers and Brown, 2000).

Employer

The state is a major employer and it is not surprising, therefore, to find that its view of employment practice should be reflected in the way in which it manages its own workforce. Given the sharp dichotomy that exists between public policy before and after 1979, significant differences in the role of the state as an employer can be observed in the periods preceding and following this date (Farnham and Horton, 1993). Although the size of public sector employment has declined, it remains significant, with a substantial proportion of the workforce employed directly or indirectly by the state. The areas of employment under government control include the civil service, HM forces, local government, the National Health Service, police, education, and public corporations such as the Post Office.

Since the First World War, governments have attempted to act as a 'model' employer. Central to this approach had been the recognition of trade unions and the extensive use of collective bargaining, following the recommendations of the Whitley Committee in 1919, as the mechanism for determining pay and terms and conditions of employment. Organisations in the public sector encouraged their employees to join appropriate, recognised trade unions so that decisions over wages and other matters of employment should receive broad support among their workforces. Public sector employees, who enjoyed relatively high job security, were among the first to have pension and sick pay schemes and to have in place procedures covering such matters as discipline and grievances. This is not to say that employment relations in this sector were without criticism:

> Until the 1980s, strong institutional support for trade unions and collective bargaining, relatively good conditions of service (e.g. pensions and sick pay), and the rapid expansion of public sector employment concealed the less generous policies of governments concerning internal and external pay relativities and other conditions of employment.   (Winchester and Bach, 2003: 287)

As well as adopting this specific employer role as a model of best practice for the private sector to follow the government went beyond mere encouragement by requiring private sector contractors from whom it purchased goods and services to pay fair wages when engaged on government work.

The changes to the state's role as an employer since 1979 can be seen in many parts of the public sector. First, it became an employer of fewer staff. Primarily this was through the privatisation of the utility companies (gas, water and electricity) and the nationalised industries and corporations such as British Steel, British Shipbuilders, British Airways, British Telecom and the Royal Ordnance Factories. In all, this removed some

1.5 million employees from the public sector. Second, in the National Health Service, which employs over 1 million people, the creation of the 'internal market', the appointment of general managers and the development of trust status for health authorities has attempted to bring the 'disciplines' of the market into the service and to direct management attention to the need for cost savings (which include those to be made in labour costs).

Similar changes have been observed in local government where more than 2 million people work. The government encouraged the adoption of local-level determination of pay in contrast to the centralised Whitley Council structure. In addition, significant changes have occurred for both manual and white-collar workers from the introduction of initiatives such as Compulsory Competitive Tendering (CCT) and 'Best Value'. Jobs have been lost and employees' terms and conditions altered significantly.

In their review of these developments, Bach and Della Rocha (2000) suggest that a new form of public sector management has emerged, comprised of three characteristics. First, the growth of a strengthened and more assertive management function. Second, mirroring changes in the private sector, the devolution of decision-making to managers of business units. Third, a greater focus on the market for public services since competitive pressures should lead to an improvement in their quality.

EUROPEAN SOCIAL POLICY

As a member of the European Union (EU) employment relations in the UK are subject to the EU's supranational policy-making processes, although there is considerable controversy over the extent to which standardisation across the EU is desirable. Two features distinguish the formulation and implementation of European policy from that in the UK. First, the EU approach to the development of policy rests heavily on the active participation of the 'social partners', representatives of employers and employees, in the process. Second, unlike the tradition of voluntarism in the UK, EU decisions are implemented through the passage of law, typically in the form of Directives. Perhaps the most controversial element of EU employment policy is the Social Chapter of the Maastricht Treaty. The Labour government signed the Chapter soon after coming to power in 1997, thus reversing the decision of its predecessor, which opted out because it believed the provisions were detrimental to a free-market approach to employment. However, it is important to note that employment relations are affected by some EU decisions irrespective of the Social Chapter's contents. This may be seen in the following ways. First, the UK had already signed up to a number of Directives passed before the Maastricht Treaty was agreed, including equal pay and equal treatment at work, and health and safety at work. Under the latter, changes to maternity leave and payments were introduced in the Trade Union Reform and Employment Rights Act 1993. Similarly, this Directive was used by the EU to propose a maximum 48-hour working week and minimum periods of daily rest and paid holidays (*see* Chapter 13). Second, decisions by the European Court of Justice, which acts as a final appeal court on matters covered by Directives, can force the UK government to amend existing employment laws. For example, the adjudged failure of the UK to conform to the requirements of the Collective Redundancies and Transfer of Undertakings Directives forced the government to amend the law with regard to consultation with employee representatives (*see* Chapter 19).

Once the UK had signed the Social Chapter, it was required to implement any Directives introduced under Social Chapter authority, in addition to those emanating from those already in force. A number of Directives have had an impact on UK employment relations. First, the European Works Council (EWC) Directive 1994 requires multinational companies with 1000 or more employees within the member countries of the EU, including at least 150 employees in at least two of these countries, to establish an information and consultation body covering the whole of its workforce. Each EWC must meet at least once a year to allow managers and elected employee representatives to discuss company plans and prospects. Second, the Parental Leave Directive 1996 requires employers to provide 13 weeks of leave for each parent up to the child's fifth birthday. The key elements of the Directive were included in the Employment Relations Act 1999 which provided for employers and employees to agree their own scheme to implement these key elements, through either a collective agreement with recognised trade unions or a workforce agreement, the latter being an agreement made between an employer and the employees or their representatives in non-union businesses. If such an agreement is not made then the Act contains a model scheme that will apply. Third, the Part-time Work Directive 1997 aimed to remove discrimination against part-time workers, improve the quality of part-time work and facilitate the development of part-time work on a voluntary basis. Again, the UK law giving effect to the Directive is the Employment Relations Act 1999. The first two aims of the Directive recognise that, traditionally, part-time workers have not necessarily enjoyed the same benefits as their full-time counterparts, for example in terms of sick pay provision and access to training. The third aim is designed to contribute to the flexible organisation of working time by making part-time work more attractive to workers, thereby easing employers' operation of a more flexible workforce. Fourth, the Fixed-Term Workers Directive has similar aims to that on part-time work for those employed on fixed-term contracts. In addition, legislation requires the following: objective reasons for the renewal of fixed-term contracts; a limit on the number of renewals; and/or a limit on the total duration of successive fixed-term employment contracts. The fifth Directive concerns Equal Treatment in Employment and Occupations and came into force in 2000. Following similar principles to those dealing with race and sex discrimination (*see* Chapter 8), it prohibits both direct and indirect discrimination on the grounds of religion or belief, disability, age or sexual orientation.

In addition, the National Information and Consultation Directive 2002 provides for information and consultation arrangements among firms employing 50 or more workers. It seeks to ensure firms operating in only one country operate similar practices to those companies that are covered by the European Works Council Directive. The details of this Directive are considered in the next chapter. The Directive on Temporary Agency Work was finally agreed in 2008, some six years after it was first proposed. This Directive requires, subject to certain conditions, that agency-supplied workers should receive terms and conditions of employment that are comparable to those given to permanent members of staff.

The impact of each Directive or decision will vary depending on the employment characteristics of the individual business. It is clear, however, that European social policy will continue to have a significant impact on UK employment relations and that managers responsible for making people resourcing decisions in organisations will need to take account of its increasing influence on these matters.

MANAGEMENT STRATEGIES AND EMPLOYMENT RELATIONS

The previous section has indicated how public policy can influence the conduct of employment relations. Nonetheless, employers still retain significant scope in deciding how the employment relationship will be managed. In what can be seen as a seminal work on approaches to employment relations, Fox (1966) drew a distinction between two 'frames of reference' which underpin managerial action – the unitary and the pluralistic. The unitary view supposes an identity of interests between employer and employee with a single source of authority (managerial) and a sole focus of loyalty (the organisation's goals). Drawing on the team analogy, the unitary view perceives conflict to be irrational, the result of misunderstandings or poor communication. Trade unions are seen as an intrusion into the organisation which competes with management for the loyalty of employees. Pluralism, on the other hand, assumes that the organisation is composed of groups of individuals who have legitimate, competing interests. Conflict is seen as an inevitable result of these groups seeking to further their own interests. Trade unions exist as the legitimate representative agent of employees, expressing the inherent conflict in their relationship with management. The role of management is therefore one of seeking to reconcile these inevitable conflicts in their decision-making.

Influential as these theories remain, the 'debate has moved on' (Edwards, 2003: 12). In particular, some writers claim to have identified a *neo-unitary* (Farnham and Pimlott, 1995) or *sophisticated unitary* (Scott, 1994) perspective. Here the loyalty of employees cannot be assumed as implied by the traditional unitary view, but commitment needs to be fostered by employers, typically through the adoption of contemporary human resource management techniques (Storey, 1992a). Characterising neo-unitary theory, Farnham and Pimlott argue that:

> Its main aim seems to be to integrate employees, as individuals, into the companies in which they work. Its orientation is distinctly market centred, managerialistic and individualistic. By gaining employee commitment to quality production, customer needs and job flexibility, employers embracing this frame of reference have expectations of employee loyalty, customer satisfaction and product security in increasingly competitive market conditions. **(Farnham and Pimlott, 1995: 46)**

One key feature that emerges from this approach is a focus on the individual employee rather than concern with the collective relationship. This would seem to be compatible with the rise of contemporary HRM practices and the direction of public policy throughout the past 30 years. However, there is evidence that the collective relationship remains significant in many organisations (Millward *et al.*, 2000).

Building on the implications of this view for management style, Purcell and Ahlstrand (1994) argue that individualism and collectivism are not necessarily polar opposites but rather two dimensions which, when combined, can illustrate ideal types of employee relations management style. According to these authors, individualism refers to:

> the extent to which the enterprise views its employees either as individuals with needs, aspirations, competencies and particular skills of their own, or treats them as homogeneous blocks of people, with personnel and payment policies unable to distinguish between individuals and individual performance.
>
> **(Purcell and Ahlstrand, 1994: 179)**

Collectivism, on the other hand, is closely related to the pluralist perspective and the question for management is:

> whether to oppose, condone, or encourage the emergence of the collective labour organisation, and to ask what sort of relationship should be developed with it. Pluralism in this sense is about power sources and power sharing.
>
> (Purcell and Ahlstrand, 1994: 183)

Individualism, they suggest, has three distinct points on its dimension. At the lowest level the cost of labour is to be minimised: employees simply have commodity status, to be bought from the external labour market when demand requires and to be shed if demand for services declines. At the top of the scale, employees are regarded as a valuable resource, to be trained and developed accordingly, since greater emphasis is placed on the internal labour market. In between these, Purcell and Ahlstrand suggest a paternalist approach where companies have a tradition of welfare-based policies which seek to elicit loyalty from the employees.

Similarly, the collectivism dimension has three points on its scale. At its lowest point it refers to the classic unitary position of resisting union involvement, with (active) discouragement of employees to form any independent collective grouping. The centre position is characterised as an adversarial one. In the negotiating sense it implies a distributive form of bargaining (*see* Chapter 16) where compromise agreement between exaggerated positions is reached. A cooperative relationship implies a partnership between management and unions where joint, formal and informal approaches are taken to resolve problems between employees and employers. Combining these two dimensions produces a matrix with resulting management styles, as shown in Figure 15.1.

Figure 15.1 The management style matrix

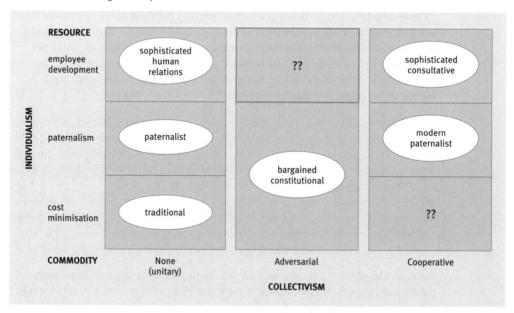

Source: Purcell and Ahlstrand (1994) *HRM in the Multi-divisional Company*. Reproduced by permission of Oxford University Press.

Each of the boxes is given a short title which seeks to capture the essence of the resulting management style. Two of the boxes, however, contain question marks, since Purcell and Ahlstrand argue that these approaches are 'inherently unstable'. In the bottom right-hand corner a situation is posited of collective cooperation but exploitation of the individual – a position that is unlikely to remain viable for any period of time. Similarly, treating employees as a resource (as portrayed in the top middle box) while collective relations are adversarial is likely to be untenable in the long term. Although this model has been criticised, particularly in relation to the stages on the individual dimension (Marchington and Parker, 1990; Storey, 1992b), it does offer a useful analytical framework for understanding the complexity (and possible tensions) of managerial style in employment relations. In particular, Purcell and Ahlstrand recognise the dynamic nature of the process and suggest that it is possible to use the matrix to trace changes in managerial style. For example, an organisation which de-recognises trade unions and adopts strategies typical of contemporary HRM may be seen to be moving from, say, an adversarial to a sophisticated human relations style. On the other hand, the adoption of practices designed to develop the existing workforce while seeking a more cooperative relationship with recognised unions may suggest a move from an adversarial to a sophisticated consultative style; perhaps characteristic of partnership agreements (*see* Chapter 16).

TRADE UNIONS

The changes evident in the field of employment relations have had far-reaching implications for trade unions. In 1979 some 55 per cent of the workforce were in union membership, collective bargaining was the primary method in the UK of determining terms and conditions of employment, and unions were a key party in the development of public policy on economic and social matters as well as on industrial relations itself. By the early part of this century, union membership had fallen dramatically, and it is estimated that in firms employing 10 or more workers only some 34 per cent of workers are members of a trade union (Kersley *et al.*, 2006). Collective bargaining now sets rates of pay for 40 per cent of employees (Kersley *et al.*, op. cit.) and trade unions have been largely excluded from the determination of public policy. The decline in union membership is most notable in private sector workplaces. Here, the *Workplace Employment Relations Survey* (WERS) 2004 (Kersley *et al.*, 2006) estimates that only 22 per cent of workers are in a union, while 64 per cent of those working in public sector jobs are union members. A number of explanations have been put forward to explain the decline in union membership. Williams and Adam-Smith (2005: 180–1) summarise them as follows:

- the decline of male manual jobs in the manufacturing industries where unions were traditionally well organised
- a weakening of the 'collective identity' among workers which underpins union solidarity
- the growth in unemployment during the 1980s which led to an initial, significant decline in membership
- greater employer hostility towards trade unions
- relatedly, the political climate created by Conservative governments which allowed managers to bypass unions or exclude them from the workplace

● the apparent unwillingness of unions to be more proactive in seeking to recruit new members.

The authors point out that none of these developments alone can explain the decline in union membership. They suggest that a complex interrelationship of the factors is at work with some being more significant, at different times, over the last two decades. The combination of these factors has led to questions being asked as to whether unions have any future role to play, at least outside the public sector. Not all commentators, however, share the view of the inevitability of union decline, particularly when a Labour government was elected in 1997:

> Given . . . an easing of the hostile political climate and the efforts they themselves are making to expand their organizational capabilities, it seems clear that the trade unions will continue to maintain a presence in the future and may well even expand their influence.
> (Bradley *et al.*, 2000: 168)

Certainly, it appears that unions have stemmed the decline in their membership and some have achieved an increase in numbers (Blyton and Turnbull, 2004: 157). In this final section some of the prescriptions for overcoming the malaise in which unions find themselves will be explored.

Union mergers

Although union membership had been on a generally upward trend throughout the twentieth century until 1979, the number of trade unions had steadily declined, primarily through a process of merger and amalgamation. Since 1979 this has continued and there are now around 170 trade unions recorded by the Certification Officer for Trade Unions and Employers' Associations (Certification Officer, 2008). This offers one long-term solution for the unions. That is, the creation of a small number of very large, and potentially powerful, unions covering a range of occupations and industries able to negotiate with employers from a position of numerical strength. However, the process to date has been generally *ad hoc* and thus some form of strategic basis, perhaps emanating from the Trades Union Congress, would be needed. As the TUC (1991) noted nearly 20 years ago:

> the underlying motives of most contemporary mergers are defensive, or consolidatory, rather than expansionist . . . the merger process will continue and grow . . . Yet it will not lead to any discernible ideal 'model' or optimum union size . . . [the structure of] British unions will look as illogical and unplanned as before [although] . . . they will be much leaner and fitter; with more effective and improved services.
> (in Kessler and Bayliss, 1998: 171)

However, the trend towards larger unions seems set to continue, and several significant mergers have occurred in the 2000s. The outcome of this process will be a small number of very large unions with highly diverse memberships. However, as Blyton and Turnbull (2004: 161) note, 'while centralized financial control may improve the administrative efficiency of these "super-unions", problems of representative effectiveness may actually be exacerbated'.

New partnerships

A number of variants of this approach can be discerned. What is broadly in common is that:

> . . . social partnership with employers assumed that areas of 'common interest' between unions and employers could form the basis of partnerships of mutual benefit.   (Waddington, 2003: 235)

This view suggests that unions will need to accept the shift in power towards employers and engage in new forms of relationships with them. In its guise of 'new realism' this might include partnership agreements (*see* Chapter 16). For unions the approach can be portrayed as offering employers benefits through recognising (or continuing to recognise) a trade union. As organisations adopt contemporary HRM techniques (with or without a strategic focus), Guest (1995) argued that unions should champion the cause rather than oppose it. Many of the core elements of contemporary HRM, at least in its 'soft' formulation, are compatible with the objectives of trade unions and offer fertile ground for unions, thus:

> By seeking partnership at the company level, unions may work to their own strengths and influence policy at the level where the important issues still seem to be decided. HRM may provide unions with one of their best chances of survival.
> (Guest, 1995: 136)

Certainly there is growing evidence that the initial hostility of unions towards contemporary HRM practices is softening and it is being seen as offering new grounds for bargaining.

The servicing model of trade unions

This strategy requires unions to develop a range of services to their members which may partly reflect the decline in the collectivist dimension in employment. Acceptance of the individualisation of the employment relationship may provide opportunities for unions to offer assistance on individual grievances, disciplinary and dismissal cases, as well as advice to those working on individual contracts. For example, the right of workers to be accompanied at formal grievance and disciplinary interviews by a union representative offers unions a route to demonstrate to workers the benefits of membership. However, services can be offered beyond the immediate workplace and include:

> discounted insurance on holidays, cars and housing; credit card facilities; personal loans and mortgage arrangements; and independent tax, financial and pensions advice.   (Waddington, 2003: 240)

Although the contemporary nature of some services (travel and finance, for instance) may reflect growing affluence, the adoption of the principles of traditional services is not new to unions. Indeed Webb and Webb (1896) identified the provision of such benefits of 'mutual insurance' as one method used by unions to protect their members' interests. While recognising the wider aspirations of workers, Hyman (1994: 134) suggests caution is needed in terms of the primary function of unions: 'an organisation whose sole or dominant identity is to provide commercial services to discrete customers is not easily recognizable as a trade union'. Further, Waddington (2003) suggests that the provision of such services has had no significant effect on increasing union membership.

Organising unionism

One further strategy that remains open to trade unions as their traditional membership among manual, full-time employees in the manufacturing sector declines, is to seek to build membership from among new groups of employees. If there is some compatibility between union objectives and 'soft' HRM, then equally there are grounds for arguing that those workers exposed to its 'hard' variant, those treated as 'commodity' status, could benefit from union membership.

Organising unionism is a term often applied to deliberate campaigns launched by unions to increase their membership through recruitment, sometimes of groups of workers neglected by the union in the past. However, as Heery *et al.* (2000) point out, this approach is not just about recruitment: rather, 'organising' requires resources to be devoted to building the workplace organisation of the union. This, it is argued, will not only help retain membership, but may also provide the basis for extending membership even further. A further feature of this approach is the use of specialised union-trained recruitment officials, often with experience of managing campaigns outside the union movement, in contrast to using existing union officials.

As a strategic response by unions, the organising approach owes much to the successful experience of unions in Australia and the United States. Some evidence that these lessons are being recognised by the union movement is shown in the analysis of the then Transport and General Workers Union (now part of UNITE) 'Link Up' campaign of the early 1990s (Snape, 1994). This was designed to recruit into membership those groups, including part-time and contract workers, that were traditionally unorganised. Although limited in its success, the campaign had a clearly articulated aim which was:

> to present a positive image to the wider community, playing down the view of unions as representatives of a narrow sectional interest group, linking recruitment with the social aims of the union, and emphasising community as well as workplace involvement.
> (Snape, 1994: 231)

However, the findings of Wrench and Virdee (1996) show that there may be a need for unions to go beyond their traditional areas of concern if they are to be successful in demonstrating the value of unionism to previously under-represented groups of workers. They report the findings of two case studies where trade unions had sought to recruit predominately female ethnic minority workers in low paid, insecure employment. The limited success achieved led them to conclude that:

> the trade union movement has no hope of bringing unionisation to these workers unless it works in co-operation with communities and links unionisation to broader issues such as workplace discrimination, sexual and racial harassment at the workplace, health and safety, cultural, linguistic and religious rights, harassment by the police and immigration authorities and so on.
> (Wrench and Virdee, 1996: 273)

The limited success of these initiatives suggests that trade unions have some distance to travel before these elements of the 'peripheral workforce' see any benefits in union membership. Clearly these strategies of structural adjustment, new partnerships, benefits and new membership markets are not mutually exclusive. What they have in common is the need for unions to become more proactive in their approach to recruitment and to demonstrate positively the benefits that unions offer workers and employers.

SUMMARY LEARNING POINTS

1 The past 30 years have witnessed radical changes to British employment relations. A series of governments hostile to trade unions and the principle of collective relations have, through legislation and economic and social policy, dramatically weakened trade unions and shifted the power in the employment relationship in favour of management.

2 Following the election of Labour governments in 1997, 2001 and 2005, employment relations have witnessed further changes. It remains unlikely, however, that these will lead to a return to the corporatist approach characteristic of the 1970s.

3 Those managers within organisations responsible for people resourcing decisions need to consider the impact of legislation providing a National Minimum Wage and statutory provisions for union recognition.

4 The signing of the Social Chapter by the UK government, together with further Directives from Europe, mean that developments in European social policy will continue to affect resourcing decisions.

5 Faced with greater choice resulting from the shift in bargaining power in the employment relationship, organisations have been able to adopt an employment relations style which may retain a role for trade unions or signal a move towards a more individualistic relationship.

6 In these circumstances trade unions have been forced to seek new directions for their role as the representative of workers.

REFERENCES AND FURTHER READING

Adam-Smith, D., Goss, D. and Bairstow, S. (2001) 'Coming to terms with New Labour('s) laws', *Employee Relations Review*, 12, 3–9.

Adam-Smith, D., Norris, G. and Williams, S. (2003) 'Continuity or Change? The implications of the National Minimum Wage for work and employment in the hospitality industry', *Work, Employment and Society*, 17(1), 29–45.

Auerbach, S. (1990) *Legislating for Conflict*. Oxford: Clarendon Press.

Bach, S. and Della Rocha, G. (2000) 'The management strategies of public service employers in Europe', *Industrial Relations Journal*, 31(2), 82–96.

Barley, S. and Kunda, G. (2004) *Gurus, Hired Guns, and Warm Bodies*. Princeton NJ: Princeton University Press.

Beatson, M. (1995) 'Progress towards a flexible labour market', *Employment Gazette*, February, 55–66.

Blyton, P. and Turnbull, P. (2004) *The Dynamics of Employee Relations*. Basingstoke: Macmillan.

Bradley, H., Erickson, M., Stephenson, C. and Williams, S. (2000) *Myths at Work*. Cambridge: Polity.

Brown, W., Deakin, S., Hudson, M. and Pratten, C. (2001) 'The limits of statutory union recognition', *Industrial Relations Journal*, 32(3), 180–94.

Central Arbitration Committee (2008) *Annual Report 2007–08*. London: Central Arbitration Committee.

Certification Officer (2008) *Annual Report 2007–2008*, www.certoffice.org/annual-report, accessed May 2009.

Crouch, C. (1982) *The Politics of Industrial Relations*. London: Fontana.

Crouch, C. (1995) 'The State: economic management and incomes policy', in Edwards, P. (ed.) *Industrial Relations: Theory and practice in Britain*. Oxford: Blackwell.

Dickens, L. and Hall, M. (1995) 'The State: labour law and industrial relations', in Edwards, P. (ed.) *Industrial Relations: Theory and practice in Britain*. Oxford: Blackwell.

Edwards, P. (2003) 'The employment relationship' in Edwards, P. (ed.) *Industrial Relations: Theory and practice in Britain* (2nd edn). Oxford: Blackwell.

Farnham, D. and Horton, S. (eds) (1993) *Managing the New Public Services*. Basingstoke: Macmillan.

Farnham, D. and Pimlott, J. (1995) *Understanding Industrial Relations*. London: Cassell.

Fox, A. (1966) 'Industrial sociology and industrial relations', *Royal Commission Research Paper No. 3*. London: HMSO.

Fredman, S. and Morris, G. (1989) 'The state as employer: setting a new example', *Personnel Management*, August, 25–9.

Gall, G. (2007) 'Trade union recognition in Britain: an emerging crisis for trade unions?' *Economic and Industrial Democracy*, 28(1), 78–109.

Giddens, A. (1998) *The Third Way*. Cambridge: Polity.

Gregg, P., Knight, G. and Wadsworth, J. (2000) 'Heaven knows I'm miserable now: job insecurity in the British labour market', in Heery, E. and Salmon, J. (eds) *The Insecure Workforce*. London: Routledge.

Guest, D. (1995) 'Human resource management, trade unions and industrial relations', in Storey, J. (ed.) *Human Resource Management: A critical text*. London: Routledge.

Hall, M. (1994) 'Industrial relations and the social dimension of European integration: before and after Maastricht', in Hyman, R. and Fenner, A. (eds) *New Frontiers in Industrial Relations*. Oxford: Blackwell.

Heery, E., Simms, M. Delbridge, R., Salmon, J. and Simpson, D. (2000) 'Union Organizing in Britain: a survey of policy and practice', *International Journal of Human Resource Management*, 11(5), 986–1007.

Howell, C. (2005) *Trade Unions and the State*. Princeton NJ: Princeton University Press.

Hyman, R. (1994) 'Changing trade union identities and strategies', in Hyman, R. and Fenner, A. (eds) *New Frontiers in Industrial Relations*. Oxford: Blackwell.

Hyman, R. (1995) 'The historical evolution of British industrial relations', in Edwards, P. (ed.) *Industrial Relations: Theory and practice in Britain*. Oxford: Blackwell.

Kersley, B., Alpin, C., Forth, J., Bryson, A., Bewley, H., Dix, G. and Oxenbridge, S. (2006) *Inside the Workplace: Findings of the 2004 Workplace Employment Relations Survey*. Abingdon: Routledge.

Kessler, S. and Bayliss, F. (1998) *Contemporary British Industrial Relations*. Basingstoke: Macmillan.

Leadbeater, C. (1999) *Living on Thin Air*. London:Viking.

Low Pay Commission (LPC) (2001) *The National Minimum Wage: Making a difference: The next steps*, Third report, June, www.lowpay.gov.uk/lowpay/rep_a_p_index.shtml.

Marchington, M. and Parker, P. (1990) *Changing Patterns of Employee Relations*. Hemel Hempstead: Harvester Wheatsheaf.

Millward, N., Bryson, A. and Forth, J. (2000) *All Change at Work? British employment relations 1980–1998, as depicted by the Workplace Industrial Relations Survey series*. London: Routledge.

Nuti, D. (1999) 'Making sense of the Third Way', *British Strategy Review*, 10(3).

Purcell, J. and Ahlstrand, B. (1994) *Human Resource Management in the Multidivisional Company*. Oxford: Oxford University Press.

Scott, A. (1994) *Willing Slaves? British Workers Under Human Resource Management*. Cambridge: Cambridge University Press.

Sisson, K. (1991) 'Industrial relations', *Employee Relations*, 13(6), 3–10.

Smith, P. and Morton, G. (2001) 'New Labour's reform of Britain's employment law: the devil is not only in the detail but in the values and policy too', *British Journal of Industrial Relations*, 39(1), 119–38.

Snape, E. (1994) 'Reversing the decline? The TGWU's Link Up campaign', *Industrial Relations Journal*, 25(3), 222–33.

Storey, J. (1992a) *Developments in the Management of Human Resources*. Oxford: Blackwell.

Storey, J. (1992b) 'HRM in action: the truth is out at last', *Personnel Management*, April, 28–31.

Towers, B. and Brown, W. (2000) *Employment Relations in Britain: 25 years of the Advisory, Conciliation and Arbitration Service*. Oxford: Blackwell.

TUC (1991) *Unions in Europe in the 1990s*. London: TUC.

TUC (1999) *Partners in Progress: New Unionism in the Workplace*. London: Trades Union Congress.

Trades Union Congress (2003) *Trade Union Trends: Recognition Survey*. London: TUC.

Undy, R. (1999) 'Annual review article: New Labour's "Industrial Relations Settlement": the Third Way?' *British Journal of Industrial Relations*, 37(2), 315–36.

Waddington, J. (2003) 'Trade Union Organization', in Edwards, P. (ed.) *Industrial Relations: Theory and Practice* (2nd edn). Oxford: Blackwell.

Webb, S. and Webb, B. (1896) *The History of Trade Unions*. London: Longman.

Williams, S. and Adam-Smith, D. (2005) *Contemporary Employment Relations: a critical introduction*. Oxford: Oxford University Press.

Winchester, D. and Bach, S. (2003) 'Industria Relations in the Public Sector', in Edwards, P. (ed.) *Industrial Relations: Theory and practice in Britain*. Oxford: Blackwell.

Wrench, J. and Virdee, S. (1996) 'Organising the unorganised: race, poor work and trade unions', in Ackers, P., Smith, C. and Smith, P. (eds) *The New Workplace and Trade Unionism*. London: Routledge.

Younson, F. (2000) 'How to handle a union recognition claim', *People Management*, 20 July, 44–6.

ASSIGNMENTS AND DISCUSSION TOPICS

1 Choose an organisation with which you are familiar, or an organisation whose employment matters have been documented in the press, and assess what style of employment relations management (*see* Figure 15.1) has been adopted. You should identify specific illustrations for both the collective and individual dimensions. Is there any evidence that management are attempting to change their style? If so, how are they changing and for what reasons?

2 Do trade unions still have a role in contemporary employment relations or are they an institution which is past its 'sell by date'? Why?

3 What benefits do employers gain from recognising trade unions as the representative of employees?

4 Has the balance of power in the employment relationship swung too far in favour of management?

5 Is the statutory trade union recognition procedure a defence of the human rights of workers or an unnecessary and intrusive interference of managers' right to manage?

6 Assess the advantages and disadvantages for employers, trade unions and employees of the National Minimum Wage.

7 To what extent, and for what reasons, is it now more appropriate to talk about *European* employment relations rather than British employment relations?

Chapter 16

Employment Relations Processes

by Derek Adam-Smith

LEARNING OUTCOMES: TO BE ABLE TO

- Explain the role employment relations processes have in the effective resourcing of organisations

- Assess the key changes that have taken place in collective bargaining and pay determination

- Identify and explain the ways in which employment relations is managed in organisations that do not recognise trade unions

- Evaluate the contribution that employee involvement practices can make to organisational performance

- Appreciate the nature and process of employment relations negotiations

INTRODUCTION

The previous chapter explored some of the ways in which the British context of employment relations has changed over the past 30 years, and the responses of both employers and trade unions to the new environment within which they operate. As a result of these developments the processes of employment relations, particularly the structure of collective bargaining, have been modified to meet new organisational circumstances and objectives. At the same time, new approaches to managing the employment relationship have been introduced. Nonetheless, it is possible to detect some continuity in the way in which decisions over the wage for work bargain are made.

EMPLOYMENT RELATIONS POLICIES AND PEOPLE RESOURCING

Employment relations issues can be viewed as one particular aspect of the broader decisions that relate to the effective resourcing of organisations with people. Decisions regarding the recognition of trade unions and the way in which that relationship is structured, how non-union employees' terms and conditions will be determined, and the relevance and choice of forms of communication and involvement should logically flow from the broader HR strategies pursued by the organisation. The clear message is that in order to provide for consistency there needs to be a framework of general principles to aid managers in day-to-day decision-making. At the same time, a codified employment relations policy can be evaluated continuously to ensure its appropriateness as internal and external circumstances change. However, employment policies do not operate in isolation from other parts of the business. Over 35 years ago the Commission on Industrial Relations argued that an organisation's strategy for the management of people at work should flow from and be closely allied to its overall business strategy (CIR, 1973). The advent of contemporary HRM philosophies as an alternative conceptualisation of the employment relationship proposes a greater emphasis on the need for organisations to integrate employment and business strategies. Commenting on the movement from formalisation and collectivism to flexibility and individualism implicit within the contemporary HRM practice, Salamon notes that:

> this shift . . . has been the product of a strategic review by management of its industrial relations system to meet external pressures and constraints (in particular its economic environment) and, not least, to support and integrate more closely with its business objectives.
> (Salamon, 1998: 455)

However, it is important to recognise the complexity associated with setting medium- to long-term strategies. As Sisson and Marginson (2003: 160) note: 'strategies . . . may simply be a series of vague statements or a few key financial ratios'. Nonetheless, it is claimed that HR managers can make a difference to organisational success by operating at a strategic level within organisations (see Ulrich, 1997; Ulrich and Brockbank, 2005). In these cases, it is reasonable to expect those in these roles to be in a position to guide the organisation in the development of employment relations policies.

Where there is some form of proactive organisational policy for employment relations, Salamon (1998) suggests that the issues requiring consideration can be grouped under five headings.

Managerial principles – Primary importance here is the issue of the managerial prerogative, that is, the extent to which management seeks freedom of action to make operational decisions. If there is a policy not to recognise trade unions then the only constraint affecting management is that contained in legal provisions. Even if unions are recognised then management may seek to limit formally the matters which will be subject to collective bargaining. In addition, employers may seek to ensure that they retain the right for managers to communicate directly with employees rather than through trade union channels.

The relationship between management and employees – The second group of issues is concerned with the extent to which employees are valued as an asset of the organisation, their right to be treated fairly in grievance and disciplinary matters, and their right to join a trade union. The basis on which trade unions will be recognised may form part of such considerations.

The determination of terms and conditions of employment – Issues to be addressed here include the development of equitable payment systems, the relationship between productivity and terms of employment, the use of collective bargaining, consultation and other mechanisms for dealing with employment matters.

Meeting mutual expectations – The application of appropriate methods of human resource planning, recruitment, training, motivation, promotion and termination which will achieve an appropriate balance between organisational requirements for a trained and experienced workforce with employees' needs for employment security.

The role of procedures – The use of procedures, perhaps developed with employee and/or trade union involvement, to resolve effectively employment differences between the parties.

Clearly the nature and content of an organisation's employment relations policy will be influenced by a number of factors. These include technological and economic circumstances, ownership (public service or private profit-making), organisation size, and market and business objectives. An understanding of the choices open to organisations is consequently of importance to managers responsible for people resourcing decisions. As Sisson and Marginson (2003: 182) argue:

> Management industrial relations practice in Britain is characterized by immense variety . . . [reflecting] the fact that British managers have had considerable scope to exercise choice in what they do. Such practice is not entirely random, however. Much of it can be related to specific structural features.

COLLECTIVE BARGAINING STRUCTURE

Collective bargaining may be defined as the method of determining terms and conditions of employment through the process of negotiation between representatives of employers (normally management) and employees (typically trade union officials). It is thus a method of 'joint' decision-making which implies a need for agreement to be reached between the two negotiating parties. The outcomes of such negotiations are termed collective agreements.

Where organisations recognise trade unions for the purpose of collective bargaining managers have a degree of choice over how they structure this relationship. Of course, since collective bargaining involves reaching an agreement, it is important to bear in mind that the interests of unions and workers, and the power they are able to exercise may constrain management's freedom. Three key features of collective bargaining structure are important to an understanding of this formal relationship, and which help explain the different arrangements which may be found in organisations – 'bargaining levels', 'units', and 'scope'.

The first element is the *level*, or levels, at which bargaining takes place. This may involve multi-employer bargaining between employers' associations and trade unions at industry level and produce national collective agreements. While still common in parts of the public sector, the use of multi-employer bargaining has almost completely disappeared from the private sector. Bargaining may also take place at the company level or at the level of the establishment (in multi-site organisations). Of course, an employer's choice is not confined to only one level. An employee's terms of employment may be made up of elements from national, company and establishment agreements. For example, a company level agreement may set sickness pay entitlement and annual holidays, while pay rates may be the result of bargaining at the establishment level. In this example, staff working at different sites would receive the same annual holidays, but receive different rates of pay. The second element is the bargaining *unit* (or units). The bargaining unit refers to the group of employees covered by a particular agreement or set of agreements and may vary in number from company to company. As we saw in the previous chapter, the determination of the bargaining unit may be critical to the decision of whether a union is successful or not in a claim under the statutory recognition procedure. In the example above, holiday entitlement is negotiated for all employees and thus there is only one bargaining unit within the company for that matter. However, since pay rates are determined at each site there will be a number of bargaining units covering each group of workers in each site.

The final element in the bargaining structure concerns the *scope* of collective bargaining. This refers to the subject matter covered by the collective agreements. Again, the content of collective agreements will vary from organisation to organisation and, perhaps, within different bargaining units. While pay rates are common items covered by negotiation, a wide range of other topics may also be the subject of collective bargaining. These include hours of work, staffing levels, physical working conditions, the introduction of new technology and redundancy matters. The broad strategy of trade unions is to extend the scope of collective bargaining by seeking to negotiate over an increased range of topics, while management may wish to limit the matters which are subject to joint regulation. Where the scope of collective bargaining ends, the right to manage, or the managerial prerogative, begins. Thus the degree of managerial resistance to the extension of collective bargaining will depend upon their wish to make decisions without obtaining trade union agreement, and their ability to enforce this intention.

TRENDS IN COLLECTIVE BARGAINING

As a dynamic process it is likely that the arrangements for collective bargaining will change over time to take account of new circumstances. As bargaining power has swung in favour of management there have been managerial initiatives to tailor bargaining structures more closely to business objectives. As far as the scope of matters is covered, there appears to be little change in recent years in the topics over which bargaining takes place. Data from the 2004 *Workplace Employment Relations Survey* (WERS) (Kersley *et al.*, 2006: 194) shows that 'mainstream' topics dominate the bargaining agenda: 'Sixty-one per cent of workplaces which recognized unions normally negotiated over pay, one half negotiated over hours and holidays, more than one-third negotiated over pensions and over a quarter negotiated grievance and disciplinary procedures.' Other issues that were negotiated by management with trade unions include equal opportunities, health and safety matters and performance appraisal schemes; a small minority of firms also bargained over training, staffing planning and recruitment and selection. However, the *WERS* data reveal that these other matters were negotiated in a very small number of workplaces. This would tend to suggest that employers are largely able to restrict bargaining to a narrow range of items, reflecting the way in which power has swung in favour of management including to those that retain a collective relationship with trade unions. Thus the extent and changes over time in the 'scope' of collective bargaining provides us with an indicator of shifts in the bargaining relationship.

A far more significant trend in collective bargaining has been the decline in the coverage of collective bargaining in the UK, both in terms of its incidence and the number of employees covered by collective agreements on pay and other terms and conditions of employment. The *WERS* findings on collective bargaining coverage are shown in Exhibit 16.1.

A number of key points can be made from the data shown in Exhibit 16.1. Most notably, collective bargaining occurs only in a little over a quarter of all workplaces; in the previous survey in 1998, the corresponding figure was 30 per cent. However, the continuing decline in the overall incidence masks a significant difference between the public and private sectors. In the former, collective bargaining took place in 83 per cent of all workplaces, but in the private sector the corresponding figure was only 14 per cent, down from 17 per cent in 1998. Outside the public sector there are wide variations in the coverage of collective bargaining. While its incidence remains high in gas, water and electricity, in hotels and restaurants, wholesale and retail, and other business services it is markedly low, reflecting the problems unions have faced in recruiting workers in these industries, and in persuading management of the value of union recognition.

The *WERS* also reported on the way the extent of collective bargaining varied in relation to the numbers employed in the workplace, and the size of the organisation. As the size of each increases, so does then incidence of collective bargaining. Collective bargaining occurs in more than half of all workplaces with over 200 employees (two-thirds in those over 500 employees), and covers well over half of all employees. In comparison, in workplaces with between 10 and 24 employees, only 19 per cent of workplaces reported the use of collective bargaining, and here it covered only 19 per cent of workers. As far as organisation size is concerned, collective bargaining covers over half of all workers in firms employing a thousand or more workers.

It is possible to see collective bargaining as a process of declining importance in the landscape of employment relations, confined to large private sector employers and the public sector. While this is not an unreasonable conclusion to draw, the decline needs to be put in perspective. Although not as significant as 30 years ago, collective bargaining

EXHIBIT 16.1 Collective bargaining coverage by sector and industry

Sector or industry	Workplaces with any collective bargaining (%)	Employees covered by collective bargaining (%)
All workplaces	27	40
Private sector	14	26
Public sector	83	82
Manufacturing	20	39
Electricity, gas and water	96	87
Construction	17	26
Wholesale and retail	9	17
Hotels and restaurants	2	5
Transport and communication	43	63
Financial services	63	49
Other business services	10	12
Public administration	93	90
Education	67	58
Health and social work	36	60
Other community services	32	46

Source: Kersley *et al.* (2006: 180).

still determines many of the central elements of the employment contract, such as pay, for nearly half of those at work. Further, since pay rates in these organisations may set a benchmark for other businesses, the influence of collective bargaining on employment terms remains significant. As Kersley *et al.* (2006: 181) note: '[the] wide variations in the coverage of collective bargaining at the workplace level is an important feature of pay setting in Britain, one that is often overlooked by those who simply dismiss joint regulation over pay and conditions as a thing of the past.'

Pay review bodies

While collective bargaining remains the dominant method of pay determination in the public sector, a notable feature here has been the introduction of pay review bodies

(PRB) to cover a number of public sector occupations. These bodies are established by government, but operate, in theory at least, independent of the government, and are charged with making recommendations on pay increases for specific groups of workers. The proposed pay increases are determined based on submissions from trade unions, employers and other interested parties. The review bodies covering doctors, dentists, senior civil servants and the armed forces have existed since the 1960s. Additional bodies were created to cover nurses, midwives and health visitors in 1983 and schoolteachers in 1991. A pay review body was created for prison officers in 2001.

For governments, concerned with ensuring order in the delivery of public services, PRBs are attractive since they appear to offer a more rational approach to pay determination than may be found in the more conflict-based process of collective bargaining (White, 2000). It is perhaps no surprise that the PRBs for nurses and related occupations, and schoolteachers were established following major industrial disputes. Those public sector workers covered by PRBs have tended to fair better in the pay increases than those where collective bargaining remains the method of wage determination. However, employers, for example health trusts and local authorities, tend to lose influence in the setting of pay rates for groups of their staff while still having to fund their cost.

However, as a form of pay determination, whether PRBs are distinct from collective bargaining or a particular type of it, has been the subject of debate (see, for example, Kersley *et al.*, 2006; Burchill, 2000). For those who see them as a variant of collective bargaining, their argument is that the review bodies mediate between the pay increase proposed by the unions and the case put forward by employers: 'mediation' being the substitute for face-to-face negotiation. The final recommendation is rarely far from each of the views of each of the parties.

Decentralised and single-table bargaining

While national or industry level collective bargaining remains influential in much of the public sector, a further noticeable trend over recent years in the private sector has been the move away from industry level bargaining to agreements being made at the level of the employer or site (in multi-site organisations). With very few exceptions, multi-employer bargaining no longer exists in the private sector. The ability of employers to shift the level of collective bargaining much closer to operational decision-making has been facilitated by the declining power of trade unions, discussed in the previous chapter. The main driving force behind the move to decentralised bargaining appears to be the need for management to tailor their pay policies and decisions more closely to wider organisational considerations which are themselves influenced by contextual factors (Brown and Walsh, 1991). Thus, where decisions over production, marketing and budgets have been decentralised, it is likely that managers at the business unit will take some responsibility for pay negotiations and other employment relations issues, albeit within limits set by higher management. Where bargaining has been located at lower levels in the organisation, unit managers are able to relate pay decisions to particular business circumstances, including the performance of the unit, productivity improvements and local labour market characteristics. The benefits that decentralised bargaining may provide as a means to improve labour productivity are summarised by Brown *et al.* (2003). They also draw attention to the link it has to the individualised employment relationship characteristic of HRM: 'When much skill acquisition is on-the-job, and when technological change is constant and incremental, there are advantages in having fluid job titles, predictable career trajectories, and stable internal salary structures. Enterprise bargaining fits in with the more individualistic treatment of employees . . . and it provides a ready base for enterprise-related incentive schemes' (Brown *et al.*, 2003: 200). Thus recent changes suggest that employers are more carefully considering the relationship between collective bargaining, and employment and business strategies.

Movements in the level of collective bargaining to a point closer to where other operational decisions are made are an illustration of managerial attempts to regain control over employment relations processes. However, collective bargaining arrangements are more complex where a number of bargaining units exist within an organisation. In these cases managers may find themselves having to negotiate separate pay increases with several different trade union representatives. Not only does this take time and involve repetitive meetings, but it may also be difficult for managers to coordinate the outcomes of a series of negotiations. In part these difficulties have been eased by the continuing process of merger and amalgamation of unions, but there is evidence that managers have sought additional ways to reduce the number of bargaining groups with which they have to deal (Millward *et al.*, 2000).

One managerial initiative aimed at securing simplified bargaining structures in multi-union firms is to introduce a single negotiating forum for all employees, manual and non-manual, covered by collective bargaining – an arrangement that has been called 'single-table bargaining' (STB). Although potentially strengthening the bargaining position of recognised trade unions and making the consequences of any industrial action far more serious, it appears that the advantages resulting from simplified bargaining arrangements and the prevention of 'leapfrogging' claims – as one bargaining group seeks to maintain its differential over another – outweigh these disadvantages. In a review of a number of companies that had introduced single-table bargaining, Incomes Data Services (IDS, 1995) found that, although often linked to major organisational change, there was no one specific reason for their introduction. Among those cited by companies were a move to decentralised pay bargaining providing the impetus to simplify the negotiating process; the breakdown of national bargaining arrangements creating a vacuum which allowed employers to establish STB; a need to survive in increasingly competitive markets prompting a review of working practices and STB being seen as a means to facilitate their introduction; a blurring in the distinction, first, between many manual jobs and, second, between white collar and manual work; and the move to STB being part of a policy to harmonise terms and conditions of employment.

There is strong evidence of an increase in the move to STB among many employers as part of a strategy to simplify bargaining arrangements:

> **Amongst workplaces where collective bargaining was the dominant form of pay setting, the proportion with single-table bargaining rose from 40 per cent in 1990 to 77 per cent in 1998. This shift, most marked in the public sector, but still very apparent in the private sector,** *possibly represents one of the most striking changes in the nature of British industrial relations in the 1990s.*
>
> **(Millward *et al.*, 2000: 203, emphasis added)**

Although the incidence of single-table bargaining appears to have declined to 60 per cent of all workplaces (Kersley *et al.*, 2006), it remains a prominent feature of contemporary bargaining structure. Trade unions appear broadly in favour of single-table bargaining since it may offer opportunities to widen the scope of collective bargaining. However, the process requires the unions to reach a consensus on their claim before meeting management, and this may prove difficult if each union has different priorities for the negotiations.

Partnership at work and partnership agreements

The past few years have witnessed a growing interest in 'partnership at work'. The precise meaning of partnership is the subject of some debate (Tailby and Winchester, 2000), as is the role, if any, that trade unions play in the process. For example, the Chartered Institute of Personnel and Development sees partnership being concerned more with 'an approach to the employment relationship between employees individually, than it has to do with trade unions' (IPD, 1997: 4). However, in the light of the decline in the coverage of collective bargaining, the particular feature of partnership agreements has led to attention being given to this development in employment relations. The key element appears to be a commitment from employees and unions to greater flexibility in working practices in return for improved employment security. Three main drivers for the development of this approach can be identified. First, the Labour government's attempt to find a formulation of its Third Way (*see* Chapter 15) appropriate to workplace relations. Second, the need of trade unions to demonstrate to employers that they continue to have a valuable role to play in the changed world of employment. Third, where employers chose to maintain a relationship with recognised trade unions, they have sought ways in which this relationship could assist in enhancing their competitiveness. Evidence from the experience of such arrangements in the United States, for example, suggests partnership approaches can facilitate the introduction of new working arrangements and lead to improved organisational performance.

An understanding of the principles of partnership at work can be gleaned from the views of the Trades Union Congress and the Involvement and Participation Association, an organisation with a long history of promoting partnership and involvement at work. Although there are some differences in emphasis between the two bodies, the key principles can be summarised as follows:

- shared commitment to the success of the business
- employment security for workers and workforce flexibility, coupled with appropriate training
- an emphasis on the quality of working life
- informing and consulting employees
- employee representation
- sharing of organisational success.

In assessing the evidence so far on partnership agreements in practice, Tailby and Winchester (2000) point out that while their content is not radically different from existing employment relations and HRM practices, the process of negotiating such agreements contains some atypical features. These include joint management and union presentations to employees and workplace representatives, the use of outside consultants to assist in developing the framework of the agreement, and a focus on longer-term horizons. They go on to state:

> In combination, these features of different phases of the negotiation process amount to the most distinctive characteristic of recent partnership agreements. In many cases, the language and rhetoric of agreements, and the close involvement of trade union officials in the management and legitimation of organisational culture-change programmes, imply an ideological break with past practice.
>
> (Tailby and Winchester, 2000: 383–4)

However, others have reservations regarding the significance of such agreements. Sisson and Marginson (2003: 173) note that it is 'very much a minority movement', that key aspects of the typical features are not commonly used, and conclude that 'The significance of partnership for British Industrial Relations is difficult to assess, in the light of its novelty and the imprecision with which the term is often used.' Similarly, based on his own research, Waddington (2003: 236) argues that 'many new agreements . . . have the title "partnership agreement" attached to them simply because of the political climate rather than the content of the agreement', and questions whether they are a useful measure of change in employment relations. Thus, whether partnership agreements herald a new permanent basis for collective relationships or are merely the latest 'fad' will need to await the judgement of time. As one full-time union officer, involved in developing a partnership approach at a company, commented: 'I don't think our members should fear it, but, I mean, you can't have 150 years of the gaffer putting the boot in and then all of a sudden expect everybody to flip over' (Marks *et al.*, 1998: 218).

INDIVIDUAL BARGAINING

All employees have an individual contract of employment, but where trade unions are recognised by the employer, pay and some other terms of employment may be determined through collective bargaining. In such cases the terms of the collective agreement or agreements are incorporated into the employee's contract of employment. However, in keeping with the growing *individualisation* of the employment relationship, those responsible for human resource matters need to decide how pay, and other terms and conditions of employment are to be determined: how will management's unilateral right be exercised?

Chapter 9 provides an examination of a range of alternatives, including performance-related and competency-based pay. While the outcome of such arrangements is often referred to as individual contracts, the extent of bargaining that takes place between the employer and individual employee is likely to be limited. It is unlikely that managers are willing to invest the time needed to review and negotiate terms with individual members of staff. Brown *et al.* (2000) have sought to clarify what individualism, in the context of settling terms and conditions of employment, means in practice. They draw attention to the distinction between 'procedural' and 'substantive' individualism. The former is linked to the trend, noted above, in the decline of collective bargaining as the procedure for agreeing terms and conditions of employment. Substantive individualism, on the other hand, refers to the extent to which differences can be indentified in contractual terms of individual employers within the same organisation, particularly those working in the same grade. The authors conclude that 'substantive individualism' is rare, and that 'a high degree of standardization of employment contracts [exists] within British workplaces, so far as both pay and non-pay entitlements are concerned' (Brown *et al.*, 2000: 627).

CONCILIATION, MEDIATION AND ARBITRATION

A key assumption of the negotiating process is that the two parties will reach an agreement to resolve the differences between them. However, it must be recognised that there will be circumstances where management and trade union representatives will not find a mutually acceptable solution and will register 'a failure to agree'. In these cases, conciliation, mediation and arbitration can be used as an alternative to industrial action. Each involves the introduction of a third party to assist in the resolution of the dispute. The differences in the three processes are shown in Exhibit 16.2. The key distinction is between conciliation and arbitration. In the former the conciliator seeks to help the parties negotiate their solution to the dispute, while the use of arbitration suggests that the negotiators are unable to resolve the matter themselves and request a third party to decide on the issue. Mediation can be seen to be something of a 'halfway house' between the other two.

EXHIBIT 16.2 **Third-party dispute resolution**

	Role	Approach to dispute resolution	How settlement reached
CONCILIATOR	'A CATALYST' seeking to narrow disagreements	Support negotiating process: help parties clarify objectives, extent of differences, identify possible solutions and find formulae to settle dispute; keep the parties talking	Responsibility for settlement rests jointly with the parties to the dispute
MEDIATOR	'A PROPOSER' of recommendations	More proactive approach than conciliation; from assessment of parties' written cases mediator makes proposals which may resolve dispute or provide basis for further negotiation	Responsibility with parties but mediator's views may be influential
ARBITRATOR	'An AWARD-MAKER' to end a dispute	Arbitrator or panel of arbitrators have agreed terms of reference from parties; take written and oral evidence and make an award based on the issues	Arbitrator decides on resolution of dispute; award usually binding on both parties

Pendulum arbitration

Some interest has emerged in the use of pendulum arbitration as a means of resolving disputes. In conventional arbitration the arbitrator may make an award anywhere between the management offer and union claim at the point at which the negotiations broke down. It is open to the criticism that arbitrators can be tempted to 'split the difference' between management and unions. Thus both parties have an incentive to keep their positions as close as possible to their preferred solution. However, in pendulum arbitration the arbitrator is required to find in favour of either the company or the trade union: a compromise solution is not allowed. Such a process, it is claimed, provides a strong incentive for both parties to reach a negotiated settlement rather than lose their case at arbitration: at least their respective final positions will be reasonable and equitable. In addition, should pendulum arbitration be used, the parties' final offer and final claim are likely to be fairly close so that neither is substantially dissatisfied with the award made.

There are, however, some difficulties associated with the process, including the following.

- If bargaining has not proceeded in 'good faith' then the arbitrator may be forced to choose between two unreasonable positions.

- There may be some difficulty in clarifying the precise final positions of the two parties – can these be changed between the breakdown of negotiations and submission of the reference to the arbitrator?

- Where a dispute concerns a group of items, deciding on one package may mean that the merits of each individual item are ignored. However, allowing the arbitrator to deal with each issue would mean that the arbitrator is producing his or her own package, thus undermining the key principle of pendulum arbitration.

There seems to be little evidence of the widespread adoption of pendulum arbitration in Britain. It can be argued, however, that pendulum arbitration forces a more realistic view to be taken by both management and unions and provides an alternative to industrial action in dispute resolution.

EXHIBIT 16.3 **Back to the future?**

In an engineering company in the north-east of Britain that had a collective agreement with the General, Municipal and Boilermakers Union, the agreement provided for the use of pendulum arbitration as an alternative to strikes as a means to resolve disputes. It had been used on five occasions to determine the annual pay awards when no negotiated settlement could be reached. Four of the five arbitrators' decisions had gone in favour of the trade union. Dissatisfied with this position management gave notice of their intention to end the agreement. The union's response was to threaten industrial action to protect the 'no-strike' agreement!

Source: *The Independent*, 30 August 1991. Reproduced by permission of *The Independent*.

THE NON-UNION ORGANISATION

While trade union presence and collective bargaining remain important features of employment relations in the public sector and parts of the private manufacturing industry, its decline in other parts of British industry and commerce has led to attention being focused on the way in which relations are conducted in non-union organisations. It is important to note that firms that do not recognise unions are not a homogeneous entity, but may vary considerably in the way that employment relations is managed. At one end of the spectrum are small, independent companies in which employment terms and working conditions are often poor: what Sisson (1993) characterised as 'bleak houses'. Even here, however, we should recognise that there may be considerable diversity between individual firms. At the other end are those businesses that are typically described as the 'household name' group of companies. These organisations, held up as examples of an alternative model for the conduct of employment relations, include IBM, Marks & Spencer, Hewlett Packard and Mars. Although recognising the possibility of over-generalisation, according to Blyton and Turnbull (2004) the characteristics of these non-union firms tend towards:

> a sense of caring, carefully chosen plant locations and working environments, market leadership, high growth and healthy profits, employment security, single status, promotion from within, an influential personnel department (and a high ratio of personnel staff to employees), competitive pay and benefit packages, profit sharing, open communications, and the careful selection and training of management, particularly at the supervisory level. (Blyton and Turnbull, 2004: 286)

In these firms there would appear to be evidence that the techniques associated with contemporary HRM are not only present but provide a clear guide to the development of employment policy and practice. It would seem, therefore, that each stage of Purcell and Ahlstrand's (1994) individualism axis – traditional unitary, paternalism and sophisticated human relations (*see* Chapter 15) – can be found in the non-union organisation.

In an attempt to expand on the nature of employment relations in the non-union firm, Guest and Hoque (1994) developed a typology of management approaches to employment relations. Although care needs to be taken with generalising from their work, since it was based on a survey of new firms in a particular sector and relied on management respondents, it does offer a useful framework for developing an initial understanding of characteristics of such organisations. These authors distinguish between employers that do not recognise trade unions as *good, bad, ugly* or *lucky*. Their distinction is based on whether the firm has a clear strategy for managing its human resources or not, and the extent to which it operates a range of human resource policies, such as employee involvement schemes, performance-related pay and sophisticated recruitment, selection and socialisation practices.

According to this distinction, *good* firms have both a clear HR strategy and make extensive use of HR policies designed to provide employees with an alternative to trade union membership: in this sense contemporary HRM is used as a substitute for trade unions. Such companies would be typified by the household names identified above, and would portray themselves as non-union rather than anti-union. According to Williams and Adam-Smith (2005: 164) two key features of large non-union firms can be identified. The first relates to the idea of the use of HR policies as a substitute for union organisation. The benefits offered, it is argued, exceed those that could be achieved by employees through union membership, thus making unions both unnecessary and a disruptive influence on the carefully nurtured harmonious relationship between the employer and employees. The second feature is the emphasis placed by such firms on managing employees as individuals. The philosophy of individualism permeates the whole culture of the organisation, and the collectivism inherent in union–management relations runs counter to this. However, the authors go on to sound some notes of caution about the extent to which this contemporary HRM model can be commonly applied. They note that the examples typically offered to support this view rely on the use of the same companies. Also, they question the practicalities of managing employees individually, at least in regard to most terms and conditions, and present evidence that many firms have highly standardised contractual terms.

Neither *bad* nor *ugly* organisations would provide much, if anything, by way of HR policies. Such firms are often suppliers to larger businesses, often competing on price, and thus would consider the cost of such practices not to be viable. Their non-union status derives from the belief that unions would limit flexibility and seek to push up wages, so threatening their survival. The distinction between them is that *ugly* firms, unlike *bad* ones, would be more likely to have a conscious HR strategy based on treating labour as a commodity, perhaps indicative of a hard HRM approach. Why, then, would workers put up with such treatment, when they could leave or seek a union to represent them? The answer is most likely to stem from their position in the labour market. Typically, those working in such firms are likely to have little, if any, specialised skills, or be on the fringes of the formal economy, without work permits or claiming state benefits. Alternatively, they may have domestic responsibilities which limit the hours during which they can be in paid employment.

Businesses characterised as *lucky* are those without a strategy that may well have some practices that have been introduced on a piecemeal basis. There is little, therefore, by way of sophisticated HR management but equally no attempt to manage by fear. Thus their non-union position arises through luck rather than by deliberate management practice. Some evidence for the existence of this style of management is offered by Goss (1991). He termed one of the managerial approaches his study of employment relations in small firms revealed as 'fraternalism'. In businesses such as professional services or specialised IT, where the employer typically works alongside the staff, and is highly dependent upon the skills of the employees in a tight labour market, a picture of harmony and egalitarianism may emerge. Workers here receive favourable pay and other terms of employment, and the opportunity to practise and develop their specialised skills. Thus there is a strong sense of mutuality in the employment relationship with both parties achieving much of what they want from the relationship.

It would seem, then, that the pattern of employment relations in non-union organisations is complex. While some companies appear to be following 'best HR practice' and have utilised contemporary HRM approaches as a means of investing in their employees as a resource, in others the more negative connotations of 'resource exploitation' seem more appropriate.

EMPLOYEE INVOLVEMENT, COMMITMENT AND HIGH PERFORMANCE WORK

Contemporary HRM is claimed to offer a different and distinctive approach to the management of the employment relationship. Guest (1987), for example, suggests that

HRM has four policy goals: integration, commitment, flexibility and quality. Of these, 'securing the commitment of individual employees . . . is at the heart of many of the recipes of HRM' (Sisson and Marginson, 2003: 167). Indeed, Goss (1994) suggests that commitment is the 'Holy Grail' of HRM. Given its importance, considerable interest has been shown in those employment relations processes that may offer enhanced worker commitment to the organisation, its business objectives and their own work. HR managers thus need to be aware of the types of practices available and the circumstances where their use may be appropriate, such that a greater fit between the organisation's objectives and its employment policies might be achieved.

Processes of work organisation designed to secure greater employee commitment have been variously described as 'employee involvement', 'high commitment' and 'high performance' practices. Legge (2000) suggests that the following techniques may be associated with seeking worker commitment: trainability; extensive communication systems; teamworking; an emphasis on training and learning; involvement in decision-making; performance appraisal linked to rewards; and a policy of job security. Many of these are dealt with in detail in other chapters of the book, and the emphasis here will be on employee involvement and communication.

As an employee relations process, employee involvement (EI) differs from collective bargaining in that the latter is a joint power-sharing strategy in which trade unions are incorporated into the organisational decision-making process. EI practices, on the other hand, are rarely trade union-based, are primarily concerned with building individual employee commitment to the organisation and offer little by way of shared decision-making. Although some techniques have been used by organisations for many years, it is their recent fusing into a more concerted approach by managers in some organisations that has attracted renewed interest in their possibilities. As Rose (2004: 379) concludes:

> The take-up of EI has been fairly comprehensive and widespread in a growing number of organisations . . . companies use EI practices as an integral part of a wider HRM strategy geared towards increasing employee identification with, and commitment to, the organisation and are at least partially successful in this.

Although serious doubts have been raised concerning the ability of EI techniques to deliver increased employee commitment to the organisation and the extent to which employee expectations and business objectives are being met through such initiatives, there is evidence to suggest that techniques associated with employee involvement have grown in both importance and scope over recent years (Millward *et al.*, 2000; Kersley *et al.*, 2006). While employee involvement takes a variety of forms they can, according to Marchington (1995), be categorised into five groups: *downward communication*, *upward communication and problem-solving*, *task participation*, *consultation and representative participation*, and *financial participation*.

Downward communication

In this form EI is characterised as a means by which management provides information to employees in order to develop their understanding of managerial plans and objectives. Such means include formal and informal communications between managers and their staff, employee reports, company newspapers, videos and annual presentations to employees by senior executives. Team briefings, used by many organisations, are regular meetings between supervisors and their work group at which primarily local but also wider organisational information is communicated to employees.

Upward communication and problem-solving

This group of techniques is designed to utilise the knowledge and opinions of employees, either as individuals or in small groups. Marchington suggests that:

> The objective is to to increase the stock of ideas within an organisation, to encourage co-operative relations at work, and to legitimise change.
>
> (Marchington and Wilkinson, 2008: 405)

Suggestion schemes have a long history in Britain but they have seen a resurgence in recent years. Here, employees who have made a suggestion for improved performance or cost savings may receive a financial reward from the organisation. Total quality management and quality circles are strategies which Japanese experience suggested might assist British companies in their search for improved quality and competitive advantage. Attitude surveys are a structured means to explore the opinions and views of employees on work and employment issues. Employee willingness to participate is likely to be conditional upon whether management are expected to, and do, act on the feedback received.

Task participation

This third approach focuses on schemes designed to encourage employees to expand the range of tasks they undertake. It has close links with the quality of working life movement and may involve job rotation, job enrichment and teamworking practices. In these forms it contrasts with the Tayloristic approach to job design and underpins such initiatives as empowerment and semi-autonomous work groups. Here employees are granted greater authority to make decisions and accept responsibility for such matters as adherence to quality standards.

Consultation and representative participation

Unlike previous forms, this approach to EI is an indirect form of involvement in that processes such as joint consultation are based on discussions between management and representatives of employees drawn from among them. Representatives are usually elected for a fixed period of time. Joint consultation differs from collective bargaining, since the final decision on any matter rests with management and is not the subject of a joint decision-making process. From a managerial perspective it can operate as a forum for grievances to be raised (particularly where unions are not recognised) and as a way of 'sounding out' employee representatives on managerial plans and proposed organisational change. According to the *Workplace Employee Relations Survey* (Kersley *et al.*, 2006), there has been a continued decline in the use of consultative forums. The survey also notes that these forums are much more common in larger workplaces than smaller ones.

However, many organisations will be required to give greater attention to consultation following the introduction of the EU Information and Consultation Directive into UK law. This requires companies with 50 or more employees to inform and consult with employee representatives over a range of issues. As a minimum, the process will need to cover: current and future business prospects; current and planned employment within the establishment, particularly if there is any threat to jobs; and decisions that may lead to changes in the organisation of work or terms of employment.

Financial participation

The final category of EI techniques are those designed to relate the employee's overall pay to the success of the organisation and include profit-sharing schemes and employee share ownership plans. These schemes are discussed in Chapter 9, but the assumption behind them is that employees will work harder if they receive a personal financial reward from the organisation's success.

Clearly the types of EI outlined here are not mutually exclusive. In a case study research of 25 organisations, Marchington *et al.* (1992) found a wide range of different schemes being utilised. The choice of techniques needs to be made upon an assessment of their ability to assist in the meeting of business and employment relations objectives and the organisation's individual circumstances. What are the managerial purposes behind the introduction of employee involvement schemes? Three are worthy of particular note in terms of this chapter's learning outcomes. The first they call *HRM participation* and note that two versions may exist. Version 1 is where trade unions are recognised but in their current weakened position. Here some form of direct communication with employees is used to bypass union communication channels. Version 2 is seen in non-union firms as part of a union avoidance strategy, typified perhaps by practice in the *good* companies noted above. The second set of circumstances they define as *market participation* and, again, two versions can be identified. The circumstances associated with version 1 relate to competitive product market pressures, and EI schemes are designed to enhance the quality of the product or service offered with the aim of inducing customer loyalty. These would include such techniques as quality circles or customer care programmes. The second version is most often seen where the external labour market is tight and firms need to retain and recruit workers but where there is little scope to achieve this through major pay rises. The aim here is to enhance the quality of employees' working life and thus increase employee loyalty to the firm.

However, Ackers *et al.* (1992) also note the possibility of *faddish participation* where managers introduce EI schemes as a result of following fashion or 'being seen to be doing something'. For example, Kersley *et al.* (2006: 91) report that almost three-quarters of their employer respondents claimed to operate teamworking in their organisations. However, the autonomy of the teams was often limited: 'In 83 per cent [of these were] . . . teams given responsibility for specific products or services; and in 61 per cent team members jointly decide how work was done. But in just 6 per cent were teammembers allowed to appoint their own team leaders.' This illustration would suggest that in some cases the rhetoric of EI may be somewhat removed from the reality.

Nonetheless, there is evidence that the appropriate application of high commitment/ involvement practices does boost performance (Guest *et al.*, 2000), but this is most likely to occur where they are used in 'bundles' rather than randomly or in isolation. For example, individual PRP, profit sharing and share ownership appear complementary, as do training, teamworking and supervisor training. What needs to be avoided is the idea that any one employee involvement technique will necessarily provide an advantage to the organisation.

THE NEGOTIATION PROCESS

Negotiation is a process that is used by managers in a variety of workplace circumstances where there is some degree of conflict between a manager and another party. It occurs in discussions with suppliers or customers over the price, quality and timing of delivery of a product or service. Managers may regularly find themselves in negotiations with other managers over the allocation of responsibilities within an organisation. Where trade unions are recognised, negotiations with their representatives over pay, work allocation and other terms of employment are a feature of organisational life. While there are a number of common features in these different types of negotiation, the focus here is on negotiations over aspects of the wage for work bargain.

Contrasting approaches to conflict resolution

Negotiation takes place in those circumstances where there is a degree of conflict between the parties over the allocation of a resource. The aim of the process is to persuade the other party to move from their original position to one which is acceptable to both parties. It thus implies a need for compromise. This can most clearly be seen over pay negotiations, where employee representatives wish to maximise the return for the labour employed while managers will seek to limit the impact of additional cost to the provision of goods or services.

Two broad approaches to the resolution of conflict can be identified: competitive and collaborative bargaining. Competitive bargaining is characterised by 'I win – You lose, I lose – You win' where gains by one party will be at the expense of the other. The power or energy generated by the conflict is used to advance one particular sectional interest: management or employees. Collaborative bargaining, on the other hand, is characterised by 'I win – You win, I lose – You lose', suggesting that it is possible for both parties to benefit from the resolution of the differences. Here the energy is moulded to seek mutually satisfactory solutions in changing circumstances. Which approach will be chosen depends on a number of factors which are summarised in Exhibit 16.4.

Where there is a greater commonality of interest, for example over a health and safety matter, it may be more appropriate to employ a collaborative approach than where there is a more obvious conflict of interests. The latter might include managerial attempts to impose redundancies while the union is seeking security of employment. Different approaches may be more appropriate at different stages of the negotiations. Where productivity improvements are being sought as part of pay negotiations, a collaborative model may be more suitable for identifying sources of cost savings, but the actual distribution of the savings between the organisation and pay increases for employees may call for competitive tactics. Where there is a high level of trust between

EXHIBIT 16.4 Key factors determining the approach to negotiation

- The issue
  - conflict of interest
  - common interest
- Stage of negotiations
- Quality of existing relations
  - trust
  - actions of others
- Preferred style and values
- Impact of external influences

management and employees, it may be possible to treat matters as problems requiring a joint problem-solving approach rather than to view them as divisive issues. Clearly the personal values and the preferred style of the negotiating members are influential – some people may view all issues as competitive irrespective of the actual merits of the case. Finally, external influences such as technological and economic contexts may determine which approach is used.

Phases of negotiation

A useful framework for analysing the negotiating process is to identify that it passes through five related phases.

1 Preparation.
2 Opening presentation.
3 Development and bargaining.
4 Closing.
5 Implementation and review.

Preparation

Thorough and thoughtful preparation by both parties is the key to ensuring that negotiations provide an effective and mutually satisfying agreement for both employees and managers. In this phase a number of important activities take place in advance of any meetings with the other party. For the management team the identification and clarification of the issue or issues to be dealt with during the negotiations needs to be undertaken before any detailed consideration can be made. This may involve the collection and evaluation of relevant information. Importantly, managers should be aware of the organisation's policy and any constraints this places on the negotiations. Once these activities have been completed, it is possible for the negotiating team to set their objectives for the meetings that are to follow. Since negotiating implies an element of compromise, these objectives can be thought of as a range – from the preferred or ideal solution to a fallback position. The latter may represent, for example,

Figure 16.1
Negotiating
objectives: conditions
for a settlement

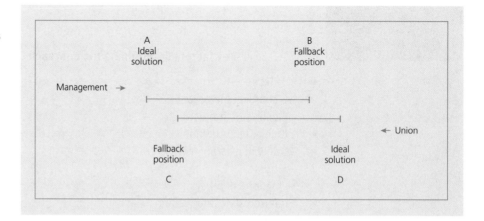

the limits of a manager's authority. Setting a range of objectives is important to effective negotiations, since the union team will be undertaking a similar exercise and the settlement will be found within the area where the two sets of objectives overlap. This is portrayed in Figure 16.1. The settlement of the issue will lie in the area between points B and C where the parties' negotiating objectives overlap. Where precisely the agreement will be reached will depend, in part, on the skills of the negotiators and the balance of power between management and the trade union.

Once objectives have been set, it is possible to develop arguments which support management's view of the case. At the same time, if there is some indication of the union's objectives and view of the case (perhaps because a formal claim has been submitted in advance of the meeting) then counter-arguments can be developed. Finally, particular responsibilities among the management negotiating team can be allocated. This may involve a consideration of the following questions: Who will lead the negotiations? Is there a need for a separate chair for the meeting? Are any managers with specialist expertise (such as health and safety, sales) needed? Will one member be responsible for note-taking? It is important that all members are agreed on the objectives and strategy to be followed, since a lack of consensus may lead to weaknesses in management's case being exposed during the negotiations.

Opening presentation

Depending on the nature and degree of formality of the negotiations, there may be a formal presentation of the respective management and union cases. Here, it is expected that each side will focus on their preferred solution. In the presentation of management's case the focus should be on why this objective is justified and there may be an attempt to set the context for the negotiations. In pay bargaining the performance of the company over the previous year may be explained in order to set the scene for the initial offer. The presentation should be relatively short and the key arguments that support management's case should be identified. If the union negotiators open the negotiations, their case should be listened to without interruption. Once this is completed, questions may be put to clarify points raised and to probe the strength of the arguments put forward. Once these presentations are completed and both parties are clear on each other's case, it may be appropriate to take an adjournment so that more detailed consideration can be given.

Development and bargaining

The third phase of the negotiations typically takes the greatest period of time as each party develops their case and assesses the merits of the arguments being placed before them. The main activity here is to seek to persuade the other party to move from their ideal solution. In general, one party should not move from their position unless there is some movement from the other. However, this can lead to stalemate, since neither is prepared to give ground for fear of making concessions without achieving some mutual shift by the other. This potential impasse can be overcome through the use of 'conditional proposals'. Management may suggest an area where they are prepared to move provided there is similar movement from the union on a matter which is of importance to the management team. For example, management may indicate that they are prepared to consider a reduction in the working week *if* the trade union representatives will reduce the size of their pay claim. If there is no movement in the latter then management have not committed themselves to shortening hours. It is important to 'signal' such proposals in advance by using such phrases as 'what if . . . then perhaps'. Negotiations induce considerable stress on the negotiators. Opportunities for adjournments should be taken appropriately, to provide not only a chance to review progress but also a break from the meeting. It is vital that the negotiations do not degenerate into personal attacks, nor that emotionally charged phrases are used: one wrong word can set the meeting back.

Closing

At this phase of the negotiations the aim is to secure the best agreement possible. This may involve a complex package of details covering a wide range of matters. It is important that this phase is not rushed, no 'loose ends' are left and that both parties are clear on what has been agreed, otherwise there may be a 'secondary dispute' over some details, necessitating another set of negotiations which may be somewhat acrimonious since the anticipated agreement has not been forthcoming. In some cases the union may wish to ballot its members on whether they are prepared to accept the negotiated settlement. Of course, the possibility of agreement supposes that there is an overlap in the respective negotiating objectives. If there is not, then there will be a need to re-examine the solutions and establish new objectives. If that is beyond the ability or the authority of the negotiating parties then a failure to agree may be recorded and the use of third-party intervention, such as conciliation or arbitration, considered.

Implementation and review

Negotiation is not an activity undertaken for its own sake, but is a process by which employees can have a voice in the decisions that affect their working lives and by which these decisions may be made more acceptable to them. Thus the effective implementation of the agreements reached is vital to the success of the process.

This action has two aspects. The first is the effective communication with and dissemination of information to those affected by the agreement. The second is the devising of a programme of implementation which includes allocating responsibility and setting time-scales.

(Corbridge and Pilbeam, 2000: 410–11)

CASE STUDY Preparing for negotiations at Sell-It-All

Sell-It-All is a retail organisation with 25 stores, mainly in the Midlands area of the UK. The stores sell a wide range of household goods, DVDs and stationery products. Part of its head office function includes an administration department, headed by an administration manager, and is responsible for two main activities. First, dealing with information requests from its stores and handling customer enquiries and complaints – a customer and store liaison team. Second, inputting statistical information on to a database in order that monthly reports on stock movements, etc. can be prepared for senior managers – the data processing team. There are separate teams of six staff with a team leader for each of these two teams. The average salary is £16 000 per year and average cost of employment is £18 500. A trade union is recognised by the company and membership within the department is estimated at about 75 per cent. Over the past year, the administration manager has become increasingly concerned about problems within her department. On the data processing side, information is received from the stores over the month and the team leader has indicated that during this time staff are able to cope easily with work demands. However, there is a significant increase towards the end of the month, and in order to meet deadlines it has been necessary to authorise overtime working that has cost £5000 over the past year. The team leader has also reported that the pressurised nature of the work with its accompanying need for accuracy has made staff less keen to work overtime.

The customer and store liaison team is also not without its problems. The manager has had several complaints from store managers that they or their staff have not been able to contact a member of the team despite repeated telephone calls; and faxes and emails are sometimes not answered for several days. The manager has also received a number of letters from customers expressing similar experiences. She has discussed the problems with the team leader for this group of staff, who has confirmed that the telephone call waiting time has increased significantly at peak times. This appears to be primarily during the first couple of weeks of each month when new products are introduced into the store and personnel at the outlets need additional information. The union representative has raised the problems his members have encountered with uneven work demands including the pressure to input data at month end and the difficulties answering customer and store enquiries at the beginning of the month when new products are introduced into the store. The latter includes abusive customers and store managers. The pressure the data inputting staff feel at month end, he feels, may result in increased sickness levels due to the stress generated – thus increasing the workloads of those who are at work. He has stated that data processing staff are unhappy about working overtime at peak periods and that more staff are needed in the department. Both team leaders have said that they each need an additional member of their team to cope with work demands. However, given the somewhat cyclical nature of the demands, the manager believes that another half post for each team would suffice. The problem with such a solution, she feels, is that for part of the time these additional half posts would not be fully employed and there would still be the possibility that workload demands will cause delays. In addition, two half posts would generate a cost of employment some 10 per cent higher than that for one full-time post. As a result, the manager is considering proposing a flexibility deal to the staff to avoid the need for recruiting any additional staff. This would involve staff in each team assisting their colleagues in the other section when demand is greatest. Thus, at month end some customer and store liaison staff would assist with data processing and during the first two weeks of the month the data processing team would help with customer and store enquiries. Longer term, she believes this could lead to a fully flexible operation. The direct cost of training staff in their new roles is estimated at £1500 initially, with another £400 needed in the second year for follow-up training. The manager recognises that staff are only likely to agree to this if they see an improvement in their pay.

Question

The manager is now preparing to meet the union representative to put this proposal to him. The task is to prepare a set of negotiating objectives for the manager. Taking account of the cost of employment and salary information provided above, and the guidance offered in the negotiation section of this chapter, you should identify:

1 Management's ideal solution.

2 Management's fallback position.

Each of the positions should be justified with reasons and from this you should be able to determine a range of possible solutions between these extremes.

The implications of the agreement need to be communicated to other managers and supervisors not involved in the negotiations, and the impact of the agreement on employees will have to be explained. How this latter responsibility will be apportioned between managers and union representatives will need to be decided, and consideration given to what action employees can take if they are unclear or unsure of its impact.

SUMMARY LEARNING POINTS

1 The effective resourcing of organisations requires careful consideration of the range of employment relations processes which need to be tailored to the organisational objectives and its broader resourcing strategies.

2 Where trade unions are recognised, management is faced with a number of choices regarding the structure of collective bargaining. Whether bargaining should be centralised or decentralised is likely to be determined by reference to the size and geographical spread of its business units, and its product and labour markets.

3 New forms of collective relationships such as single-table bargaining and partnership agreements are being adopted by employers who are seeking greater control over work processes.

4 In the non-union firm, or for categories of employees for whom unions are not recognised, management have greater freedom in determining the shape of the

employment relationship, although employment practices in non-union firms are highly variable.

5 Although collective bargaining has declined in coverage there is little evidence of this being replaced by individual employment contracts featuring variation in substantive terms.

6 The adoption of employee involvement techniques is evident in both unionised and non-union firms. These techniques are designed to elicit a greater level of employee performance and commitment to organisational objectives.

7 Reaching mutually acceptable agreements with trade union representatives requires managers to develop an understanding of the complexity of the negotiating process and the relevant problem-solving and communication skills.

REFERENCES AND FURTHER READING

Ackers, P., Marchington, M., Wilkinson, A. and Goodman, J. (1992) 'The use of cycles: explaining employee involvement in the 1990s', *Industrial Relations Journal*, 23(4), 268–83.

Blyton, P. and Turnbull, P. (2004) *The Dynamics of Employee Relations*. Basingstoke: Macmillan.

Brown, W. and Walsh, J. (1991) 'Pay determination in Britain in the 1980s: the anatomy of decentralisation', *Oxford Review of Economic Policy*, 1, 44–59.

Brown, W., Deakin, S., Nash, D. and Oxenbridge, S. (2000) 'The employment contract: from collective procedures to individual rights', *British Journal of Industrial Relations*, 38(4): 611–29.

Brown, W., Marginson, P. and Walsh, J. (2003) *The Management of Pay as the Influence of Collective Bargaining Diminishes*, in Edwards, P. (ed.) *Industrial Relations: Theory and practice in Britain* (2nd edn). Oxford: Blackwell.

Burrows, G. (1986) *'No-Strike' Agreements and Pendulum Arbitration*. London: IPM.

Burcill, F. (2000) 'The pay review body system: a comment and consequences', *Historical Studies in Industrial Relations*, 10, 141–57.

CIR (1973) 'The role of management in industrial relations', *CIR Report 34*. London: HMSO.

Corbridge, M. and Pilbeam, S. (2000) 'Negotiation, grievances, discipline and redundancy', in Farnham, D. (ed.) *Employee Relations*. London: CIPD.

Goss, D. (1991) 'In search of small firm industrial relations', in Burrows, R. (ed.) *Deciphering the Enterprise Culture: Entrepreneurship, petty capitalism and the restructuring of Britain*. London: Routledge, 152–75.

Goss, D. (1994) *Principles of Human Resource Management*. London: Routledge.

Guest, D. (1987) 'National ownership and HR practices in greenfield sites', *Human Resource Management Journal*, 6(4), 50–74.

Guest, D. and Hoque, K. (1994) 'The good, the bad and the ugly: employment relations in the new non-union workplace', *Human Resource Management Journal*, 5(1), 1–14.

Guest, D. and Pecci, R. (1998) *The Partnership Company: Benchmarks for the future*. London: Involvement and Participation Association.

Guest, D., Michie, J., Sheehan, M. and Conway, N. (2000) 'Getting inside the HRM-performance relationship', *Human Resource Management and Performance: First Findings from the Future of Work Study*, Birbeck College, School of Management and Organizational Psychology.

IDS (1995) *Introducing Single Table Bargaining*, Study 584, August. London: IDS.

IPD (1997) *Employment Relations into the 21st Century*. London: IPD.

Kennedy, G., Benson, J. and McMillan, J. (1980) *Managing Negotiations*. London: Business Books.

Kersley, B., Alpin, C., Forth, J., Bryson, A., Bewley, H., Dix, G. and Oxenbridge, S. (2006) *Inside the Workplace: Findings from the 2004 Workplace Employment Relations Survey*. Abingdon: Routledge.

Kessler, I. and Undy, R. (1996) 'The new employment relationship: examining the psychological contract', *Issues in People Management* (12). London: IPD.

Kochan, T. and Osterman, P. (1994) *The Mutual Gains Enterprise*, Cambridge MA: Harvard Business Press.

Legge, K. (2000) 'Personnel Management in the "lean organisation",' in Bach, S. and Sisson, K. (eds) *Personnel Management: A Comprehensive Guide to Theory and Practice*, Oxford: Blackwell.

Marchington, M. (1995) 'Involvement and participation', in Storey, J. (ed.) *Human Resource Management: A critical text*. London: Routledge.

Marchington, M. and Wilkinson, A. (2008) *Human Resource Management at Work: People Management and Development* (4th edn). London: CIPD.

Marchington, M., Goodman, J., Wilkinson, A. and Ackers, P. (1992) 'Recent developments in employee involvement', *Employment Department Research Series No. 1*. London: HMSO.

Marks, A., Findlay, P., Hine, J., McKinlay, A. and Thompson, P. (1998) 'The politics of partnership? Innovation in employment relations in the Scottish spirits industry', *British Journal of Industrial Relations*, 36(2), 209–26.

Millward, N., Bryson, A. and Forth, J. (2000) *All Change at Work? British employment relations 1980–1998, as depicted by the Workplace Industrial Relations Survey series*. London: Routledge.

Monks, J. (1998) 'Trade unions, enterprise and the future', in Sparrow, P. and Marchington, M. (eds) *Human Resource Management: The new agenda* (2nd edn). Oxford: Blackwell.

Purcell, J. and Ahlstrand, B. (1994) *Human Resource Management in the Multidivisional Company*. Oxford: Oxford University Press.

Rose, E. (2004) *Employment Relations*, Harlow: Pearson.

Salamon, M. (1998) *Industrial Relations: Theory and Practice* (3rd edn). Hemel Hempstead: Prentice Hall.

Sisson, K. (1993) 'In search of human resource management', *British Journal of Industrial Relations*, 31(2), 201–10.

Sisson, K. and Marginson, P. (2003) 'Management: Systems, Structure and Strategy' in Edwards, P. (ed.) *Industrial Relations: Theory and practice in Britain* (2nd edn). Oxford: Blackwell.

Tailby, S. and Winchester, D. (2000) 'Management and trade unions: towards social partnership', in Bach, S. and Sisson, K. (eds) *Personnel Management: A comprehensive guide to theory and practice*. Oxford: Blackwell.

Ulrich, D. (1997) *Human Resource Champions: The Next Agenda for Adding Value and Delivering Results*. Boston: Harvard Business School Press.

Ulrich, D. and Brockbank, W. (2005) *The HR Value Proposition*, Boston: Harvard Business Press.

Waddington, J. (2003) 'Trade Union Organization', in Edwards, P. (ed.) *Industrial Relations: Theory and practice in Britain* (2nd edn). Oxford: Blackwell.

White, G. (2000) 'The pay review body system: its development and impact', *Historical Studies in Industrial Relations*, 9, 71–100.

Williams, S. and Adam-Smith, D. (2005) *Contemporary Employment Relations: a critical introduction*. Oxford: Oxford University Press.

ASSIGNMENTS AND DISCUSSION TOPICS

1 Undertake an analysis of the way in which pay increases are determined within your organisation. If trade unions are recognised, the analysis should cover the levels at which agreements are made, the different bargaining units and agents that are involved, and how the pay of non-union employees is determined. If the organisation is non-union, the analysis should focus on the criteria and means that are used to decide the level of pay increases and the extent to which employees are able to individually negotiate their pay increases.

2 Identify the employee involvement practices used in your organisation. For what reasons do you believe they have been introduced? Are they effective?

3 Should the legal requirement for employers to recognise a trade union if a majority of employees are in favour be retained, abolished or amended? Give reasons for your view.

4 Discuss the view that employee involvement techniques are simply a means by which an employer manipulates employees into believing they have a say in the organisation's decisions when the reality is that power remains with management.

5 Observe an employment relations negotiation within an organisation. What skills were used by the parties involved? Did the negotiations appear to be of a competitive or collaborative nature and what factors led you to this view?

Chapter 17

Conflict Resolution: discipline and grievance

LEARNING OUTCOMES: TO BE ABLE TO

- Evaluate the role of disciplinary procedures in remedying dysfunctional conflict in the employment relationship

- Contribute to the design and operation of disciplinary procedures that not only comply with the standards of reasonable behaviour expected under the law but also have a corrective action philosophy

- Analyse the disciplinary hearing and the interviewing skills required

- Engage with a positive approach to the resolution of employee concerns and grievances

- Contribute to the design and operation of a grievance procedure

INTRODUCTION

It is unrealistic to expect that relations between employers and employees will always be harmonious and inevitably there will be conflict within individual employment relationships. At some stage it is possible that either the employer will be dissatisfied with an employee or an employee will be dissatisfied with the employer, or both parties can be dissatisfied at the same time. The informal resolution of dissatisfaction is an essential and natural part of good day-to-day management and most difficulties can be resolved at this level, but more formal arrangements are necessary when dissatisfaction in the employment relationship becomes unresolved conflict. Disciplinary and grievance procedures are formal mechanisms for resolving individual conflict and represent positive opportunities for corrective action and concern resolution. Fairness in disciplinary and grievance matters and a managerial focus on conflict resolution are fundamental features of performance-focused employment relationships and effective procedures have the potential to protect the organisation's investment in human capital.

INDIVIDUAL CONFLICT-RESOLVING MECHANISMS

Employer dissatisfaction may relate to employee performance, conduct, attendance or any other unfulfilled elements of the contract of employment. If the employee is not meeting the employer's legitimate expectations in the performance of the contract, there is potential for conflict between the two parties and it is reasonable for the employer to seek corrective action to resolve an unsatisfactory situation. Formalised corrective action is embodied in a disciplinary policy and procedure. Employee dissatisfaction may relate to employer treatment, demands, expectations or any other enactment of the contractual relationship which is perceived to be unreasonable, inequitable or illegitimate. Employee dissatisfaction may impact negatively on motivation, commitment and work performance. Unresolved conflict rooted in employee dissatisfaction can also destroy the contract of employment, either through the employee regarding it as being constructively terminated or through employee resignation. The formal opportunity to remedy employee dissatisfaction and resolve the consequential conflict is provided by an effective grievance procedure.

Unresolved conflict is therefore likely to be dysfunctional to an employment relationship. Disciplinary and grievance procedures have the potential to remedy dissatisfaction, resolve conflict, promote organisational equity and facilitate mutual adjustment within the contract of employment (*see* Figure 17.1).

A positive approach to resolving conflict is possible if discipline is viewed as an opportunity for corrective action and a grievance is viewed as an opportunity for the resolution of an employee concern. This approach will not exclude the application of managerial penalties and sanctions when necessary and appropriate.

THE NATURE OF DISCIPLINE AT WORK

Discipline at work means different things to different people and incorporates the concepts of self-discipline, peer discipline and managerial discipline. Self-discipline can

Figure 17.1 Mutual adjustment in the contract facilitated by disciplinary and grievance procedures

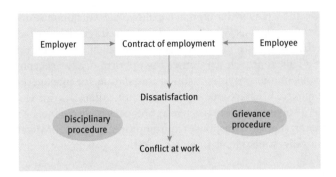

be encouraged and developed through employment relations practices which seek to secure the commitment of employees to organisational objectives. Peer discipline, pressure from work colleagues, can be an effective remedy to substandard performance or conduct where teamworking prevails. Managerial discipline is the exercise of control over employee performance and behaviour based on the legitimate organisational authority provided by the contract of employment. Managerial dissatisfaction with employee performance or conduct potentially produces conflict in the employment relationship. The formal disciplinary process is a procedural way of managing this conflict, through emphasising managerial values and standards, and seeking employee consent within the employment relationship. The primary concern in this section is with managerial discipline.

Discipline at work can have the different objectives of retribution, deterrence and rehabilitation. Retribution implies some form of punishment, deterrence infers dissuading the employee, and other employees, from repeating the unsatisfactory conduct or performance, and rehabilitation suggests the pursuit of improvement and reconciliation between the parties to the employment relationship. Managerial behaviour in disciplinary matters is influenced by perceptions of what is meant by discipline. If it is perceived as punishment or the application of sanctions then a predisposition to a punitive approach is probable. If discipline is perceived as an opportunity to constructively correct an unsatisfactory situation then a predisposition to positive managerial interventions, including problem-solving, support, training and clarification of employer expectations, is more likely.

> Managerial discipline is a constructive process instigated by management against an employee who fails to meet reasonable employer expectations in terms of performance, conduct or compliance with rules.

Managerial disciplinary action can be constructive and rehabilitative and need not necessarily be retributive or punitive, although when encouragement, guidance or development does not resolve managerial dissatisfaction then sanctions against the employee may be necessary and legitimate.

> A disciplinary procedure is the means by which rules are observed and standards are maintained. The procedure should be used primarily to help and encourage employees to improve rather than just as a way of imposing punishment. It provides a method of dealing with any apparent shortcomings in conduct or performance and can help an employee to become effective again.   (ACAS, 2009b: 13)

Fairness and equity in the approach to discipline will minimise disagreements and benefit employment relations. A professional and ethical approach to discipline is neatly summed up in the statement, 'problem-solving to be the first resolve and punishment the last resort'. This approach maximises the opportunity for acceptance and correction of the problem and provides a sound foundation for managerial policy on discipline. In summary, effective managerial practice argues for an emphasis on prevention, problem-solving and constructive approaches to discipline, because this is more likely to generate a positive response from employees and is more likely to protect the organisation's investment in its human capital.

ORGANISATIONAL RULES

A prerequisite to effective managerial discipline is the existence of organisational rules on conduct and performance. Rules set standards and define acceptable and unacceptable behaviour. Rules are necessary to let employees know where they stand and provide a framework for the employment relationship. Rules underpin managerial prerogative and aim to secure employee compliance to instructions which are deemed necessary to achieve organisational objectives. Rules are normally initiated, defined and communicated by management, although where the right to manage is circumscribed by individual or collective employee representation the rule-making process will be shared to some extent. If rule-making is subject to consultation, negotiation or co-determination, the rules may have greater acceptance and authority through having solicited a degree of employee consent and rules should be designed with the aim of voluntary compliance rather than a reliance on retribution for non-compliance. If rules are to be effective they need to be perceived as reasonable by employees and accepted as workable by line managers who have to enforce them. The managerial expectation that rules will be observed is legitimised by the common law duties of the employee which are implied into the contract of employment; these duties include being ready, willing and able for work, the exercise of care and competence in the performance of the work and obedience to reasonable instructions. The contract of employment may also include express terms relating to the expected standards of employee conduct and performance. The employer is therefore contractually entitled to specify performance, attendance, timekeeping and conduct standards. Managers cannot just rely on those rules which are overtly expressed, as rules evolve and become legitimised through custom and practice. For example, an unwritten but tacitly agreed arrangement where staff who work at a faster pace than the generally accepted norm are permitted to leave work an hour early on a Friday may become a contractual entitlement, through custom and practice. This may override management's written rule that employees should remain at their place of work until the contractual finishing time.

In addition to rules which are determined principally by management, and those arising out of custom and practice, rules emerge out of legal enactment and precedents. Examples of this include the statutory and case law associated with health and safety at work, unlawful discrimination and harassment. Societal standards, in so far as they can be defined, are also incorporated within the rules of the organisation. This incorporation is based on the concept that as a microcosm of society, work organisations will reflect generally accepted standards. These may include, for example, societal values associated with violence, drunkenness, dishonesty and sexual impropriety (Figure 17.2).

Figure 17.2 Sources
of organisational rules

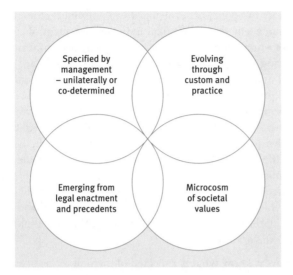

Recognising that organisational rules are generated from several sources encourages a flexible and dynamic interpretation of the rules and this is more compatible with a problem-solving approach to any employee failure. As suggested earlier, for rules to be effective they must be understood and accepted as reasonable by those who are to be covered by them and they also need to be acceptable as reasonable and workable to the managers who have to operate them. Disreputable rules will be difficult to operate and enforce. While it is not possible to specify a rule for every eventuality:

> Fairness and transparency are promoted by developing and using rules and procedures for handling disciplinary and grievance situations. These should be set down in writing, be specific and clear. Employees and, where appropriate, their representatives should be involved in the development of rules and procedures. It is also important to help employees and managers understand what the rules and procedures are, where they can be found and how they are to be used.
>
> (ACAS, 2009a: 3)

The consequences of not conforming to rules should be clearly communicated to employees, particularly where the breaking of a rule will threaten continued employment.

DISCIPLINARY PROCEDURES

While rules set the standards, disciplinary procedures provide a means for ensuring that standards are met and a method for dealing with a failure to meet them. Disciplinary problems can frequently be resolved by the team leader, supervisor or first line manager through counselling or through informal corrective action, and it is clearly desirable to resolve any conflict at the lowest possible level. It is only when this managerial intervention fails that it becomes necessary to escalate the disciplinary matter and to enter a formal disciplinary procedure. A preamble in a disciplinary procedure to the effect that management will aim to resolve issues through counselling and other action outside the formal process will underpin this low level approach, and this is complementary to a policy of devolving HR responsibility to line managers, but identifies a need for management development in the management of conflict.

There are a number of compelling reasons why organisations should be concerned with producing and operating sound and effective disciplinary procedures. First, there are around 1 million disciplinary cases annually, so the magnitude of the problem makes it worth tackling. Second, the importance of procedural fairness has been firmly established as a principle by employment tribunals. Third, employment legislation specifies that the principal statement of employment conditions should make reference to disciplinary rules, procedures and appeal mechanisms. Fourth, the consistent application of fair and effective disciplinary procedures will minimise the potential for disagreements and misunderstandings in matters of discipline and reduce the probability of employee dismissal. According to the CIPD (2009), 'disciplinary and grievance procedures provide a clear and transparent framework to deal with difficulties which may arise as part of their working relationship from either the employer's or the employee's perspective' and are needed:

- So employees know what is expected of them in terms of standards of performance or conduct and the likely consequences of continued failure to meet these standards.

- To identify obstacles to individuals achieving the required standards – training needs, lack of clarity of job requirements, additional support needed – and take appropriate action.

- As an opportunity to agree suitable goals and time scales for improvement in an individual's performance or conduct.

- As a point of reference for an employment tribunal should someone make a complaint about the way they have been dismissed.

Disciplinary procedures, as well as enabling employers to demonstrate reasonableness at a tribunal – *the compliance HR role* – also enable employers to set standards of conduct and performance and agree suitable goals and time scales for the employee's improvement, thereby resolving the conflict and protecting the organisation's investment in human capital – *the added-value HR role*.

Principles of natural justice

There are advantages in disciplinary procedures conforming to the principles of natural justice: 'When drawing up and applying procedures employers should always bear in mind the principles of fairness' (ACAS, 2009b: 13). These principles of natural justice have evolved from societal norms and case law and are associated with fairness and equity in the treatment of people. Disciplinary procedures which include the principles of natural justice will benefit from increased moral authority, will command more respect and are more likely to lead to just outcomes. Natural justice in discipline will also enhance perceived equity and foster a voluntary compliance to organisational rules.

> These principles of natural justice have emerged from ideas of equity, due process and model legal practice and are therefore associated with citizen consent to the rule of law within civilised societies. In the employee relations context the advantage is in the employee, as a corporate citizen, consenting to abide by managerial rules because justice will be dispensed fairly. **(Pilbeam and Corbridge, 2000)**

Procedures which incorporate the principles of natural justice, and which are applied correctly, will significantly contribute to a demonstration of reasonableness, should an employer need to defend an allegation of unfair dismissal or unreasonable treatment at an employment tribunal. The principles of natural justice are understood rather than specified, and a useful way of viewing them is as 'the way I would like to be treated if I were the subject of managerial discipline'. An expression of the principles, in the context of employment, is included in Exhibit 17.1 and organisational disciplinary procedures should be tested against them.

EXHIBIT 17.1 Principles of natural justice in employment

In employment these incorporate:

- a knowledge of the standards or behaviour expected
- a knowledge of the alleged failure and the nature of the allegation
- an investigation to establish a *prima facie* case, which should normally precede any allegation
- the opportunity to offer an explanation and for this explanation to be fairly heard and considered
- the opportunity to be accompanied or represented
- the penalty should be appropriate in relation to the offence and take mitigating factors into account
- the opportunity and support to improve, except when misconduct goes to the root of the contract
- a right of appeal to a higher authority.

ACAS code of practice and guide on discipline and grievance at work: 'back to the future' on handling disciplinary procedures?

The much criticised statutory minimum disciplinary and grievance procedures were repealed in 2009. Employers and employees are now required to follow the '*ACAS Code of Practice: Disciplinary and Grievance Procedures*' (2009). The Code applies to disciplinary situations, including both misconduct and poor performance, but does not apply to dismissals for redundancy or the non-renewal of fixed term contracts – although employers should still follow a fair and reasonable process before any dismissal. The new ACAS Code is a reincarnation of the Code that existed before the introduction of the statutory procedures. The Code is accompanied by a guidance handbook, '*Discipline and grievances at work: the Acas guide*', which again is very similar in principles and content to the old ACAS Advisory Handbook. The Code sets out the basic requirements of fairness that will be applicable and provides the standard of reasonable behaviour expected of the employer and the employee in disciplinary and grievance matters. A failure to follow the Code does not in itself make a person or organisation liable to proceedings, but employment tribunals will take the Code into account when considering cases. Unlike the Code, employment tribunals are not required by law to have regard to the ACAS guidance booklet. However, the ACAS Guide provides more detailed advice for employers, and employees, both in general terms and in individual cases, and in view of the almost biblical status of the ACAS

Advisory Handbook which preceded the introduction of the statutory minimum procedures, employment tribunal decisions are likely to revolve around adherence to the ACAS Guide as well as the Code. Breach of the Code does not mean that a dismissal will be automatically unfair, but compensation awards may be adjusted by up to 25 per cent where the tribunal considers either party has unreasonably failed to comply with a provision of the Code.

The Code sets out a framework for conducting disciplinary proceedings fairly and for resolving workplace disputes. The general requirements are that the employer should:

- Raise and deal with issues without unreasonable delay.
- Establish the facts of each case through proper investigation.
- Inform the employee of the allegation of either misconduct or unsatisfactory performance, and the potential consequences, in writing and provide evidence for the allegation.
- Hold a meeting with the employee to discuss the problem and allow the employee the opportunity to explain.
- Allow the employee to be accompanied at the disciplinary meeting.
- Decide on appropriate action.
- Provide employees with an opportunity to appeal.

The Code (2009a) sets out the features of a good disciplinary procedure and these are founded on the principles of natural justice (*see* Exhibit 17.2) and the Code emphasises that:

> **Employers and employees should always seek to resolve disciplinary and grievance issues in the workplace. Where this is not possible employers and employees should consider using an independent third party to help resolve the problem.**

One major addition to the conflict resolution process has been the introduction of the ACAS pre-claim conciliation helpline where employers and employees can take advice from conciliators on settling the disciplinary or grievance 'dispute'. Pre-claim means before an ET1 is submitted. The aim is to avoid escalation which might result in a claim being made to an employment tribunal through employers and employees resolving their differences. ACAS (2009a) also recommend informal resolution:

> **Many potential disciplinary or grievance issues can be resolved informally. A quiet word is often all that is required to resolve an issue. However, where an issue cannot be resolved informally then it may be pursued formally.**

Where an employee raises a grievance during a disciplinary process the disciplinary process may be temporarily suspended in order to deal with the grievance. Where the grievance and disciplinary cases are related it may be appropriate to deal with both issues concurrently.

The Polkey principle (*Polkey* v *A E Dayton Services Ltd* [1987] IRLR 503) was effectively reintroduced in 2009. Prior to *Polkey* an employer could have argued that it would have made 'no difference' to the outcome of the dismissal even if a procedure has been followed and the employment tribunal could find the dismissal fair and reasonable in these circumstances. The Polkey principle means that if an employer does not use the correct disciplinary procedure when dismissing an employee then the dismissal

EXHIBIT 17.2 Features of disciplinary procedures

Good disciplinary procedures should:

- be in writing
- be non-discriminatory
- provide for matters to be dealt with speedily
- allow for information to be kept confidential
- tell employees what disciplinary action might be taken
- say what levels of management have the authority to take the various forms of disciplinary action
- require employees to be informed of the complaints against them and supporting evidence, before a disciplinary meeting
- give employees a chance to have their say before management reaches a decision
- provide employees with the right to be accompanied
- provide that no employee is dismissed for a first breach of discipline, except in cases of gross misconduct
- require management to investigate fully before any disciplinary action is taken and ensure that employees are given an explanation for any sanction and allow employees to appeal against a decision
- apply to all employees, irrespective of their length of service or status, or say if there are different rules for different groups

The employee should be heard in good faith with no pre-judgement and a disciplinary penalty should not be imposed until the case has been investigated, and there is a reasonably held belief that the employee committed the act in question.

Source: ACAS, *Discipline and Grievances at Work: The ACAS Guide 2009*.

will be unfair, even if following the correct procedure would have still resulted in dismissal. Consequently, it is important for an employer to follow a correct disciplinary procedure in dismissing an employee. Failure to follow the disciplinary procedure will be seen as unreasonable by an employment tribunal and result in a finding of unfair dismissal on the basis of procedural defect (BERR, 2008: 9). However, the employment tribunal is under a statutory obligation to award compensation that would be 'just and equitable in the circumstances' and although finding that a dismissal was unfair, the tribunal may reduce compensation if an employer can demonstrate that following the procedure would have made no difference to the dismissal decision.

The structure of a disciplinary procedure

The ACAS model of a procedure (Exhibit 17.3) incorporates the notion of three incremental disciplinary stages based on the nature and seriousness of the performance

EXHIBIT 17.3 Indicative model of a disciplinary procedure

1 Purpose and scope

This procedure is designed to help and encourage all employees to achieve and maintain standards of conduct, attendance and job performance. The company rules (a copy of which is displayed in the office) and this procedure apply to all employees. The aim is to ensure consistent and fair treatment for all in the organisation.

2 Principles

Informal action will be considered, where appropriate, to resolve problems. No disciplinary action will be taken against an employee until the case has been fully investigated. For formal action the employee will be advised of the nature of the complaint against him or her and will be given the opportunity to state his or her case before any decision is made at a disciplinary meeting. Employees will be provided, where appropriate, with written copies of evidence and relevant witness statements in advance of a disciplinary meeting. At all stages of the procedure the employee will have the right to be accompanied by a trade union representative, or work colleague. No employee will be dismissed for a first breach of discipline except in the case of gross misconduct, when the penalty will be dismissal without notice or payment in lieu of notice. An employee will have the right to appeal against any disciplinary action. The procedure may be implemented at any stage if the employee's alleged misconduct warrants this.

3 The Procedure

First stage of formal procedure

This will normally be either:

- *an improvement note for unsatisfactory performance* if performance does not meet acceptable standards. This will set out the performance problem, the improvement that is required, the timescale, any help that may be given and the right of appeal. The individual will be advised that it constitutes the first stage of the formal procedure. A record of the improvement note will be kept for . . . months, but will then be considered spent – subject to achieving and sustaining satisfactory performance

  or

- *a first warning for misconduct* if conduct does not meet acceptable standards. This will be in writing and set out the nature of the misconduct and the change in behaviour required and the right of appeal. The warning will also inform the employee that a final written warning may be considered if there is no sustained satisfactory improvement or change. A record of the warning will be kept, but it will be disregarded for disciplinary purposes after a specified period (eg, six months).

Final written warning

If the offence is sufficiently serious, or if there is further misconduct or a failure to improve performance during the currency of a prior warning, a final written warning may be given to the employee. This will give details of the complaint, the improvement required and the timescale. It will also warn that failure to improve may lead to dismissal (or some other action short of dismissal) and will refer to the right of appeal. A copy of this written warning will be kept by the supervisor but will be disregarded for disciplinary purposes after . . . months subject to achieving and sustaining satisfactory conduct or performance.

Dismissal or other sanction

If there is still further misconduct or failure to improve performance the final step in the procedure may be dismissal or some other action short of dismissal such as demotion or disciplinary suspension or transfer (as allowed in the contract of employment). Dismissal decisions can only be taken by the appropriate senior manager, and the employee will be provided in writing with reasons for dismissal, the date on which the employment will terminate, and the right of appeal. If some sanction short of dismissal is imposed, the employee will receive details of the complaint, will be warned that dismissal could result if there is no satisfactory improvement, and will be advised of the right of appeal. A copy of the written warning will be kept by the supervisor but will be disregarded for disciplinary purposes after . . . months subject to achievement and sustainment of satisfactory conduct or performance.

Gross misconduct

The following list provides some examples of offences which are normally regarded as gross misconduct:

- theft or fraud
- physical violence or bullying
- deliberate and serious damage to property
- serious misuse of an organisation's property or name
- deliberately accessing internet sites containing pornographic, offensive or obscene material
- serious insubordination
- unlawful discrimination or harassment
- bringing the organisation into serious disrepute
- serious incapability at work brought on by alcohol or illegal drugs
- causing loss, damage or injury through serious negligence
- a serious breach of health and safety rules
- a serious breach of confidence.

If you are accused of an act of gross misconduct, you may be suspended from work on full pay, normally for no more than five working days, while the alleged offence is investigated. If, on completion of the investigation and the full disciplinary procedure, the organisation is satisfied

(Box continued)

that gross misconduct has occurred, the result will normally be summary dismissal without notice or payment in lieu of notice.

Appeals

An employee who wishes to appeal against a disciplinary decision must do so within five working days. The senior manager will hear all appeals and his/her decision is final. At the appeal any disciplinary penalty imposed will be reviewed.

Source: ACAS, *Discipline and Grievances at Work: The ACAS Guide 2009*, Appendix 2.

or the conduct of the employee. ACAS does not recommend the use of oral or verbal warnings, in fact ACAS dispensed with this type of warning some years ago. If a disciplinary issue is not resolved at an informal level, it may become necessary to enter the formal disciplinary procedure. The first stage of the formal procedure may be either *an improvement note* for unsatisfactory performance or *a formal written warning* for misconduct. An improvement note provides an opportunity to set out the performance problem, the improvement required and the time scale for achieving the improvement, together with a review date and details of any support to be provided to the employee. Even in performance matters the employee needs to know that the improvement note represents the first stage of the formal disciplinary procedure and that failure to improve may lead to a final written warning and, ultimately, dismissal. The improvement note is used for monitoring and reviewing performance over a specified period. In cases of misconduct, employees are given a written warning setting out the nature of the misconduct and the change in behaviour required. The warning should also inform the employee that a final written warning will be considered if misconduct is repeated. The second stage of the procedure may be *a final written warning*. The final stage may be either *ASOD* (action short of dismissal, including disciplinary transfer, or reduction in status and responsibility) or *dismissal*. The three stages are represented in Figure 17.3.

While providing a useful guide to employer action, the stages should not be viewed as a strict sequence as it is reasonable for an employer to have the flexibility to enter the procedure at any stage, depending on the seriousness of the conduct or performance matter. The earlier stages will normally be executed by team leaders, supervisors and first line managers, with more senior management becoming involved as the disciplinary matter escalates. The participation and role of a specialist HR function will be contingent on organisational circumstances and also senior management policy and attitude towards the devolution of HR responsibilities to line managers. There are examples of organisations in retailing and catering where an active HR presence occurs at a very early stage in the disciplinary process, and in contrast there are examples of blue-chip organisations where the role of the HR function is advisory and remote from the application of the disciplinary procedure.

Figure 17.3 The principal incremental stages of a disciplinary procedure

	Nature of the disciplinary matter and the procedural stage	Management response and action	Level of management (with advice from HR specialist as required)
1	**Unsatisfactory performance**	Improvement note	Team leader/Supervisor
	Misconduct which is not serious	Written warning	Team leader/Supervisor
2	**Continued unsatisfactory performance** for which an improvement note has already been issued or **Repeated misconduct** for which a written warning has already been issued or **Serious unsatisfactory performance or serious misconduct**	Final written warning	Line manager
3	**Further unsatisfactory performance** for which a final written warning has been issued or **Further misconduct** for which a final written warning has been issued or **Gross misconduct**	Dismissal or action short of dismissal • Transfer • Demotion • Suspension • Reward decrement	Senior manager

Disciplinary procedures – operational issues

Case law has established the importance of thorough investigation in disciplinary matters. The initial aim of an investigation is to gather factual information which establishes whether or not there is a *prima facie* case for making an allegation. An investigatory meeting with the employee may be held to establish the facts of the matter, but it should be made clear to the employee that it is not a disciplinary meeting. The disciplinary meeting subsequently provides an opportunity for the employee to explain or respond to an allegation. Further investigation may be necessary following the disciplinary meeting. Proper and objective investigation is an important element in establishing employer reasonableness at an employment tribunal, should this be necessary. The disciplinary matter should be dropped if investigation fails to establish a *prima facie* case to answer or if the employee's explanation is satisfactory. The employer does not have to prove beyond reasonable doubt that an employee has committed an offence or that the employee is 'guilty' of misconduct or substandard performance; case law has established that the burden of proof is one of 'establishing reasonable belief' based on the balance of probabilities, taking into account the information available at the time (*see* Chapter 18). It may be appropriate to suspend the employee from work during an investigation, particularly in cases of alleged gross misconduct. Suspension should normally be on the basis of paid leave unless the contract specifies unpaid suspension. Even where unpaid suspension is contractually legitimate, suspending an employee prior to providing an opportunity to explain may be perceived as premature punishment through loss of pay. Unpaid suspension in these circumstances may not only be perceived as unfair, but also be to the detriment of a workable employment relationship, if there is no case to answer or the employee provides a satisfactory explanation. Suspension, whether paid or unpaid, needs to be used judiciously because of the potential for the employee to suffer from the 'no smoke without fire' syndrome. Sometimes it will be essential to use suspension in the interests of the employee or other employees or customers, clients and members of the public, or to protect the objectives of the organisation.

The reasonableness of employer action, more specifically addressed in the next chapter, is a guiding principle in the operation of disciplinary procedures and involves the assessment of whether disciplinary action falls within the range of responses of a reasonable employer. The concept of even-handedness, meaning that employers are normally expected to treat employees similarly in similar disciplinary matters, unless differences in treatment can be objectively justified, is also a well-established disciplinary principle. In order to be able to demonstrate reasonableness and even-handedness, it is important for employers to document disciplinary matters fully in terms of records of investigation, disciplinary meetings, warnings, monitoring and support.

In operating disciplinary procedures, are managers and HR managers required to be impartial or objective? This is a problematic question. Impartiality suggests a lack of bias towards or against any particular side, but can management ever do anything but ultimately make decisions from a managerial perspective, and even if managers are impartial will employees believe it? The disciplinary procedure is a quasi-judicial process where, contrary to normal legal practice, the prosecution and judiciary are not separated and the employer is acting as both prosecutor and judge; this militates against impartiality. Objectivity, in contrast, implies an interpretation of the facts and a decision-making process not distorted by emotion or personal bias. Objectivity acknowledges managerial prerogative but affords some protection to the employee against managerial whim, and in practice it is objectivity rather than impartiality which is normally incorporated into disciplinary procedures.

Warnings and warning letters should normally spell out the nature of the offence or behaviour, the remedy or improvement required, and the support, guidance and monitoring to be provided, and should specify a review time scale (*see* the ACAS *Guide* for examples of letters). The objective of a warning is to ensure that the employee not only understands and accepts the problem but is able to commit to resolving it by appreciating exactly what is required by management. The employee should be left in no doubt about the potential consequences of failure to resolve the problem, and such consequences should be specified as well. The seriousness of a warning is indicated by whether it is given as a first written warning or as a final written warning. Normally warnings will be disregarded or considered spent after a specified period of satisfactory conduct or performance. This is in the interests of natural justice so that the employee, having made a mistake and paid the appropriate penalty, has the opportunity to 'wipe the slate clean' in due course. The period for which the warning is to remain 'live' should be reasonable and determined by the particular merits of the case. There is an inherent tension in deciding upon the warning time limit between the desire to encourage employees to put the matter behind them, in the interests of re-establishing a positive employment relationship, and the provision of the opportunity for the 'repeat offender' to exploit the expiry of a warning by quickly lapsing into the unsatisfactory conduct or performance. The ACAS Code provides guidance on time limits, suggesting 6- and 12-month periods for first written warnings and final written warnings respectively, while the CIPD (2009) suggest one year and two years respectively. The employer is entitled to set a time limit which is reasonable in the particular circumstances:

> There may be occasions where an employee's conduct is satisfactory throughout the period the warning is in force, only to lapse very soon thereafter. Where a pattern emerges and there is evidence of abuse, the employee's disciplinary record should be borne in mind in deciding how long any warning should last. (ACAS, 2009b: 33)

Exceptionally there may be circumstances where the misconduct is so serious, verging on gross misconduct, that it cannot be realistically ignored for future disciplinary purposes. In such circumstances, it should be made clear that the final written warning can never be removed and that any recurrence of the misconduct will lead to dismissal. Such instances should be rare, as full rehabilitation is clearly difficult when an employee is permanently under threat of dismissal. In endeavouring to ensure that an employee fully understands a warning, it is useful to ask for a copy of the warning letter to be signed. This does not preclude the employee from responding to a warning in writing, or disagreeing with it. This opens up a debate about whether the employee is being asked to sign a letter in order to:

(a) acknowledge receipt, *or*
(b) indicate that the content of the letter has been read and understood, *or*
(c) signify agreement with the content of the warning.

From a managerial perspective, achieving (a), (b) and (c) may be desirable, but unrealistic to achieve because the employee may think that they are compromising their position by signing something. There is no obligation on the employer to achieve (a), (b) or (c), but a reasonable employer will be expected to make every demonstrable effort to ensure that a warning letter is received and that it is capable of being understood by the recipient. As an alternative to a signed warning letter an accurate record of a disciplinary hearing may be provided for employee signature, but (a), (b) and (c) still apply.

To avoid automatically attaching the disciplinary label to a managerial concern about the work performance of an individual, a distinction can be created between misconduct and work performance concerns through having separate disciplinary and capability procedures. This distinction, which is embedded in the ACAS Code through the notion of an improvement note for performance matters, is intended to encourage an even more positive approach to performance problems by focusing on managing a return to acceptable standards of performance. ACAS (2009) does not explicitly recommend separate conduct and capability procedures and states that disciplinary situations include misconduct and poor performance. However, ACAS recognises that if employers have a separate capability procedure they may prefer to address performance issues under this procedure but 'the basic principles of fairness set out in this Code should still be followed'. There are, for example, restoring-efficiency procedures in the civil service, in order to communicate a more positive, problem-solving and partnership approach to managing the return to effective performance, although ultimately a failure to improve leads to the next stage of the disciplinary procedure. The positive approach to managerial concern about employee performance involves:

- identifying a performance gap through the objective specification of performance standards and the measurement of current performance;
- an analysis of the reasons for the performance gap and deciding upon a suitable response which may include training, supervision, greater or lesser empowerment, clearer definition of objectives, re-balancing of the psychological or economic contracts, or indeed warnings and disciplinary action (*see also* Chapter 11).

Disciplinary hearings

It is important to carry out investigations of potential disciplinary matters to establish the facts of the case and this involves the collation of evidence. This may require an investigatory meeting with the employee before proceeding to any disciplinary hearing. ACAS (2009a: 6) recommend that in misconduct cases, where practicable, different people should carry out the investigation and disciplinary hearing. The investigatory meeting should not result in any disciplinary action and although there is no statutory right for an employee to be accompanied at an investigatory meeting, the employer can allow it.

When a *prima facie* case for the expression of a concern or an allegation has been reasonably established, a disciplinary meeting should take place. The employee should be informed in writing about the nature of the allegation or concern, be forewarned about the disciplinary status of the meeting and where it fits into the procedure, be told of the right to be accompanied or represented, and given the time, date and place of attendance, ensuring that there is sufficient, but not excessive, time for preparation. As well as the right to a companion at a grievance hearing, section 10 of the ERA 1999 gives workers (not just employees) the right to make a reasonable request to be accompanied at a formal disciplinary meeting. The worker chooses the companion, who can be a fellow worker or a certified trade union official (who need not be employed by the same organisation). The companion can be a trade union official even where a trade union is not recognised and therefore non-unionised organisations may have to accept a trade union official as the worker's companion when requested by the worker. Even where a trade union is recognised, the companion does not have to be an official of that union and could come from a trade union of the worker's choice. The statutory role is one of companion rather than representative. The companion should be allowed to address the hearing to put and sum up the worker's case, respond on behalf of the worker to any views expressed at the meeting and confer with the worker during the hearing. The companion does not, however, have the right to directly answer questions on the worker's behalf, address the hearing if the worker does not wish it or prevent the employer from explaining their case. The worker may propose an alternative date for the meeting if the chosen companion is not available on the date proposed for the meeting. In this case the employer is required to postpone the meeting to the date proposed by the worker, provided that the alternative date is reasonable, has regard for the availability of the manager and falls before the end of five working days of the date proposed by the employer. The companion is entitled to reasonable time off during working hours in order to fulfil his or her responsibilities (Temperton, 2000; Lewis and Sargeant, 2000; Aikin, 1999; ACAS, 2009a, b).

Disciplinary hearings will rarely progress in neat, orderly stages, but a systematic framework can be helpful in contributing to fairness and in encouraging constructive discussion. At the meeting the employer should normally:

- introduce those present and clarify their respective roles

- explain the purpose and process of the meeting

- state the allegation or concern unambiguously, support it with any relevant facts or evidence, and allow the employee to clarify the allegation through questions

- offer the employee the opportunity to respond or to offer an explanation, to which the employer should listen attentively and sensitively, and allow the employee to consult with the companion

- question the employee in order to gather further particulars and confirm factual information

- consider carefully the employee's response or explanation

- make the decision, normally in adjournment, to ensure and demonstrate that proper consideration is being given to all the circumstances, including mitigating factors and previous work record

- accept that there is no case to answer or that it has been answered, in which case the disciplinary process ceases, or, alternatively, decide that disciplinary action is necessary and inform the employee of the decision in writing, and also of the right to appeal (which ACAS recommend should normally be lodged within five working days) should there be dissatisfaction with the decision

- ensure that the employee knows what is now expected and by when, normally in writing

- agree to provide reasonable support, training and feedback and to review the matter within the specified time scale.

These relatively straightforward guidelines disguise the fact that the meeting is potentially a highly emotional encounter. The interviewer can be confronted with a range of responses, from aggression or distress on the one hand to passiveness and disinterest on the other; the employee may exhibit devious ingenuity or engage in self-denial behaviour. Professionalism, objectivity based on facts and rationality need to be demonstrated. The skills to be utilised include open and probing questioning, active listening, summarising, managing angry responses, sensitivity to feelings of devastation and the ability to focus on the facts in order to progress the meeting to a logical conclusion. All of this means that the disciplinary meeting can be as challenging for the manager as it is for an employee. The meeting should not be treated merely as a means of confirming suspicions or concerns, but as an opportunity to resolve any conflict in the employment relationship through improving conduct or performance on both sides. Fairness and natural justice at the disciplinary meeting and in individual matters of discipline generally will ultimately contribute to good employment relations. Perhaps a corrective action procedure is a more appropriate name for a disciplinary procedure.

CASE STUDY   Discipline at work – Jobs for the Toys Limited

You are employed as the HR officer at Jobs for the Toys Limited. It is a wholesale operation and supplies gifts, stationery and toys to the retail trade. There are approximately 120 employees. You recently advertised for a sales office manager and, as the successful applicant would be required to call on clients a couple of times each week, a pool car would be made available when required. In view of this driving requirement, the job description and the person specification, and the application form, made it clear that applicants would need to have a current and clean driving licence. The recruitment and selection process was successful and you appointed what you considered to be a good-grade candidate. Her name is Betty Garland. Betty has now been working for the organisation for several months and, although she is meeting the minimum job requirements, she is not realising her potential as quickly as anticipated. In particular, her communication skills appear limited and at times she can give the impression of being either evasive or a little confused.

Since Betty started with the organisation there have been several occasions when a pool car has not been available. In these circumstances employees who need transport can hire a vehicle from The Self-Drive Company, with whom you have a long-standing business relationship. On checking the invoices it became apparent to the accounts supervisor that the cost of hiring a car for Betty was greater than for other employees in the organisation. The accounts supervisor checked with The Self-Drive Company, but did not receive a satisfactory explanation. She therefore drew it to your attention. You contacted the car hire firm and discovered that the reason for Betty being charged a higher amount for the hire of a car was that, on inspecting her driving licence, The Self-Drive Company noted that the licence contained a current endorsement for driving without insurance. This resulted in an additional premium being charged for the hiring of a car. Naturally this concerns you and you check Betty's personal file. The application form contains the following question: 'Do you hold a clean driving licence?' Betty has answered 'Yes'!

Questions

1 What impact does this situation have on the employment relationship between Jobs for the Toys and Betty, and what particular issues do you need to consider before embarking on a course of action?

2 What alternative forms of action, or inaction, are available to you?

3 Taking account of the principles of natural justice, what will be your approach if you decide to hold a disciplinary meeting?

4 Be prepared to undertake the disciplinary meeting in a role-play situation with somebody taking the role of Betty.

5 Having undertaken the disciplinary meeting in which Betty confirms that she does have a current endorsement, which she failed to declare, what action will you take and why?

You can assume that Jobs for the Toys has a disciplinary policy and procedure which is based on ACAS principles and guidelines.

Disciplinary procedures and employment tribunals

UMIST research (Earnshaw, 1997) found that the main cause of employment tribunal claims being found in favour of the applicant is procedural defect. The continuing focus on remedying procedural defects suggests that Earnhaw's findings are still relevant. Where employees are successful in their claim for unfair dismissal, the success is often related to procedural shortcomings by the employer. Common procedural defects include:

- employees not being made fully aware of the allegation and any supporting evidence
- employees not being given the opportunity to respond to the allegation or the absence of a disciplinary meeting
- warnings not being sufficiently explicit
- insufficient time being given to the employee to remedy a problem
- inadequate or insufficient investigation
- a concern with speed of action rather than proper consideration of the facts
- dismissal occurring in the course of an argument
- a failure to apply the disciplinary procedure in full
- the decision not to have or to use a formal disciplinary procedure.

Despite well-documented, sound HR practice, and the legitimacy of the principles of natural justice, there remains scope for education and advice to employers in relation to procedural fairness. A dismissal process need not necessarily be slow, or paper bound, but remedying procedural defects is a way to reduce claims for unfair dismissal and for making dismissals legally safe. Good disciplinary procedures will not eliminate all claims, but will make them easier to defend.

GRIEVANCES – EMPLOYEE CONCERN RESOLUTION

Employees may have concerns about treatment relating to terms and conditions of employment, health and safety, work relations, equal opportunities, bullying and harassment, working practices, the work environment and organisational change, *inter alia*. It is important to recognise, acknowledge and resolve concerns and issues that leave employees feeling unfairly treated because failure to do this can result in employees deciding to take action to redress the perceived unfair treatment. This employee action may range from poor attendance or poor quality work, to leaving the organisation, which is costly in terms of losing the organisation's investment in its human capital and also unsatisfactory as the problem remains unrecognised and unresolved. A concern with healthy employee relations and good communication will encourage the informal resolution of problems, but the climate of the organisation will affect the extent to which employee grievances are presented to management. An absence of employee grievances does not necessarily mean that there are no problems; it may mean that employees believe that their concerns will not be taken seriously or that they are afraid of repercussions. A grievance is the formal expression of dissatisfaction or injustice that an employee feels towards the employer. It is based on the legal and procedural right of individuals at work to formally express dissatisfaction with elements of the work situation, to have that dissatisfaction acknowledged and heard and a managerial attempt made to resolve the situation. In expressing a grievance the employee is highlighting an issue of dissatisfaction which is considered sufficiently serious to present formally to management and therefore warrants managerial attention regardless of any statutory grievance procedure obligations.

The terms dissatisfaction, complaint, grievance and dispute represent a hierarchy of the strength of employee feeling and willingness to present the issue formally to management. Dissatisfaction is felt, complaints are expressed informally, grievances are presented formally, and disputes may be internal or external and collective or individual. Not every employee dissatisfaction or complaint results in a grievance or a dispute; whether it does depends on the willingness of the employee to present the issue, the managerial response and whether it is resolved to the employee's satisfaction. The progression from the informal to the formal machinery may be seen in some organisations as a failure to address the issue at the informal level, resulting in the employee feeling that 'enough is enough' and there is no alternative but to use the formal procedure.

The employment relations climate and the culture of an organisation are significant in the way in which grievances are received and handled. In a unitary or neo-unitary organisation (*see* Chapter 15) there are assumptions that common values and common objectives are held by all employees and that the 'right to manage' is generally accepted by all (Farnham, 2000). In these organisations internal conflict may be perceived as dysfunctional and as a consequence individuals may feel inhibited about raising a formal grievance because of the effect it may have on their career prospects or for fear of being labelled a 'deviant'. In a pluralist organisation, conflict is accepted as inevitable, with employees having a right to question managerial policies and decisions. The formal grievance procedure is more likely to be used, and the need for a formal mechanism for resolving conflict is taken for granted in pluralistic employment relationships.

As suggested earlier, employee concerns and grievance subjects vary. They can range from issues affecting one individual with no organisational implications, to issues affecting a group of workers which challenge management decisions and with the potential to escalate to a collective dispute before being settled. Common issues that give rise to formal grievances include:

- terms and conditions of employment
- health and safety
- work relations
- bullying and harassment
- new working practices
- working environment
- organisational change
- discrimination.

Grievance procedures

Grievance procedures provide a formal mechanism for the presentation and resolution of employee dissatisfaction. ACAS (2009a) defines grievances as 'employee concerns, problems or complaints' and in relation to grievance matters advise that:

- The employee should raise the concern in writing with a manager.
- The employer should hold a meeting to discuss the grievance.

- The employer should allow the employee to be accompanied.
- The employer should decide on appropriate action and inform the employee of the decision in writing.
- The employer should allow the employee to take the grievance further – effectively allowing an appeal.

The Employment Rights Act 1996 obliges the employer to provide the name or job title of the person to whom individual employees should present the grievance. ACAS advice is for employers to respond to an employee's grievance within a reasonable time. The employer should hold a meeting, normally within five working days, to discuss the grievance and allow the employee to be accompanied. The employer should decide on appropriate action and inform the employee of the decision in writing and allow the employee to take the grievance further – effectively allowing an appeal. The ACAS guidance is aimed at resolving conflict in the employment relationship internally and is in accord with the ambition of avoiding recourse to litigation as a first resort because this litigation is not good for the employer, for the employee or for tribunal caseload (Dickens, 2002).

Grievance procedures set out the stages through which a grievance progresses within the organisational hierarchy. This recognises the authority and responsibility of the parties at the different organisational levels and allows for a structured approach. The stages should also define the time scale for the resolution of the problem. This allows for a review of the decision by both parties at each stage. The number of stages in a procedure is largely determined by the organisation structure, but in practice no more than three internal stages are workable. More than this can lead to a procedure that is unwieldy, slow and potentially confusing in the way it operates. A three-stage procedure may operate at departmental, functional and senior levels.

1 The departmental level provides the first hearing of the grievance through the line manager of the aggrieved employee.
2 The functional level conducts the next hearing of an unresolved grievance and involves the line manager's manager or the functional manager.
3 The senior level conducts the third hearing of an unresolved grievance and involves a member of the senior management team or the managing director or the chief executive.

Exhibit 17.4 illustrates a potential grievance hearing structure.

The time scale for resolution, from receipt of the written grievance to its settlement, should be clearly defined and the aim should be to settle the grievance in the shortest

EXHIBIT 17.4 Hearing structure for grievance or dispute for larger organisations

Stage One	Line manager
Stage Two	Functional manager or manager's manager
Stage Three	Senior manager or director
External	ACAS pre-claim helpline or mediation

EXHIBIT 17.5 Example of a grievance procedure

If you feel unhappy about any aspect of the application of agreements, procedures or terms and conditions of your employment and its impact on you or if you feel you have been treated unfairly, you have the right to raise the issue formally through the grievance procedure. You may raise issues informally with your line manager at any time. If a situation is not dealt with to your satisfaction informally you should take it up immediately through the grievance procedure. You have the right to be accompanied at a grievance meeting by a trade union official or by a fellow employee of your choice. Your grievance will be given serious consideration and the proceedings will be kept as confidential as is reasonably practicable.

Stage 1   You should inform your line manager immediately in writing of any situation you feel is unfair. Your manager will meet with you within five working days.

Stage 2   If the issue remains unresolved, you may progress the matter by appealing to your functional manager or your manager's manager. A meeting will be held within a further five working days.

Stage 3   If the situation remains unresolved to your satisfaction a further appeal meeting will be held with a senior manager. This meeting will be held within a further ten working days.

At each stage of the grievance procedure you will be advised of the outcome within three working days. Situations of a sensitive nature such as discrimination or harassment or which directly involve your line manager may be raised in the first instance with the HR manager.

possible time. The outcome of the grievance should be notified to the aggrieved employee in writing, stating their right to take the grievance to the next stage of the procedure if there is dissatisfaction with the decision of the reviewing manager. The grievance procedure should identify the type of issues that can be raised, but this should not be used as a means of restricting the use of the procedure. An example of a grievance procedure is shown in Exhibit 17.5.

Discrimination and harassment are sensitive issues, needing careful handling, and may require a different procedure. The person doing the harassing or discriminating may be the aggrieved employee's line manager and this is problematic for the issue to be raised and resolved through the standard grievance procedure. In these cases the grievance may need to be reported to a designated, and trained, person and there is therefore an argument for having a separate procedure to deal with these sensitive issues (*see* Chapter 8).

Grievance hearings

The importance of management taking any grievance seriously cannot be over-emphasised. If employees feel strongly enough to use the formal grievance procedure to raise complaints they have the right to a fair and respectful hearing. Dissatisfactions and complaints raised outside the formal procedure also need to be treated with priority to reduce the likelihood of formal processes being invoked. Indicators of a potential problem with unresolved dissatisfaction may be high levels of labour turn-over, absenteeism, resistance to change and low morale. Failure to investigate or attempt to identify internal causes may result in unfair treatment being unreported and unresolved, and may lead to longer-term problems for the organisation. A number of skills and conditions are required for grievance hearings.

Provide an appropriate physical environment. It is important to the employee that the situation is being taken seriously and therefore a room where the complaint can be heard in private, free from interruption, should be made available. The employee should be given notice of the date, time and venue and informed of the right to be accompanied.

Listen to, and hear, what is being said by the aggrieved individual. Any hearing requires good active listening skills, appropriate body language and eye contact if the aggrieved employee is to feel that the issue is being listened to and heard.

Ask appropriate questions in a non-threatening way. Empathetic questioning is essential to understanding the nature of the grievance and how the aggrieved person feels. The complaint must be fully exposed and this may need careful probing and questioning so that all the facts can be identified and clarified. Questions should be asked in a non-threatening way to encourage the employee to speak openly without feeling that it will disadvantage the case. It is valuable to identify the outcome the aggrieved is looking for, because it is not uncommon for the situation to require a negotiated settlement – compromise may be the only way forward: 'Invite the employee to re-state ther grievance and how they would like it resolved' (ACAS, 2009b: 45).

Prepare. A grievance is employee-initiated and, apart from reading the written grievance carefully and gathering the facts of the matter, there may be little the manager can do to prepare for the first hearing. It is at the subsequent stages that managerial preparation is mainly undertaken.

Analyse the facts and take a decision. Having heard all the facts of the case, consulted the relevant policy, sought advice from another manager or an HR specialist and looked at similar situations that may have set precedents, the manager takes a decision. A manager works within the framework of organisational policies and procedures and the grievance decision may set another precedent, in effect contributing to 'organisational case law'; therefore, any managerial interpretation of the grievance must be one that the employer can live with. If further time is needed for investigation, employee agreement should be sought for extending the procedural time scale to avoid the further complaint of not adhering to the agreed procedure.

Communication and monitoring of decisions

An individual grievance ends with an outcome that is accepted by the individual or the procedure is exhausted, but the situation does not end there. It is important that the grievance decision is communicated clearly to the employee within the procedural time scale and that both parties understand exactly what has been agreed. There is value in monitoring grievances in terms of issues raised and outcomes agreed because issues that frequently give rise to grievances may highlight an organisational problem. Some of the terms and conditions of employment may need to be rewritten in a format that is more easily understood by employees and managers, or training may be needed to explain the implementation of policies. Grievance decisions can be analysed for the more general organisational implications and the establishment of precedents. The decisions can be aggregated, evaluated and communicated, anonymously if necessary, to relevant managers and used positively in management development.

There is potential for managers to feel threatened by employee use of the formal grievance procedure. Managers therefore require support to develop a full knowledge of the application of policies and procedures and to have the confidence to take difficult decisions and a manager with a higher incidence of formal grievances may have a development need. Flatter organisational structures and managerial empowerment may result in managers increasingly being in decision-making situations which require discretion. Managerial discretion requires confident and competent line managers who communicate well with employees, both informally and formally. Employee concerns will only be resolved if managers know about them. In summary, Exhibit 17.6 articulates the key professional and ethical characteristics of a grievance procedure.

EXHIBIT 17.6 **The key professional and ethical characteristics of a grievance procedure**

1   Clearly communicated and staged procedures.
2   Short time limits for resolution which enable matters to be dealt with quickly and at the lowest possible level.
3   A process which is based on listening and concern resolution.
4   A means of effectively communicating outcomes to the aggrieved employee.
5   An awareness that finding out what an employee actually wants to achieve can often lead to resolution.
6   A preparedness to admit to making a mistake if that is actually the case.
7   An awareness that managerial decisions in grievance issues can create precedent and thereby alter the organisational rules.
8   An overall analysis of employee grievances may point to the need for rule or policy revision or management development.
9   Honesty, integrity and confidentiality.

MEDIATION AS AN ALTERNATIVE TO TRIBUNAL PROCEEDINGS

Following the repeal of the statutory disciplinary and grievance procedures in 2009, the government was keen to promote mediation as an effective alternative way of resolving employment disputes. Mediation is based on the principle of collaborative problem solving with a focus on the future, rather than allocating blame. An independent mediator can be appointed who talks to both the employer and the employee, often separately, and suggests ways for them to reach agreement. It is informal and flexible and aims to restore the employment relationship. As mediation is confidential parties are encouraged to have an open and honest discussion. It also avoids the cost and time of tribunal proceedings. A guide on mediation for employers has been jointly prepared by ACAS and the CIPD (CIPD, 2008) and provides employers with practical help in deciding if mediation could work for them and highlights the factors and processes to be considered in its implementation.

> Grievances most obviously lend themselves to the possibility of mediation. Managers may not always see it as appropriate to surrender their discretion in relation to disciplinary issues where they believe a point of principle is at stake, such as misconduct or poor performance. However, disciplinary and grievance issues can become blurred, and the employer may prefer to tackle the underlying relationship issues by means of mediation.
>
> (ACAS, 2009b: 7–8)

SUMMARY LEARNING POINTS

1 Disciplinary and grievance procedures can be positively viewed as individual conflict-resolving mechanisms. They allow mutual adjustment within the contract of employment through corrective action and concern resolution. Good disciplinary and grievance procedures not only ensure compliance with the law but also make an added-value contribution through protecting the organisation's investment in human capital.

2 Organisation rules relating to employee conduct and performance need to be clear, and disciplinary procedures should provide for fairness in dealing with employees who break the rules or fail to meet legitimate performance standards. Disciplinary procedures gain credibility and potential for effectiveness through the incorporation of the principles of natural justice and the ACAS features.

3 The ACAS Code of Practice and Advisory Guide on discipline at work provide guidance for the design and operation of disciplinary procedures.

4 Conducting a disciplinary meeting is a highly skilled activity requiring resilience and professionalism. Although it is not typical for meetings to progress smoothly and through orderly stages, the elements and structure of an effective disciplinary meeting can be identified and analysed.

5 The law requires that grievance reporting procedures are communicated to employees and employees have a right to be accompanied at a grievance hearing. Different levels of employee dissatisfaction are in evidence in organisations and not all result in the employee using a formal grievance procedure. The formal procedure should support the speedy resolution as close to the problem as possible, and the time scales for a hearing should be expressed and adhered to.

6 Managers need to be skilled to hear grievances in an open and positive way. Some sensitive issues require particularly careful handling and may need other mechanisms for reporting and hearing.

7 Managerial decisions emerging from grievances should be monitored for organisational implications and the creation of precedents.

REFERENCES AND FURTHER READING

Advisory, Conciliation and Arbitration Service (2009a) *Code of Practice 1: Disciplinary and Grievance Procedures*. London: ACAS.

Advisory, Conciliation and Arbitration Service (2009b) *Discipline and Grievances at Work: The ACAS Guide*. London: ACAS.

Aikin, O. (1999) 'The differences the Employment Relations Bill will make to individual employees' rights in the workplace', *People Management*, 11 March, 27–8.

BERR (2008) 'Resolving disputes in the workplace: Government response'. Department for Business, Enterprise and Regulatory Reform. BERR/05/08/NP. URN 08/359 www.berr.gov.uk

CIPD (2009) *Discipline and Grievance Procedures*. Factsheet. London: CIPD.

CIPD and ACAS (2008) *Mediation: an employer's guide*. London: CIPD.

Dickens, L. (2002) 'Individual employment rights since 1997: constrained expansion', *Employee Relations*, 24(6), 619–37.

Earnshaw, J. (1997) 'Tribunals and tribulations', *People Management*, May, 34–6.

Employment (Conflict Resolution) Act (2002). London: HMSO.

Employment Digest 270 (1989) *Preparing for a Disciplinary Interview*, June. Croner CCH Group.

Employment Relations Act (1999). London: HMSO.

Employment Rights Act (1996). London: HMSO.

Farnham, D. (2000) *Employee Relations in Context*. London: CIPD.

Farnham, D. and Pimlott, J. (1995) *Understanding Industrial Relations*. London: Cassell.

Fowler, A. (1994) 'How to handle employee grievances', *People Management Plus*, October.

Fowler, A. (1996) 'How to conduct a disciplinary interview', *People Management*, November.

Lewis, D. and Sargeant, M. (2000) *Essentials of Employment Law*. London: CIPD.

Pilbeam, S. and Corbridge, M. (2000) 'The skills of employee relations', in Farnham, D. (ed.) *Employee Relations in Context*. London: CIPD.

Public Interest Disclosure Act (1998). London: HMSO.

Salamon, M. (2001) *Industrial Relations: Theory and practice* (4th edn). Hemel Hempstead: Prentice Hall.

Temperton, E. (2000) 'Disciplinary procedures: the right to moral support', *People Management*, 16 March, 21–2.

ASSIGNMENTS AND DISCUSSION TOPICS

1 Discuss with student or work colleagues what they perceive to be the meaning of discipline at work; identify the retributive, deterrent and rehabilitative elements.

2 Obtain one or more disciplinary procedures and test them against the principles of natural justice and the ACAS features.

3 Obtain copies of several disciplinary procedures and compare and contrast them in relation to:
   - the number and specification of stages
   - the managerial responsibilities at each stage
   - the time limits on warnings
   - the requirements to sign warning letters and the significance of the signature.

4 Critically evaluate the role of the HR specialist in matters of employee discipline in several organisations and explain any similarities or differences.

5 What are the arguments for having a grievance procedure and what are the key professional and ethical characteristics of an effective grievance procedure?

6 Investigate the number of formal grievances in your organisation over a specified period. Analyse the subjects of the grievances and the outcomes of the hearings. Write a brief report on your findings, paying particular attention to any organisational implications.

Chapter 18

Termination of Employment

LEARNING OUTCOMES: TO BE ABLE TO

- Explain the five potentially fair reasons for dismissal and the concept of reasonableness in the circumstances

- Advise on the termination of a contract of employment in line with relevant legislation

- Contribute to the avoidance of successful claims for unfair dismissal

- Describe the employment tribunal process in relation to dismissal

INTRODUCTION

Employees who have been resourced into the organisation will at some stage disengage or be released from the contract of employment. Termination of employment, whether through dismissal, resignation or retirement, is a crucial function of the people resourcing aim of having the right people, in the right place, at the right time. It is necessary to understand the legal framework for dismissal, as it provides an effective practice guide and enables employers to act reasonably and fairly. In addition to statutory provision, case law establishes or redefines dismissal principles, and it is therefore necessary for managers to scan the legal environment. The effective management of termination of employment adds value through contributing to protecting an organisation's investment in people by ensuring that the right people remain in employment, and also in avoiding the financial and other costs associated with successful employee claims for unfair dismissal. Redundancy is given particular consideration in the next chapter.

INTRODUCTION TO DISMISSAL

The legal framework relating to dismissal is continuously evolving, not only through statute but also through principles which emerge from decisions in specific cases. The search for right and wrong answers in the management of employee dismissal is elusive, but this does not absolve HR practitioners and managers from needing to know when more knowledgeable or expert advice is required. This is the rationale for a focus on dismissal in this chapter, because pitfalls await the unwary who may think a dismissal progresses smoothly and naturally. A more appropriate view is that:

> A dismissal consists of collecting relevant information, a sequence of decision points and informed judgement based on a knowledge of the legal framework, the principles of natural justice and considerable skill.

Dismissal cannot be divorced from the procedures for conflict resolution discussed in the previous chapter.

The legal environment needs be continuously scanned for dismissal developments. This scanning provides guidance on current thinking in employment law, gives insights into how legislation is being interpreted, and identifies difficulties in which other employers have become entangled. A cautionary note is valid. Rather than searching for particular precedents, perhaps the domain of lawyers, it is advocated that dismissal decisions are guided by the general concepts of fairness, reasonableness and respect for the employee. This integrates an ethical dimension with the legal framework and contributes to good employment relations (Exhibit 18.1). Good dismissal practice and principles are preferable to mechanistic subservience to the law, and courts recognise that employers are not always perfect.

THE ORIGINS AND AIMS OF UNFAIR DISMISSAL LEGISLATION

Prior to the Industrial Relations Act (IRA) 1971 there was little constraint on employers who wished to dismiss employees and, with a few exceptions, dismissal could be for

EXHIBIT 18.1 **An ethical approach to dismissal within the legal framework**

- Is the employee ready, willing and able?
- Is the employer able to provide work?
- Is the employee responding reasonably to the genuine needs and demands of the employer?
- Is the employee being treated with respect?
- Is the mutual trust and confidence necessary to the performance of the contract intact?

any reason or for no reason. The IRA created a limited job property right for employees and attributed a specific legal meaning to the concept of unfair dismissal. The main dismissal provisions are now consolidated in the Employment Rights Act (ERA) 1996, supplemented by provisions in the Employment Act 2002. The law is intended to afford some protection to employees against unreasonable treatment by employers which ends in loss of employment. There is a debate about the extent to which the law was aimed at encouraging fair practice in dismissal, with the legal remedies as a backstop, and the extent to which the law had the objective of enabling unfairly dismissed employees to be reinstated in their jobs. Which of these two perspectives is adopted will influence a judgement about whether the law has been successful (*see* Summary learning points 2, 3, 5 and 6).

The right of employees not to be unfairly dismissed was feared by employers as a significant infringement of managerial prerogative. These fears are largely unrealised, because the legislation does not deprive employers of the freedom to dismiss employees, and employers cannot be required to re-employ dismissed employees. The legal protection provides for some financial sanctions against employers who dismiss employees unfairly and unreasonably. In reality:

> The law actually legitimises dismissal by defining it as fair and reasonable in certain circumstances through providing a set of rules and guidelines, in effect a highway code, which allow employers to dismiss employees without fear of adverse consequences – the right of managers to dismiss is effectively made legitimate.

TYPES OF DISMISSAL

Distinctions need to be drawn between different types of dismissal to avoid incorrect usage and application. Wrongful and unfair dismissal have different meanings. Wrongful dismissal relates to a fundamental breach of contract, normally because of improper notice periods or failure to make notice payments. Wrongful dismissal claims were formerly heard by county courts, but can now be adjudicated by an employment tribunal, by an employment judge sitting alone. The remedy for successful claims of wrongful dismissal is normally limited to an amount equal to the payment due from the date of the wrongful dismissal to the date when the employment would have been lawfully terminated.

Unfair dismissal, in contrast, has a distinct legal meaning and is a dismissal which is not for one of the potentially fair reasons, as defined by the ERA 1996, or is not reasonable in the circumstances.

Claims for unfair dismissals are heard by an employment tribunal.

Dismissal with notice, summary dismissal and instant dismissal also have different meanings. Employees are normally entitled to be given proper notice of termination of the contract by the employer; this is termed dismissal with notice. Frequently an employee will receive payment in lieu of notice, because the employer no longer wants the employee at work. Whether this payment in lieu of notice is contractually legitimate or whether it constitutes damages for failure to give proper notice is subject to legal debate, but in practical terms the employee faced with the prospect of being paid and not having to work for it frequently finds this an attractive option.

Summary dismissal is dismissal without notice and will be lawful when an employee breaches a fundamental term of the contract of employment. This will normally be the case if the employer establishes a reasonable belief that the employee has committed an act of gross misconduct or when there is a wilful refusal to obey a legitimate and reasonable instruction. Gross misconduct and refusals to obey instructions go to the root of the employment relationship and destroy the contract; in these circumstances the employer is not obligated by the contractual term to give contractual notice, and summary dismissal occurs. Instant dismissal, which is often confused with summary dismissal, describes an immediate dismissal *without* proper investigation and *without* incorporating the principles of natural justice. Instant dismissal, unlike summary dismissal, has no legal standing and is likely to be judged by an employment tribunal as procedurally unfair; it should therefore be avoided.

DISMISSAL DEFINED

There are three principal dismissal occurrences.

1 The employer terminates the contract of employment, with or without notice.
2 The employee terminates the contract of employment by reason of the employer's behaviour (commonly known as constructive dismissal).
3 A fixed-term contract expires and is not renewed.

Where there is unambiguous employer action to terminate employment, the fact of the dismissal may be relatively easy to establish. Employer intention to dismiss must be clear and the employee cannot unreasonably interpret as a dismissal an ambiguous statement, a dismissive comment or a dismissal attempt by an unauthorised person. The test is whether there is a genuine and legitimate intention to dismiss the employee. It is an obvious truism that dismissal needs to be established before any claim for unfair dismissal can proceed, but there is frequently debate on whether a dismissal has taken place and often a difficulty in identifying an effective date of termination with precision. Agreements to terminate the contract do not constitute dismissal, but are only valid if the employee agrees to terminate with full knowledge of all the implications. An invitation to resign, as a preferable alternative to being dismissed, or the persuasion to resign under duress, or the tricking of an employee into resigning, are likely to constitute dismissals.

If the employee resigns there is no dismissal, but employee intentions must be clear. A 'throw-away' comment by an employee, either in a provocative situation or when under pressure, cannot be snatched by the employer as a resignation. An unreasonable interpretation of employee words or actions will constitute a dismissal rather than a resignation, and proper investigation is needed to establish the real employee intention if 'reasonableness' is a managerial concern. Where the resignation is unambiguous the employer is not obliged to agree to a subsequent employee request to withdraw the resignation, although the employer can choose to do so. An employer can also choose to withdraw a dismissal if an error is made.

In the case of 'constructive dismissal' it is the employee who resigns, but claims that the contract of employment has been terminated by the employer's unreasonable treatment or behaviour. The elusive question is – under what circumstances can an employee resign and claim constructive dismissal? This is explored later in this chapter. Dismissal can also occur through the expiry and non-renewal of a fixed-term contract. Dismissal at expiry will be lawful if there is a genuine employer need for a fixed-term contract, for example in the case of a project or a limited amount of work. Dismissal at the expiry of a fixed-term contract may be unreasonable if the contract is merely being used to limit statutory employment rights. To demonstrate reasonableness an employer is obligated to show that when a fixed-term contract expires the employee is fairly considered for other employment opportunities. An employer cannot lawfully avoid a continuous service requirement for statutory employee protection through a succession of fixed-term contracts. Attempts to avoid continuous employment through a succession of contracts which incorporate breaks in employment may be interpreted as 'a cessation of work within continuous employment'. It is the ratio of employment to unemployment with the same employer that will be significant in determining continuous employment. These complications are introduced because there is sometimes an uninformed view that fixed-term contracts, in supporting numerical flexibility, are largely free of legal constraint. Despite the generally positive mood of employment tribunals towards the employer's need to run enterprises flexibly and efficiently, employer freedom to use fixed-term contracts is circumscribed. First, it is no longer lawful for fixed-term workers to waive their rights to claim unfair dismissal (Employment Relations Act 1999). Second, the European Union Fixed Term Work Directive enacted in the Fixed Term Workers Regulations (2002), through protecting these workers against less favourable treatment than those on permanent contracts, gives fixed-term workers the same rights as those on unlimited contracts and seeks to control 'the abusive use of fixed-term contracts' (Aikin, 2001). In addition, fixed-term contracts will normally become permanent after four years. Fixed-term contracts are an area where further and better advice may be desirable.

EMPLOYEE QUALIFICATION FOR UNFAIR DISMISSAL PROTECTION

To qualify for protection against unfair dismissal an individual must first be an employee, with a contract of employment. Currently, an individual with a contract for services will not qualify. The distinction between a contract of employment and a contract for services is becoming less easy to define, and specialist reading is necessary for those interested in the distinction. The courts tend to apply a 'multiple test' to determine employment or self-employment status (Selwyn, 2000). A mutual agreement for an employee to become self-employed is not conclusive and, in the context of this chapter, the 'self-employed' individual may retain statutory protection against unfair dismissal. Teleworking trends generate further complexity for employment status and protection.

Until 2006 employees also needed to be less than 65 years of age or, where it was different, the normal and lower retirement age for the organisation. From 2006, and in order to implement the requirements of the European Equal Treatment Directive outlawing age discrimination in employment, a default retirement age of 65 years was set, effectively making compulsory retirement before 65 years of age unlawful. Also from 2006 employees have had the right to request working beyond 65 years of age, rather like the process for requesting flexible working for parents, and where an employer agrees to continued working the right of the employee not to be unfairly dismissed also continues. The government is committed to a further review of the default retirement age, and its implications and the default retirement age is subject to legal challenge.

Employees normally require one year's continuous service with the same employer, although some reasons for dismissal are inadmissible and do not have a service require-ment. The continuous service qualification period for protection against unfair dismissal has been six months (in 1974) and two years (up to 1999), and sometimes up to five years for part-time workers. In striking a balance between equal treatment objectives, particularly concerns about the potential for indirect discrimination against female employees, and employer flexibility to run businesses efficiently through being able to dismiss employees during the first year, the government settled on the one-year qualification period. There is no reason why the one-year period should not be subject to further challenges.

INADMISSIBLE REASONS FOR DISMISSAL

Dismissal for an inadmissible reason will render it automatically unfair and the one-year service requirement will not normally apply. *Potentially* inadmissible reasons include dismissal on the grounds of:

- pregnancy or maternity
- sex or race or disability or age
- spent convictions
- refusal to work on a Sunday
- health and safety activities or actions
- asserting a statutory employment right
- trade union membership, activity or non-membership
- the relevant transfer of an undertaking
- making a protected public interest disclosure
- exercising rights under the Working Time Regulations 1998
- *no* reason being given.

The scope of these inadmissible reasons may appear disproportionate in relation to the scope of the five potentially fair reasons (*see* below), but in practice the converse is the case. Inadmissible reasons are discussed briefly because managers need to recog-nise that special considerations apply.

Dismissal on the grounds of pregnancy, or for any reason connected to pregnancy, is effectively outlawed (ERA 1996: 599). This applies during pregnancy, during maternity leave or on return from maternity leave. It is unfair to select an employee for redundancy on the grounds of pregnancy or maternity leave. Attempts to construct a hypothetical 'pregnant-man' comparison to justify dismissal on the grounds of non-availability for work have failed (*Webb* v *EMO* [1995] IRLR 645 and *Tele Danmark* v *Brandt-Neilsen* [2001] IDS Brief 696, ECJ). By implication, it may be unlawful to refuse to employ a pregnant woman or a woman of childbearing age because she may become pregnant. Dismissal on the grounds of sex, marital status, race or ethnic origin is effectively outlawed by the Sex Discrimination Act 1975 and the Race Relations Act 1976, as amended. Sexual orientation and religion or belief were added to this list in 2003, and age in 2006. The legislation covers acts of direct discrimination and also acts of indirect discrimination which are to the detriment of the employee and which cannot be objectively justified. Indirect discrimination may occur, for example, if employees are selected for redundancy on the basis that they work part-time hours, because this may have a disproportionate impact on women who make up the majority of part-time workers. Dismissal as a result of pressure from other employees on the grounds of sex, marital status, race or ethnic origin is not justifiable. The burden of proof is now on employers to demonstrate that unlawful sex or race discrimination did *not* take place. Dismissal on the grounds of a disability, as defined by the Disability Discrimination Act 1995, may be automatically unfair unless it is justifiable within the terms of the Act.

Under the Rehabilitation of Offenders Act 1974 a spent conviction is not a proper reason for dismissal, although certain occupations are exempted. Under the Sunday Trading Act 1994, consolidated in ERA 1996, 'protected workers' who refuse to work on a Sunday cannot be fairly dismissed on the grounds of the refusal. Employers are not able to fairly dismiss employees for carrying out authorised health and safety duties or who alert the employer to a reasonable health and safety concern. It is normally unfair to dismiss an employee for ceasing work or taking other appropriate protective steps because of a genuine belief of being in serious and imminent danger. Employees will be unfairly dismissed if the principal reason is related to the assertion of a statutory employment right. This assertion may be an allegation that a right is being denied or other employee action, for example commencing employment tribunal proceedings, to enforce the right. The statutory right does not have to apply to the employee asserting the right. Also, it is immaterial whether the asserting employee qualifies for the right; the test is whether the employee has a genuine belief of qualification and whether the allegation is made in good faith.

A dismissal will be unfair if it is for one of the following reasons:

- for becoming or proposing to become a member of an independent trade union
- for taking part or proposing to take part in the activities of an independent trade union at appropriate times
- for not being a member of a trade union or refusing to become a member or refusing to remain a member of a trade union.

Where a business or a part of a business, in legal terms an economic entity, is transferred from one employer to another, through sale or externalisation, a dismissal, by the old or the new employer, will be considered unfair if the reason for the dismissal is principally connected with the transfer of the undertaking. Dismissal relating to business transfers needs to be treated with considerable care, particularly as the guiding principles keep changing through case law. The Working Time Regulations (1998) provide workers with the right to paid leave and to rest periods, and also limit the number of hours they can be required to work on average in each week. Employees will be unfairly dismissed where they refuse to comply with an employer instruction which is in contravention of the regulations. The Public Interest Disclosure Act (1998) provides protection for 'whistleblowers' – workers who are dismissed or victimised for making a qualifying disclosure. Finally, a dismissal is automatically unfair where no reason is given.

FAIR REASONS FOR DISMISSAL

Under ERA (1996) an employee can be lawfully dismissed for one of five potentially fair reasons:

- misconduct
- lack of capability
- redundancy
- statutory bar to employment
- some other substantial reason.

Effectively a sixth potentially fair reason for dismissal has been created by the default retirement age, because an employer can fairly dismiss an employee at age 65, subject to having conformed to the set procedure.

For a dismissal to be fair, not only must an employer have a fair reason (substantive justice), but also the dismissal must pass the test of 'reasonableness in the circumstances' (principally procedural justice).

Misconduct dismissals lead to many complaints for unfair dismissal, and specific types of misconduct are explored later in this chapter. Lack of capability relates to the skill, aptitude, physical and mental abilities, health, flexibility and qualifications of the employee in relation to contractual duties. Redundancy will normally be fair and reasonable where selection for redundancy is based on an objective procedure, where consultation arrangements have been appropriate and where alternative employment options have been explored. A statutory bar applies where the continued employment of an employee would result in a contravention of a legal duty, and in these circumstances an employer may fairly dismiss. The fifth potentially fair reason for dismissal is some other substantial reason (SOSR) of a kind that justifies dismissal, an acknowledgement that the previous four reasons are not exhaustive. These potentially fair reasons provide the employer with comprehensive scope for dismissal through legitimising it where:

- the employee's behaviour is unacceptable
- the employee cannot do the job
- there is no work for the employee
- the employee cannot legally be employed
- there are other substantial impediments to employment.

For a dismissal to be fair, an employer needs to show that it was for one of the five potentially fair reasons. This forms the basis for resisting any allegation of unfair dismissal. It is not always a simple matter to categorise correctly a dismissal and, although there should be a genuine effort to do so, an incorrect categorisation will not automatically invalidate the employer's argument that the dismissal was for a fair reason. As well as having a legal purpose, the five fair reasons for dismissal provide a useful framework for dealing with problems at work.

REASONABLENESS

Even where dismissal is for a fair reason, the substantive issue of whether the dismissal is fair rests on whether the action of the employer is 'reasonable in the circumstances'.

> The question of reasonableness will be determined in accordance with equity and the substantial merits of the case. (ERA, 1996)

Reasonableness is not determined by a judgement of whether the dismissal was correct, but 'whether the dismissal fell within the range of responses of a reasonable employer'. If the circumstances of the dismissal place it within this range, then it will be considered reasonable by an employment tribunal. Reasonableness in the circumstances is not an objective standard and the question of whether an employer acted reasonably involves consideration of the way in which the dismissal was carried out, in the context of the organisation's size and resources, and whether the reason for dismissing the employee was a sufficient reason. Figure 18.1 provides a framework for considering this concept of reasonableness.

Figure 18.1
Reasonableness in the circumstances

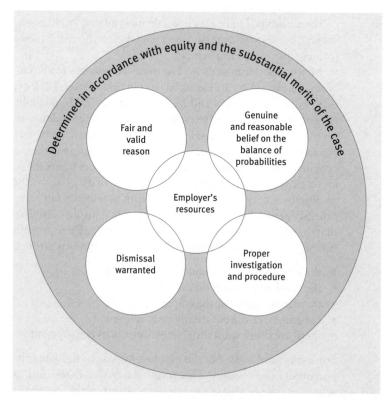

The legal framework, the ACAS Code of Practice on discipline and grievance procedures, supplemented by the ACAS guide on discipline and grievances at work, and tribunal decisions recognise that the size, the nature of the work activity and the resources of an organisation are material factors in determining reasonableness in the circumstances. A disciplinary procedure appropriate to a large organisation may be inappropriate for a much smaller one. The length of time and extent to which sub-standard employee performance can be accommodated will be influenced by the nature of the work and the impact of the individual performance on organisational effectiveness. Opportunities for redeployment, disciplinary transfer or other action short of dismissal will similarly be facilitated or limited by the employer's resources.

> Where some form of formal action is needed, what action is reasonable or justified will depend on all the circumstances of the particular case. Employment tribunals will take the size and resources of an employer into account when deciding on relevant cases and it may sometimes not be practicable for all employers to take all of the steps set out in this Code.
>
> (ACAS, 2009a: 3)

Procedural fairness involves thorough investigation, a proper hearing, the opportunity for an employee to offer an explanation, accompaniment, and the right of appeal. Good documentation of the procedural steps in dismissal cases is important in establishing the reasonableness of employer action. Until 1987 there existed a principle known as the 'no difference rule'. Even where a proper procedure had *not* been followed in a dismissal, it was open to an employer to argue that even if a proper procedure *had* been applied it would have made 'no difference' to the dismissal decision. This principle was effectively exploded in the case of *Polkey* v *A E Dayton Services* ([1987] IRLR 503), where dismissal was found to be unfair because of procedural failure. The procedural failure in that instance related to redundancy consultation, but the 'Polkey principle' has been extended by tribunals to other dismissals; thereby reasserting the importance of following a fair procedure. Consequently, procedural failure by the employer will normally result in a finding of unfair dismissal. However, the employment tribunal is under a statutory obligation to award compensation that would be just and equitable in the circumstances and may reduce compensation if an employer can demonstrate that following the procedure would have made no difference to the outcome.

Employers do not have to *prove* that a dismissal offence or incident actually occurred, nor does the employer have to prove that an employee was 'guilty'. ACAS (2009a: 18) avoids the use of the word 'guilty', instead preferring: 'Where misconduct is **confirmed** or the employee **is found to be** performing unsatisfactorily . . .' (emphasis added). The burden of proof is not one of *beyond reasonable doubt*, as in criminal law, but on 'the establishment of a genuine and reasonable belief' and 'the balance of probabilities'. This is a vital distinction. The question to address is whether the employer is entitled to hold a genuine and reasonable belief that the offence or incident occurred based on the factual information available at the time following proper investigation (*see* Exhibit 18.2, *BHS* v *Burchell* [1980] IRLR 379). Contrary information which becomes available subsequent to the dismissal will not normally invalidate the decision to dismiss.

Consideration of whether dismissal is actually warranted is another element of reasonableness. There are three principles to emerge from case law:

1 Is it reasonable to treat the reason as sufficient grounds for dismissal or would action short of dismissal have been a reasonable alternative (does the penalty fit the crime)?

EXHIBIT 18.2 The Burchell test in misconduct cases

It is the establishment of a genuine and reasonable belief following proper investigation that is the basis of the employer's decision in misconduct cases, there is no requirement for proof of guilt.

The case of *London Ambulance Service* v *Small* 2009 reminded employment tribunals of what they should do when assessing the fairness of a misconduct dismissal. The claimant was a member of an ambulance crew. A formal complaint was made about the claimant's treatment of a patient. The claimant's evidence, and that of his colleague on the scene, conflicted with that of the patient's family. The employer also took into account an expert medical report on the patient's condition before deciding to dismiss the claimant for misconduct. The employment tribunal decided that the dismissal was procedurally and substantively unfair, concluding that the employer did not have reasonable grounds for believing the claimant was guilty of misconduct as, although the claimant had failed in some respects, many allegations were not proved.

The EAT thought the tribunal, although wrong on some issues, was not wrong enough for the decision to be overturned. The Court of Appeal concluded the employment tribunal had failed to apply the law correctly. The principles laid down in the case of *British Home Stores* v *Burchell* in 1980 applied:

- Did the employer genuinely believe that the employee had been guilty of misconduct?
- Did the employer have reasonable grounds for that belief?
- Had the employer carried out a proper investigation before dismissing the employee?

If the answer is 'yes', the dismissal will be fair.

When dealing with misconduct dismissals, tribunals should focus their fact-finding on the way in which the employer dealt with the allegation of misconduct. Fact-finding about the misconduct itself will only be relevant in considering the extent to which the employee contributed to their own dismissal. In misconduct cases, it is not a requirement for employers to **prove** misconduct for a dismissal to be fair. If the employer follows the Burchell test and the decision to dismiss falls within a 'range of reasonable responses' it will be fair. It is not for an ET to substitute its own opinion.

2 Have employees in similar circumstances been treated similarly? This is the concept of being even-handed, but it is based on the merits of the case as the employer is not legally bound by organisational precedent.

3 Are there mitigating circumstances? Examples include previous good record, length of service, external pressures, aberration, or employer contribution to the circumstances of the dismissal.

FIVE FAIR REASONS EXPLORED

The five potentially fair reasons referred to earlier are now examined from a practical and managerial perspective. Prescriptive guidance is inappropriate, because each case will need to be considered on its substantial merits, but dismissal examples are explored and attention is drawn to related issues. The intention is to provide a focus for investigation when these issues arise at work.

Misconduct

It is necessary to differentiate between misconduct and gross misconduct. Misconduct which is not gross may not warrant dismissal until the disciplinary procedure has been exhausted and may therefore be dealt with incrementally under that procedure. Gross misconduct may go to the root of the contract and warrant summary dismissal. The employer has a duty to determine and to communicate those types of misconduct that may lead to loss of employment.

> Some acts, termed gross misconduct, are so serious in themselves or have such serious consequences that they may call for dismissal without notice for a first offence. But a fair disciplinary process should always be followed, before dismissing for gross misconduct. Disciplinary rules should give examples of acts which the employer regards as acts of gross misconduct. (ACAS 2009a: 22/23)

Therefore, employers need to provide indicative examples of gross misconduct, without making them exclusive or exhaustive, as case law demonstrates that people are creative in identifying and enacting new forms of gross misconduct. Automatic dismissal for incidents of gross misconduct is not justified and natural justice principles should still apply. Seven examples of misconduct will be specifically addressed in the following sections:

- theft and dishonesty
- violence
- alcohol abuse
- breach of confidence
- refusal to obey instructions
- absenteeism
- misconduct outside the workplace.

These are potentially fair reasons for dismissal, but the focus of attention needs to be on the circumstances under which they warrant fair and reasonable dismissal. The crucial question will frequently be whether the mutual trust and confidence necessary for the performance of the contract has been destroyed by the conduct of the employee. If it has then dismissal will follow. An important consideration for employers is that action short of dismissal for very serious misconduct may send signals to the workforce that certain types of behaviour, although disapproved of, do not result in loss of employment.

Theft and dishonesty

If an employee is suspected of theft or dishonesty, the employer is not obliged to prove guilt beyond reasonable doubt. The employer's obligation is to establish a genuinely held and reasonable belief that the theft or dishonest act is attributable to the employee, following appropriate investigation. It is important to adhere to a proper procedure even where theft or dishonesty may appear to be an open and shut case. In a *prima facie* case of dishonesty the usual sequence of prior investigation, the opportunity for the employee to explain and the consideration of the explanation should still be followed. It is often appropriate to suspend the employee during the investigatory process.

Allegations of theft or dishonesty may result in criminal proceedings. There are several issues here. First, the employer may wish to establish a reasonable belief, depending on the nature of the offence, before involving the police, as simultaneous investigations with different burdens of proof may add complexity to the dismissal question. Second, once criminal investigations are initiated, freedom may be constrained because employer action may interfere with or prejudice judicial proceedings. Third, the employer is not obliged to await the outcome of a criminal trial before making a decision, although where a reasonable belief has not been established it may be appropriate to do so. Fourth, the employer can consider information not admissible in a criminal trial. Fifth, even if a dismissed employee is acquitted in a court of law the dismissal is not rendered unfair, provided the employer acted reasonably; in such circumstances the court proceedings are considered to be largely irrelevant. A serious breach of rules or regulations is normally associated with an act of dishonesty and it is this breach that may warrant dismissal, not an alleged criminal offence (*see* Exhibit 18.3).

EXHIBIT 18.3 An illustrative case of dishonesty dismissal and the burden of proof

Peter is a supervisor with Bright Lights, an electrical wholesaler, and has been employed for three years. Part of his job is to transfer electrical components to a subcontractor, Tom, using official company documentation. Tom is a legitimate company subcontractor who repairs faulty electrical appliances. On two occasions Peter, using official documentation, has transferred to Tom more electrical components than was justified. The surplus components have been sold to the trade and the money given to Peter by Tom. The estimated value of the surplus components is £300.

The employer discovers this arrangement. It is a breach of administrative procedures and clearly undermines the degree of trust and confidence the employer can have in Peter. A reasonable belief is established that the illegitimate transfers have taken place; in fact strong evidence exists. During the disciplinary hearing Peter realises that the employer can substantiate the allegation and he admits to it.

Peter's explanation is that he was merely responding to pressure from his friends in the trade to supply components at short notice, that he had no dishonest intention and he intended to arrange for the cost of the components to be charged to his employee account so that he could pay Bright Lights retrospectively. The employee account system enables employees to purchase electrical components by signing charging slips at the point of purchase and receiving a demand for payment at the end of each month. Bright Lights did not accept Peter's explanation as legitimate and after due consideration dismissed him summarily. Criminal proceedings were also instigated following a reporting of the matter to the police. At the same time, Peter initiated a claim for unfair dismissal.

The decisions of the respective judicial bodies provide an interesting contrast. The employment tribunal was satisfied that the dismissal was fair and reasonable because the employer established a reasonable belief that a serious breach of rules had occurred and that the dismissal was justified because mutual trust and confidence in the contract of employment had effectively been destroyed. In the criminal proceedings, Peter elected trial by jury and was acquitted on the charge of theft. The judge was influential in the verdict as he pointed out to the jury that Bright Lights may have contributed to the situation because the principle of retrospective employee payment was condoned by Bright Lights. The criminal issue was whether or not Peter intended to pay for the electrical components retrospectively, and it could not be established beyond all reasonable doubt that he did **not** intend to do so. He was therefore found 'not guilty'. This case brings into sharp relief the different issues and burdens of proof associated with employment law and criminal law. The 'not guilty' verdict does not invalidate the legitimacy of dismissal.

Under what circumstances is an act of theft or dishonesty not gross misconduct? This is problematic, but the question is posed because there may be an inclination to consider all acts of theft or dishonesty as gross misconduct – can such an inclination be justified? The seriousness of the act may be a determining factor, but how can the degree of seriousness be established? The following points need to be taken into account:

- the triviality or gravity of the offence, based on considerations of value, volume, frequency and impact on the business
- custom and practice relating to the offence and the extent to which rules are made clear and actually enforced
- the even-handedness with which offenders are treated; for example, it may be unreasonable to clamp down on a dishonest practice by making an example of one individual
- the organisational position of the offender; for example, responsibility for others, seniority and the level of trust necessary
- previous record, length of service and any substantive mitigating circumstances.

Some acts of theft or dishonesty will clearly be gross misconduct. However, depending on the organisational circumstances, the use of telephones for personal calls, sending personal email, using the Internet for non-business reasons, the freeloading of stationery, or the unauthorised removal of materials or equipment no longer required by the organisation may be less clear cut.

Violence

A serious view is normally taken of violence by or between employees at work. Violence is not only a physical act, since threatening behaviour or harassment may constitute psychological violence. Although it is reasonable to rule that fighting will normally result in summary dismissal, this still needs to be communicated unambiguously. Even in the case of serious and overt violence, it remains necessary to investigate it thoroughly to establish reasons and motivation, but those involved should only be interviewed when they are in a fit state, emotionally and physically. If it emerges that there is an aggressor and a victim, the latter only acting in self-defence, the employer can treat the aggressor and the victim differently. Where it is not possible to distinguish between an aggressor and a victim, and where the violent incident warrants summary dismissal, it may be reasonable for the employer to dismiss both parties. Although this may not appear to be fair, it is a demonstration of how an employer is entitled to protect the interests of the undertaking, if necessary to the detriment of the employee. Other issues which may be material to an investigation into violence include:

- the degree of violence
- the degree of provocation
- the location of the violent act
- custom and practice; for example, condoned horseplay or initiation rituals
- the position, length of service and record of those involved, together with any substantive mitigating circumstances
- implications for the standing or reputation of the organisation.

Consideration of these factors will enable a reasonable employer to reach a decision about whether dismissal or action short of dismissal is appropriate when dealing with violence at work.

Alcohol abuse

Merely being under the influence of alcohol at work may not be a sufficient reason for dismissal, unless some other act is committed while under the influence, such as an act of violence, damage, abuse or insubordination, or where there are serious safety implications or where the employee's position is such that the alcohol-related conduct goes to the root of the contract and destroys mutual trust and confidence. It is important to distinguish between the act of drinking, smelling of alcohol, being under the influence and being unfit for work, as they may warrant different managerial responses. The employee should always be asked to provide an explanation for any alcohol-related incidents, but only when in a fit state to do so. An alcohol-related incident should be considered in the context of the organisational alcohol policy that defines the rules on alcohol consumption, which may range from a total ban, to drinking that is legitimate and socially acceptable (*see* Chapter 14). An aircraft pilot and a train driver have been fairly dismissed for relatively small amounts of alcohol consumption, but in contrast it may be entirely acceptable for employees in some occupations to entertain professional clients and consume alcohol as part of the hospitality activity. The provision of alcohol at authorised social functions may make an employer an accessory to alcohol-related misconduct. The alcohol rules should be clear and the employer is entitled to expect responsible behaviour from the employees even where the consumption is sanctioned.

Alcoholism and alcohol dependency may constitute a medical problem, with implications for support and treatment, and need to be treated differently from an incident of alcohol abuse. Failure by an employee to respond to alcohol counselling or treatment will be a fair reason for dismissal, probably on the grounds of incapability rather than misconduct. The test will be the reasonableness of the dismissal in the particular circumstances.

Breach of confidence

Employers are entitled to take a serious view of breaches of confidence by an employee, and the seriousness of these matters is recognised by tribunals. The employee owes a common law duty of fidelity to the employer. There are two principal ways in which confidence can be breached: first, by disclosing confidential information to a competitor or other unauthorised persons and, second, through seeking to bring the organisation into disrepute. In a case of disclosing confidential information the factors to consider are the significance of the information itself, the means by which it was obtained, the motivation for disclosure, the position of the employee and the nature and extent of any potential or real damage to the organisation. Similarly, in bringing the organisation into disrepute, the issues will relate to significance, motivation, position and damage. Organisation culture and managerial values may influence the extent to which employees are 'permitted' to complain about or disparage the organisation, but it is unreasonable to expect employees not to express some discontent, and mutual trust and confidence will need to be destroyed before dismissal is reasonable.

Refusal to obey instructions

An implicit obligation of the contract of employment is that an employee will obey the employer's instructions. A refusal to obey, enacted as either insubordination or disobedience, may amount to gross misconduct and be a fair reason for dismissal. The instructions must be legitimate and reasonable and there is no employee contractual obligation to conform to unlawful or unreasonable orders. Safety instructions can illustrate these points. Refusal by an employee to work safely, following proper instruction, may constitute gross misconduct, while refusal to work in an unsafe situation may be legitimate. If an employee refuses to obey a managerial instruction, the issues to consider are the clarity and comprehensibility of the instruction, whether it is legitimate to insist that the instruction be carried out, and whether the employee is fully aware of the consequences of continued refusal.

> The principle is that instructions have to be reasonable and refusals have to be unreasonable.

In cases of a refusal to obey instructions the employer needs to consider redeployment or other action short of dismissal as an alternative to terminating employment. Where the employee genuinely questions the legitimacy of instructions, a reasonable employer will take time to consider and explain, but the right to manage and the requirement to obey are fundamental features of the contract, and tribunal decisions tend to recognise that a refusal may result in loss of employment for the employee. A contemporary question is the extent to which an employer can insist that an employee works 'beyond contract'. Is a refusal to work beyond contract legitimate or obstructive to the performance of the contract? The issue is again one of reasonableness – how much performance beyond contract is being required and what is normal practice? The position of one employee who refuses to work extra uncompensated hours or take on additional work may be undermined where the majority of employees conform to such an order.

Absenteeism

Absenteeism in a misconduct context relates to unauthorised absence from work and not to ill-health absence which is a capability issue. Absenteeism is a difficult area because an employee may claim that the absence is due to sickness, and therefore implicitly authorised within the terms of the sick absence arrangements. The manager needs to establish the validity of sickness claims, but this is problematic. A false claim that absence is for reasons of sickness amounts to deception and, particularly where sick pay is concerned, can amount to dishonesty.

Unauthorised absence goes to the root of the contract because the employee is not ready, willing and able for work. The issues to consider include:

- the recorded level of absence
- whether the employee is aware of the standard expected and the consequences of a failure to meet an attendance standard
- whether the organisational implications of the absence are minor, serious or major
- whether employees are being treated similarly.

Monitoring systems are essential and lateness information should be integrated with absence data to provide a fuller picture (*see* Chapter 11). One incidence of wilful and unauthorised absence may effectively destroy the contract, but custom and practice are important. If, for example, the employer maintains a level of staffing to provide cover for absent employees and occasional unauthorised absence is implicitly accepted, dismissal for one incidence of absenteeism may be unreasonable. There remain occupations and patterns of work, perhaps involving early or late starts or unsociable hours or shift work, where absence is condoned to a limited extent and this is material to dismissal decisions. In addition, there remain some organisations where employees perceive sick absence up to a certain level to be an entitlement to be used.

Conduct outside the workplace

To what extent is employee conduct outside employment the legitimate concern of the employer? Tribunal decisions indicate that where employee conduct outside employment has adverse consequences for the employer it becomes of employer concern. Some guiding principles and examples are available. In principle, conduct outside employment has implications for the contract of employment if it significantly lowers confidence in the integrity of the employee, if the ability or work capacity of the employee is compromised, or if the conduct is substantially detrimental to organisational performance or reputation. A reasonable belief that the particular conduct has occurred needs to be established. Illustrative examples of conduct outside employment which may, in certain circumstances, warrant dismissal include:

- conviction for a criminal offence, although an automatic dismissal rule would normally be unreasonable
- working for another employer, if that employment results in a reduction in the effectiveness of the individual or in a conflict of interest or where other employment is prohibited

- continuing to engage in legitimate activities which seriously spill over into employment, for example duties as a police special, territorial army service or political candidacy and activities
- membership of interest groups or pressure groups where the objectives are incompatible with those of the employer.

Those in the public eye, public servants and those working with vulnerable groups can legitimately anticipate a greater employer concern with conduct outside employment.

CASE STUDY   Christmas spirit and the amorous kitchen porter

Is dismissal within the range of responses of a reasonable employer taking account of equity and the substantial merits of the case, or is action short of dismissal the response of a reasonable employer?

It is Christmas Eve in a department store and you are the HR manager. You have had a busy Christmas trading period, having worked extremely long and unsocial hours, and you are looking forward to a few days' break, although you do have a management research report to complete for your Postgraduate Diploma in Human Resource Management course. At 3.00 pm the managing director (MD) storms into your office with a distressed catering manager in tow. The MD reports that he has just discovered the kitchen porter lying comatose on the staff staircase clutching a bottle of brandy, having reached this prone position only after trying to kiss and cuddle anyone in the proximity. These amorous advances were also made towards the MD himself, much to the merriment of a collection of other employees who observed the incident. Apparently this state of affairs had been going on for about an hour and was the talk of the store among the staff.

The kitchen porter has been employed for three years and normally works part-time hours, but has worked full time during the Christmas trading period. There is no other known incidence of alcohol abuse. His work is just satisfactory, although his performance gives cause for concern from time to time, and as a prank he recently barricaded himself in the washing-up area using cooking pots to construct a wall. The warning for this is still live. There is a shortage labour market for reliable and effective kitchen porters, both as direct employees and through employment agencies. The MD says he has matters of greater importance to deal with and makes it clear to you that he wants the matter sorted out before the end of the day.

Questions

1 What action would you take immediately?

2 What issues would you need to consider?

3 What would be your decision on disciplinary action?

4 Would it make any difference if it was the (female) catering colleagues of the kitchen porter who, with the knowledge and tacit agreement of the catering manager, presented the kitchen porter with the bottle of brandy at lunchtime as a Christmas present; the kitchen porter was then encouraged, probably enticed, by a couple of mischievous colleagues, spurred on by knowledge of his recent erratic behaviour with the potwash barricade, to have a drink from the brandy bottle?

> It would seem, then, that employees may do what they like outside working hours,
> as long as it does not affect their ability to do the job under a contract of employment.
> It is therefore important . . . that the employer is able to make a convincing
> demonstration of the impact such behaviour will make.   (Williams, 1996)

Lack of capability

This section deals with capability concerns relating to incompetence, lack of qualifications and ill health.

Incompetence

Competence encompasses skill, knowledge, flexibility and other attributes. The concern of the employer is whether competence is sufficient for the effective performance of the contract. Where incompetence results in substandard performance, it is useful to distinguish between remedial incompetence, non-remedial incompetence and a failure to exercise competence, because they need to be treated differently. Figure 18.2 displays these three types of incompetence as overlapping areas, and managerial judgement to determine which applies is necessary.

Remedial incompetence signifies that, through genuine and joint action, competence can be developed and an acceptable standard of performance can be achieved. The following steps are required:

Figure 18.2
Incapability or substandard work: incompetency typology

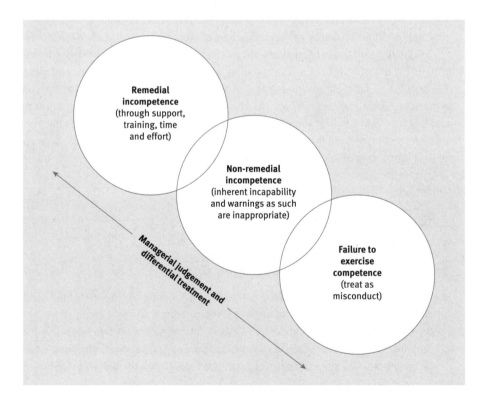

- ensure the employee understands the expected standard of work
- identify the gap between employee performance and the expected standard, focusing on the knowledge, skill and other attributes required
- provide sufficient time, opportunity, training and other support where practicable
- inform the employee of the consequences of a failure to achieve the required standards
- keep the matter under review and feed back on progress.

Non-remedial incompetence exists where, despite the best efforts of the employee and the employer, an acceptable standard of performance is not achievable. This is also termed inherent incapability. Warnings as such are not appropriate because they will not make any difference, but this does not negate the value of identifying a performance shortfall, pointing out the potential consequences and examining opportunities for contractual changes or redeployment, although there is no obligation to create a special job.

Failure to exercise competence, through carelessness, wilfulness or negligence, is a misconduct (and not a capability) issue and needs to be treated accordingly.

Changing skill and knowledge demands may render incompetent an employee who was previously performing satisfactorily. This is no fault of the employee and significant changes in job demands may constitute job redundancy. Where job demands change but the identity of the job remains and the employee becomes incompetent, the employer is entitled to ensure that the business is not adversely affected. This may ultimately result in the fair dismissal of the employee for incapability. Employee competence can also be an issue when a newly appointed manager demands higher standards of competence and performance than had previously been the case, resulting in the redesignation of an employee as incompetent. To what degree is the new manager entitled to demand higher standards? The answer is 'to a reasonable degree', as the right to manage is respected in the contract of employment. These two illustrations demonstrate that competence is continuously redefined in response to reasonable managerial demands because organisations are not compelled to retain employees who are not competent to perform the contract.

Lack of qualifications

Academic, technical or professional qualifications may be deemed necessary for performance in the job and if qualifications are required prior to commencement of employment, they should be checked out. Where they are required to be achieved within employment, a reasonable time scale and a reasonable number of attempts should be allowed. For dismissal to be reasonable the following points are also relevant:

- The qualifications required must be unambiguously determined by the employer.
- A contractual obligation to achieve the qualification must exist.
- The qualification must be essential to the performance of the contract.

Ill health

Lack of capability through ill health, because of unacceptable performance or absence levels, is difficult to manage and each case needs to be considered on its particular

EXHIBIT 18.4 Principles for dealing with ill health

1 The employer's objective is fact-finding to establish capability, or otherwise, to perform the contract.
2 The employee, who has a duty to remain contactable, should know of any employer concern.
3 The employer should normally seek a medical prognosis.
4 The employee should know whether the job is at risk.
5 The employer should consider alternative work or contractual changes which provide continued employment, where practicable.
6 Employees with similar ill-health performance or absence records should receive parity of managerial attention, unless there is a valid reason for disparate attention.
7 Dismissal is not a medical decision, but a managerial decision with a medical input.
8 The decision to dismiss can be based on the 'enough is enough' principle.

merits. The managerial judgement is objective and not emotive and treats the employee reasonably.

> The ill-health process consists of a series of steps or decision points leading to a conclusion which frequently cannot be predicted early in the proceedings.

If there are doubts about the validity of absence, the matter should be dealt with as misconduct, not ill-health incapability. A common framework of ill-health dismissal principles can be utilised (Exhibit 18.4). The managerial focus is not on diagnosing the ailment, but on the implications for the job. Warnings, in a conventional sense, are inappropriate because employees cannot be warned back to health, but employer concern, particularly where loss of employment is possible, must be conveyed. The purpose of the medical prognosis is predictive, and the aim is to establish the probability of improvement or deterioration in the health of the employee in so far as it may affect employment. Employer access to medical information needs employee consent under the Access to Medical Records Act 1988 and the Data Protection Act 1998 (*see* Chapters 5 and 11). The Data Protection Act 1998 classes information on health as sensitive information requiring more overt employee consent to its collection, security and use. The employer also needs to be able to demonstrate that the health information is going to be used for a legitimate purpose – such as consideration of the employee's fitness to perform the contract of employment. This poses some challenges for the employer, but it would appear that a distinction can be made between 'medical information' and 'attendance records', with only the former being subject to employee consent constraints (Information Commission, 2002). Employee refusal to allow an employer access to relevant medical information or refusal to be consulted by an organisational medical practitioner presents a difficulty, but refusals to cooperate in these ways do not prohibit the employer from proceeding on the basis of the information that is available. A medical prognosis is more of an art than a science and involves uncertainty and sometimes conflicting predictions. The employee's medical practitioner, with legitimate claims to intimate professional knowledge of the employee, may provide one scenario, and the employer's medical practitioner, with legitimate claims to intimate professional knowledge of the work, may provide an alternative and contrasting scenario. In this situation the employer can seek a 'tie-break', which may only create a third alternative, or more pragmatically elect to follow the opinion of the practitioner who has been appointed by the organisation for the purpose. The decision to dismiss is always a managerial decision. The decision is informed by medical opinion, but takes account of the nature of the work, the impact on the organisation, the length or frequency of any absence, the resources and potential of the organisation to accommodate absence or reduced performance, and the employee's record and length of service.

An employee with ill-health problems may be able to return on reduced hours or with different responsibilities to facilitate rehabilitation to work. Unless transitional arrangements can be accommodated on a permanent basis, the employer is only expected to offer these contractual alterations for a limited and reasonable period. Whether an absent employee is receiving sick pay is largely irrelevant to the reasonableness of a dismissal. It is not necessary for an employer to await the expiry of any sick pay before dismissing where it is evident that the employee will not return to normal work, although it may be compassionate to do so. There is, however, potential for a wrongful dismissal claim where contractual sick pay terms are breached. Conversely, the expiry of sick pay is not a legitimate reason for dismissal; and paradoxically the expiry of sick pay in reducing the financial burden of absence on the employer may make lawful dismissal more difficult.

Frequent short-term sick absence is often more disruptive than a longer period of ill-health absence and in practice attracts less managerial and co-worker sympathy. Medical opinion is still valid in cases of frequent short-term absence in identifying underlying health issues which may respond to treatment. Medical certificates are not indisputable evidence of being unfit for work, although there is understandable hesitancy about challenging their legitimacy. There is a distinction between being unwell and being unfit for work (*see* Chapter 11, Exhibit 11.3); the unwell but apparently fit employee brandishing a certificate of unfitness is provocative to other employees. There is a paradox here also, because in cases of psychological ill health the employee may be fit for work until actually returning to work.

Dismissal for incapability due to a disability will not automatically be unfair, but employers will need to justify a dismissal decision. Where an employee is unable to manage the essential elements of a job, even where reasonable adjustments have been made, and contractual changes and alternative employment are not practicable, then dismissal may be justified. In effect a more stringent test of reasonableness is applied to the ill-health dismissal of an employee classified as disabled under the Disability Discrimination Act 1995.

The 'enough is enough' principle is the point at which the reasonable employer has exhausted alternatives to dismissal and is entitled to dismiss, however painful this may be for the employee or the employer. This principle applies equally to frequent absence and long-term ill health. In seeking to balance the need of the organisation to achieve its objectives efficiently and the need of the employee for further time to regain capability, the issue is whether 'the time has arrived when the employer can no longer reasonably be expected to keep the employee's post open for him' (*Hart* v *Marshall* [1977] IRLR 51). Effectively this is a test of whether the employee is able to give continuous and effective service.

Redundancy

Redundancy handling is given comprehensive treatment in Chapter 19. The purpose here is to demonstrate briefly that a framework exists to enable employers to dismiss fairly and legitimately for the reason of employee redundancy in the pursuit of organisational efficiency. When a business ceases, the result for the employee is termination of employment through redundancy and this will normally be a fair reason for dismissal. Redundancy through reorganisation and restructuring is also potentially fair. In addition to obligations to consult with employees and their representatives, to follow a fair procedure, to consider alternative work and to make statutory redundancy payments, employers are required to apply an objective and reasonable selection procedure if redundancy dismissal is to be fair. The training and enabling of the managers to handle individual redundancy situations is vital to ensuring procedural fairness.

Statutory bar to employment

A bar exists where employment contravenes a statutory duty or restriction and it would be unlawful to continue to employ the person in the position for which they are contracted. The loss of a driving licence by an employee employed in a driving capacity may constitute a fair reason for dismissal, but the dismissal still has to pass the test of reasonableness. This requires consideration of the seriousness of the driving offence, and whether it results in a loss of confidence and trust in the employee, the length of a driving ban, the extent of the driving required for the job, the viability of the employee making alternative transport arrangements and the practicability of redeployment. The loss of a driving licence is a serious matter but there are differences, for example, between a chauffeur who is banned for three years for drunken driving and a warehouse worker occasionally required to make deliveries who loses a driving licence for three months under the totting up of penalty points. Each case must be assessed on its merits.

The absence of a licence to practise in some positions in the legal, accountancy or medical professions, or the absence of a certificate of technical competence in, for example, occupations associated with electricity or power presses, may be a fair reason for dismissal, if it is reasonable in the circumstances. An employee failure to renew a work permit will normally be a statutory bar to continued employment.

Some other substantial reason (SOSR)

This safety net reason for dismissal effectively recognises that the previous four reasons of misconduct, lack of capability, redundancy and statutory bar are not exhaustive. Sometimes referred to as an 'employer's charter', it enables employers, and tribunals, to exercise discretion by identifying dismissal reasons which do not conveniently fall into other more specific categories. The essential consideration is that the reason must be substantial in nature and must warrant dismissal.

The most frequent 'other substantial reason' is dismissal of an employee because of their refusal to agree to a variation to contractual terms and conditions necessitated by organisational change, economic survival or other sound business reason. Although

EXHIBIT 18.5 Variation to contract: changing terms and conditions

Whether it is fair and reasonable to dismiss an employee who refuses a change to terms and conditions of employment depends on all the circumstances, including whether the employer has sound business reasons for the change and whether it has acted reasonably in the way in which it has dismissed the employee. The factors to be taken into account include: the extent of any detriment to the employee, the importance of the changes to the effectiveness of the business, whether the employee was consulted about the changes, whether other employees accepted the changes and whether alternatives to dismissal were considered.

The employee, Juliet Fiona, was an area sales manager covering south-east England. The employer wanted to increase the sales area to the whole of the south of England for reasons of continued viability of the organisation in difficult trading conditions. The employee was fully consulted, but in a typically contrary style, she objected to the change. Although initially working under protest she later refused to work to the new terms. After a disciplinary hearing and the opportunity to restate her objections the employer remained convinced that the expanded sales area was necessary to the health of the business. The employee was dismissed for some other substantial reason. The employment tribunal ruled that the dismissal was fair and reasonable, as the needs of the employer were commercially sound and there was no significant disadvantage to the employee in covering a larger geographical area.

made some time ago, the following statement by Aikin epitomises the primacy given to business needs.

> The reasonableness [of the change] is to be considered from the employers' and not from the employees' point of view and is based on business needs. (Aikin, 1984)

The contract of employment is dynamic and if commercial imperatives demand changes in employment terms, even if disadvantageous to the employee, the changes may be reasonable and a refusal to accept them may warrant dismissal. For a dismissal to be reasonable an employer needs to demonstrate a sound reason for the change, consult with the employee, consider alternatives to dismissal, and facilitate any changes through time scale, training, compensation and other support as necessary and practicable. This gives considerable latitude to the employer, reinforces the right to manage and recognises that quite substantive changes in the contract can be made unilaterally. A majority of employees accepting a unilaterally imposed change in terms and conditions may undermine the reasonableness of a refusal to cooperate by a small number of individuals. There are many cases which uphold the employer's right to make unilateral changes in certain circumstances. The cases of the sales manager in Exhibit 18.5 and the chicken catcher in Exhibit 18.6 are illustrative of some of the considerations associated with changing terms and conditions of employment for operational reasons. The SOSR test is always whether the reason for dismissal is substantial, whether alternatives to dismissal have been exhausted and whether the dismissal falls within the range of responses of a reasonable employer.

EXHIBIT 18.6 The employer, the chickens and the chicken catcher and the balance of disadvantage – some other substantial reason (SOSR) for dismissal

Faccenda Chickens Ltd produced fresh chickens for large multiple suppliers. Mr Wilson was employed as a chicken catcher with normal working hours of 4 am to 12 noon from Monday to Friday. Three years after Mr Wilson was employed the growth of the business necessitated an extension to the number of hours during which chickens were caught. A commercial decision was made to vary the starting and finishing times of the chicken catchers. The organisation informed the employees of the proposed changes which would involve working an eight-hour shift, but with starting hours varying between 2 am and 10 am. The chicken catchers were given notice of the termination of their existing contracts and offered new contracts with revised terms. Employees were consulted individually about these changes.

Mr Wilson was not prepared to accept the new working arrangements. The employer listened to his objections, but ultimately he was given a week to make his decision about whether he would accept or reject the new contract. He clearly indicated that he was not prepared to accept it and he was dismissed. Mr Wilson lodged a claim for unfair dismissal and stated that he had two principal objections. First, his early shift from 4 am to 12 noon enabled him to spend time with his children, whereas the new contract would make it difficult for him to do this. Second, his existing hours enabled his wife to go out to work and this was an economic necessity.

At the employment tribunal it emerged that his wife had not worked for nearly a year and the tribunal did not consider this a substantial reason for objecting to the new working hours. The tribunal also examined the proposed working pattern under the new contract for a period of one month and concluded that it would not significantly reduce the number of times that Mr Wilson would be able to see his children.

The tribunal considered previous cases where an employee's dismissal for a refusal to accept new terms of employment necessitated by a reorganisation of a business was found to be for some other substantial reason and of a kind which justified dismissal in the circumstances. The tribunal declared that Mr Wilson's dismissal was for some other substantial reason because Faccenda Chickens faced rapid expansion and the reorganisation was necessary to improve efficiency. The dismissal was held to be fair.

Mr Wilson made an appeal to the Employment Appeal Tribunal on a point of law but the EAT did not support his view. The EAT was convinced that the employer had fully considered the pressures on the organisation, the needs of the chickens and the interests of the employee, and ultimately and on balance the employee would have to be inconvenienced.

Source: Wilson v Faccenda Chickens Ltd, EAT 98/86.

Other illustrative SOSRs judged to have been fair and reasonable in particular circumstances include:

- irreconcilable personality clashes
- customer complaints or pressure
- employee plans to join a competitor

- office affairs
- severe body odour and failure to improve personal hygiene
- failure to disclose a material fact or making false statements on application for employment.

CONSTRUCTIVE DISMISSAL

Under what circumstances can an employee resign and successfully claim constructive dismissal? There are two key concepts – *conduct* and *repudiation*. It is the conduct of the employer which is material, not whether there is an intention to cause the employee to resign, and the conduct must be such that it can be reasonably construed as repudiating the contract of employment. Employer conduct will only constitute repudiation if it is a significant breach of an express or implied term and it goes to the root of the contract, effectively destroying it. This inhibits employees from success-fully claiming constructive dismissal merely on the grounds that they do not like some-thing; the unreasonable treatment by the employer must be fundamental to the contract. Repudiation of the contract is accepted by the employee through the resignation, but where there is no resignation it can be inferred that the conduct of the employer has been tolerated and implicitly accepted. However, the employee is not excluded from registering an objection at the time and continuing to work. The registration of this objection reserves the right of the employee to subsequently claim constructive dismissal on the basis that the incident or behaviour was not on its own sufficient to warrant resignation, but when taken with other subsequent occurrences can be construed as destroying the contract. Therefore, in addition to a single repudiatory act resulting in constructive dismissal, for example failing to pay wages or a significant and unjustified change in terms and conditions, there can be cumulative constructive dismissal. Indicative illustrations are provided in Exhibit 18.7 to give a flavour of constructive dismissal. In all cases the employee needs to demonstrate unambiguously that the employer's behaviour was not only unreasonable, but also that it forced a resignation. It is a question of degree in each case and ultimately whether mutual trust and confidence is fatally wounded.

EXHIBIT 18.7 Indicative examples of employer conduct which may be construed as constructive dismissal

- Issuing unjustified warnings or undermining authority or expressing unwarranted suspicions
- Using provocative or defamatory language or engaging in physical or psychological abuse
- Preventing access to pay increases, promotion or development opportunities
- Making unreasonable and substantial changes to job duties or terms and conditions
- Failing to respond effectively to genuine grievances
- Failing to provide effective support to victims of harassment, bullying or unfair discrimination
- Insisting on unsafe working practices
- Insisting on excessive workloads

CASE STUDY Wacker Payne and the Royal Naval Reserve training weekend

This case concerns an incident relating to the portering staff within the General Services and Maintenance (GSM) department of a Goodwins department store. The budget for this department has been devolved to the GSM manager, and the head porter has been made increasingly aware of the cost implications of the decisions he is making.

The General Services and Maintenance department

The GSM department provides a range of general services to the store, including portering, warehousing, stock movement, cleaning, maintenance repairs and security. The GSM porters work shifts designed to give optimum cover for 7-day trading. The shifts are:

Early: 07.00–16.00 or Late: 09.00–18.00

Week 1 – Monday to Friday
Week 2 – Tuesday to Saturday
Week 3 – Wednesday to Sunday

In addition to the GSM manager and the head porter there are 2 team leader porters, who undertake some supervisory duties such as work allocation as well as portering duties, 18 general porters and a department administrator.

The management, William (Wacker) Payne and the shop steward

The GSM manager, Geri Smiley, has worked at Goodwins for just over a year, and prior to that was an officer in the WRNS. Her duties include the planning of the work and setting the performance standards for the GSM department. The head porter, Harry Pilbeam, has worked at Goodwins for 15 years, and has been head porter for six years. He is responsible for the day-to-day running of the department, the organisation of duty rosters and the management of the staff. William (Wacker) Payne has been a porter at Goodwins for six years, having joined after 15 years as an able seaman in the Royal Navy. He is an active member of the Royal Naval Reserve and spends as much time as he can pursuing this interest. Helen Romsey is the HR manager and responsible for providing HR advice to all the managers. Sarah Symonds is the GSM department administrator and also a shop steward for USDAW, the shop-workers' trade union. She provides advice and support to USDAW members.

Union agreement on time off

The GSM department is unionised and Wacker Payne is a member of USDAW. The union has a collective agreement with Goodwins concerning the maximum number of employees allowed time off at any one time. This agreement states that 'in addition to those porters not rostered for a particular day no more than three porters will be granted time off at any one time'. This number is seen by management as the maximum to enable the GSM department to meet customer service standards while minimising overtime costs. It is custom and practice that no member of staff should be rostered to work a double shift – i.e. stay on duty for the shift immediately following the one he/she has just finished. In relation to this case study the staff handbook states that 'Goodwins employees should normally be granted time off, with pay, for reserve forces duties, subject to the essential needs of the business.'

Wacker and the Royal Naval Reserve training weekend

On Friday 28 May Wacker Payne asked to see Harry Pilbeam, the head porter, and explained that he had just received details of an RNR training weekend for Saturday and Sunday 5 and 6 June. He was due to work on those days, and requested time off to attend the RNR training, particularly as his commanding officer had indicated that attendance was essential for maintaining the currency of Wacker's CPD record. The head porter explained that he would need to check rosters for that weekend and let him know. Later in the day Harry Pilbeam saw Wacker Payne and told him that he had scrutinised the work schedules for 5–6 June, and in addition to those not rostered to work four porters were on leave that weekend. As a consequence he would not be able to grant Wacker the time off for RNR duties. Harry also explained that a request for annual leave from another porter had already been refused for that same weekend. It was the first time in the six years Wacker Payne had worked for Goodwins that he had been refused leave to attend RNR training and he was aggrieved, seeing the management decision as inflexible and not in keeping with the Goodwins claim that 'people are the most valuable resource'. He controlled his anger and disappointment and asked to see Geri Smiley and requested her to allow him the necessary time off. She checked on the situation but confirmed the decision of the head porter.

The grievance

Wacker Payne expressed his dissatisfaction to Geri Smiley and went to see his shop steward. After speaking to her he returned to his manager and told her that he wished to raise a formal grievance. The grievance alleged that he was being victimised by Harry Pilbeam and that Harry did not have the authority to refuse the request for time off, as the employee handbook required management to grant time off for RNR duties. He again requested time off on 5–6 June. He attached a copy of a letter from the Secretary of State for Defence, addressed to employers, urging them to support employees who were members of the reserve forces in the work they did and praising the essential and patriotic role of these volunteers. The MOD letter also stated that because of the importance of this training weekend 'leave should only be refused where the employee's absence would cause serious harm to the business'. Geri Smiley and Helen Romsey arranged to meet Wacker Payne and his shop steward on the following Monday, 31 May, to hear the formal grievance. The grievance was heard, the issues were discussed and the request for time off was again refused. A further two stages of the grievance procedure were heard during the week culminating in a meeting with the store director. All the requests were refused and Wacker Payne was informed that he was required to work on the weekend in question.

The alleged disciplinary situation

On the Saturday morning, 5 June, at 08.30, half an hour before Wacker Payne was due on duty, the team leader porter on duty received a telephone call from Wacker's wife saying that Wacker was sick and unfit to attend work that day. The team leader porter had no alternative but to telephone off-duty porters to arrange for someone to work overtime to keep the GSM department operational. Later in the day he received a further telephone call from Wacker's wife saying that he was still indisposed and would not be

(Box continued)

at work the following day. Further cover was arranged for the Sunday. Wacker Payne was not due to work on the Monday or Tuesday (because of informal rota adjustments) and he reported for duty as planned on the Wednesday.

Questions

You can assume that Goodwins has disciplinary and grievance procedures which are based on ACAS guidelines and the principles of natural justice.

Role-play

On his return to work on Wednesday 9 June Wacker Payne has been asked to attend a meeting with management to explain his absence from work. Students, or tutors, should be allocated to the roles of Geri Smiley, Helen Romsey, Wacker Payne and Sarah Symonds. The remaining students can join the management or employee teams to assist with preparation and the development of strategies during periods of adjournment. After periods of separate preparation by both the management and employee teams Geri Smiley and Helen Romsey should undertake a disciplinary meeting with Wacker Payne and Sarah Symonds. The meeting should be as realistic as possible and either party can adjourn at any time to consult with their respective teams. The role-play is complete when management communicate a decision to Wacker Payne.

Grievance discussion group or assignment

What advice would you give the GSM manager, Geri Smiley, in preparing for the first grievance hearing? What facts do you think ought to provide the focus of the meeting? Prepare a briefing paper which Geri Smiley could use in conducting the grievance hearing.

Disciplinary discussion group or assignment

What action would you advise the GSM manager, Geri Smiley, to take when Wacker Payne returns to work? What investigations would you undertake? If you discovered that Wacker Payne attended the RNR weekend camp what action would you take? Prepare a briefing paper for Geri Smiley outlining the issues to be covered in a disciplinary hearing.

EMPLOYMENT TRIBUNALS

Employment tribunals (ETs) are independent judicial bodies originally intended to provide an informal, accessible and non-legalistic process for dealing with individual employment disputes. It is debatable whether these intentions are being achieved, with legal representation the norm for employers and delays of months in cases reaching tribunals because of caseloads. Overell (2004), in his characteristic forthright style, is vehement about the role of lawyers in moving the tribunal process away from the informal, non-legalistic and accessible ideal: 'All parties unite in their collective animus toward the system's victors – the lawyers. Bodies that were set up to administer swift, informal workplace justice appear to be turning it into the playground of Pharisees. Once the lawyers get to work, the idea of objective justice is quickly twisted into a malleable, interest-relative substance that feeds on enmity and revenge.' Something of a hyperbole, but it makes the point.

An ET consists of a legally qualified employment judge and two lay members. The appointment of lay members is to create a more impartial and practical approach, but there continues to be a trend of ET decisions being supportive of managerial pre-rogative. In some circumstances an employment judge may sit alone, although this is not normally the case in claims for unfair dismissal. An escalation of ET cases is evident, with 100 000 in 2004 rising to 190 000 in 2008 (ACAS, 2008), 25 per cent of which are claims for unfair dismissal. This trend has coincided with a decline in collective bargaining coverage, changes to structures in the economy (with small non-unionised service sector employers more likely to generate ET claims), the extension of individual employment rights and the greater willingness of individuals to seek redress for a grievance through the courts. Only around 30 per cent of all unfair dismissal claims actually reach a tribunal, 40 per cent are settled through ACAS intervention and 30 per cent are withdrawn. Of the 30 per cent of employee claims that reach a tribunal only about a third are found in favour of the employee, representing a success rate for the employee of 1 in 10. Although, in the large number of cases settled by ACAS or withdrawn by the applicant there will have been instances where a mutually accept-able agreement was reached which gave some satisfaction or compensation to the employee. This is, however, a difficult area to penetrate because ACAS involvement is protected by confidentiality in conciliated settlements. The large number of ET cases is a matter of some concern. This prompted the revision of the ACAS Code on disciplinary and grievance procedures, together with the introduction of the ACAS pre-claim conciliation service, in order to shift the focus on resolving employment dis-putes back into the workplace.

Employment tribunal process

The parties to the process are the employee bringing the claim (the claimant) and the employer resisting the allegation (the respondent). To bring a claim of unfair dismissal the employee normally completes the claim form ET1, obtainable from the Employment Service. The claim has to be made within three months of the effective date of termin-ation or the date upon which the employee genuinely believes unfair dismissal took place. Where it was not reasonably practicable for the applicant to present the case within the three-month period, a tribunal may exceptionally exercise discretion to extend the time limit where it is considered just and equitable. The ET1 requires the applicant to state the complaint, identify the employer and indicate the remedy being sought. The remedy can be reinstatement or re-engagement or compensation. The ET1 will be registered and acknowledged on receipt by the Central Office of the Employment Tribunals. If the complaint falls outside those which may be considered or is out of time or the employee does not qualify for protection, then the case will not be heard and the applicant will be informed. If jurisdiction is established, copies of the ET1 will be sent to the respondent and to an ACAS conciliation officer. The respondent is required to reply to the allegation of unfair dismissal, normally by completing the response form

ET3, within 28 days. If an employer fails to lodge its response within the time limit, the employment judge must decide the case without a hearing and issue a default judgment, meaning that the employee will often win the case automatically. Employers will be able to apply to review the default judgment in some cases, but only after the decision has been made. In the ET3 the employer is required to confirm that dismissal took place, the dates of employment, salary details and whether there is an intention to resist the claim. The employer is also required to specify the grounds on which a claim is being resisted. A failure to respond to a notice of appearance may result in the right to take part in the tribunal proceedings being forfeited.

The ACAS role is characterised by impartiality and confidentiality. Conciliation officers have a duty to promote a settlement at the request of either party or on their own initiative. The promotion of a settlement will be the focus of concern for the conciliation officer, not the attribution of blame or guilt. Information given to a conciliation officer cannot be introduced at a tribunal hearing without the consent of the party who gave the information. Conciliated agreements reached through ACAS, or with the advice of independent legal representation, are binding and the applicant waives the right to continue with the claim.

The ET may instigate a preliminary hearing to establish whether it has the power to consider a complaint. Other preliminary hearings may be arranged to grant applications for 'further and better particulars' in relation to the claim or to make 'document discovery orders' or to make 'witness orders' compelling attendance at a hearing. This prior investigation aims to facilitate the process and avert surprises and courtroom antics at the hearing. A pre-hearing review may be arranged by the ET if it appears that either party has a weak case. This is intended to filter out any unmeritorious cases, and where the ET considers that a party has no reasonable prospect of success it can order that party to make a financial deposit as a condition of continuing to take part in the case. If the party against whom the order of a deposit is made decides to continue with proceedings, costs against that party may be awarded in certain circumstances and the deposit may be lost.

Tribunals have the power to strike out an originating application or notice of appearance where the proceedings are conducted in a manner which is 'scandalous, frivolous or vexatious'. These rules in relation to costs, deposits and striking out of cases are intended to dissuade disaffected and dismissed employees from making claims which are devilish and have no chance of success. Costs can be awarded where a party acts abusively or disruptively either before or during a tribunal hearing.

The procedure at an ET hearing is flexible and not bound by strict rules of evidence. The parties may give evidence, call witnesses to give evidence, question their own witnesses and those of the other party and address the tribunal. The tribunal members can question both parties and witnesses at any time. The case can be presented and defended by the parties involved or by named representatives. The tribunal decides on the order of proceedings and the hearing will normally be in public, although there can be reporting restrictions in cases of sexual harassment or sexual misconduct.

Oral evidence plays a key part in establishing facts or refuting allegations and it is generally in the interests of both parties to attend the hearing. The oral evidence is heard under oath or affirmation and written documents in support of an argument should be available at the hearing. It is recommended that each party sends to the other party, and to the tribunal, either a list or the 'bundle' of documents which are to be used at the hearing in order to simplify or shorten the hearing. Having heard the evidence the tribunal makes a decision, which may be unanimous or by majority vote, and the decision is usually announced at the end of the hearing. Written reasons for the decision, normally in summary form, are sent to the parties. There are certain circumstances in which a tribunal can be asked to review a decision, although this is exceptional, and a review will not be warranted merely because one party wants to re-argue its case. Appeals against a decision can only be made on a point of law and are normally made to the Employment Appeal Tribunal (EAT). ET decisions are not binding on other tribunals, but tribunals are bound by precedents established by superior courts.

Remedies for unfair dismissal

If a tribunal finds that there has been no unfair dismissal the matter ends, subject to any appeal. Where the dismissal is found to be unfair the remedies are re-employment or compensation. The tribunal has the power to order reinstatement (re-employment in the same position with continuous service) or re-engagement (re-employment under a new contract in an alternative but similar and suitable position). In deciding whether to order re-employment the tribunal will consider:

- the wishes of the employee
- the practicability for the employer
- the extent of employee contribution to the dismissal.

The employer cannot be forced to re-employ a dismissed employee and re-employment occurs in less than 1 per cent of cases. A failure to comply with an order for reinstatement or re-engagement will normally result in the employee receiving additional compensation. If the tribunal decides that re-employment is not an appropriate remedy, compensation will be awarded. The compensation may be reduced by any employee contribution to the dismissal or if an employee unreasonably rejects a suitable offer of re-employment. Breach of the ACAS Code on discipline and grievance procedures does not mean that a dismissal will be automatically unfair, but compensation awards may be adjusted by up to 25 per cent where the tribunal considers either party has unreasonably failed to comply with a provision of the Code.

The awards fall into three categories – a basic award, a compensatory award and an additional award.

The basic award is calculated on the basis of the number of years of continuous service and the age of the employee at dismissal, in the same way as redundancy payments. It is basic financial compensation for loss of employment and the maximum number of weeks' pay that can be awarded is 30. The statutory maxima used to calculate the basic award put the maximum award at £11 400 in 2009.

A compensatory award is intended to take account of any financial loss which is a consequence of the dismissal. It embraces loss of pay, up to the date of the hearing and in the future, and loss of other employment benefits. The compensatory award is set at a level which the tribunal considers to be just and equitable in the circumstances. The employee is expected to make reasonable efforts, mainly through seeking other employment, to mitigate any loss, and part of the award may be recouped to offset any income support which has been paid. The limit on the compensatory awards was significantly increased in 1999 to £50 000 and this figure is index-linked – in 2009 it was £66 200. In cases of unlawful discrimination there is no limit.

The additional award is payable when an employer refuses an ET order to re-employ and can be up to 52 weeks' pay.

Although the compensatory potential of these various awards may appear complex and extensive, the median employee compensation for dismissal is only around £4000 (Employment Tribunal and EAT Statistics, 2008: http://tribunals.gov.uk/), putting the job loss remedy in a rather different perspective. Awards in discrimination cases have been unlimited since 1993 but the median settlement in 2008 ranged from less than £2000 in age discrimination cases to around £8000 in race discrimination cases. The tribunal decision in all cases includes a statement of the compensation awarded and specifies how it was calculated. Injury to feelings compensation is not paid in dismissal cases; it is only financial loss to the employee that is taken into account (*Dunnachie* v *Kingston-Upon-Hull* CC [2004] IRLR 727 HL); this contrasts with the position in discrimination legislation which states that damages may include compensation for injury to feelings.

CASE STUDY   Ellie and the Oasis concert

You are the HR officer for a reputable high-street retailer, Goodwins Department Store Group. A line manager has come to you for advice. He tells you that a member of his department, Ellie, was absent from work yesterday and Alice, a friend, had telephoned to report that Ellie was sick with an 'upset stomach' and would not be attending work that day. Ellie is 18 years old, is in her first job since leaving full-time education and has 11 months' full-time service. Her performance level is acceptable. On Ellie's return to work today the line manager enquired about her health and was informed that she was feeling much better and perfectly able to undertake her duties.

The reason the line manager has come to see you is that there is something of a kerfuffle going on in the store because at lunchtime today the local newspaper had been printed and the front page contained a picture of a music concert featuring Oasis. The concert had taken place the previous day. The reason for this being of interest is that the picture includes a clear and distinct image of Ellie among the adoring fans. There is, therefore, a *prima facie* case (Ellie has no known twin) that, instead of being ready, willing and able for work, Ellie was attending the concert. You agree with the line manager that he should interview Ellie to seek an explanation. It is difficult to do this with any degree of confidentiality because Ellie is now infamous, the newspaper picture having gained very wide publicity among employees. A consequence of this is that 'the eyes and the ears' are on the store management to see what they will do, and what precedent will be established, in the case of Ellie.

At the interview with the line manager, in which Ellie has a companion, Ellie admits to being at the concert, but claims that the concert was in the afternoon. She qualifies this by stating that she had been genuinely ill with a 'stomach upset' in the morning, but she felt sufficiently recovered to attend the concert in the afternoon. She offers an apology for misinterpreting the rules as she thought that once she had reported sick she was not obliged to return to work that day even if she felt better. She asserts that she will know better in future. The line manager adjourns the hearing in order to consider the explanation. The line manager seeks your advice and it is agreed that you will check with the newspaper in the pursuit of 'further and better particulars'. On contacting the newspaper it is discovered that the photograph which captured Ellie was actually taken before midday. This can be verified because the digital camera records the exact time of the photograph.

The line manager is in a quandary and your input to the decision is appropriate because of organisation-wide implications in terms of precedent. You have checked with the occupational health professional who categorically states that there is no way that she can prove *or* disprove whether Ellie had an upset stomach the day before. You therefore need to make a managerial decision.

Questions

1 What would be your decision and why?

2 What message would your decision send to other employees?

3 To what extent does natural justice allow us all (including Ellie) to make a serious mistake?

4 Would your decision be any different if an extra piece of information is fed to the line manager by a senior member of his team to the effect that Ellie had purchased her ticket for the concert two weeks previously and that this fact can be verified?

SUMMARY LEARNING POINTS

1 There are no certainties in dismissal; statute law and case law provide principles but each case needs to be considered on its merits. Employers need sufficient understanding of dismissal law 'to know when more expert advice is necessary'. To be legitimate, dismissals need to be for a fair reason **and** reasonable in the circumstances. The existence of the contract is dependent on the continued existence of mutual trust and confidence between the employer and the employee. Employers are in no way deprived of the freedom to dismiss employees.

2 If the original intention of the legislation was for the primary remedy to be re-employment for the unfairly dismissed employee then the legislation has been an abject failure. Unfair dismissal legislation does not provide employment security, but only limited compensation for the loss of that security. The only way to provide employment security is to ensure that a dismissed employee is kept in employment until a claim is determined, hence the increasing emphasis on internal dispute resolution.

3 The retrospective nature of the tribunal process offers huge potential for the elimination of re-employment as a potential remedy because:
   - the passage of time associated with the ET process and its adversarial nature provide considerable scope for attitudes to harden
   - the tribunal hearing provides an opportunity for the parties to recognise that the employment relationship has irretrievably broken down

- the tribunal process can kill the desire of the employee to work for the employer because of perceived objectionable behaviour in resisting a claim
- the duty, and economic necessity, to mitigate any loss may result in the employee obtaining another job before the case is decided
- the employer may have covered the job by replacing the employee, making re-employment less practicable.

4 If an employer acts reasonably and follows a proper procedure, dismissal is legitimised and there is nothing to fear from unfair dismissal legislation. In general, the needs of the business will override the needs of the individual and tribunal decisions are very respectful of the right to manage.

5 The purpose of the legislative framework can be subjected to an alternative interpretation, that of encouraging good practice, and it is possible to be more optimistic in determining success. The principles applied by tribunals, the ACAS involvement and the publicity associated with unfair dismissal claims have combined to act as a conduit for disseminating effective practice.

6 It may not be the legal remedies available to employees that encourage employers to engage in fair and reasonable treatment. It is the pursuit of good employment relations, the undesirability of negative publicity, the time and costs involved in resisting unfair dismissal claims and, in some cases, a concern with ethics and professionalism in the management of people.

REFERENCES AND FURTHER READING

Advisory, Conciliation and Arbitration Service (2008) *Annual Resource and Accounts 2007/08*. London: ACAS.

Advisory, Conciliation and Arbitration Service (2009a) *Code of Practice 1: Disciplinary and Grievance Procedures*. London: ACAS.

Advisory, Conciliation and Arbitration Service (2009b) *Discipline and Grievances at Work: The ACAS Guide*. London: ACAS.

Aikin, O. (1984) 'Law at work: a need to reorganise', *Personnel Management*, February, 37–9.

Aikin, O. (1994a) 'Procedures for staff dismissal', *Personnel Management*, March, 55–6.

Aikin, O. (1994b) 'Law at work: unreasonable behaviour', *Personnel Management*, July, 51.

Aikin, O. (1999) 'The differences the Employment Relations Bill will make to individual employees' rights in the workplace', *People Management*, 11 March, 27–8.

Aikin, O. (2001) *Employment Law Update*. Aikin Driver Partnership, June, 6–7.

Arkin, A. (2004) 'The claim game', *People Management*, 15 July, 40–1.

Banerji, N. and Wareing, A. (1994) 'Unfair dismissal cases: 1987 and 1992 survey results compared', *Employment Gazette*, 102(10), 359–65.

Barnett, D. (2002) *Tolley's Managing Dismissals: practical guidance on the art of dismissing fairly*. Oxford: Tolley.

CIPD (2004) *Managing conflict at work: a survey of UK and Ireland*. London: CIPD.

CIPD (2009) *Discipline and Grievance Procedures*. Factsheet. London: CIPD.

Deeks, E. (2000) 'Lawyers plan in-house alternative disputes resolution (ADR) scheme', *People Management*, 3 August, 17.

Dickens, L. (1982) 'Unfair dismissal law: a decade of disillusion?' *Personnel Management*, February, 25–7.

Dickens, L. (2002) 'Individual employment rights since 1997: constrained expansion', *Employee Relations*, 24(6), 619–37.

DTI (2000) *Fair and Unfair Dismissal: A Guide for Employers*. PL714 (Rev 13). London: DTI.

Earnshaw, J. (1997) 'Tribunals and tribulations', *People Management*, May, 34–6.

Employment (Conflict Resolution) Act (2002). London: HMSO.

Employment Department (1993) *Fair and Unfair Dismissal: A guide for employers*. PL 714 (Rev 2). London: DTI.

Employment Gazette (1994) 'Industrial and employment appeal tribunal statistics 1992–93 and 1993–94', 102(10), 367–71.

Employment Relations Act (1999). London: HMSO.

Employment Rights Act (1996). London: HMSO.

Employment Rights (Disputes Resolution) Act (1998). London: HMSO.

Goodwyn, E. (1995) 'Will there be a flood of new claims for dismissal?' *People Management*, September, 53.

Industrial Relations Review and Report 555 (1994) 'Guidance on identifying reasons for dismissal', March, 11–14.

Industrial Relations Review and Report 556 (1994) 'EC equality law secures rights for part-timers', March, 2–4.

Industrial Relations Review and Report 566 (1994) 'Sunday Trading Act 1994: employment protection rights', August, 2–6.

Industrial Relations Review and Report 570 (1994) 'Inconsistent treatment not decisive in itself', October, 12–13.

Industrial Society (1999) *Managing discipline and grievance*. London: Industrial Society.

Information Commission (2002) *Data Protection Code of Practice: Employment Records*. Wilmslow: Information Commissioner's Office.

IRS Employment Review 575 (1995) 'EAT addresses limits of "Polkey" reductions', January, 12–15.

IRS Employment Review 727 (2001) 'Managing discipline at work', 5–11.

IRS Employment Review 759 (2002) 'Don't nurse a grievance: resolving disputes at work', 7–13.

Jackson, T. (2001) *Handling discipline*. London: CIPD.

Jackson, T. (2001) *Handling grievances*. London: CIPD.

Kersley, B., Alpin, C., Forth, J., Bryson, A., Bewley, H., Dix, G. and Oxenbridge, S. (2005) *Inside the Workplace: First Findings of the Workplace Employment Relations Survey (WERS 2004)*. London: DTI.

Leadership and Organisation Development Journal (1995) 'Record year for ACAS: more solutions to more problems', 16(6), 41–2.

Lewis, P. (1981) 'An analysis of why legislation has failed to provide employment protection for unfairly dismissed employees', *British Journal of Industrial Relations*, 19(3), 316–26.

Lewis, D. and Sargeant, M. (2004) *Essentials of Employment Law*. London: CIPD.

Milne, S. (1995) 'Tribunals see a doubling of unfair firings', *The Guardian*, 16 August, 15.

Mordsley, B. (1998) 'Tribunals: system overhaul', *People Management*, 14 May, 23–4.

Muir, J. (1994) 'Alcohol and employment problems', *Work Study*, 43(7), 16–17.

Overell, S. (2004) 'UK leaves appeals on the shelf', *Personnel Today*, 21 September, 14.

Pilbeam, S. and Corbridge, M. (2000) 'The skills of employee relations', in Farnham, D., *Employee Relations in Context*. London: CIPD.

Selwyn, N. (2000) *Selwyn's Law of Employment*. London: Butterworth.

Suter, E. (1997) *The Employment Law Checklist* (6th edn). London: IPD.

Willey, B. (2003) *Employment Law in Context*. Harlow: FT Prentice Hall.

Williams, A. (1995) 'Pregnant pause while Lords rethinks discrimination case', *People Management*, November, 45.

Williams, A. (1996) 'Coming to terms with extra-curricular sinners', *People Management*, January, 46.

ASSIGNMENTS AND DISCUSSION TOPICS

1 Read Exhibit 18.3 and discuss why the burden of proof is different under criminal and employment law. What implications does this have for the way that dismissals are handled by managers?

2 Are there any cases of condoned dishonest acts in your organisation? How did they come into being? Do they warrant dismissal? How could they be prevented or stopped?

3 Broken promise and high spirits – what is 'reasonable' in the context of dismissal is rarely a simple question and never reducible to an unequivocal response, so test yourself on this one. An employee had 11 years' unblemished service and no disciplinary record, and her performance was good. She got drunk at the Christmas party but promised it would never happen again. In the following July she concluded a successful deal and spent the rest of the afternoon entertaining the supplier at the bar on the employer's premises. She then slid down the first floor banisters but fell halfway, breaking a tooth and fracturing her skull. She did not have a general drink problem and was only mildly drunk. The employer dismissed her and the employment tribunal decided that the dismissal was within *the band of reasonable responses*. An important factor was that they felt she could not be trusted after breaking her promise. The employee appealed. What would you have done in the circumstances, and why?

4 Attend an employment tribunal which is hearing a claim of unfair dismissal. Write up your experience with reference to the legal framework of dismissal, commenting on whether:
   (a) a proper procedure was followed;
   (b) the employer acted reasonably in the circumstances;
   (c) the employee contributed to the dismissal.

   Present an executive summary of the main points to your class.

5 Periodic surveys of unfair dismissal applications have identified the following characteristics of claims:
   - The largest source of claims was in the distribution and hotel and catering industries.
   - Most of the claims were from private sector employees, although the public sector share increased significantly between the surveys.
   - Women are heavily under-represented in the number of claims.

   Discuss the reasons for these findings.

Chapter 19   Managing Redundancy

LEARNING OUTCOMES: TO BE ABLE TO

- Describe the causes of redundancy

- Explore the measures which employers can consider in order to avoid redundancy

- Examine relevant legislation and consider the rights and responsibilities of the employer and the employee

- Analyse the effectiveness of alternative selection methods for compulsory redundancy

- Contribute to the development of policies for the effective management of redundancy, including the development of the managerial skills needed to handle redundancy effectively

- Examine the concept of survivor syndrome and consider action necessary to rebalance the organisation post-redundancy

INTRODUCTION

In order to achieve effectiveness in people resourcing a change in the composition of the workforce is likely to be needed from time to time.

> British industry requires constant review of products and methods of work, and the successful application of new technology. The ability to maintain competitiveness in world markets depends on this. It is inevitable, however, that the redeployment of labour and redundancies will sometimes be necessary. A poorly thought out approach to change can result in a level of uncertainty which damages company performance and, should redundancies be unavoidable, may lead to financial and emotional costs to the individuals affected. (ACAS, 2009: 3)

The pursuit of competitive advantage or the need for increased productivity or efficiency gains may result in fewer workers being needed to do work of a particular kind, and this may lead to some employees being made redundant. This can take the form of a reduction in the number of employees required or a change in the skill base of the workforce through the release or retraining of employees who do not have the required skills together with the recruitment of employees who do. This can be a challenging time for any organisation and this chapter examines the ways in which the process of redundancy can be managed effectively. The rebalancing of the organisation following redundancies is also examined because the principal objective of a redundancy programme is to resource the organisation with the quantity and quality of employees to enable the organisation to survive and to be successful, and the surviving employees will be fundamental to achieving this aim. People make the difference to organisational performance and are a source of competitive advantage, but a redundancy situation can unbalance the organisation and destroy the motivation, trust and commitment of the people upon whom the organisation will rely for future success. In short, redundancy often engenders fear and insecurity which damages the psychological contract between employers and employees, and this is detrimental to the organisation. From being told that they are 'talent' and 'the most valuable asset', people can perceive themselves as 'the most disposable resource'.

DEFINITION OF REDUNDANCY

Redundancy is one of the potentially fair reasons for dismissal (*see* Chapter 18) and the statutory definition is contained in the Employment Rights Act 1996. Redundancy occurs if the employee's dismissal is wholly or mainly attributable to the fact that:

> the employer has ceased or intends to cease to carry on the business for the purposes for which the employee was employed;
> or
> the employer has ceased or intends to cease to carry on that business in the place where the employee was so employed;
> or
> the requirements of that business for employees to carry out work of a particular kind, or for employees to carry out work of a particular kind in the place where the

employee was employed by the employer, have ceased or diminished or are expected to cease or diminish.

The key words are *cease* and *diminish*, and the key phrase is *work of a particular kind*. The statutory definition translates into any situation where the whole organisation or part of it closes down or where the organisation has a reduced need for a particular kind of work. An essential feature of a redundancy situation is that it stems from causes which are external to the individual. It involves conflict of interest between the managerial objective of maintaining an efficient and profitable organisation and the employee's objective of protecting their job. However, the principal aim of redundancy activity is to ensure organisation survival and therefore the organisation needs a clear picture of the organisational structure necessary to achieve this. High-level leadership skills will promote employee confidence, enable them to engage with the new vision and work to ensure that the effect on customers is minimised.

CAUSES OF REDUNDANCY

A significant factor for modern businesses is the pace of change. This makes human resource planning and the accurate projections of the quantity and quality of workers more challenging. There are measures that can be taken by employers to increase worker flexibility, and a range of patterns of work are available to enable the employer to respond effectively to the need for change. However, there will be times when the employer will need to shed labour and restructure the organisation to accommodate internal or external pressures. In this scenario the requirement for the number of employees in employment decreases and a redundancy situation occurs. The four main causes of redundancy can be categorised as structural decline, decreases in economic activity, technological changes and reorganisation/restructuring.

Structural decline in a sector or industry causes a decline in the demand for the product or service with a consequent reduced demand for labour. This will tend to affect all organisations within the sector. Examples include the general decline in the UK manufacturing base and from 2009, the financial services industry.

Decreases in the level of economic activity which affects sales or income; either through a general economic recession, which impacts upon all sectors, or a cyclical and specific downturn in a particular area of economic activity, such as house building or the tourist industry; for example, the global economic downturn between 2008 and 2010. The percentage of organisations stating an intention to decrease staff levels rose from 18 per cent to 40 per cent between the autumn of 2008 and the spring of 2009 (CIPD, 2009a).

Technological changes can take place within a single organisation or across a sector. The introduction of new technology may reduce the demand for the labour necessary to achieve the same level of output or it can change the skill requirements of the job thereby making some skills redundant. This results in the redundancy of workers who do not have the required skills or the ability to acquire them. Changes in the world of work may lead to changes in the requirement for a different skill set and hence may lead to redundancies. For example, the increased use of the Internet for customer purchase on-line in the retail sector may have led to a loss of jobs in retail outlets, but to an increase in jobs in warehousing and dispatch. The increase in on-line banking may have led to branch closures, but to an increase in banking call centres and also in the bank IT function driven by the need for robust on-line systems.

Reorganisation or restructuring within an organisation in order to make more efficient and effective use of plant, machinery or the workforce, with the aim of improving competitiveness, profitability or return on investment. This receives much attention in contemporary organisations.

These causes of redundancy can be interrelated. A reduction in macroeconomic activity may produce inflationary pressures, causing higher interest rates with upward pressure on domestic prices. This can contribute to an accelerated structural decline because imported goods and services become cheaper. In the face of foreign competition it may be necessary to seek to maintain viability through both restructuring the organisation and the introduction of new technology.

THE AVOIDANCE OF REDUNDANCY

The avoidance of redundancy is a commendable goal, but the idea of a full employment policy or a no compulsory redundancy agreement is no longer realistic. Organisations can strive, through their strategic and human resource planning activities, to develop and implement resourcing policies that reduce the need for compulsory redundancy.

> Management is responsible for deciding the size and most efficient use of the workforce. By carefully developing a strategy for managing human resources, disruption to company performance can be minimised, job losses avoided or reduced and the process of change eased. Effective human resource planning can help to determine existing and future staffing needs. In turn this can lead to an improvement in job security for employees and to the avoidance of short-term solutions which are inconsistent with longer term organisational needs. **(ACAS, 2009: 5)**

The human resource plan (*see* Chapter 4) should anticipate internal and external pressures for change and guide people resourcing decisions to ensure incremental adjustments to workforce composition, which avoid the organisational 'shock' of redundancies. This may be difficult to achieve at a time of rapid change or economic recession when reduced labour mobility and low turnover rates may mean that numerical human resource targets cannot be achieved through natural wastage. Employers should also be mindful of ways to adjust workforce composition at no or low cost. Options for avoiding redundancy include:

- seeking new markets and business solutions
- reviewing the position of those working for you who are not employees
- freezing of recruitment and allowing natural wastage
- introducing innovative HR practices such as sabbaticals or extended time off
- reducing or eliminating overtime working
- the retraining and redeployment of employees
- short-time working or lay-offs.

Managers can pursue new markets and business solutions as a response to a downturn in the requirement for employees, for example the development of on-line sales to provide an increased market or the introduction of new products or services. These responses are likely to be longer-term measures and may not eliminate the need for redundancy in the short to medium term. The business solution is an option in a competitive environment, but adjustments to the workforce in terms of numbers and skills may be inevitable if the organisation cannot react to market pressures and make business changes sufficiently quickly. Organisations facing a redundancy situation should normally review the position of non-employees and contractors first. There is no redundancy payment entitlement for workers who do not have a contract of employment and the feasibility of releasing these workers is a logical first consideration, and can send a message to employees that everything possible is being done to protect their jobs. The position of employees on temporary or fixed-term contracts should also be reviewed to target those which are due to finish and ensure that they are not extended if there is someone under threat of redundancy, who could be offered suitable alternative employment.

Another managerial option is the freezing of recruitment. If the aim is a reduction in costs through reducing the workforce and if the problem is relatively short term, a recruitment freeze may be the solution. The dilemma that arises with this option is that the freezing of recruitment affects the organisation in an arbitrary way and its impact is very difficult to predict. It is dependent solely on who resigns and from which job, and is therefore not based directly on business needs. A compromise approach is to scrutinise carefully each vacancy with the aim of limiting recruitment to posts that are vital to the achievement of organisational objectives. This may ultimately achieve the headcount target, but the cost savings may not be achieved within an acceptable time scale. An alternative employment practice, which may help in reducing costs, is to offer a sabbatical or a period of extended time off with the payment of a retainer. This may be attractive to those with a young family who would welcome time at home, or those wishing to travel who could embark on this with a reduced risk.

The need for redundancy may be reduced through limiting or eliminating overtime working. Surplus labour in one part of the organisation can be used to eliminate overtime working in other parts. This common-sense approach, while being attractive through the retention of employees, is difficult to implement in practice. If the organisation has employees with specialised but not transferable skills, this option may not be practical. An organisation making some employees redundant while operating a policy of significant overtime working will be sending contradictory messages to the workforce. A strategy to avoid redundancy in this situation is to retrain employees. If employees with the ability to undertake the necessary training and to acquire the new skills are identified and trained quickly, this can be a successful method of avoiding redundancies. Anticipating the skill change requirements is crucial and sufficient time must be allowed for the retraining and re-skilling to take place.

The use of short-time working or lay-offs is also an option to avoid redundancy, but organisations have no automatic right to lay off employees without pay or impose short-time working even if there is no work for them to do. A lay-off is where there is no work for the employees and no payment of wages is made. Short-time working is defined as where less than half of a normal week's pay is earned. To use short-time working or lay-offs without repudiating the contract of employment, either there needs to be an express term in the contract, or a unilateral change to the working arrangements by the employer and this must not be for an unreasonably long period. If it is for an unreasonable period, which may be only four weeks, employees may justifiably consider themselves to be made redundant and claim redundancy payments. Lay-offs and short-time working are short-term responses to a temporary reduction in demand for a product or service which may be resolved by temporarily cutting the wage bill, but it will not provide a long-term solution to overstaffing.

REDUNDANCY DRIVERS

Although a range of potential causes of redundancy and alternatives to redundancy have been identified it is worth considering why organisations are driven to redundancy. The primary purpose of an organisation is to provide the goods or services that it was established to do, *and to continue to do that*. Each organisation has a range of stakeholders who rely on its survival and the stakeholders have an interest in the viability of the organisation. Therefore, the driving force in any organisation is to survive and succeed and with careful planning, good management, high quality goods or services, loyal customers and a committed workforce the stakeholders expect the organisation to flourish. However, external factors such as the global economic situation at the end of the first decade of the twenty-first century create extreme pressures. The lack of investment capital, the fall in consumer spending, high levels of uncertainty and a destabilised world economy creates organisational risk. It is not only private sector organisations that are at risk; the availability of public money is also reduced, placing pressures on public sector organisations to be more economically efficient. Despite effective planning and sound management, external factors may generate a situation where it is difficult to continue without reprofiling the workforce. Falling orders and financial pressures may threaten survival and management action becomes imperative, and as a consequence organisational survival may become dependent on reducing staffing levels.

A CBI survey (2009) of organisations employing almost 3 million people reported how the world of work had changed since the recession of 1990s: 'the employment landscape has changed markedly . . . flexible working practices have given organisations and their staff more freedom to adapt to changing demands and individual needs'. The CBI reported that more than half the surveyed organisations opted for a pay freeze and interestingly 44 per cent reported no change in investment in training, with 9 per cent actually reporting increased training investment. The survey also reported that more than two-thirds of employers:

> **have taken, plan to take or are considering a wide variety of measures to reduce labour costs while saving jobs and retaining skilled employees. Increasing the use of flexible working can help employers to reduce working hours or make better use of existing staff resources while benefitting employees by helping them to balance work with their outside lives.**

Although alternatives to redundancy can be considered (*see* Exhibit 19.1), redundancy may still be the only option when organisational survival is at stake.

EXHIBIT 19.1 Responses to threats of redundancy: illustrative examples

The CBI survey reported that employers have taken, plan to take, or are considering a wide variety of measures to reduce labour costs while saving jobs and retaining skilled employees.
CBI and Harvey Nash (2009) *Employment trends 2009: work patterns in the recession*

BA have asked thousands of staff to work for nothing, for up to one month, to help the airline survive.
http://news.bbc.co.uk/go/pr/fr/-/business/8102862.stm

The four-day week has now spread from the factory floor to the heart of the City . . . KPMG has become the first of the 'big four' accountancy firms to offer a voluntary four-day working week . . . 11000 staff, including partners, were invited to apply for a four-day week and/or partially paid leave of between four and twelve weeks.   http://business.timesonline.co.uk/tol/business/economics

Employees are now very willing to consider anything that ultimately might save their own job, at a time when other jobs might be difficult to find.
http://business.timesonline.co.uk/tol/business/economics

1   Consider these statements as responses to redundancy threats and identify the situations when these responses might be appropriate.

2   Discuss the advantages and disadvantages of these initiatives and identify the factors that need to be taken into account when implementing any of them.

3   Identify any other alternatives to redundancy.

REDUNDANCY AND THE LAW

Redundancy is one of the fair reasons for dismissal specified in the Employment Rights Act 1996. Employers have a statutory duty to inform the DTI, within the time scales laid down for consultation, that they intend to make more than 20 employees redundant, even when all the redundancies are voluntary. This is to allow the DTI to provide assistance in finding alternative employment or training opportunities for the affected employees.

The legal framework for redundancy can be considered in four parts:

1   The requirement for consultation with employees.
2   The payment of compensation for job loss.
3   Protection against unfair selection for redundancy.
4   Other statutory rights.

CONSULTATION WITH EMPLOYEES

There is a requirement for consultation between the employer and the employees in a redundancy situation regardless of the number of employees to be made redundant. The aim of managerial consultation with the employees is to listen to what the employees have to say and to provide an opportunity for discussions on ways of avoiding the redundancies. Information on the numbers and type of staff to be made redundant, as well as ways to minimise the effects of redundancy, are also essential dimensions of the consultative process. Consultation should occur when redundancy proposals are still in a formative stage because employees, and their representatives, will need adequate information and proper time to respond. There is a legal requirement to disclose in writing to the employee representatives the information needed to guide the consultation. This information includes the reasons for the redundancies, the number and type of employees to be made redundant, the total number of this type of employee employed in the organisation, the proposed method of selection for redundancy, the proposed procedure for the redundancy dismissals (including the period over which they will take place) and the proposed redundancy payment arrangements. ACAS (2009) recommends that employers also include in the consultation the process for the management transfers and downgradings (including the effect on employee earnings) where these are accepted in preference to redundancy. It has become clear from case law that employers are obliged to reveal the business reasons behind the decision to make employees redundant. This is because of the requirement to consult over the ways of avoiding redundancy dismissals and this necessarily requires the employer to consult over the business decisions that make the redundancies inevitable (*Coalmining Limited* v *NUM*: EAT/0397/06/RN, 2007). Other factors for discussion include the application of the selection methods, whether it will be on a departmental basis or organisation-wide basis, arrangements for relocation where that is an option, the timing of those leaving, especially those who may wish to leave during the redundancy notice period, the retention of company benefits and the arrangements for a trial period in a new job.

Collective redundancies

The Collective Redundancy and Transfer of Undertakings (Protection of Employment) Regulations 1995 require employer consultation with 'appropriate representatives' when 20 or more employees are to be made redundant over a 90-day period. The employer is obliged to consult with the trade union, where one is recognised. The Collective Redundancies and Transfer of Undertakings (Protection of Employment) Regulations 1999 require employers to consult with employee representatives not only about those being made redundant, but also about others who might be affected by the dismissals by, for example, taking on additional duties left over from the redundant positions. Where a trade union is not recognised, employee representatives must be elected. The election of employee representatives needs to ensure that employees have the appropriate number of representatives and that they are elected from the employees affected. Employers are required to take an active role in, first, ensuring that proper elections take place and, second, in protecting representatives from detrimental treatment. Sufficient representatives are required to represent the interests of all affected employees and, in addition, the term of office of representatives must be sufficient to enable the effective dissemination of information and for proper employee consultation to take place. The election of employee representatives should be held within a time scale that allows sufficient time subsequently to meet the legal requirements for consultation periods. Elected representatives have rights in law to enable them to fulfil their duties. These rights are similar to those of TU representatives and include access to the employees who are affected by the redundancy proposals, reasonable time off with pay to carry out their duties and to undertake appropriate training, and a right not to be dismissed because of their status as employee representatives. A genuine attempt must be made to consult in a meaningful way and where possible with 'a view to reaching agreement'. While collective consultation is a statutory requirement, case law makes it clear that employers are still obliged to consult individually with those affected by redundancy. Collective consultation is therefore in addition to, and not in place of, individual consultation. The number of employees to be made redundant determines the timing of consultation with employee representatives:

- Where 20–99 employees are to be made redundant at one establishment over a period of 90 days or less, consultation should take place at least 30 days prior to the first dismissal.

- Where 100 or more employees are to be made redundant at one establishment over a period of 90 days or less, consultation should take place at least 90 days before the first dismissal.

Small-scale redundancy

Where fewer than 20 employees are to be made redundant, case law has reinforced the importance of the employer's duty to consult individually with each employee, and the employer should use the consultation process as a means of explaining and considering the individual's situation. Redundancy is a 'potentially fair' reason for dismissal, but the employer is still statutorily obliged to follow a reasonable procedure and this includes consultation with the individual threatened with job loss. Failure to consult may result in the reasonableness of the dismissal being challenged at a tribunal. The individual consultation should discuss why and how the individual has been selected, examine ways of avoiding redundancy and explore the possibility of suitable alternative work within the organisation.

REDUNDANCY PAYMENTS

Redundancy legislation provides for statutory payments for the loss of employment which is 'wholly or mainly' due to redundancy. Those entitled to receive redundancy payments are employees who have a contract of employment and have more than two years of continuous employment (although a reduction to one year is currently being considered). Statutory redundancy payments are based on age bands, a weekly figure multiplier, a maximum statutory weekly figure and length of continuous service, with the number of years' service currently restricted to a maximum of 20. The maximum weekly pay figure used for the redundancy pay calculation is restricted by statute – £380 in October 2009, making the statutory payment (because it is possible to accrue entitlement to 30 weeks' pay) a maximum of £11 400. The age bands are of course discriminatory on the grounds of age, but permitted under the law, as are employer-enhanced redundancy payments as long as they mirror the statutory scheme. Under the Age Equality Regulations 2006 the former upper and lower age limits of 18 and 65 were removed and statutory redundancy payments are no longer tapered after the employee's 64th birthday.

According to CIPD (2009b), quoting the CIPD/KPMG labour market survey, autumn 2008: 'half the organisations surveyed offer redundancy payments above the statutory minimum. The average redundancy payment is found to be £10,575, though a quarter of employers pay less than £5,000.' At best, a statutory redundancy payment provides a bridgehead or temporary financial respite for an employee who is effectively between jobs. Where an employer fails to make a statutory redundancy payment, the employee can take a claim for payment to a tribunal. A redundant employee has the right to a written statement of how a redundancy payment has been calculated, and a dispute about the calculation of the payment can be referred to a tribunal. An employer can elect to make redundancy payments above the statutory minima.

SELECTION FOR REDUNDANCY

The selection criteria to be used by an employer in a redundancy situation are not defined in law. However, the employer must follow customary arrangements or agreed procedures or, if there are no customary arrangements or procedures, selection should be based on objective criteria and also be reasonable in the circumstances. Selection for redundancy gives rise to many claims for unfair dismissal and managers need to be fair, reasonable and objective, ensuring that selection criteria are discussed and agreed during consultation, stated in the redundancy policy and applied in an even-handed way. The reason for having objective criteria is to ensure that employees are not unfairly selected for redundancy. Case law is clear that the application of subjective criteria based on a manager's judgement, and unsupported with objective evidence, will be unfair (*E-Zec MedicalTransport Services* v *Gregory*: EAT/0192, 2008). Some selection criteria will almost inevitably be considered to be unfair by an employment tribunal. These unsafe criteria include selection based on trade union activity or membership, part-time working, unless it can be clearly demonstrated that the work cannot be done on a part-time basis, asserting a statutory employment right, such as rights under Sunday Working and Working Time Regulations, National Minimum Wage, maternity and parental leave, public interest disclosure, Part-Time Workers Regulations, Fixed-Term Workers Regulations, exercising the right to be accompanied at a disciplinary hearing and requesting flexible working. The Maternity and Paternity Regulations 1999 clarified the position regarding the nature of the contract of employment during the extended period of maternity leave, and as long as there is a genuine redundancy situation and the employee is consulted in accordance with legislation, there is nothing to stop that employee being selected for redundancy on the basis of the application of the agreed criteria. Selection is also unfair if it is based on sex, marital status, race, disability, religion or belief, sexual orientation or age. An employee selected for redundancy has a statutory right to be fairly selected, and if the employee considers that selection is unfair or not in line with agreed criteria, or if the criteria lack objectivity, then a claim can be made to an employment tribunal.

Redundancy can be non-compulsory or compulsory. Non-compulsory redundancy is more widely acceptable because employees elect job loss rather than being forced out. However, they may need to be enticed by more attractive financial arrangements, thereby minimising the damaging and demotivating effects of redundancy. Clearly non-compulsory redundancy may increase the short-term financial cost, but it may also achieve the reprofiling and rebalancing of the workforce in a shorter time than where adversarial relationships develop because of compulsory redundancies.

Non-compulsory redundancy

Voluntary redundancy

This occurs when the employer seeks volunteers for redundancy from the workforce. In this situation it is effectively the employee rather than management who makes the redundancy decision. Problems can occur if there are more volunteers from the workforce than are required, because the employer will still need objective criteria to select for redundancy in order to make an appropriate selection from the volunteers, as the probability of achieving the precise number of volunteers required by the employer is low. The advantage of voluntary redundancy is a reduction in the potential for conflict between management and employees, as well as the reduction of the negative impact of redundancies on the total workforce. A disadvantage, however, is that it is likely to be a more costly option because of the need to offer an enhancement to statutory redundancy payments as an employee incentive to volunteer for redundancy. Another potential disadvantage is the lack of control over who volunteers; the most valuable and skilled employees may opt to go because they find it easier to secure new employment. Refusing voluntary redundancy to those who want to leave can have a negative impact on their morale and motivation, and allowing the weak performers, or lower-skilled employees, to go can be perceived as rewarding them through an attractive severance package. This can lead to resentment among remaining employees and as a consequence be detrimental to employment relationships. Handling voluntary redundancy requires as much managerial skill as that required for compulsory redundancy situations. Also, asking for volunteers who are subsequently rejected for voluntary redundancy is very disappointing for the employees concerned and has negative implications for the employment relationship.

Early retirement

This can also constitute redundancy, and the redundant worker will be eligible for redundancy payments as well as access to their occupational pension. It is necessary to ensure that the reason for dismissal is 'purely' redundancy and not just early retirement, because there are income tax implications. Redundancy payments are tax free up to a maximum of £30 000 in 2009, but if the HM Revenue & Customs judge the termination of employment to be early retirement rather than redundancy then payments made to the employee may be liable to income tax. Offering redundancy to employees nearing normal retirement age can be less contentious within the workforce but high levels of early retirement can lead to a skewed age profile and little natural retirement for several years, making career progression difficult for those who remain. Selecting people for redundancy on age criteria will be deemed in breach of the Employment Equality (Age) Regulations 1996 and therefore unfair selection for redundancy.

Compulsory redundancy

Last in first out (LIFO)

As the name suggests this selection method is based on the length of service of employees. It is a method that is transparent, easy to apply and easy for the workforce to understand. It has a 'felt fair' appeal and effectively rewards loyalty to the organisation. It can give rise to skill-mix problems where the most recent recruits have the most up-to-date skills, and electing to lose those first may not be commercially sound. LIFO has the advantage of being a quantifiable criterion and is resistant to a charge of favouritism or managerial bias. It is also a lower-cost option because long-service staff with a greater redundancy pay entitlement are retained. LIFO can lead to a skewed age profile where those employees with shorter service are the younger employees. ACAS (2004) has not been convinced about the LIFO selection method for some time:

> If all other selection methods have failed selection on LIFO can be used as a last resort . . . Employers need to be aware of the potential dangers of losing workers with key skills using the method of selection.

Effectively a LIFO death knell was sounded by the introduction of age discrimination legislation in 2006 and, although there are debates about the connection between length of service and age, it is becoming recognised that length of service as the sole criteria for redundancy selection may constitute unlawful age discrimination. However, length of service, as one of a number of selection criteria in a redundancy process, is capable of being justified even though, on the face of it, it is discriminatory against younger employees. The case of *Rolls Royce PLC* v *Unite* (CA, 14 May 2009) is instructive. Under a collective agreement, and using a measured factor approach, employees were awarded one point for every year of service. Points were also awarded for achievement of objectives, self-motivation, knowledge and expertise, versatility and contribution to the team. The Court of Appeal ruled that length of service as one criterion in redundancy selection was not unlawful under the Employment Equality (Age) Regulations 2006. Although it was *indirectly discriminatory* on grounds of age, having such a criterion was justified in that it was 'a proportionate means of achieving a legitimate aim' in accordance with the regulations. The legitimate aim was to reward loyalty and to achieve a stable workforce in the context of a fair process of redundancy selection; and it was proportionate because it was only *one of a number of criteria and was by no means determinative*. The proportionality element of the test was therefore satisfied by the fact that length of service was only one of a substantial number of criteria used to make the redundancy decisions. This strongly suggests that LIFO on its own would not be justifiable, and should therefore be avoided. In any case, in terms of effective human resource planning and talent management it seems to make little sense in relation to achieving the aim of redundancy, which is the survival and success of the organisation.

Measured factor selection criteria and talent planning

If the overriding reason that organisations embark on a redundancy process is to ensure their survival and success, the retention of skilled employees is clearly a commercial priority in order that an efficient and effective workforce remains post-redundancies. The required employee and skills profile should therefore be decided on and articulated prior to individual redundancy decisions being taken. A matrix of measured factors can be produced to include key competencies, skills and experience, as well as performance standards. Performance standards include not only work efficiency and effectiveness measures but may also include attendance and disciplinary records (*see* Exhibit 19.2). The higher the score on the measured factors, the more the individual

EXHIBIT 19.2 Measured factor criteria for redundancy selection

Selection criteria and weighting	Worker 1	Worker 2	Worker 3
1 Customer focus 20%	(80) 16	(40) 8	(80) 16
2 Acquisition of core competencies 25%	(60) 15	(60) 15	(72) 18
3 Team skills 20%	(80) 16	(30) 6	(50) 10
4 Absence record* 10%	(20) 2	(0) 0	(90) 9
5 Appraisal rating 15%	(30) 4.5	(20) 3	(50) 7.5
6 Timekeeping 10%	(40) 4	(40) 4	(50) 5
Total	57.5	36	65.5

* Absence incidents – the number of incidents in one year attracts a points rating:
>10 = 0; 8–10 =10; 6–7 = 20; 4–5 = 30; 2–3 = 50; 1 = 70; 0 = 90.

meets the needs of the organisation and the more valuable the employee is to the business. The factors included in the matrix flow from the human resource plan which specifies the talent profile required following the restructuring of the organisation. This selection method therefore aims to match employee skills, abilities and attitudes to the organisational objectives. It may be problematic to define skill requirements in sufficient detail for systematic measurement, and the objective process relies heavily on the organisation holding sufficient data on individual employee skills, abilities, competencies and attitudes to be able to make objective assessment. Where a full employee data set is unavailable some form of competency testing or an assessment centre may be necessary.

This systematic ranking approach, as long as it is reasonably objective and non-discriminatory, tends to find favour with tribunals and is relatively transparent to employees who can see how they are being assessed. Whatever selection criteria are decided upon, they need to be applied fairly and equitably. The employer that applies a measured factor approach using performance criteria and competencies combined with a weighting and scoring system should ensure that neither the criteria nor the weightings are themselves discriminatory. The tribunal will not normally require the scores to be disclosed to anyone other than the individual. The employer should provide an appeals procedure in line with the agreed grievance procedure. The advantage of the appeals procedure is that it potentially allows for complaints about unfair selection to be resolved internally and therefore reduces the likelihood of complaints to an employment tribunal. However, the message is clear: employers need to identify and apply selection criteria for redundancy objectively.

OTHER STATUTORY RIGHTS

In addition to consultation, redundancy payments and fair selection for redundancy, the law also provides that the employee under notice of redundancy, first, qualifies for a statutory right to reasonable paid time off to seek work or training opportunities, second, the right to be offered suitable alternative work within the organisation and, third, a trial period in an alternative job within the organisation.

An employee who qualifies for statutory redundancy payments is entitled to 'reasonable' time off with pay to look for future employment. The law does not define reasonable time off, but an employer refusing time off to an employee under notice of redundancy for seeking alternative employment would need to demonstrate to a tribunal that the time being taken was unreasonable. Redundant employees are entitled to their statutory notice period or to payment in lieu of notice when they are not required to attend work during their period of notice. Failure by the employer to honour the notice period may result in a claim for wrongful dismissal. The Employment Rights Act requires that an employee who is under threat of redundancy should be considered for any job within the organisation which is considered 'suitable alternative work'. Case law has established what, in principle, constitutes suitable alternative work and when it may be unreasonable for the employee to reject it. To be suitable, the alternative work should normally provide similar rewards, have similar status, be within the employee's capability and not involve excessive inconvenience. The employee is also entitled to a trial period in the job. The reason for the trial period may be either for the employer to assess the employee's ability to do the job or for the employee to try the job to decide whether or not it is suitable for his or her skills and experience. If, at the end of the trial period, which can last up to four weeks, either the employer or the employee legitimately and reasonably considers the job unsuitable, the employee retains the right to redundancy payments based on the original job.

THE EFFECTIVE MANAGEMENT OF REDUNDANCY

Organisations can seek to manage any redundancy situation in a systematic way to minimise resentment, and to ensure that redundancies are handled fairly and reasonably within the statutory framework. This involves having a redundancy policy and thinking about the practicalities of how redundancy can be handled effectively. An analytical framework for systematically managing redundancy is exposed in Figure 19.1 and consideration of these elements will direct managerial action at each stage of the process.

The redundancy policy

Management can plan ahead for redundancy, not only through human resource planning, but also through having an agreed redundancy policy in place. A policy defines

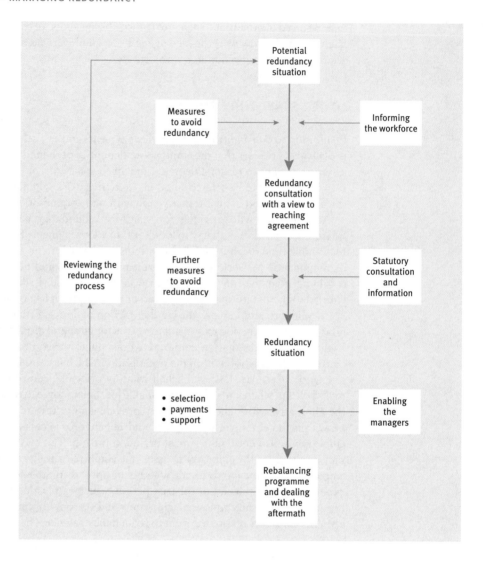

the parameters for managerial action and enables redundancy to be dealt with in a more objective way. A redundancy policy, which is agreed, regularly reviewed, effectively communicated and clearly understood by employees is essential to the successful management of redundancy. The following elements can be included in a redundancy policy.

- *An opening statement* – makes a positive organisational statement about the commitment to maintaining employment levels and job security, while acknowledging that the organisational need for employees and for skills of a particular kind changes over time and management may need to take action from time to time to align employment levels and skills profiles with business needs and objectives.

- *Consultation arrangements* – state the consultation arrangements to be used in individual and collective redundancy situations, commit to providing information in a timely way, acknowledge the time scales that will be followed: these may be the statutory minimum or enhanced, and specify the election arrangements for employee representatives in a collective redundancy situation.

- *Actions to be taken to reduce the need for redundancy* – refer to the alternative courses of managerial action that will be considered in order to avoid the need for employees to be made redundant.

- *Selection criteria* – define objective, fair, non-discriminatory and transparent selection criteria to include the method that will be used and the process that will be followed; specify any eligibility and the terms of voluntary severance, but acknowledge that too few or too many volunteers will mean that the selection will have to take place and that compulsory redundancies will be necessary.

- *Redundancy payment arrangements* – specify statutory requirements for payments together with any enhancement to redundancy payments which will be implemented.

- *Redeployment procedures* – refer to organisational redeployment procedures and identify the process through which employees will be considered and selected for suitable alternative employment.

- *Appeals procedure* – state the employee's right to appeal internally against the operation of the redundancy policy together with an outline of the appeals process and procedure.

- *Support systems* – specify organisational support such as outplacement services, counselling, training and the right to time off for job search.

- *Policy review* – details of the process and the time scales for policy review.

The handling of redundancy

Often the first indications of organisational difficulties result in the informal communications system, the grapevine, coming into operation, with rumour and misinformation exaggerating the redundancy threat and creating workforce tensions. The managerial fear of these tensions can result in attempts to keep things from employees. Organisations may try to conceal a threat of redundancies for several reasons including the negative effect it may have on the business, the decline in staff morale, the adverse effect on the customers and shareholders, the potential for decline in market share and the loss of key workers. The timing of an announcement to employees is important and needs to be well judged. Telling employees that their continued employment is threatened is a difficult thing to do. However, once the business decision to consider the redundancy option has been taken, employees need to be informed in a sensitive and professional way. Employees will want answers to difficult questions and managers need to be in a position to provide accurate information. Redundancy often occurs at a time of organisational change and redundancy itself can intensify the change required by the organisation, because those employees remaining may be employed on different jobs and with different systems of work. It is important therefore that employees are persuaded of the need for change and that they accept the way in which redundancy fits into the change process. Individuals are, in general, resistant to change, but there can also be the desire for change and for new challenges. Change can be successfully managed (*see* Chapter 12) and the organisation can move to a position of strength. If change is not managed well, low morale and a decline in confidence can adversely affect the organisation and undermine the efforts of management to rebalance the organisation. A systematic approach to the management of a redundancy situation contributes to ensuring that appropriate actions are taken at the relevant time and that problems are minimised.

The announcement to employees should be made at the same time as the communication of measures initiated to avoid redundancy and this should also coincide with the arrangements for consultation with employees. This initial consultation may lead to an exchange of information and then to the statutory consultation process. The outcome of the statutory period of consultation may be agreement on further avoidance measures or ideally for the redundancy requirement to be avoided, but this is uncommon and the organisation may have to acknowledge formally that a redundancy situation exists. An agreed redundancy policy will not only facilitate the redundancy selection process and provide information on redundancy payments, but will also focus attention on *the training and enabling of managers* to deal with the redundancy process, the development of *a communication strategy*, and the arrangements needed for the *counselling and support* of redundant employees.

The training and enabling of managers

This is fundamental to the effective management of the sensitive and emotionally charged situation of redundancy. Many managers will not have dealt with this previously and may not be appropriately skilled. Managers need to be competent in handling the variety of employee responses and recognise the importance of treating each employee as an individual. A redundancy situation creates general concerns about security of employment and all employees will want to know if jobs are threatened. Common concerns and feelings are likely to be experienced by employees and managerial awareness of these will help to predict reactions and allow for appropriate responses to be planned. However, individuals vary and stereotypical assumptions should not be made.

The financial implications of redundancy are normally significant to the individual, but work provides other rewards and satisfactions which are also threatened by job loss. Employment may be central to an individual's social life, not only in providing opportunities for interactions at work, but also in providing access to social events. Job loss through redundancy or a change in hours or location through redeployment can significantly affect work–life balance. Extended travel, revised hours or a change to shift working may mean that the employee is too tired or is denied the opportunity for outside social activity. Individuals derive status and self-esteem from work and therefore any change in the working arrangements may affect individual morale. An employee may be afraid that job loss will result in a loss of status in the community, and there have been instances of redundant employees being afraid to inform family members and continuing to leave for work to give the impression of still being employed. Another common employee concern is the fear of the unknown. The fear of change, or the anticipation, may have a more negative effect than the change itself, because many people are resistant to change, like familiarity and avoid situations that are threatening. Therefore, managers, in dealing with redundancy, need to recognise this emotional dimension and have the sensitivity skills necessary to respond appropriately.

Managers should also recognise that individual circumstances and characteristics, such as age, gender and personality, affect individual responses. For example, young workers who suffer job loss may find it difficult to relate to their peers and be concerned about the effect on their social life, if the majority of their friends are in employment. Older workers may fear never working again and the real threat of age discrimination may demoralise the individual. Some employees may be concerned about the threat to their status as a 'bread winner' because this may be a source of recognition, security and self-esteem; others may fear having to return to domesticity and the consequent loss of social and financial independence. An individual's financial situation, such as mortgage commitments, credit liabilities and family circumstances, will also have a significant impact on the individual response. Disproportionate publicity about large redundancy packages has contributed to the myth of large redundancy payments, but most redundant employees receive little more than the statutory minimum payment. Redundancy payments are therefore best viewed as a bridging arrangement to another job, rather than providing financial security for a long period.

Personality characteristics will influence individual responses to the threat of job loss. Some people will be resigned, some react angrily and others withdraw. Others may perceive redundancy as a challenge and an opportunity to do something new, or of being forced into accepting an opportunity that they have been afraid of previously. Those without external support, from the family or elsewhere, may find it helpful to have someone with whom to discuss the situation. There can be feelings of self-blame and these can be destructive. If other people are also being made redundant, the individual may be able to externalise the negative feelings and accept that the reason for job loss is attributable to circumstances beyond their control, and less stigma may occur or be perceived. The employee's length of service may influence feelings in a redundancy situation; those with a long period of employment may feel betrayed and have intensified feelings of anger, making it more difficult to adjust to what is happening.

Managers need to be able to recognise and to handle individual responses of anger, denial, fear and anxiety. There is rarely a place for humour in the redundancy encounters between management and employee. Good listening skills are necessary and employees should be allowed and encouraged to express their feelings. The redundancy consultation interview should not be hurried and sufficient time should be allotted for the manager to speak, listen and provide the information needed by the employee. Important information should be given in writing because the stressful circumstances of the interview may mean that information given orally is not accurately recalled by the employee. Information specific to the individual employee should be prepared prior to the interview, talked through during the interview and ideally handed to the employee soon after the interview. Line managers will often be anxious in a redundancy situation as they may also feel under threat. This needs to be recognised by those training the managers. In summary, training the managers involves developing the skills necessary to deal with the redundancy encounters with individual employees and providing information on the redundancy policy, the reasons for redundancies, the timing of redundancies and the individual entitlements in terms of payment, time off and support.

A communications strategy

This should guide managerial action and several steps are involved. The timing of the initial disclosure of the redundancy threat is crucial and therefore individual or group announcement strategies need to be critically reviewed to determine which will work best. A senior management announcement is more likely to project an image of a concerned organisation that is not just passing the buck to lower levels of management. The reasons for the redundancy threat should be communicated clearly and accurately, together with the alternative solutions being considered. Information on the prospect of any redundancy package should be outlined, be consistent with the policy and be communicated effectively. Opportunities to talk on an individual basis should be made available. Employees affected by redundancy decisions, both leavers and survivors, can perceive the process to be unethical if redundancy information is withheld, if inadequate advance notice is given, if redundancies are announced near or during holiday seasons, or if they learn about an impending downsizing from sources outside the organisation (Hopkins and Hopkins, 1999). In terms of practical implications, managerial actions which are perceived to be unethical can lead to reduced productivity and morale and therefore to competitiveness and profitability problems.

Counselling and support

The organisation needs to consider the support that professional counselling can give to employees. There needs to be a system of employee access to staff who are trained and who know how to deal with individual responses to redundancy. Access to a counselling service should be communicated and sufficiently resourced to minimise waiting time. Counsellors can be either trained staff from within the organisation or specialist external consultants. If external consultants are chosen, the way in which they are deployed is important. Consultants should be placed with discretion, as there can be employee feelings of being 'taken over' by outsiders, which may lead to increased resentment. Having said this, the displacement of emotion and anger on to external consultants may be able to be used constructively by the organisation and allow managers and employees to relate to each other in an objective way, and without the emotional dimension. These external outplacement consultants provide a wide range of services. The outplacement role is to facilitate the transition from the redundant job to the next employment or self-employment, and outplacement specialists have the skills, resources and contacts to assist in a variety of situations. The range of services may include: financial planning and advice, which increases in importance if large severance payments are involved, career counselling, including an appropriate battery of assessments to facilitate discussions and widen job options, skills assessment and development, job search skills, including application and CV advice, interview techniques and networking opportunities as well as the setting up of a 'job shop', if there is a significant number of redundancies. Outplacement services can help the redundant worker to progress through the stages of shock and disbelief towards success and hope in securing a new job.

The effective management of redundancy is difficult and organisations do not get it right all the time, but a well-thought-out policy and procedure which recognises the business, legal, professional and ethical issues is more likely to be seen in a positive light and to contribute to organisational survival.

REBALANCING THE ORGANISATION AFTER REDUNDANCY

The restructuring and rebalancing of the organisation following a redundancy situation is essential to organisational survival and success. Prior to the start of a redundancy situation the organisation needs a clear picture of what it is striving to achieve in reducing the number of employees, what vision and strategic direction is required to succeed and what organisational structure is needed to achieve the strategy.

> The immediate priority, if redundancies become unavoidable, is the fair and sensitive treatment of employees who are losing their jobs. Once this has been achieved, the organisation's effectiveness in today's competitive market is largely dependent on the morale of the survivors. Clumsy redundancy handling is bad for the employer's business and long-term reputation. A demoralised workforce, anxious about job security and critical of the handling of the redundancies, is not likely to display commitment, enthusiasm and initiative.
>
> (CIPD, 2009c)

The key activities in managing the transition to the new organisation for those who remain include communicating the vision for organisational success, supporting people to adjust to the change, understanding the performance requirements for success and communicating the changes to the structure and how they will be managed. While redundancy affects those being made redundant, it also affects those remaining, and the negative feelings associated with surviving redundancy and remaining with the employer is termed 'survivor syndrome'. Survivor syndrome denotes the emotional, psychological and organisational repercussions faced by those employees who survive a redundancy programme – Figure 19.2 identifies some of the potential repercussions (*see also* the end of chapter case study). These survivors are, after all, the employees who will be driving forward the organisation to achieve its defined objectives and to ensure its success. While the surviving employees may experience relief at avoiding redundancy, it is important to

Figure 19.2
Redundancy survival:
potential
repercussions

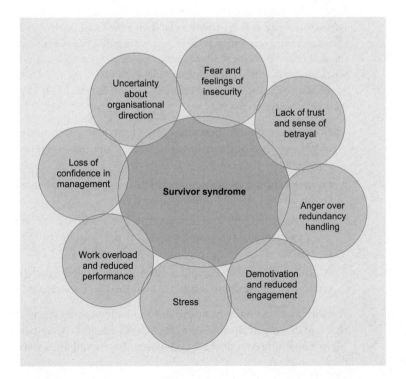

recognise that redundancies can contribute to a destabilisation of the workforce as a whole, and concerns which remain after those made redundant have left the organisation need to be addressed if the organisation is to be successful.

Managerial effort therefore needs to be focused not only on those leaving, but also on those remaining. Early consideration needs to be given to the shape, design and structure of the organisation post-redundancy. Strategic and human resource planning can anticipate how the organisation will be affected, not only in numbers of jobs but also in skills and structure. The development of a rebalancing plan and its communication to the workforce are vital if feelings of teamwork and confidence are to return. Research conducted by Baruch and Hind (2000) indicate that careful handling of redundancy can limit the effect of survivor syndrome. For example, the following factors were seen to be important in reducing the fears and anxieties of those surviving redundancy: open communication, positive and constructive employee relations, the offer of early retirement and enhanced redundancy payments, full involvement of employee representatives, full explanation of the reasons for redundancy, open and rigorous selection process, which was conducted quickly and decisively, positive messages to those who elected to leave but who were deemed essential, which increased morale and commitment, well-trained managers who could deliver uneasy messages and, finally, a specific outplacement programme which enabled those being made redundant to do well in their transition from the organisation. In short, this research supports the view that redundancies which are well managed reduce the adverse effects on the survivors. Uncertainty and lack of organisational direction may mean that those remaining will continue to experience insecurity and seek employment elsewhere, resulting in the loss of key skills and compromising the recovery of the organisation. Wolfe (2004) identifies two primary issues which are seen as key factors for survivors: first, *knowledge and understanding of the process together with fair treatment of their peers who are leaving* as this provides clarity for past and present events and confidence for the future, and, second, a feeling that *managers, and the organisation as a whole, are aware of the problems that may arise from downsizing,* such as job redesign, increased workloads and different working teams. Appelbaum and Donia (2001) suggest that to rebalance the organisation effectively and address the effects of survivor syndrome, four actions are necessary:

1 Effective communication strategies – to reduce uncertainties, clarify the reasons and the process of the redundancies, develop survivor cohesiveness and provide direction.

2 Human resource planning – to reflect the vision for the newly structured organisation and the business objectives.

3 The redesign of jobs and restructuring the work – to maximise the skills and experience of remaining employees in the context of the business objectives.

4 A skills analysis and training needs analysis – to ensure that skills are utilised effectively and training needs are identified and addressed.

A positive managerial response to the post-redundancy organisation sends the message that a planned and considered approach is being taken, contributes to the confidence of the remaining employees, builds commitment and ultimately enables the organisation to succeed.

CASE STUDY   Coping with redundancy (if you stay)

Last week 30 people left the *Financial Times* after opting for voluntary redundancy. On Monday, a party was held for them. There was nice food and nice drinks and nice speeches and a band played. You could say this was a happy occasion for all concerned. Each was leaving by choice. They had weighed up the relative merits of slogging on with the day job, and leaving now with a very large cheque in their back pockets. Each had decided the latter looked the more tempting option.

What interests me, though, is not how good this must be for those who have gone, nor how smug the company is feeling. I am interested in the emotions of those left behind. 'Survivor guilt' is what business schools call the response to mass firings of workmates. But when your colleagues leave voluntarily, the emotional response is more subtle and more shameful. This week I have taken my own emotional temperature, and asked about a bit, and I have come up with seven different survivor syndromes following redundancy.

1 **Survivor envy**. When 30 colleagues have taken their lives by the horns, you cannot help but wonder if you are a hopeless, spineless wimp not to have done the same with yours. We have looked at the numbers and either seen that they do not add up or concluded that we are not brave enough to give it a go and have returned to the harness – which feels rather heavier than before.

2 **Survivor bereavement**. This is the big one: the sight of so many people going is sad and unsettling. People you have worked with for years are not there any more; the person who edited my first story on the paper is gone forever. There has been a string of emails saying goodbye. It feels intense at the time but it lasts an indecently short period of time. Although often you see these work colleagues more often than members of your family, the relationship is based on your working together and, once you no longer do, the point of it is gone.

3 **Survivor 'premature ageing' syndrome**. This happens when the people who leave are older and more experienced than you. Last week, the *FT* lost more than 600 years of experience. This is alarming for those of us on the next rung down. I find myself one of the oldest and most experienced people around, which is a bit more exposed than I would like to be, ideally.

4 **Survivor 'existential crisis' syndrome**. This is by far the most worrying of the syndromes! Watching those people say goodbye, I started to wonder what it had been about. They had worked hard for all those years and then walked out of the door for the last time with some money but with what else? What was the point of all those years? What did they have to show for it? The trouble with these questions is that they apply equally to those who remain. What is the point of what we do? This is a big question and I am not prepared to examine it.

5 **Survivor 'I'm-too-valuable-to-go' syndrome**. This applies to those who asked to leave but were turned down. Handled badly this can be disastrous. If you are told that you cannot take the money and run by dint of your superior performance, you may feel that you are being punished for your hard work and end up feeling very bitter indeed.

6 **Survivor 'I'm-glad-to-see-the-back-of-you' syndrome**. The great thing to aim at when looking for voluntary redundancies is to make sure that you lose those who are unhappy in their jobs. They are

(Box continued)

more of a problem than those who are not very good as they spread misery and bitter ones should be shown the door at once.

7 **Survivor 'How-long-do-I-have-to-wait-before-nabbing-that-office' syndrome**. Now there is a nice office up for grabs. I know for a fact that at least two people have their eye on it. I would not mind it myself, come to that!

Questions

1 Evaluate each of the survivor syndromes identified and discuss the validity of each as a legitimate assessment of survivor feelings.

2 Take each syndrome in turn and develop a strategy to minimise the impact of the syndrome in a voluntary redundancy situation.

Source: adapted from 'Coping with redundancy (if you stay)', *Financial Times* 6 March 2005 (Kellaway, L.).

SUMMARY LEARNING POINTS

1 A legislative framework exists to afford limited protection and compensation for employees who lose their job through no fault of their own. The legislation does not specify selection criteria for redundancy, but requires that fair and objective criteria are agreed and adhered to in any redundancy situation.

2 Organisations should strive to avoid the need for compulsory redundancy by careful consideration of a range of alternative actions. An agreed policy for the effective management of redundancy should be in place and communicated prior to a redundancy situation occurring. The policy should provide guidelines and information for managers to enable them to handle redundancy fairly, skilfully and consistently. The policy also lets employees know how they will treated.

3 Employees display different responses to the threat of redundancy, making managing the process difficult and stressful for all concerned. Collective and individual consultation are key features of effective redundancy handling.

4 The timing of the communication of the threat of redundancy is vital. Poor managerial timing can adversely affect the organisation commercially and also reduce the confidence of employees in managerial effectiveness. It may also lead to the organisation losing key staff because they seek alternative employment.

5 A range of services can be provided to assist the employee in the transition to the next employer, or to retirement. Support or outplacement services for those leaving can also contribute to more positive feelings in those who remain with the organisation.

6 After redundancy the organisation needs to plan for the future. This strategic planning should occur prior to the redundancies and be communicated and implemented following redundancies. The organisation needs to be rebalanced,

not only in terms of numbers but also in terms of structure, work allocation and skills. Survivors need as much consideration as those who leave.

7 Employees who remain with the organisation following a redundancy programme may have a reduced feeling of job security, and the fair treatment of those leaving and the effective communication of future plans and objectives are essential to building future organisational success.

8 Organisations which recognise the business, legal, professional and ethical considerations in handling redundancy situations are more likely to be seen in a positive light and achieve business success.

REFERENCES AND FURTHER READING

Advisory, Conciliation and Arbitration Service (2004) *Redundancy Handling: Advisory Booklet 12*. London: ACAS.

Advisory, Conciliation and Arbitration Service (2009) *Redundancy Handling: Advisory Booklet*. London: ACAS.

Appelbaum, S. and Donia, M. (2001) 'The realistic downsizing preview: a management intervention in the prevention of survivor syndrome', *Journal of Career Development International*, 6(1), 5–19.

Baruch, Y. and Hind, P. (2000) 'Survivor syndrome – a management myth', *Journal of Managerial Psychology*, 15(1), 29–45.

Beardwell, I., Holden, L. and Claydon, T. (2003) *Human Resource Management: A contemporary approach*. Harlow: Financial Times Prentice Hall.

Beylerian, M. and Kleiner, B.H. (2003) 'The Downsized Workplace', *Management Research News*, 26, 97–101.

CBI and Harvey Nash (2009) *Employment trends 2009: work patterns in the recession*. London: CBI.

Chiumento, R. (2003) 'How to support survivors of redundancy', *People Management*, 9(3), 6 February, 50–1.

CIPD (2002) *Redundancy Survey Report*. London: CIPD.

CIPD (2009a) *Labour Market Outlook: Quarterly Survey Report*. London: IPD. Spring.

CIPD (2009b) 'The cost to employers of redundancy'. *Impact: quarterly update on CIPD policy and research*. Iss: 26 February.

CIPD (2009c) *Redundancy: Factsheet*. London: CIPD.

CIPD and KPMG (2009c) 'Labour Market Outlook'. *Quarterly Survey Report*. Spring.

Cowie, J. (2005) *Managing redundancy and guide to suppliers*. London: IDS.

Daniels, K. (2004) *Employment Law for Business Students*. London: CIPD.

Department of Trade and Industry (2003) *Redundancy, Consultation and Notification*. London: DTI.

Doherty, N. and Horsted, J. (1995) 'Helping survivors to stay on board', *People Management*, January, 26–31.

Hopkins, W. and Hopkins, S. (1999) 'The ethics of downsizing: perceptions of rights and responsibilities', *Journal of Business Ethics*, 18, 145–56.

Incomes Data Services (2005) *Managing redundancy*, HR Study Plus. London: IDS.

Incomes Data Services (2007) *Managing redundancy and guide to suppliers*, HR Study Plus. London: IDS.

IRS Redundancy Survey (2004) 'Communicating bad news: managing redundancy'. *IRS Employment Review Issue 803*.

Labour Force Survey (2005) Office for National Statistics, www.statistics.gov.uk.

Leopold, J. *et al.* (2005) *The strategic managing of Human Resources*. Harlow: FT Prentice Hall.

Merrick, N. (2000) 'A natural preparation', *People Management*, 26 October, 50–4.

Office of National Statistics (2005) *Redundancies*. London: ONS, www.statistics.gov.uk.

Penna, Sanders and Sidney Career Consulting (2001) *Redefining Redundancy: Research Report 7*, April, 1–12.

Pilbeam, S. and Corbridge, M. (2000) 'The skills of employee relations', in Farnham, D. (ed.) *Employee Relations in Context*. London: CIPD.

Rothwell, J. (2000) 'How to break the news of redundancies', *People Management*, November.

Suff, P. and Warner, J. (2003) *Managing redundancy*, IDS Studies Plus. London: IDS.

Tait, R. (2005) *Survivor Syndrome: What is it, will your organisation catch it and what's the cure?* The Taylor Partnership Ltd, www.taylorclarke.demon.co.uk/survivorsyndrone.htm.

Welfare, S. (2004) 'Communicating bad news: managing redundancy', *IRS Employment Review 803*, July, 11–17.

Wolfe, H. (2004) *Survivor syndrome: Signs, symptoms and strategies*. Brighton: IES.

ASSIGNMENTS AND DISCUSSION TOPICS

1 Critically review the redundancy policy of your organisation. How fair, effective and workable are the selection criteria identified in the policy?

2 What employee data is needed to use a measured factor approach as a credible and objective redundancy selection process? What difficulties might managers encounter?

3 Critically evaluate the alternative measures that may be taken by an organisation in order to avoid compulsory redundancy.

4 Analyse the skills and competencies that managers need in order to manage the individual redundancy encounter effectively. How can the skills be acquired in this sensitive area of managerial action?

5 Evaluate the effectiveness of the support your organisation offers to employees who are being made redundant.

6 Prepare a briefing paper for your management team on how to recognise and respond effectively to 'survivor syndrome'. Use the briefing paper as the basis for a short presentation to a small group of colleagues or fellow students.

Index

Fluid Mechanics

Sixth Edition

Frank M. White

University of Rhode Island

Higher Education

Boston   Burr Ridge, IL   Dubuque, IA   New York   San Francisco   St. Louis
Bangkok   Bogotá   Caracas   Kuala Lumpur   Lisbon   London   Madrid   Mexico City
Milan   Montreal   New Delhi   Santiago   Seoul   Singapore   Sydney   Taipei   Toronto

Higher Education

FLUID MECHANICS, SIXTH EDITION

Published by McGraw-Hill, a business unit of The McGraw-Hill Companies, Inc., 1221 Avenue of the Americas, New York, NY 10020. Copyright © 2008 by The McGraw-Hill Companies, Inc. All rights reserved. No part of this publication may be reproduced or distributed in any form or by any means, or stored in a database or retrieval system, without the prior written consent of The McGraw-Hill Companies, Inc., including, but not limited to, in any network or other electronic storage or transmission, or broadcast for distance learning.

Some ancillaries, including electronic and print components, may not be available to customers outside the United States.

This book is printed on acid-free paper.

1 2 3 4 5 6 7 8 9 0 DOC/DOC 0 9 8 7 6

ISBN 978–0–07–128645–9
MHID 0–07–128645–4

About the Author

Frank M. White is Professor Emeritus of Mechanical and Ocean Engineering at the University of Rhode Island. He studied at Georgia Tech and M.I.T. In 1966 he helped found, at URI, the first department of ocean engineering in the country. Known primarily as a teacher and writer, he has received eight teaching awards and has written four textbooks on fluid mechanics and heat transfer.

From 1979 to 1990 he was editor-in-chief of the *ASME Journal of Fluids Engineering* and then served from 1991 to 1997 as chairman of the ASME Board of Editors and of the Publications Committee. He is a Fellow of ASME and in 1991 received the ASME Fluids Engineering Award. He lives with his wife, Jeanne, in Narragansett, Rhode Island.

To Jeanne

Contents

Preface

General Approach

The sixth edition of *Fluid Mechanics* sees some additions and deletions but no philosophical change. The basic outline of eleven chapters, plus appendices, remains the same. The triad of integral, differential, and experimental approaches is retained. Many problem exercises, and some fully worked examples, have been changed. The informal, student-oriented style is retained. A number of new photographs and figures have been added. Many new references have been added, for a total of 418. The writer is a firm believer in "further reading," especially in the postgraduate years.

Learning Tools

The total number of problem exercises continues to increase, from 1089 in the first edition, to 1674 in this sixth edition. Most of these are basic end-of chapter problems, classified according to topic. There are also Word Problems, multiple-choice Fundamentals of Engineering Problems, Comprehensive Problems, and Design Projects. The appendix lists approximately 700 Answers to Selected Problems. The example problems have been newly restructured in the text, following the sequence of steps outlined in Section 1.3.

The Engineering Equation Solver (EES), described in Appendix E, is bound-in with the text and continues its role as an attractive tool for fluid mechanics and, indeed, other engineering problems. Not only is it an excellent solver, but it also contains thermophysical properties, publication-quality plotting, units checking, and many mathematical functions. The author is indebted to Sanford Klein and William Beckman, of the University of Wisconsin, for invaluable and continuous help in preparing and updating EES for use in this text.

Content Changes

There are some revisions in each chapter. Chapter 1 has been revised so that the history of fluid mechanics comes earlier, in Section 1.2. Problem-solving techniques have been moved to Section 1.3. The discussion of the velocity field, Section 1.7, has been shortened, and the mathematical material moved to Chapter 4. The brief but useful discussion of nonnewtonian fluids has been improved. A reviewer helped the author improve the treatment of experimental uncertainty, Section 1.13. The discussion of the Fundamentals of Engineering (FE) Exam has been updated, and the text contains 85 FE-type problems.

Chapter 2, thanks to reviewer requests, has been relieved of the heavy Navier-Stokes discussion, now put back into Chapter 4. The emphasis returns to plain hydrostatics. The treatment of manometers has been improved. Instead of relying entirely on moment-of-inertia hydrostatic-force formulas, a new example shows how to work directly with pressure distributions. The treatment of rigid-body motion has been shortened to avoid excessive three-dimensional excursions, and section 2.10 on pressure measurement introduces digital manometers.

In Chapter 3, the development of control volume analysis has been significantly shortened. Example 3.5, a $\mathbf{V}(x, y, z)$ field integration example, has been replaced by one less sophisticated, a sluice gate. Bernoulli's equation still comes last and is not broken out into a new chapter. I try to stress that the Bernoulli relation is dangerously restricted and often misused by both students and graduate engineers. The reviewers have suggested a better way of explaining when the Bernoulli equation is invalid. Example 3.22, a complicated and unsatisfying transient-flow case, has been replaced by a better example.

Chapter 4 now begins the treatment of the acceleration vector, removed from Chapter 2. At the persuasive suggestion of the reviewers, Section 4.10, *Illustrative Potential Flows,* has been moved to Chapter 8. Twenty new problems have been added here.

Chapter 5 continues to emphasize the *pi theorem* method of finding dimensionless groups. But I have added a discussion, an example, and some problems, for the method of Ipsen (a 1960 textbook), which is a terrific alternate approach that yields all the pi groups at once. At the reviewers' request, I added four new examples, and "more air, not so much water."

Chapter 6 has added a *Type-4* pipe-flow problem treatment: finding the correct pipe length. Under minor losses, new data on diffuser losses has been added. Under flow measurement, a treatment of particle image velocimetry has been added.

Chapter 7 adds new data on automobile drag, including the world record for high mileage, 12,665 miles per gallon! A discussion of the Airbus A-380 is also added.

Chapter 8 now contains all the potential-flow material that had been in Chapter 4. New data on the lift and drag of rotating cylinders has been added, which casts much doubt on the accuracy of the classical figure used in earlier editions and in other books.

Chapter 9 needed few changes, in the writer's opinion. *New Trends in Aeronautics* was updated, and 25 new problems were added.

Chapter 10 benefits from new and updated references and a thought-provoking new chapter-opener photo. Eighteen new problems have been added here.

Chapter 11 was aided by reviewer suggestions. A new section, with problems and data, has been added on the performance of free propellers. More discussion and data have been included on wind turbines, which certainly have a great future.

Appendix B, *Compressible Flow Tables,* has been greatly shortened by using coarser increments in Mach number. The tables give the flavor of a function, and the flow functions can easily be obtained from Excel, MATLAB, or an ordinary calculator.

Supplements

A number of supplements are available to students and/or instructors. A print version of the Student Study Guide has been developed by Jerry Dunn of Texas A&M University. Students may also obtain, in DVD format, EES, fluid mechanics videos developed by Gary Settles of Pennsylvania State University and CFD images and animations prepared by Fluent Inc. In ARIS format for students, Fundamentals of Engineering (FE) Exam quizzes, prepared by Edward Anderson of Texas Tech University, and some algorithmic problems are available.

Instructors may obtain a series of PowerPoint slides and images, plus the full Solutions Manual, in pdf format. The Solutions Manual provides complete and detailed solutions, including problem statements and artwork, to the end-of-chapter problems. It may be photocopied for posting or preparing transparencies for the classroom.

Acknowledgments

As usual, so many people have helped me that I cannot remember or list them all. Sheldon Green of the University of British Columbia, Gordon Holloway of the University of New Brunswick, Saeed Moaveni of Minnesota State University Mankato, and Tapan K. Sengupta of the Indian Institute of Technology at Kanpur gave many helpful suggestions. Samuel S. Sih of Walla Walla College and John Borg of Marquette University were especially helpful with the solutions manual. Many other reviewers and correspondents gave good suggestions, encouragement, corrections, and materials: Larry Belfiore of Colorado State University; Paulo Vatavuk of Unicamp University, Brasil; Bertrand Côté of the Université de Sherbrooke, Canada; Elizabeth J. Kenyon of EJK Technical Publishing Services; John Ladd of Integrated Defense Systems, St. Louis, MO; Andris Skattebo of Scandpower A/S; Jeffrey S. Allen of Michigan Technological University; Peter R. Spedding of Queen's University, Belfast, Northern Ireland; Cristina L. Archer of Stanford University; Fulvio Bellobuono of the University of Naples; Debendra K. Das of the University of Alaska Fairbanks; Kevin O'Sullivan of the Associated Press; Lennart Lüttig and Nina Koliha of REpower Systems AG, Hamburg, Germany; Jesse Shoemaker and Gina Mabbott of Dwyer Instruments; Pirouz Kavehpour of UCLA; Johan Stander of the University of Stellenbosch, South Africa; Sukanta K. Dash of The Indian Institute of Technology at Kharagpur; David Chelidze, Richard Lessmann, and Donna Meyer of the University of Rhode Island; Craig Swanson of Applied Science Associates, Inc.; Ghanem F. Oweis of the American University of Beirut, Lebanon; Cliff Moses of the University of Texas at San Antonio; Ephraim Sparrow of the University of Minnesota; Deborah Pence of Oregon State University; Dale Hart of Louisiana Tech University; Georg Huber of Klagenfurt, Austria; Ken Craig of the University of Pretoria, South Africa; Lino Guzzella of ETH Zurich; Edmund Robertson and John O'Connor of the University of St. Andrews; Gary L. Peak of McCauley Corp.; Haecheon Choi of Seoul National University; and Nevan C. Hanumara of M.I.T.

The McGraw-Hill staff was, as usual, enormously helpful. Many thanks are due to Bill Stenquist, Amanda Green, Melinda Bilecki, Kelley Butcher, Jonathan Plant, Megan Hoar, Carrie Burger, John Leland, Tracy Konrardy, Suzanne Jeans, Brenda Ernzen, Michael Weitz, Christine Walker, Louis Poncz, Brenda Rolwes, Pamela Carley, Jenny Hobein, and Christina Nelson. Finally, the continuing support and encouragement of my wife and family are, as always, much appreciated. Thanks are also due to our dog, Sadie, and our cat, Harry.

Fluid Mechanics

Hurricane Rita in the Gulf of Mexico, Sept. 22, 2005. Rita made landfall at the Texas-Louisiana border and caused billions of dollars in wind and flooding damage. Though more dramatic than typical applications in this text, Rita is a true fluid flow, strongly influenced by the earth's rotation and the ocean temperature. [*Photo courtesy of NASA.*]